Constructing
Democratic Governance
in Latin America

THE JOHNS HOPKINS UNIVERSITY PRESS

An Inter-American Dialogue Book

Constructing

Democratic Governance

in Latin America

SECOND EDITION

Edited by

Jorge I. Domínguez

Michael Shifter

THE JOHNS HOPKINS UNIVERSITY PRESS
Baltimore & London

© 1996, 2003 The Johns Hopkins University Press
All rights reserved. First edition 1996
Second edition 2003
Printed in the United States of America on acid-free paper
9 8 7 6 5 4 3 2 1

The Johns Hopkins University Press
2715 North Charles Street
Baltimore, Maryland 21218-4363
www.press.jhu.edu

Library of Congress Cataloging-in-Publication Data

Constructing democratic governance in Latin America / edited by
Jorge I. Domínguez and Michael Shifter.—2nd ed.
    p. cm. — (An Inter-American Dialogue book)
Rev. ed. of: Constructing democratic governance.
Includes bibliographical references (p   ) and index.
    ISBN 0-8018-7119-0 — ISBN 0-8018-7120-4 (pbk.)
    1. Latin America—Politics and government—1980–
2. Democracy—Latin America.   I. Domínguez, Jorge I., 1945–
II. Shifter, Michael.   III. Constructing democratic governance.
IV. Series.
    JL966 .C6768 2002
    320.98'09'049—dc21

2002001839

A catalog record for this book is available from the British Library.

Contents

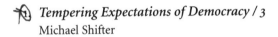

PART III   COUNTRY STUDIES

PART IV   CONCLUSION

Preface

In the early 1990s, the Inter-American Dialogue launched a systematic effort to analyze one of the hemisphere's most significant challenges: how to build effective democratic governance. Jorge I. Domínguez, professor at Harvard University and a founding Dialogue member, and Abraham Lowenthal, president of the Pacific Council on International Policy and the Dialogue's founding executive director and current board member, provided invaluable intellectual leadership for that effort. The resulting first edition of *Constructing Democratic Governance,* which appeared in 1996, reflected the best thinking of a set of first-rate analysts from Latin America, the Caribbean, Canada, and the United States.

This second edition represents an attempt to review the progress that has been made in the Americas in moving toward more effective democratic governance since the studies in the first edition were prepared. Using the first edition as the reference point or baseline, we thought it was important to take careful measure of the advances and setbacks in a variety of key dimensions, including the performance of political parties, civilian control over the armed forces, and the fundamental protection of human rights. All of these were central to the original conceptualization of the project as well.

As in the first edition, we believed it would be most illuminating to blend both country and thematic studies. Although slightly scaled down and more modest, the result—seven country studies and six chapters on relevant crosscutting themes—offers a similarly in-depth and wide-ranging interpretation of democratic governance throughout the region. This updated effort featured a comparably impressive and diverse group of analysts, some of whom contributed to the original exercise as well. We appreciate the fine work of all thirteen authors.

We were extremely fortunate to benefit once again from Jorge Domínguez's superb intellectual direction. His role in every phase of the project was absolutely vital. It was an enormous pleasure to collaborate with Domínguez, whose formidable skills and vast experience in conceptualizing, organizing, and producing a volume of this sort are without peer. We are grateful as well to Harvard University's Weatherhead Center for International Affairs and to its David Rockefeller Center for Latin American Studies, which provided support to Domínguez during the course of this project, and to Kathleen Hoover, for her excellent assistance.

The chapters went through several drafts and were substantially informed and enriched by a conference held in Washington, D.C., in September 2000. We were pleased by the ample, high-level, and diverse participation from Washington's policy community during a set of lively discussions. The Dialogue firmly believes that a productive exchange among key decision makers and analysts about democratic governance challenges helps bridge the worlds of policy and academia. For their valuable perspectives and thoughtful comments, we wish to thank: Margaret Sarles of the Agency for International Development; Christopher Sabatini of the National Endowment for Democracy; Ricardo Lagorio of the Argentine Embassy; Chilean political leader Andrés Allamand (then with the Inter-American Development Bank); Cynthia McClintock of George Washington University; and former ambassador and assistant secretary of state for Inter-American Affairs, Viron P. Vaky, now a senior fellow with the Dialogue.

We want to express our deep appreciation to Henry Tom of the Johns Hopkins University Press for his unfailing patience and his critical and constructive feedback on the draft chapters. Tom's support in undertaking both editions of *Constructing Democratic Governance* has been indispensable. We are grateful as well to Kenneth Potter for his fine translations of several chapters.

At the Dialogue, we are particularly indebted to Victoria Wigodzky, who managed and coordinated this effort with exceptional skill, efficiency, and good cheer. Her contribution in providing comments, editing, and translating various chapters was invaluable. Peter Hakim, the Dialogue's president, also added his characteristically sharp critique on several drafts. Jennifer Burrell deserves special thanks for her fine role during the project's initial stage. We are grateful to several interns who ably performed a variety of tasks essential to the production of this volume: Christine Lawson, Daniel Mack, Alvaro Herrero, and LeeAnn Liu.

The Inter-American Dialogue's research and publications are designed to improve the quality of public debate and decision on key issues in Western Hemisphere affairs. The Dialogue is both a forum for sustained exchange among leaders and an independent, nonpartisan center for policy analysis on U.S.-Latin American economic and political relations. The Dialogue's one hundred members—from the United States, Canada, Latin America, and the Caribbean—include prominent political, business, labor, academic, media, military, and religious leaders. At periodic plenary sessions, members analyze key hemispheric issues and formulate recommendations for policy and action. The Dialogue presents its findings in comprehensive reports circulated throughout the Americas. Its research agenda focuses on four broad themes: democratic governance, inter-American cooperation, economic integration, and social equity.

The Inter-American Dialogue wishes to express its gratitude to the National Endowment for Democracy and its senior program officer for Latin America and the Caribbean, Christopher Sabatini. The Endowment's generous support not only helped underwrite the original project, but also enabled the Dialogue to commission the papers for this volume and organize the September 2000 conference in Washington, D.C. We are also pleased to acknowledge the broader support that the Dialogue has obtained from the Ford and William and Flora Hewlett foundations.

Michael Shifter
Vice-President for Policy
Inter-American Dialogue

Contributors

Felipe Agüero is associate professor of political science and director of graduate studies at the School of International Studies at the University of Miami. He previously taught at Ohio State University, and has been fellow at the Institute for Advanced Study in Princeton and the Helen Kellogg Institute at the University of Notre Dame. He is editor with Jeffrey Stark of *Fault Lines of Democracy in Post-Transition Latin America* (Miami, Fla.: North-South Center Press, 1998), which received a Choice 1999 Award for Outstanding Academic Book.

John M. Carey is associate professor of political science at Washington University in St. Louis. His research focuses on the effects of constitutional design on the performance of democracies. He is currently working on a cross-national study of party and coalition strength within legislatures.

Fernando Cepeda Ulloa teaches political science at the Facultad de Administración de la Universidad de los Andes. He has recently published several books and reports about democratic governability and corruption as well as an evaluation of the mandate of the Summit of the Americas on the fight against drugs. Dr. Cepeda is a former ambassador to the Organization of American States and former minister of government.

Michael Coppedge is associate professor in the Department of Government and International Studies at the University of Notre Dame and serves as director of the Quality of Democracy Working Group at the Kellogg Institute. His research projects concern the political, institutional, economic, and social conditions that promote stable democracy, approaches to democratization, democratic diffusion, and the causes and consequences of party-system characteristics in Latin America.

Javier Corrales is assistant professor of political science at Amherst College in Amherst, Massachusetts. During 2000–2001, he was a fellow at the Woodrow Wilson International Center for Scholars in Washington, D.C. His area of interest includes the politics of economic policy reform in developing countries. He is currently writing a book on the role that ruling parties play in the implementation of economic reform and launching a new research project on the politics of education reform in Latin America.

Carlos Iván Degregori is a political analyst and senior researcher at the Lima-based Instituto de Estudios Peruanos (IEP). An anthropologist by training, he has taught at a number of universities in Peru and abroad, including the Universidad Nacional Mayor de San Marcos, Columbia University, the University of Wisconsin at Madison, and the Ecole des Hautes Etudes en Sciences Sociales in Paris. His current projects focus on the theme of memory and political violence, and on the political impact of President Alberto Fujimori's second reelection.

Rut Diamint teaches international conflict and international negotiations at Universidad Torcuato Di Tella in Buenos Aires, Argentina. At UTDT, she coordinates the project "The Civil-Military Issue in Latin America: Training a Civil Network of Specialists." Dr. Diamint writes numerous articles and edited *Control Civil y Fuerzas Armadas en las Nuevas Democracias Latinoamericanas*. Currently, she is writing a book on security-sector reform in Latin America.

Jorge I. Domínguez is the Clarence Dillon Professor of International Affairs and director of the Weatherhead Center for International Affairs at Harvard University. He has been the co-editor for both first and second editions of *Constructing Democratic Governance*. Dr. Domínguez is a founding member of the Inter-American Dialogue.

Denise Dresser is visiting fellow at the Pacific Council on International Policy at the University of Southern California, on leave from her post as professor of political science at the Instituto Tecnológico Autónomo de México (ITAM). Dr. Dresser has been a visiting research fellow at the Center for U.S.-Mexican Studies, University of California, San Diego, and a senior visiting fellow at the Inter-American Dialogue. She is the author of *Neopopulist Solutions to Neoliberal Problems: Mexico's National Solidarity Program* and of numerous articles on Mexican politics and U.S.-Mexico relations.

Mala N. Htun is assistant professor of political science at the Graduate Faculty of Political and Social Science of New School University. She is author of *Democracy, Dictatorship, and Gender Rights in Latin America* (New York: Cambridge University Press, forthcoming) and several articles on women in politics and women's rights in Latin America. She is adviser to the Women's Leadership Conference of the Americas and the Inter-American Dialogue.

Marta Lagos is director of Latinobarómetro, a yearly opinion survey on socio-political subjects in seventeen countries of the region. Since 1995, she has been the World Association for Public Opinion Research (WAPOR) representative for Chile, and was founding member and first president of the Chilean association of Public Opinion Research. She is a founding member of a new organization called Global Survey, which coordinates comparative work from the four regional barometers: Eastern Europe, Africa, Asia, and Latin America. She is also major owner of MORI Chile, a Market and Opinion Research company (part of the international group MORI International), and one of the leading opinion pollsters in the country.

Bolívar Lamounier recently established a new consulting firm, Augurium: Análise, Consultoria e Empreendimentos S/C Ltda. Previously he was founder and research director of the Instituto de Estudios Económicos, Sociales y Políticos de São Paulo (IDESP) in Brazil. A member of the Inter-American Dialogue, he has been a partner at MCM, one of Brazil's leading consulting firms, since 1995. He was also a member of the drafting constitutional commission appointed by President José Sarney.

Steven Levitsky is assistant professor of government at Harvard University. His research interests include political parties, changing patterns of political organization and representation in Latin America, and democracy and democratization. Dr. Levitsky is currently completing a book manuscript on the transformation of labor-based parties in contemporary Latin America.

M. Victoria Murillo is assistant professor of political science at Yale University. Her book, *Labor Unions, Partisan Coalitions and Market Reforms in Latin America* (New York: Cambridge University Press, 2001), analyzes union-government relations in Argentina, Mexico, and Venezuela during the implementation of market-oriented reforms. Her current research focuses on the relationship among consumers, providers, and the state in privatized public utilities in Latin America as well as on the dynamics of teachers' unions facing educational reforms.

Michael Shifter is vice-president for policy at the Inter-American Dialogue. He develops and implements the Dialogue's program strategy in the area of democratic governance and human rights. He also commissions policy-relevant articles and edited books, and prepares policy reports and other documents. Mr. Shifter is an adjunct professor at Georgetown University's School of Foreign Service.

Acronyms and Abbreviations

General

ERA   Equal Rights Amendment
NAFTA   North American Free Trade Agreement
NGO   non-governmental organization
SOE   state-owned entity

International Organizations

CEDAW   Convention on the Elimination of All Forms of Discrimination Against Women
ECLAC   Economic Commission for Latin America and the Caribbean
IDB   Inter-American Development Bank
ILO   International Labour Organization
IMF   International Monetary Fund
MERCOSUR Southern Cone Common Market
OAS   Organization of American States
OECD   Organization for Economic Cooperation and Development
OPEC   Organization of Petroleum Exporting Countries
UN   United Nations

Argentina

ANSSAL   National Administration of Health Insurance
ARI   Argentines for a Republic of Equals
CGT   General Labor Confederation
CTA   Congress of Argentine Workers
FG   Big Front
FREPASO   Front for a Solidaristic Country

MODIN	Movement for National Dignity and Independence
NUD	Necessity and Urgency Decree
OA	Anti-Corruption Office
PAMI	Program of Integral Medical Attention
PJ	Peronist Party
SOMISA	Argentine Steel and Iron Industry
UCR	Radical Civic Union
UCEDE	Center Democratic Union
YPF	Yacimientos Petrolíficos Fiscales

Bolivia

COB	Bolivian Workers' Confederation
MRN	National Revolutionary Movement

Brazil

ABIN	Brazilian Intelligence Agency
CUT	Single Workers' Confederation
CVRD	Companhia Vale de Rio Doce
MP	provisional measures
MST	Landless Workers Movement
PFL	Liberal Front Party
PMDB	Brazilian Democratic Movement Party
PPA	Pluriannual Investment Plan
PPB	Brazilian Progressive Party
PRN	Party of National Reconstruction
PSDB	Brazilian Social Democracy Party
PT	Workers' Party
PTB	Brazilian Labor Party
SFC	Supreme Federal Court
SNI	National Intelligence Service

Chile

CONADI	National Corporation for the Development of Indigenous People
CUT	Unified Workers' Confederation
RN	National Renovation
SERNAM	National Women's Service
UDI	Independent Democratic Union

Colombia

AD M-19	Democratic Alliance M-19
ANAPO	Popular National Alliance
ANDI	National Industrial Association
CGTD	General Confederation of Democratic Workers
CTC	Workers' Confederation of Colombia
CUT	Unified Workers' Union
ELN	National Liberation Army
EPL	Popular Army of National Liberation
FARC	Revolutionary Armed Forces of Colombia
MRL	Liberal Revolutionary Movement

Costa Rica

PLN	National Liberal Party

Ecuador

DINE	Department of Industries of the Ecuadorian Army
ENCIS	Civilian Personnel

El Salvador

ARENA	National Republican Alliance
FMLN	Farabundo Martí National Liberation Front

Honduras

DNI	National Intelligence Directorate

Mexico

CROM	Mexican Regional Workers' Confederation
CTM	Mexican Workers' Confederation
EZLN	Zapatista Army of National Liberation
FSTSE	Federation of Public Services' Unions
IFE	Federal Electoral Institute
PAN	National Action Party
PLM	Mexican Labor Party
PNR	National Revolutionary Party
PRD	Party of the Democratic Revolution
PRI	Revolutionary Institutional Party
PRONASOL	National Program of Solidarity

STRM   Union of Telephone Workers of Mexico
UNT   National Workers' Union

Nicaragua

AGRESAMI   San Miguel Farming Enterprise
CONAGRA   Commercial Farming Association
FSLN   Sandinista National Liberation Front

Paraguay

UIP   Industrial Union of Paraguay

Peru

AP   Popular Action
APRA   American Popular Revolutionary Alliance
CGTP   Peruvian General Workers' Confederation
C90   Change 90
FREDEMO   Democratic Front
IU   United Left
JNE   National Board of Elections
MRTA   Tupac Amaru Revolutionary Movement
NM   New Majority
SIN   National Intelligence Service
SP   Shining Path
TGC   Constitutional Guarantees Tribunal
UPP   Union for Peru
VV   Come Along, Neighbor

United States

CIA   Central Intelligence Agency
DEA   Drug Enforcement Agency
WHINSEC   Western Hemisphere Institute for Security
                Cooperation

Uruguay

FA   Broad Front
PIT-CNT   Inter-Union Workers' Plenary–National Workers'
                Convention

Venezuela

AD	Democratic Action Party
ANC	National Constituent Assembly
CNE	National Electoral Council
COPEI	Social Christian Party
CSE	Supreme Electoral Council
CTN	National Tactic Command
CTV	Venezuelan Workers' Confederation
DISIP	Directorate of Intelligence and Prevention Services
FBT	Bolivarian Workers' Front
IRENE	Integration and Renovation New Hope
MAS	Movement to Socialism
MBR-200	Bolivarian Revolutionary Movement
MEP	People's Electoral Movement
MVR	Fifth Republic Movement
PPT	Fatherland for All
PROVEA	Venezuelan Education Program—Action in Human Rights

PART I

Introduction

1

Tempering Expectations of Democracy

Michael Shifter

Over recent years, analysts and policy makers alike have been drawn to the idea of systematically tracking the progress of effective democratic governance in Latin America. They have generally pointed to the inadequacy of descriptive "snapshots" or rankings according to some scale of selected criteria. There is a natural interest in trying to determine whether conditions of democracy are improving, deteriorating, or staying just about the same. The exercise has intellectual value, but in fact goes considerably beyond that. It is also worthwhile, in a more practical sense, to generate public policy recipes that are more sensitive to and grounded in political realities and, therefore, ultimately more effective.

In this respect, at least three critical questions should be kept clearly in mind. The first is, democratic progress compared to when? In conducting such appraisals, it is important to recognize what the reference point is. The second critical question, in consideration of the highly variegated nature of the region, is which Latin America, which subregion or particular country, do we have in mind? And, finally, what are the dimensions most relevant for assessing democratic governance? The first edition of *Constructing Democratic Governance* attempted in some measure to respond to these questions. It sought to provide a benchmark survey of the mid-1990s, highlight relevant regional and country differences, and spell out a more nuanced and wide-ranging conceptualization of the key elements of democratic governance.

As with the first edition, the authors investigating individual countries were asked to address a common set of issues. This time, however, the authors examine the latter 1990s, when the optimism associated with the end of the Cold War and a succession of democratic transitions gave way to a markedly more sober perspective. The issues examined on each occasion are, however, substantially unchanged. They include the nature of the electoral process; the condition of parties and other political institutions; executive-legislative and civil-military relations; the rule of law, human rights, and the state of the judiciary; corruption; the roles of civic, professional, business, and labor organizations and of the media; the treatment of minorities and women; and the impact of socioeconomic inequities. To be sure, some of these issues are considerably more salient in some countries than in others.

The select set of seven country cases—Brazil, Mexico, Argentina, Peru, Chile, Venezuela, and Colombia—are complemented by six chapters that seek to highlight cross-national analysis. Themes concerning the role of public opinion, women's political participation, the military, labor, the political effects of market reforms, and relations between the executive and legislature are particularly germane and in fact yield important comparative insights about the nature of democratic governance.

Half a dozen years later, the three critical questions that guided the initial inquiry remain more pertinent than ever. The responses given then, although preliminary and tentative, reflected a more promising political moment. This time the responses are appreciably more tempered, especially when viewed in relation to the perhaps unrealistically high expectations for democratic advance that characterized the early 1990s.

According to the classic, conventional criterion for democracy—the holding of free and competitive elections—the region's political performance (with the exception of the January 2000 coup in Ecuador) has been remarkably positive. Few serious analysts would challenge the claim that the quality of democratic governance in some countries—Mexico and Peru stand out—notably improved from the early 1990s to the beginning of the next decade. The chapter on Argentina, too, highlights some important steps toward greater democratic consolidation. Other chapters are particularly sobering, however. The treatment of public opinion, for example, reveals growing and troubling levels of public dissatisfaction with the functioning of democracy in many countries of the region. Even the percentage of citizens who regard democracy as the preferred form of government has declined. More strikingly, there is an increasingly strong correspondence between economic performance and the support of democratic governments. Surveys consistently reveal declining confidence about the prospects of getting on sound economic footing. In short, the comparative public opinion data at least offer some grounds for challenging any assertion about the deepening, or consolidation, or improved quality of democracy in Latin America in general.

In addition, levels of poverty and inequality have remained persistently high since the mid-1990s. Just as elections regularly take place, inflation continues to be under control. But even moderate economic growth still eludes most countries.

⌐At the century's turn, the cluster of countries that make up the Andean region, Colombia and Venezuela included, is in greatest turmoil and most problematic for satisfying standards of effective democratic governance. In this regard, deterioration over recent years can be seen most dramatically in the case of Colombia. As the chapter in this volume makes clear, the country is enduring multiple and profound crises—in this case, the frequently overused term is most apt—that, uncharacteristically for Colombia, have failed to elicit a coherent and effective response from the country's now corroded political system. Yet, despite the country's drug-fueled violence, rampant corruption, and institutional decay, some democratic traditions—regular elections included—remain intact. The ambiguities and paradoxes of Colombia's predicament are amply discussed.⌐

⌐The notion of representative democracy, marked by independent powers of government and a system of checks and balances, may still prevail throughout much of the region, and even in besieged Colombia. But it is being fiercely contested and challenged in the case of Venezuela, under the government led by President Hugo Chávez. In that country, with civilian, constitutional government in place since the late 1950s, an alternative, competing concept that might be called "popular sovereignty," developed in this volume, is being advanced by the Chávez government. Such a notion is explicitly based on and inspired by majoritarian principles, and prizes broad social support more than checks and balances. In various hemispheric forums since 1999, the Chávez government has made its case in opposing the dominant, consensual idea—a convergence in embracing representative democracy—that especially marked the early 1990s. The broad disenchantment with both political and economic performance in many countries may well give Chávez's alternative view growing resonance and appeal.⌐

Peru, in contrast, offers some measure of hope. In November 2000, the country witnessed the astonishing meltdown of the decade-long regime led by President Alberto Fujimori and his national security chief Vladimiro Montesinos. Progressively, during the 1990s, there were serious and substantial setbacks on an array of critical indicators of democratic governance in Peru, including press freedom, the role of the military, the functioning of the electoral system, and the separation of powers. By any standard, the task of democratic, institutional reconstruction is a formidable one, as the Peru chapter amply illustrates.

Although the other countries treated in this volume present slightly more sanguine political scenarios, they also underscore the continuing and significant obstacles toward building effective democratic governance. Profound economic problems in Brazil, Mexico, and especially Argentina have substantially dimmed prospects for favorable political performance.

At the same time, when one assumes a longer-term perspective—comparing prevailing conditions to those that marked the region several decades ago—the progress in these countries is unmistakable and impressive. Despite enormous difficulties, the legacy of the two presidential terms of Brazilian President Fernando Henrique Cardoso was, on balance, positive in terms of democratic governance. And the current political challenges in Mexico and Argentina, however formidable, should be viewed in relation to the more than seven decades of single-party rule in Mexico and long stretches dominated by military governments in the case of Argentina.

In part, the puzzle of continuing vitality in key aspects of democratic practice—in this volume, for example, the impressive strides made by women in political participation stand out—can be explained by the region's resilient civil society. Although the landscape has changed considerably in recent years, a mapping of Latin America's civil society would highlight the proliferation of innovative initiatives, many at the local, community level. In addition, non-governmental groups concerned about such questions as human rights and environmental protection have matured and become more sophisticated and more closely connected with effective global networks marked by shared agendas. Professional and business associations, too, have played increasingly prominent roles in organizing and pursuing their own interests. A more independent and vigilant media has sought to keep both public and private institutions accountable and ensure and promote reasonable degrees of transparency. Despite enormous problems and difficult circumstances faced in some countries, the media on balance has made exemplary progress compared with a few decades ago.

Still, it is important to try to account for the region's considerable shortcomings in moving toward more effective democratic governance. Serious discussions of political failures often, for example, lead to the catchall explanation of bad leadership. However, few if any analysts of democratic governance have treated this as anything more than a residual category, and have so far not carried out systematic and serious studies about the margin of maneuver of Latin American leaders in responding to critical situations and making key decisions. If negative political results can be in part dismissed as bad leadership, then it is reasonable to suppose that there is such a thing as good leadership that can, albeit on the margins, make a difference in the daily lives of Latin American citizens. While there is every indication that most Latin Americans seek and expect both democratic politics and effective economic performance and social advance, there are serious questions about the extent to which such aims are compatible with one another, and can be successfully and simultaneously pursued.

Leadership, of course, is also important in the United States, and can have a significant bearing on the fundamental goal of building effective democratic governance in Latin America. In November 2000, the presidential elections in the United States were highly controversial and contentious, raising questions about the soundness of the country's electoral practices and institutions. And, of course, the terrorist attacks on September 11, 2001, not only exposed the vulnerability of the United States but also highlighted the centrality of effective presidential leadership.

In the context of a sharp downturn in the U.S. economy, coupled with deepening economic and social problems throughout the region and declining public confidence in political institutions, the task of energizing multilateral institutions on behalf of effective democratic governance becomes even more compelling. The political role of the Organization of American States (OAS) and its relevant bodies, along with the institution-building function of the Inter-American Development Bank, are crucial to such an effort. But given the asymmetry in power relations that has long characterized—and continues to characterize—the hemisphere, it is hard to see how much progress can be made if the United States does not attach the highest priority to a coherent and sustained strategy aimed at democracy promotion.

A continuing and systematic review of the state of democratic governance throughout Latin America can not only generate a richer and more nuanced understanding of the region's complex political challenges and dilemmas, but can also help point to a more productive policy agenda. The authors of this volume have, one hopes, contributed, even in some small measure, to advance such worthy goals.

PART II

Themes and Issues

2

Presidentialism and Representative Institutions

John M. Carey

The performance of presidential systems in Latin America during the past decade has been, for the most part, encouraging when compared to that of preceding decades. Most countries held regular elections that were judged fair and competitive by international observers, and that often transferred power to opposition candidates and their parties. Mexico and Nicaragua experienced the growth—and Chile the restoration—of competitive party systems after prolonged periods of authoritarian and/or one-party rule. Governments in Guatemala, Nicaragua, and El Salvador reached peace agreements that incorporated into electoral competition groups that had been adversaries in long and bitter civil wars. Aggregate economic indicators improved in many countries relative to the abysmal 1980s, while presidential democracy survived in many others even in the face of economic hard times.

This is not to suggest that presidentialism in Latin America was without problems in the 1990s. Economic performance was uneven, inequality increased almost everywhere, and political violence remained a plague, particularly in Colombia, as guerrilla groups, paramilitaries, and the government have fought to a standoff that leaves the viability of the state itself open to question. Without discounting the importance of these crises of governance, however, this chapter focuses more narrowly on the current state of representative institutions. Even within this realm, two ominous trends in Latin American presidentialism are particularly noteworthy. One involves elected presidents willing to trample institutional opponents of their agendas and their perpetuation in office. Alberto Fujimori in Peru is the prime example, based on his 1992 *autogolpe*, his subsequent manipulation of the 1993 constitution, his intimidation of political adversaries, and his strong-arm tactics during the 2000 election in his effort to secure a third term. There is reasonable concern about a similar pattern by Venezuelan President Hugo Chávez. A second exceptional phenomenon of the 1990s is the removal of presidents from office by extraordinary legislative action—impeachment or quasi-impeachment—during their constitutional terms, as witnessed in Brazil in 1992, Venezuela and Guatemala in 1993, Ecuador in 1997, and Paraguay in 1999. Whether these cases represent failures or vindications of presidentialism is debatable. Each involved conflict between the elected branches and the disruption of normal constitutional procedure. Yet democratic rule was preserved in each case, and one could argue that the assertion of legislative authority over the executive marks a regional resurgence of checks and balances over *presidencialismo*.

It is worth noting a distinction between these potential maladies and the academic diagnoses prevalent during the 1980s, which held that presidentialism was more prone than parliamentarism to constitutional crises and democratic breakdown. Based largely on the experiences of the 1960s and 1970s, scholars in Latin America and the United States held that legislative-executive conflict encouraged members of one branch or the other to trump their opponent's intransigence by inviting coups and military rule. The preoccupation with military usurpation of government has declined since the wave of democratizations that began in the late 1970s. Adam Przeworski et al. and Karen Remmer have demonstrated statistically the resilience of democracies in middle- and higher-income countries to coups, even during periods of economic crisis.[1] Based on surveys and interviews in the early 1990s, Fitch found low regard among the Ecuadorian officer corps for constitutional procedure and civilian rule, which appears prescient in light of the military's role in toppling President Jamil Mahuad in January 2000.[2] Equally noteworthy, however, is that censure of the military's actions, from both domestic and international actors, deterred the extension of military rule and encouraged the transfer of office to the elected vice-president.

To sum up, there were some signs of trouble in the performance of Latin American presidentialism as the twentieth century drew to a close, but they have manifested themselves in unexpected ways. The problems do not fit the conventional scenario of regime breakdown through a military seizure of power. Moreover, the issue of performance has come to supersede that of stability in the study of Latin American democracy.

In what follows, I identify a range of issues that are central to the performance of representative institutions in Latin America at the beginning of the twenty-first century. The scope of the chapter precludes a comprehensive review of institutions, and critical topics such as decentralization to subnational governments, judicial reform, and the enhancement of comptroller and ombudsman offices are not discussed. The focus is limited to recent and ongoing changes in the presidency and the context in which it operates, particularly the balance of power between the executive and legislative branches.

To the extent that this chapter has a normative component, the bias throughout is in favor of strengthening legislatures relative to executives, for various reasons. First, I regard the executive branch as the more potentially dangerous of the two in terms of agency problems between citizens and public officials. Legislatures frustrate citizens with glacial decision making, but this provides something of a safeguard against capricious action or the abrupt policy reversals that have characterized many Latin American presidencies in recent decades.[3] Second, legislatures tend to be more inclusive institutions than executives, particularly in presidential systems, where even multiparty coalition cabinets are subordinate to the chief executive. Legislatures tend to reflect societal diversity more accurately, to accommodate deliberation, and to allow for negotiation and compromise among competing groups more effectively than do executives. Third, decision-making procedures in the legislative branch are potentially more transparent than in the executive, in part because of the presence of opposition watchdogs, but also because legislative procedure requires voting. Voting records can—and increasingly do—provide a public record of who favored which policies and who opposed them. To the extent that such records enter public political discourse, they can potentially increase the accountability of elected officials. Finally, most legislatures in Latin America have long been underfunded, understaffed, and ill-equipped to compete on an even footing with presidents as policymaking actors. The preference for strengthening legislatures inherent here has less to do with establishing the dominance of that branch than with moving toward parity. This betrays a more fundamental bias, toward effective checks and balances, for which I do not offer theoretical justification.

The rest of the essay proceeds as follows. First, I review a range of institutional arrangements governing the selection and survival of executives and legislatures. With respect to presidents, these include the adoption of runoff elections and primary elections, restrictions on reelection, and removal from office before the expiration of the presidential term. Then I broaden the scope of analysis to examine the institutional context in which presidents bargain with legislatures—issues of parliamentary confidence in the cabinet, the cameral structure of the legislature, and restrictions on legislative reelection. Finally, having discussed how the composition of the executive and legislature shapes their predispositions toward conflict and cooperation, I turn to procedures by which they make policy decisions, the budget process and legislative voting, examining the effects of these arrangements on the relative bargaining power of the branches and the transparency of governance. The conclusion takes stock of recent changes in the institutional context of executive-legislative relations.

Selecting Presidents

Runoff Elections

The two most common methods of electing presidents are the plurality and the majority runoff systems. Under plurality rule, there is one election, and the candidate with the most votes is elected. Under the majority runoff system, if no candidate wins an outright majority of the vote in the first round, there is a second-round election pitting the top two first-round candidates against each other. Much of the literature on presidentialism in the wake of transitions to democracy directs attention toward methods of presidential and legislative election, their impact on partisan support for the president, and legislative-executive relations. One of the central conclusions from this literature is that, relative to plurality elections for president, the majority runoff format contributes to the proliferation of presidential candidates and the fragmentation of the first-round presidential vote.[4] That is, whereas plurality elections for president tend to discourage vote fragmentation, runoffs do not. In turn, where presidential and legislative terms coincide, presidential candidates' electoral coattails can affect fragmentation in legislative elections. Therefore, whereas plurality elections for president can reduce fragmentation of legislative party systems, this effect is absent under the runoff format. All this suggests that majority runoff elections for the presidency can enhance the unpredictability of presidential elections and encourage divided government. The former effect follows from the ability of candidates with relatively narrow popular appeal to emerge from first-round contests in divided fields, perhaps even with second-place finishes, then consolidate support in the runoff against the other first-round survivor.[5] The latter effect is based on the reduced likelihood of single-party majorities as fragmentation of the legislative party system increases.[6]

By the late 1990s, standard majority runoff systems were in place in Chile, Colombia, Brazil, the Dominican Republic, Ecuador, El Salvador, Guatemala, Paraguay, Peru, and Uruguay; Argentina and Nicaragua had established first-round victory thresholds of 45 percent of the popular vote, and Costa Rica 40 percent.[7] The irony here is that a prominent rationale for shifting to the majority runoff format was the fear that plurality (or plurality-like) rules risked the election of presidents opposed by majorities of voters and legislators, which in turn could trigger constitutional crises.[8] By this logic, the attraction of majority runoff is that it ensures majority endorsement of presidential winners. It may, however, have opened the door to the election of outsiders such as Fernando Collor in Brazil in 1989, and Jorge Serrano in Guatemala and Alberto Fujimori in Peru in 1990. Each ran against the traditional party system in his country, survived the first round with less than one-third of the vote, and won the presidency in a runoff. Despite their second-round "mandates," each of these quickly found themselves mired in interbranch conflicts, which culminated in the premature deaths of Collor's and Serrano's presidencies and Peru's Congress. The rapid rise of Alejandro Toledo against Fujimori himself in the first round of the 2000 Peruvian election suggests that the runoff format still has the capacity to catapult outsiders into contention, primarily as "anyone-but-X" candidates.

Party fragmentation under runoff elections, however, has been counteracted in various instances by incumbency advantage, the adoption of primary elections, or the establishment of formal multiparty coalitions. Running for reelection as incumbent presidents, for example, Fujimori (twice), Carlos Menem in Argentina, and Fernando Henrique Cardoso in Brazil all profited from the stature and the formidable resources of office, commanding broader support than candidates in races not involving incumbents generally can. I discuss the broader significance of presidential reelection and of the rise of primary elections in Latin America below, but it is worth noting here that broad electoral coalitions have formed behind presidential candidates in a number of cases, even in the first rounds of runoff systems.

Coalition Politics in Chile

Chile is prominent in this respect, particularly given the deep historical roots of its multiparty system and the extent to which the failure of cross-party accommodation was associated with the breakdown of democracy in 1973.[9] The politics of coalition in post-transition Chile inherited the momentum of the broad movement united behind the "No" vote to block General Augusto Pinochet's perpetuation in office in 1988. Ironically, that momentum was sustained throughout the 1990s in part by the two-member district electoral system designed by Pinochet's advisers with the specific intention to disenfranchise the radical Left and over-represent the general's supporters on the Right. Under this system, only the top two candidate lists in any district win representation. For any party in the Chilean system, therefore, abandoning the coalition strategy and going it alone is potentially suicidal. This stark calculus encouraged the maintenance of both the Concertación (the coalition of parties spanning the Center–Left of the ideological spectrum), which has governed since the transition, and the major coalition of the Right.[10] The first two elections under the two-member district rule coincided with presidential elections in which coalitions behind the major candidates mirrored those in legislative races, and the Concertación candidates won first-round victories. To the extent that the legislative electoral system provided greater incentives than the presidential system for coalition, it may be that coalition coattails extended from the former to the latter during these years rather than the reverse.

After 1993, however, a constitutional reform that changed presidential term length uncoupled presidential and legislative elections, removing one of the institutional underpinnings of the coalition system.[11] The coalitions survived the 1997 legislative and 1999 presidential elections, although not without considerable strain over selecting and supporting common presidential candidates within the Concertación, and over finding common ground on contentious policy issues such as retrospective justice and labor reforms. By 2000, a number of potentially important institutional reforms were being seriously considered. On one hand, the two largest parties in the coalition of the Right were openly discussing the possibility of merging into one, formally consummating the electoral marriage they have maintained since the transition.[12] At the same time, leaders of all parties were voicing tentative support for a package of reforms that would certainly include the elimination of non-elected senators—a move long opposed by the Right—and may also eliminate two-member districts in favor of a more proportional electoral system.[13] The latter would greatly reduce the imperative to coalesce, or to merge parties. Although the broader package of reforms indisputably represents a move toward greater democratization, it is worth keeping in mind that the move back toward proportional representation might well spell the end of the broad party coalitions that characterized the first decade of post-transition politics in Chile.

Primary Elections

Primary elections were adopted by parties and coalitions in a number of Latin American countries during the 1990s. These have mainly been used to nominate candidates for president, not those farther down the ballot. Latin American primaries are all nationwide, simultaneous affairs, precluding the controversy over sequencing and the disparities of regional influence that mark the U.S. process. Equally important for Latin America in the 1990s, presidential primaries appear to have served as commitment devices, helping to hold together coalitions and parties marked by substantial centripetal forces. By turning the decision on candidate selection over to voters, primaries relieve party leaders and coalition partners of the prickly task of choosing a common candidate, and they legitimize the anointed candidate in the eyes of those partners who do not get the nod.

In 1999 alone, the Chilean, Argentine, Mexican, and Uruguayan experiences demonstrate this effect. During interpartisan negotiations over the Concertación's nomination, for example, the threat by a bloc of Chilean

Christian Democrats to bolt from the coalition and support a candidacy by Andrés Zaldívar was averted by an agreement to hold primary elections. The primary campaign itself, by encouraging candidates to make public appeals beyond the ranks of party militants, helped defuse tension, most notably when Lagos asserted in a televised debate that he would "be the third president of the Concertación, not the second Socialist president," emphasizing his commitment to the coalition and distancing himself from the administration of Salvador Allende.[14] Finally, Lagos' overwhelming primary victory, with over 70 percent of the vote, made the Socialist's candidacy easier to accept, or at least more difficult to renounce, for Christian Democrats. Similarly in Argentina, Radical candidate Fernando de la Rúa's primary victory over the Front for a Solidaristic Country's (FREPASO) Graciela Fernández Meijide legitimized his candidacy in the eyes of Meijide's supporters. In both cases, primaries served to consummate marriages of the Center and the moderate Left behind common candidates who prevailed in the general election, but for whom less unified support prior to the first round might have proved disastrous.

Primaries were held at the party, rather than coalition, level in Uruguay and Mexico in 1999, but in both cases appeared to pull together—or at least to mitigate discord within—parties that were substantially factionalized. In Uruguay, part of the motivation for adopting primary elections was to counteract nearly a century of institutionalized factionalism encouraged by Uruguay's unique double simultaneous vote electoral system, under which votes *within* the major parties were almost always split among multiple candidates, not one of which—not even the winner—commanded widespread support.[15] In Mexico, the Revolutionary Institutional Party (PRI) experimented with various forms of candidate selection in gubernatorial elections during the 1990s, including the traditional *dedazo* (the president's capacity to hand-pick his successor), conventions for party members, and primary elections. The success of primaries in producing effective candidates at the state level encouraged the decision to employ this device for the first time to select the party's 2000 presidential candidate.[16] The potential for primaries to dampen conflict was evident both within the PRI and in its contrast with the opposition. Within the PRI, despite complaints that the party's leadership surreptitiously supported winning candidate Francisco Labastida, Labastida's convincing margin of victory prompted the grudging acceptance of the result by runner-up Roberto Madrazo.[17] Among the opposition, in contrast, the failure of the National Action Party (PAN) and the Party of the Democratic Revolution (PRD) to form a unified anti-PRI coalition stemmed at least in part from the parties' inability to agree on a method for conducting a primary by which both would be bound.[18] In the end, of course, this division among the opposition did not prevent the PAN's Vicente Fox from ending seven decades of PRI control of the executive in the July 2000 election. Yet up until the last moment, the opposition's failure to select a common candidate generated doubt about its ability to unseat the PRI and sustained bitter recriminations between Fox and the PRD's Cuauhtémoc Cárdenas.[19]

To sum up, primaries have been rare in Latin American presidential elections, but their use is spreading. They undoubtedly open up the process of candidate selection to broader popular participation. They also appear to enhance the ability of parties and coalitions to generate candidates who are internally acceptable, even in contentious environments.

Reelection

The most conspicuous change in electoral institutions in Latin America in the 1990s was the reversal of the long-standing tradition barring immediate reelection in Peru (1993), Argentina (1994), Brazil (1996), and Venezuela (1999). The current status of rules on presidential reelection is shown in Table 2.1.

The high-profile changes to allow incumbent reelection notwithstanding, it is worth noting that, during the same period, the Dominican Republic, Nicaragua, and Paraguay moved in the opposite direction, prohibiting reelection, which had previously not been restricted at all. Other countries also made smaller adjustments to the restrictions associated with presidential terms, with no clear pattern visible. Colombia (1991) disallowed reelection after an intervening term out of office, which had previously been permitted. Panama (1994) increased the required "sitting out" period from one to two terms. Ecuador (1998) allowed reelection after one intervening term, which had previously not been allowed.[20] In short, the particulars of presidential reelection—for example, whether restrictions are permanent or interim— are potentially important, and one should exercise caution before concluding that there is a uniform trend toward reelection in Latin America. Nevertheless, the prominence of the countries that moved toward relaxing restrictions, and the compelling personalities with which each of these reforms is closely associated, are fundamental changes and warrant further consideration.

What does the provision for immediate reelection mean for presidencies in Latin America? In the most straightforward sense, eliminating the restriction allows voters an increased measure of discretion in retaining a popular incumbent for a second term. This is an argument that reelection enhances choice, and therefore the quality of democracy, rectifying one of the central shortcomings of presidentialism cited by Juan Linz,[21] that the no-reelection rule prevents the retention of a competent and popular chief ex-

Table 2.1. Rules on Presidential Reelection

No Reelection	After One Interim Term	After Two Interim Terms	Two Consecutive Terms, Then No Reelection	Two Consecutive Terms, Then One Interim Term
Colombia	Bolivia	Panama	Brazil	Argentina
Costa Rica	Chile		Venezuela	Peru
Guatemala	Dominican Republic			
Honduras	Ecuador			
Mexico	El Salvador			
Nicaragua	Uruguay			
Paraguay				

ecutive. The point would appear to be supported by the resounding reelection victories won by Presidents Fujimori in Peru and Menem in Argentina in 1995, and Cardoso in Brazil in 1998. Reelection may also improve democratic responsiveness, to the extent that the prospect of reelection encourages first-term presidents to be more attentive to citizens' preferences.[22]

The inverse problem, of course, is the abuse of power by presidents seeking to ensure their reelectoral success. Indeed, each of the countries that banned presidential reelection during the past decade had endured extreme cases of such *continuismo* in its recent history—under Alfredo Stroessner in Paraguay, various Somozas in Nicaragua, and Joaquín Balaguer in the Dominican Republic. Prior to the abrupt collapse of Fujimori's presidency, Peru appeared to be moving along this path, and the extraordinary circumstances surrounding the president's removal in November 2000 should not distract us from the danger of *continuismo* that case represented. It is worthwhile, therefore, to review the issues surrounding Fujimori's attempt to hold onto his office.

First, Fujimori's very candidacy in 2000 violated the limit of two consecutive terms embodied in the constitution he himself introduced in 1993. He justified his third candidacy by declaring that his *first* term as president (1990–95) did not count, for having begun under the previous constitution (which allowed no consecutive reelection at all!). When Peru's Constitutional Tribunal rejected Fujimori's creative interpretation of his own charter, the president's compliant congressional majority fired the offending judges—a blatantly unconstitutional move. During the 2000 campaign, Fujimori's supporters systematically intimidated opposition candidates and disrupted their campaign rallies; his administration used state resources to pressure the Peruvian media to slant its campaign coverage; and there were irregularities in the vote count, particularly in the first round. The second round was marred by Toledo's withdrawal from the race. His rationale, that guarantees for clean elections were still not in place, was plausible, but his position was undermined by opinion polls suggesting that Toledo's momentum had crested and that Fujimori would win the runoff. In the end, even acknowledging Fujimori's genuine electoral support and the prospect that he might have been beaten by a more resolute opponent, his 2000 victory must serve as a warning that presidential *continuismo* by means of intimidation and fraud has not been relegated decisively to the past.

The case of Argentina's President Carlos Menem illustrates other institutional subtleties that can accompany presidential reelection. In his initial term, Menem had successfully stacked the Argentine Supreme Court with compliant justices, who subsequently ratified his constitutionally dubious expansions of presidential power. In order to secure the necessary legislative support for constitutional reform allowing reelection, however, Menem acquiesced to opposition demands to restore the Court to its original size, removing many of his cronies and thus restoring greater balance to the Court. One upshot was that Menem's attempt to read Argentina's two-consecutive-term clause in a way analogous to President Fujimori in Peru faced a double institutional obstacle. First, many politicians in Menem's own party preferred the president's rival, Eduardo Duhalde, as the Peronist candidate. Emboldened by the political opposition to the president's overtures, the Supreme Court ruled unanimously in March 1999 against appeals that would have allowed a third consecutive Menem candidacy. The Court's action, which was supported by a congressional majority consisting of pro-Duhalde Peronists and all other parties, thus deterred Menem from further pursuing the Peronist nomination. In short, the bargain Menem struck in 1994 secured his first reelection, but the longer-term effect was to restore the potential for judicial independence from the executive, balancing power more evenly among the executive, the legislature, and the courts than had been the case earlier in the decade.[23]

A couple of other points warrant consideration with respect to presidential reelection. First, ending presidents' automatic status as lame ducks should increase the authority of incumbent presidents over other public officials by extending the prospective control of incumbents over patronage and prospects for advancement farther down the political career ladder. In Venezuela in early 2000, for example, President Chávez's impressive public support, coupled with the adoption of his new constitution allowing for successive six-year presidential terms, suggests he could hold the presidency for up to twelve more consecutive years. Within his party, the Movimiento Quinta República (MVR, Fifth Republic Movement), his personal discretion over candidate nominations appears to be even greater than that of incumbent presidents under the ancien régime, as described by Michael Coppedge.[24] This encouraged deference among lower-level politicians within the MVR in the run-up to the 2000 "mega-elections." Chávez and the MVR's Comando Táctico Nacional (CTN, National Tactic Command, the party's central committee) were generally coordinated in their announcements of endorsed candidates, but not always. When Chávez made announcements on his radio program of endorsements that did not correspond to the CTN's, the latter subsequently scrambled to amend its candidate list and ratify the presidential decision.[25] The contrast with the status of incumbent Costa Rican presidents with respect to their parties' aspirants and nominees is striking. In the latter country, once a new presidential nominee is selected, that candidate's expected future control over executive power and patronage allows him to supplant the incumbent president's authority over other politicians.[26] In Venezuela, by contrast, the prospect of Chávez's extended control over the executive elicits deference from subordinates in his party.[27]

One final thought with respect to presidential reelection has to do with a potential problem associated with "punctuated" reelection, or requirements for presidents to sit out interim terms before being eligible to run again. In most cases, the required sitting out period is one term. This opens up the possibility that an incumbent president prohibited from immediate reelection may be privately inclined to undermine his own party's immediate electoral success. If another politician from the incumbent's own party wins control of the executive, with all the policymaking and patronage powers that entails, then the outgoing president will almost certainly be eclipsed as the party's leading figure. If the incumbent's party *loses* the next election, however, the outgoing president may retain prominence as leader of the opposition, as well as an aura as the champion capable of winning a national election. Sitting out requirements, therefore, present potential moral hazard problems for ambitious politicians and their parties. This tension was evident in Venezuela, among former Presidents Jaime Lusinchi, Carlos Andrés Pérez, and other aspirants within Acción Democrática (AD, Democratic Action), under the 1961 constitution, which allowed reelection after two interim terms.[28] It was also widely believed that two-term Argentine President Carlos Menem failed to support the candidacy of his party's nominee, Eduardo Duhalde, in 1999 in part because Menem aspires to retain leadership of the Peronist Party (PJ) and attempt to regain the presidency in 2003. The moral hazard problem is particularly acute under the Peruvian and Argentine formats, because an outgoing incumbent whose party retains the presidency will confront a co-partisan *who is eligible for reelection* at the end of the required sitting out period. There is every reason to expect this arrangement to generate perverse incentives within parties.

Removing Presidents

Impeachment and Quasi-Impeachment

In terms of drama, no development in Latin American executive-legislative relations over the past decade surpasses the removal of presidents from office—not by military coup, but by parliamentary action. Indeed, for all the attention Fujimori's 1992 *autogolpe* in Peru and Chávez's plebiscitary attack on Venezuela's Congress and courts have rightly attracted, it is important to note that legislatures deposing presidents have been more common over the past decade than the reverse.

Table 2.2 outlines the cases in which the term of one or the other branch has been prematurely terminated, along with a couple of near misses, during the past decade. In each of these cases, charges of corruption were levied by one side, or both, against the other. The allegations against Collor, Samper, and Alemán, moreover, were (or are) sufficiently well documented as to be compelling. In these instances, one could reasonably conclude that the corruption issue itself is sufficient as a cause of the crisis. It is also noteworthy that, in two of the three cases, both branches survived the crisis—and even in Brazil, Collor was later acquitted of the corruption charges on appeal to the Supreme Court because the overwhelming evidence against him was acquired illegally.[29] Corruption alone, then, does not appear to be sufficient to bring conflict between the branches to the most decisive conclusion.

Most of these cases, however, are also marked by severe conflict over policy, and over the relative powers of each branch to implement its preferred economic plan. Presidents Collor, Pérez, Fujimori (in 1992), Bucaram, Mahuad, and Alemán all faced substantial legislative opposition, as well as popular protests, against their imposition of economic austerity policies.[30] Pérez's removal, although legally based on irregularities in appropriating government funds, is widely believed to have been motivated by opposition to the president's sudden imposition of neoliberal shock therapy, which alienated even his own co-partisans in Congress. Bucaram's removal was similarly motivated, and Mahuad's was triggered by his move to dollarize Ecuador's economy. Alemán's troubles were preceded not only by reports of illegal enrichment, but also by bitter resentment of his plan to privatize the social security system, and the method by which he pushed that reform through the National Assembly.[31] President Chávez's economic posture is more difficult to discern, but he appears, if anything, less inclined toward neoliberalism than the Congress he replaced, and the steadfast legislative opposition to his political reform agenda was certainly central to his insistence on its dissolution. Cubas Grau's crisis was triggered by objections by

Table 2.2. Curtailment of Presidential and Legislative Terms in the Past Decade

Country	Year	Survivor	Circumstances
Peru	1992	President	*Autogolpe* by President Fujimori, supported by military, disbands Congress and courts.
Brazil	1992	Congress	President Collor, having been impeached by the chamber for corruption, and facing certain conviction by the Senate, resigns.
Guatemala	1993	Congress	President Serrano attempts an *autogolpe* against Congress; his action prompts strong popular protests and repudiation by the Constitutional Court, whose decision is supported by the military. The incumbent Congress selects a replacement for Serrano, and subsequently agrees to dissolve itself and face new elections a year early, in 1994.
Venezuela	1993	Congress	Congress removes President Pérez from office on charges of misappropriation of funds and embezzlement. After prolonged legal preceedings, Pérez is convicted by the Supreme Court of misappropriation, but the embezzlement charges are dropped.
Colombia*	1996	Both	The Chamber of Deputies, dominated by President Samper's own Liberal Party, and many of whose members are also suspected of having accepted payments from drug traffickers, votes not to pursue impeachment proceedings against the president, despite solid evidence that Samper's 1994 campaign had received over $U.S.4 million from the Cali cartel.
Ecuador	1997	Congress	Congress votes, 44–34, to remove President Abdalá Bucaram from office for "mental incompetence"; installs congressional President Fabio Alarcón as president. The military chief declares his forces "absolutely apolitical," and states that "We are leaving it to the politicians to find a prompt solution to this problem." Bucaram flees the country in the face of popular protest.
Paraguay	1999	Congress	President Raul Cubas Grau's pardon of former coup-plotter, General Lino Oviedo, is countermanded by the Supreme Court. The president's refusal to recognize the Court decision prompts impeachment preceedings in Congress. With an impeachment vote pending, and facing escalating street protests

(continued)

Table 2.2. *(continued)*

			over the assassination of the vice-president and attacks by Oviedo supporters on demonstrators, the president resigns and is replaced by the president of the Senate.
Venezuela	1999	President	The Constituent Assembly, convoked by newly elected President Chávez and dominated by his supporters, declares itself sovereign over both policy and matters of constitutional reform, thus rendering the existing Congress superfluous. Congress objects to what it regards as a unsurpation of power by Chávez, but acquiesces in the face of popular opposition.
Ecuador	2000	Congress	In the face of massive protests by indigenous groups, junior military officers lead a coup, removing President Mahuad from office. Immediately thereafter, acquiescing to international pressure, the officers renounce any intention to govern and turn power over to former Vice-President Noboa, who is sworn into office before Congress.
Nicaragua*	2000	Both	Assembly opponents attempt to remove President Alemán on charges of corruption and illegal enrichment, but fail to muster sufficient votes.
Peru	2000	Congress	A leaked videotape of President Fujimori's security adviser bribing a legislator triggers a crisis marked by charges of fraud and intimidation of opposition political forces. Fujimori initially agrees to call early elections and leave office after an interim of ten months. As revelations of corruption build, however, Fujimori tenders his resignation from abroad. The emboldened Congress rejects the resignation, removes Fujimori from office on grounds of "moral incapacity," and replaces him with the president of Congress, drawn from the opposition, to serve out the interim term.

*Cases of significant procedural moves toward removal of presidents that stalled.

both Congress and the Supreme Court over his use of the presidential authority to issue pardons.

What are we to make, then, of the executive-legislative standoffs that reached crisis proportions in the 1990s? I suggest three central conclusions.

First, although Table 2.2 presents a useful box score, examining these cases alone would risk drawing faulty inferences due to selection on the dependent variable: constitutional crisis. That is, executive-legislative conflict may be present in these crises, but such divided government is not necessarily a recipe for constitutional crisis. In the most comprehensive analysis of the issue, José Cheibub[32] finds no statistical relationship between partisan deadlock between the branches and regime failure. Most presidential administrations in Latin America confront divided government,[33] and since the wave of democratization beginning in the 1970s, the vast majority has governed without constitutional crises.

Second, when conflict between the branches *has* reached crisis proportions, Congresses have prevailed more often than presidents. This statistic should not be interpreted to imply that Latin American legislatures are evenly matched with presidents in their influence over policy under conditions of normal politics, but it does cast doubt on the long-standing and widespread reputation of Latin American legislatures as ineffectual and dominated by executives. The quasi-constitutional manner in which many of the crises were resolved is not encouraging for those who value procedural consistency (although most would probably regard these results preferable to military rule), but the outcomes suggest that, when constitutional crises present themselves, Congresses in Latin America are formidable presidential opponents.

Third, the two cases where presidents have prevailed were instances of widely popular anti-politicians confronting legislative opposition from already-discredited traditional parties. The point is highlighted in relief in the justification offered by the architect of President Chávez's efforts to stack the Venezuelan judiciary. Responding to criticisms of the judicial selection process, Manuel Quijada explicitly defended the political bias with reference to the bankruptcy of the party system Chávez had displaced: "What do you want? If you remained silent during forty years of magistrates [beholden to the two traditional parties], then you should be able to put up with those of the Fifth Republic Movement for twelve years [the period Chávez intends to remain in power]."[34] Fujimori exhibited similar scorn for Peru's established parties during his showdown with Congress in 1992, and opinion polls subsequent to the *autogolpe* indicate that the public shared his opinion on this count.[35] Where parties retain even modest levels of support, in contrast, legislative-executive conflict has generally been tempered, and divided government has proven workable (if not pretty), as in Argentina, Bolivia, Brazil, Chile, El Salvador, Mexico, and Uruguay. Thus, measures aimed at strengthening the links between voters and legislators, such as the extension of primaries, smaller-magnitude electoral districts, and the elimination of prohibitions on reelection (discussed below) may deter presidential penchants for *autogolpes*.

Recall

One other institutional development pertaining to the removal of presidents worth noting is the recall provision in Article 72 of the Venezuelan constitution of 1999. Recall provisions are not uncommon in comparative constitutions, but their exercise is rare and the threshold for removing elected officials is generally a majority vote. The Venezuelan recall is innovative, and unique, in that the threshold for removal is the number of votes cast for the president (or any other elected official) in the original popular vote. Thus, given that Chávez won with almost 60 percent of the vote in 2000, the obstacles to remove him (assuming similar turnout) during the 2000–2006 term through this procedure are formidable. But if a president were elected with a plurality in a divided field (e.g., a vote split 35 percent-30 percent-25 percent-10 percent), the threshold could be quite low, and the prospect of recall might be not at all remote.

The Venezuelan brand of recall allows for the retention of presidential election by plurality, with the accompanying incentives for party system consolidation, but also provides a safety valve in the event of an "Allende scenario," in which a plurality winner faces intransigent opposition. In this sense, Venezuelan recall addresses Linz's[36] criticism of presidentialism as generating false majoritarian mandates. If recall is a credible scenario, particularly for those elected by narrow pluralities, then it should discourage such presidents from taking actions that might alienate majorities, and encourage them to cultivate support across a broad cross-section of the population.

Legislative Capacity

The Parliamentary and Hybrid Options

The basic thesis that presidential regimes are more prone than parliamentary regimes to democratic breakdown is supported by broad cross-national data,[37] lending credence to the more specific claim that the uneven record of democracy in Latin America is in part attributable to constitutional design.[38] In the initial period of transition away from military government, academics and political reformers alike devoted considerable attention to whether presidentialism ought to be replaced by parliamentarism, or by some sort of hybrid regime in which cabinets would depend on assembly confidence. In Argentina, a presidential commission appointed during the Alfonsín administration recommended a hybrid constitutional design modeled on the French system. Similar ideas circulated widely in Chile, and Brazil went so far as to submit the option of a pure parliamentary system to a popular vote in 1993. Voters soundly rejected the option (along with that of constitutional monarchy), however, in favor of the presidential status quo. Proposals for fundamental changes of regime type fizzled elsewhere as well.

Whatever the merits of parliamentarism, and notwithstanding its appeal to academics, Latin American constitutions remain fundamentally presidential. Within Latin American presidentialism, however, requirements of assembly confidence for ministers are not unheard of. Such provisions were prominent in Chile a century ago, and in Ecuador, Uruguay, and Peru more recently.[39] Moreover, recent constitutional reforms in both Argentina (1994) and Venezuela (1999) moved these countries one step closer to hybrid regime status, creating the positions I will characterize as *first ministers* (called chief of the cabinet of ministers in Argentina, and vice-president in Venezuela). Peru maintained this position (called prime minister) in its new constitution of 1993. These first ministers are constitutionally designated as chairs of the cabinet, and are removable by Congress—an absolute majority in Peru's unicameral body, 60 percent in Venezuela's, and by concurrent absolute majorities in bicameral Argentina. Theoretically, this provision may encourage presidential negotiation with, and deference to, legislative majorities by tying the survival of at least part of the executive to assembly confidence.

None of these constitutions represents a substantial move toward a French-style hybrid regime, however, for a couple of reasons.[40] First, presidents in every case can name *and* remove the first minister, whereas the legislature can only remove the minister. Thus the first minister is really more a creature of the president than a joint, intermediate actor. In comparative perspective, then, these charters are much more like Russia under Yeltsin's 1993 constitution than like the French Fifth Republic, Finland, Portugal, or, for that matter, Poland. Second, and also like Russia, the Venezuelan and Peruvian constitutions include provisions that allow the president to dissolve the assembly if it dismisses the first minister repeatedly (two times in Peru, three in Venezuela). The arrangements by which first ministers are subject to assembly confidence are relatively new, so it is difficult to gauge their impact. However, based on the constitutional details, these do not appear to be serious steps toward establishing assembly confidence in cabinets anywhere near akin to that in parliamentary, or even the long-standing hybrid, regimes of Western Europe.

Unicameralism

In terms of altering the institutional environment of executive-legislative bargaining, a more striking development than the creation of first ministers is the replacement of bicameralism with unicameralism. In both Peru and Venezuela, the change was initiated by presidents in the name of streamlining government and increasing efficiency. Many opponents of Presidents Fujimori and Chávez greeted the reform skeptically, basing arguments on the classical ideas of Montesquieu and *The Federalist*[41] that unicameralism removes a potential layer of restraint on executive authority, and hence is a step toward tyranny. Former Venezuelan Constituent Assembly member Ricardo Combellas'[42] reservations about unicameralism, in contrast, are based on the logical complement of the classical understanding. Combellas argues that, under unicameralism, a swing to control of the single chamber by a majority in opposition to the president—in midterm elections, for example—spells a head-on clash between the branches, whereas bicameralism holds out the possibility that the president can triangulate, building alliances with legislators in the less hostile chamber. By providing a lifeline for an embattled president, then, bicameralism might encourage negotiation and moderation.

The specific effects of a shift to unicameralism depend, of course, on whether the preferences and behavior of the (eliminated) upper chamber would have differed systematically from that of the (surviving) lower chamber. If the composition of the two chambers would be identical or nearly so, then the argument against bicameralism on the grounds of waste and duplication is more compelling, and any argument about the effects of unicameralism on the effectiveness of checks and balances—whether the traditional *Federalist*-type interpretation or Combellas' inverse—is less so.

A key factor affecting whether composition of chambers is likely to be similar is the method by which seats are apportioned. In many Latin American bicameral systems, Senate seats are apportioned on a federal-style principle, with equal representation of geographical subunits—whether states, provinces, or departments. Such Senates tend to be severely malapportioned—more so than lower chambers, where seats are generally distributed more or less according to population. A second group of Latin American Senates are elected from single, national districts, rendering the issue of malapportionment for the upper house moot. Chile is a residual case, as the two-member districts designed by the outgoing Pinochet regime do not correspond to previously existing political or administrative units for either the Chamber or the Senate.

Table 2.3 summarizes the apportionment structure of the bicameral systems in Latin America, including Peru and Venezuela prior to the unicameral reforms. In the Peruvian case, the method of apportionment would lead one to expect minimal difference in the composition of the chambers, whereas in Venezuela federal-style apportionment left open the possibility for incongruence between chambers. In both systems, upper and lower chamber term lengths were the same, and both chambers were renewed at each election in their entirety.

Table 2.4 shows that, notwithstanding Venezuela's apportionment struc-

Table 2.3. Relative Levels of Malapportionment in Bicameral Systems

Country	Year	Federal System	Lower Chamber Malapportionment[a]	Upper Chamber Malapportionment	Upper minus Lower
Federal Style					
Argentina	1995	Yes	0.14	0.49	0.35
Bolivia	1997	No	0.17	0.38	0.21
Brazil	1998	Yes	0.09	0.40	0.31
Dominican Republic	1986	No	0.08	0.38	0.30
Mexico	1997	Yes	0.06	0.23	0.17
Venezuela	1998	Yes	0.07	0.33	0.26
National District for Upper House					
Colombia	1994	No	0.13	0.00	−0.13
Paraguay	1993	No	0.04	0.00	−0.04
Peru	1990	No	0.00[b]	0.00	0.00
Uruguay	1992	No	0.03	0.00	−0.03
Unique Two-Member Districts in Both					
Chile	1997	No	0.15	0.31	0.16

[a]The malapportionment index, and scores, are from Samuels (2000). The index runs from 0 to 1—0 representing perfect correspondence between the distribution of population across districts and the distribution of seats; 1 representing a hypothetical arrangement by which all seats represent the vote of a single voter while all other voters are accorded no representation.
[b]The lower chamber index reported is that for the unicameral assembly for the 1995 election. It is apportioned by the same method as had been the Chamber of Deputies prior to the cameral reform.

ture, the partisan distribution of seats correlated strongly across chambers in both countries during most of the period preceding the cameral reforms. In no case for either country do the two chambers produce contending plurality —much less majority—parties across chambers, and the overall distributions of seats always follow each other closely. In both cases congruence declined somewhat as the traditional party systems disintegrated in the elections immediately preceding constitutional reforms.

Based on both the apportionment principle and electoral results, one could reasonably consider the Peruvian Senate to have been superfluous. Electoral results suggest a similar conclusion about the Venezuelan Senate, although its apportionment suggested a federal-style representation of the states. In this sense, the timing of the switch to unicameralism is puzzling. A series of reforms initiated in the late 1980s established direct elections for Venezuelan state governors, who had previously been presidential appointees, thus encouraging greater independence from national politicians. Reforms in the revenue sharing system between federal and state gov-

Table 2.4. Partisan Representation in the Peruvian and Venezuelan Congresses (by chamber)

	Peru					
	1980		**1985**		**1990**	
Party	Chamber	Senate	Ch	Sen	Ch	Sen
APRA	32	30	59	50	29	27
Acción Popular	54	43	6	8	14	13
Ptdo. Pop. Cristiano	6	10	7	12	14	8
Izquierda Unida	6	15	27	25	9	10
Front of Independents	2	2	1	2	2	2
Cambio '90					18	23
Mov. Libertad					5	10
F. Indpt. Moralizador					4	
Izq. Socialista					2	5
Other				3	3	2
Correlation Coefficient	0.97	0.97	0.92			

	Venezuela									
	1978		**1983**		**1988**		**1993**		**1998**	
Party	Ch	Sen	Ch	Sen	Ch	Sen	Ch	Sen	Ch	Sen
Acción Dem.	44	48	57	64	48	48	27	32	30	35
COPEI	42	48	30	32	33	43	26	28	13	14
MAS	6	5	5	5	9	7	11	2	11	9
La Causa Radical							20	18	2	2
Convergencia							13	20	2	7
Mov. Quinta Rep.									18	14
Proyecto Ven.									10	7
Patria Para Todos									6	7
Other	9	0	9	0	10	2	3	0	8	5
Correlation Coefficient	0.99		0.99		0.97		0.92		0.94	

ernments also increased the resources and responsibilities of state governments. In short, reforms that predated the Chávez period had substantially increased the substance of Venezuelan federalism, making states more important units of representation. Although President Chávez has touted decentralization and local accountability, his elimination of the Senate would appear to be a step away from guaranteeing the Venezuelan states meaningful representation under the new constitution.

In sum, based on partisan distributions of legislative seats, bicameralism had not previously been a critical element of Peru's institutional design; neither did it have much impact in Venezuela in practice, despite federal-style apportionment for the Senate. By the 1990s, however, changes in the Venezuelan party system, coupled with reforms aimed at strengthening state governments, offered the potential that Venezuelan bicameralism could have been increasingly consequential. Ironically, and perhaps by design, it was at precisely this moment that bicameralism was replaced in Venezuela by unicameralism.

Legislative Term Limits

Legislative term limits are another feature of institutional design with important implications for the strength of political parties and of legislatures more generally. In contrast to restrictions on presidents, prohibitions of any sort on the reelection of legislators (term limits) are relatively rare. Only Mexico, Costa Rica, and the Philippines constitutionally prohibit the reelection of legislators at the national level.[43] The future of legislative term limits in Mexico and Costa Rica is uncertain, particularly in the former, where the end of one-party dominance opens the possibility that Congress might challenge the supremacy of the executive. If this is to happen, it will be necessary to encourage electoral independence and the development of policy expertise among legislators. Neither of these is likely as long as reelection is proscribed.

In Costa Rica, the Philippines, and many of the U.S. states, prohibitions on legislative reelection were adopted by forces *outside* the traditional party system—by a post-civil war constituent assembly, by a commission appointed by a provisional government, and by direct democracy through citizen initiatives, respectively. In each case, the move to term limits was motivated by the sense that unlimited reelection had generated a class of professional legislators who used the advantages of incumbency to perpetuate themselves in office. These were, then, cases of term limits by "insurgency." In Mexico, by contrast, leaders of the Partido Nacional Revolucionario (PNR, National Revolutionary Party) initiated the adoption of legislative term limits in 1933 in order to strengthen the dependence of legislators on the national party and weaken their ties to local constituencies.[44]

The impact of term limits on legislative parties depends on the relative control by party leaders over *legislature-specific* goods that legislators want versus their control over *non-legislative career paths*. First, legislators are

Table 2.5. Resources Controlled by Party Leaders and Valued by Ambitious Legislators

Legislature-specific	Non-legislative
• Nomination for reelection	• Nomination for election to other offices
• Reelection campaign funding	• Campaign funding for other offices
• Offices and staff	• Appointments to government positions
• Committee assignments	• Access to non-governmental, post-legislative
• Promotion in the hierarchy of legislative leadership	employment
• Control over the legislative agenda	

politically ambitious, meaning that they desire reelection if it is allowed, or other political office if it is not.[45] Second, leaders in different political parties —and in different countries—vary in the control they exercise over the resources that aid political careers. These resources, outlined in Table 2.5, may be legislature-specific or they may pertain to non-legislative career advancement.

If party leaders exercise substantial control over legislature-specific resources but less over the resources that facilitate non-legislative careers, then we should expect term limits to diminish the authority of party leaders over rank-and-file legislators. For example, in the United States, at both the state and federal levels, legislative party leaders generally exercise substantial control over legislature-specific resources but relatively little over non-legislative resources. Thus, prohibiting reelection in the United States undermines the value of the legislature-specific resources that parties control, whereas party control over non-legislative goods is minimal to begin with. Therefore, term limits in the United States weaken the influence of legislative party leaders over career-oriented legislators.[46]

Along similar lines, consider the case of Costa Rica. The prohibition on consecutive reelection eliminates the possibility of legislative careers, undermining the value to deputies of legislature-specific goods. What matters to politically ambitious deputies are post-legislative political career opportunities which, in Costa Rica's unitary system of government, mean executive branch appointments which, in turn, go almost exclusively to the president's co-partisans, generating dependence on executive-controlled patronage for post-legislative career prospects.[47] In this sense, Costa Rica appears to resemble Mexico. The critical difference, however, is that the identity of the executive who will control patronage is far more uncertain in Costa Rica than has been the case in Mexico until just recently. First, Costa Rican presidential terms are perfectly concurrent with legislative terms, and presidents cannot be reelected. Thus no incumbent president ever controls appointments relevant to any incumbent deputy. Second, the Costa Rican presidency has been subject to close competition during the entire term limits period, so deputies cannot count on their party controlling access to patronage after their service in the legislature ends. Finally, within parties, competition over presidential nominations is open and fierce, and presidential aspirants solicit endorsements and support from incumbent deputies. Thus, even if a deputy's co-partisan wins the subsequent presidential election, one's factional affiliation during the previous nomination battles affects one's prospects for a post-legislative appointment.

Term limits adopted by insurgency in Costa Rica and the United States undermine party discipline because they reduce the value of the legislature-specific resources that leaders control while non-legislative resources controlled by party leaders are scarce and in uncertain supply. As the leader of the Assembly's National Liberal Party (PLN) delegation put it: "Because of term limits, as minority leader, I have no stick to beat anyone with."[48] Term limits were adopted in Mexico at the initiative of the PRN leadership with a different calculus in mind. The national party expected, rightly, to exercise firm control for an extended period over the non-legislative resources valuable to ambitious politicians—nominations to other offices, campaign finance, and an abundance of political appointments at all levels. In the Mexican context, term limits strengthened the control of central party leaders over rank-and-file legislators.

The conditions under which legislative term limits fostered party discipline in Mexico, however, appear to be eroding quickly. Most important, no party can expect indefinite control over executive patronage, so the value of a promise that party loyalty will be rewarded with future patronage is increasingly dubious. Electoral competitiveness, moreover, increases the appeal to all parties of a strengthened Congress, as a hedge against losses in presidential elections and an effective counterweight to the executive branch. This motivation suggests abandoning term limits, which by definition rob legislatures of the policy expertise that accrues with years of lawmaking experience. The decline of one-party dominance in Mexico, therefore, undermines the rationale for legislative term limits on two counts: by making control over post-legislative patronage less secure, and by increasing the attractiveness to all parties of a strong and autonomous legislature.

Policymaking Procedures

So far, I have reviewed elements of institutional design pertaining to the origin and survival of executives and legislatures. I turn attention now to two matters of policymaking procedure: the budgetary process, and the connection between legislative voting and transparency.

Budgets

Budgets are natural objects of interest for students of political institutions for a number of reasons. First, they obviously matter—politicians, bureaucrats, and interested parties fight tenaciously over both aggregate levels and the distribution of appropriations. Second, they must be created and passed every year, so they provide a steady stream of data that can be compared over time. Third, budgetary allocations can be counted, and so offer a precise look at the trade-offs among competing values that are at the heart of politics. In other work, summarized briefly here, I develop and test models of how budgetary procedures in Latin America affect spending decisions. My principal argument is that the procedure by which budget legislation is drafted, amended, and passed into law directly affects the tendency of regimes toward fiscal restraint and the relative bargaining strength of executives versus legislatures on spending policy.

Consider budgetary policymaking under four formats found in presidential democracies: the package veto, item veto, aggregate ceiling, and item-by-item ceiling formats. The first is a simplified version of budgetary policymaking in the United States and elsewhere, in which the Congress presents the president with a budget law, which the president must either accept in its entirety or veto, in which case spending is set at some reversion point known to both players. Under the item veto format, found in Latin American countries such as Argentina and Brazil, the Congress passes a budget and the president then has the option of vetoing specific spending provisions while promulgating the rest, with spending on those vetoed items set at the known reversion point. Under the aggregate ceiling format, the president proposes a budget that establishes the overall maximum level of spending; amendments in the legislature can increase spending on some programs only if those increases are offset by cuts to other items. Congressional amendments to spending legislation that shuffle funds among programs may then be subject to presidential veto, which implies some reversion policy in the absence of agreement (e.g., Uruguay, Philippines); or, in the absence of a veto that requires a supermajority override (e.g., Peru), congressional majorities may be able to make their amendments stick. Finally, under the item-by-item ceiling format, used in Chile, the president proposes the budget, but only amendments that reduce specific items are allowed. Again, amended budget bills may or may not be subject to a presidential veto, and if they are, the location of the reversion spending policy becomes central to bargaining.[49]

I refer readers interested in the details of the spatial model and empirical tests of its hypotheses to Lisa Baldez and John Carey, and Carey.[50] For present purposes, I simply review the basic logic of bargaining under each procedure across two spending programs—guns versus butter, for example—assuming the president wants higher spending than Congress on one program, and Congress prefers more than the president on the other.

Under the package veto format, Congress will offer a bill setting spending on both programs as close to its own ideal as possible, constrained by the president's willingness to sign the bill rather than accept the policy that pertains if no agreement is reached (no spending in some countries; in others, spending at the previous year's level). Under the item veto format, the president has the ability to unpack congressional proposals, effectively considering each program separately. Congress, then, can think of itself as making two separate proposals. For the program on which Congress prefers less than the president, it should propose its own ideal spending level, which the president should accept rather than risk getting even less spending as a result of deadlock. For the program on which Congress prefers more than the president, Congress can propose spending somewhat higher than the president's ideal, constrained by the president's willingness to accept the deadlock outcome on that program.

Under the aggregate ceiling format, any proposal the president makes establishes a budget ceiling, which defines the possible trade-offs among all spending programs. If Congress' ideal combination of spending policies across all programs is located below this ceiling (i.e., it prefers less overall spending than the president proposes), it can simply amend the proposal to its ideal policy. If Congress prefers more spending than the proposal, then its best response is to amend the president's budget to the point on the ceiling that is closest to its ideal.[51] Theoretically, there should be one such best response for every possible ceiling set by the president's proposal. If the president knows the Congress' preferences, then she knows what each of those best responses would entail. Thinking ahead, the president should tailor her initial proposal so as to elicit the response that produces a budgetary outcome closest to her own ideal. The catch is that the president's *strategic* proposal may very well *not* be the same as her *sincere* proposal—that is, the combination of spending levels she most prefers. Specifically, the president should propose less than her ideal under the aggregate ceiling format, to prevent a Congress with different spending priorities from hijacking the budget proposal to its own ends.

Finally, under the item-by-item ceiling, the president proposes an entire budget; Congress can amend specific items downward only. The president can simply propose her ideal spending level on all programs. There is no advantage to proposing less. Congress, in turn, accepts the president's proposals on programs where it prefers *higher* spending (because it cannot appropriate more), and uses its amendment power to reduce spending to its own ideal where it prefers less. The outcome is spending on every program that reflects the preferences of whichever branch, Congress or the executive, is most parsimonious.

The model illustrates the importance of proposal authority, restrictions on amendments, veto powers, and the nature of the deadlock (or reversion) policy on bargaining between the branches. It also generates hypotheses about the effects of specific configurations of powers on spending policy. For example, overall spending should be highest under the package veto format, which encourages logroll-type compromises in which each branch consents to some spending preferred by the other in exchange for funding for its own programs. Spending should be lowest under the item-by-item ceiling format, which privileges moves to cut spending, discouraging logrolls. Spending levels should fall between these extremes under the item veto and aggregate ceiling formats, each of which allow budgetary actors limited means to strike deals at compromise spending levels, while discouraging grand logrolls. It is worth noting that the procedural formats most common throughout Latin America provide presidents commanding authorities, either as holders of the item veto or as budgetary ceiling setters, or both.

Controlling for economic growth rates and the availability of credit to finance government spending, data from thirteen presidential democracies over a ten-year period demonstrate that presidential powers to set spending ceilings through their budget proposals discourage deficits.[52] The effect is compounded when combined with restrictions on legislative amendments to the president's proposal. The same data show no measurable effect of the item veto on deficits. The format by which the presidential proposal establishes item-by-item spending ceilings, as in Chile and South Korea, is most conducive to fiscal austerity.

Legislative Transparency

A final matter of institutional design to which I want to direct attention is legislative voting procedure—specifically, whether votes are recorded and the votes of individual legislators are publicly available. Public availability of legislative voting records is easy to provide through the adoption of relatively inexpensive electronic voting technology, and it contributes to the overall transparency of government, which is a democratic good. Improvements in transparency, moreover, do not require the average citizen to pore over legislative bulletins or surf government Web sites. Politicians and journalists appear willing to do the heavy lifting, once the information is in the public domain. On the other hand, legislators—particularly those in the majority—are not naturally inclined to make voting records public, and will often resist efforts to do so. There appears to be an overall trend, however, toward the publication of legislative voting records, which should be welcomed and encouraged.

To illustrate these points, consider the following. Legislative voting records have been a staple of Brazilian congressional campaigns since the reestablishment of democracy in the mid-1980s, which coincided with the installation in Congress of electronic voting equipment. Voting records are simultaneously points of collective and individual responsibility. Prior to the October 1998 Brazilian congressional elections, billboards around Rio de Janeiro listed names of legislators who had cast votes in favor of President Fernando Henrique Cardoso's economic policies. Cardoso's efforts to privatize state-owned industries, trim the civil service, and cut social security were endorsed by the International Monetary Fund (IMF), opposed vehemently by parties on the Left, and supported only with trepidation by members of an uneasy multiparty coalition spanning the Center and Right that nominally backed Cardoso in Congress. Legislators who voted yes were rewarded by the executive with targeted policy concessions and with patronage, but were excoriated on the billboards as *traidores da Pátria* and *entreguistas*—traitors who would sell the country out to foreign domination.[53]

In 1998, as part of a modernization plan endorsed by President Fujimori, the Peruvian Congress installed electronic voting equipment, allowing legislators to vote with the push of a button. The new technology presented a dilemma for Peruvian legislators in that the electronic system automatically produces a record of each legislator's vote. The traditional method of handraising, on the other hand, had the convenient property of maintaining the anonymity of individual legislators (except to those physically present and watching) and obscuring the partisan breakdown of support and opposition.[54] The dilemma came to a head on September 24, 1998, as Congress debated a motion to interpellate the minister of the presidency over allegations of corruption.[55] Opposition legislators called for an electronic vote so as to make each legislator's, and each party's, position public. The president of the Congress, Ricardo Marcenaro Frers, of the majority Nueva Mayoría party, demurred, arguing that the electronic method was slow and unwieldy, drawing derision from Henry Pease of the opposition Unión por el Perú (UPP, Union for Peru): "You cannot argue against the electronic system because it's slow. The whole reason for electronic voting is so citizens know how their congresspeople voted, so [votes] can be publicly justified. It's an instrument of democracy and transparency, which is why Congress spent as much as it did [to have it installed], not so we can use it on some votes and not on others. It has to be used, sir."

When Marcenaro pressed on with handraising, Pease summoned a rule allowing a qualified minority to slow legislative procedure to a near standstill, continuing to hammer on the transparency issue: "What the country is going to notice is that the parliamentary majority is afraid that, through the Internet and other mechanisms, its votes on some matters will be made visible."

During a prolonged debate, some of Marcenaro's co-partisans eventually broke ranks. Sandoval Aguirre (Nueva Mayoría) wanted the record to be clear that it was a Nueva Mayoría majority that had the electronic voting system installed in the first place, and that "One reason for this system is that it leaves a record of votes for current political analysts and for history, so that how each one of us voted is known; and those congresspersons that run for reelection, when they face the voters, they'll have to explain how it is that on each of the issues they voted as they did. . . . This process of modernization puts us among the most developed parliaments in Latin America, among other things due to the use of technology that favors democracy."

Finally, Marcenaro allowed a motion to take subsequent votes electronically, which passed unanimously (by show of hands!). Shortly thereafter, the Peruvian Congress began posting records of all electronic votes on its Web site.

Compare the Brazilian and Peruvian cases with that of Venezuela. Electronic voting machines were installed in the Venezuelan Congress in 1998, but they have been left idle by four successive legislatures: the Congress that initially installed them; the Asamblea Nacional Constituyente (ANC, National Constituent Assembly) of 1999; the interim "Congresillo" (officially, the Comisión Legislativa Nacional [National Legislative Commission]), a body of twenty-one members appointed by Chávez to exercise legislative authority between the dissolution of the ANC and the establishment of a new Asamblea Nacional; and the new Asamblea Nacional, elected in 2000.[56] The record of floor debates from the ANC demonstrates that opposition legislators petitioned for recorded votes on the grounds of transparency and to establish a record of legislative intent, but that the requests were perceived as threatening and were rejected by legislative leaders.[57]

The Venezuelan case illustrates the obstacle that legislative leaders can present to transparency, even in the face of demands from the rank and file. On similar grounds, voting records are not public in Argentina, Bolivia, Colombia, Costa Rica, Ecuador, El Salvador, or Guatemala. Yet resistance by legislative leaders is susceptible to steady—and public—pressure. In Peru and Mexico, the majority party leaders eventually acceded to requests from opposition politicians and from academics, making electronic vote records available on the Internet. A similar dynamic may be at work in Colombia, pursuant to the exposure in spring 2000 of a massive corruption scandal that prompted President Andrés Pastrana to propose the publication of legislative voting records as part of a massive legislative reform package.[58] Although the fate of the reforms is unclear at the time of writing, the proposal to publish votes has attracted support from academics and non-governmental organizations (NGOs), who have continued to press for its realization.[59]

It is reasonable to expect a ratchet effect in making votes public, in that once the practice is instituted, for whatever reason, it becomes difficult to justify eliminating it, either on political or logistical grounds. This should discourage backsliding. We should regard it as promising that, during the 1990s, the following Latin American countries either regularly used, or at least installed, electronic voting systems: Brazil, Chile, Mexico, Nicaragua, Peru, and Venezuela; and that the adoption of electronic voting is under consideration in the Dominican Republic, Ecuador, El Salvador, and Guatemala.

Trends in Institutional Performance and Recommendations for Reform

Presidentialism in Latin America at the turn of the century is far from problem free. In the Andean region, in particular, crises of governance are daunting, with widespread protests against austerity policies in Ecuador and Bolivia, a devastating civil war in Colombia, apprehension about presidential aggrandizement in Venezuela, and a wholesale crisis of regime legitimacy in Peru. In these latter two cases, the viability of legislatures as checks against presidential usurpation of authority are clear and immediate concerns. In the former cases, the crises reflect policy conflicts that transcend executive-legislative relations, and it is less straightforward what effect alternative arrangements of representative institutions would have.

Beyond these current flashpoints, it is important to note some more promising trends in the performance of the elected branches and in their interaction with each other. Where relevant, I also take stock of the effects of institutional reforms over the past decade and their connection to these trends. First, the pretensions and the ability of Latin American militaries to step in and govern in place of elected civilian politicians has continued to decline. Second, in a number of countries, the 1990s witnessed the development —or, in some cases, the reestablishment—of political parties and coalitions with relatively broad electoral appeal, some stability, and a willingness to sustain negotiation over policy with adversaries, whether from a position in government or in opposition. These countries include Argentina, Bolivia, Brazil, Chile, the Dominican Republic, El Salvador, Honduras, Mexico, and Uruguay; and despite their uneven records of late, even Nicaragua and Guatemala must be regarded as having improved on this count relative to the 1980s and earlier.

Institutional reforms that strengthen the connection between citizens and elected officials have played a role here. One example is the adoption of primary elections for presidential candidates, which represents a step toward greater electoral openness, and has contributed to holding together otherwise fractious parties and coalitions. Another example is the removal of prohibitions on presidential reelection. A couple of things are important to note with respect to constraints on presidential reelection. First, reforms in the past decade have not been uniform. The cases in which restrictions were relaxed—Argentina, Peru, Brazil—are prominent and have attracted the most attention, but other countries have increased restrictions. Second, the manner in which Fujimori's third candidacy was engineered rightly invites skepticism about relaxing prohibitions on reelection. Nevertheless, in my judgment, as mechanisms to safeguard fair elections improve, the advantages of presidential reelection outweigh the disadvantages.

Another general pattern has to do with the outcomes of legislative-executive conflict. Most partisan deadlock situations over the past decade have produced solutions of the muddling through variety, in accord with the guiding principle behind separation of powers systems. In conflicts that have escalated beyond that point, interbranch conflicts over policy have generally been accompanied by charges—often credible—of corruption. In constitutional crises that have curtailed the constitutional terms of presidents or legislatures, what is perhaps most striking is that it is almost always the legislature that prevails. This is a crude indicator, but it is encouraging insofar as it suggests reconsideration of Latin America's reputation for presidential dominance.

A number of reforms over the past decade have focused on the structure of executives and legislatures. The creation of limited requirements for parliamentary confidence in cabinets, through the creation of first ministers, is not sufficient to change fundamentally the presidential nature of Latin American executives. The actual reforms implemented in Latin America over the past decade fall well short of establishing hybrid regimes. The configurations of appointment and dismissal powers, together with the trigger mechanisms for assembly dissolution, more closely resemble those of post-Soviet constitutions than the European models of shared confidence, which are advocated by many proponents of hybrid systems.

Another institutional change that is outwardly dramatic, but of potentially limited consequence, is the shift to unicameralism. In Peru, in particular, the apportionment principle under bicameralism, together with the historical pattern of partisan representation across chambers, suggest that the Senate was largely redundant to begin with. Thus, the most important effects of eliminating the Senate may be the administrative cost savings associated with elections and running that chamber, without much impact on policy or government performance. In Venezuela, patterns of partisanship, by themselves, suggest a similar conclusion. However, the apportionment principle in Venezuela was more clearly federal than in Peru. In conjunction with other decentralizing reforms in the late 1980s and early 1990s, bicameralism appeared poised to contribute to effective federalism in Venezuela—a trend that was smothered by the constitutional reform of 1999. In short, Peruvian bicameralism should not be mourned because it was never of much consequence; Venezuelan bicameralism was cut down before its potential could be assessed.

There are a number of potentially important reforms for executive-legislative relations that may move to the center of the reform agenda in the near future. One is the restriction on legislative reelection, particularly in Mexico, where legislators have been limited to a single term for most of this century, but where the end of PRI dominance may stimulate interest in reelection as a means of developing a more autonomous and capable legislature. Parliamentary careers are essential to the development of policy and procedural expertise, which in turn reduce the informational asymmetries between the branches, allowing legislatures to confront executives on more equal footing. Legislative reelection, like presidential reelection, also strengthens the connection between citizens and officeholders. For both these reasons, eliminating prohibitions on legislative reelection where they exist—in Mexico and Costa Rica—would be salutary for the institutional performance.

Another set of potentially important reforms involves the process by which executives and legislatures bargain over government spending. The various configurations of proposal and amendment procedures found throughout Latin America have distinct consequences for aggregate spending levels and for the relative powers of the branches over policy. In the interest of facilitating compromise between the branches while limiting the tendency of budget negotiations to produce grand spending logrolls, the configuration I have identified here as the aggregate ceiling format is particularly attractive. Effectively, it encourages the president to set a fairly modest overall spending level, but then allows the legislature full discretion in allocating funds across programs.

A final, increasingly prominent, procedural issue is that of legislative transparency, particularly as it pertains to voting. Party leaders are occasionally recalcitrant about making this information public, but the spread of Internet technology and the availability of electronic voting machines make it increasingly difficult to justify conducting legislative business behind a veil of anonymity. This trend should be regarded as a plus for quality of democracy, and the spillover effects for the academic study of comparative legislatures are substantial as well.

The reforms advocated here aim at two general goals: strengthening the links between citizens and elected officials, and strengthening legislatures relative to executives. These properties are widely admired in the academic literature, but it is equally widely recognized that it is politicians, citizens, and their respective organizations—not academics—who engineer institutional reforms. The goals of strengthening the electoral connection and strengthening legislatures, however, should have appeal among such actors. Opposition groups, in particular, have a natural interest in holding elected officials accountable for their actions, and in strengthening legislatures, where they are likely to have some representation even when they are not contenders to control the executive.

Toward these ends, the following reforms should feature prominently in the agenda of opposition groups. First are reforms that encourage the development of legislative resources and expertise, such as allowing legislative reelection where it is prohibited, to encourage parliamentary careers. Along similar lines, increasing the physical resources of legislatures is crucial. Latin American legislatures are, for the most part, chronically understaffed and underequipped relative to executives and their Ministries. Increasing funding for skilled staff, library and data archives, and access to information technology is essential to developing legislatures capable of checking executive authority. Procedurally, the aggregate ceiling budget procedure should be attractive to opposition groups that have secured legislative representation, insofar as it maximizes legislative discretion over the distribution of funds across government programs while retaining a general incentive for executives to exercise restraint on overall spending levels. Of the reforms discussed in this chapter, perhaps the one most easily within reach of opposition groups is the publication of legislative voting. Technological obstacles to this reform are not formidable, opposition to it is difficult to defend publicly, and in some cases only a qualified minority (i.e., the legislative opposition itself) is formally required to demand publication of the record.

3

The Military

Rut Diamint

The gradual decrease of militarism in Latin America did not result automatically from democratization. Persistent coup-making is no longer part of the regional political landscape, but the military retains a preeminent role in the resolution of domestic political conflicts. Government institutions remain unable to represent effectively various demands from civilians, thereby allowing the armed forces to mediate and their political influence to reappear under new forms.

In this chapter, I discuss some of the elements that currently characterize the military problem in the democracies of Latin America. Relationships between civilians and the military have changed as a consequence of the political and economic reforms of the past decade and the noteworthy reassessment of the concept of security that these reforms precipitated. The current relationship between governments and the armed forces is, nevertheless, far from the theoretical model of civil supremacy. The incomplete reorganization of power and authority, the persistence of unchecked military prerogatives, and pending institutional reforms allow for diverse forms of military power. This weakens incipient democratic controls and paralyzes the embryonic ability of society and the government to manage security issues.[1]

Latin American democracies are afflicted with shortcomings that encourage novel forms of military participation, while employing procedures that preserve a democratic image. For example, military officers manage considerable economic resources, intelligence agencies still serve the administration in power, military coup plotters espouse populist causes, paramilitary forces are instruments of social control, and a militarized police also undertakes social control. Against this backdrop, the role of the military tilts the balance of social forces to weaken democracy.

Military organizations have lost importance as corporate entities, but their alliances with dominant social sectors allow them to continue to bargain over power. The exchange of favors with civilian elites grants officers corporate prerogatives within a democratic framework. The military has sought to adjust to the reform of the state by trying to preserve the sources of its power and the economic and personnel resources it had hitherto commanded. It adjusted to democracy as a corporation, defending its institutional privileges. The ability of military officers to question civil authority is more restricted than in the past, even though most social structures lack means and capacities to manage relations between civilians and the military through institutional channels.

Recent scholarship on military issues has not yet clearly defined the civil-military interrelationship within the new democracies of Latin America. For example, Wendy Hunter considers that there was an accommodation by omission in Argentina, Brazil, and Chile.[2] Hunter explains that this tacit agreement attenuates conflicts between civilians and the military; competition between them for power and influence remains within limits set by both parties when democracy is at risk. The formula that says, "we shall not meddle in your affairs if you do not meddle in ours," leaves the door open for a probable repoliticization of the military.[3] It also eases pressures on civilians to assume their responsibilities over public policies. Hunter's revealing research alerts us to the hazards of that omission but it does not analyze the political game or the specific pacts between the government and military officials. Nor does it consider the deinstitutionalizing effects of military prerogatives, nor the external factors that impel civil and military actors to maintain those prerogatives for the sake of governability.[4]

Other authors believe that military influence declines with the increased albeit unconsolidated exercise of political power by civilians. The research of David Pion-Berlin and Craig Arceneaux presents a sort of naïve and instinctive perspective: "But the long-term prognosis for civilian control can, we maintain, be improved should civilian decision-makers assert their own authority over specific operations in the short to medium term and, by so doing, stem military encroachment."[5] J. Samuel Fitch, however, points to the difficulties of maintaining civilian control, taking into account the Hispanic tradition in which the military is considered guardian of the homeland.[6] To counteract the absence of political leadership, Fitch proposes, "the U.S. may be able to provide technical assistance in certain areas, but the real need is likely to be to assist civilians in Congress and the defense ministry, rather than the military."

Both Pion-Berlin and Hunter believe that professionalization and the search for institutional objectives for the armed forces suffice to facilitate the military's withdrawal from politics.[7] Yet, political instability results mainly from the inability to subordinate the armed forces to a new framework of governance and to establish institutional rules of the game to reshape corporatist prerogatives.[8] Neither military goal statements nor the allocation of resources and equipment are enough to guarantee a proper role for the military profession without the military's recognition and institutionalization of its accountability to civilian authorities.

The National and International Role of the Military

The end of the Cold War had a direct impact on the military's missions. Edward Luttwak's convincing essay on the shift from geopolitics to geoeconomics highlighted a series of changes in the area of security.[9] These changes led to a significant reduction of the military's role in regional integration processes. Powerful and influential private civilian agents assumed new leadership positions, often overshadowing government officials.

A state-centric conception, in which the nation's sovereignty and defense were more important than the citizen, is giving way to an emphasis on the value of the individual. As a consequence, the concern over the state's security is amended to include concern for sustainable human security. The issues on the new security agenda are societal: population displacements, ethnic conflicts, human rights violations, environmental degradation, and endemic poverty. These are already security concerns in developed countries. In Latin America, the inclusion of these social issues as concerns regarding political stability and governability expands the security agenda, turning social problems into state security issues.[10]

The armed forces had long been accustomed to seeing their own citizens as the enemy. They have had to learn to protect the citizenry and even to participate in international peacekeeping operations. These peacekeeping missions, known as "operations-other-than war" by the U.S. military, have a strong civilian component. During a peacekeeping mission, the military typically works alongside NGOs, health providers, observers from multilateral organizations, and other soldiers. The work of providing humanitarian aid and health care or of demobilizing combatants involves them in activities contrary to their roles as warriors. It also compels governments to think along different political lines, expanding their strategic visions from the national to the global arena.

This altruistic profile is new to the history of the armed forces in Latin America, where the civilian/military divide is still haunted by the unresolved issues of human rights abuses and various forms of military influence contrary to democratic governance. This points to an important difference from the democratic transitions of Eastern Europe, where the armed forces, faithful to the one-party system and accustomed to following the politician's orders, were more easily subject to civilian control. Many Latin American armed forces are still not fully subordinate to their governments because their primary loyalty is to their own institutions rather than to their societies. Instead of redefining military issues in the context of a new institutional framework, Latin America's public space becomes militarized, as the structure, models, and doctrines of the military are applied to police tasks.

One of the most significant changes in Latin American democracies has been this overlap between the functions of the military and the police, further confusing institutional controls. The government's inability to provide adequate security for its citizens has prompted distrust in the institutions responsible for public order. Individual citizens at times take matters into their own hands, hiring private companies to ensure their security.

Several Latin American governments have enlisted the military in the fight against drug trafficking and organized crime or to stop protests by newly disempowered social actors. The mandate to incorporate civilian missions into the military leads to a contradiction: in actions intended to preserve global or regional peace, the military must include civilian missions, but when these are carried out at the national level, they constitute a new challenge to democratic consolidation.

Power and Government in South America

For many years, Latin American societies were under either military rule or a civilian government where the armed forces reserved power to enable them to mediate between political contenders. The transformations of the past decade established a new covenant to provide for civilian rule that, although still incomplete, allows political forces to compete for office without the arbitration of the armed forces. In some countries this hegemonic rearrangement is successful, while in others it triggers uncertainty and disruption in the political regimes.

The progress of democratic reconstruction has been irregular at best. In Brazil, President Fernando Collor de Mello tried to establish a new civilian order while the bourgeoisie continued leaning on the military to reestablish the old balance of power. The agreement signed between Presidents Collor de Mello and Carlos Menem (Argentina) in 1990, leading to mutual disclosure of nuclear activities, the closing of the Cachimbo nuclear test facility, and the decision not to develop a nuclear-powered submarine, was interpreted as a measure to diminish the weight of the military complex in Brazilian politics.[11]

Nevertheless, Brazil's military retains prerogatives under democratic rule that resemble those under the military government.[12] The Brazilian military is a powerful political actor and a state agency that retains numerous functions, privileges, and bargaining ability, assuring its influence in the decision-making process. The most basic tenet of civilian control over the military, the allocation of the leadership and management of the nation's defense policies to a civilian Ministry, involved a complex and tense process between the government and the military. For example, in December 1988 the minister of the navy, Mauro César Pereira, presented three serious objections to the creation of a Ministry of Defense: (1) the possible loss of identity of the individual forces, (2) the logistical difficulties of integrating the forces, and (3) the lack of competent civilians.[13] At the time, five high-ranking military officers were members of the president's cabinet, including the ministers for the army, the navy, and the air force as well as the head of the military cabinet and the chief of the intelligence service. The political recomposition at the end of the 1990s seemed aimed at sustaining new reforms leading to establishing Brazil as a global player: "Global player is an expression common to Brazil's diplomacy and foreign policy formulation that refers to Brazil's significant, if limited, role to play in world politics."[14]

Fernando Henrique Cardoso's administration reorganized the bases of presidential power. In September 1999, a constitutional amendment went into effect authorizing the establishment of a new Ministry of Defense.[15] However, a number of presidential decrees concerning military issues provided evidence that some civil-military conflicts remain. First, the government decided to replace the Department of Civilian Aviation, controlled by the air force, with the National Agency of Civilian Aviation. Second, the government sold 20 percent of the shares of Embraer, the state's airplane company directed by the air force, to a consortium of French companies. Third, the government privatized airport administration. The resistance of the air force led the president to request the resignation of the chief of the air force, Brigadier Walter Werner Brauer, which was followed soon after by the dismissal of the minister of civil defense, Elcio Alvares.[16]

These developments are striking considering the strong link between the Cardoso government's strategic plans and the geopolitical concepts of the army.[17] For example, the secretary for strategic affairs and the armed forces assess technological competition similarly.[18] The president's speeches echo military concerns about the country's vulnerability and inability to defend the Amazon region.[19] The programs to attain great power status in twenty-five years are publicly supported by high-ranking government and military authorities in the design of strategies for 2005, 2010, and 2020. There is in Brazil no military strongman, as there is in Venezuela or Chile, but the leadership role of the military in the Brazilian political system remains undisputed.

In Peru, it proved impossible for President Alberto Fujimori to include longtime elites in his modernizing project. As a result, the political weakness of the presidency required an alliance with sectors of the armed forces, while the political parties disintegrated. Thanks to the internal reorganization, President Fujimori was able to utilize the usual political and social control methods employed by authoritarian governments: manipulation of public opinion, strategies of voter persuasion, and persecution of political opponents.[20] All this took place under the command of Vladimiro Montesinos, former adviser of the National Intelligence Service and Fujimori's closest aide, at the time in charge of mounting a sort of technological espionage and, above all, of knitting a spider's web to entangle the armed forces.[21] The use of the armed forces to break up workers' strikes, combat guerrillas, and support presidential despotism fragmented and ruptured the chain of command within the military, planting seeds of doubt regarding the future behavior of the military in subsequent administrations.[22]

Starting in the 1970s, the Peruvian armed forces—the only ones in Latin America that undertook a process of social and structural reforms—faced the traditional elite as well as the leftist sectors, whose causes they had partially taken as their own. The modernization process undertaken by the Peruvian armed forces differed from those of the other military governments of the 1970s that were based on a patrimonial, authoritarian, and conservative model. According to Juan Rial, the example closest to the Peruvian case is that of Guatemala.[23] In Ecuador, in contrast, the armed forces also had a bureaucratic-modernizing Left-leaning project as well as a technocratic one, but they failed to obtain support for these programs, further rupturing the social fabric.

Consistent with this assessment, in January 2000 a legitimacy crisis terminated the constitutional government of Jamil Mahuad in Ecuador. The privileges of the armed forces in Ecuador are eternal and they are transmitted from generation to generation. The military's proclamation during the January 2000 uprising gives an account of those privileges: "The armed forces will not allow its honor to be sullied by those who have betrayed the trust of the Ecuadorian people, leading hundreds of thousands of families into misery, and that have used their economic power with impunity to manufacture a scandal concerning the armed forces so as to distract attention from processes that urgently need to be carried out."[24]

The target of the January coup alliance was the "neo-liberal economic model, in particular, the proposed dollarization of the economy."[25] The Ecuadorian armed forces maintain a remarkable balance between a rejection of economic reforms and a convenient adaptation to free market rules and competition with the private sector. This participation in business activities has given the Ecuadorian armed forces the highest credibility rating, above those of the Church and the media.[26] This enables them to maintain their strong power and control, allowing them to mediate the political crises of Presidents Abdalá Bucaram and Jamil Mahuad. In Ecuador, trust in po-

litical democracy has decreased sharply thanks to the recurring political failures of the 1990s and the frequent instances of government corruption that
contributed to the population's impoverishment. The credibility of the military has endured, free from accusations of human rights violations. This
broad societal support for the military compares only to the similar, if
smaller, support in Bolivia. In Bolivia, the Church and the media win the top
ratings for institutional credibility, but the armed forces retain a significant
degree of acceptance in comparison with other political players that are
blamed for botched government reform and the costs of regionalization
efforts.[27]

On January 21, 2000, a coup in Ecuador, perpetrated by a small and
disorganized group, overthrew the constitutionally elected president. This
group included 16 elite colonels, 195 officer-candidates of the army's Superior Polytechnic School and the army academy, and 150 "heroes of Cenepa"
(officers who served in the 1995 war with Peru). This coup put the future of
democratic governance in Ecuador at risk. First, it marked a significant
break in the army's chain of command, further weakening the institution
and leading to decreased control by the civilian authorities.[28] Second, it underscored the alliance between the armed forces—that did not engage in the
repression of citizens—and the indigenous community that represents 30
percent of the population. Third, it inflamed the old internal divisions between two regions that have been at odds since the birth of the nation: the
conservative landowners of Quito and the liberal merchants of Guayaquil.
In this case, the alliance between the military and one elite had not weakened, and democratic reconstruction was unsuccessful.

Colombia is the most conflict-ridden country. Its government lacks a monopoly on power. In addition, the illegal narcotics trade risked turning the
country into a narco-state, where authorities from the three constitutional
branches were financed by drug money and where drug dealers directly controlled certain government agencies. The case of Colombia shows some success, namely, a weak military institution that has not participated in politics.
Yet that political accomplishment does not result in a strong democracy, but
rather in the failure of a nation-state and the destruction of a distributive
model of political alliances. The armed forces have increased their relative
political autonomy to carry out repressive activities, while the peace policies
promoted by civilian authorities contributed to armed confrontations instead of demilitarizing the conflicts.[29] Plan Colombia augments military
power, notwithstanding President Pastrana's claim that it would "strengthen
democracy, improve citizen participation, achieve peace, effectively fight
drug trafficking, modernize and expand access to the justice system, protect
human rights and carry out social programs."[30] It is not clear how Plan
Colombia will strengthen the justice system, improve civilian security, or

punish criminals.[31] On the other hand, this plan could trigger numerous side conflicts. One controversy is developing over the impact of massive poppy field fumigation on neighboring countries. Another may be the institutional disarray that could be engendered by using the military to combat a police problem, without drawing a clear distinction between counterinsurgency and counternarcotics. In addition, peace negotiations are conducted between the government and the guerrillas, excluding the paramilitaries (who were included in the case of El Salvador) because military sectors consider them to be strategic allies in the fight against guerrillas.

Considering the dispersal of national power, the Colombian government's current lack of legitimate capacity to wield power is alarming. The Revolutionary Armed Forces of Colombia (FARC) guerrillas, the largest subversive group on the American continent, number between 10,000 and 15,000 combatants. The FARC is present in some 450 of the 1,075 municipalities in the country. The National Liberation Army (ELN) has between 3,000 and 5,000 members; its specialty is actions directed at weakening the economy.[32] Paramilitary groups were responsible for three-quarters of the extrajudicial deaths in the late 1990s.[33] Also in the late 1990s, the police increased their resources, clearly competing with the military for their share of power. Furthermore, the police acquired facilities and technology at times superior to those of the military. In 1999, without the Colombian government's participation, General Rosso José Serrano, then the chief of National Police, personally lobbied the U.S. Congress. The police are almost functionally independent of the armed forces despite the fact that they fall under the jurisdiction of the Ministry of Defense, not the Ministry of the Interior or of Public Security, as is the case in other Latin American countries. The police's high profile is a consequence of the severe internal violence: Colombia has the highest number of kidnappings (1,678 in 1998) and the highest homicide rate in the world (77 per 100,000 inhabitants between 1987 and 1992).[34]

Curbing the military's autonomy is not one of the government's priorities in part because there is no significant coalition pressing for substantial social change; today's landlord bourgeoisie includes drug dealers who have become cattlemen. Relations between civilian and military authorities exist in a context of deteriorated public order.[35] The Colombian situation poses risks beyond this nation's boundaries. On February 7, 1999, Peru deployed two additional battalions of about 1,200 men each to its northern border. Also in 1999, Ecuador reassigned units that had been stationed on the Peruvian border to its border with the Colombian Department of Putumayo in order to dissuade incursions by Colombian guerrillas and drug dealers. President Fujimori addressed the OAS, alerting it of the imminent danger of war on the border. Venezuela stationed nearly 12,000 troops at about seventy points along its border with Colombia. There were reports that more than a thousand guerrilla fighters attacked Port Inirida, a town on the Brazilian border, causing concern in the Cardoso government.[36] These troop movements could develop into military confrontations in the future as handy diversions from political or economic crises. Similar circumstances led to war between Ecuador and Peru in 1995.

Venezuela's situation was not much better as the twenty-first century began. Hugo Chávez's election to the presidency in February 1999 generated a high degree of internal tension and external unease because he revived fears of a potential military dictatorship. The number of voters who favor him does not suffice, as Michael Coppedge states in his chapter of this book, to assess Chávez's legitimacy. Despite thirty-five years of a tacit agreement that regulated civil-military relations, Chávez's tactics to form a hegemonic coalition have strayed far from normal democratic procedure. This has occurred in part in response to a long crisis characterized by extremely high levels of civilian violence and the inexplicable and widespread impoverishment of the population.[37] The new constitution concentrates power in the executive branch and grants prerogatives to the armed forces in different political areas, from education to economic development. Chávez's reliance on the armed forces raised the fear of the government's militarization, a fear further exacerbated by a 13 percent increase in the military budget (despite an overall cut in the government's budget of 10 percent) and a provision in the new 1999 constitution that deprived Congress of the right to oversee military promotions.[38] Military officers have been assigned to strategic positions. They manage the state-owned oil company and are increasingly involved in police work. However, the alliance within the military that had favored political reform has been weakened. For example, Jesús Urdaneta, former director of the political police, Chávez's prison cellmate, and an early inner-circle member, accused Chávez of devious administrative handling.[39] Chávez's old ally, Francisco Arias, competed against Chávez in the July 23, 2000 presidential elections.

Venezuela is entangled in a contradiction. Its political system, devoid of legitimacy, tries to regain it through another political arrangement that lacks democratic legitimacy but enjoys popular support. The leader of this political ploy is (not fortuitously) a military man who resorts to the rhetoric of restoration and order as he breaks all the rules of the political game, while still unable to create a new basis for legitimacy. The president justifies the lackluster record of his administration, claiming that, during the first year, the task was that of institutional consolidation and the removal of the bourgeoisie from the structures of power. But he had less luck than Fujimori in sustaining economic growth in an authoritarian situation; moreover, his objectives certainly diverged from those outlined in the so-called Washington Consensus, that is, the set of free market policies that acquired worldwide intellectual and policy hegemony in the 1990s. The Venezuelan case under Chávez exemplifies how the failure of political parties can lead to a messianic project in which a populist leader bets on a miraculous salvation while he dilutes democracy.

Bolivia, too, has raised international concerns about the possibility of yet another democratic failure. In 1997, a military coup leader of years past, Hugo Banzer, returned to power by democratic means. Bolivian military officers also spread throughout the structure of government and consider themselves the custodians of democracy.[40] As Adrián Bonilla points out, "A central theme in the security agenda of Andean nations is the nature of civil-military relations. . . . In every country the armed forces remain key actors in domestic political processes, playing decisive roles in the origin and solution of political crises."[41]

Paraguay, paragon of the institutional imperfections that characterize Latin American democracies, also faced a deep crisis of legitimacy in the late 1990s. The assassination of Vice-President Luis María Argaña and the forced exile of President Raúl Cubas to Brazil in March 1999 give evidence of the violence employed to resolve political differences in Paraguay, where the armed forces are privileged participants. Paraguayan politics faces either the prospects of an old-fashioned coup ("A budding desire exists in that direction [of carrying out a coup], a desire which we follow")[42] or the possible electoral victory of General Lino Oviedo, a coup leader seeking to emulate Chávez. There is no legitimacy in either the official ranks or the opposition. The military are still the guarantors of "order." There is a lack of agreement on clear rules of the game. Instead, strongman personalist leaders prevail. The role of the Colorado Party is also disconcerting. It is at the same time a possible source of legitimacy, crisis, and confrontation. It is practically impossible to forge a new institutional consensus with this peculiar party system. Moreover, the military rebellion that attempted to depose President Juan Carlos Wasmosy was stopped not by an organized citizenry determined to defend democracy but by pressure from the international community and the threat of Paraguay's suspension from the Southern Cone Common Market (MERCOSUR).[43]

In Uruguay, the military problem seems comparatively minor, but there are still remnants of the privileges conquered by officers in power. The political regime functions without having reviewed its military history. The fears of the military were revived probably because of the break with the two-party system and the increasing power of a third socialist-leaning Frente Amplio (FA, Broad Front) party. In this context, an isolated event such as the case of the restitution of identity to the daughter of a *desaparecido* (a disappeared person, presumed murdered), granddaughter of a well-known Argentine poet, effectively removed the separation between society and the military. Nevertheless, the statements of General Manuel Fernández, head of the Joint Chiefs of Staff, demonstrate the endurance of old concepts: "The enemy seeks to obtain through democratic means the victory that it could not achieve by force." He forecasted that the armed forces "will have to fight again. The situation is changing from bright to dark."[44] He also noted that the armed forces would not ask forgiveness for their actions against the Tupamaro guerrillas. There are no military demands against the democratic system, but neither is there unquestioned subordination to its authority.

In Argentina, a new civilian hegemony was established as a consequence of the military's failed efforts at government administration and economic reforms and its defeat in the war with the United Kingdom in 1982 over the South Atlantic islands. This collapse of the armed forces did not by itself fully restore civil-military relations, however. The liabilities generated by President Raúl Alfonsín's judicial agreements and President Menem's amnesty brought about new lawsuits while preserving a significant distance between civilians and the military.[45] Compared to Chile, however, Argentina has made exemplary changes to consolidate democracy.[46]

Chileans still put up with a highly autonomous military abetted by a constitution made to order, which generates profound discord in society while the government furtively avoids confrontation. In Chile, the army has been willing to yield power in exchange for concessions, such as amnesty for those officers implicated in the abuses committed during General Augusto Pinochet's dictatorship and control over the military budget.[47] President Ricardo Lagos, however, has been firmer than previous administrations in carrying out his intention to limit military autonomy. Lagos insisted that the courts would decide Pinochet's future; Lagos has also sought to change the constitution. The Chilean political reform process has been notably slow and ponderous. Only in the late 1990s, thanks to international factors, did there develop the conditions necessary to legitimize civilian authority without the censorious mediation of the military, which still considers itself the guarantor of the state. The tension between subordinating the armed forces to the civilian government and the need to consolidate governability is influenced by the existence of a broadly supported political coalition allied to the military. The ruling democratic Concertación coalition and the opposition right-wing parties have not been able to carry out a full political reform, but they are in basic agreement on their vision for the country. This agreement on the military issue is reflected in implementation of defense policies through a civilian-controlled Defense Ministry. Nevertheless, divisions of opinion among civilians regarding the role of the armed forces contribute to maintain military prerogatives.[48]

Power and Government in Central America

Central America has overcome militarism, but its people have become increasingly disenchanted with the meager economic achievements of the new democratic administrations. In the security issue area, there is a growing overlap between national defense and public order tasks. The reduction in the number of military personnel on active duty, a cause for celebration, dropped in El Salvador from 63,175 in January 1992 to 31,000 in February 1993; in Guatemala, from 53,000 in September 1996 to 31,000 in December 1997; and in Nicaragua, from 86,810 in January 1990, to about 14,500 in 1999.[49] This encouraging news, however, does not prevent the military from maintaining its influence and privileges relative to the rest of the citizenry.

For forty-three years Nicaragua suffered the Somoza dynasty, buttressed by a repressive apparatus that served the interests of the family and its allies. The next eleven years the revolutionary government of the Sandinista National Liberation Front (FSLN) governed. It repudiated somozista principles while nonetheless militarizing society. The Sandinistas were defeated as a result of the deterioration caused by the economic crisis, the war with the "contras" (armed opposition bands strongly backed by the U.S. government), and the public's urgency to achieve peace. The preferences of the citizenry scattered, but nonetheless permitted a reconstitution of capitalist dominance. Since 1990, Nicaraguan citizens have had freely elected leaders of different political persuasions, shifting from socialists to right-wing liberals. In spite of the population's political uncertainty, democracy has prevailed in Nicaragua. In the final moments of Sandinista rule, Sandinista leaders incorporated a sector of the military into the party system. Budget restrictions and international pressures to reduce the size of the army undermined the role of the armed forces as key players in the political arena. The military does not feel defeated, however; it still maintains institutional strength.

The process of *civilianizing* internal security led to the (still unfinished) creation of a Civil Defense Ministry. A new police force was also created; legislation enacted in August 1996 mandated both civilian control and the professionalization of the police. These demilitarizing measures rested on the Central American democratic security agreements as a frame of reference.[50] But just as there was no military victory in the Sandinista era, in the 1990s there was no civilian victory to establish the rule of law among all the sectors. The conflicts that generated the war of the 1980s were not fully resolved.[51] Despite social trauma and the precarious economic situation, however, in the 1990s political forces came to accept peaceful pluralistic political competition, having lost their taste for combat. "It is the first time in the history of the Nicaraguan Republic that political opponents do not resort to violence to settle their differences."[52]

The emergence of democracy in Guatemala owes more to the failure of the authoritarian regime than to the success of pro-democracy forces. It was achieved through peace negotiations that revealed deep internal conflicts. In addition, the exclusion of a large segment of the mostly indigenous population highlights the lack of consensus between the government and society. The attempt to establish control over the armed forces has proven to be a serpentine process of advances and setbacks.[53] The program to restructure the army could not eliminate all the injustices of the authoritarian regime. Trust between society and the military is still a distant goal. Some Guatemalans still believe that bullets are legitimate forms of obtaining power.

The Guatemalan state is intrinsically weak because a segment of society does not feel represented by government authorities. This segment credits the government with ending the internal war, but blames the government for failing to bring about social inclusion and structural reform. The legacy of the war has not yet been fully overcome even though the Truth Commission, called "Comisión de Esclarecimiento Histórico" (Commission to Clarify History), seeking to reconcile Guatemalan society, documented numerous cases of abuse that occurred during the civil war.[54] Implementation of the peace accords has only been partially successful. The size of the military was reduced by 33 percent, but other pending agreements have not been implemented, or only partially so. Examples include the assignment of the Civilian Intelligence Agency to the Ministry of Government, the creation of the Security Advisory Council, the transfer of the Weapons and Ammunition Registry to civil authorities, the army restructuring program, the reorganization and redeployment of the armed forces, and the reevaluation of the military budget.[55] Alvaro Arzú's government began the important process of transferring control of the powerful military intelligence apparatus to civilian hands, but it was left to the government of Alfonso Portillo to finish it. The military's role is not likely to expand in the future, but in the short term it will be difficult to achieve a process of reconciliation, civil supremacy, and social inclusion capable of nurturing a sustained democracy.

El Salvador's governability crisis was not solved at the negotiating table, as Ricardo Córdova notes. None of the competing sectors obtained a clear victory. El Salvador's armed forces had been the region's most violent, yet it became a democracy and transformed its military policy thanks to strong multilateral support.[56] Pressure exerted by, and assistance from, the international community, especially the United Nations, defined the rules for the drastic reduction of the size of the military and achieved the successful disarmament of the guerrilla movement. As in Argentina, the scale of the crisis and the level of daily violence—the Truth Commission report was entitled "From Madness to Hope"—had a purifying effect. The military could not continue a war it could not win, and the guerrillas, having lost their social objectives, became a political party competing in open elections. The government had sufficient internal and external backing to disengage the areas of national defense from those of internal security and thus regulate the lawful tasks of the military. It replaced the militarized political police with a civilian police, enacted a law on compulsory military service, created the Human Rights Legal Defense Office and a national council to oversee the courts, with a mandate to purge the judicial branch. Despite resistance from some officers, a broad civilian coalition has triumphed in El Salvador thanks to the militancy of the victims of repression. Nevertheless, social conflict is still marked by frequent violence, high crime rates, the inefficiency of the justice system, and high levels of social inequality.[57] The survival of the new political regime is not at stake, but such turmoil demonstrates an explosive dissatisfaction with which a still weak state cannot cope.

The realignment of power in Latin American countries has paralleled the reconfiguration of the state. The state has long been defined as requiring a territorial entity and a population under a single legal system. Nonetheless, processes of integration have modified the criteria of territoriality through a real or metaphoric redrawing of borders. Border permeability evokes freedoms independent of a national frame of reference. Citizens believe that they accrue new rights and duties as members of supranational communities. This situation generates a need for adjustment between local and global law and requires a clearer specification of authoritative state jurisdiction. In this new "order," institutions are organized under different criteria that include both the concerns of states and the concerns of national and international societies. Military thinking generally rejects the reach of globalization. Yet the issue of civilian control of the military, seeking to end the role of the armed forces as the intermediaries in internal political conflicts, has become a regional and global concern as well.

The Entrepreneurial Logic

Changes within the armed forces of several of the region's countries responded more to the need for government reform than to a redefinition of the role of military defense within the framework of democratic governance. Criteria of efficiency and rationality were applied to all armed forces, including those of developed nations. Executive and legislative branches of government took proactive control of the military through the powerful budget appropriations process. Yet, as a negative by-product of the same process, new forms of military power emerged under the rules of the game for the new economy.

The military carried out political-administrative tasks during the authoritarian regimes and managed companies that the state either wholly or partially owned. This allowed the military access to the most powerful sectors, maintaining contacts and gathering information on private economic activities. The arrival of democracy found them well positioned to retain and sharpen their managerial skills.

The participation of the military in private-sector production and marketing represents the handling of considerable resources without congressional supervision or guidelines from the Ministry of Defense. This autonomy allows the military to compete with the civilian government (as in Ecuador) or affect civilian decision-making processes (as in Honduras). In Ecuador, for example, national security legislation allows the military to compete with the government as a social services provider. Article 38 of this legislation establishes that the armed forces "without damage to its fundamental mission will collaborate on the country's social and economic development." Article 48 further establishes that the military should "advise on the organization, preparation, and planning of telecommunications, transportation, construction, and other companies."[58] These provisions were interpreted to give the Ecuadorian armed forces a strong presence in various firms. The armed forces provide both employment and patronage: their reach exceeds that of the civilian government itself, politically co-opting the citizenry, willingly or unwillingly. As Bertha García Gallegos has noted: "The government and the political class have delegated, more or less explicitly, an excessively wide spectrum of social responsibility to the military (in areas of education, health, community development, forestry, and the environment). But the military has also usurped such responsibilities, acting autonomously as an institution that faces no effective civilian control."[59]

The Ecuadorian armed forces continue to increase their economic power. The Department of Industries of the Ecuadorian Army (DINE) owns iron and steel industries, a footwear factory, an agro-industrial firm, a flower business, a hotel and tourism network with sophisticated hotels (Marriott), a multipurpose factory that produces backpacks and tents for tourists, a local General Motors plant, a mining company, a shrimp harvesting enterprise, a men's and women's clothes manufacturing company, the Rumiñahui bank, a company to manufacture pickup trucks, electromechanical tools, household items, water and sewage pipes, a foreign exchange financial services company, and several factories related to military production, in addition to partnerships in other companies.[60] This army is modeled on very peculiar defense criteria. Contrary to the United States, where the private sector competes for defense contracts, ensuring greater transparency and control, in Ecuador, the military acts as a holding company that not only has a monopoly on armed force but also on economics. The director of DINE, Ramiro E. Ricaurte, has said: "DINE has pursued diverse areas of economic activity in order to satisfy the requirements of the armed forces and of the community, generating wealth, development, employment and the well-being of thousands of Ecuadorians."[61] Is this the peacetime mission that we should want for the armed forces?

This situation is similar to the one described by Arnoldo Brenes and Kevin Casas for Central America: "The Central American generals traded political influence for two things: impunity from human rights violations and non-disclosure of their personal and institutional finances."[62] These activities are outside existing oversight statutes and therefore are not plausibly punishable.

The banks of the Honduran and Guatemalan armed forces, this study shows, are some of the main banking institutions in Central America. The military welfare institutions throughout the region have traditionally been autonomous financial entities, funded from the public treasury but not subject to fiscal oversight. They took advantage of years of military dictatorships to increase their wealth. In both Honduras and Guatemala, military institutions participate in the agricultural, livestock, communications, transportation, manufacturing, and real estate sectors of the economy. In Honduras, the armed forces are the eighth largest business entity in the country.[63] Leticia Salomón points to the malaise that this situation creates within the business community, whose members complain of the uneven playing field because of the favorable treatment that the armed forces get from the government, allowing them to lower their production costs.[64]

In Nicaragua, as a result of the changes in the 1980s implemented by the Sandinista government and in the 1990s modified by President Violeta Chamorro, numerous public-sector and military enterprises were privatized. Nevertheless, the military still owns companies and enjoys an elitist distribution of urban and rural properties among members of the high command, awarded as postwar compensation to individuals,[65] not to the military institution. Members of the high command have become partners of companies possessing vast extensions of land in the northern, central, and western parts of the country, such as Consorcio Comercial Agropecuario or Commercial Farming Association (CONAGRA) and Empresa Agropecuaria San Miguel or San Miguel Farming Enterprise (AGRESAMI), land acquired from demobilized soldiers.[66]

The penetration of Central American armed forces into the business world is not an exception but rather the result of political agreements granting them immunity and privileges in exchange for accepting elected civilian rule. No multilateral agreement, or pressure from an international institution, or legal action can reverse the personal and institutional enrichment of the military. Governments can attempt to build controls so that armed forces accustomed to privilege and dedicated to narrow professional objectives, such as the fight against drug trafficking and smuggling, accept and respect the control of civilian authorities. Yet there is little doubt that it will be more difficult to dismantle an economic organization built on legal loopholes.

Corruption has also played its part in the accumulation of military wealth. In 1998, the Argentine press reported on the involvement of Fabricaciones Militares (Military Industries), a dependency of the Ministry of Defense and the Argentine army, in a weapons sales scheme to Ecuador and Croatia. The army profited from the secret lease of weapons to Military Industries, which exported them. In effect, the army sold on the open market goods that properly belong to the nation. The use of the revenues from these sales remains unknown. The sales were arranged illegally with the complicity of members of the executive branch; there was obviously no external audit. The courts have been handling this case. The case surprised the citizenry. It exposed government corruption and brutal, mafia-like methods, such as the induced explosion of a gunpowder factory and the blowing up of a helicopter that carried Argentine and Peruvian military passengers.

In Peru, too, the corrupt handling of national resources has been denounced. Javier Velásquez Quesquén, an opposition deputy from the American Popular Revolutionary Alliance (APRA) party, called on Congress to appoint an investigating committee. Should high military officers be found to have participated in corrupt government deals, he argued, they should be charged with treason: "Neither the Comptroller's office nor the internal audit departments of the armed forces or of the National Police, much less the Congress, have audited or investigated anything; for that reason I believe that it would be timely to investigate."[67] On October 29, 2000, Lieutenant Colonel Ollanta Humala Tazo led a military uprising in opposition to the persisting influence of Vladimiro Montesinos. The military rebels justified their actions as an attempt to cleanse Peruvian politics: "The montesinista-led generals became rich from participating in drug trafficking, weapons smuggling, and other businesses. They seriously compromised the well-being of the army, the Peruvian people, and the very existence of Peru as a sovereign nation."[68] When the *Liberación* newspaper disclosed that Montesinos had a $2 million account in the Swiss bank Wiese, President Alberto Fujimori said that "the revenues correspond to the earnings reported by a consulting law firm in which Montesinos is a partner, which operates independently of the advisor's activities in the National Intelligence Agency."[69] A few months later, Montesinos became a fugitive, having provoked the crisis that toppled the Fujimori regime. A videotape surfaced in which Montesinos is seen giving money to an opposition deputy to switch allegiance to Fujimori's party. Once Montesinos was no longer at Fujimori's side, the press printed a report from the Swiss Embassy in Lima that he had $48 million in Swiss banks.[70] This was no longer a case of military but of government corruption, sheltered by the shady alliance of the president with a sector of the armed forces. The officers loyal to Fujimori did not have a political agenda; they had economic ambitions. They did not need a coup to reach their objectives, just a president who required a spurious alliance to stay in office.

In Paraguay, according to analyst Carlos Martini, President Alfredo Stroessner based his power on engaging a group of officials whom he made partners in the "great business of corruption." Stroessner called it the "price of peace": corruption in exchange for loyalty, business deals in exchange for devotion.[71] This thinking permeated the entire economy, rapidly generating wealth for the military leadership. The government "relied on discretionary administrative practices that led to corrupt acts carried out with impunity."[72] The young leader of the conscientious-objector movement against the compulsory military draft, Camilo Soares, stated, "The army must be abolished for the sake of the country. We will then avoid generals that are both corrupt and untouchable, officers who decimate our forests and commit all types of injustices with impunity."[73] Another sign of military corruption was the proliferation of landing strips in regions under military jurisdiction, with an unusually high rate of activity attributed to smuggling and drug traffic.[74]

This type of competition in the marketplaces of societies with clear institutional shortcomings further weakens transparency and public control. Personal protection, economic security, or business "insurance" are bought from individuals who use their institutional power to compete unfairly with the private sector and, at the same time, use their leverage to increase their dominance in society. The military-businessmen are not taxpayers; the blurred relationship between public institutions and private enterprises allows military-businessmen to remain exempt from paying taxes.

In Brazil, circumstances differ. Its military industry is highly competitive and managed under a government budget. Its products have civilian as well as military application. The military-industrial complex accounts for an important proportion of the country's exports, giving the armed forces a strong voice in economic policies. The U.S. Arms Control Disarmament Agency ranked Brazil among the ten leading arms suppliers to Third World countries in the 1980–87 period. Aircraft manufacturer Embraer, armored-car industrialist Engesa, and rocket and ballistic missile systems manufacturer Avibras accounted for most Brazilian arms exports.[75] In Argentina, military prerogatives were cut when the military-industrial complex firms were liquidated. To be sure, unlike in Brazil, these companies were not competitive, were poorly managed, and did not have an export market. The decision to dismantle them, however, was not a response to their inefficiency; rather, it was an effort to restrict the military's independent resource base.

In Brazil and Chile, the armed forces still manage their own enterprises while they receive funds from taxpayers for their institutional purposes. In comparison to the previous cases, this form of accumulating power is more rational and in closer alignment with the law. This does not mean, however, that professional armed forces, with specific missions, are less corrupt. The critical factor is not in the level of professionalism of the armed forces but in the political system, the courts, and the institutional configuration of power. Military missions do not eliminate economic prerogatives—note that the armed forces of Peru are quite professional. The key change depends on the democratic exercise of authority, respect for the separation of powers, and citizen oversight.

The military's incursion into the private sector is one of the characteristics of the period of state reform. Its consequences have not been fully analyzed, but they most likely cripple the development of institutional capabilities of new Latin American democracies. The military's autonomous financial prerogatives are contrary to the concept of civilian supremacy, that is, the democratically elected government's capacity to set national defense priorities and oversee their implementation. Only then will doubts disappear regarding the long-term loyalty of the armed forces to civilian authorities.[76] In Fitch's words: "In the extreme case, the armed forces operate a miniature government on their own—receiving petitions from various civilian groups, making policy decisions, allocating resources to different programs, and implementing those programs as they see fit. This military 'state within the state' is not subject to democratic control, nor is it accountable to the nation through any democratic mechanisms except for superficial oversight by the president."[77]

In the meantime, the armed forces obtain more power relative to the government and more privileges over civilians. Once the armed forces lost the discretionary use of the state's economic resources that they had enjoyed when they were in power, they looked for financial alternatives to use at will. They developed business capabilities. This instrument is more dangerous than its predecessor. In the past, the constitution deemed them violators of national laws although there was no political will to bring them to trial. Now, within the rule of law but without standards for punishment, they have greater immunity to reach their corporate goals without the risk of a future penalty.

The Institutional Logic

The existence of properly functioning institutions, with transparent procedures and accountability, is a key indicator of the quality of a democracy. If we were to grade the Ministries of Defense using these criteria, the scores would be pretty low. Governments have not invested resources to counteract the tradition of military autonomy that marked Latin American societies. The defense ministers of many countries continue to be active or retired military officers. In countries with civilian defense ministers, they often function as intermediaries between military and civilian authorities; they do not set defense policy, determine the mission of the armed forces, oversee policy compliance, or correct deficiencies as they arise.

In almost all countries, Defense Ministries have a limited role as policy makers. This results in part from fear of antagonizing the armed forces, thus hampering governability. It also stems from the lack of civilian expertise on defense issues, a subject that has always been in the hands of the military. This lack of proficiency undermines the capacity of civilians to function as professional peers relative to the military.

Mexico was long characterized by the efficiency of a bureaucratic apparatus in agreement with the ruling party's needs. Its National Defense Ministry embodied a tacit accord between the PRI and the armed forces, each acknowledging respect for the other's rights. There are no civilian employees in the National Defense Ministry or the Navy Ministry. Officers on active duty lead both of them. Civilians working in military schools are under "piecework contracts," which is a legal way to hide these governmental activities. In effect, state authorities do not set Mexico's defense policy. It is set by military authorities. The army manages the National Defense Ministry just as the navy manages the Navy Ministry. Each Ministry reports directly to the president and each represents military interests in the executive branch. Mexico does not have a Ministry of Defense.

In Paraguay, in 1999 Nelson Argaña, son of assassinated Vice-President Luis María Argaña, was named minister of civil defense in an attempt to reinforce civilian rule. This Defense Ministry has civilian officials, but the military brass assigned to the top managerial posts makes the key decisions. In addition, the armed forces high command is at the same hierarchical level as the Defense Ministry; the high command decides institutional policy.

In Bolivia, "the Ministry of Defense is neither a policy-making institution nor a forum for debate. It has become a residual entity for inter-party agreements. The appointment of its top officials depends more on inter-party politics than on the strategic preservation of national interests."[78]

Ecuadorian Ministry of Defense employees are mainly active-duty or retired military personnel. No civilian occupies a technical or management position. Civilian personnel in Empleados Civiles (ENCIS) are in middle management administrative positions (mainly mid-level advisory positions in specific areas such as the environment, development, and law). Military personnel fill approximately 89 percent of all jobs. Staff from the army's Polytechnic Institute, one of the country's top schools, also participates directly in the administrative system (they control computer networks, for example), which gives them a strong voice in public administration. In the Defense Ministry, each military branch has its own standard operating procedures. In general, interservice relations are quite weak; the military services share little information between themselves and even less with other government agencies.

In El Salvador and in Guatemala, defense ministers are always generals. The peace agreement reforms did not change this situation. Military officers fill all posts that set and implement military doctrine. In Honduras, in contrast, a civilian was named defense minister, notwithstanding military resistance, eliminating the position of commander-in-chief, which came to correspond with the presidency. In response, the army's commander-in-chief, Colonel Rodolfo Portillo Interiano, rallied the military leadership against Defense Minister Edgardo Dumas Rodríguez, the first civilian to occupy this position. Acting as the new commander-in-chief, President Carlos Flores Facussé responded firmly. He dismissed or reassigned all officers who opposed civilian control of the armed forces in order to send a clear message regarding civilian supremacy.[79]

In countries with civilian defense ministers, such as Argentina, Chile, Brazil, and Uruguay, there has been a change. Civilian management of defense policy is considered a prerequisite of democracy. The best data are Uruguay's. The Ministry of Defense reports that it employs 27,676 military and 2,377 civilians. Although not explicitly stated, the Ministry counts the members of the armed forces as Defense Ministry personnel.[80] Yet not even in Uruguay, one of the countries where civilian state institutions remained strongest, was the establishment of full civilian supremacy in setting defense policy achieved. For example, President Julio María Sanguinetti created the National State Directorate for Intelligence to replace the Defense Information General Directorate. The new directorate's task is to advise the executive branch on national and international intelligence and counterintelligence issues. This new institution still depends on the Ministry of National Defense. An armed forces general heads it, and its executive director is also a high-ranking military officer.[81]

In Brazil, the military increased their participation in President Itamar Franco's government (1992–94). Franco expanded the number of military officers appointed as ministers from five to seven: the three military Ministries (Army, Navy, and Air Force) and also Transportation, Communications, Federal Administration, and the Strategic Affairs Secretariat. Members of the armed forces also headed two state companies (Sudene and Telebras) as well as the federal police.[82]

Brazil established a civilian Ministry of Defense in 1999. In its first year, the Defense Ministry did not have a full administrative staff. Only in 2000 was it assigned a building. Many tasks still remain in the hands of the armed forces. The significance of the state bureaucracy, especially that of the Foreign Ministry, suggests that Brazilian government strategic policy will remain remarkably coherent. Little resistance is expected from the military so long as Defense Ministry objectives coincide with military interests.

In the southern cone of South America, the publication of the White Papers on Defense in Chile and in Argentina represented a significant step forward in setting defense policy as the policy of the state.[83] These official documents were based on agreements reached at the hemispheric summits of defense ministers. They were a first, imperfect, albeit politically very significant attempt to set defense policy formally. The Chilean draft emphasized concepts while Argentina's was mostly factual, reflecting the characteristics of each country's defense community. The comparison of these two documents reveals the Chilean military's influence over defense-related issues. For example, what Argentina sees as "globalization" with various positive and negative consequences, Chile sees as "unipolarity" under U.S. hegemony. The evidence also shows that increased political control over the armed forces results in more democratic values, principles, and interests in the sphere of national defense and in the assignment of very different tasks to Defense Ministries.[84]

From 1953 to 1990, Colombia's defense ministers were military officers. The first task of the first civilian minister was to win the trust of the military establishment and, at the same time, regain public respect for the military, which had deteriorated during the previous administrations because of scandals linked to corruption and the narcotics trade.[85] But defense policy in Colombia transcends the responsibilities of a civilian defense minister. Colombian defense policy must include the design of basic strategies toward guerrilla counterinsurgency, peace negotiations, and international relations. In the late 1990s, the armed forces acquired more power and autonomy, yet the danger to the Colombian state makes security issues not so much a concern about military subordination to civilian authority as one of the issues of greatest importance for state survival.

The main obstacle to the design of defense policy as the policy of the state has been the lack of government investment in training qualified public officials. Several countries of the region have defense schools, run mostly by the armed forces. These schools do not train a permanent corps of qualified civilian public officials for the Defense Ministry, however. Rather, they create a social club whose members share ideas and interests. Some countries have set up public policy schools to improve public administration skills, and most have institutes to train the diplomatic corps. None of these offer specialized courses in areas of defense, security, or strategy, however, nor do the universities. A clear and steadfast political decision to improve the civilian government's capacity is the only way to address these problems. An investment in the skills of those in charge of formulating defense policy and strategy will only begin to yield results in the medium term.

The lack of democratic change is even more evident in the intelligence services. The attempts to circumscribe these agencies within a legal framework, through Congress, with the objective of exercising civilian control over their activities, have only been partially successful. Argentina succeeded in curtailing its intelligence services. In 1987, new legislation on defense separated the areas of defense and security, but legislation regulating the intelligence sector was not enacted. President Fernando de la Rúa's government carried out the most important personnel reduction program affecting the intelligence services, dismissing 1,070 agents; the army retired 600 other civilian intelligence agents.[86]

In Brazil, the shift from the Brazilian National Intelligence Service (SNI), which had been the dictatorship's most powerful agency, to the Brazilian Intelligence Agency (ABIN), created during the government of Collor de Mello, resulted from a process marked by stressful relations with the military and the reluctance to eliminate an instrument useful for gathering domestic political information.[87]

In most Central American countries, the intelligence services had functioned as authoritarian enclaves to persecute citizens. The peace processes required the reform of intelligence services to align them with the new postulates of civilian security. In Guatemala, the September 19, 1996 agreements to strengthen civilian rule and set the function of the army within a democratic society achieved this objective. In Honduras, the National Intelligence Directorate (DNI) was eliminated. It had exercised military control over the population for thirty years. In Nicaragua, the Popular Sandinista Army's general reduction and restructuring plan also featured a decreased number of personnel engaged in intelligence activities. In every case, new laws were enacted to subordinate the intelligence services. Civilian governments did not achieve significant reforms, however, nor did they reach consensus on the proper role of these agencies under democratic governance.

Two serious institutional deficiencies have been the lack of well-qualified civilians and of effective control over the intelligence services. A third has been the inability of the legislatures to oversee defense policy. Legislatures have the right to ratify or deny military promotions. In Argentina and Honduras, for example, legislatures have used this power to prevent the promotion of military personnel who have violated citizens' rights. The worst case has been Venezuela. Congress rejected the promotion of thirty-four officers who had participated in coup attempts, but the executive granted the promotions anyway despite the legislative veto.[88]

A common characteristic in the region is that Congress has a nominal capacity to monitor public-sector spending. In a democracy, fiscal policy is the tool that sets public administration priorities according to the government's political preferences. Yet in most cases, Finance Ministries lack the tools to assess in detail the proper use of appropriated funds once these have been allocated to each military service. Congress is even less capable of auditing expenditures.[89]

Some countries in the region increased their defense spending from the 1980s to the 1990s, but most have experienced a decrease linked to the rise of democracy and the end of ideological confrontation (see Table 3.1). Nonetheless, the long-standing guidelines of budgetary allocation have persisted.[90] The rise in defense spending in Colombia and Mexico is a direct consequence of new threats, such as drug trafficking and terrorism. In Central America, there has been a marked reduction in outlays. The increases in Chile and Brazil are attributed to the cost of modernizing the armed forces. Ecuador and Peru had an upward spike linked to their war in 1995. U.S. military assistance, very significant in some cases, should be added to these totals (see Table 3.2).

Civilian expertise on defense issues will take many years to develop. Military management of a nation's defense and security, carried out as if the armed forces own these policies, cannot be reversed immediately. Legitimate civilian leadership depends on the knowledge and training of a corps of public officials, congressional and political party advisers, and the slow but necessary development of academic work to address these issues. This is

Table 3.1. Defense Expenditures

Country	Defense Expenditures (in $U.S. millions)			Defense Expenditures per Capita			Percent of Gross Domestic Product		
	1985	1997	1998	1985	1997	1998	1985	1997	1998
Argentina	5,157	4,972	5,157	169	143	147	3.8	1.8	1.8
Bolivia	181	155	147	28	18	17	2.0	2.0	1.8
Brazil	5,515	18,546	18,053	41	112	108	1.8	3.3	3.2
Chile	2,287	2,922	2,952	189	200	200	10.6	3.8	3.7
Colombia	604	2,542	2,474	21	71	68	1.6	3.3	3.2
Ecuador	405	692	522	43	57	42	1.8	3.5	2.6
Paraguay	85	134	128	23	26	24	1.3	1.5	1.4
Peru	913	1,276	970	49	52	39	4.5	2.2	1.6
Venezuela	1,174	1,540	1,281	68	67	55	2.1	1.8	1.5
Guatemala	167	182	153	21	16	13	1.8	1.5	1.2
Honduras	103	101	95	23	16	15	2.1	2.1	2.0
Mexico	1,768	3,664	3,755	22	39	39	0.7	1.0	1.0
Nicaragua	314	36	29	96	8	6	17.4	1.4	1.1

Source: The Military Balance, 1999–2000.

Table 3.2. U.S. Military Aid, 1998 (in U.S. dollars)

Country	FMS*a*	FMSC*b*	DCS*c*	IMET*d*	E-IMET*e*
Brazil	43,560,000	3,436,000	133,457,170	220,000	24,933
Colombia	68,226,000	11,775,000	79,808,925	607,000	316,814
Venezuela	30,852,000	6,427,000	187,346,453	400,000	388,000
Mexico	2,722,000	20,317,000	182,327,876	921,000	1,008,000
Argentina	7,298,000	215,000	213,404,551	607,000	196,559
El Salvador	7,016,000	271,000	3,962,187	512,000	333,462
Ecuador	1,761,000	2,746,000	56,638,503	534,000	108,289
Bolivia	238,000	3,285,000	3,365,755	570,000	134,196
Honduras	4,659,000	370,000	2,945,018	425,000	69,559
Peru	1,031,000	14,462,000	19,284,136	462,000	199,642

Source: Adam Isacson and Joy Olson, *Just the Facts: A Civilian Guide to U.S. Defense and Security Assistance to Latin America and the Caribbean* (Washington, D.C.: Center for International Policy, 1999). Also see "Arms UN-Control: A Record for U.S. Military Exports," in *Dictators or Democracies? U.S. Arms Transfers and Military Training*, 4th ed. (Washington, D.C.: Democratization for Demilitarization Project, April 1999).
a FMS: Foreign military sales: p. 157.
b FMCS: Foreign military construction sales: p. 143.
c DCS: Direct commercial sales: p. 160.
d IMET: International military education and training program: p. 130.
e E-IMET: Expanded international military education and training program: p. 133.

how a new leadership is built, based on the suitability of its members, which eliminates civilian inadequacy in the eyes and minds of the armed forces.

New Threats and Old Armed Forces

In Europe, Japan, and North America, there are strong trends to conceptualize defense in terms of what has become known as the new security agenda within a framework of assertive multilateralism. In the hemisphere, the acceptance of these missions is in tension with the limited capacity of the armed forces to face threats that have greater political and social implications. None of the South American military institutions have modernized their doctrine. Weapons and equipment purchases generally do not derive from centralized planning (Chile excepted); such purchases take place within the constraints imposed by the reform of the state yet still maintaining traditional guidelines of deployment and mobilization.

Latin American governments have signed numerous global agreements, such as the UN Armaments Registry (reproduced by the OAS) and the Chemical Weapons Convention. They have signed bilateral memorandums of understanding on security as well as agreements on subregional defense, confidence building, border issues, and control over customs houses. Except for rare examples linked to training for peacekeeping missions or human rights courses of questionable effectiveness, these agreements do not add up to a new doctrine that reflects the new postulates of human security or regional cooperation.[91]

Traditional missions, however, continue to exist. As Jorge Domínguez points out, "There has been at least one militarized inter-state dispute per year in Latin America and the Caribbean since 1991; the frequency of militarized disputes actually increased in the second half of the 1990s. Though the worst incident was the full-scale war between Peru and Ecuador in 1995, interstate disputes are also common within Central American countries and between Venezuela and Colombia."[92] The military considers that its main function is the defense of the nation's sovereignty and territory.

Participation in peacekeeping missions has helped to relegitimize officers who had lost the due deference of citizens. This is one of the most promising ways to democratize and control the armed forces. Argentina is the most active Latin American country working with the UN. It went from 20 observers in 1988 to over 1,400 soldiers in 1994. By the end of 2002, more than half of its permanent military personnel had served under the UN flag. Uruguay is the second largest Latin American contributor of military personnel to the UN. In 1998, almost 900 Uruguayans participated in the UN mission to Mozambique. Up to 1999, Brazil had sent close to 12,000 soldiers to peacekeeping operations. At the end of the Gulf War, the Chilean air force sent a squadron of helicopters to monitor the Iraq-Kuwait border, and since 1991 it has participated in six missions. Bolivia, Ecuador, and El Salvador have also sent troops for these operations, and some of their officers train at the Argentine Joint Training Center for Peace Missions. Paraguay's former ambassador to the UN, José Félix Fernández Estigarribia, tried unsuccessfully to involve his country's military in peace missions in order to reduce the likelihood that the military would interfere with the country's fragile democratic transition.[93] Notably, in spite of its declared intention of collaborating with the democratization of the military in Latin America, the U.S. Southern Command has not included the promotion of peace missions among its recommendations for the region.[94]

This auspicious participation of the Latin American military is offset by the risks entailed in the fight against drug trafficking. Counternarcotics operations tend to blur the distinction between security and defense, once again giving the military custody of its own citizens and involving the armed forces in areas for which they are neither suited nor under congressional supervision.

Drug trafficking fosters the "securitization" of defense, that is, increased financial resources, equipment acquisitions, and security forces personnel while levels for the same items decrease within the armed forces. The armed forces of the Southern Cone countries rejected U.S. suggestions to refocus their military missions on what the United States perceived as most important, based on its own drug problem: "The impact of the drug industry has been devastating on U.S. society. Annual imports of 300 million tons of cocaine, 70 percent of Colombian origin, have caused 100,000 deaths and $300 billion in costs in the last 10 years. Cocaine imports feed the habits of 12 million drug users in the United States, including 3.6 million addicts, contribute to 14,000 drug related deaths per year, and lead to untold economic costs for health care, public safety, and the loss of productivity."[95]

In the late 1990s, despite this initial reluctance, some countries took a more flexible attitude while in others drug trafficking came to be touted as the most urgent threat. In Argentina, for example, the former head of the Joint Chiefs of Staff, Vice-Admiral Jorge Enrico, said that the armed forces "cannot remain inactive or passive" about the narcotics trade, and added, "I don't see the armed forces doing police work. This should be left in the hands of the security forces. There are several areas in which we can participate, however, such as coordination and the command and control of large scale operations."[96] In Brazil, this is already happening. On November 29, 1999, 1,200 men from the army, navy, air force, and police participated in Operation Mandaçaru to eradicate marijuana plantations and trade.[97] The Brazilian military's intervention in internal security is neither legal nor illegal.[98]

The situation in Uruguay is similar. Dr. Juan Luis Storace, former minister of defense, affirmed that the armed forces are the "most effective resource against" drug trafficking: "I don't deny the participation of the Ministry of the Interior (in charge of the police force) but . . . it would seem that the armed forces have greater reach outside the country's boundaries."[99]

The situation in Central America is different. Some traditional military issues related to unresolved border disputes linger, but there is also no reluctance from either civilian authorities or military officers to make the fight against drug trafficking the military's central mission. With a deficient judicial system, limited budget resources, and inadequately prepared security forces, it is logical that the military be assigned to these tasks. In 1982, President Ronald Reagan declared the "War on Drugs" as a principal national security objective, but this did not imply that the United States would put its armed forces in charge of this fight. Mexico fears the "colombianization" of the drug issue because this course of action expands the power of the military while it neglects the search for political solutions.

The risk to be highlighted is this behavior's destabilizing potential to democracies. Pion-Berlin and Arceneaux concur that this is the predominant vision: "In sum, the dominant presumption is that operations located outside traditional military roles are more difficult to contain, and ultimately harmful to civilian control." But they also consider that "the variety of civil-military experiences throughout South America alone is enough to falsify the simple correlation between internal security and military role-expansion on the one hand, and the erosion of civilian authority on the other."[100] I do not agree with this analysis based on the ill-advised extension of Huntington's concept of subjective/objective control to the military in Latin America. Fitch shares my assessment: "The persistence of the 1960s American notion that Third World militaries should be actively engaged in 'civic action' and 'nation building' encourages the military view of themselves as multipurpose state institutions, rather than a specialized profession with a specific military function."[101] Drug trafficking issues tend to weaken the inchoate formation of normative channels to design defense policies, increase the range of military autonomy, and produce de facto military participation without civilian government oversight.

In 1992, an expert advised the U.S. Congress not to center its Latin America policy exclusively on the war on drugs:

> Some observers warn that a concentration on drug-related issues obscures other fundamental long-term policy goals such as stability, democracy, respect for human rights, the environment and overcoming poverty. In this vein, they suggest that by promoting host nation military involvement in Andean counter-drug operations, the United States is promoting a policy that could strengthen the power of the military at the expense of often fragile civilian democratic political institutions in the region.[102]

Destabilizing effects are generated by the policies of a powerful state bearing on politically fragile democracies in the process of consolidation. There is a contradiction, moreover, within the U.S. government between an agenda that promotes respect for human rights, governability, and institutional strength, and another driven by the pragmatic policies of the U.S. military. In pursuit of its anti-drug campaign, the U.S. Southern Command tends to emphasize intramilitary contacts, exacerbating the imbalance between civilian and military authorities in Latin America.

This lack of coherence is also evident in the difficulties of attempting to establish policies to combat crime, which is one of the biggest threats to security in Central America. In 1997, there were 300,000 assault weapons in circulation; the murder rate was 140 homicides per 100,000 inhabitants, the highest in the continent. Also in 1997, Guatemala reported 100 lynchings or attempted lynchings.[103] This public security crisis prompted the reassignment of the armed forces to internal security activities. The problem in this instance is not the inability to define military missions, but rather the lack of authority to maintain public order, aggravated by the residual violence from the authoritarian regimes.

Conclusion: The Americas Running at Two Speeds?

In Latin America, the mechanisms to establish interstate subregional trust have been more effective than those to foment trust among the government, the citizenry, and the military. The failure to control the armed forces does not imply a return to the era of military coups. The issue in the twenty-first century is the different forms of military influence over politics. Rational policy assessment is any government's goal but it has not been achieved regarding defense issues. Human rights issues are also still pending. Different situations in Argentina, Chile, Uruguay, Bolivia, and Guatemala show that political annulment of lawsuits against the military or plans to demobilize troops do not suffice to erase memory or create trust. Security forces are not considered impartial, accountable before the law, or respectful of human rights and democratic procedures.

U.S. military structures exacerbate these deficiencies. U.S. military assistance programs only deepen the region's institutional imbalances and undermine civilian capacities to formulate defense policy. Many Latin American military officers continued to receive professional training in U.S. military academies to the end of the 1990s (see Table 3.3).[104] They become the counterparts of the Pentagon and the U.S. Southern Command, thus gaining a measure of autonomy in handling defense matters.

The commander-in-chief of the U.S. Southern Command, General Henry Shelton, explained the importance of maintaining intermilitary contacts: "In many parts of the world, the military is often the most cohesive institution and wields significant power and thus can influence the outcome of events during a crisis and affairs of the government."[105] This vision does not help to build the civilian leadership that the region needs.

Christopher Gibson and Don Snider have studied the dynamics of civil-military relations in the United States, focusing on the decision-making process. They demonstrate that the armed forces acquired a greater capacity to participate at the highest levels of decision making, developing experience in making political decisions.[106] This is also the case in Latin America. The armed forces are not only undertaking missions of a civilian nature, but are also enhancing their ability to influence decisions in other government institutions. Research into the decision-making processes of several South American countries shows that the principal demand of the military is for greater inclusion in the government's decision-making process.[107]

In another extended study of civil-military relations in the United States, Peter Feaver and Richard Kohn found that the military tend to reject civilian culture. With some amazement, they find that military officials believe "that civilian leaders have a right to be wrong." These authors believe that this conception runs contrary to the premises of civilian control. Yet this

Table 3.3 School of the Americas Students, 1998

Country	Number of Students	Percent of Total
Argentina	20	3
Bolivia	52	8
Brazil	0	0
Chile	153	23
Colombia	150	23
Ecuador	10	2
Honduras	24	4
Mexico	60	9
Peru	42	6
Venezuela	30	5

Source: Adam Isacson and Joy Olson, *Just the Facts 2000–2001: A Civilian Guide to U.S. Defense and Security Assistance to Latin America and the Caribbean* (Washington, D.C.: Center for International Policy, 2001), 91.

conception has been a constant factor in the relations between the military and politicians in Latin America. The authors add: "Contrary to the traditional understanding of civilian control, a majority of elite military officers today believe that it is proper for the military to insist rather than merely advise (or even advocate in private) on key matters."[108]

If these behaviors are worrisome in countries with a strong democratic tradition, what implications do they have for the political regimes of Latin America? Most Latin American governments have not confronted issues of inadequate civilian control or the lack of civilian competency to set defense policies. Nor have political and social leaders invested in training well-informed political party counterparts of military officers. Only such capable civilians could eventually institutionalize a dialogue with the military.

What are the consequences of this diagnosis? Latin America is running at two speeds. In Europe, the two speeds refer to the differences between countries whose societies are more developed and convergent and that have similar economic indicators (rate of inflation, level of unemployment, etc.), on the one hand, and those that are less developed and whose economic indicators are less positive, on the other. In Latin America, the level of institutional development must be added to the assessment. Thus some countries have implemented economic reforms, joined the global marketplace, and restructured their political order. Despite many challenges, Argentina, Brazil, Chile, Costa Rica, El Salvador, Mexico, and Uruguay are on the path to democratic consolidation. In contrast, Paraguay, Guatemala, Honduras, Nicaragua, and the Andean countries are stuck at the slower speed. In the second set of countries, no pact guarantees the unhindered operation of political forces or the military's withdrawal from taking part in government. Moreover, this "fault line" between the two Americas does not imply that the military question is solved at either of the two speeds. As Patrice McSherry points out, "Throughout Latin America, the armed forces remain convinced of their right to intervene in politics and society, and such missions give the militaries justifications for maintaining large forces in the absence of credible threats."[109]

Institutional imbalances will persist as long as there remains a discrepancy between legal authority and political power. This generates an unending struggle for the control of the state apparatus, where either the military joins the dominant coalition or their reaction provokes political instability. The best strategy to discourage this perverse logic is to create a civilian defense community. This paves the way back to Karl Deutsch's concept of a security community: a territory with deeply rooted and pervasive practices and institutions, which generate long-term expectations that changes will be peaceful and that disagreements and disputes will be resolved eschewing violent conflict.[110] The inclusion of various national and regional civil society organizations will strengthen this civilian community, contain the autonomy of the armed forces, and properly set the military question as a matter of state policy. Ultimately, security issues belong in a new public sphere, where all governmental institutions are configured and questioned. The result will be a civil society willing to control and improve the state's performance and the health of democracy.

4

Market Reforms

Javier Corrales

Starting in the 1980s, Latin America embarked on one of the most sweeping processes of economic change since the 1930s. Most nations in the region began to introduce tough policies to cure macroeconomic maladies and, more significantly, restructure the economy to make room for market forces. The goal was to transform the region's decades-old model of economic development—characterized until then by heavy state interference in the economy to promote an inward-oriented industry—into a new model committed to free markets and devoid of state-induced distortions.

By the end of the 1990s, it became clear that this transition to the market, where it occurred, produced an unexpected outcome: the simultaneous rise of competitive and non-competitive institutions. This was evident at the level of both economics and politics. Economically, reformers produced some of the most market-oriented institutions that the region has ever seen. But at the same time, they produced or retained institutions and practices that hinder economic competition. Politically, Latin American nations have developed some of the freest and most competitive political institutions in their history. But at the same time, old-style illiberal practices such as state-sponsored favors to privileged groups, restrictions on competition, and non-transparent rules have also flourished.

In the 1980s, advocates of market reforms predicted that market reforms would displace illiberal forces for good, or at least cause them to lose prominence. Political liberalism would follow economic liberalism "with seeming inevitability."[1] By the late 1990s, quite the contrary, some illiberal practices have actually become entrenched. This chapter seeks to explain this unexpected outcome. It seeks to understand why Latin America's reforms produced competition-enhancing and competition-curtailing forces.

This outcome was, in some ways, the political cost of peaceful change. When state leaders embarked on the process of reforms, they encountered significant political resistance. Reformers first attempted to dismiss and sometimes even repress this resistance. Yet, some of this resistance proved to be unbending, forcing reformers to make political concessions. The result was a political entente between reform-minded state actors and market-resistant societal actors. Reform-hesitant groups consented to the reforms in return for concessions.

The payoff of this negotiation was nothing short of a permit to conduct sweeping economic transformations—all in record time. The downside was that some of these concessions violated the very spirit of the reforms. The concessions made market reforms politically digestible, but they also diluted the competition-enhancing objectives of the reforms.

The chapter begins with a brief description of the economic situation prior to the reforms. Latin America was suffering from an acute deficit of stateness. The state ceased to perform well many of its requisite roles. Although the explicit goal of the reforms was to retrench the state from the economy and make room for the private sector, the real objective was to correct this deficit of stateness. States wanted to restore their capacity to govern, rather than be pummeled by, economic forces.

The chapter then describes some of the political obstacles encountered by reform-minded state officials. Overcoming these political obstacles led to solutions that shaped the outcome of reforms. Illiberal concessions were offered, paradoxically, in order to make room for liberal economics.

The final part of this chapter switches focus. It assesses the impact of reforms on the economic and political life of the region. Are Latin Americans better off economically as a result of the reforms? Are Latin American democracies stronger? Answering these questions requires classifying countries in terms of degree of reform implementation. Not all Latin American nations reformed with equal zeal in the 1990s. Those that proceeded slowly were clearly the worst performers, both economically and politically. Those that proceeded more aggressively exhibited a more mixed record. On the one hand, they have made strides in correcting the deficit of stateness of the 1980s, which has brought political and economic payoffs. However, they have not restored state capacity fully. Aggressive reformers have retained some of the vices of the old statism while simultaneously failing to achieve the virtues of more streamlined states. In short, aggressive reformers have only partially restored stateness, and this has had both positive and negative consequences.

The State and the Economy Prior to the Reforms

Increasing Statism, Declining Stateness

Latin America prior to the 1990s was an example of increasing statism accompanied, paradoxically, by declining stateness. *Statism* refers to the tendency of states to intervene in the economy. State intervention can include many facets: (1) direct ownership of firms that produce goods and services; (2) regulation of prices; (3) creation of barriers to entry in different markets; (4) establishing external tariffs to make imports more expensive; (5) subsidizing credit and channeling special grants to specific sectors and interest groups; (6) spending beyond revenues; (7) excessive taxation of profit-making sectors such as exporters; (8) using the state as an employer or banker of last resort; and (9) creating limits in the number of, and participants in, private transactions.

Stateness refers to the capacity of states to assert themselves over the national territory. Stateness is a measure of the extent to which states can design policies and elicit the necessary consensus—at home and abroad—to ensure implementation. Scholars tend to disagree about how best to gauge stateness, but there seems to be a consensus that the following four criteria are crucial:

1. bureaucratic cohesion (emphasized by Max Weber): the extent to which state officials achieve the necessary cohesiveness, skills, and rationality to formulate policy

2. extractive capacity (emphasized by Charles Tilly): the extent to which states succeed in taxing the population in a way that meets the revenue needs of the state without penalizing too heavily the competitive sectors of the economy

3. international links (emphasized by Theda Skocpol): the extent to which states find backing from other actors in the external sector

4. capacity to govern the economy (emphasized by Peter Hall): the extent to which the state is able to design policies that are adequate to meet any given economic challenge[2]

As the following section shows, Latin American states in the postwar period reached increasing levels of statism and declining levels of stateness.

The Postwar Period: Gerschenkron Gone Awry

The relationship between the state and the economy in Latin America prior to the 1990s was an example of Gerschenkron gone awry. Alexander Gerschenkron (1904–78) was a Russian-born Harvard economist who, in the 1950s, argued that late developers had little option but to rely on the state in order to industrialize. The state, Gerschenkron argued, was the only entity with the political muscle necessary to overcome the structural impediments to industrialization in late-developing countries. These impediments included both economic factors (e.g., the large technological leap that was necessary to catch up and the scarcity of capital) and political factors (e.g., the political stronghold of agrarian interest and risk-aversion of domestic investors).[3]

By the 1960s, most of Latin America had turned decidedly Gerschenkronian. States were intervening heavily in almost every aspect of the economy,[4] always justified by the need to promote industry.[5] States were expanding the size and number of state-owned enterprises (SOEs), nationalizing foreign-owned firms, regulating markets, imposing trade restrictions, setting interest rate ceilings, subsidizing credit to selected sectors, and so on. Initially, these measures produced their intended results. The larger Latin American nations achieved rapidly very high levels of industrialization, and often, increases in socioeconomic standards.

In the late 1960s, serious economic distortions began to emerge. Statism turned out to be too expensive. Fiscal spending chronically exceeded revenues, which generated continuous fiscal deficits, and import bills chronically exceeded export revenues, which generated continued external deficits.[6] Despite these problems, Latin American nations decided to deepen, rather than relax, statism. In contrast to East Asia, where newly industrializing nations were turning toward a more export-oriented model accompanied by macroeconomic discipline, Latin American nations opted in the 1960s–70s to deepen import-substitution and to disregard macroeconomic discipline.[7] On average, public-sector outlays in Latin America expanded from 28 percent to 42 percent of GDP between 1970 and 1982. In some countries, SOEs became the dominant economic actor. In Peru, the number of public-sector employees almost doubled between 1968 and 1978; SOEs absorbed 36 percent of all investments in 1976, up from a mere 6 percent in 1968.[8] In Brazil, there were 571 SOEs operating in 1976, accounting for 29 percent of total sales,[9] and 28 of the 30 largest companies were SOEs.[10] Even states that had been fiscally conservative (e.g., Mexico, Venezuela) developed fiscal and external deficits in the 1970s. The speed of state expansion and the degree of state intervention were high for world standards.

The paradox of Latin America's state-centric model, to use Marcelo Cavarozzi's label,[11] was that, although inspired by Gerschenkronian thinking, it nonetheless violated fundamental Gerschenkronian precepts. For instance, state intervention occurred indiscriminately, often in disregard of whether the intervened sectors would truly promote industrialization. In Mexico, state intervention began to be characterized more by bailing out failed private businesses than by any rationale to generate profits.[12] In Brazil, the state owned assets of questionable industrialization values, such as nightclubs, horse racetracks, hotels and motels, and the like. Rather than promote social welfare or efficiency gains, states were promoting either the particular interest of vested groups or those of politicians in office.

One result of this indiscriminate statism was to spoil private actors. Private economic actors began to think of the state as an insurance agent. If something went wrong, the state could be lobbied to provide relief. Hence, economic actors turned reckless in their investment or simply over-reliant on state favors. The result was an expansion of the market for rents: economic actors became addicted to state favors, or rents, and the state became increasingly eager to furnish those rents[13] in the hope of securing political support.[14]

States became so overstretched that they lost their capacity to generate savings, thus violating Gerschenkron's main justification for state intervention: the state's presumed advantage in mobilizing capital. By the end of the 1980s, the state's ability to generate and invest resources, never too impressive, became negative.[15] Consequently, the largest owner of assets in the country, the state, became the leading cause of industrial decay. The quality and output of goods and services deteriorated, directly harming citizens. In Argentina in the late 1980s, for example, only one of seven generators was operating in the state-owned company that provided power to Buenos Aires. Daily blackouts became customary, seriously inconveniencing patients in hospitals, students at school, and workers at factories, not to mention the costs on the national output.

And yet this investment neglect was not enough to prevent fiscal deficits. Tax revenues were low while state spending remained uncontrollable. This revealed the extent of the decline of stateness. States had become too weak. They controlled neither their own staff (bureaucrats, SOE managers, and provincial authorities who pushed for this spending) nor their societies (interest groups remained starving for state-rents).

To cover rising fiscal deficits, Latin American states traditionally followed two roads: borrow more money and print more money. With the 1982 debt crisis, borrowing ceased to be an option. This too was symptomatic of declining stateness in the form of declining international backing. Although the West applauded the region's transition to democracy in the 1980s, it reacted with aghast at the region's economic performance. International financial markets virtually closed their doors to Latin America following the debt crisis in 1982, foreclosing the possibility of private financing. Private capital inflows went from positive in the 1970s to negative in the 1982–90 period (outflows related mostly to debt servicing far outpaced inflows from private capital and export revenues).[16]

The only option left was to cover deficits by printing money. The result was a dramatic monetary expansion without a commensurate rise of productivity, leading to a dramatic surge of inflation in the 1980s. Hyperinflation—an uncommon economic pathology in which prices rise at a rate of 35 percent per month or more—became commonplace in Latin America.[17] The high inflation of the 1980s was particularly taxing on low- and middle-income groups, becoming the leading cause of poverty in the region in the 1980s.

Fading Credibility, Fading Civicness

Serious as they were, these violations of Gerschenkronian principles paled in comparison to what was probably the worst violation of all: the demise of what Gerschenkron called "faith": "To break the barriers of stagnation in a backward country . . . a stronger medicine is needed than the promise of better allocation of resources or even of the lower price of bread . . . [or] the prospect of high profits. What is needed . . . is faith—faith, in the words of Saint-Simon, that the golden age lies not behind but ahead of mankind."[18] Faith is Gerschenkron's word for what contemporary political economists label "credibility." At a time when few economists talked about credibility, Gerschenkron was already arguing that economic prosperity was dependent on the "faith" variable.

By the 1980s, Latin American states had become the biggest destroyers of credibility. Years of economic mismanagement and distortionary policies led to pervasive mistrust among economic agents, who lost confidence in the state's ability to fulfill any promise. They began to defect by buying dollars en masse, which placed enormous devaluation pressure on local currencies. Despite state efforts to resist, Latin America's real exchange rates devalued an average of 23 percent (in some countries surpassing 60 percent) in the 1982–87 period.[19]

The decline of credibility took a heavy toll on the democratic life of the region. Although many Latin Americans were enjoying the greatest number of political and civil rights ever, they were surrendering a wide array of economic rights: citizens faced a shrinking supply of consumer goods, social services, employment opportunities, and purchasing power. Equally deleterious for democracy was the decline of transparency in the state's management of economic matters. Nobody had a clear idea of public finances. Nobody could speak confidently about the level of prices, wages, and production in the coming months. Not even the managers of SOEs knew exactly the amount of assets and liabilities they managed. To this day, Argentina's Ministry of the Economy is unable to furnish information about the amount of electricity demanded and supplied between 1980 and 1991. In Cuba, SOEs had never even bothered to provide figures about their budgets. In the 1980s, nobody could predict confidently when the state would pay its bills next. One of the most important pieces of legislation in any democracy—the national budget —became a piece of fiction in many countries. In Argentina, the president even stopped drafting an annual budget. Economic disinformation was pervasive.

Economic agents responded to this dual situation of economic hardship and lack of state transparency by becoming predators of public assets and cheaters of the state, what some have classified as "defensive" strategies.[20] Employees of SOEs, for instance, cheated the state by stealing supplies, reducing productivity, and increasing absenteeism. Private firms cheated the state by failing to pay taxes, stealing telephone lines, overcharging SOEs for services rendered, and underreporting profits. Financiers cheated the state by provoking financial scares to profit from exchange rate instability. State officials, in turn, responded in kind. They tried to cheat economic agents by generating increasing levels of inflation, delaying payments, announcing surprising decrees, and mandating spending cutbacks and freezes in bank deposits.

In short, the 1980s was the era of pervasive mutual cheating. State and societal actors were in the business of muddling through the crisis by trying to outsmart or cheat each other, which in the end, ate away public assets. Indexes of political and civil liberties were thriving in many countries, but indexes of public mindedness were collapsing. Latin America was suffering the consequences of a deficit of stateness. Crucial standards of stateness—bureaucratic competence, extractive capacity, international backing, and control over economic affairs—were wiped out, paradoxically, by excessive statism. State presence in the economy was pervasive, but ineffective and perverse. Rather than promote savings, investment, and economic well-being, states became creators of distortions, disavings, and special privileges. Rather than inspire faith, they destroyed credibility. Citizens turned into pirates of public assets, and states, into agents of disinformation. Latin America in the late 1980s faced an urgent need to restore stateness.

Market Reforms Since the 1980s

More Markets as a Recipe for More Stateness

In desperation, Latin American nations in the late 1980s launched some of the most market-oriented programs of economic stabilization and structural adjustment ever (see Table 4.1).[21] Ostensibly, these programs entailed rolling back the state. But in reality, states were seeking to rebuild themselves —to restore stateness. The idea was that by correcting overstretch, states would become better at governing the economy.[22] The catchy phrase of the period was "from the fat to the fit state."[23] States proceeded to withdraw from carrying out productive activities (i.e., privatize SOEs) and to reduce what Anne O. Krueger calls the "restrictiveness of controls" in the economy (i.e., liberalize trade and deregulate markets).[24] States also began to try to reallocate spending more rationally (i.e., budget restructuring), relieve taxation on competitive sectors (i.e., eliminate distortive taxes), provide subsi-

Table 4.1. Foreign Exchange Raised through Privatization in Developing Regions, 1990–1997

Region	Total (in $U.S. millions)	Percent
East Asia and Pacific	17,642	17.9
Europe and Central Asia	25,599	26.0
Latin America and the Caribbean	47,742	48.4
Middle East and North Africa	1,216	1.2
South Asia	2,681	2.7
Sub-Saharan Africa	3,671	3.7
All Developing Countries	98,551	100.0

Source: World Bank (1999).

dies exclusively to disadvantaged households, not to disadvantaged firms or interest groups (i.e., reduce indirect subsidies), and spend only in consonance with revenues (i.e., fiscal discipline).[25]

The scope of the reforms was enormous. They entailed nothing short of a complete overhaul of the Gerschenkronian model of development. Some analysts compare this process with "the Great Transformation," the term used by Karl Polanyi to describe the eruption of modern capitalism in the West in the late nineteenth century.[26] Others compare it to the process of change that took place in the 1930s to 1940s, when Latin America embarked on an equally monumental process of change—from an outward-oriented development to an inward-oriented model.[27] Politically, the parallels between the 1930s–1940s and 1980s–1990s periods are indeed striking. In the late 1980s, as in the 1930s, economic change was triggered by a deep economic crisis (the Great Depression of 1929 and the debt crisis of 1982) and implemented from above. In both periods, the change entailed a confrontation between the state, which sought to dismantle the status quo, and very powerful societal groups, which sought to preserve some elements of the status quo. Thus, the reform process of the 1990s, like that of the 1930s, pit the state against societal forces, rendering the reforms an essentially political enterprise.[28]

The Impetus for Change and the Autonomy of the State

A debate exists concerning how autonomously, if at all, Latin American states acted when they decided to embark on market reforms. Some scholars discount this autonomy, pointing to two pressures exogenous to the state that compelled states to move in this direction. One pressure is the international system: the panoply of transnational firms, bond traders, multilateral lending institutions, international academics, and Western leaders who advocated market reforms in the 1980s. Many scholars argue that, confronted with pressure from abroad, Latin American states had no option but to yield.[29] The penalty for not yielding was simply too high: transnational businesses refused to invest in the absence of privatizations; international lenders refused to lend money in the absence of fiscal discipline.

The other exogenous pressure was domestic business, or more specifically, export-oriented domestic businesses. While the bulk of the private sector in Latin America was inward-oriented, inefficient, and thus opposed to economic opening, a small minority of capitalists emerged in the early 1980s who were export-oriented and thus confident about their capacity to compete. This latter group saw statism and protectionism as an obstacle to growth. For some scholars, when Latin American states decided to liberalize, they were catering to this sector. As evidence, these scholars typically point out that most privatizations ended up in the hands of these firms.

Yet, there is a tendency to exaggerate the power of each of these pressures. Despite similar international pressure, some Latin American states introduced modest reforms while others went deeper. Mexico, for instance, liberalized trade with the United States to a degree that no one in the 1980s imagined or expected. Argentina chose an exchange rate regime that was far tighter than the IMF recommended. Rather than yield to international pressure, Latin American states emulated seemingly successful international models, which in the 1980s, appeared to be the East Asia Tigers, Chile, and Spain.[30] One could even make the argument that state leaders often manipulated international constraints to their advantage: they voluntarily sought onerous international commitments in order to increase their bargaining leverage vis-à-vis domestic actors.[31] In addition, the claim of business pressure is often overstated. That competitive businesses ended up as reform winners does not necessarily make them reform pushers. In fact, when most states decided to embark on reform, they found very little support domestically. Even businesses that sympathized with the reforms hesitated in making investments: the reforms appeared too politically risky and uncertain.[32]

More powerful than these exogenous pressures, however, was the deficit of stateness. The desire to escape this deficit is the motivating force that led so many states to confront the risks and political obstacles of economic reform. What were those risks and obstacles?

The Politics of Market Reforms

Implementing market reforms confronted major political obstacles. Understanding these political obstacles is crucial to understanding the outcomes of reforms. The first major political obstacle was the *preexisting credibility gap*. A credibility gap occurs when actors do not believe the policies that states announce.[33] When the reforms were announced, Latin American states were at the peak of their credibility deficit. This was enormously crippling for reforming officials. It meant that economic agents were unwilling to cooperate with the reforms, not necessarily because they opposed them, but because they distrusted those in charge. Economic agents demanded assurances of state commitment as a precondition for cooperating.[34] For instance, agents would not accept fiscal reform (tax increases) without assurances that the state would not misspend. Citizens were unwilling to pay higher fees for services without assurances that services would improve. After decades of faltering on their promises, states found themselves at a loss to provide the demanded assurances, and hence, obtain the cooperation of society.

A second problem was the *asymmetrical distributive consequences* of the reforms. Whereas the economic transition of the 1930s entailed many winners (mobilized workers, middle classes, and industrialists) and few losers (landed elites),[35] the reforms of the 1990s had many losers, or cost-bearers— at least in the short term.[36] The reforms were deliberately intended to generate what Joseph Schumpeter once described as "creative destruction": inefficient modes of production (e.g., uncompetitive firms) needed to give way to more efficient systems of production.[37] This process of "destructuration" and "restructuring" had a deep social impact.[38] It would generate winners, of course, but who the winners would be was not easy to ascertain beforehand.[39] In addition, the gains made by many winners would be too diffuse and perceptible only in the medium term.[40] The losers, on the other hand, were easy to identify a priori—namely, non-competitive economic agents[41] and actors who depended heavily on the central government: provincial governments, technologically backward and capital-scarce firms, subsidized agricultural producers, low-skill workers, firms doing businesses with the state, and middle-class citizens enjoying subsidized services. In essence, potential losers encompassed the bulk of the economy. The perception that there would be unclear winners and many clear losers complicated the politics of reform. The tactic normally used by policy makers to win political support, mobilizing the support of potential winners, was simply unavailable.

A third problem was what could be labeled as the *crisis paradox*. Some scholars argue that preexisting economic crises facilitate reform implementation, in part because they render state officials and societal groups more willing to accept the risks and costs of reform.[42] On the other hand, economic crises can impede reform implementation.[43] Cost-bearing groups do not necessarily become more accepting of sacrifices simply because times are bad. In Venezuela, the Dominican Republic, Ecuador, and various Central American nations, for instance, raising bus prices in the midst of economic crises provoked riots. Not everyone suffers during moments of economic crises. In Brazil in the 1980s, many economic agents managed to protect themselves from inflation (through indexation and capital flight), and to even profit from it (through financial speculation based on price, exchange, and interest rate fluctuations).[44] These groups did not automatically become ardent demanders of change. Crises can encourage attitudes of non-cooperation, or at least of cost-exporting—agents such as provincial governors pass the costs of adjustments to other actors such as central states.[45] During the 1998–99 economic recession in Latin America, protectionist pressures exploded in Mercosur countries (Argentina, Brazil, Uruguay, and Paraguay), an anti-market president was elected in Venezuela, a pro-market president was overthrown in Ecuador, and senators demanded more spending instead of austerity in Colombia. During the 2000–2001 recession, workers and farmers blocked major highways (*cortes de ruta*) to protest spending cutbacks in Argentina, Colombia, Guatemala, and Paraguay. Finally, once a crisis abates, governments confront yet a new problem: the rebirth of pro-spending pressures, which reform-minded states find difficult to contain.[46] If fiscal discipline is a "lifestyle, not a one-time-only affair," to quote Mexico's Finance Minister José Ángel Gurría Treviño (1998–2000),[47] then the return to normalcy acts as a temptation to stray from that lifestyle. In Chile, for instance, containing the pro-spending demands of societal groups was one of the most difficult political dilemmas that the first democratic government after the Pinochet regime (1973–90) confronted.[48] Resisting these pressures inevitably produces societal resentments, or "post-adjustment blues," to borrow Moisés Naím's phrase.[49] Thus, the essence of the crisis paradox is that, on the one hand, crises make citizens and politicians more risk-taking, and thus, more willing to accept change, but crises do not necessarily enhance tolerance for sacrifice, especially among cost-bearers. Moreover, once the crisis abates, pressures to relax austerity return with a vengeance.

Another problem is the *dislocation in executive-ruling party relations*.[50] One of the most important cost-bearers of market reforms are members of the ruling party themselves.[51] Ruling parties fear that the reforms will hurt their constituents, and thus, jeopardize their electoral chances. They also fear that shrinking the state will reduce the number of state offices that the party can staff, and consequently, reduce the leverage of professional politicians in society in general. If the ruling party happens to be statist (a historical advocate of state intervention) or laborist (a party with historical links to labor unions), resistance can be even more acute.[52] Paradoxically, most reform-minded presidents in Latin America in the 1990s came from either statist or laborist parties.[53] This gave rise to an intense executive-ruling party conflict. Unhappy sectors of the ruling party soon began to challenge the executive, often taking the upper hand within the party and transforming it into a semi-opposition force. A resentful ruling party, more so than other societal interest groups, is well poised to undermine the reforms. Ruling parties have strong links to legislators, cabinet members, governors, bureaucrats, unions, civic groups, and campaign strategists, all of whom are well positioned to veto or sabotage reforms. Overcoming the opposition from ruling party members is thus a pressing challenge for every reform-minded administration.

The Political Solutions

Implementation of market reforms required finding solutions to each of these political obstacles, a path that was often much harder than solving the economic maladies themselves. The way in which states addressed these problems significantly shaped the outcome of reforms. Specifically, the solutions provided by states help to explain why market reforms in Latin America were not always as technically correct or even market-oriented as technocrats had wanted.

Overcoming the credibility gap gave rise to two outcomes in particular. One was *overshooting*, that is, the implementation of policies that were far more intense than economically necessary.[54] States figured that overshooting was the only way to regain societal trust.[55] The goal was to overturn actors' expectations by announcing policies that went beyond everyone's expectations. Examples of overshooting include: "big-bang" packages,[56] deep devaluations followed by herculean attempts to uphold very tight exchange rate regimes,[57] rushed and sweeping privatization of risky and symbolic public utility companies,[58] severe budget cutbacks, drastic freezing of deposits, and rapid decentralization of social services to the provinces.

The other outcome of confronting the credibility deficit was the *hyper-technocratization* of the state, at least its economic wing.[59] Squadrons of highly specialized economists, often trained in the United States, took charge of the cabinet. These "technopols" became the real, often untouchable, protagonists of the reforms. They bombarded the political system with highly complex projects. They obtained autonomy from the president to operate politically, designing ingenious institutional innovations to make reform possible.[60] In Mexico, for instance, different reform-resistant Ministries had jurisdiction over state-owned enterprise. Minister of Finance Pedro Aspe managed to change rules in order to transfer those firms to the jurisdiction of his own Ministry, and thus take them away from the control of reform-resistant Ministries. Bureaucratic concentration thus preceded privatization. As with overshooting, the logic was more than simply economic. States were hoping to signal strong commitment via hyper-qualification. On the one hand, this helped the state find solutions to difficult economic problems and regain the confidence of investors.[61] On the other hand, this made some civic groups feel detached from the state: as non-experts, they found it harder to communicate with state leaders who were not used to "talking" to actors outside their profession.

Overcoming the asymmetric distributive costs also shaped the reform process. First, it led to an obsession with *international recognition*. Once the reforms were announced, nations typically adopted very pro-Western, pro-U.S. foreign policies, even if they had once been proud members of the non-aligned movement. The most dramatic example was the 1990 petition by Mexico, one of Latin America's preeminent balancers of the United States, to enter into a preferential trade agreement with the United States. Almost every reforming state in Latin America, not just Mexico, pursued deep trade liberalization. Again, this was more than just a response to the economic situation. It was a political move: states were trying to use free trade in order to gain international recognition, which was especially necessary to compensate for the weakness of domestic support. By reaching binding trade agreements with their neighbors, states sought to impress their neighbors and also lock in the reforms, that is, to make it harder for domestic reform enemies to undo the policy course. The strategy paid off. Reformers who obtained "privileged levels of international support" were more likely to implement reforms.[62]

An example of this obsession with international recognition is Carlos Menem, two-term president of Argentina (1989–95, 1995–99). When Menem came to office in 1989, he announced one of the most far-reaching market reforms in Latin America. It is not coincidental that he took twenty-two trips abroad, visiting twenty-nine countries, in his first year and a half in office. These were more trips and more countries than his predecessor, Raúl Alfonsín (1983–1989), had visited in his first two years in office. Menem spent 14 percent of his first six months in office traveling, twice the amount of time spent by Alfonsín in his first year. The reason for this difference was that Menem, unlike Alfonsín, began his administration by launching a profound market reform effort in the context of insufficient domestic political support. His numerous trips abroad, in conjunction with his vigorous trade liberalization, was an attempt to fill this domestic political void.

Another strategy to compensate for the weakness of domestic political support was to offer *targeted favors to both potential winners and actual losers*. On the side of potential winners, the key issue was to encourage investors to invest. When governments began to privatize, they often faced a scarcity of domestic buyers, mostly because investors were too risk-averse and economic conditions were uninviting. Governments had to find ways to entice them to invest. States needed to privatize quickly to signal commitment, but investors' hesitance—due to the credibility gap—kept them from moving ahead.[63] Creating favorable conditions for investment such as transparent rules was not enough. Governments thought it necessary to offer induce-ments, which came to include concessions of exclusivity, barriers to entry of competitors, weak regulatory mechanisms, lax enforcement of anti-trust laws, various forms of state subsidies, and guarantees.[64] These concessions, or "rents-as-baits,"[65] were politically fruitful in the short term, insofar as they allowed governments to earn the cooperation of initially apathetic would-be-winners.[66] But the cost was the rise of illiberal economic practices ("crony capitalism"), paradoxically, in the midst of a serious program of economic liberalization.

Losers, too, became the target of special favors ("compensation schemes").[67] One way was to insulate potential losers (such as peripheral provinces) from suffering the impact of reform.[68] A typical pattern was to channel large sums of revenues from privatization to low-income sectors that did not necessarily benefit from market reforms. In Mexico, for in-stance, President Carlos Salinas de Gortari (1988–94) used some revenues from privatization to fund the National Program of Solidarity (PRONA-SOL), a huge $U.S.3 billion program nominally intended to fight poverty through public works. In reality, PRONASOL became a de facto populist machine to enhance the ruling party's electoral chances.[69] Likewise, shortly after disbanding Congress temporarily in 1992, Peru's three-term president, Alberto Fujimori (1990–2000), began to fund all kinds of social and infra-structure development projects with revenues from privatization,[70] thereby accomplishing three goals dear to him: helping the poor, delegitimizing op-position parities, and enhancing his chances of getting reelected.[71]

The pressure to increase spending on social sectors came not just from within but also from international actors. By the mid-1990s, multilaterals began to recommend spending more on social service delivery, and to make those services more efficient, setting aside handsome loans for these pur-poses. World Bank funds for education projects in Latin America in the 1990–95 period, for instance, were 8 times higher than in the early 1980s.[72] Reforming governments gladly followed this recommendation to spend, but with one crucial modification: they ignored the advice to make social spend-ing more efficient. Social spending increased in almost every Latin Ameri-can government in the 1990s,[73] but few governments showed signs of spend-ing more efficiently.

Three types of vices characterized this renaissance of social spending in Latin America. The first was the use of funds for private gain (corruption). The second was the use of funds for neopopulist gains (compensation of re-form losers).[74] The third was the use of funds for partisan gains (subsidiza-tion of the electoral prospects of the ruling party).[75]

The result of these concessions for both winners and losers was the trans-formation of many governing coalitions. Presidents transformed their ini-

tial laborist/populist bases of support into new coalitions comprised of reform winners (mostly export-oriented actors, which were offered incentives
to participate in privatization) and reform losers (the very poor, rather than
mere workers, who received direct compensation). This was the kind of
coalition that reelected reform-oriented ruling parties in Argentina, Chile,
Colombia, Mexico, and Peru in the mid-1990s.

Overcoming the problem of executive-ruling party dislocation also
shaped the contours of the reforms. In the late 1980s, few presidents thought
that ruling parties were a problem at all. In fact, few presidents actually worried about negotiating at the level of political parties, much less the ruling
party. Instead, governments focused on two models of state-society negotiation. One model emphasized dealing primarily with technocrats and business elites (the Pinochet model from 1983 to 1988).[76] The other model focused on direct negotiations with peak interest groups, intended to produce
tripartite pacts among the state, federations of protected industrialists, and
national labor unions (the Mexico model).[77]

When attempted in more democratic contexts such as in Argentina,
Brazil, and Venezuela, the Pinochet model of working mostly with technocrats and businesses elites was too exclusivist, and thus, highly irritating
to societal groups. Outside Mexico, the model of state-business-labor pacts
also failed as an antidote to inflation,[78] in part because pact-signers could
not trust each other to hold prices down, in part because the state was too
weak to enforce compliance.[79] It also failed because the real cause of inflation was not labor wage demands and business price hikes, but monetary
and fiscal looseness.[80]

A third model of state-society bargaining focused on both ruling and opposition political parties. Bolivia followed this model in the mid-1980s,[81] but
it was not until the 1990s that it became more common in the region. Scholars became interested in the conditions under which this model of state-
party negotiation would succeed. Stephan Haggard and Robert R. Kaufman
offered the powerful argument that opposition party cooperation with reforms is more likely in countries where party polarization and party fragmentation are low.[82] This explains why Brazil (where fragmentation was
high) and Argentina (where polarization was high) had trouble implementing reforms in the 1980s.

However, the inroads made by Argentina and Brazil in the 1990s suggest
that reforms can proceed even when the conditions for interparty negotiation are inauspicious.[83] Perhaps the reason for this is that the most important difficulty to solve was not so much opposition issues per se, but rather
ruling party distress. Presidents discovered that trying to circumvent or undermine the reform-resistant sectors within their own party (or "dinosaurs,"

as they were pejoratively labeled in Mexico) was counterproductive, leading to more rather than fewer obstacles to implementation. Thus, presidents in Argentina, Mexico, Colombia, and Chile began to accommodate them, to offer them concessions in the form of political space. In Mexico, Salinas went as far as to agree to give the old guard substantial influence over the electoral campaign of 1994 to the detriment of loyalists within his own party.

The result of all this accommodation was a masterful political bargain: presidents gained substantial autonomy in economic policy in return for allowing orthodox sectors of the ruling parties to survive and hold on to certain organizational prerogatives. There is no question that the reforms assaulted some of the privileges of these dinosaurs, but even dinosaurs were able to retain far more prerogatives than neoliberal *técnicos* wanted. On the positive side, this led to the creation of what I label the "state-with-party" condition, which enormously enhanced the chance of reform implementation.[84] On the negative side, accommodating orthodox sectors ended up oxygenating, rather than displacing, groups that were averse to reforms.

States that failed to obtain the support of a ruling party—because the ruling party rebelled (Paraguay, 1994–98), disintegrated (Venezuela, 1996–98), or was not allowed to become institutionalized (Peru, 1995–99)—found themselves facing greater difficulties implementing reforms. Inevitably, these executives turned to extra-partisan forces for support, usually closer alliances with the military as a way to compensate for the political isolation of the state.

It is now easy to understand some of the features of market reforms in Latin America in the 1990s. In some ways, this is a period of reform *in extremis.* Overcoming the credibility gap led to reforms that were deeper than elsewhere in the world. Big bang approaches prevailed, including dramatic privatization programs, to the point where Latin America achieved the most impressive privatizing record in the world and the largest proportion of revenues of all developing countries (see Tables 4.2 and 4.4). It also explains the region's fast and profound trade opening, together with its pro-Western realignment, one of the most dramatic in the post–Cold War period outside Eastern Europe.

Furthermore, overcoming the distributional impact of reforms and the dislocations in executive-ruling party relations produced the simultaneous coexistence of competition-enhancing and competition-curtailing institutions. The special favors offered to winners, losers, and party members led to cartels of winners, pockets of neopopulism, and protection for reform-leery politicians, all of which contradicted the spirit of the reforms. The reforms of the 1990s produced more market forces in Latin America than at

Table 4.2. Privatization Revenues in Latin America and the Caribbean, 1990–1997 (in $U.S. millions)

	1990	1991	1992	1993	1994	1995	1996	1997	Total
Argentina	7,532	2,841	5,741	4,670	894	1,208	642	4,366	27,894
Brazil	44	1,633	2,401	2,621	2,104	992	5,770	18,737	34,302
Chile	98	364	8	106	128	13	187	NA	904
Colombia	NA	168	5	391	170	NA	2,075	2,876	5,685
Mexico	3,160	11,289	6,924	2,131	766	167	1,526	4,496	30,459
Peru	NA	3	212	127	2,840	1,276	1,751	1,268	7,477
Venezuela	10	2,278	140	36	8	39	2,017	1,387	5,915
All Latin America and the Caribbean	10,915	18,723	15,560	10,488	8,199	4,616	14,142	33,897	116,540
Percent of All Developing Countries	86.2	77.2	59.4	44.3	37.8	21.1	55.7	50.9	52.4

Source: World Bank (1999).

any time since the 1940s, but they did not exactly extinguish illiberal economic and political practices.

The Political and Economic Impact of Reforms

Are Latin Americans better off as a result of the reforms? Are Latin American democracies stronger? Answering these questions requires looking at the record of market reform implementation. Not all countries in the region reformed their economies with equal zeal. Those countries that experienced more implementation difficulties or delays are, no doubt, the worst economic performers, and in some cases, the most politically troubled nations. More aggressive reformers, on the other hand, exhibit a more mixed record.

Shallow, Intermediate, and Aggressive Reformers

There were three types of reformers in the 1990s: shallow, intermediate, and aggressive reformers (see Table 4.3). This classification is drawn from an evaluation of accomplishments in various reform categories dear to free-marketeers: inflation reduction, trade opening, financial liberalization, fiscal deficit reduction, privatization of money-losing SOEs, and deregulation of markets.

The areas in which most countries achieved the greatest accomplishments by 1999 were trade liberalization, domestic financial liberalization, inflation abatement (except Ecuador), and debt reduction (except Argentina).[85] These are astounding accomplishments. Latin America was world-renowned for its high inflation, indebtedness, and protectionism. By 1999, the average annual inflation rate for Latin America as a whole was 9.5 percent, the first time in decades that it was single-digit.

However, in other areas of reform, there were major variations. At one extreme are shallow reformers. These are countries that moved slowly on most other domains of reform. Their pace in privatizing in general, reducing deficits, and deregulating markets was slow, haphazard, or nonexistent. Examples include Venezuela, Ecuador, Paraguay, Haiti, and Cuba.

Then there are intermediate cases. These are countries whose privatization, fiscal reform, and liberalization record is mixed—not as stagnant as slow reformers but not sweeping either. Brazil and Colombia are good examples, although Brazil in the late 1990s was moving closer to the aggressive-reform category (in terms of the acceleration of privatization), whereas Colombia was moving closer to the shallow-reform category (in terms of rising deficits).

Finally, there are aggressive reformers. These countries went the farthest in reducing and controlling fiscal deficits (see Table 4.4) for more than five consecutive years and in privatizing money-losing SOEs (see Table 4.2). Chile and Bolivia since the 1980s, and Argentina, Mexico, and Peru in the 1990s are good examples.

Table 4.3. Type of Reformers, 1985–1999

	Inflation Abatement	Trade and Domestic Financial Liberalization	Deficit Reduction	Privatization of Money-losing SOEs	Privatization of Profit-making SOEs and Degree of Competition in Various Sectors
Aggressive (Argentina, Mexico, Peru, Chile, Bolivia)	Yes	Yes	Yes	Yes[a]	Mixed
Intermediate (Brazil, Colombia)	Yes	Yes	Low	Mixed	Mixed
Shallow (Cuba, Ecuador, Venezuela, Paraguay, Haiti)	Yes[b]	Yes	Low[c]	Low	Low

[a]Bolivia "capitalized" rather than "privatized" SOEs.
[b]Inflation in Cuba has never been overt because the price system is tightly controlled. Scholars instead treat "lines to get consumer goods" as a proxy of inflation. There are few signs of improvement in this area. Inflation declined in Venezuela and Ecuador in 1999–2000, but mostly as a result of economic contraction.
[c]Cuba is an exception: fiscal deficits have been significantly reduced.

Table 4.4. Latin America's Growth and Fiscal Performance, Before and After Reforms

Country (timing of deepest market-oriented stabilization program)	Average Annual Growth Rates			Average Annual Fiscal Balance		
	1950–1980	Five Pre-reform Years	1991–1999[a]	Five Pre-reform Years	Five Post-reform Years[a]	1999[b]
Aggressive Reformers						
Argentina (1991)	3.8	0.8	4.7	−1.1	−0.6	−2.1
Bolivia (1985)	3.5	0.0	3.9	−13.5	−1.7	−4.2
Chile (1985)	3.9	0.0	6.0	0.3	1.5	−1.5
Mexico (1988)	6.5	2.8	3.1	−10.3	−0.3	−1.3
Peru (1990)	4.9	2.8	4.7	−5.3	−0.8	−2.6
Intermediate Reformers						
Colombia (1991)	5.1	3.8	2.5	0.5	−1.4	−4.6
Brazil (1994)	7.0	1.4	2.5	−2.3	−6.2	−9.0
Shallow Reformers						
Ecuador (1992)	6.2	4.4	1.9	1.3	−1.5	−4.0
Paraguay (1989)	5.4	2.7	2.1	0.5	0.3	−1.5
Venezuela (1989)	5.2	2.7	1.9	−1.3	−1.1	−4.0

Source: Barbara Stallings and Wilson Peres, *Growth, Employment, and Equity: The Impact of Economic Reforms in Latin America and the Caribbean* (Washington, D.C.: Brookings Institution, 2000).
[a] Preliminary estimates.
[b] Preliminary estimates of non-financial public-sector deficit based on Economic Commission for Latin America and the Caribbean (ECLAC) data. For Argentina, figures do not include provinces and municipalities. For Peru, figures include central government.

Although on the whole, these aggressive reformers went the farthest in liberalizing their economies, their record was not entirely consistent. Sometimes, for instance, aggressive reformers failed to privatize money-making or money-catching SOEs (copper mines in Chile, oil SOE in Mexico, the Banco de la Nación in Argentina). Other times, they failed to deregulate/liberalize fully certain sectors. If one uses a complete measure of liberalization—including not just the introduction of private ownership (privatization) but also competition (market structure)—one finds that countries exhibit different scores on each of these dimensions across different sectors. The electricity sector is illustrative. Table 4.5 classifies Latin American nations according to degrees of privatization and competition in the electricity sector. Several points become clear. First, simply privatizing a sector does not ensure economic competition (e.g., Venezuela). Second, some non-aggressive reformers at the general level actually privatized and introduced competition (e.g., Colombia, in the electricity sector). Third, not all aggressive reformers liberalized all sectors fully: for example, Mexico had neither privatized nor introduced competition in electricity.

Aggressive reformers often privileged liberalization of ownership rather than liberalization of competition. This failure to inject sufficient competition in certain markets is one major drawback of the reform process. Where this failure occurs, the sector is often plagued with higher prices, concentrated ownership, and imperceptible improvements in services. The need to solve the political obstacles to market reforms described previously—specifically, the need to entice investors with guaranteed markets—helps explain many of these gaps. This argument still cannot explain the sectoral variation in liberalization, within and across countries. This is a pending topic of research.

Politics and Economics among Shallow Reformers

Economically, shallow reformers are, unquestionably, the worst performers. Gross domestic product per capita declined in most shallow reformers in the 1990s (see Table 4.6). Shallow reformers are cursed with the worst of both worlds. They carried over into the 1990s the economic problems associated with the deficit of stateness of the 1980s, while adding new ones, namely, the trauma associated with failed or incomplete reform attempts. Some shallow reformers desisted altogether from pursuing deep market reforms by the end of the 1990s (e.g., Cuba, Haiti, and Paraguay). Others became stuck in a pattern that, in reference to Venezuela, I have labeled "ax-relax-collapse."[86] The

Table 4.5. Latin America's Electricity Markets in 1999

		Market Liberalization			
		None	Planned	0–50 percent	+ 50 percent
	State	Paraguay Mexico			
	Limited private	Nicaragua Venezuela	Brazil Uruguay		
Ownership		Ecuador Costa Rica Honduras			
	Mixed		Guatemala	Colombia El Salvador	Peru Bolivia
	Private			Panama Chile	Argentina

Source: Evanan Romero, "Latin America's Electricity Markets," presentation at the Conference on Venezuela's Democracy, Harvard University, April 2000.

Table 4.6. Per Capita Gross Domestic Product

	1981–1990[a]	1991–1999
Aggressive Reformers		
Argentina	−2.1	3.3
Bolivia	−1.9	1.4
Chile	1.3	4.4
Mexico	−0.3	1.3
Peru	−3.3	2.9
Intermediate Reformers		
Brazil	−0.7	1.0
Colombia[b]	1.6	0.5
Shallow Reformers		
Cuba[c]	2.8	−2.6
Ecuador	−0.9	−0.2
Haiti	−2.4	−3.1
Paraguay	0.0	−0.6
Venezuela	−3.2	−0.3

Source: ECLAC (2000).
[a]Calculated on the basis of figures at constant 1990 prices.
[b]Values for the 1997–99 period were estimated on the basis of provisional figures.
[c]Calculated on the basis of constant prices in the local currency. Most of the contraction occurred in the 1989–94 period.

country reaches a severe economic crisis, prompting the state to launch severe adjustments (the ax phase). Suddenly, the reform process gets interrupted (the relax phase), mostly for political reasons. This culminates in yet another economic crisis, often more severe than the previous one (the collapse phase). The ax-relax-collapse pattern of reform was common in the Southern Cone and Peru in the 1970s–1980s, and in Venezuela, Ecuador, and, increasingly, Colombia in the 1990s.

Shallow reformers are afflicted with severe political maladies at the state and society levels. At the state level, repeated reform failure perpetuates, maybe even accentuates, the institutional feebleness of the state. States remain unable to govern. They implement policies haphazardly. Attempted policies produce pain, but are never sustained long enough to yield intended results. Fiscal revenues are precarious and fiscal outlays, uncontrollable. Opportunities abound to sabotage the state or to find allies willing to sabotage the state. Presidents, in turn, feel insecure, institutionally trapped, and impatient with the opposition. These are quintessential assailable or insecure states.

At the level of society, shallow reformers are characterized by deep polarization—an entrenchment of a deep political cleavage on the question of market reforms. Reform enemies (usually the majority) blame the prevailing economic travails on the move toward the market; reform advocates (usually a sizable minority) blame the travails instead on the incompleteness of the reforms. Each group finds evidence to justify its position.

The combination of vulnerable states and polarized political cleavage creates the right conditions for major political upheavals, sometimes even constitutional crises. These have come in many forms: insecure presidents have threatened to disband Parliaments, Supreme Courts, or elections (Venezuela, 1994; Colombia, 2000), sometimes making good on their threats (Venezuela, 1999; Haiti, 1999; Peru, 1992). Other times, Congresses are the ones that succeed in removing market-oriented presidents (Brazil, 1992; Venezuela, 1993; Ecuador, 1996). Other times, the pressure against presidents comes from the military (Argentina, 1990; Venezuela, 1992 and 2002; Paraguay, 1996; Ecuador, 2000) or from the electorate itself, which resoundingly defeats market-oriented administrations (Venezuela, 1993 and 1998).[87] As long as slow reformers continue to lag in solving the problems of deficit of stateness, they will be subject to this type of political instability.

Politics and Economics among Aggressive Reformers: More Stateness, But Not Enough

The political situation of shallow reformers contrasts sharply with that of aggressive reformers. First, aggressive reformers made substantial progress in addressing the deficit of stateness that prevailed in the 1970s–1980s.[88] With the rise of hyper-technocracy, for instance, these states achieved higher levels of bureaucratic competence (meeting Weber's standard of stateness), at least in economic affairs. Because of tax reforms, they have developed a better capacity to raise revenues (meeting Tilly's standard). By regaining access to cheaper international credit and capital flows, they are in stronger international footing than in the 1980s (meeting Skocpol's standard). And by removing inflation, restoring budgets, stabilizing exchange rates, and fortifying economic institutions, reform-aggressive states have developed a stronger capacity to govern the economy (meeting Hall's standard).

In addition, the political cleavage on economic issues at the society level has softened. By the end of the 1990s, no significant political party in aggressive reforming countries seriously advocated dismantling market reforms. "The point is to reform, not change, the model," proclaimed the Alianza, a Center–Left coalition that won the 1999 presidential election in Argentina. This acceptance of market economics and fiscal discipline is now typical of most Center–Left parties in aggressive reforming countries.[89] Aggressively reforming countries might still face the challenge of pressures from interest groups and specific politicians lobbying for subsidies and protection, but not the challenge of political parties calling for the return to the old ways. Political conflicts will center on how to "cushion the impact of the market (i.e., provide relief for 'losers,' and soften market-generated insecurity) rather than how to block"[90] market forces. While market reforms have heightened ideological debates on economic issues among shallow reformers, they have ameliorated them among aggressive reformers.

The restoration of stateness and the decline of political polarization in many ways explain why aggressive reformers performed better economically in the 1990s. These countries grew economically, attracted foreign investment, managed external shocks better, and devoted resources to social services.

However, aggressive reformers have not achieved economic nirvana. Part of the problem is that stateness has been restored only partially. Some old vices of statism endure (e.g., neopopulism, favoritism, weak application of anti-trust norms). Other features of stateness remained unrealized. There are two important ones.

High exposure to, and insufficient defense against, external shocks. Aggressive reformers have become highly exposed to external market forces, and thus, to external shocks. To use a common household term, these nations are more globalized. Although they have managed external shocks better than in the past (e.g., all aggressive reformers except Argentina recovered quickly from the effects of the 1998–99 Asian crisis), they have yet to develop mechanisms for managing successfully their external sector. Most lack diversified, technology-intensive exporting sectors. This constitutes a deficit of a major component of stateness—what Joseph Stiglitz and other students of East Asia's development call the capacity to pursue "export promotion activities."[91] Most exports still consist of either agricultural/primary commodities, which are susceptible to uncontrollable price fluctuations, or low-skilled labor-intensive manufacturing, which does not generate multiplicatory technological effects. Their economies continue to be centered on old-economy "land-based production," rather than on higher-valued "products of the mind," typical of states that tend to perform better in the new international economy.[92]

In addition, aggressive reformers are more susceptible to the volatility of international financial markets. One of the rewards of successful reform implementation is access to portfolio investments: bond buyers become more willing to buy local bonds when macroeconomic fundamentals improve. This is good news, because developing countries need all the capital they can raise. The problem occurs when two types of external shocks occur. One is a financial panic in some other region of the planet, leading bondholders to turn indiscriminately risk-averse. The other is a shrinking of the global supply of money, for example, when Organization for Economic Cooperation and Development (OECD) countries raise interest rates. At either moment, bondholders leave Latin America in search of safer havens or higher interest rates elsewhere. Raising interest rates at home to stop these outflows rarely works: it produces a domestic recession without necessarily deterring capital outflows.[93]

Pro-cyclical spending. In the era of globalization, no state can be master of its own fate entirely. International economic forces are beyond the control of even the most powerful states. Yet, states vary in the extent to which they can manage fluctuations in the economy. Some countries are better at cushioning the impact of economic cycles than others. Historically, Latin American nations have belonged to the latter categories. Their public finances have had a strong pro-cyclical bias: fiscal spending accelerates during economic good times, but contracts during bad times, depriving states of the fiscal means to counteract fluctuations in business cycles.[94] Market reforms might have worsened this distortion. The need to maintain tight fiscal discipline discourages governments from increasing spending during recessions to either stimulate aggregate demand or at least provide relief to displaced workers. In addition, revenues decline (and international credit becomes more expensive) during bad times, which pressures governments to cut spending.[95] As a result, aggressive reformers feel the impact of external shocks quite intensely.

The main conclusion is that two major criteria of stateness—Skocpol's international backing and Hall's governing the economy—have been restored only partially in Latin America. The relationship between aggressive reformers and the external sector is now a source of both strength and fragility. And the capacity of states to manage business cycles, and thus govern their economies, remains in question. Aggressive reformers are thus facing the paradoxical outcome of having restored substantial stateness on many dimensions, but still lacking stateness in many others.

Conclusion: Three Decades of Extremism, Reform Boundary, and Future Reforms

The reform agenda in the early 2000s is centered precisely on filling the gaps and fixing the mistakes of the market reforms of the 1990s. This so-called second wave of reforms seeks to inject more competition into all markets, address the pro-cyclical nature of fiscal discipline, enhance the independence of state regulatory services, and improve the efficiency of state institutions responsible for social services.[96] The point is to increase both market forces and state presence, while ensuring that the state is streamlined.[97] Aggressive reformers have stronger market and state institutions than in recent times, but at the same time, they have retained or generated imperfections in how these institutions operate. They have achieved partial restoration of stateness and markets. Whether Latin America will make equally impressive inroads in the new round of reforms remains to be seen. What is clear is that this second wave of reform is likely to be as politically painful as the first one.

Clearly, shallow reformers remain ill-equipped to embark on this second wave of reforms. Their macroeconomic problems remain too serious to permit state officials to focus on non-economic affairs. Aggressive reformers, on the other hand, ought to be institutionally and politically better prepared to move ahead. And yet, thus far, they have shown less zeal in pursuing the second wave of reforms than expected.

A common explanation for this is "reform fatigue," the idea that after fifteen years of momentous economic reforms state elites have lost the energy to push for more change, and society, the stomach to assimilate it. This is not a trivial point. Latin America enters the twenty-first century having undergone three decades of *in extremis* political economy: the extremist statism of the 1970s, the extremist decline of the 1980s, and the extremist reformism of the 1990s. We are no way near understanding the full ramifications of three decades of roller-coaster political economy on Latin America's society.

Yet, fatigue with reform and with economic change in general is not the only or most serious political obstacle for further reform. Reformers in Latin America do not appear to be tired or deprived of ideas, especially at the beginning of the 2000s, when so many new political forces, with new energies, have come to office. In addition, voters seem willing to elect politicians with innovative proposals for strengthening the public sector.

This chapter suggests that, rather than reform fatigue, the main impediment to the second wave of reform is reform boundary. Market reforms were the result of a political negotiation between audacious reformers and risk-averse politicians to alter a specific area of national life: the economy. The agreement had clear parameters. Orthodox sectors were quite insistent about the areas that were off-limits to technocrats: labor issues, the internal workings of the bureaucracy, the management of social services. To move to the second wave of reforms requires going beyond the boundaries of this agreement. This requires a new round of negotiations.

The problem is that risk-averse politicians today are less willing to grant reform permits as ample as those of the 1990s. More than anything, market reforms might have left them in a stronger bargaining position vis-à-vis the state. As this chapter has shown, the reforms of the 1990s granted reform-resistant sectors substantial political protection, that is, assured positions within parties and bureaucracies, access to and control of state resources, participation in policymaking, freedom to build clientelistic/electoral machines, and monopolistic control of markets. These actors have stronger reasons to oppose new change (they are now the main beneficiaries of the status quo) and the power to resist effectively (their stronghold over political resources). Now that many Latin American nations suffer less onerous economic conditions, reformers might have lost bargaining leverage over reform-resistant sectors. The second wave of reforms is thus launched in a context in which the balance of power has shifted decidedly in the direction of reform-cautious groups. It is unlikely, therefore, that this wave of reforms will proceed as aggressively as market reforms were.

The era of big bang, extremist reform politics, so typical of the early 1990s, is probably over. The next wave of reforms will be more piecemeal. Perhaps this is fortuitous. Big bang change produced far too much political trauma for anyone to miss it dearly. But if reformers and politicians lose the willingness to compromise that characterized the 1990s, the region risks losing more than just big bang politics. It could well lose the capacity to enact needed change, leaving the region with flawed markets and flawed states. It would be a pity that Latin America, having made so much progress in reordering its economy, would remain stuck with this sorry combination.

5

Latin American Labor

M. Victoria Murillo

At the beginning of the twentieth century, Latin American workers in early industrializing nations organized in a hostile political environment, while in other countries, labor unions were almost absent or incipient. At the end of the twentieth century, labor unions enjoyed more freedom to organize in new democracies, albeit challenged by capital mobility, economic liberalization, and state retrenchment. This chapter analyzes the new challenges faced by organized labor in Latin America at the turn of the century, with special attention to South America and Mexico. In doing so, it emphasizes the previous development of labor political strategies in closed economies with highly interventionist states. These strategies become less effective in open economies with shrinking public sectors. However, at the time of economic liberalization and institutional transformation, the political influence of labor unions still serves to affect the design, implementation, and schedule of market reforms. At the same time, partisan loyalties between unions and labor-based political parties shape the interaction between organized labor and the government. Partisan loyalties generate trust and increase the willingness of labor unions to bear some of the costs of reforms. Additionally, competition for leadership within the union movement explains labor militancy against market reforms, whereas union fragmentation influences labor effectiveness in shaping policy implementation during the period of economic liberalization.

The temporal coincidence between democratization and economic liberalization imposed further challenges for organized labor. Whereas labor unions had usually been at the forefront of political liberalization protests, democratization reduces the influence of labor mobilization once elections became the principal means of expressing citizen preferences. In the context of this dual transition, labor unions try to deliver better wages and more secure employment to their members, but they encounter new challenges, such as increasing economic volatility. Even when they realize the need for innovative strategies to deal with new issues, strategic innovation develops slowly. It can take one of three forms: new alliances, organizational autonomy, or industrial participation. In the first case, labor unions break with old allies and seek new partners, including political parties and other sectors of the population also hurt by economic liberalization. In the case of organizational autonomy, they concentrate on the survival of the organization through the acquisition of new resources created by the opening of the economy, such as the provision of new services in competitive markets or the acquisition of privatized property. Industrial participation involves labor unions adopting a more proactive role in the implementation of new technologies to increase labor productivity in a competitive economy. Strategic innovation is important because the traditional strategies of labor unions have become less effective. The chapter concludes by arguing that institutional reform and leadership competition can accelerate the slow pace of strategic innovation while providing a new role for labor unions in new democracies.

From the Labor Market to the Political Market

In the twentieth century, labor organized first in mutualist associations and later through unions. It started earlier where foreign investment in extractive activities and the association of employers prompted labor organization as well as in the urban centers of early industrializing nations. Immigration waves, which contributed to the supply of labor, imported labor organizers and provided new ideologies, such as anarchism and socialism. These imports contributed to the organization of labor unions. For the most part, governments and employers resisted and repressed labor organization, fearing distortions in labor markets, attacks on private property, and the threat of large-scale social conflicts. State repression curtailed workers' bargaining power on the shop floor while the limitations to universal suffrage restricted their citizenship rights in many countries. Thus, workers fought to organize for collective bargaining in the labor market, but did not pursue political strategies.

During the first half of the twentieth century, political liberalization changed workers' options. The expansion of suffrage made workers an electoral constituency for political parties. Elites' concern with the "social question" brought even non-labor-based governments toward the institutionalization of industrial relations. Moreover, in countries experiencing high political volatility, organized labor could become an important ally for aspiring political elites. The partnerships between politicians and labor unions provided the latter with channels to reach the state and the former with political constituencies. The value of labor political strategies became apparent once labor partisan allies gained power.

In Mexico, the House of the International Workers of the World organized Red Battalions during the Mexican Revolution. In return for their military support, the 1917 constitution included labor rights. By 1919, the Mexican Regional Workers' Confederation (CROM) had chosen a political strategy to compensate for its industrial weakness and organized the Mexican Labor Party (PLM) to support the candidacies of Presidents Álvaro Obregón and Plutarco Ellías Calles. In exchange, Calles appointed CROM labor leader Luis Morones as the minister of industry, trade, and labor. Morones was explicit in the use of a political strategy as an alternative to industrial action under the label of "tactical flexibility" (acción múltiple).[1] This strategy was followed by subsequent union leaders after the establishment of the Mexican Workers' Confederation (CTM) during the administration of pro-labor President Lázaro Cárdenas (1934–40).[2]

A decade later, in Argentina, Colonel Juan Perón used his position as secretary of labor to build a political support base in an alliance with labor leaders tired of dealing with hostile governments.[3] Many Argentine labor leaders dropped previous political identities, from syndicalism to socialism, to embrace a strategy that, as in Mexico, was labeled "tactical flexibility." This strategy included the compensation of industrial weakness with political influence and the provision of services that workers were not receiving from employers.[4]

Despite the predominance of labor political strategies, there was variation in their effectiveness. Political strategies did not guarantee success. These strategies were most effective when labor unions were strong enough to define favorable terms of exchange with their allies and when these allies gained power. The partisan relationship with organized labor, politicians' need for workers' support, and the strength of organized labor defined the degrees of "inducements" and "constraints" for labor organization in the labor code.[5] Strong labor movements were able to obtain better terms in their political exchange with politicians building up their support coalitions. Allies in power often facilitated unionization, and sometimes made it compulsory, as in the Argentine and Mexican public administrations. If allies were in the opposition, the state could curtail unionization or limit it to the company level, as in Chile and Peru.

Labor market regulations further reinforced the value of political strategies because they provided the benefits that were not achieved through collective bargaining. As a result, even when allies had not yet reached power, the promise of access to the state made political strategies more appealing. Hence, organized labor followed political strategies even when allies were not in power. During the 1920s, labor unions were affiliated with APRA and the Socialist Party in Peru, the Communist and Socialist parties in Chile, and the Communist Party in Brazil. Political strategies brought further repression when labor allies were in the opposition. In Peru, the Peruvian General Workers' Confederation (CGTP) was dissolved by President Luis Sánchez Cerro after a failed Aprista insurrection in 1932. Nonetheless, Aprista labor leaders would increase their influence at the expense of communist leaders during the administration of José Luis Bustamante (1945–48). In Brazil, President Getúlio Vargas also repressed communist labor leaders after a failed series of attempted insurrections in 1935. However, he would later move to control labor unions, co-opt labor leaders, and enact a labor code favorable to urban workers in 1943. In Chile, the labor-based parties were allowed to be elected to Congress first and to the executive later as part of the Chilean Popular Front in the 1930s. However, communist leaders were persecuted from the end of World War II until the late 1950s.[6]

During the Great Depression, Latin American governments began to adopt trade protectionism and currency-appreciating exchange rate policies, building the conditions that would facilitate domestic industrialization even before import substitution industrialization and state intervention became public policies.[7] In a context characterized by closed economies and state intervention, organized labor's use of political strategies became more effective. Protectionism reduced the pressure on labor costs while state expansion facilitated unionization because public managers with soft budget constraints were more concerned with labor peace than with productivity. Moreover, state-owned companies were large and involved sectors with relatively skilled labor, which facilitated unionization. Additionally, the weak bargaining power of labor unions in small and medium-size private companies further increased their support for state intervention into labor markets. Finally, in addition to the economic context and employers' resistance to workers' organization, state-driven ideologies of social change further contributed to labor preferences for political strategies.[8]

Concerns about labor unrest and a simultaneous search for labor constituencies prompted Latin American governments to regulate labor markets even in the absence of explicit alliances. The movement toward labor market regulation increased labor's attention to political developments. Once regulations were in place, labor unions found that state intervention in industrial relations made the appeal to labor peace or electoral support more effective with politicians than with private employers. This situation resulted in politicized labor movements trying to achieve by regulations what they could not reach through collective bargaining. As described by Silvia Sigal and Juan Carlos Torre,[9]

Except in some particular cases of unions whose productive location made them strategic, industrial unionism was, in general, too weak to follow an economic strategy centered at the company level. Due to this weakness and the scope of state intervention, labor relations issues, such as work time, vacations, job mobility, and minimum salary have been subject to regulation rather than to collective bargaining between unions and employers (author's translation).

Not even the wave of authoritarianism that spread through the region in the second part of the twentieth century eroded labor preference for political strategies. Instead, when military rulers and repressive regimes hindered political strategies, labor unions politicized industrial action to counteract political repression. Because democratization became, in many cases, a precondition for workers' organization and collective bargaining, labor unions used strikes and mobilizations to resist military regimes. Their mobilization contributed to create a climate of social unrest during the process of political liberalization that preceded democratic transitions.[10]

There were early instances of anti-authoritarian mobilization. Venezuelan labor unions mobilized against the dictatorship of Marcos Pérez Jiménez, and in support of political liberalization, leading to the Punto Fijo pact and the inauguration of democracy in 1958. Twenty years later, Brazilian military rulers faced a "new unionism" (*novo sindicalismo*), which became an important democratizing force through the formation of the Workers' Party (PT). In Chile, Uruguay, and Argentina, organized labor also appealed to general strikes to protest against military rulers in the wake of the 1982 debt crisis.[11]

In sum, political volatility, economic protectionism, and state intervention favored the politicization of Latin American labor unions. In turn, governmental elites perceived labor unions as one of the few organized groups in weak civil societies. Their reactions ranged from co-optation of political constituencies to repression of challengers to the established order. In either case, state reactions confirmed the importance of political strategies for labor unions, demonstrating that they could not ignore politics even if all they wanted was to bargain collectively in the industrial arena. Therefore, union politicization was not provoked solely by left-wing ideologies or partisan co-optation. It was the response to a context that made political strategies more useful than industrial action. However, at the end of the twentieth century, economic liberalization and increasing capital mobility challenged the political strategies of Latin American labor.

Economic Liberalization: Transformation and Challenges

The Latin American debt crisis and the recession of the 1980s triggered a process of economic liberalization in the region that challenged both labor political strategies and their industrial bargaining power. In an effort to cope with the crisis, most Latin American countries began opening their economies and retrenching their states through privatization, deregulation, and decentralization of the provision of services.[12] Additionally, capital mobility increased at a much faster rate than labor mobility around the world. This situation increased labor insecurity even in countries with scarce capital due to growing financial volatility and competition for attracting mobile capital with cheaper labor costs.[13] These processes challenged labor unions' emphasis on states and national public policies. Meanwhile, union members suffered the costs of the transitions toward open and competitive economies as well as the dramatic changes in the organization of work provoked by the crisis of Fordism.

At the turn of the century, economic and industrial transformations were weakening the power of traditional labor unions. Economic liberalization and state reform particularly affected formal-sector workers, that is, the natural constituencies of labor unions. Trade liberalization sharpened differences among workers, in particular between those in tradable and non-tradable sectors and more and less competitive firms. This heterogeneity made it harder to organize workers based on horizontal solidarity. International competition and privatization also provoked labor restructuring and layoffs in sectors that had been among the most highly unionized in the past, thus reducing the relative influence of unions. Despite cross-national differences, higher unemployment, starting during the recession of the 1980s, further hurt labor bargaining power by increasing job insecurity for workers, as shown in Table 5.1. Even as the region emerged from the recession in the 1990s, unemployment continued to be high in Argentina, Colombia, Panama, Peru, Uruguay, and Venezuela. Indeed, even Chile, which had experienced a dramatic reduction in unemployment after the end of the 1980s recession, had an unemployment rate of more than 10 percent by 2000. The effect of unemployment is dual because it erodes the ranks of unions while increasing the competition between those employed and those searching for a job. This hinders the bargaining position of unionized formal workers as a result of the absence or insufficiency of unemployment insurance systems.

Perhaps more important, market reforms made workers more uncertain about their future labor market position, particularly in the protected and public sectors, which were the most unionized. Formal- and public-sector employment with the highest degree of unionization experienced the sharpest decline during the period of market reforms. During the 1990s, the informal sector grew by more than 3 percent as a percentage of urban employment.[14] Argentina, Colombia, Ecuador, Honduras, Mexico, and Peru, however, have informal sectors that are larger than the average. Additionally, the public sector shrank by almost 3 percent in the region (Table 5.2). The

Table 5.1. Open Unemployment (annual averages)

	1985	1990	1995	1997	1998
Argentina	6.1	7.5	17.5	14.9	13
Bolivia	5.7	7.2	3.6	4.4	—
Brazil	5.3	4.3	4.6	5.7	7.7
Chile	17	7.4	6.6	5.3	6.2
Colombia	13.8	10.5	8.8	12.4	15.1
Costa Rica	7.2	5.4	5.7	5.9	5.4
Ecuador	10.4	6.1	6.9	9.3	8.1
El Salvador	—	10	7	7.5	7.6
Honduras	11.7	6.9	6.6	5.2	5.8
Mexico	4.4	2.8	6.2	3.7	3.2
Panama	15.7	20	16.4	15.4	15.5
Paraguay	5.1	6.6	5.5	6.4	13.9
Peru	10.1	8.3	7.9	8.4	8.2
Uruguay	13.1	9.2	10.8	11.6	10.1
Venezuela	14.3	11	10.3	11.4	11.3

Source: International Labour Organization, *OIT Informa: Panorama Laboral* (Lima: International Labour Organization, Statistical Annex, 1998).

Table 5.2. Changes in Urban Employment

	Informal Sector (percent urban employment)		Public Sector		Other Formal Urban Employment	
	1990	1998	1990	1998	1990	1998
Latin America	44.4	47.9	15.8	13	40.1	39.1
Argentina	52	49.3	19.3	12.7	28.7	38
Brazil	40.6	46.7	11	9.3	48.4	44
Chile	37.9	37.5	7	7.2	55.1	55.3
Colombia	45.7	49	9.6	8.2	44.7	42.8
Costa Rica	41.2	45.4	22	17	36.8	37.6
Ecuador	55.6	58.6	18.7	14.8	25.7	26.6
Honduras	57.6	57.9	14.9	10.3	27.5	31.8
Mexico	47.5	49.6	25	21.7	27.5	28.7
Panama	36	38.5	32	21.8	32	39.7
Peru	52.7	53.7	11.6	7.2	35.7	39.1
Uruguay	39.1	41.2	20.1	16.8	40.8	42
Venezuela	38.6	43	22.3	19	39.1	38

Source: International Labour Organization, *OIT Informa: Panorama Laboral* (Lima: International Labour Organization, Statistical Annex, 1998).

Table 5.3. Unionization as a Percentage of the Formal Sector Wage Earners

	Year	Union Density (in percents)
Argentina	1995	65.5
Bolivia	1994	59.7
Brazil	1991	66
Chile	1993	33
Colombia	1995	17
Costa Rica	1995	27.3
Ecuador	1995	22.4
El Salvador	1995	10.7
Guatemala	1994	7.7
Honduras	1994	20.8
Mexico	1991	72.9
Nicaragua	1995	48.2
Panama	1991	29
Paraguay	1995	50.1
Peru	1991	13.3
Uruguay	1993	20.2
Venezuela	1995	32.6
USA	1995	14.2

Source: International Labour Organization, *World Labour Report* (Geneva: International Labour Organization, 1998), 237.

reduction of the public sector was more dramatic in Argentina, Costa Rica, Ecuador, Honduras, and Panama, whereas Chile had already a slim state because the shrinkage had taken place before 1990. These variations are important for understanding that, despite common traits, the region's union experiences are very different.

The variation in union experiences can also be perceived in the diversity of unionization of formal-sector wage earners in the region. Table 5.3 confirms the diversity in unionization across countries. However, it is important to note that figures on union density can be deceptive because they tend to be self-reported and Ministries of Labor only compute membership when they register unions. Moreover, they are taken as a percentage of formal workers, yet the informal sector grew substantially, as shown in the previous table.[15]

In summary, market reforms created new challenges for Latin American labor. Open economies made labor costs salient because they could not be transferred to consumers, thereby heightening productivity concerns for international competition. Latin American labor unions (and employers) have relatively little experience in dealing with productivity and training to make workers more competitive in order to keep their jobs in an open economy. State retrenchment increases the number of private employers relative to public managers or state bureaucrats dealing with labor unions. Strict budget constraints and production costs became more important than social unrest and political support. Thus, political influence lost relevance vis-à-vis labor market strength after the economic transition. Labor unions have to learn to deal with these new conditions while their members are suffering the cost of economic transition. Labor political strategies need to be reassessed in light of the new economic conditions, where collective bargaining may be more useful than pressure on a retrenching state.

However, because there is a difference between open and opening economies, political strategies and access to government can still be effective during the period of institutional reform commonly associated with trade liberalization and state reform. Governments wanted to implement the changes as quickly and smoothly as possible to make their economies attractive for capital. In this context, organized labor can demand input in institutional reforms or compensation for the costs of the transition. Hence, although in an already open and privatized economy unions' political influence loses effectiveness, organized labor could use its political clout during the process of institutional change. For this reason, partisan loyalties between labor unions and governments implementing market reforms were able to provide labor unions with policy input and compensations even as economic liberalization and deregulation reduced the influence of politics on economic activities and industrial relations.

Partisan Loyalties and Labor Competition

The legacy of previous political strategies and alliances influenced the response of organized labor to economic liberalization. Previous interactions between labor unions and political parties created mutual expectation, which, in turn, shaped their interactions at the time of stabilization and market reforms. Labor unions trusted their allies when they claimed the need to implement these policies despite their costs to their constituencies. Hence, when partisan allies were in government, organized labor usually cooperated. Most labor unions accepted market reforms in Mexico under PRI President Carlos Salinas (1988–94), in Argentina under Peronist President Carlos Menem (1989–99), and in Chile during the administration of Concertación President Patricio Aylwin (1990–95). In contrast, when partisan allies were in the opposition, organized labor distrusted the government's goals with the new policies and usually rejected market reforms. The Brazilian Single Workers' Confederation (CUT), associated with the opposing PT, boycotted the stabilization attempts of President José Sarney (1985–90) and tried to sabotage the privatization efforts of Presidents Fernando Collor (1990–92) and Fernando H. Cardoso (1995–2002). The Bolivian Workers' Confederation (COB), controlled by left-wing groups, resisted market reforms under Víctor Paz Estenssoro (1985–89) and Gonzalo Sánchez de Lozada (1993–97), following a long history of hostility with the National Revolutionary Movement (MRN). In Uruguay, the Inter-Union Workers' Plenary—National Workers' Convention (PIT-CNT) associated with the FA also resisted adjustment efforts under Colorado President Julio María Sanguinetti (1985–90) and market reforms attempts under Blanco President Luis Alberto Lacalle (1990–95).

Although market reforms created similar challenges for organized labor in different countries, partisan loyalty or hostility to the governing party provoked different reactions to these policies. Partisan loyalties influenced the interaction between labor unions and governments implementing market reforms. The trust placed in labor allies or the distrust of long-term adversaries shaped labor perceptions of the trade-offs associated with market reforms and the unions' disposition for negotiating with the government. Labor unions were predisposed to collaborate with labor-based parties implementing market reforms although these policies created uncertainty and distress for their membership. They trusted the long-term benefits of these policies based on previous interactions with the governing party when political influence effectively compensated for industrial weakness to the benefit of union constituencies. Partisan loyalties also provided communication channels to inform labor leaders about the constraints faced by governing politicians.[16] Labor-based parties, therefore, had a comparative advantage in implementing market reforms because they were less likely to face labor opposition. Because labor-based parties wanted to keep this comparative advantage, they tried to avoid reforms that could facilitate the replacement of their labor allies from leadership positions within the unions. For that reason, they were less likely to reform the institutions that regulate collective bargaining and labor organization.[17]

In Mexico, during the administrations of Presidents Carlos Salinas (1988–94) and Ernesto Zedillo (1994–2000), and in Argentina, under President Menem (1989–99), several discussions and proposals sought to reform the regulations on labor organization and collective bargaining. In Mexico, a single labor code regulated individual and collective labor law and labor organization. Both the Salinas and Zedillo administrations left the labor code untouched. In Argentina, different laws regulated individual labor contracts, collective bargaining, and labor organization. This separation allowed the government to modify individual labor law regarding temporary contracts without touching the laws on collective bargaining and labor organization until 1998. That same year, Menem passed a reform that strengthened the power of national unions by centralizing collective bargaining, opposing demands of decentralization made by businesses and international financial institutions.[18] Despite the zeal with which these administrations implemented market reforms and the fact that opposition political parties and private businesses also demanded changes in those regulations, reform of collective labor rights and regulations of labor organization did not occur. In these cases, labor-based administrations used their links with unions to facilitate economic liberalization and state retrenchment. Hence, they did not want to face the risk of breaking with labor allies that had supported the process of market reform.

Conversely, governments hostile to labor or competing with labor-based parties had more incentives to reform labor legislations. In Chile, military ruler Augusto Pinochet pioneered economic liberalization and state withdrawal from economic activities after he ousted Socialist President Salvador Allende in a 1973 coup. Pinochet banned a large number of unions and suspended collective bargaining and the right to strike. In 1979, under international pressure, he reformed the labor code to permit worker organization only at the company level as well as collective bargaining without unions. Although the law authorized unionization, it introduced important limitations in the activities and scope of unions. For instance, the 1979 law imposed restrictions on the organization of the public sector and temporary workers as well as banning confederations and any form of collective bargaining beyond the company level. In 1994, after the democratic transition, the Center-Left coalition Concertación, which controlled the Chilean Unified Workers' Confederation (CUT), reformed labor regulations. This reform facilitated collective bargaining and labor organization in an effort to reward labor allies that restrained their militancy and supported further economic liberalization and privatization. The 1994 law authorized unions within the public sector and abolished the prohibition on intercompany collective bargaining. It also protected union leaders from dismissal and facilitated union financing by demanding that workers who benefited from collective bargaining contribute 75 percent of union fees to avoid free riding.[19]

The influence of partisan loyalties in generating trust and facilitating collaboration between labor unions and governing parties was more apparent for the cases where labor allies were in the opposition. The lack of trust and communication between governments and labor unions usually resulted in labor resistance to market reforms. In Brazil, labor union resistance hindered the stabilization efforts of President José Sarney and boycotted market reforms under his successors. The mutual distrust of labor unions and non-labor-based administrations often resulted in repression of the former in order to implement market reforms. In Bolivia, President Paz Estenssoro resorted to a state of siege in order to impose structural adjustment on the bellicose COB. In Peru, President Alberto Fujimori (1990–2000) undertook market reforms against the resistance of left-wing and Aprista unions. Furthermore, to counteract labor hostility, Fujimori passed labor reforms targeted at liberalizing the labor market and weakening labor unions. Therefore, partisan loyalties and trust influenced the interaction between organized labor and governments during the process of economic liberalization and state retrenchment.

In addition to partisan loyalties, leadership and interunion competition also shaped union-government interactions. Leadership competition within the unions weakened their tendency to collaborate with their partisan allies in the government during the period of economic opening. If opposition to market reforms attracts the electorate and union members, it may result in the growing influence of militant union activists who threaten to replace allied labor leaders. In this case, leadership competition could make allied labor unions more militant against market reforms. This was the case of the Venezuelan Workers' Confederation (CTV). Although a proportional representation electoral system allowed other parties in the executive committee, AD union leaders who had supported President Perez in the party primaries controlled the CTV. However, after Perez's announcement of market reforms provoked urban riots showing popular discontent, AD union leaders ceded to the pressures of left-wing activists in the CTV and called a general strike less than six months into his administration. Additionally, the growing influence of union challengers, associated with the left-wing Causa R, which opposed market reforms, continued to induce the militancy of AD union leaders later into Perez's administration. In contrast to the experience of Argentina's Menem and Mexico's Salinas, who were able to sustain labor support for the process, the opposition of the CTV contributed to the demise of Perez's market reforms.

Interunion competition or organizational fragmentation weakened labor bargaining power, and thus the capacity to achieve concessions of economic liberalization. Coordination problems made collective action of rival organizations more difficult and weakened their bargaining power. For instance, the Mexican labor movement was divided into several national confederations, all associated with the PRI, but competing for members outside the public administration (where the Federation of Public Services' Unions, or FSTSE, had a monopoly of representation). During the Salinas administration, government officials manipulated the competition among these rival confederations for scarce resources. Interunion competition allowed the government to make fewer concessions in return for labor quiescence, support in social pacts, and campaigning for the North American Free Trade Agreement (NAFTA).

Union monopoly, in contrast, strengthened labor bargaining power at the time of institutional reforms because it reduced coordination problems in the exchange of labor support for concessions. In the case of Argentina, the

General Labor Confederation (CGT) faced no interunion competition since its unification in 1992. Whereas before its unification, Peronist President Carlos Menem was able to play one faction against the other, after unification union monopoly strengthened CGT bargaining power and policy input. Organized labor succeeded in changing several laws, creating union pension funds, and modifying social security reform in order to restrict private providers from competing with union-run health funds. Additionally, privatizations included a provision for employee ownership with union administration that facilitated union purchase of companies in their sectors. Likewise, the reform of individual labor regulations introduced clauses that required union agreement for the use of short-term temporary contracts.

Therefore, partisan loyalties, partisan leadership competition, and interunion competition are important variables in understanding the interaction between unions and governments during a period of economic liberalization. We cannot assume a uniform labor reaction to the common challenges created by market reforms without considering these variables and their effect on labor influence in the process of economic liberalization.[20]

Democratization and Leadership Competition

The simultaneous development of market reforms and democratization had important political consequences for the region's citizens, who gained access to government during the 1980s recession. The economic downturn and later the costs of the transition toward open economies frustrated citizens in new democracies and made democratic consolidation a more difficult task.[21] Organized labor not only faced the costs of economic liberalization but also discovered the erosion of its political strategies, which had been hidden during the democratic transitions, when politics became legal again.

The mobilization of labor unions and other organized groups (such as social movements) had more visibility during political liberalization undertaken in the final phase of authoritarian regimes.[22] Labor unions organized strikes and mobilized workers in public demonstrations against authoritarian rulers, pushing for the acceleration of transitions toward democracy. After democratic transition, elections rather than mobilization became the primary means of expressing citizens' preferences in new democracies. Labor protests were redirected toward policy implementation, but democratic elections focused on counting numbers rather than measuring the intensity of preferences. Moreover, economic liberalization made the number of workers in the most "unionizable" sectors shrink while business concerns and "free market" ideologies became predominant. Thus, aspiring politicians sought to gain the votes of a growing unorganized informal sector rather than those of a shrinking formal working class that had already established partisan loyalties. Weak democratic institutions further reinforced this process by facilitating the emergence of "new populisms" whose political support base was the informal sector as opposed to the traditional populist link with organized labor.[23]

Political liberalization also affected the internal dynamics of labor unions by providing more options for electoral allies and by creating an environment more favorable to the democratization of unions themselves. The experience of the *novo sindicalismo* in displacing the *Varguista* leadership in the Brazilian labor movement was linked to the process of political liberalization. In fact, in those countries where labor political strategies had been more effective, "incorporating" governments had regulated leadership competition to make the replacement of their loyal allies more difficult, thus controlling labor unrest. In those cases, the process of internal leadership competition was restricted and required legal changes. In Mexico, where labor unions had been associated with the seventy-year governing party, unions feared that democratization would reduce their access to the state and facilitate their replacement. Mexican union leaders thus resisted democratization because this process challenged the efficiency of their political strategies by increasing the risk of having the PRI lose power while prompting internal leadership competition within their unions.

In short, dual transitions toward open politics and economies created conditions that made the traditional political strategies of labor less effective. Economic liberalization reduced the bargaining power of organized labor whereas democratic politics reduced their political influence due to the emergence of new constituencies, shrinking ranks, and increasing independence of voters. Therefore, it was not only harder, but also less meaningful, to gain access to the state. Hence, the influence of organized labor declined in electoral politics and its access to the state became less effective in shaping work conditions.

Labor Prospects in the New Millennium

Labor mobilization and political influence were able to affect the pace of economic and political transitions, but elections and industrial relations became more important once the transitions were over. However, because labor unions used political strategies during periods of political and economic liberalization, they were slow in adapting their behavior to open politics and economies. In fact, numerous unions resisted economic liberalization while refusing to change their strategies and discourses even in a context of dramatic institutional transformation and political decay. In cases where change in strategies occurred, they took one of three non-exclusive forms: (1) new political and social alliances, (2) organizational autonomy, (3) industrial participation. The change in the environment and leadership competition create incentives for strategic innovation, albeit if at a slow pace.

The first strategy involved the formation of new political and social alliances. These alliances broke old partisan loyalties and resulted in workers participating in the creation of new political parties, extending their alliances to other popular sectors, particularly in the informal sector. These new labor groups rejected corporatist mediations and state control of labor unions. Subordination to state regulations offered less rewards than at the time of the original "incorporation." Moreover, these labor activist ranks were challenging incumbent labor leaders who had maintained their control of labor movements helped by state regulations on union governance. In fact, due to the existence of such regulations, these new labor leaders had to break formally with the unions recognized by the state and claimed "autonomy" from the state. In Venezuela and Brazil, they called themselves "new unionism" and refused to join the national confederations associated with corporatism. In Argentina, they broke with the Peronist CGT and founded the Congress of Argentine Workers (CTA). In Mexico, the National Workers Union (UNT) joined union leaders with a long tradition of "independence" from the PRI with others who just had broken with PRI corporatism.

These new labor unions defined alliances with sectors of the population previously excluded by unions and with emerging political parties. They made efforts to reach out to the growing informal sector, the landless peasants, and the unemployed. They joined their efforts in popular protests against the uneven distribution of the costs created by adjustment and economic liberalization. Their relationship with political parties, though, was more diverse. Brazilian union leaders in the *novo sindicalismo* were at the core of the founding group of PT and their Venezuelan counterparts followed their example when organizing Causa R. The Argentine CTA union leaders participated in the creation of FREPASO and Mexican "independent" union leaders, for the most part, joined the Mexican PRD when it emerged. However, because the latter two were not labor-based parties as the PT and Causa R, labor played a minor role in defining the internal dynamic of these parties. Moreover, although these new parties enjoyed reasonable electoral success, they were unable to match the labor-based parties founded in the 1930s and 1940s. During the 1990s, the PT always came in second in presidential elections. In its best nationwide performance, Causa R won a fourth of the votes for the 1993 presidential election.[24] The PRD has remained the third party in Mexico, and although the FREPASO won the 1999 presidential elections, it did so in alliance with the traditionally middle-class-based Radical Civic Union (UCR).

A second strategy was organizational autonomy. It did not require breaking partisan loyalties or building new ones, but rather concentrating on useful resources for the survival of the labor union organization after state retrenchment and economic opening. Unions offered services previously provided by the state to their members. To cover these services, they took advantage of their influence at the time of market reforms. Unions in privatized sectors that were most challenged by the economic transition have adopted this strategy in Argentina and Mexico. Some Argentine unions, for example, have participated in the privatization of state enterprises in their sectors. In Argentina, the oil workers' union owns the oil fleet of the former state-oil company Yacimientos Petrolíficos Fiscales (YPF). The electricity workers' union bought various public utilities and electricity transmission companies and received the concession of a coal mine while the railroad workers' union was granted the concession of a railroad. Along with other unions, they have created their own pension funds after the government enacted a pension reform, and have also reorganized their health care funds to improve competition. These new union-run "business" activities emerged from the market reforms implemented by President Menem and provided unions with resources to compensate for declining union dues while serving their members.[25] In Mexico, too, the teachers' union and the telephone workers' union abandoned their dependence on state-regulated social security. Instead, after breaking their official links with the PRI, they developed their own provision of services for members, including credit unions and other social benefits.

The third strategy, industrial participation, involves adopting new ways of implementing productivity and competitiveness with the involvement of labor unions and workers' input. The Union of Telephone Workers of Mexico (STRM) participated with management in the training of workers and the measurement of productivity while joining quality circles.[26] Causa R unions have introduced member voting on collective contracts.[27] In Brazil, the automobile unions of the *novo sindicalismo* led a process of mid-level corporatism with automakers', autoparts', and autodealers' organizations around long-term restructuring programs that included union participation.[28] Despite these examples, most unions were either slow or failed to participate in the productive process with the aim of increasing productivity to keep their members' jobs. The reasons are twofold. First, market reforms lacked institutional incentives, such as worker councils, to foster such participation while employers were reluctant to share company information or decisions with labor unions. Second, labor unions accustomed to mechanisms of mobilization and political influence were slow to build the professional expertise necessary to sustain this third strategy. Furthermore, the costs of the economic transition made this strategy very difficult to follow in those areas where increases in productivity involved more layoffs than training.

Strategic innovation evolves only at a slow pace even though labor unions have become aware of the limitations created by traditional strategies. Even traditional unions are starting to distance themselves from their allied parties and strikes can still result in labor gains, particularly in the public sector. In Mexico, after the PRI lost the 2000 presidential elections, public-sector employees went on strike for the first time and were successful in obtaining a special bonus from the lame-duck administration of President Ernesto Zedillo. In Venezuela, despite the dramatic decline of AD and President Chávez's continuous attempts to co-opt unions, AD union leaders still controlled the labor movement and organized a successful strike in the oil sector, taking advantage of high oil prices in early 2000.[29] However, these were exceptions rather than the rule. For workers producing tradable products and in the private sector increasing international exposure curtailed the effectiveness of strikes. What are the elements that can facilitate strategic innovation in this context?

Leadership competition in open economies can accelerate innovation while increasing the voice of workers as citizens of new democracies, thus potentially reducing the political distress that increasing economic exposure creates. Liberalizing governments attempted to increase competitiveness by deregulating labor markets and reducing labor costs (e.g., by curtailing payroll taxes). However, there has been little institutional innovation to foster labor unions' involvement in increasing the productivity of the company (e.g., through work councils). Additionally, labor market deregulation, for the most part, did not target the rules related to leadership competition within unions.[30] Reducing the cost of leadership competition within trade unions to deal with Michels' "iron's law of oligarchy" would foster competition on what leaders can offer members in open economies, thus leading to innovation. However, governments seem to fear that militancy against economic liberalization would be the new "offer" provided by leadership competition to union constituencies.[31]

Leadership competition and rotation imply a trade-off regarding labor strategic innovation. Labor involvement in productivity and training or in the development of organizational autonomy requires specialization, which often creates an asymmetry of information. Asymmetries of information usually empower incumbent leaders and make leadership competition more costly. However, the fear of replacement can make leaders responsive to workers who should be involved in new work technologies associated with increasing productivity and worker involvement in production (e.g., flexible specialization, quality circles).[32] Moreover, at a time when workers face growing insecurity due to increasing exposure to international shocks in opening economies, union democracy offers workers the possibility to voice their concerns and have them expressed by their leaders. That is, union democracy improves the quality of leaders (and probably provides checks on corruption) while giving voice to workers as part of an organized civil society.[33] In new democracies that are undergoing enormous institutional change and have weak civil societies, the inclusion of organized groups such as labor unions in the public debate could help to avoid disillusionment with the political process and provide more time for democratic consolidation.

Conclusion

Latin American organized labor adopted political strategies at a time when these were more effective than industrial action. Political strategies were still somewhat effective during economic and political liberalization because labor unions could obtain concessions in return for facilitating the development of these processes. After the dual transition, these strategies lost effectiveness because labor costs became more important than labor peace for policy makers. At the same time, citizens' votes (including those of the unorganized poor) became more necessary to win elections than the mobilization of organized labor, further weakening labor unions' bargaining power vis-à-vis politicians.

Despite the decline in the effectiveness of their traditional political strategies, labor unions were slow to adapt to new circumstances. The reasons for the delay can be found in the institutional inertia of labor organizations after so many years of operating in a context where political strategies were useful. Additionally, labor leaders were concerned with maintaining leadership positions that risked being challenged by experimentation and innovation. At the same time, policy makers did not provide institutional incentives because their agenda sought to neutralize labor opposition rather than promote union innovation. In this context, the promotion of leadership competition could serve as an instrument for fostering innovation. However, government officials fear its effect on increasing militancy and managers worry about efficiency losses derived from the ensuing specialization. Nevertheless, because the challenges for Latin America in the early twenty-first century include democratic consolidation and competitive economies, the risk implied in leadership competition may be worth taking. Although the role of labor as umpires of some political systems has declined, responsive labor unions can give workers a voice in the workplace and in a strong civil society needed for democratic consolidation. Thus, dual transitions toward democracy and markets in the region may gain from similar changes in labor unions. Workers are being exposed to increasing economic competition. Political competition can strengthen their voice in the workplace and in the policy discussion of new democracies.

6

Women and Democracy

Mala N. Htun

Latin American democratic transitions were expected to bring about progress toward gender equality in state and society. Women's movements had mobilized extensively against authoritarian rule and developed close ties to grassroots movements, labor unions, and human rights groups. During the transition, feminists achieved positions of political leadership and demanded that political parties address gender issues. In response to pressure from these activists, many of the democratic governments that assumed power in the 1980s and 1990s made commitments to boost women's political representation, legislate gender equality, and introduce public policies to improve women's lives. Have democratic governments achieved these objectives? Although in no democracy do women participate in and influence public life equally to men, by the end of the 1990s, women's visibility and influence had risen dramatically. Democracy expanded women's opportunities to participate in politics as elected officeholders, in social movement and interest group organizations, and as voters. The region's elected officials adopted quota laws establishing a minimum level for women's participation as candidates in national elections, introduced legislation to eradicate domestic violence, and created hundreds of women's police stations to receive victims of violence.

This chapter offers an overview of women's participation in democratic politics in Latin America and analyzes the policy performance of democratic governments on women's rights issues. Democracy enabled women to gain access to positions of power in record numbers and created a climate receptive to demands for gender equality. Yet even when national governments approved new policy frameworks or discursive shifts, they rarely allocated funds and adapted institutions to implement new laws and policies. Latin American democracies have been more successful integrating women into formal structures of political power than modifying political structures to meet the demands of gender equality. While the number of women in positions of power has grown, democratic performance on women's rights laws and policies has been uneven. Even when a "critical mass" of women is in power, they are not always able or willing to unite and bring about advances in women's rights. In most cases, women owe their primary loyalty to their parties, not to other women politicians. Democracy, moreover, has facilitated the mobilization of coalitions opposed to change on certain gender issues, particularly abortion. Although democracy has given much to celebrate in terms of women's achievements, democratic performance also offers grounds for disappointment. Women are better off than before, but gender equity remains a distant ambition. ⌡

Democratic Inputs: Modes of Women's Participation in Politics

Democratic governance has expanded women's opportunities to participate in politics and made women's rights issues increasingly prominent on national policy agendas. Yet the nature and outcomes of women's participation are complex. Record numbers of women are present in national decision making, although there continues to be significant variation across countries. Latin American civil societies have spawned numerous women's groups and movements with diverse interests and objectives. Yet the diversity of women's interests makes collective action toward a common agenda more difficult. Women make up more than half the electorate in most countries, and studies reveal some distinctive tendencies in women's voting. Still, there is little evidence that gender gaps or gender issues are decisive in determining electoral outcomes.

Women in Decision Making

The consolidation of democratic procedures in Latin America has coincided with impressive increases in women's presence in political decision making.[1] The gains are most dramatic in national legislatures. In 1990, women occupied an average of only 5 percent and 9 percent of the seats in the Senate and in the lower house of Congress, respectively; by 2002, this had increased to 13 and 15 percent. As Table 6.1 shows, however, there is significant variation across different countries. Women's presence among ministers has grown as well: in 1990, women made up 9 percent of ministers, in 2000, 13 percent. In several countries, including Chile, Colombia, Costa Rica, El Salvador, Honduras, Panama, and Venezuela, women occupied one-fifth to one-quarter of ministerial posts in 2000. Women's representation among mayors and governors, however, is still low. Women were 5 percent of mayors in 1990, and 6 percent in 2000. In global terms, the Latin Ameri-

Table 6.1. Women in Political Office in Latin America

Country	Women Ministers, 2000 (in percents)	Women in Chamber of Deputies (or in unicameral Parliament), 2002 (in percents)	Women in Senate, 2002 (in percents)
Argentina	8	31	36
Bolivia	0	12	4
Brazil	0	7	6
Chile	25	13	4
Colombia	19	12	13
Costa Rica	18	35	—
Cuba	10	28	—
Dominican Republic	8	16	7
Ecuador	7	15	—
El Salvador	25	10	—
Guatemala	8	9	—
Honduras	26	9	—
Mexico	16	16	16
Nicaragua	8	21	—
Panama	25	10	—
Paraguay	8	3	18
Peru	7	18	—
Uruguay	0	12	10
Venezuela	21	10	—
Average	13	15	13

can average lags behind that of the Nordic countries, is comparable to Asia and the rest of Europe, slightly ahead of Sub-Saharan Africa, and well ahead of the Arab states.

Women's growing presence in national political decision making is attributable to several factors. The first is an overall expansion in women's capabilities and opportunities. Women's life expectancy increased from 54 years in the 1950s to 73 years in 1999. In 1970, women made up 23 percent of the labor force; by 1999, women represented 35 percent of the labor force overall. Fertility dropped from six children per woman in the 1950s to 2.6 in 1999. Women make up half of secondary school students and half of post-secondary students.[2] Second, the transition to democracy in the region created conditions for the emergence of women's social movements. During the transition period, political parties reached out to include and co-opt these movements, drawing many women into leadership ranks.

The final factor influencing women's opportunities to gain access to power is public attitudes about women's leadership. In a study of public opinion in five Latin American countries conducted by Gallup on behalf of the Inter-American Dialogue and the Inter-American Development Bank in

October 2000, 57 percent of those surveyed said that having more women in political office would lead to better government. People also held women to be superior to men in dealing with a range of issues and problems, including historically male-dominated areas like economic policy and foreign affairs. Sixty-two percent expressed the belief that women leaders would do better than men at reducing poverty, 72 percent at improving education, 57 percent at combating corruption, 64 percent at protecting the environment, 59 percent at managing the economy, and 53 percent at conducting diplomatic relations.

Yet these factors suggest that women's presence in power should register gradual increases. In fact, in the mid- to late 1990s, and early 2000s, there was a dramatic surge in women's representation in several countries. In Argentina, women's presence in the Chamber of Deputies skyrocketed from 6 to 30 percent, and in the Senate, from 3 to 36 percent; in Costa Rica's Congress, women's representation increased from 14 to 35 percent; in Ecuador from 4 to 17 percent; and in Peru's Congress, from 11 to 18 percent. The surge suggests that other factors besides the gradual growth in women's capabilities, changing attitudes, and the pace of democratization are at work. Indeed, a growing number of Latin American governments are acting consciously to boost women's presence in power by introducing quotas and other affirmative action measures. In the 1990s, 11 Latin American countries adopted quota laws establishing a minimum level of 20 to 40 percent for women's participation as candidates in national elections, and Colombia enacted a law requiring that women comprise 30 percent of senior public sector decision makers (Venezuela, however, has since rescinded its quota law).

Table 6.2 shows that, with the exception of Argentina, the region's quota laws were passed within a very short period of time. This simultaneity of policy change across many countries points to an international or regional explanation. In fact, most countries adopted quotas in the years following the Fourth World Conference on Women held in Beijing in 1995 and a series of key regional meetings between Latin American women politicians. In May 1995, Latin American congresswomen gathered at the Latin American Parliament in São Paulo to discuss Argentina's quota experiment and quota politics around the world. The regional meeting served as "the spark that ignited a call to action" on behalf of quotas for women politicians in many countries.[3] Later in the year, the Platform for Action adopted by the world's governments in Beijing endorsed the goal of ensuring "women's equal access to and full participation in decision-making." Among other measures, the Platform called on governments to adopt affirmative action policies to achieve the equal representation of women and men.[4] The Beijing and São Paulo conferences of 1995, as well as other regional meetings, generated policy ideas in the minds of Latin American women politicians, helped unite

Table 6.2. Quota Laws in Latin America

Country	Date of Law	Legislative Body	Quota (in percents)	Women before Law (in percents)	Women after Law (in percents)	Change (in percent points)
Argentina	1991	Chamber	30	6	30	+24
		Senate	30	3	36	+33
Bolivia	1997	Chamber	30	11	12	+1
		Senate	25	4	4	0
Brazil	1997	Chamber	30	7	6	−1
Costa Rica	1997	Unicameral	40	14	35	+21
Dominican Republic	1997	Chamber	25	12	16	+4
Ecuador	1997	Unicameral	20	4	15	+11
Mexico	1996	Chamber	30	17	16	−1
		Senate	30	15	16	+1
Panama	1997	Unicameral	30	8	10	+2
Paraguay	1996	Chamber	20	3	3	0
		Senate	20	11	18	+7
Peru	1997	Unicameral	25	11	18	+7
Average				9	17	+8

Source: Mala Htun and Mark Jones, "Engendering the Right to Participate in Decisionmaking: Electoral Quotas and Women's Leadership in Latin America," in *Gender and the Politics of Rights and Democracy in Latin America,* ed. Nikki Craske and Maxine Molyneux (London: Palgrave, 2002) and author's calculations based on recent election results.

women around the idea of the quota, and legitimized the idea of quotas at the global level.[5] Presidential interest has also been important. Presidents and other male politicians supported quotas out of embarrassment over the low levels of women's representation in their countries, the desire to court women's votes and the support of women politicians, and the need to meet commitments made in the Beijing Platform for Action and other international documents such as the Convention on the Elimination of All Forms of Discrimination Against Women (CEDAW).[6]

On average, quotas have helped to boost women's presence in the legislature by 8 percentage points, an impressive increase from one election to the next. Yet the effects of quotas have varied significantly across countries. In only four circumstances (the Argentine Chamber of Deputies and Argentine Senate, the Costa Rican Congress, and the Paraguayan Senate) did women's presence rise to approach the level contemplated in the quota law. In other cases, such as the Chamber of Deputies of Bolivia, Brazil, Mexico, Panama, and Paraguay, and the Senates of Bolivia and Mexico, quotas coincided with only minimal gains in women's representation.[7] The variation in the success of quotas in getting women elected depends on the details of the laws themselves and the nature of the electoral system to which the laws are applied.

To be most effective, the quota law must be obligatory, must offer details of how the quota is to be implemented by political parties, and must contain a placement mandate for women candidates. This is not the case in all countries. For example, Brazil's quota law amounts to a recommendation rather than an obligation. The law requires parties to *reserve* 30 percent of positions on party lists for women, but does not oblige parties to actually *fill* these slots with women candidates. Since Brazilian electoral regulations allow parties to offer 50 percent more candidates than seats disputed in a district, a party can theoretically run a full slate without any women on the ticket.[8] As a result, in Brazil's 1998 elections, women made up, on average, a mere 10 percent of candidates. Similarly, because it is vague, the Mexican quota law does not prohibit parties from complying with the quota by including women on the ballot as alternates or *suplentes*. In the Mexican elections of July 2000, parties and coalitions complied with the quota, but only because women made up a disproportionate number of the *suplentes* for legislative elections. For example, in the race for the 200 seats in the Chamber of Deputies filled through proportional elections, about 60 percent of the *suplentes* on the lists of the three main parties/coalitions were women.[9]

Finally, to be effective, quota laws must contain a placement mandate forbidding parties from clustering women candidates at the bottom of party lists. The Argentine Ley de Cupos, or Quota Law (1991), requires that women be placed in *electable* positions, which has been interpreted to mean that every third (and sixth, ninth, etc.) slot on the list be occupied by a woman. Party compliance with these placement mandates is largely responsible for the success of the Argentine law in boosting women's presence in the Chamber of Deputies from 6 to 30 percent, and in the Senate, from 3 to 36 percent.[10] The Bolivian and Paraguayan quota laws also contain placement mandates; the law in the Dominican Republic does not. The Costa Rican law originally contained no placement mandate, although in 2000, the Supreme Electoral Court issued a ruling interpreting the law to mean that women must be placed in electable positions on lists for legislative elections.[11] After the ruling establishing placement mandates, women's presence in Costa Rica's Congress climbed from 19 to 35 percent.

A country's electoral system also conditions the impact of quotas. Quotas work best in proportional elections when legislators are elected through closed lists in large districts. In closed-list systems, voters vote for a party list, not an individual candidate. The party list contains a rank ordering of candidates set by party leaders that determines the order in which candidates from the list gain a seat. In this system, party leaders can place women in high positions on the party list to maximize their chances of getting elected. In open-list systems, by contrast, voters vote for individual candidates, whose chances of gaining a seat depend on the individual votes they receive. Open-list elections involve competition among candidates within each party for individual votes in addition to competition across parties, which tends to put women candidates at a disadvantage. Furthermore, quotas tend to work better in higher district magnitudes; that is, when more candidates are elected from a single electoral district. The larger the district, the larger the number of candidates from any single party who will get elected, and the greater the opportunities for women who may be in lower positions on party lists. The open-list system helps to explain the disappointing results of quotas in Brazil and Panama. In countries with mixed electoral systems (Bolivia and Mexico), where part of the legislature is elected through proportional representation and part through plurality elections in single-member districts, quotas do not apply to plurality elections, reducing their impact on the composition of the legislature as a whole.

Collective Action

Gender-related collective action in Latin America has historically come in two forms. In the first place, women have used their gender identity as a resource to mobilize around issues of common political concern. "Women's traditional roles as wives and mothers stimulate and legitimate their social protests and political participation."[12] In Brazil in the early 1960s and Chile in the early 1970s, groups of women deployed their gender identities in protests against the rising cost of living and food shortages. In Argentina in the 1980s, the Madres de la Plaza de Mayo (Mothers of Plaza de Mayo) used gender identities as a resource to demand government accountability in human rights. The 1985 Mexico City earthquake provoked the formation of women's groups to provide emergency assistance and restore basic services to devastated neighborhoods, and women organized to create communal kitchens in Peru during the economic crisis of the 1980s.[13] These women's groups have policy objectives that are not gender-specific, yet they use gender as a resource to generate political mobilization and to enhance their legitimacy.

Second, issues of women and gender have served as the focal point for the political mobilization of citizens including, but not limited to, women. During the political battles surrounding the legalization of divorce in Argentina, Brazil, Chile, and Colombia, both the partisans and opponents of divorce organized public demonstrations, marches, petition campaigns, and elite lobbying networks. Public debates about abortion provoked the mobilization of liberals favoring the expansion of the grounds of legal abortion as well as conservatives seeking constitutional prohibitions on abortion under all circumstances. In the 1990s, national and international networks emerged to increase public awareness and lobby on behalf of issues like domestic violence, women's reproductive health, the implementation of the Beijing Platform for Action, and women's legal rights.[14]

[How has the consolidation of democratic procedures affected these two modes of gender-related mobilization? To a certain extent, conditions of authoritarian rule in Latin America proved conducive to the mobilization of women on the basis of their gender identities. By proscribing political parties and labor unions, authoritarian governments created incentives for citizens to organize around identities such as gender. Women mobilized around gender to defend human rights, demand greater social service provision in low-income neighborhoods, and protest population control programs. The military's assumption that women were "apolitical," moreover, exempted women's organizations from the repression exercised by the state against other groups.[15] As numerous scholars have documented, women's groups served as crucial interlocutors in the broader coalitions seeking to bring about a return to civilian rule in the region.

The return to civilian rule and the consolidation of democratic governance lifted restrictions on political organization and citizen mobilization. This created many more opportunities for women to be politically active, but also reduced the comparative advantage of gender-specific organizations as conduits for social demands. As a result, many women who had entered politics during the struggle against authoritarian rule left gender-specific organizations for political parties and other "traditional" organizations like labor unions. As Chilean politician Adriana Muñoz puts it, "Whereas previously one could speak of a 'women's movement,' now it is more appropriate to speak of 'women in movement.'"[16] The dispersal of politically active women throughout political and civil society generated the impression that with the democratic transition women's movements lost strength and vitality. Moreover, the disappearance of the overarching objective of the return to civilian rule, which had previously served to unite diverse groups of women, led to greater fragmentation among women's movements.]

Many of the women's groups that persisted into the 1990s were not the spontaneous political organizations of the authoritarian period but NGOs with a professional staff. "NGO-ization," a term coined by Sonia Álvarez to refer to the "increased specialization and professionalization" of feminist sectors of the women's movement, is one of the most prominent trends identified by scholars in the 1990s. Women's NGOs involved in the provision of services to women, the lobbying of governments, and consultation with state agencies and international institutions have multiplied across Latin America. Some observers complain that NGO-ization, by building financial linkages between women's organizations and the state, mutes the former's capacity for critical political interventions. There are also concerns that the increased professionalization of women's groups has jeopardized their connections to "popular" women.[17]

In summary, although the consolidation of democratic procedures reduced the competitive advantage of gender-specific organizations, it also expanded opportunities for women's participation in both women's and mixed groups. Although some observers lament the fragmentation and dispersion of the women's movement of the past, the multiplication of the venues and forms of women's collective action in the 1990s attests to the diversity of women and their interests in Latin America.

Voting

Besides serving as elected officeholders or working in civil society organizations, women participate in the political process by voting. How do women's votes affect democratic politics? This section analyzes the question of whether there are any discernible tendencies in women's voting and then examines the impact of these tendencies on national elections. There is some evidence that women's historic tendency to vote for parties of the Right has shifted in some countries, although it is not clear that this gender gap makes a difference for electoral outcomes.

The Gender Gap?

Electoral research has long confirmed the existence of a small but persistent "gender gap" in many countries. Initially remarked upon by European and North American scholars such as Maurice Duverger and Seymour Martin Lipset in the 1950s and 1960s, the gender gap referred to the fact that while women tended to support Center–Right parties and candidates, men were more likely to endorse parties and candidates of the Left. Data from the early 1970s revealed that the difference between male and female support for parties of the Left was as great as 14 percentage points in Italy, 13 percentage points in Germany, and 9 percentage points in Great Britain.[18] Scholars commonly explained female conservatism as a function of their greater religiosity, longer lifespans, and lower trade union membership.[19] Beginning in the 1980s, however, there were signs that women in many established democracies were realigning away from the Right and toward parties and candidates of the Left. Ronald Inglehart and Pippa Norris characterize women's electoral realignment as a movement from a "traditional gender gap" to a "modern gender gap," and attribute the transition to value changes provoked by a transformation in sex roles in postindustrial societies. Meanwhile, "traditional" gender gaps persisted in many developing countries.

Evidence from some Latin American countries affirms the existence of a "traditional" gender gap. The thesis of female conservatism reaches back into the early history of Latin American electoral politics. "Progressive" leaders such as Lázaro Cárdenas in Mexico withdrew their support for woman suffrage on the grounds that it would strengthen the electoral position of conservative parties. Ecuadorian liberals were similarly afraid of women's allegiance to the Roman Catholic Church and believed that women would be susceptible to the influence of priests at election time. In Ecuador and in Chile, conservative parties, and in Mexico, a conservative administration, granted women the vote in order to expand their electoral bases. In other countries, namely, Brazil, Peru, the Dominican Republic, Nicaragua, and Paraguay, woman suffrage was adopted through decrees issued by dictators.[20]

In Chile, women have tended to vote for parties and candidates of the Right, leading to the most pronounced gender gap in the region. In the 1960s, 73 percent of women, compared to 56 percent of men, voted for parties of the Right or for the Christian Democrats.[21] Inglehart and Norris' data from the World Values Survey indicate that in the early 1990s, the gender gap in voting preferences in Chile was among the most pronounced among the thirty-six countries in the sample, and continued to be visible even when controlling for social structure and cultural beliefs.[22] The gender gap persisted through Chile's 1999 presidential election. Right candidate Joaquín Lavín received 51 percent of women's votes, while 49 percent of women voted for Socialist Party leader Ricardo Lagos. The Lagos–Lavín gap was even more pronounced among men, however, with 54 percent casting their votes for Lagos and 46 percent for Lavín.[23]

Data from Mexico and Brazil show that women are less likely to support parties of the Left than are men, although male and female support for parties of the Right is about equal. Polling data gathered around the time of Mexican elections in 1988 and 1991 revealed that the left-wing PRD drew considerably more support from men than from women, while the traditional PRI drew more support from women. (Support for the Right-of-Center National Action Party [PAN] was about equal.)[24] This trend continued into the later 1990s. Poll data gathered around the time of the 1997 elections for the mayor of Mexico City demonstrated that even when one controls for education, religiosity, political interests, and other variables, women were more reluctant to support the PRD than men.[25] In Brazil's 1998 presidential elections, 29 percent of men claimed to support the candidate of the Left (Workers' Party leader Luiz Inácio Lula da Silva), compared to a mere 24 percent of women. Male and female support for President Fernando Henrique Cardoso was about equal (49 percent of men polled supported him, compared to 48 percent of women).[26] In Argentina, World Values Survey points to a gender gap, but in the opposite direction from Chile, Mexico, and Brazil.[27]

The small gender gap characterizing the preferences of the mass electorate in these countries is at odds with the behavior of politicians and political parties. Politicians and parties of the Left historically snubbed by women voters have served as the most forceful advocates of gender equality issues. Mexico's PRD, for example, was the first party to adopt women's quotas for internal elections and for candidates in popular elections. The PRD quota policies produced a spillover effect into other parties. The PRI adopted similar quota rules and women activists initiated internal debates about quotas in the PAN.[28] Chile's Socialist Party, also more likely to be snubbed by female voters, has incorporated many feminist activists into its ranks and promoted women to senior decision-making positions within the party. Chilean President Ricardo Lagos (a Socialist) in early 2000 appointed five women to his sixteen-member cabinet, a historic high for Latin America.

Nonetheless, there is growing evidence that parties of the Right are attempting to incorporate, if not "feminist," then "pro-women" principles into their agendas. In the 1990s, parties and candidates adopting Right-of-Center positions on economic issues were increasingly likely to emphasize gender issues in their campaigns. One politician from the Chilean Right, for example, developed a slogan stating that "if the twentieth century was the time for women to enter the workforce, the twenty-first is the time for men to rejoin the family." Former Argentine President Carlos Menem endorsed electoral quotas for women and allocated millions of dollars of federal money to create a network of provincial women's councils. Peruvian President Alberto Fujimori traveled to the Beijing Women's Conference, appointed an unprecedented number of women to senior decision-making positions, and introduced policy projects directed at lower-income women such as day care centers, literacy drives, and microcredit programs.

Gender Gaps and Electoral Outcomes

Latin America's small gender gaps are worth taking into account if they matter in electoral outcomes. Media hype in the United States about the 1992 "Year of the Woman" that helped elect Bill Clinton to the presidency, the "Angry White Men" who restored a Republican majority to Congress in 1994, and the "Soccer Moms" who reelected Bill Clinton in 1996 generated speculation that gender gaps may be decisive in elections. In theory, gender gaps can influence elections in two ways: through the mobilization of women as a "swing vote" and through the emergence of gender-related "issue voting" among the electorate. Yet there is little evidence that women are a self-conscious voting bloc in Latin America or that the electorate chooses candidates on the basis of their positions on gender issues.

First, socioeconomic and ideological differences among women often prevent them from uniting to maximize their leverage in electoral politics. In the United States, the interaction of class, race, and values generate political differences among women that "make it difficult, and inaccurate, to declare the existence of any sort of women's consciousness or women's voting bloc."[29] In the U.S. presidential elections, for example, women voted for Bill Clinton more than men *on average*, but "women's disproportionate support for Clinton and the Democratic Party in 1996 was driven by certain groups of economically vulnerable and socially liberal women, while Dole drew upon upscale and socially conservative women."[30] In Latin America, pronounced socioeconomic, regional, value, and race differences among women similarly militate against women's organization into a self-conscious voting bloc. In a survey of popular views about women in politics conducted in Peru in 1997 and 1998, Cecilia Blondet found tremendous variation in responses among regions.[31] These and other differences among women historically impeded the consolidation of a "united" women's movement, and have generated political disagreements at national and regional meetings of women's groups.[32]

The second question is the extent to which gender-related "issue voting" characterizes Latin American elections. Issue voting refers to "policy-conscious voting decisions" by the electorate.[33] To date, there is little evidence that gender-related issue voting has emerged in Latin American politics, although politicians may campaign on some gender issues in order to enhance their appeal. In fact, issue voting of any sort, even on economic issues, is still a nascent phenomenon in Latin American elections. Domínguez and McCann's studies of Mexican voters in the early 1990s, for example, found that voter positions on the performance of the economy and on party positions were "only marginally related to voter intentions."[34] In the Mexican elections of 1994 and 1997, however, retrospective economic judgments mattered more: Mexicans were more likely to vote for the PRI if they approved of the country's economic performance and tended to support the opposition otherwise.[35] This suggests that in the Mexican case at least, issue voting on the economy may have emerged toward the later 1990s, although traditional party loyalties continued to significantly influence voter choice. For various reasons, a transition toward gender-related issue voting may be longer in coming.

In their classic study of U.S. politics, Campbell et al. established that issue voting requires three conditions: (1) the public be divided on the issue; (2) the issue be salient to voters; and (3) candidates or parties adopt distinctive positions on the issue.[36] Each of these three conditions poses challenges to the emergence of gender-related issue voting in Latin America. With the exception of controversial issues like divorce and abortion, most gender-related policy issues lack political prominence and fail to generate significant political discord. Although representatives of all Latin American governments endorsed the Platform for Action generated by the United Nations Fourth

World Conference on Women held in Beijing in 1995, only small segments of the general public reported knowledge of the Beijing Conference or its provisions. The adoption of women's quota laws by so many governments within a short period of time was unprecedented, but few voters knew about the quotas. A Peruvian survey revealed that 75 percent of people were unaware of quota law.[37] Ethically charged issues like divorce and abortion, on the other hand, have had high visibility and the potential to divide voters. Yet most parties and leaders have not adopted clear and contrasting positions on these issues. During the debates over the legalization of divorce in Brazil and Argentina in the 1970s and 1980s, for example, no party adopted a firm position on the issue and instead freed legislators to vote their conscience.[38]

One country where issue voting around gender may have emerged is Chile. Gender-related issues are politically prominent and clear differences of opinion exist. Only in Chile was the Beijing Women's Conference, for example, a hotly contested issue in Congress and the media. Public controversy also surrounded the creation of the National Women's Service (SERNAM) in the early 1990s as well as the government's introduction of some sex education programs into public schools.[39] Political parties have adopted firm positions on gender issues like the legalization of divorce. Although the Center–Left Christian Democrats and Center–Right Renovación Nacional (National Renovation) failed to adopt an explicit party line,[40] the Independent Democratic Union (UDI) on the far Right and the Democratic and Socialist parties on the Left endorsed clear, and contrasting, positions.

Nonetheless, it is not clear whether the politicization of gender in Chilean politics accurately reflects underlying voter dispositions, since there is often a big gap between public opinion and the position of parties. On divorce, for example, the vast majority of the public supports legalization, but the divorce bill approved by the Chamber of Deputies has been stalled in the Senate since late 1997 because of opposition from conservative senators. It is also unclear whether gender issues have been decisive for electoral outcomes. Although Joaquín Lavín and Ricardo Lagos had contrasting positions on the legalization of divorce and permission for therapeutic abortion, most analysts believe that these issues mattered less for the election than did the arrest of General Pinochet in Britain and the association of Lavín's party with Chile's authoritarian past. In summary, although important for other reasons, there is no overwhelming evidence that women's votes or gender issues are decisive for electoral outcomes.

Democratic Outputs: Policy Performance on "Women's Issues"

In the 1990s, Latin American governments adopted many new laws and policies to address problems of inequalities and to improve women's status.[41] At least sixteen countries enacted legislation on domestic violence. Every country created special agencies within the government to propose, advise, and coordinate public policies to improve women's rights. Legislators reformed national constitutions to incorporate new articles declaring equality between men and women, and modified discriminatory property rights regimes and other sections of family law to grant women more rights. Some governments introduced literacy drives, day care services, and microcredit programs directed at poor women. Other governments improved programs for women's reproductive health such as cervical cancer screening and family planning services.

This policy record appears impressive until one takes a closer look. Governments have introduced policy changes on some issues, but not all issues. A great deal has been accomplished in the area of domestic violence, such as the creation of women's police stations, battered women's shelters, new legal options such as restraining orders, and the recognition of marital rape. However, considerably less has changed in the area of women's reproductive health. Abortion is considered a crime across the region and, although rarely punished, pushes women to resort to clandestine procedures at great risk to their health. Yet most governments have not taken action to decrease the high frequency of illegal abortion by ensuring comprehensive access to voluntary family planning services. Countries such as Chile and Argentina have done very little to provide women with access to family planning on a national scale. On the other hand, the government of Alberto Fujimori in Peru attempted nationwide family planning but in such a reckless manner so as to provoke severe criticism from feminist NGOs and from Roman Catholic bishops due to reports about the involuntary sterilization of women in rural areas.

Moreover, there is frequently a large gap between the spirit of gender equitable laws and policies and their actual implementation. Judges are reluctant to apply the new devices granted to protect women victims of violence under new domestic violence legislation. Constitutional declarations of sex equality coexist with discriminatory sections of civil and criminal codes. National women's health programs and campaigns are poorly implemented and executed. Projects directed at poor women such as day care services and literacy drives have uneven coverage and frequently overlap with clientelistic endeavors directed at ruling party supporters.

Why are Latin America's gender-related policy changes not deeper and more expansive? In the first place, many recent policy measures are rapid responses to commitments made by governments at the international level. In agreements such as the United Nations Convention on the Elimination of all Forms of Discrimination against Women, endorsed by the UN General Assembly in 1979, the Inter-American Convention on Violence against Women

(1994), the Declaration of the Summit of the Americas held in Miami in 1994, and the Beijing Platform for Action (1995), Latin American governments committed themselves to a wide array of policy measures to promote gender equality. In the late 1990s, the region's leaders acted quickly to fulfill their international obligations without contemplating seriously all the institutional and procedural changes necessary to carry out the new initiatives. For example, many governments adopted legislation creating policies to eradicate violence against women without adapting the national budget to allocate funds for these policies. Similarly, some countries approved quota laws without the implementing legislation or electoral reform necessary to make quotas work.

Second, women's participation in leadership is not always effective, and women's political alliances are not sufficiently powerful or durable to pressure for change in all areas and to oversee implementation of new policies. To be sure, in the 1990s, as women's presence in decision making grew to reach a "critical mass" in some countries, women from different political parties and social sectors came together in political alliances to push for law and policy advances on gender issues. Yet women's participation is not sufficient to guarantee effective policy changes benefiting women. To explain the causes and conditions of sustainable policy, we must explore the possibilities and limitations of women's expanded participation in leadership. Even when women decision makers are present in greater numbers, they will not always be interested in promoting women's issues or able to ally with women from other parties. Nor do women necessarily have the power to promote change.

The Effects of Women's Presence in Leadership on Policy Outcomes

Evidence demonstrates that women's greater presence in power shifts the terms of legislative debates and introduces new items to the policy agenda. Studies from the United States have shown that women are more likely than men to raise concerns and sponsor legislation related to the family, equal opportunity, childcare policy, and reproductive health.[42] Linda Stevenson's study of bills on domestic violence and quotas in Mexico showed that legislative activity on these women's rights issues was related to changes over time in the number of women in the Congress.[43] Htun and Jones' data on committee membership and bill introduction in Argentina revealed that women are more likely than men to sit on congressional committees dealing with issues deemed to be of traditional concern to women and to sponsor bills in the "women's rights" and "children and families" issue areas.[44] A survey of legislators in the Brazilian Congress affirmed that women were significantly more likely than men to support the continuation of quota laws in

Congress and the extension of quotas to the executive branch, the criminalization of sexual harassment, the allocation of more public funds on gender equality policies, the payment of maternity leave by social security service, and the granting of tax incentives to businesses in exchange for hiring more women workers.[45]

These studies suggest that women's presence in power has served an agenda-setting goal. Yet there is a large gap between agenda setting and policy outcomes. Even when many women are present in power, they do not always act together on behalf of other women. Why? First, party discipline frequently prevents women from different parties from uniting in cross-partisan coalitions. Party loyalty may overpower gender identity in legislative politics. Based on interviews with eighty Mexican women in politics, Victoria Rodríguez concludes that "women's political loyalties, first and foremost, rest with the political party or organization to which they belong. Gender loyalty, for all practical purposes, comes in (a distant) second."[46] Another study of Mexico found that multipartisan alliances of women were successful in achieving their objectives only when these did not contradict party interests. When party interests diverged, as in the case of quota laws, protection of women in the workplace, and abortion, women's alliances were significantly weakened and legislation was not enacted. Gender-related policy changes came about only when the interests of the various parties coincided, as in the case of domestic violence.[47]

Second, questions of gender equality have not been among the top priorities of most women in decision-making positions. In Argentina, data show that 33 percent of women legislators presented a third or more of their bills in the women's rights area and 11 percent in the children and families area, but 58 percent of the women legislators presented no bills in women's rights and 61 percent presented no bills in children and families.[48] Moreover, almost no one makes gender equality issues a centerpiece of their political campaign. One Argentine politician noted that "men have convinced women that talking about women's issues is of little importance. Women, in order to be important politically, can't talk about gender issues."[49] Moreover, most women who have achieved power owe their positions to mentors—usually male party leaders or relatives—and not to other women. Rodríguez maintains that in Mexico, women's "solidarity and loyalty rest with policies and programs, political patrons and mentors, career plans and ambitions—not with the other women in the party."[50]

Third, women in power have different positions on policy issues and different ideas about what constitutes women's interests. In the United States, for example, political movements of women have taken sharply opposing sides on some of the key policy issues affecting women, such as the proposed Equal Rights Amendment (ERA) to the U.S. Constitution as well as the constitutional status of first trimester abortions.[51] In Latin America, women have been active in both feminist reproductive rights movements advocating an expansion of the conditions of legal abortion as well as in pro-life movements lobbying for constitutional bans on abortion under all circumstances.[52] The existence of a common gender identity in no way implies that women have uniform interests, even on issues that affect women.

Finally, few women in elected office actually wield significant power.[53] Although there are some notable exceptions, party presidents, the presidents of important congressional commissions, leaders of party blocs in Congress, and other key posts have continued to be held by men. Few women have been present in the groups and settings where behind-the-scenes decisions are made. One Mexican politician observed that the circles of power were constructed over the course of many years, and trace their roots to an era when women did not enjoy the social position and opportunities they do today. The rules of the political game were constructed as men's rules, and their endurance marginalizes women in practice without the need for men to discriminate actively.[54] Even when many women enjoy formal titles and offices, the fact that the nature of power remains predominantly masculine means that few women have it.

Explaining Gender-related Policy Changes

If the presence of a critical mass of women in power is not sufficient to guarantee effective policy changes on women's rights issues, how can policy be explained? Understanding the causes and conditions of law and policy changes requires exploring the institutional configurations that enhance or decrease the influence of *all* actors with a stake in gender issues. My own study, which attempted to account for policy change on family law, the legalization of divorce, and the conditions of legal abortion in Argentina, Brazil, and Chile, found that women's participation was important for policy change, but did not tell the whole story.[55] Some progressive advances in law and policy were brought about by professional lawyers, liberal politicians, and even dictators. Nor was democratic governance always associated with policy advances on women's rights. In Argentina and Brazil, for example, reforms benefiting women were introduced under both military and democratic rule. The authoritarian government of Getulio Vargas in Brazil in the 1930s and 1940s not only granted women the vote but also expanded the conditions of legal abortion to include women who had been raped, a move that went beyond existing laws in most of Europe as well as the United States. The Brazilian military government of General Geisel legalized divorce in 1977 and altered the marital property regime to grant women more rights. Civil code reforms granting married women full civil capacity and equalizing property relations within marriage were promulgated by the government of General Juan Carlos Onganía in Argentina in 1968.

The study demonstrated that gender-related reforms depended on the opening of institutional "policy windows" allowing issue networks of feminists, professional lawyers, and liberal politicians to enact changes in the law. In the case of divorce, windows opened when governments clashed with Roman Catholic bishops. In the case of family law reforms and early-twentieth-century reforms to abortion law, windows opened when state leaders appointed expert commissions to propose modernizing laws to civil and criminal laws in line with international standards. By contrast, abortion became more difficult to reform by the late twentieth century. Although democratic governance enabled advocates of abortion law liberalization to lobby public authorities, democracy also created conditions for anti-abortion groups to organize and expand their influence. The simultaneous mobilization of the feminist reproductive rights movement and the pro-life movement raised the stakes and reinforced the obstacles to policy change. In short, explaining policy change requires studying, not merely the presence of women in the state, but sequences of interactions among various social groups and institutions including Roman Catholic bishops, feminist activists, liberal lawyers, reformist politicians, conservative interest groups, and dictators.

Conclusion

Women's participation in democratic politics in Latin America gives cause for celebration and concern. The growth in women's presence in decision making, the explicit commitments made by governments to principles of sex equality, and official attention to gender-related problems like domestic and sexual violence are reasons to celebrate. The situation of many Latin American women has improved from decades ago. On the other hand, new policies suffer from mediocre implementation, making women's rights more abstract than concrete. The gap between law and practice and the failure of many new female decision makers to exercise effective leadership constitute deficiencies in democratic politics. Although partially a function of women's diverse interests and the dynamics of democratic party competition, the difficulties faced by women leaders in organizing more durable political coalitions reflects continued male bias in political institutions and the masculine culture of power in the region.

What will it take to enhance women's influence and deepen the policy changes under way? The adaptation of the culture of power to women's presence in decision making is a long-term process. Transformations in the social practices surrounding gender relations provoked by demographic, socioeconomic, and technological changes may eventually "filter up" to influence men's and women's willingness to submit to women's authority. In the shorter term, male leaders can help to forge new norms of power by demonstrating in public that they take women seriously as decision makers. Overall, improving democratic performance on women's rights issues depends on the consolidation of democratic governance in general. Poor governance—institutional failure, poor law enforcement, corruption, inefficiency, lack of accountability—thwarts policy implementation. Profound social inequalities, including variation in the status of women across region, class, and ethnic group, limit the reach of new policies designed to improve women's lives. Translating women's abstract rights into concrete rights demands that these dilemmas of democratic governance be resolved.

7

Public Opinion

Marta Lagos

After a long history of instability, military rule, and repression, democracy has, for the first time, become the dominant form of government in Latin America.[1] In most countries, with the exception of Uruguay and Chile, democracy has been established for the first time, or has been reestablished after decades of military hegemony. The latter is the case in Argentina, where democracy finally took hold after a series of failed redemocratization attempts in the late 1950s and early 1960s.[2]

The redemocratization process in Latin America has been possible as a result of the failure of authoritarian regimes, particularly those that emerged since the 1960s (the "new authoritarianism") and because there has been an international trend toward democracy (the "third wave"), especially in Southern and Eastern Asia.[3] Also, intense international surveillance by governments, parties, trade unions, and NGOs, which stresses the need for civilian rule and respect for human rights, fosters adherence to democratic norms. When reference is made to "new democracies," this description does not negate a previous pluralist experience, such as the case of Germany after 1949, an "old" democracy interrupted by a non-democratic regime. Rather, the adjective indicates that for the first time in most countries throughout the region, universal suffrage and the rule of law are applied, elected governments recognize opposition forces fulfilling the political role of checks and balances, and the ruling party can be ousted from power through elections.

These political goods that characterize democracy are not sufficiently taken into account when analyzing democratic consolidation in the region. As Dankwart Rustow has pointed out, the factors that give birth to a democracy and the factors needed to develop it are not the same.[4] The legitimacy of the system as a whole—the legitimacy of an elected parliament or judiciary—cannot be taken for granted simply because democracy has been established in a given country. A democracy must earn its legitimacy not only through institutions, but also through the social and political actors that are identified with the system.

The new democracies coexist with democracies that have long pluralist traditions, many of which were already well established by the end of the 1950s, such as Colombia and Venezuela. These countries, however, also face serious political and social challenges: violence and narcotics flourish in Colombia; in Venezuela, an elected ex-military man and coup leader has imposed an extreme form of democracy by plebiscite, severely restricting the power of opposition parties and distancing the country from Robert Dahl's concept of a polyarchy.[5]

Old and new democracies face many challenges. Not only do they need to anchor political institutions and set up the necessary political resources to sustain them, they must also formulate inclusive public policy, rather than the restricted agendas of the elitist democratic governments of the past, which were so easily ousted by the military.[6] Many new democracies were established by an electorate that, for the first time, included illiterates and members of the rural and urban poor populations.[7] With these circumstances, in tandem with the economic problems of widespread poverty and inequality, the consolidation process has encountered many new challenges that were not initially evident to researchers and analysts. Although it is true that simplistic or over-enthusiastic views were not adopted with regard to the region's political evolution, researchers and analysts failed to predict the enormous difficulties and to see the differences between the political resources needed for the inauguration and those needed for the consolidation process.

The new democracies face an additional external element not present before this third wave: the international monitoring[8] of democratic performance in any given country and the pressure that this puts on elites and populations. For example, while the military in Ecuador removed President Mahuad from office, they restrained themselves from remaining in power, as they had habitually done in the past.[9] In Paraguay, the military has been on the verge of seizing power on several occasions, but fear of international retaliation, that the cost of such a step would be greater than that of tolerating the current regime, has held them in check. Although in Peru and Venezuela, significant and basic democratic components have been excised, in the case of Peru, international pressure convinced Fujimori to call for presidential elections allowing the country to return to democratic rule.[10]

This picture of democracy in Latin America, with its triumphs and challenges, is not complete if one does not consider recent and past history. Recent history reveals long and painful military experiences that left deep wounds in society, not only due to human rights violations, but also because these regimes undermined the social fabric of democracy.[11] Economic reforms, on the other hand, an integral part of the political agenda of the 1990s, have created new challenges and difficulties.

In addition to the legacy of debt left by the military regimes, it should be kept in mind that the restoration of democracy took place under extremely difficult economic circumstances. The military, particularly the "new authoritarians,"[12] had promised to remove the obstacles to development that previous civilian governments were unable to rectify. Despite these promises, the return to civilian rule forced democratic governments to cope with complex and simultaneous adjustment processes to organize the economy, take care of the basic needs of the citizenry, and deal with the expectations of a majority of the population that now expected democracy to solve all their problems. In fact, Latin America's democratic third wave faced in one decade what established democracies typically experienced in five. Above all, new democracies have to face a variety of events simultaneously without having the necessary time to build the political resources needed to support the shocks of social and economic reforms in order to bring about stable development.

The legitimacy of the democratic system was often presented as a function of its performance, creating high expectations. For example, in a 1983 presidential campaign speech, Raúl Alfonsín stated that "with democracy you eat, you educate, and you cure."[13] Given the fact that its legitimacy is tied to deliverable goods, both political and economic, the performance of democracy has become a major indicator of consolidation. While economic reform creates high expectations, privatization soon brings about fatigue and frustration. After a decade, it seems that politicians and technocrats have failed to communicate the real impact of privatization on economic performance. Given these circumstances, I agree with Carol Graham and Nancy Birdsall's remarks that "acceptance of continued market reform could be the short-run outcome of the limited political voice of those excluded from new opportunities, and time and greater accountability of public policy to the median voter could generate a political backlash against market policies."[14] This is true not only against market policies, but also against democracy. If military and democratic governments fail to solve a country's problems, citizens turn away and look for either collective or more individualistic solutions. Venezuela is a good example of an ad hoc solution.

Data available in industrialized democracies prove that the legitimacy of the system does not rest solely upon its economic performance. Political benefits—elections and government alternation—are also considered an element of its legitimacy.[15] However, in Latin America, fatigue from the privatization process, poor economic performance, and a failure to narrow the income gap has tarnished the legitimacy of democracy. With this limited legitimacy, solutions are often offered and bought at any price, as indicated by the authoritarian albeit popular appeals of Presidents Alberto Fujimori and Hugo Chávez in Peru and Venezuela, respectively.

The establishment of democracy raises expectations in three main areas: a cultural expectation that seeks the determination of societal game rules; an economic expectation, in the sense that people expect it to deliver economic and social benefits such as health, education, jobs, and housing; and a political expectation in the form of stability and the fair and orderly handling of conflicts of interest. These expectations have to be resolved simultaneously with the problems of post-authoritarian trauma, whereas Western democracies of the first and second waves had several decades of political and economic development in which to heal their wounds and grow.

In an effort to shed new light into the challenges and difficulties facing new democracies in Latin America, public opinion surveys have been conducted across seventeen countries since 1995 by the Latinobarómetro. The survey data, a sample of the adult population from the Rio Grande in northern Mexico to Cape Horn in southern Chile, represent the over 400 million inhabitants of Latin America.[16] Public opinion surveys are subjective instruments that statistically summarize what are often volatile opinions, attitudes, and behavior, and whose results have to be taken as a static measurement at a specific point in time.[17] It is only through successive measurement of the same subjects from different perspectives that the researcher can get a clear picture of any given social phenomenon. No single data point is conclusive, and it is only over time that we can observe the presence of permanent relationships between different elements of collective behavior. Nevertheless, public opinion data do bring us nearer to an understanding of social phenomena because they provide us with a perspective of the overall population as opposed to that of an elite segment or of the media.

To redress this neglect, this chapter reviews and contrasts basic aspects of modern democratic theory with data from public opinion polls, analyzing the most important issues that affect democratic consolidation. This analysis is based on the examination of attitudes, opinions, and values held by most Latin Americans. The principal issues addressed in the following pages include low interpersonal trust, levels of legitimacy vis-à-vis democratic efficacy, civic attitudes in which the majority of those polled express a desire for more rights than obligations, and high expectations for the future among the citizenry. Although these variables substantially affect democratic consolidation in Latin America, their real significance has traditionally been left out of conventional studies.

The opinions of the population are often seen as contradictory and inconsistent, and the researcher's task is to understand the causes of these (sometimes apparent) contradictions and inconsistencies. This is especially true of what is understood by the concept of democracy. The content of the word *democracy,* if we take words as "mental products"[18] for most intervie-wees, is not the complex concept used by analysts, but simply the sum of in-teractive experiences within a given culture. Democracy as a word has cul-turally dependent content; it is in fact a perception. Public opinion surveys measure perceptions and "perceptions are truth, because people believe them" (Epictetus). A perception as a mental product can be true or false when measured against an objective indicator, yet this does not change the content of the believed truth.

Public opinion may judge a country to be democratic without its ac-tually complying with the necessary elements of a democratic system. The perceived concept of democracy, therefore, may have different contents in different countries with different historical experiences. To explore these varying meanings, I use opinion surveys. The data cover a wide set of ques-tions dealing with politics and economics. In this essay, data will be pre-sented dealing with basic behavioral attitudes toward democracy that are useful in understanding the complexities involved in democratic consoli-dation.

The historical analysis of these data allows us to identify both a starting point and the rate of change in addition to absolute magnitudes.[19] How do political benefits correlate with democratic stability in other societies? Al-though most Latin American countries have enjoyed democratic govern-ments in the past, these cases, often encompassing a brief time period, are a trap for the analyst, creating a temptation to rely on a diffuse "democratic culture" which, in reality, cannot be sustained by the meager cultural her-itage of short democratic periods.[20]

In fact, due primarily to the lack of comparable survey data, the study of political culture has not been at the core of the analysis of the problems of democracy in Latin America. Democracy today is "the only game in town" and its problems and crises can be analyzed through the expansion or regres-sion of its main components.[21] The current focus is on determining the dom-inant components of the democratic culture and establishing how many of these are in play in any given country where the population perceives itself as a "democracy." For at the end of the day, the different types of democracies es-tablished around the world deny more than they confirm the existence of a model democracy.[22] They may not be "democracies by-the-book," but may in fact be the only types of democracy the existing political cultures are able to sustain. Their main political resources may not be evolving toward a better stage that could theoretically sustain a consolidated democracy.

What are the characteristics that underlie these different manifestations of democracy? Do they help to explain the difficulties these Latin American countries have encountered? Do they shed light on new difficulties on the horizon, on paths that these democracies may follow?

Considering the events of the 1990s, is it wise to expect significant changes in the components of Latin American democratic regimes in the current decade? How can we face this decade without being overly optimistic or pessimistic about how democracies will develop? Will the new democracies that have emerged around the world develop mutations of the components of democracy, giving birth to different types of democracies? Or will they converge toward one model with an increasing number of components to confirm its democratic vows? In other words, what are the rates and the elements of change in these new democracies, and where do these changes lead?

At every point in the analysis, it is important to bear in mind that we are speaking about two concepts: the theoretical intellectual understanding of democracy (democracy as a set of rules) and the culture-dependent concept of democracy (the public opinion perception). As Larry Diamond correctly points out, "despite considerable theoretical grounds for expecting that political culture plays an important role in the development and maintenance (or failure) of democracy, the post-1960s generation of work on democracy has tended to neglect the phenomenon, particularly at the mass level."[23] The following pages will attempt to disentangle the different components of democratic and political support[24] and their meaning using a five-year series of Latinobarómetro data (all the tables and statistics cited in this chapter come from the Latinobarómetro).

Interpersonal Trust

After the seminal article by Seymour Martin Lipset and throughout the 1960s, economic development was correlated with the development of democracy, assuming that a certain degree of welfare was a prerequisite for such a system.[25] Efforts to overcome underdevelopment attempted to create favorable conditions for the democratization of Latin America, and many of the development assistance programs, particularly in the United States, were based on this notion. The failure of democratic performance showed that this interpretation was restrictive and that economic factors, although relevant, were not sufficient to explain political development. Other factors needed to be considered, among which political culture was of great relevance.[26]

It was Emile Durkheim[27] who, over a century ago, stated in his inaugural address at the Sorbonne that it was people who shaped institutions and that these institutions could not do what was beyond the nature of their members. Therefore, before judging the performance of institutions, it is necessary to know about the people that comprise those institutions. Durkheim goes on to say that societies are what we make of them, we need not ask what they are.

Table 7.1. Interpersonal Trust, 1996–2001

Q. Generally speaking, would you say that you can trust most people, or that you can never be too careful when dealing with others?

	Totals for Latin America (in percents)				
	1996	1997	1998	2000	2001
You can trust most people.	20	23	21	16	17
You can never be too careful when dealing with others.	77	75	76	82	80
No response	3	2	3	2	3
Total	100	100	100	100	100
N	18,717	17,767	17,901	18,125	18,135

Source: Latinobarómetro.

It is the basic interaction among citizens that provides the grounds and shapes the nature of the institutions in any given society, according to Durkheim. It is not surprising to find interpersonal trust to be a basic precondition to confidence in institutions in the study of Western democracies. Political culture is rooted in a wide and complex set of values, beliefs, attitudes, and behavior in which interpersonal trust plays a major role. If trust is weak, there is less willingness to trust democratic institutions.[28] You cannot trust Parliament, Congress, government, or the justice system if you cannot trust in your neighbor, your colleague at work, or your classmate.

Latin America is characterized by a low degree of interpersonal trust (see Table 7.1). Only 17 percent of the adult population admit that "you can trust people," down from 20 percent in 1996.[29] This downward slope is very significant if one considers that is backed up by over 18,000 interviews in 17 countries, over 5 years, altogether amounting to 90,000 observations. This is not an accident of the present time, but a main cultural trait of the region as a whole that distinguishes it significantly from industrialized Western democracies.

Does this thwart the efforts to strengthen democracy and foster its consolidation? Or is this a major permanent trait, which will have to be built into the democratic culture of the region? Unlike European countries, where economic well-being and scientific and technological development have strengthened individualism and weakened association networks, citizens in Latin America are distant from each other, not because of economic or technological pressures, but because lifestyles and society are organized in such a way that interrelationships with others tend to be biased toward closed networks rather than an open society. This lack of trust in third parties is not a consequence of, but rather a hindrance to, modernity. Poverty also works as a hindrance to an open society.[30] If we also consider the broader historical context, including long and painful military episodes, then the consolidation of democracy becomes a challenge far beyond institutional reconstruction; it emerges as a major transformation of the basic structure of the interpersonal relationships of society as a whole. To what extent is it possible to expect, and in what period of time, given the fact that in the recorded five years the downward slope has been confirmed? If future behavior is the continuation of past behavior, interpersonal trust may remain low in Latin America for decades to come.

The rate of interpersonal trust is low throughout Latin America. There is slightly higher than average trust in Mexico, at 36 percent, and Uruguay, at 24 percent. However, trust is especially low for countries like Chile (15 percent).

Trust has been related to economic development in many countries. The countries included in the World Value Study[31] show a positive correlation between the level of interpersonal trust and economic growth. The level of interpersonal trust in industrialized societies is more than double the average for Latin America and reaches its highest score in countries like Sweden.

The Latinobarómetro shows that low levels of trust increase poverty and thwart development. In fact, low interpersonal trust translates into a lack of confidence in institutions. Political parties and Parliaments are the most affected entities, although the justice system is also harmed. The lack of interpersonal trust further diminishes an already feeble capacity for association, indicated by the reluctance to join neighborhood committees, parents associations at school, and volunteer groups. This environment fails to foster the conditions for association, envisioned by de Tocqueville in *Democracy in America*. Rather, mistrust creates a pluralist order in which citizens stand alone before the authorities and a political order made up by individualities, where association networks and interest groups capable of influencing the authorities have not been an instrument of progress and development.

Latinobarómetro measures trust in institutions, where we observe a decreasing level of trust from 1996 to 2001 (see Table 7.2). The Church stands out at 49 percent as the most trusted institution in Latin America for one out every two citizens. Trust in the Church is particularly high in Paraguay (66 percent), El Salvador and Guatemala (63 percent), and Bolivia (60 percent). Trust in the Church in a lay country such as Uruguay is 27 percent. There is a correlation between the level of trust in the Church and the per capita income of countries: the higher the trust in the Church, the lower the per capita income. In fact, average trust in the Church is higher in Central America than in South America for all years. Trust in this institution is a remarkable exception, 3 times higher (in the category, "a lot") than trust in any other political

Table 7.2. Trust in Institutions, 1996–2001

Q. Please look at this card and tell me how much confidence you have in each of the following groups, institutions, or persons mentioned on the list: a lot, some, a little, or no confidence?

	Totals for Latin America* (in percents)				
	1996	**1997**	**1998**	**2000**	**2001**
Church	49	52	54	52	49
Armed Forces	16	19	14	15	14
Judiciary	8	12	9	8	8
President	—	15	12	12	9
Police	8	12	8	9	9
National Congress	5	10	6	6	6
Political Parties	3	7	4	4	4
TV	13	15	12	10	15
N	18,717	17,767	17,901	18,125	18,135

Source: Latinobarómetro.
*Only the "A lot of confidence" data are shown.

institution measured. Political institutions and the mass media have a low level of trust, even compared to the level of interpersonal trust. How can people trust an institution more than they trust their neighbors?

At the same time, it is possible to observe an important variation in the levels of trust per country and year, indicating that they are performance-dependent. The police, for example, have increasing levels of trust in some countries, especially in those where they played a repressive role during the authoritarian period (Chile, for example). Similar phenomena occur with the military: other data in the survey indicate that it is seen as a valid institution, in spite (or because?) of its role in military governments.

The trust question has four categories, of which two are positive. When we observe the two positive categories, measured "a lot" and "some," the order of trust levels changes in some cases, but the main finding remains.

For the sum of these two categories, the contrast between any other institution and the Church is still more than twofold, at 77 percent. Indeed, political institutions are poorly trusted: the judicial system, 27 percent; the presidency, 30 percent; the police, 30 percent; Congress, 24 percent; and political parties, with the lowest level, at 19 percent. Meanwhile, the armed forces score 38 percent.

It is also important to observe the evolution of the level of trust per institution in the region as a whole. Here, the 2001 data show a striking drop across the chart: the Church drops from 77 to 72 percent; the judicial system, from 34 to 27 percent; the presidency, from 39 to 30 percent; the police, from 39 to 30 percent; Congress, from 28 to 24 percent; and political parties, with the lowest level, from 20 to 19 percent. Trust in the armed forces drops from 43 to 38 percent. This decrease in trust indicates the way institutions have been punished by the public as a consequence of poor economic performance in the region in 2001 with respect to 2000.

Trustworthiness of Institutions in Latin America

This trust profile is representative of most of the nations, with the exception of Uruguay, the country with the highest average trust in all political institutions in the region. It is also possible to find countries with high levels of trust in some institutions (here considering "a lot" and "some"), such as Venezuela in the presidency at 60 percent, Chile at 51 percent, and Uruguay at 46 percent. Trust in the police is at 52 percent in Uruguay, 51 percent in Chile, and 50 percent in Venezuela. Venezuela's democracy by plebiscite explains the very high degree of trust accorded to President Hugo Chávez, which surpasses that of Chile's President Ricardo Lagos.

Political parties, the institutions with the lowest average trust in the region, enjoy the highest levels in Uruguay (46 percent) and Venezuela (37 percent).

At the same time, it is especially interesting to observe levels of trust in the armed forces. The highest trust in the armed forces in the region is Ecuador, at 60 percent, Venezuela with 54 percent, Brazil with 53 percent, Chile with 46 percent, and Uruguay with 44 percent. The lowest trust in the military is in Central America, with an average of 26 percent. In contrast, Ecuador, Paraguay, Bolivia, and Brazil show the lowest average of trust in political institutions altogether.

These examples, along with the evolution and level of trust in political institutions, show that, on the basis of a given level of trust that is distinctive to each country, there is a clear relationship to past performance as well as to the historical role played in the recent past by each specific institution. In other words, countries can be ranked by the averages of their levels of trust in institutions, which vary little from year to year. Uruguay and Venezuela occupy the top of the list, while Paraguay and Brazil, the last places. The exceptions show that the traits of those countries were more or less stable throughout the years, except for Venezuela, which had important increases in trust in political institutions after Chávez's election. In fact, with the exception of Venezuela, changes in levels of trust in institutions are not evolving in a permanent upward trend that would indicate an increasing legitimacy as democracy grows older in any given country. On the contrary, the level and evolution of trust in institutions show unstable variations linked to performance more than a stable upward trend.

By contrast, average institutional trust in Europe in the 1990s was 57 percent for the legal system, 67 percent for the educational system, 75 percent for the police, 50 percent for Congress, 58 percent for the armed forces, and 35 percent for the press.[32]

These data show that this mistrust is an entrenched trait and not merely a temporary situation due to current difficulties. New democracies in Latin America experience low confidence in the region's institutions. The situation is not comparable to the problem of declining trust facing the United States.[33] Unlike established democracies, the main differences rest upon the various types of regimes. Because there are no opinion data available, we do not know if greater institutional trust existed in previous democratic regimes in Chile and Uruguay or during the short democratic experiences of other countries. What can be said is that new democracies must now deal with citizens possessing a low sense of trust. This negative sentiment is not a consequence of the failure of the democratic regimes, or of the consolidation process itself, but is rooted in permanent cultural traits that existed prior to the establishment of new democracies. The democratic consolidation processes, therefore, must contend with the additional challenges of creating open societies and breaking down existing barriers of mistrust.

We certainly need more data to determine the causes of this phenomenon. Different arguments can be adduced. A consideration of the historical preconditions of new democracies—military rule, repression, and economic underdevelopment—rules out facile explanations. The explanations given for the declining levels of trust in some advanced democracies do not necessarily apply to Latin America as a whole. One could easily argue that the average citizen of these advanced democracies has a higher level of education as well as much greater access to information, and is therefore better able to make informed, critical evaluations of public officials based on documented performance.[34] This would also imply that higher levels of education and more information would be necessary elements to increase trust levels. Unfortunately, data show that there is not necessarily a positive relationship, or correlation, between higher levels of education and trust in institutions, except for post-graduate studies. It can also be argued that those countries (Western industrialized democracies) had higher levels of trust prior to the establishment of national states, and therefore, developed democratic societies with a different original position, so that trust could be seen not as a consequence of democracy but maybe democracy develops more effectively in trusting societies.

In the case of Latin America, one could argue that Spanish colonial rule (with a hierarchical authority structure) and the native population produced a completely different original position of segmented trust networks, where people exercised trust within closed, unorganized groups. In fact, the development of a state bureaucracy and formal communications even in the private sector is based on mistrust, which is embedded, exercised, and spread through the formalities of daily life. This, in turn, confirms once again Durkheim's description of the nature of the legitimacy of any given institution, reflecting the behavior of their people. What remains as hard evidence is the fact that these differences between established Western democracies and Latin America are relatively permanent, so that the development of political goods has to look for other sources of trust that can be used to substitute for this important deficiency. Higher levels of trust exercised within informal, closed networks of people (family, friends, co-workers) can be a source of trust, deeply rooted in the culture of the region. This may end up being more powerful than education and information, which will most probably take generations to produce a significant massive impact on trust levels.

The low degree of interpersonal trust correlates strongly with the negative view toward fellow citizens. Individuals are seen as lacking honesty (barely 29 percent are considered honest), and as uncaring of their obligations (only 44 percent are considered reliable [see Table 7.3]). Citizens do, however, have a clear idea of their many rights and of the fact that laws are not being complied with (79 percent say "a little" or "not at all" lawful). Low interpersonal trust contributes to a negative view of individuals. It does not create a discriminating citizen, but a cynical one that demands rights with as few obligations as possible.

These attitudes, opinions, and behaviors of citizens toward one another and toward institutions in Latin America are consistent traits of the civic culture that appear to have undergone little evolution. This civic culture weighs heavily in explaining some of the problems of consolidation that these democracies are encountering. Without a major transformation, these traits are unlikely to evolve into a more positive outlook, similar to those existing in established democracies, which would provide needed political resources for stability. On the other hand, we do not know how much trust each culture must have in order to produce the needed political resources for stability, because in spite of these very low levels of trust, democracies continue to exist. The idea that it may be possible to build stable democracies with sources of legitimacy other than the known high interpersonal trust common to open societies in Western democracies remains an open query.

From a public opinion point of view, it is a fact that more open and prosperous societies have a more sophisticated, complex understanding and perception of the content of the word *democracy,* while less prosperous, less educated, more closed societies have a simple, sometimes mono-causal perception and understanding of the term. At a particular point in time, democracy can be one single element that produces one single significant change.

Table 7.3. Latin American Civic Culture Traits, 1996–2001

Q. Do you think that the [nationality] are very, quite, a little, not at all . . . ?

	Totals for Latin America* (in percents)				
	1996	1997	1998	2000	2001
Lawful	25	30	27	23	21
Demanding of their rights	53	56	56	53	52
Conscious of their obligations and duties	37	40	40	36	44
Supportive of each other	52	54	55	—	—
Honest	36	40	37	32	29
N	18,717	17,767	17,901	18,125	18,135

Source: Latinobarómetro.
*The "Very" and "Quite" categories are combined.

Once again, the case of Venezuela illustrates this phenomenon very well. The general public in Venezuela considered the Chávez election as a major step forward that eliminated important restrictions and produced a more democratic society. All other consequences are, at this point, irrelevant for the perception of democracy in that country. It can be tagged as a "false perception of democracy," but it is false to the analyst, not to the citizen. The perception of democracy is always true for the general public, regardless of the fact that this may be "false" or "correct" with respect to democratic theory.

Legitimacy and Efficacy of Democracy

From a public opinion point of view, measuring perceptions of democracy has to consider the possibility of it being a "false" perception. This can be a false understanding of efficacy or of performance as in the case of populist regimes.

From a theoretical perspective, a new democracy poses a question of legitimacy and efficacy of the political order.[35] Legitimacy involves a positive stance toward pluralist institutions and a belief that democracy is the most appropriate form of government for the country. Efficacy is a more restrictive concept dealing with the ability of democracy to solve the most important problems. It attempts to evaluate the performance of governments, pluralist institutions, and the country's elite.[36] Democracy may enjoy a high degree of legitimacy, but at the same time, citizens may criticize its efficacy. This could lead to political dissatisfaction, giving rise to expressions of political cynicism. Discontent or malaise toward the political system and the administration can occur, affecting attitudes. It is possible that a permanent and prolonged perception of inefficacy may tend to erode the legitimacy of democracy, although this entails two analytically different concepts. The degree of independence of these two concepts indicates how much bad performance a population is willing to accept before citizens start to blame the system.

The first dimension of legitimacy involves general and abstract attitudes toward a democratic regime, what Leonard Morlino and José Montero call "diffuse" legitimacy, which is very relevant in countries with previous authoritarian regimes.[37] Attitudes toward the democratic regime are revealed by the survey question of whether democracy is preferable to any other kind of regime.[38] This indicator gives respondents three dimensions of the type of regimes—democratic, authoritarian, or neutral—from which to choose. The second dimension is the indicator of the efficacy of democracy, or its capacity to manage socioeconomic order. It is measured by the level of satisfaction with democracy. These questions that are designed to interpret analytical concepts express perceptions that may be true or false with respect to the theory they intend to represent, having apparently (if this distinction is not made) rather contradictory or illogical results.

The results in Table 7.4 show stable support for democracy from 1996 to 2000, 60 percent, with a striking drop in 2001 to 48 percent. Compared to Europe, 78 percent prefer democracy. In Southern Europe, support for democracy is even higher at 84 percent.

Poor economic performance in the region as a whole has significantly impacted the legitimacy of democracy. On the other hand, it is possible to observe (especially in countries in Southern Europe) that legitimacy of democracy constantly increased as the consolidation process took place, where citizens made a much broader and wider distinction between the performance elements of any given government and the main traits of the democratic system. Citizens of Western democracies distinguish alternation in power as an element of efficacy and a political good of the democratic system, and therefore do not withdraw support for the democratic system when performance of the government in office is bad.

In Latin America, there is considerable variation among countries in the level of support for democracy. Uruguay and Costa Rica, both with long democratic traditions, witnessed a significant drop in support for democracy: from 84 to 79 percent and from 83 to 71 percent from 2000 to 2001, respectively. On the other hand, several countries have very low levels of support for democracy, including Brazil (dropped from 39 to 30 percent) and Paraguay (dropped from 49 to 35 percent). There is no country in the region where the drop in support between 2000 and 2001 is not very significant, with the exception of Mexico, where alternation in power after seventy years produced a stable support of 46 percent in 2001, no significant change compared to 45 percent in 2000. This is an important characteristic of the phe-

Table 7.4. Support for Democracy, 1996–2001

Q. Which of the following statements do you agree with the most?
Democracy is preferable to any other kind of government.
In certain situations, an authoritarian government can be preferable to a democratic one.
It doesn't matter to people like me whether we have a democratic government or a non-democratic government.

	Totals for Latin America (in percents)				
	1996	1997	1998	2000	2001
Democracy is preferable.	61	63	62	60	48
Authoritarian government is preferable.	17	18	17	17	19
It doesn't matter.	17	14	16	17	21
Do not know	4	3	3	4	9
No response	2	2	1	1	3
Total	100	100	100	100	100
N	18,717	17,767	17,901	18,125	18,135

Source: Latinobarómetro.

nomena observed, for it indicates an impact that goes beyond individual countries, showing the weight and importance of economic performance throughout the region.

Not even past democratic experience seems to be a reliable predictor of democratic support, as would be expected, for example, in the case of Chile. Democratic support starts at the inauguration of democracy in 1990 at 65 percent, falling to 54 percent in 1995 and 45 percent in 2001. In Chile, support for democracy dropped 20 points in a decade (from 1990 to 2001). This is precisely the opposite trend as exhibited in Spain during the first decade after Franco's death, where support for democracy increased steadily, catching up with average European levels.

At the same time, support for democracy is relatively high when compared to the low levels of trust toward institutions. Latin Americans are, in general, not willing to trust their institutions, but half of the population supports democracy after a decade of slim performance. The only institution that is more trustworthy is the Church. Relatively speaking, the gap between Latin America and Europe with respect to support for democracy is minor compared to the gaping lack of trust in institutions and interpersonal trust. Nevertheless, democracy has its own strengths in spite of the negative impact of performance upon its reputation. It could be argued that democracy's strength lies precisely in the fact that faith in the political system has not been lost.

Culturally speaking, democracy is a higher good, greatly valued by the majority of the population, which in turn places high expectations on it. Latin Americans want to live in a democracy. Even when a regime is not technically considered democratic, citizens still classify themselves as living in a democracy. In accord with this view, having an imperfect democracy is better than not having one at all.

Authoritarianism received significant and stable support (17 percent) throughout the five years measured. This percentage is considerably higher than in Southern Europe.[39] There are, however, important differences among countries. We find countries with growing support for authoritarian systems: Paraguayans, for example, prefer this form of government (increasing from 39 to 43 percent between 2000 and 2001); countries where no changes occur (Mexico[40] with similarly unchanged percentage—35 percent in 2001); and countries where there is decreasing support (Brazil and Venezuela, from 24 to 18 and 20 percent, respectively, between 2000 and 2001). Central America has on average lower support for authoritarian regimes, 15 percent, compared to South America and Mexico with 21 percent.

The contrast reveals that Latin America's support for authoritarianism exceeds that of Southern Europe at the moment of transition. In Spain it was 10 percent immediately following the death of General Franco and it has been decreasing ever since. If Latin America parallels this evolution, these percentages should tend to decrease over time.

Finally, those that are indifferent to any type of regime show an upward slope, increasing from 14 percent in 1997 to 21 percent in 2001. In 1997 (a good year for Latin America in economic terms, prior to the Asian crisis, and with still high expectations for economic reform), the general public rewarded democracy with its highest scores. Highest levels of indifference are found in general in Central America with an average of 25 percent, precisely because those populations support less authoritarian rule and democracy. While South America and Mexico show a lower average of 19 percent, it is in South America that authoritarian rule has more support. Differences are enormous in South America: while Uruguay, by far the most democratic country in the region, has only one percent in this dimension, Brazil has 31 percent, Chile 28 percent, and Ecuador 26 percent.

The causes of these differences from country to country involve the content of the meaning of democracy. While Chile, a country with a long democratic tradition, has suffered from a disenchantment about democracy due to the maintenance of "authoritarian enclaves," it could be argued that citizens with higher hopes for what democracy means could have expected major institutional reforms that would restore the more democratic institutional setting prior to the Pinochet regime. Increases in indifference would then be an indication of positive views of the content of democracy, more than a rejection of the regime type. Increases would indicate a rejection of the present form of democratic rule by the older population as well as a new form of non-citizens produced in the younger generations. Ecuador, on the contrary, suffers from primarily economic performance problems. Altogether the effect is the inverse of the process of consolidation of democracies in Southern Europe.

For the first time (in 2001), there are data available with open-ended and closed questions about the meaning of democracy that give us important light for understanding this inverse development in Latin America. It is most striking to find one out of every two people in Latin America cannot answer the question about the meaning of democracy, which implies that the content of the word can be easily filled with perceptions that contain false truths. This is especially true in Central America, 52 percent, and lower in South America and Mexico, 43 percent. For those that can answer the question, the term *liberty* defines the word for 9 percent, *equality* for 5 percent, *voting* for 3 percent, *social and economic development* for 2 percent. Content seems diffuse and widespread, indicating the absence of basic components as its major traits. Democracy is in fact a diffuse concept, not developed or nurtured by the democratic process. The absence of a strong presence of political goods renders the percentages of support for democracy in the region quite significant, although low in number. It could be said that people do not recognize all of democracy's traits although they perceive its potential strength and therefore still support it, believing more than actually supporting. It would seem that survey results measure belief in democracy more than support.

This line of reasoning is confirmed when observing other perceptions of the content of the word that people have. When asked about the most important element that democracies should have, elections come in first place (26 percent), an economic system that ensures a fair income to all, 19 percent, equality before the law, 16 percent, and freedom of speech, 14 percent. Countries like Venezuela and Peru identify elections as "the" distinctive qualifying element to classify themselves as a democracy (36 and 44 percent respectively). Have elections been transformed into the single political good that distinguishes democracies from non-democracies in people's perceptions? And is this precisely because of the diffuse content of the word *democracy*?

It is possible to identify different single qualifying elements for different countries: for Brazil it is the economy (41 percent), for Mexico it is equality before the law (25 percent), for Bolivia it is elections (39 percent). Chile is again an exception, viewing democracy as comprised of three main components: elections (23 percent), the economy (21 percent), and freedom of speech (19 percent). Most of the other countries follow the average combination of elections and the economy. Finally, when asked whether economic development or democracy is more important, 51 percent of respondents chose economic development. This is a further indication of the absence of the necessary political goods as content of democratic perception.

There are currently also data available from the Afrobarometer and the Eastern European barometer, and there will be data available in the near future from the Asian barometer. Using these data, trends can be identified and a correlation between support for democracy and satisfaction with democracy can be established. In general, regardless of the level of support and the level of satisfaction in absolute terms, the average span between the level of support and the level of satisfaction for democracy is about 20 to 25 points. It seems that all democracies have a more or less stable proportion of dissatisfied democrats. Thus, the problem lies in the number of supporters of democracies.

In Latin America there is a low degree of satisfaction with democracy (see Table 7.5). Satisfaction drops from 41 percent (adding very and fairly satisfied) in the good economic year of 1997 to 25 percent in 2001. Although both satisfaction and support for democracy fall, the 22 and 23 point difference (respectively) between them remains, confirming findings in other parts of the world where the number of dissatisfied democrats is related to the amount of support for democracy.[41] In turn each region (Africa, Eastern Europe, Latin America) shows specific levels of support that differ from region to region and are historically and culturally dependent.

There are significant differences among the surveyed countries. While Uruguay shows the highest degree of satisfaction, all countries experienced a fall in satisfaction in 2001 with respect to 2000 (from 69 to 55 percent) followed by Venezuela (from 55 to 41 percent). Especially striking are those countries where satisfaction is extremely low and falls farther: Peru (from 23 to 16 percent) and Paraguay (from 12 to 10 percent). However, there are countries with low satisfaction that experienced an increase over the previous year, such as Brazil (from 18 to 21 percent) and Nicaragua (from 16 to 24 percent). All these variations are explained by country-specific developments within the previous two years. The high level of satisfaction with democracy in Venezuela is better understood when looking at the components of the perception of the word explained above, where elections as its main component (36 percent) doubles the importance of economic performance (18 percent). Furthermore, as is the case in the regional comparison, countries also show a more or less constant difference between the level of support and satisfaction for democracy, that is, they produce relatively stable numbers of dissatisfied democrats. Countries with a higher level of satisfaction also have higher levels of support for democracy.

Democracy in Latin America, as perceived the population, is more a belief than concrete support of known elements. The diffuse content of the word allows for false perceptions of its components, producing effects like

Table 7.5. Satisfaction with Democracy, 1996–2001

Q. In general, would you say that you are very satisfied, fairly satisfied, not very satisfied, or not at all satisfied with the way democracy works in [country]?

	Totals for Latin America (in percents)				
	1996	1997	1998	2000	2001
Very satisfied	8	12	11	12	6
Fairly satisfied	19	29	26	25	19
Not very satisfied	45	39	41	42	42
Not at all satisfied	20	17	18	18	22
Do not know	2	2	2	2	8
No response	6	1	1	1	2
Total	100	100	100	100	100
N	18,717	17,767	17,901	18,125	18,135

Source: Latinobarómetro.

those in Venezuela and Peru. In these two cases, there is an absence of the necessary political goods that would enhance democracy's legitimacy and would allow for it to be distinguished from the efficacy of any given government, as is the case in industrialized democracies.

The efficacy of democracy is also tied to the performance of the government, primarily in coping with economic issues. Decades of frustrated development can only lessen the legitimacy of a democracy. Expectations determine the satisfaction levels with the performance of a democracy, and in Latin America these data show a common trait. Expectations for a better personal future (see Tables 7.6 and 7.7) are positive while expectations for a country's future are less positive or even negative. The people feel better off than the country, leading to dissatisfaction with the country.

The data show that in most countries, people have a negative view of future economic development (subtracting "worse" from "better"). This view changes significantly between 2001 and 2000, but it is still mostly negative (see Table 7.8). This is particularly so in Bolivia, where percentages of negative future expectations drop from 24 to 20 percent, and in Ecuador, from 19 to 13 percent. It also drops in Venezuela from 43 to 19 percent, and in Chile from 37 to 3 percent. Personal future economic expectations are positive in all cases, with the exception of El Salvador (-1 percent). This economic indicator experiences important changes as well between 2000 and 2001. Altogether, the gap between the negative future country expectation and the future personal expectation has shortened on average. Poor economic performance has produced lower expectations from the people toward the system, with the exception of Venezuela, where pressure of economic expecta-

Table 7.6. Intergenerational Economic Expectations

Q. Imagine a 10-step stairway, with the poorest people standing on 1 and the richest people standing on 10. Where would you stand? And where would your parents stand? And where do you think your children will stand?

Totals for Latin America (averages)	
Past generation	5.76
Present generation	4.66
Future generation	7.66

Source: Latinobarómetro 2000.

Table 7.7. Intergenerational Economic Expectations (averages)

Q. Imagine a 10-step stairway, where the poorest people stand on 1 and the richest stand on 10. Where would you stand? And where would your parents stand? And where do you think your children will stand?

	Past Generation	Present Generation	Future Generation	Difference Future − Present
Venezuela	5.83	4.62	9.24	4.62
Brazil	6.66	4.53	8.89	4.36
Peru	5.73	4.21	8.20	3.99
Chile	5.68	4.82	8.68	3.76
Argentina	5.62	4.47	7.84	3.37
Bolivia	6.47	4.83	8.19	3.36
Colombia	5.40	4.36	7.52	3.16
Ecuador	5.95	4.29	7.45	3.16
Uruguay	5.13	4.54	7.17	2.63
Paraguay	5.22	4.35	5.95	1.6
Mexico	4.88	4.85	6.20	1.35
Latin America	5.76	4.66	7.66	2.98

Source: Latinobarómetro 2000.

tions has almost doubled in the last year, implying the limited duration of the perceived values of political goods that Chávez's government produced in its election. Expectations have also increased in Peru as a result of the new government.

In spite of this trenchant assessment of the economic situation, a more positive view of the long-term future is found in the intergenerational trend. On a scale of 1 to 10, where 1 is very poor and 10 very rich, the average score of the economic situation in the present generation is 4.66, while that of the previous generation is 5.76 and the next generation is 7.66. There is a pessimistic view of the economic situation in the present, an optimistic view of the future, and a nostalgic view of the past. The present generation is squeezed between the nostalgia of the past and the enormous pressure that rests upon their children.

Strikingly, throughout South America and in Mexico, the current generation feels that their economic situation is worse than that of their parents, and worse than the anticipated situation of their children. The current generation perceives the greatest differences between the present economic situation and that of their children. On a scale of 1 to 10, with 1 being the poorest and 10 being the richest, Venezuela and Brazil have the highest future score at 9.24 and 8.89, respectively, with Paraguay coming in last at 5.95.

These data show that the long-term prospects in each country are viewed optimistically and seem to contradict the pessimism noted in the data that focused on the issue of future personal and national economic prospects. Brazil stands out as the country with the widest gap between generations.

Table 7.8. Future Economic Expectation, Personal and Country, 2000–2001

Q. In general terms, do you think that in the next 12 months the economic situation of your country will improve, stay the same, or get worse compared to the way it is now?

Q. And likewise, do you think that in the next 12 months your economic situation and that of your family will improve, stay the same, or get worse compared to the way it is now?

	Future Economic Situation of the Country (net*)		Personal Future Economic Situation (net*)		N	
	2000	2001	2000	2001	2000	2001
Bolivia	−24	−20	14	16	1,080	1,075
Costa Rica	−21	−20	14	15	1,001	1,000
Ecuador	−19	−13	−6	9	1,200	1,200
Colombia	−18	−36	19	2	1,200	1,200
El Salvador	−13	−22	1	−1	1,001	1,000
Mexico	−7	3	17	26	1,208	1,317
Paraguay	−6	−23	21	9	602	604
Honduras	−4	−40	27	1	1,003	1,006
Nicaragua	−2	−17	10	14	1,001	1,005
Venezuela	43	19	53	37	1,200	1,200
Chile	37	3	42	15	1,183	1,174
Panama	19	−19	35	14	1,000	1,000
Argentina	19	1	28	12	1,200	1,200
Peru	13	7	25	20	1,046	1,200
Brazil	6	4	42	47	1,000	1,075
Uruguay	2	−1	12	9	1,200	1,231
Guatemala	−1	−29	21	4	1,000	990

Source: Latinobarómetro, 2000–2001.
*The net is calculated by subtracting "Worse" from "Better."

Brazilians evaluate the previous generation at 6.66 (0.9 point above the average) and the next generation at 8.89 (1.23 points above the average). Venezuela evaluates its next generation the highest at 9.24 (1.58 points above the average). While Venezuelans have high expectations for their children, the people of Paraguay and Colombia have low expectations for the future economic situation. The high degree of optimism expressed by Venezuelans can be attributed to Chávez's charisma, to the failure of the previous party-based administrations of the Democratic Action Party (AD) and the Social Christian Party (COPEI), and to the dismal government of Rafael Caldera, who won the presidency in spite of his party's (COPEI) preference for Eduardo Fernandez. This future optimism also has to be seen as a demand for economic goods that will in turn produce effects on whatever each one understands constitutes the meaning of democracy.

The efficacy of democracy does not rest solely on its ability to solve economic problems. It must also be able to provide essential non-material goods such as security, access to health services, and adequate opportunities to obtain education, employment, and housing. One prominent feature of Latin American reality is its massive process of urban development, resulting in the accelerating growth of its cities that lack the necessary infrastructure or the human and institutional resources to fight crime. There is a strong general awareness of the rapid increase in crime, drug addiction, and corruption, according to the surveys taken in 2000. This awareness is almost to the point of unanimity in countries such as Honduras and Argentina, with very high percentages in other countries, as shown in Table 7.9.

These results need to be carefully analyzed, keeping in mind the political context of a democracy, where the free press reports extensively on crime, versus an authoritarian regime, where this type of information has traditionally been censored by the military, the assumptive authority against crime, due to "national security" concerns. The same logic applies to drugs and corruption. Democracy brings transparency to a wide range of social problems, often making the public aware of their existence for the first time. Given the extensive corruption that existed in many military regimes, it seems that awareness (or lack of awareness) of corruption has more to do with the availability of information than with its actual levels in any given country.

To better understand the visibility of the crime problem, a question was asked about how secure/insecure the respondents felt in their neighborhoods. If such high levels of crime exist, citizens should feel extremely unsafe. However, the opposite is the case. The overwhelming majority of Latin Americans, 65 percent, feel safe in their neighborhoods. The lowest sense of security is found in Argentina (55 percent) and Brazil (56 percent). A striking statistic is the high percentage of Colombians who feel safe in their neighborhoods (72 percent), similar to Chileans (73 percent). This result

Table 7.9. Increase in Crime, Drug Addiction, and Corruption, 2000–2001

Q. Do you think that the following issues that I am going to read have increased a lot or a little, have decreased a lot or a little, or have remained the same, over the last 12 months?

Totals by Country* (in percents)

	Crime		Drug Addiction		Corruption		N	
	2000	2001	2000	2001	2000	2001	2000	2001
Honduras	92	96	92	96	91	95	1,003	1,006
Argentina	92	94	89	86	87	88	1,200	1,200
Nicaragua	91	88	90	89	92	90	1,001	1,005
Paraguay	91	95	83	87	92	96	602	604
Costa Rica	88	91	92	93	89	94	1,001	1,000
El Salvador	82	83	69	84	72	86	1,200	1,000
Ecuador	82	89	73	81	87	91	1,200	1,200
Brazil	82	88	88	91	85	85	1,000	1,000
Colombia	80	91	73	88	80	90	1,200	1,200
Guatemala	80	87	62	88	63	84	1,000	990
Chile	78	85	79	86	60	72	1,183	1,174
Panama	76	85	79	87	72	83	1,000	1,000
Bolivia	75	87	59	72	83	89	1,080	1,075
Venezuela	72	87	63	85	54	76	1,200	1,200
Uruguay	67	72	68	73	62	66	1,200	1,231
Peru	57	75	40	72	56	85	1,046	1,023
Mexico	49	91	57	65	56	59	1,208	1,317

Source: Latinobarómetro, 2000–2001.
*Only the "Increased a lot" category is shown.

contradicts the impact of violence caused by the guerrillas and the narcotics trade. Nevertheless, follow-up questions to those who do feel unsafe reveal that the overwhelming majority cite common crime (81 percent) as a cause, a percentage that is much higher than the regional median (29 percent). Only 8 percent of Colombians cite political and social conflict as a cause for insecurity. This figure is less than those of Ecuador's, 16 percent, a country with a lower sense of safety in its neighborhoods than Colombia, as reflected by the fact that only 59 percent feel safe in their neighborhoods. Fifty-eight percent of Ecuadorians consider delinquency a major cause for insecurity.

Given this critical assessment, it is not surprising to see that 63 percent believe that the police are not doing an adequate job in the fight against crime. An analysis of the efficacy of democracy must take into account the safety concerns of its citizens and democratic governments must work to solve these problems. While short-term solutions to this problem tend to be less democratic and more repressive, they may be politically more rewarding than long-term solutions.

The data show an additional window through which democracy can be understood: the demand side, that is, the attitudinal dimension. Clearly, a perfect institutional system has nowhere to go without democrats. The formal aspects of a democracy are not sufficient, in themselves, to understand democratic development. The question of exactly how democratic democrats have to be to sustain a democratic regime remains unanswered. However, democratic theory has evolved thanks to the experiences of democracies that have spread throughout the world, and will continue to do so as more nations adopt such systems. "The 25 centuries during which democracy has been discussed, debated, supported, attacked, ignored, established, practiced, destroyed, and then sometimes reestablished have not, it seems, produced agreement on some of the most fundamental questions about democracy."[42]

Elections and the economy are the two most important elements in the understanding of the diffuse meaning of democracy in Latin America. People believe in perceptions that could lead to false expectations and results. Caudillismo is one of the consequences of the democratic consolidation process when the political goods and specific content of democracy have been neglected by policy. Other consequences are yet unknown, but will surely become so, related to the economic expectations observed as the major source of change in political behavior.

Although lack of trust is not the only hindrance to the development of democratic attitudes and behavior, it is perhaps the easiest to identify and therefore tackle. There are a number of other basic components of democracy that have to be enhanced in order to fill the perception with correct content. If perceptions are truths and people act upon perceptions, then democratic development means the development of the meaning of democracy in the first place as a major reform to be undertaken by the region as a whole.

The case of Chile illustrates how a more balanced content of the word *democracy* rests upon past democratic tradition prior to authoritarian rule. Not only in the case of Chile, but also in Uruguay, Costa Rica, and Argentina, one can find elements that could be enhanced to reinforce a correct perception of democracy and thereby support more stable democratic development.

At the same time, no matter what transformations the meaning and content of democratic behavior undergo in the region, it is also more likely that democratic systems will seek to adapt to culture than cultures will adapt to the system.

Although we do know what can cause a democratic breakdown, we do not know what it takes for democracy to take root. Can there be a stable democracy with very low trust in its institutions, without trust in other fellow citizens, and without adequate economic performance? Are there substitutes for trust? The evolution of existing stable democracies suggests otherwise. Nevertheless, although the scourge of poverty has not been solved in Latin America, democratic systems have been established. Empirically based democratic theory with a multicultural perspective has only just started to analyze these new comparative data. It may be possible, at some future date, to determine the critical minimum levels of cultural traits able to engender the political resources required for stability of democracy.

The data suggest that Latin America has produced unexpected results in its democratic evolution. These results allow us to look into some of the less known aspects of its development, indicating a plural diversity of democratic forms that more or less deny the existence of a static definition of the theoretical content of democracy. Democracy in Latin America is adapting to a different cultural setting in the whole continent. These data indicate that the evolution toward Western industrialized types of democracy remains uncertain in the foreseeable future.

PART III

Country Studies

8

Venezuela

Popular Sovereignty versus
Liberal Democracy

Michael Coppedge

Opinions about the state of democratic governance in Venezuela during the
first three years of the government of Hugo Chávez Frías were polarized. On
one side, critics came close to labeling it a dictatorship. For example, Allan
Randolph Brewer Carías wrote that the 1999 constitution "lays the constitutional groundwork for the development of political authoritarianism, buttressed by regulations that reinforce centralism, presidentialism, statism,
state paternalism, partisanship, and militarism; with the danger of the collapse of democracy itself."[1] On the other side, Chávez claimed to be restoring
a truly democratic regime to Venezuela: "we will advance in the construction
of a true democracy, of a true political, economic, and social system which
we will build because they destroyed it during these last years.... We are now
going to demonstrate the daring and intelligence of the Venezuelan people
who are building with their own hands a true democracy, where justice, liberty, equality, and fraternity prevail."[2]

The truth is more complex and subtle. In order to evaluate accurately the
state of democracy during the first years of the Chávez presidency, one must
sharpen the distinction between democracy narrowly defined as popular
sovereignty versus the more conventional notion of liberal democracy. It is
also necessary to look beyond the rules and institutions of Venezuela's 1999
constitution to consider the way they were used. On first inspection, Venezuela still had a liberal democratic regime. Understood more deeply, it was
no longer a liberal democracy in every respect. Instead, it became an extreme
case of delegative democracy—a regime in which there is no "horizontal

accountability," that is, no effective check on the president by the Congress, courts, or other powers between elections.[3]

In the next two sections I explain that the president enjoyed widespread popular support for almost everything he and his followers in the Fifth Republic Movement (Movimiento V República, MVR) did, and argue that this fact qualified his government as "democratic" in the narrow sense of popular sovereignty. But I then explain how Chávez used a constituent assembly to eliminate systematically all constraints on presidential action, which increased the risk that Venezuela would cease to be a democracy by any definition in the future. I then illustrate the impact of this concentration of power on democratic governance by examining the changed roles of civil society, elections, parties, and various branches and levels of government in the Chávez regime. The chapter concludes with speculation about how this regime might end.

The attack on horizontal accountability also damaged the governability of the regime. Elsewhere I have defined governability as "the degree to which relations among strategic actors are governed by stable and mutually acceptable formulas."[4] Governability suffered because the new formulas regulating relations between government and opposition among branches of government, and between state and civil society, were both unstable and far from mutually acceptable. Chávez and his supporters saw themselves as agents of a deliberate and self-conscious revolutionary process and believed that expediency and unilateral impositions of new rules were justified by the need for a radical break with the past. Needless to say, this attitude also condoned a cavalier disregard for the rule of law, extending, as we shall see, even to the constitution.

Popular Support

Popular sovereignty—the idea that a government should do what most of its citizens want it to do—is the oldest and most literal definition of democracy, although not necessarily the best one.[5] Contemporary theorists now consider popular sovereignty neither sufficient nor strictly necessary for democracy. But even though popular sovereignty has fallen out of favor with scholars and mainstream politicians, it has a long pedigree as one legitimate standard for democracy. Furthermore, few scholars would disagree with the claim that democratic governments must respect the popular will at least some of the time, especially when it is deeply felt, widely shared, and coherently expressed.[6] Qualified in this narrow way, popular sovereignty is a necessary characteristic of democracy.

In this respect, the Chávez government's credentials were solid despite his past disloyalty to Venezuela's democratic regime. Hugo Chávez Frías rose through the ranks of the armed forces in the 1980s and 1990s. He was a star student at the military academy who considered himself an intellectual and took it upon himself to maintain a dialogue with intellectuals of the Left. As early as 1983 he had formed a conspiracy with other junior officers that was critical of the Venezuelan regime for betraying the ideals of the country's founding father, Simón Bolívar. By 1992, members of this conspiracy had risen to positions of command; Chávez had been promoted to lieutenant colonel and commanded a paratrooper division close to the capital. In February of that year, they attempted to overthrow the government of President Carlos Andrés Pérez by force, but were narrowly defeated. Nevertheless, Pérez was such an unpopular president that the coup attempt made Chávez a hero in the eyes of many Venezuelans.

Ever since March 1998, when he became the front-runner in the presidential race, Hugo Chávez was the most popular politician in Venezuela and his agenda was endorsed repeatedly in elections and opinion polls. He won the December 1998 presidential election with 56.2 percent of the vote, the most decisive electoral victory since Rómulo Gallegos' win in 1947. In April 1999, he sponsored a referendum seeking permission to summon a constituent assembly (Question 1) and to design an electoral law for the election of constituent assembly delegates (Question 2). He was the ultimate author of both questions, and both were approved with more than 80 percent of the vote (Table 8.1). When this election was actually held three months

Table 8.1. Electoral Support for Chavismo

Date	Election	Chavista	Percent of Vote	Percent of Electorate
December 1998	Presidential	3,673,685	56.2	33.4
April 1999	Referendum Q1	3,630,666	87.8	33.0
April 1999	Referendum Q2	3,382,075	81.7	30.8
July 1999	ANC candidates	3,174,226	65.5	30.3
December 1999	Constitutional referendum	3,301,475	71.8	30.4
July 2000	Presidential	3,757,773	56.9	32.2

Sources: December 1998, April 1999, and December 1999: reproduced or calculated from Margarita López Maya and Luis Lander, "La popularidad de Chávez ¿Base para un proyecto popular?" unpublished ms. (Caracas: February 2000), 4 (based on Consejo Nacional Electoral figures); July 1999: votes from López and Lander; percentages calculated from María Pilar García Guadilla and Mónica Hurtado, "Participation and Constitution Making in Colombia and Venezuela: Enlarging the Scope of Democracy?" paper presented at the XXII International Congress of the Latin American Studies Association, Miami, March 16–18, 2000, 17; July 2000: Consejo Nacional Electoral.

later, the first-place finishers in each district, all of whom were Chávez supporters, won nearly the same 3 million-plus votes that Chávez and his initiatives had won in the two previous votes. When the Chávez-dominated constituent assembly finished its work and submitted the draft constitution to a popular vote, it was ratified by nearly 72 percent of the voters. Later, in the "mega-elections" of July 30, 2000, to renew all officeholders, Chávez himself was reelected with 56.9 percent of the vote.

These figures probably exaggerate the breadth of support for Chávez because abstention ranged from 36.5 percent in the 1998 presidential election to 62.4 percent in the two-part referendum. When the pro-Chávez vote is presented as a percentage of the whole electorate, it is reduced to a quite stable but far lower 30.3 to 33.4 percent. Given the constancy of this support in the midst of extremely high abstention, this seems to be an intense one-third of the electorate that repeatedly turned out to register its support for Chávez or his agenda. One-third may seem low, but to be fair it must be compared with support for past presidents calculated in the same way. As Table 8.2 shows, Chávez's initial base of electoral support was proportionally smaller than that of six other Venezuelan presidents, but larger than that of three past presidents—Leoni and Caldera in his two governments. He was therefore in the ballpark in terms of support in Venezuela, just a bit lower than

Table 8.2. Initial Base of Electoral Support for Elected Venezuelan Presidents

President	Year	Party	Vote (as percentage of eligible voters)
Rómulo Gallegos	1947	AD	estimates minimum: 33.6 most likely: 43.6 maximum: 54.6
Jaime Lusinchi	1983	AD	47.3
Carlos Andrés Pérez	1973	AD	45.0
Rómulo Betancourt	1958	AD	43.4
Carlos Andrés Pérez	1988	AD	42.1
Luis Herrera Campíns	1978	COPEI	40.0
Hugo Chávez Frías	1998	MVR	33.4
Hugo Chávez Frías	2000	MVR	32.2
Raúl Leoni	1963	AD	28.4
Rafael Caldera	1968	COPEI	26.2
Rafael Caldera	1993	Convergencia Nacional	17.7

Sources: 1947–88: calculated from Consejo Supremo Electoral figures; 1993–98: calculated from Consejo Nacional Electoral figures.

Table 8.3. Initial Base of Electoral Support for Latin American Presidents

President	Country	Year	Vote (as percentage of eligible voters) First/Only Round	Runoff
Lagos	Chile	1999	41.9	45.9
Fujimori	Peru	1995	39.1	
Alemán	Nicaragua	1996	38*	
Zedillo	Mexico	1994	37.9	
De la Rúa	Argentina	1999	37.5	
Flores	Honduras	1997	35.9	
Cardoso	Brazil	1998	33.9	
Chávez	Venezuela	1998	33.4	
Batlle	Uruguay	1999	32.7	51.6
Chávez	Venezuela	2000	32.2	
Rodríguez	Costa Rica	1998	31.8	
Flores	El Salvador	1999	31*	
Moscoso	Panama	1999	31*	
Cubas	Paraguay	1998	25*	
Clinton	United States	1996	24.2	
Mahuad	Ecuador	1998	19.0	31.7
Fernández	Dominican Republic	1996	18*	24*
Banzer	Bolivia	1997	14.9	
Pastrana	Colombia	1998	11*	16*
Arzú	Guatemala	1995	11*	

*Estimates based on the winner's share times a recent average turnout rate for the country.

the average of 37.4 percent. One should also consider that many Venezuelan presidents have tended to enjoy broader support than presidents in neighboring countries. Chávez's base of electoral support was proportionally larger than that of ten to eleven of his contemporary Western Hemisphere presidents, and above the hemispheric (outside Venezuela) average of 28 percent (Table 8. 3). The size of Chávez's base of electoral support therefore remains solid in comparative perspective, and the intensity of this support is relatively high.

It is tempting to argue that Chávez really had only an ordinary level of support, which abstention magnified into the appearance of an extraordinary level of support. However, this interpretation is not compatible with survey evidence. Opinion polls, which are less biased by abstention, indicate that another sizable segment of the population also supported Chávez, although not intensely enough to cast an actual vote for him at every opportunity. This group, combined with the intense one-third, provided the president with clear majority support. A sampling of survey results will suffice to make this point:

- In January 2000 a survey in ten cities by Alfredo Keller concluded that Chávez would receive more votes in the next presidential election than he had received in 1998.[7]
- In February 2000, a Consultores 21 survey in sixty-six urban centers found that 71 percent of respondents would vote for Chávez if the elections were held then.[8]
- In May 2000, another Consultores 21 survey conducted in sixty-six cities reported that 55 percent would vote for Chávez against Arias Cárdenas and that Chávez had a 64 percent approval rating versus 31 percent disapproval.[9]

These indicators of the popularity of the president could also be corroborated by observing the enthusiasm with which he was received when he appeared in public and the deep respect heard in the voices of callers to his weekly radio program. Table 8.4 shows that the popular support also extended beyond personal support for Chávez. Under the Chávez government, the proportion of Venezuelans feeling positive and optimistic increased. In spite of poor economic performance, in 2000, 62 percent believed that their personal and family economic situation would improve in the next twelve months, and 57 percent believed that the country's situation would improve. Most strikingly, the percentage of Venezuelans who claimed to be very satisfied with the way democracy works in Venezuela increased from 13 percent in 1998 to 28 percent in 2000; and those "not at all" satisfied shrank from 25 percent to 7 percent.

However, not all Venezuelans held Chávez in such esteem. In fact, most middle-class and wealthy Venezuelans opposed him for the same reasons that the lower classes welcomed him: "The references to *el pueblo* [the people] as central to the process are read by these sectors as evidence of demagogic populism; his informality is equated with improvisation; his military language an expression of authoritarianism; his baseball analogies are seen as insufficiently serious and unbecoming of a statesman; his sense of humor shows boorishness; his pedagogical tone is perceived as primitive, lowbrow, and uncalled-for."[10] This polarization of opinions by class also showed up when Venezuelan newspapers conducted on-line polls, which routinely registered overwhelming contempt, among computer users with Internet access, for the president and everything he did. Despite the intensity of their opposition, these critics were clearly in the minority.

The polls therefore suggest that Chávez had a comparatively large base of

Table 8.4. Venezuelan Public Opinion (in percents)

Survey Questions	1996	1997	1998	2000
"In the next 12 months, do you think that your economic situation and that of your family will improve, stay the same, or get worse compared to the way it is now?" (percent saying it will improve)	24	34	42	62
"In the next 12 months, do you think that, in general, the economic situation of your country will improve, stay the same, or get worse compared to the way it is now?" (percent saying it will improve)	12	20	28	57
"In general, would you say that you are very satisfied, fairly satisfied, not very satisfied, or not at all satisfied with the way democracy works in Venezuela?" (percent very satisfied)	8	12	13	28

Source: Latinobarómetro, 1996, 1997, 1998, and 2000. My thanks to Marta Lagos for sharing these data.

support, but the elections suggest that only about half of this base was solid. If his fair-weather friends deserted him, he would lose his main claim to democratic legitimacy. In such a situation, this former coup leader could be tempted to govern through non-democratic means. In order to judge the likelihood of such a scenario, it is important to understand where Chávez came from, what his goals were, and why so many Venezuelans supported him.

The Crisis of Democracy and the Rise of Chávez

In the 1960s and 1970s, Venezuela earned a reputation as one of the most stable democracies in the developing world.[11] The democratic regime inaugurated in 1958 survived guerrilla movements, terrorism, and several coup attempts in its early years and continued to celebrate clean elections every five years marked by vigorous campaigning and party competition. Stability was achieved through a formula that gave a central role to the two largest political parties, the AD and the Christian Democratic COPEI. Many Venezuelans came to call this formula *partidocracia* (an amalgam of *partido* [party] and *democracia* [democracy]), which I translate as "partyarchy."[12] The guardians of the formula, so to speak, were the leading *adecos* (members of AD) and *copeyanos* (members of COPEI), whom some Venezuelans called the *"status" adecopeyano* and I will translate as the Adecopeyano establishment, or simply the establishment.

This partyarchy promoted governability in five ways. First, the two parties were broadly representative of society. They had huge numbers of party members; channeled demands from labor, peasants, and other organized groups; and from 1973 to 1988 split about 80 percent of the legislative vote and 90 percent of the presidential vote. Second, AD and COPEI practiced iron discipline: militants at all levels of the party organization risked expulsion if they disobeyed decisions made by the small inner circle of leaders, or *cogollo,* at the head of each party. Third, the two parties extended their control to non-party organizations that they had politicized. Labor leaders usually refrained from holding strikes when their party was in power, and the politicized officers of professional associations, student governments, peasant federations, state enterprises, foundations, and most other organizations used their positions to further their party's interests. The two parties therefore acted as powerful and readily mobilized blocs. Fourth, they practiced *concertación,* or consensus-seeking. The leaders of AD and COPEI made a habit of consulting one another, and usually leaders of other parties and social organizations as well, whenever controversial issues arose.[13] Policies concerning defense, foreign affairs, and the oil industry were usually made by consensus, and even when consensus proved impossible, the attempt to reach it mollified the opposition. Finally, the two parties hammered out good working relationships with other strategic actors—the military and the private sector. In exchange for non-interference in political questions, AD and COPEI governments kept benefits flowing to these other actors in the form of budget allocations, training, tax forgiveness, subsidies, protection, and other policy favors. Governability was therefore ensured by the Adecopeyano establishment which, because it controlled large, popular, and tightly disciplined parties with influence over most other organizations, had the authority to bargain with other parties and other strategic actors, and the power to enforce the deals that it made.

Oil wealth also aided governability under Venezuela's democratic formula as long as it contributed to prosperity. The rapid economic expansion and social mobility of the 1960s and 1970s contributed to the legitimacy of the governing parties; oil financed policy favors to business leaders; and it financed patronage for elites and clientelism for the masses. But the economy began a long decline in 1978. From 1978 to 1989, per capita GDP shrank 29 percent, falling back to a level not seen since 1953.[14] Venezuelans did not lose faith in their parties immediately; for the next decade, they continued to hope that a change of government would return them to prosperity. The decline began under an AD government; in 1978 they elected Luis Herrera Campíns of COPEI, and he enjoyed a second oil price surge for a while, but then the Latin American debt crisis hit. In 1983, Venezuelans elected Jaime Lusinchi from AD, who delivered only a modest reactivation of the economy, at the cost of higher inflation. In 1988, they returned to Carlos Andrés Pérez (also from AD), who had presided over the biggest boom in the 1970s; but Pérez began his administration with a radical shock program that led, in the short term, to an inflation rate of over 80 percent and an 8.3 percent contraction of the economy—the worst performance on record. It was at this point that Venezuelans became increasingly alienated from AD, COPEI, and other democratic institutions. Public anger erupted in three days of rioting and looting in all major cities in 1989.

Parties were clearly powerful actors and no other parties had governed since 1958, so when Venezuelans felt like "throwing the bums out," it was perfectly clear to them who "the bums" were. To be fair, it would be wrong to lay all the blame at the feet of AD and COPEI. The debt crisis that began in 1982 owed much to a surge in U.S. interest rates and a temporary halt to new foreign investment in the whole region. And from 1985 to 1998, Venezuela was particularly hurt by a severe decline in oil prices. Oil revenues, which used to cover 70 percent of public expenditures, now covered only 40 percent. None of this was subject to Venezuela's control. Nevertheless, the establishment parties did deserve much of the blame because they made these problems worse than they had to be and created other problems as well. They were accomplices to their own destruction.

The popular reasoning that connected the parties to the economic decline was as follows: Venezuela is a wealthy, oil-exporting country; the government's duty is to share this wealth fairly with all of us; I'm not getting my share, and neither are those around me; therefore, the party politicians who have run the state for the past thirty years must be wasting and stealing the money. Again, this is not the whole story, but there was more than a grain of truth to this popular belief. When the decline began in the mid-1970s, Venezuela was between two magnificent, closely spaced oil booms. With prudent management, this could have been a time of glorious prosperity. Instead, both Pérez (1974–79) and Herrera (1979–84) drove the country much deeper into debt despite commanding state revenues that were *several times larger* than those that any other Venezuelan governments had received. Obviously, there was massive waste and corruption. It was appropriate for Venezuelans to blame their leaders for this even if periodic overspending is virtually inevitable in oil economies.[15]

The waste and corruption—which continued throughout the decline of the 1980s and 1990s, when it was even less tolerable—was in turn made possible by partyarchy. Ironically, the same characteristics of parties that had promoted democratic governance in the first two decades of the regime worked to undermine it in the last two decades. The continuation of corruption required a climate of impunity, which was a by-product of partyarchy. The courts, like the bureaucracy, the universities, and most other institutions, were thoroughly politicized along party lines and seemed never to find sufficient evidence to justify a trial or a conviction. There has to have been complicity between AD and COPEI as well, because they behaved as though there were a secret clause in the pact of Punto Fijo prohibiting prosecution for corruption. The practice of *concertación*, intended to moderate political conflict, served equally well to conceal abuses of power by the Adecopeyano establishment. Also, in the hands of increasingly unprincipled party militants, the party founders' dedication to the moderation of conflict was transmogrified into an obsession with controlling other actors in civil society. But rather than welcoming and encouraging a newly flourishing civil society and opening the system to more genuine participation, the parties treated independent groups as threats to party control. An opportunity to deepen Venezuelan democracy was thus lost, and the independent organizations responded by linking their aims to an anti-party, anti-establishment agenda.

The parties were accomplices also in the sense that they stubbornly and tragically resisted pressures to reform themselves. Increasing disaffection with the system became evident as abstention grew from a low of 3.5 percent in 1973 to 12 percent in 1978 and 1983, 18 percent in 1988, and 39.8 percent in 1993. Many observers know that AD and COPEI, following the lead of their presidential candidates during the 1988 election year, passed an electoral reform that established the direct election of mayors and governors for the first time in 1989; this was seen as a move away from the hierarchical discipline typical of partyarchy. What fewer know is that few party leaders besides the presidential candidates were happy about this reform. They set about to nullify its effects immediately by reasserting tight *cogollo* control over nominations to these offices. AD was also primarily responsible for stalling and eventually shelving a constitutional reform bill that grassroots organizations had succeeded in putting on the agenda in 1992. The two parties flirted with reform in 1993 by nominating for president a mayor and a governor who had genuine local grassroots support and who advocated greater openness and participation and economic liberalism. But when both candidates lost in 1993—the first time neither AD nor COPEI had won the presidency in a fair election—other party leaders systematically marginalized these candidates and purged hundreds of their supporters from the ranks. The AD candidate, Claudio Fermín, was eventually expelled; President Pérez was impeached in 1993 and expelled while awaiting trial. By 1998, COPEI had no viable presidential candidate of its own and so backed one, then another, independent. AD's top boss, Luis Alfaro Ucero, forced the party machine to nominate him for president and ran a doomed race in 1998 even when his own party dumped him two weeks before the vote. AD and COPEI contributed only 9.05 and 2.15 percent of the valid votes, respectively, to the independent candidate they both backed in the end, Henrique Salas Römer.

The presidential election of 1998 that brought Hugo Chávez to the presidency was therefore the culmination of a fifteen-year process of traditional-party decline. Chávez did not destroy the old parties; rather, he filled a political vacuum. His promises were perfectly tailored to fill this particular void. His ultimate announced goal was to restore prosperity to the country—to stop the waste and corruption that Venezuelans believed had been siphoning off their wealth, and to distribute it fairly among all citizens. But his means to that goal squarely targeted the traditional parties, which he indicted for creating the mess and accused of standing in the way of the necessary reform. "We are being called to save Venezuela from this immense and putrid swamp in which we have been sunk during 40 years of demagoguery and corruption," he proclaimed in his inaugural address.[16] Although AD's popular support had already diminished and COPEI was on the verge of extinction, their militants were believed to be entrenched still in the Congress, the courts, the bureaucracy, the electoral council, and state and municipal governments. Chávez promised to remove these corrupt politicians from power and replace them with honest, hard-working, patriotic—and frequently, it turned out, military—citizens. Rooting out the corrupt partisans would require a full-scale assault on the existing democratic institutions, and the tool Chávez proposed to carry out this political revolution was a constituent assembly.

Democracy and Horizontal Accountability

It is useful to interrupt the narrative at this point to reflect a bit more on democratic theory. I have gone to some lengths to substantiate the claim that Chávez had a clear majoritarian mandate to carry out his agenda of dismantling partyarchy in order to banish corruption and restore prosperity so that the oil wealth could be widely shared once more. His diagnosis of the problems may have been simplistic, his promises demagogic, and his abilities unequal to the task; but he clearly had broad popular support to pursue these goals. In making this claim, I have no wish to become an apologist for him. Instead, I have two different goals. The first is explanatory: anyone who wishes to understand why so many Venezuelans supported Chávez and how it was possible for him to execute so much of his political agenda must recognize that his supporters granted him a kind of democratic legitimacy. I wish to describe the rationale for that legitimacy precisely. Second, I want to sharpen the distinction between democratic legitimacy based on popular sovereignty—which Chávez could reasonably claim—and democratic legit-imacy based on liberal democratic principles—which he sacrificed along the way. This distinction captures the tension between two core democratic principles in Venezuela and therefore is useful for describing and evaluating the situation. When seen against this backdrop of theory, the Chávez gov-ernment serves as a paradigmatic illustration of the tension between two standards for democracy.

Much of Chávez's popular support was derived from certain democratic ideals. There was a logic to his claims to be creating a more democratic sys-tem.[17] However, there is a different strand in democratic theory—liberal-ism—that calls for limits on the sovereignty of a popular majority. If majori-ties could be trusted never to undermine the basic procedures that make it possible to ascertain and give effect to the majority will, liberalism would be unnecessary. But the dominant strain of democratic theory for the past 150 years has assumed that majorities cannot be trusted. They easily give in to the temptation to modify the rules of the game to discriminate in favor of them-selves and against the opposition. This discrimination is not always intolera-ble: for example, it is almost universally accepted as legitimate for gov-ernments to prefer their own partisans and allies for cabinet positions, top executive branch appointments, and legislative committee appointments.[18] But the narrower the governing coalition is, and the more its discrimination extends to positions and rules that have a deep impact on fundamental in-terests of the opposition, the greater the danger of the tyranny of the major-ity.[19] If these encroachments go so far as to threaten the opposition's ability to formulate and express its views, to receive equal treatment under the laws, and ultimately to compete in the next election on an equal footing, then the minimal standards for democracy are not met.[20]

Liberal principles therefore justify and in fact require limits on the au-thority of the government of the day, no matter how clear its majoritarian mandate may be. In order to reduce the risk that a president will abuse a popular mandate, presidential constitutions provide for a diverse array of institutions with various powers to check the executive between elections. These institutions include an independent judiciary, a legislature with a dis-tinct electoral base, and, in some states, a division of powers among tiers of government and an independent electoral agency, attorney general, comp-troller, and *defensor del pueblo* (ombudsman). Liberal institutions can be thought of as a kind of democracy insurance policy. Citizens pay premiums in the present, in the form of sacrificing some of the government's repre-sentativeness and immediate responsiveness to their wishes. But these pre-miums purchase assurance that democracy will not fall below some mini-mal level in the future. Following this analogy, Venezuela's partyarchy was part of such an insurance policy: it guaranteed that the basic elements of democracy would be respected, but the price for this benefit was an excessive concentration of power in the two leading political parties (and all the abuses that followed from such concentration). Eventually, Venezuelans came to feel that the premiums were too high. They cashed in the policy and enjoyed a windfall of responsiveness from the Chávez government; but they lost their insurance that democracy would survive in the future.

Venezuela's partyarchy also aided governability, as disciplined and hierarchical parties mediated almost all relations among powerful actors. When the parties were no longer able to provide this service, governability suffered. Decades-old understandings about the role of business and labor, the Church, and especially the armed forces were questioned and had to be renegotiated, creating uncertainty and unpredictability. The most fundamental rules of all—those contained in the constitution—were debated and revised, and, as we will see, sometimes ignored.

The Elimination of Horizontal Accountability

During the first year of the Chávez government, participants on all sides seemed to agree that the constitution of 1961 somehow locked in the terms of the 1958 party-centered pact of Punto Fijo, allowed corruption, and guaranteed impunity and economic decline. This belief was baseless. The 1961 constitution was adequate for a democratic regime in Venezuela. In fact, it was a fairly standard Latin American presidential constitution, with very few provisions that could not be found in the constitutions of other democratic countries. Furthermore, the 1961 constitution provided for an amendment procedure that was feasible as long as there was sufficient political support for amendment; and what could not be accomplished by amendment could often be accomplished through ordinary legislation. For example, direct elections for governors and mayors were postponed for thirty years due to the lack of ordinary legislation, and were eventually instituted by the passage of ordinary legislation. There was no pressing institutional need to reform it.

Similarly, although the constitution of 1999 made many changes, it stayed within the range of constitutional practice in Western democracies. The presidential term was increased from four years to six, but Chile has a six-year presidential term and France had a seven-year term from 1958 to 2000. The 1961 constitution had prohibited presidential reelection for two terms, and the 1999 constitution permitted two consecutive terms. But the United States, Brazil, and Argentina allow for presidential reelection, and we must keep in mind that there are no term limits (prohibitions of reelection) on the executive at all in most parliamentary systems. Venezuela's new electoral system did exaggerate the margin of victory of the Chavistas, but in principle the first-past-the-post elections of the United States, the United Kingdom, and Canada would do so as much under comparable conditions.[21] The greater exaggeration in practice was not due to the constitution, but to the size of the Chavistas' majority and the fact that it was distributed fairly uniformly throughout the country. Also, there was nothing in the new text that prohibited further decentralization: if the government wanted to favor decentralization, it could happen (as was true under the 1961 constitution). The 1961 constitution was not an important part of the problem, and the 1999 constitution will not be an important part of a solution. The primary motivation for calling a constituent assembly was not to tinker with the constitution.

The real problem with the constitution was that it protected Chávez's adversaries' control of Congress and other institutions. AD and COPEI had cleverly arranged for the 1998 congressional and gubernatorial elections to be held one month before the presidential elections so that Chávez's powerful coattails would not affect these elections. The tactic worked: after the November 1998 elections, the pro-Chávez forces controlled only one-third of the seats in the two chambers while the anti-Chávez forces controlled two-thirds (Table 8.5). This representation created a serious obstacle to the most radical items on the president's agenda during the seven months of this legislature's existence. Intimidated by the pro-Chávez majority in public opinion, the Congress tried to appear cooperative. But the incumbent Congress did deny the president some of the emergency powers he requested in 1999, especially those that would have given him the greatest discretion for the longest periods of time. The constituent assembly was urgently desired not because the constitution was so poorly designed, but because it was the only conceivable body that would have the power to neutralize Congress, the courts, and all other guarantors of horizontal accountability.

Chávez neutralized all of these institutions' ability or desire to check his actions with breathtaking speed and efficiency. All of the key moves were executed in slightly more than one year. On December 6, 1998, Hugo Chávez was elected president with 56.2 percent of the vote. On February 2, 1999, at his inauguration, he called for a popular referendum to summon a constituent assembly. A blue-ribbon panel was appointed to draft the text of the referendum and design an interim electoral law, but Chávez disregarded its report and dictated the terms of the referendum himself. On April 25, 1999, both referendum questions were approved by over 80 percent of the voters. On July 25, 1999, legislative elections were held and the pro-Chávez alliance won 122 out of 131 seats in the ANC. The ANC began its work eight days later and finished the new constitution on November 15, a little more than three months later. At the same time, the ANC arrogated to itself the power to in-

Table 8.5. Seats Won by Parties in National Legislatures Elected 1998–2000

Party	November 1998 Chamber	November 1998 Senate	July 1999 Constituent Assembly	July 2000 National Assembly
Acción Democrática	62	29	0	30
COPEI	27	17	0	7
Proyecto Venezuela	20	14	0	7
La Causa R	5	5	0	3
Convergencia Nacional	3	1	0	2
Apertura	1	1	0	0
Independents	0	0	6	0
Primero Justicia	0	0	0	3
LAPY	0	0	0	3
Nuevo Tiempo	0	0	0	3
Others*	0	0	0	5
Opposition Total	118	67	6	63
Movimiento V República	46	21	89	78
Movimiento al Socialismo	18	10	19	20
Patria Para Todos	6	2	9	1
Partido Comunista de Venezuela	0	0	5	0
Pro-Chávez Total	70	33	122	99
Appointed indigenous delegates	0	0	3	3
Total	188	100	131	165

Sources: November 1998: Consejo Nacional Electoral; July 1999: bloc totals from Consejo Nacional Electoral, breakdown within Polo Patriótico from personal communication from Steve Ellner; July 2000: Consejo Nacional Electoral.
*In 2000, Alianza Bravo Pueblo, Movimiento Independiente Ganamos Todos (MIGATO), Constructores de un País, Encuentro con Miranda, and Pueblo Unido Multiétnico de Amazonas won one seat apiece.

tervene or dissolve other state institutions. On the day the new constitution was popularly ratified (December 15, 1999, with 72 percent of the vote), the Congress and Supreme Court were dissolved. However, the ANC continued to work as a sovereign legislature until January 31, 2000. During these six weeks, it appointed a vast number of public officials, rewrote the electoral law, and approved a "transitory regime" that served as a kind of unratified constitution until new elections could be held. The opposition howled that the transitory regime, and some decisions adopted under it, violated provisions of the constitution the ANC had just written (for example, in scheduling elections too soon); but in order to ensure that elections would actually take place, these rules were allowed to stand. Between the dissolution of the ANC and the installation of the new National Assembly, all legislative functions were performed by a twenty-one-member National Legislative

Committee appointed by the ANC. The sections below describe the role of key actors and institutions during this process and evaluate their current contributions to democratic governance (or the lack thereof).

Civil Society

Governability is favored when civil society is structured into solid, well-organized associations and these societal actors have understandings with one another and with the state that permit them to act freely and confidently.[22] This was one of the weakest areas of governance in Venezuela. There were relatively few social actors that were large and well organized, and the few that were all had a very strained relationship with the Chávez government. The most respected actor was the Catholic Church, which initially had good relations with the government. However, in July 1999 the executive cut in half its $3.4 million annual direct subsidy to the Church, and the ANC rejected proposed constitutional language that protected life "from the moment of conception."[23] By November Church officials were unofficially calling for a "No" vote in the constitutional referendum, and one bishop publicly interpreted the catastrophic mudslides in December as a sign of God's fury against the president. Chávez replied that "God is with the Revolution" and accused Church officials who opposed him of being in league with AD and COPEI and "having the devil up their cassocks."[24]

The Church's ability to mobilize opposition remains to be seen, but the private sector did not delay in expressing its lack of confidence. The one exception was the oil sector, which continued to be a private investment magnet, despite the new government's renewed determination to retain ultimate ownership and control over this key resource. Under the leadership of Venezuelan oil minister Alí Rodríguez, and with the help of growing U.S. oil consumption and refining bottlenecks, the Organization of Petroleum Exporting Countries (OPEC) succeeded in raising prices during 1999 and 2000. The oil sector therefore enjoyed a mini-boom during Chávez's first two years in office.

In all other sectors, the economic news was bad. Honda, Fiat, and Unilever were among the foreign firms that closed factories in the first two years; in all, $4 billion was transferred out of the country between July 1998 and December 1999.[25] Domestic business associations openly campaigned against ratification of the new constitution. CEOs were undoubtedly discomfited by the former guerrillas in the cabinet, the president's admiration of the Cuban model ("I feel happy to follow the path of Fidel. . . . [Venezuela is swimming] toward the same sea as the Cuban people. . . , a sea of happiness, social justice and true peace"), and his anti-business invective ("enemies of the nation," "a rancid oligarchy," "a truckload of squealing pigs," "a batch of bandits who have betrayed, pillaged and humiliated the people").[26] A lack of business confidence can certainly affect economic management: production fell 7.2 percent in 1999 and unemployment rose to approximately 20 percent of the workforce.

A third large organization, the CTV, also found itself in an antagonistic relationship with the government but lacked the leadership to launch concerted opposition. Organized labor had long been dominated by the political parties, especially AD, but now that the parties were crippled, the organization lacked direction. Nevertheless, the Chávez government made plans to separate the unions from the parties in its second year. ANC President Luis Miquilena complained that "there is an entrenched mafia of real *capos* [organized crime bosses] of labor who forgot about elections and the grass roots."[27] To root them out, the government ended the hefty state subsidies to the CTV and proposed to audit the labor leadership's assets.[28] It also held a referendum to obtain a popular mandate to dismantle the CTV by, among other means, forcing the labor federations to hold open internal elections supervised by the National Electoral Council. At the same time, Chávez promoted a parallel official union movement called the Bolivarian Workers' Front (FBT), clearly intended to mobilize workers behind the government's projects, beginning with the destruction of the CTV.[29]

Because the Establishment parties had been so thorough in their penetration of other organizations, only a small number of well-organized, autonomous, and well-known interest groups survived the parties. Human rights groups were the exception, as many organizations were founded after the violent repression of the 1989 riots. One group listed eighty human rights organizations nationwide, although it is not known how many remained active.[30] Some of these, such as the human rights group Programa Venezolano de Educación-Acción en Derechos Humanos (PROVEA) and the electoral reform group Queremos Elegir (We Want to Choose), participated in debates about constitutional reform. However, the fundamental fact is that there were comparatively few viable organizations in Venezuelan civil society. Chávez's relationship with "the people" was therefore mostly unmediated by secondary associations.

Elections

Clean elections are obviously essential for democratic governance. For decades, Venezuela's Supreme Electoral Council (CSE) enjoyed an excellent international reputation and Venezuelan elections were presumed to be pristine. However, it was well known that politicians practiced all sorts of chicanery in internal party elections, and in the popular mythology, the major parties represented at voting stations often divided up among themselves any votes cast for minor parties. Because minor parties continued to win some votes during this time, I doubt that there was systematic or widespread fraud of this nature in general elections before 1988. But with the election of governors and mayors in 1989, hard evidence of attempted fraud at this level began to turn up, and several elections had to be rerun to ensure an accurate result.[31] As these cases gained publicity, widespread cynicism about the CSE set in.[32] A reform during the second Caldera administration renamed this body the National Electoral Council (CNE) and aimed to depoliticize it by replacing some party representatives with technocrats. The CNE weathered some turbulence in the composition of its board, despite the adoption of computerized voting machines and frequent changes in electoral law, until early 2000. In January, 138 CNE officials affiliated with political parties were fired.[33] In February, the three-member board was rotated, probably due to suspicions that one board member was an "agent" for opposition presidential candidate Francisco Arias Cárdenas.[34] In the midst of this turmoil, the CNE was tasked with organizing the election of all officials, from president to local representatives, in a simultaneous election on May 28. This time, the CNE no longer had the technical capacity for the job, and these crucial elections had to be postponed. The "mega-elections" (so called because all elective offices were filled at once) were finally held on July 30 without serious technical problems. Nevertheless, informed observers considered the new council overwhelmingly *chavista* (pro-Chávez). This cannot be considered an improvement over the former multiparty council.

Political Parties

During its peak years of partyarchy, Venezuela had two well-organized, legitimate, and tightly disciplined political parties that were well suited for ensuring governability. But one concomitant of the decline of partyarchy was a popular rejection of parties structured along these lines. Consequently, after the 1998 elections, political parties became one of the weaknesses of democratic governance in Venezuela.

AD fell from one-third of the congressional seats in 1998 to 18 percent in 2000. By 2000, COPEI was diminished almost to the point of extinction. The government accelerated the collapse of the old parties by cutting off all public financing to parties, but the main cause was the loss of popular support. Neither party finally ran a presidential candidate of its own in 1998 or 2000. All members of the ANC who did not belong to a party allied with Chávez ran as independents. Nine of twenty-three governors and a respectable number of mayors were successful in the mega-elections despite being allied with opposition parties.[35] However, if there is no strong national organization, these affiliations will become increasingly meaningless.

AD initially seemed to retain enough of a foothold to reconstitute itself as a leader of the opposition, but internally it was reeling from its fall from prominence. In September 2000 it suffered a serious top-to-bottom split (the fourth in its history) that further damaged its potential to recuperate. With their co-partisans being rejected at the polls and purged from the bureaucracy, many remaining traditional politicians followed the example of Rafael Caldera, Carlos Andrés Pérez, and Claudio Fermín and abandoned their parties, some to retire and others to found new parties. Most of these politicians and new parties immediately lost political significance. They continued writing editorials and appearing on television, but had little chance of winning many votes. For example, Claudio Fermín, who even in 1998 was well positioned to be the leader of a reformed AD, won only 2.72 percent of the presidential vote in 2000—and he was the most successful of the former establishment politicians.

The largest party was Chávez's Movimiento V República (Fifth Republic Movement, or MVR), the electoral heir of the Bolivarian Revolutionary Movement (MBR-200) that organized the February 1992 coup attempt. This organization appeared to be a true party with a large membership and some organization beyond election periods. Its membership swelled rapidly after Chávez took power, which made it more internally diverse. Dominant parties, like oversized coalitions, can be hard to hold together. This one was reportedly divided between civilian and military wings that were united only by the personality of Chávez. Rumors that Chávez was distrusted by parts of its military base were confirmed in February 2000, when Yoel Acosta Chirinos accused Interior Minister Luis Miquilena of unethical contracting practices and Jesús Urdaneta Hernández was removed from the leadership of the party by its National Tactical Command. In March, these two leaders endorsed the presidential candidacy of Francisco Arias Cárdenas. All three were former military officers who collaborated with the first 1992 coup attempt. This was, in effect, a split of the MVR just fourteen months into the administration, which raised doubts about the party's future contributions to governability. Indeed, Chávez himself began undermining the MVR in 2001 by refounding his original non-party movement, MBR-200. The existence of an MVR-affiliated "José Martí group [*coordinadora*]" of thugs who provoked violence against the Arias camp and journalists raised further doubts.[36]

Some small parties participated in an alliance with the MVR called the Polo Patriótico. These included the Movimiento al Socialismo (Movement to Socialism, MAS) and, for a time, Patria Para Todos (Fatherland for All, PPT).[37] MAS was a Left or Center–Left party dating back to 1971, popular among students and intellectuals. Although it was awarded several positions in the cabinet, the Chavistas called their alliance with it "tactical" rather than "strategic" because it carried the taint of partial involvement in *concertación* under AD and COPEI administrations.[38] PPT, a ragtag Center–Left splinter from the moribund new-unionist La Causa R, nursed an increasingly unrequited love for Chávez. Although PPT was initially part of his alliance, Chávez all but excluded PPT candidates from the Polo's tickets for 2000, as he felt that this small party contributed few votes and endangered his reputation. PPT leaders had no choice but to withdraw formally from the alliance for that election, but unofficially continued to support Chávez's candidacy. The role of both parties subsequently was more that of opportunistic hangers-on than of important independent parties. These small, pragmatic parties were more easily co-opted by a president than their better-institutionalized predecessors. In this respect, party politics in Venezuela began to resemble party politics in Peru and Ecuador.

All other parties outside the Polo Patriótico were little more than personalistic vehicles with short life expectancies. Irene Sáez Conde's Integración y Renovación Nueva Esperanza (IRENE) became defunct even though she had been the leading presidential candidate before March 1998; Salas Römer's Proyecto Venezuela (Project Venezuela) was a relevant political actor only in the state of Carabobo, even though he had finished second in the December 1998 presidential race. Many believed that a new opposition party or parties could emerge from the alliance backing Arias in 2000. However, it is more likely that this will be simply one more short-lived personal vehicle. It will probably be years before the political climate makes it possible to establish a coherent, well-organized opposition party that is not based on a charismatic personality. And until then, there will be no political actor with democratic legitimacy based on a popular following that is in a position to mount effective opposition to the government.

The Executive

Democratic governance requires an executive that faithfully executes the law, maintains its autonomy from the influence of unelected actors, and yet remains accountable to other democratic actors such as a legislature and an independent judiciary. Chávez based his democratic legitimacy primarily on the first two conditions, which are derived from the logic of popular sovereignty, and sought ways to avoid the third condition, which is based on the logic of liberal democracy.

The president claimed to be promoting efficiency and honesty in the executive branch by appointing military officers to high posts and mobilizing troops to carry out some duties that would normally be assigned to civilian bureaucrats. (Polls routinely showed that the armed forces were among the least distrusted institutions in Venezuela.) In his first cabinet, six Ministries were headed by military officers and 70 percent of the vice-ministers were from the military as well. He also appointed a leader of the November 1992 coup attempt as governor of Caracas and welcomed the selection of another *golpista* (coup plotter) as president of the Congress in 1999.[39] However, what drew more attention was his "Bolívar 2000" project, which deployed 70,000 troops to build roads and bridges, distribute food, vaccinate children, clean sewers, and carry out other public works.[40] Contrary to Chávez's boasts and his supporters' hopes, the military did not appear to be immune to corruption. Eduardo Roche Lander, who served as comptroller general until his dismissal in December 1999, charged that commanders in Barcelona, Ciudad Bolívar, and Maturín billed for services not rendered and could not account for all their expenditures.[41]

Instead of increasing confidence in the executive branch, Chávez's reliance on the armed forces raised the fear of the militarization of the government. This fear was further encouraged by a 13 percent increase in the armed forces budget (despite an overall budget cut of 10 percent); the granting of suffrage to active-duty soldiers; and proposals to add a required "premilitary" curriculum in the schools and either eliminate most draft exemptions or require universal military service.[42] Nevertheless, these changes or proposals are properly understood as a not entirely welcome military role expansion initiated by a popularly elected president, not as a power grab by the military. Especially after the defection of Arias, Urdaneta, and Acosta from the Chávez camp, which was partly a reaction against this role expansion, the military's loyalties were divided. As long as the pro-Chávez tendency remains dominant, civil-military relations will be good.

But if the balance tipped against the president, the armed forces had sufficient autonomy to challenge the regime.[43] Ironically, their autonomy was increased by several changes adopted in the 1999 constitution. First, Articles 328 and 330 gave explicit constitutional responsibility to the armed forces for the maintenance of public order, participation in national development (formerly recognized only in an organic law), and some police and investigative activities. Second, the new constitution gave the armed forces complete autonomy to make military promotions, a role that had been shared with the Senate. Finally, under the 1999 constitution, all branches were united in a single command, which dampened competition for resources and would make any coup attempt easier to coordinate.

Some of the constitutional changes also raised the specter of an emerging dictatorship. However, none of these changes by itself made a dictatorship likely. Chávez's push for a six-year term with the possibility of reelection for another six years (in addition to his first year and a half in office) strongly suggested that he would *like to* stay in office a long time. But doing so would require getting reelected, and that is not assured as long as other democratic procedures are followed. The constitution gave him the new power to dissolve the National Assembly, but before he could do that, the National Assembly would have to dismiss the vice-president three times in the same period. Although Chávez's disciplined MVR majority provided him with the means to carry out such a maneuver, it simultaneously removed the principal motive for doing it: congressional obstruction of his agenda.[44] The Assembly can grant decree powers to the president, and indeed did so through a broad Enabling Law passed in October 2000. However, such delegations were also possible (and abused) under the 1961 constitution, although this one was defined more vaguely and not restricted to economic and financial matters. Nevertheless, Chávez obtained these powers following procedures defined in the 1999 constitution and with ample political support. The president is also empowered to declare a state of emergency and suspend certain constitutional guarantees, but under the new constitution he must submit such a decree to the legislature within eight days, rather than ten. Of course, if the president had a strong majority in the National Assembly, either decree powers or a state of emergency could be used to transform a government into a kind of dictatorship. But again, the crucial variable was not the constitution, which did not change significantly in either regard, but the president's intentions and the political support he could muster.

The Legislature

There were three different national legislatures in the first year of Chávez's government and a fourth elected during his second year. Each of the first three was less inclined to hold the executive accountable than the one before it. The first legislature was the bicameral Congress elected one month before the presidential election, under the 1961 constitution and the 1989 electoral law. Because it was purposely delinked from the presidential election but coincided with gubernatorial elections, the parties that had attractive gubernatorial candidates did relatively well. This helped the traditional parties and Salas Römer's Proyecto Venezuela, and denied a majority in either chamber to Chávez's Polo Patriótico coalition (Table 8.5). Although members of this Congress could not avoid being intimidated by Chávez's landslide one month later, they nevertheless refused to rubber-stamp his agenda. For example, this Congress granted the president only about 80 percent of the decree powers he requested in 1999, and the 20 percent denied him were those most wide-ranging and ill-defined. The authority Congress withheld frustrated Chávez.[45]

The next legislature was the unicameral ANC, authorized by a referendum held in April 1999 and elected in July of that year. This body might seem to have been the ultimate check on the executive, for it declared itself legally omnipotent: not bound in any way by the 1961 constitution or any existing democratic institutions. This was a controversial claim: César Pérez Vivas, leader of the parliamentary faction of COPEI, charged that "an effort is being made to stage a coup d'etat with the Constituent Assembly, which is illegally usurping the functions of Congress and the Supreme Court. Democracy is dying in Venezuela."[46] The claim of unlimited powers was supported as much by the precedent of the 1991 constituent assembly in Colombia as by any Venezuelan legal text.[47] Chávez endorsed this interpretation and promised that he would even leave the presidency if the ANC decided to remove him. The Supreme Court, however, ruled that the ANC's powers were more limited and that its decisions would have to be ratified in a popular referendum. Nevertheless, upon being sworn in, the ANC immediately tried to close down the existing Congress. After objections from the Court and the international community, the officers of the two bodies negotiated an arrangement that allowed the old Congress to extend its technical existence until a new constitution was ratified as long as it recognized its subordination to the ANC in all matters of consequence.[48] The old Congress was inactive after early August 1999.

Of course, the ANC was not inclined to check the executive, as the Polo Patriótico alliance had won 122 of its 131 seats and Chávez's MVR had a 68 percent majority all by itself (Table 8.5). This overwhelming dominance would have been impossible without massive popular support, but it was also exaggerated by two provisions of an electoral law that Chávez unilaterally decreed, ignoring the recommendations of a blue-ribbon commission he himself had convened. The first provision was that candidates could choose whether to run on a party ticket, a social movement ticket, or as independents (*por iniciativa propia*). All the Polo candidates ran on a single Polo ticket and, because the parties in the alliance had negotiated well to prevent competition within the alliance, they succeeded in pooling their votes efficiently. Tragically, all the opposition candidates ran as independents, competing against one another and dividing the opposition vote. The second provision complemented the first: voters were allowed to cast as many votes as there were seats to be filled in each district, and the candidates with the largest pluralities were elected. This was a variant of a system known as the bloc vote, which has strongly majoritarian tendencies, that is, it tends to exaggerate the margin of victory of the largest party.[49] The Polo Patriótico ran first in every single district nationwide, and because most Polo supporters cast all of their votes for candidates identified on the ballot as Polo candidates, the Polo won 95.3 percent of the elected seats with 65.5 percent of the votes, while the independents won only 4.7 percent of the seats with 34.5 percent of the votes.[50]

Although the ANC adopted rules that allowed the tiny opposition a disproportionate voice in its proceedings, the constitution inevitably favored the preferences of the governing alliance. The ANC also welcomed initiatives from interest groups but, predictably, groups advocating reforms endorsed by Chávez were far more "successful" in influencing the content of the constitution than unaffiliated groups.[51] The ANC finished its work far ahead of schedule, producing the final draft in 98 days out of the permitted 180. Chávez himself did not get a constitution that reflected his stated preferences in every respect. For example, the constitution basically endorsed decentralization even though Chávez favored greater centralization.[52] Because there was no sign that Chávez was upset by these "losses" and because Chávez pressured the ANC to finish its work quickly, I suspect that he did not care much about the text beyond a few key provisions, such as the six-year term, immediate reelection, and the extension of the suffrage to the military. He was probably more interested in what the ANC did *besides* drafting a constitution.

The ANC did a great many other things that were crucial for eliminating checks on presidential power. As already mentioned, by the end of August it neutralized any challenge that might come from the old Congress. At the same time, it created a Judicial Emergency Commission that began a purge of the entire judiciary, including the Supreme Court and the Judicial Council. After the draft constitution was ratified on December 15, the ANC (which was not dissolved until January 31, 2000) decreed a Public Power Transition Regime that dissolved Congress and the Supreme Court, and appointed the ombudsman (*defensor del pueblo*), public prosecutor (*fiscal general de la República*), comptroller (*contralor general de la República*), and the board of the National Electoral Council. It also provided for itself to be succeeded, until new elections could be held, by a National Legislative Committee consisting of eleven ANC members and ten unelected members appointed by the ANC. This Congresillo, as it was informally known, had vast powers, including the power to remove elected officials at the state and local levels.[53] Any partially appointed body with such powers is more like a revolutionary junta than a representative legislature. By the time the ANC ended its functions, there was not a single national power, other than President Chávez himself, which had not been appointed by a body that was 93 percent Chavista.[54]

The Judiciary

The Chávez government focused extraordinary efforts on purging the judiciary of allegedly corrupt or partisan officials. There was some irony in this, as the outgoing Supreme Court of Justice had handed the government a precious legal victory not long before. The constitution of 1961 made no provision for a constituent assembly summoned by a popular referendum. Without a constituent assembly empowered to neutralize the legislative and judicial branches, Chávez would have remained accountable. It was therefore crucial for his success that the Supreme Court ruled, on January 19, 1999, that a constituent assembly *could* be summoned through a referendum. This decision provided legal cover for almost everything that followed; without it, the entire process would have been patently unconstitutional. The Court's reasoning in this decision was equally important:

> The possibility of [the people] delegating sovereignty via the suffrage to popular representatives does not constitute an impediment for its direct exercise in matters for which there exists no express provision in the norm regarding the exercise of sovereignty through representatives. Thus the people preserves its sovereign [*originaria*] power for situations such as being consulted about referendum issues.... The opinion of the electorate can be sought on any decision of special national transcendence other than those expressly excluded by article 185 of the Organic Law of Suffrage and Political Participation, including a decision relating to the calling of a Constituent Assembly.[55]

This rationale endorsed the priority of democracy-as-popular-sovereignty over the logic of liberal democracy. It lent legitimacy to the profoundly illiberal notion that "supraconstitutional" means can be invented to give effect to the apparent will of a large majority of the people.

This Supreme Court was dissolved in December 1999 and replaced by a new Supreme Tribunal of Justice, which included a new Constitutional Court and inaugurated oral arguments in order to make justice more speedy.[56] Because the new tribunal was appointed by MVR majorities, it was not independent of the executive. This expectation was confirmed in June 2000, when the tribunal dismissed well-documented charges of corruption against Legislative Commission President Luis Miquilena.[57] In the meantime, the Judicial Emergency Commission, succeeded by the Commission on the Functioning and Restructuring of the Judicial System in December 1999, lost no time in replacing judges. By the end of March 2000, 294 judges had been suspended, 47 others fired, and 101 new judges appointed.[58] It was probable that most of these had ties with one of the traditional parties, as the courts had long been infiltrated by partisan or family-based "tribes." It was also credible that most of these judges were corrupt. According to Transparency International, 67 percent of Venezuelans perceived the judicial sector to be inaccessible and corrupt; the corresponding figures for Argentina, Ecuador, and Brazil (not models of propriety themselves) were 46, 47, and 56 percent.[59] Clearly a drastic change was necessary, but there was little reason to believe that the new judges would be any better.

Other Powers

The dissolution of the old institutions in December 1999 gave the government a convenient opportunity to dismiss officials who had become critical. One of these was the comptroller general, Eduardo Roche Lander, whose charges of corruption against the armed forces have already been mentioned. It also provided a new opportunity to stack some organs with loyalists. This may have been one of the problems with the CNE that led to the postponement of the mega-elections originally scheduled for May 2000. In retrospect, it was unreasonable to expect that officials appointed in January would be able to master a completely new electoral system, renegotiate with foreign contractors, and run elections at all levels with more than 6,000 candidates in less than five months. It would have been even less realistic if some CNE officials were seeking to gain some partisan advantage; there was scattered evidence of such intent.[60] Fortunately, after the postponement, the Congresillo appointed a new CNE board, but its impartiality remains to be seen.[61]

Federalism

The Congresillo quickly made use of its power to dismiss elected officials at subnational levels of government. In April 2000, acting on investigations by the comptroller general appointed just three months earlier, the National Legislative Committee dismissed Governor Alberto Galíndez of Cojedes state and seven mayors in three other states.[62] All of these were members of AD, and the only other governor threatened with dismissal was also from AD.[63] In at least one instance, heavy-handed tactics short of dismissal were used to intimidate or embarrass an opposition governor. When the Regional Legislative Committee (appointed by the ANC, like its national counterpart) conducted an investigation into the administrative practices of Governor William Dávila Barrios of Mérida state, thirty submachine-gun-toting commandos in gray fatigues from the national police (Dirección de Servicio de Inteligencia y Prevención—DISIP) accompanied the judge and two accountants who were sent to inspect the books. The premises were sealed off and traffic was blocked during their two-hour visit. This raid drew nonstop local media coverage just four days before a scheduled election in which the governor was a candidate.[64]

Conclusion

In comparative perspective, Venezuela stands out as a case of the loss of democratic governance. In the 1960s it was exemplary in both democracy and governance, but in the 1970s and 1980s both the quality of democracy and the state's capacity to govern deteriorated gradually. This trend culminated in a string of crises beginning in 1989 that climaxed with Chávez's introduction of what amounts to a different political regime, which is neither fully democratic (because it is illiberal) nor very governable.

However, it would be misleading to paint a completely negative portrait of democratic governance in Venezuela. It did not become a completely illiberal democracy during the first years of the Chávez government. There was still organized opposition, which was able to criticize the president and his ministers harshly. Despite intimidating language coming from the government, newspapers still reported scandals about both sides.[65] Individuals were still free to form and express their own political opinions and organize interest groups, social movements, and political parties. In some ways—legal protections for human rights, a lessening of impunity—the situation may even have been improving. But this regime (or, more accurately, this transitional moment) was illiberal in the sense that, for the time being, a single political movement controlled the executive, the courts, the legislature (if the Congresillo deserved the name), and hand-picked all the members of supposedly independent agencies. The institutions necessary for liberal democracy were present, but they were not sufficient, because their shared political agenda rendered them incapable of checking each other.

Although these institutions have not yet been abused very much, democracy can still suffer, because it is largely a game of expectations. Citizens who expect to be punished for acting freely cannot be truly free. It may be premature to conclude that Venezuela has already reached such a situation. But it is difficult to believe that after acting so boldly to align all these institutions politically, Chávez and his followers will refrain from using them.[66] There are few rosy scenarios for the future. After attempting a military coup, shoving aside the old Congress and Supreme Court, stacking the new ones, empowering the military, cutting off party financing, and initiating a conquest of organized labor, it would hardly be a complete shock if Chávez were to jail his critics, disband some parties, close the National Assembly, steal elections, or attempt a presidential coup. A descent into authoritarian rule cannot be ruled out.

Ironically, friends of democracy should hope for the president's continued popularity. As long as he remains popular, Chávez has no reason to subvert or destroy democratic institutions and no need to artificially boost his support by aggravating the border disputes with Guyana or Colombia. A popular autocrat is not the best guarantor of democracy, but the feasible alternatives could be much worse. As Fujimori's example suggests, Chávez's popularity will not last forever. Perhaps the chances of a peaceful departure are greater after a long government, but, despite Fujimori's example, this is not guaranteed. Before Chávez leaves there would be a risk of either a descent into authoritarianism or a sudden presidential coup. One way or another, sooner or later, he will have to go. The one certainty is that he will not go quietly.

Note: By late 2001, President Chávez had alienated three powerful groups. Business leaders were angry about the major laws he had decreed with little consultation; the CTV was provoked by his promotion of the FBT (which failed), and some key military officers were disturbed by his sympathy, and perhaps material support, for the FARC guerrillas in Colombia and his friendship with Fidel Castro. Popular support fell to no more than one-third of the population. Leaders of these three sectors plotted to force Chávez and Vice-President Diosdado Cabello to resign, opening the way for a transitional government. On April 11, 2002, a massive demonstration organized by these sectors became violent, apparently because of sniper fire coming from both sides. One-sided reporting of the killings by the opposition media swayed key commanders to join the conspiracy, and Chávez was arrested on April 12. However, the coup attempt quickly unraveled when the business sector, led by Pedro Carmona Estanga, sought to exclude their military and labor co-conspirators from the new government, and precipitously announced the dissolution of the National Assembly and Supreme Court, repudiated the 1999 constitution, and began arresting pro-Chávez governors. Latin American governments condemned the interruption of the constitutional order. (The United States backed an OAS resolution to this effect only after it appeared the coup would fail.) Military commanders around the country refused to support the coup unless the constitutional line of succession was respected, and Chávez supporters took to the streets demanding his return. Forty-three hours after Chávez was arrested, he was back in power. However, Venezuela was now much more deeply polarized than before and, therefore, less stable.

9

Colombia

The Governability Crisis

Fernando Cepeda Ulloa

How did a country that, in spite of its paradoxes and weaknesses, once boasted of its democratic stability and electoral tradition, the sensible management of its economic policies, and its strict compliance with international commitments, fall into a situation as critical as the one it has been facing every day for the past several years, and which shows every sign of further deterioration? Why is Colombia, at the beginning of the third millennium, the "problem" country of the Western Hemisphere, tormented by one of the bloodiest conflicts in the world?

The following pages undertake a systematic analysis of the principal issues that affect democracy in Colombia. An introductory discussion of the threats to the country's governability (the simultaneous crises of representation, public order, justice, and corruption) is followed by an examination of the various governmental responses that have emerged since the 1950s. The chapter continues with an analysis of the problems surrounding the 1991 constitution and an evaluation of the weaknesses of the responses undertaken by the various governments. A special emphasis is given to executive-legislative relationships, issues of decentralization and public order, the political system, and civil society. The chapter concludes by discussing several strategies or agendas that future Columbian governments should pursue in order to recover democratic governability.

Threats to Governability

Colombia is afflicted by the relative underdevelopment of its political system, which is exacerbated by both the sophistication and the inefficacy of its judicial system, as well as uneven, if sustained, economic development, particularly in territorial terms. This situation has been aggravated by the increasing power of the guerrillas and organized crime (drug cartels and mini-cartels, organized kidnapping, illegal self-defense groups, corruption cartels, etc.). On the other hand, since 1980, the peace process has weakened a military and police establishment that was already historically inadequate to deal with public unrest. The justice system, with a long trajectory of inefficacy, was simply overwhelmed by the new forms of organized crime and, in many cases, succumbed to intimidation and corruption, in spite of many examples of heroic and ennobling behavior.

The excessive predominance of a technocratic vision supported by the multilateral agencies systematically underestimated the institutional and political dimension of development policy, resulting in an even greater deterioration of an already weak state, government, and society unable to identify and overcome key problems of democratic governability. A significant aspect of this "technocratic dogmatism" was the consistent unwillingness to budget for public infrastructure in the political and institutional areas, particularly those areas responsible for the preservation of public order: the National Police, the military, the intelligence services, the judicial system, organisms of criminal investigation, civilian participation, and the prison system.

Also underestimated, if not outright forgotten, were political, legal, regional (southern Colombia in particular), and value-based realities. This attitude reflected the priorities and the mind-set of the multilateral financing agencies in the same way that now, topics related to institutions, law, the stability of the legal system, values, the administration of justice, transparency, accountability, the participation and even the quality and relevancy of education have converted the technocrats of yesterday into the technopols of today.[1] The mistakes and defects of politicians have always been publicized and analyzed. The omissions and errors of technocrats, much less so. This is one of the major sources of some of Colombia's problems.

The programs and policies adopted by the multilateral agencies played the "functional equivalent" of the output one would expect from a society's ruling group. These programs and policies, produced without the benefit of a participatory domestic process, were nevertheless presented as revealed truth. This technocratic dogmatism, unfortunately, exempted the input of the political parties into the policy formulation process. Congress, trade unions, universities, think tanks (scarce in number, to be sure) were also denied a fundamental job: the creation of an agenda through a process of discussion and consensus-building, followed by implementation, evaluation, and accountability. It is a recognized fact that the financing style of the multilateral agencies has changed significantly since the end of the Cold War, as measured by the degree of participation and advice from diverse organisms of civil society that have gone into the design of national programs. Still, the dogmatism has not completely disappeared. Therefore, no one should be surprised by the precariousness of people, institutions, and groups that should play a leadership role in Colombia today.

In short, a slow but sure process stimulated by the criminal drug trade has weakened both the establishment and the legal economy. Concurrently —and fed or exacerbated by the criminal drug trade—anti-establishment activity has been strengthened through guerrillas (who survived and even grew stronger after the Cold War), drug cartels, and later, mini-cartels, common crime, smuggling, and organized crime that drained money and goods from the government.[2]

Thus, several crises festered for quite a while, feeding off of each other and accelerating notably in the 1970s. Ultimately they converged in the critical situation that has characterized Colombia for the past several years:

- a crisis of representation and trust in political institutions and their leaders
- a crisis of public order, increasingly aggravated by the interaction of the guerrilla and illegal self-defense groups with the drug-trafficking business, which provides financing and weapons through bartering arrangements; an increase in kidnappings estimated conservatively at around 3,000 cases (not all are reported to the authorities) for the year 2000; a human rights crisis accompanied by a worrisome humanitarian crisis that is reflected in the alarming statistic of a million and half displaced people over the past ten years and an exodus of citizens fleeing the country
- a crisis in the justice system; politicization, corruption, impunity (although not to the degree pointed out in some reports)
- a crisis of corruption, caused by the increasing use of intimidation and murder by criminal organizations to get what they want
- a crisis linked to the decentralization plan due to careless, corrupt management, and the lack of opportune controls over the country's own resources as well as the very significant amounts obtained from the transfer of almost 50 percent of the nation's ordinary revenues

These crises have been aggravated by the uncommon economic recession of the past three years that has wiped out the favorable qualifications that once made Colombia desirable in the eyes of international investors and multilateral agencies. The inability of the state and civil society to identify paths of action and make concerted efforts toward consensus-building objectives has also aggravated the situation.

Responses to the Threats

A quick overview of the attempts (old and new) to overcome these crises (old and new) will help us understand the nature of Colombia's situation. The National Front (1958–74), a bipartisan agreement to reintroduce democracy and coexistence through a power sharing scheme that was initially agreed to for a twelve-year period and later for a sixteen-year period, essentially achieved these purposes. Its benevolent shade, however, incubated other problems that so far have not been overcome but have worsened: clientelism; the exaggerated factionalism of political parties; the emergence of a multiplicity of radical guerrilla movements (FARC, Democratic Alliance M-19 [M-19], ELN, Popular Army of National Liberation [EPL], Quintín Lame, etc.); production and trafficking of marijuana first, cocaine and poppies later; the weakening and the displacement of political debate by political mechanics and a worrisome political alienation. This atmosphere was caused by the conniving attitude characteristic of the National Front culture, and allowed the gestation of the very serious illicit drug problem.[3]

The first post–National Front administration, led by Alfonso López Michelsen (1974–78), undertook the task of reforming, through the Constitutional Assembly, two fundamental aspects of Colombian institutions: the justice system and the relationship between the central government and the departments and municipalities. This proposal, approved by Congress itself, was reversed by a decision of the Supreme Court in 1978 arguing that Congress could not delegate those reform powers. Julio César Turbay's administration (1978–82) reassessed the content of the initiative, expanded it, and pushed it through Congress successfully. This attempted constitutional reform was also declared unconstitutional by the Supreme Court, which found that one vote was missing in one of the sixteen voting sessions required by this process. The administration of Belisario Betancur (1982–86) tried again, but its efforts were frustrated during final congressional debate. It was said at the time that Colombia was a blocked society that could not enact urgent modifications in its institutional architecture.

The administration of Virgilio Barco (1986–90) was inaugurated without pretenses of carrying out a constitutional reform. It soon became evident that there were serious legal restrictions that impeded appropriate democratic governance. On January 30, 1988, President Barco proposed a plebiscite to lift the existing ban on summoning plebiscites (Article 13, 1957 Plebiscite). Although the proposal was almost unanimously supported by public opinion, the former presidents of the Republic were opposed, making it necessary to promote the so-called Nariño House Accord. Through this agreement, the government, the opposition, and independents could call for a referendum to adopt mutually debated and agreed upon reforms.

A magistrate of the Administrative Court (Consejo de Estado) declared the accord unconstitutional and the reformist agenda was again frustrated. Later on, the assassination of the Liberal leader Luis Carlos Galán on August 18, 1989, ordered by the drug cartels, unleashed a social uprising headed by a group of students that led to a plebiscite on May 27, 1990, in favor of a Constitutional Assembly based on the right of petition. It was the so-called seventh ballot. Based on this popular demand, presidential candidate César Gaviria promised to summon a Constituent Assembly if he was elected. On December 9, 1990, the members of the Constituent Assembly were elected. They held session until July 1991, when they proclaimed a new constitution. This time, the courts, although strongly divided, did not intervene negatively. Two facts were of influence: the serious public order situation generated by narco-terrorism and the pressure of public opinion, and, without a doubt, President César Gaviria's (1990–94) skilled handling of the situation.[4]

The 1991 constitution sought to strengthen Colombia's institutions, particularly in those areas that were long overdue for reform. These included the justice system, territorial entities, civil rights protection, mechanisms of citizen participation, the relationship between the executive and the legislative branches, and auditing institutions (General Prosecutor's Office [Procuraduría], General Comptroller, General Auditor, General Accountant). Political transparency was sought through a series of dispositions against clientelism and corruption, and the establishment of a constitutional basis on which to structure and consolidate the new economic model: openness, privatization, central bank autonomy, public utility regulatory commissions for electricity, gas, telecommunications, public services, and the like.[5]

It would not be an exaggeration to state that the new 1991 constitution left Colombia well endowed as far as the potential for democratic governance was concerned. In addition, the new economic model set the country on the right track toward integration into the global economy. A controversial anti-drug policy—based on the concept of plea bargaining—put an end to the threat posed by narco-terrorism to the rule of law, but failed to address other manifestations of the illicit drugs problem (namely, the strengthening of an illegal economy of corruption, the financing of the insurgency and other self-defense groups, etc.). Colombia was undergoing an appropriate but incomplete transition into the new post–Cold War world and the new economic model.[6]

What Happened? How Did This Transition Get Entangled?

After finishing its task of reform, the Constituent Assembly faced a difficult predicament: what to do with a Congress, elected with a high turnout in March 1990, in which the Liberals and Conservatives controlled 96 percent of the seats in both the Senate and the Chamber of Deputies, and that, in addition, had already approved an important legislative agenda? Much of the support for the Constituent Assembly was rooted in an anti-political sentiment and, therefore, was anti-Congress. How could this same Congress, substituted de facto by the Constituent Assembly, work to develop and consolidate the new institutions and the new spirit of reform? After complex negotiations, the Constituent Assembly adopted the following decisions:

- Revoke the mandate of Congress members.
- Summon new elections.
- Declare members of the Constituent Assembly ineligible for membership in the new Congress.
- Allow the reelection of revoked Congress members.

Critics have formulated four significant points against the constitution of 1991:[7]

1. It weakened the political system by fomenting a multiparty system with so-called electoral micro-enterprises—presidential candidacies or "independent" governorships and mayorships based on anti-politics or on purely situational circumstances (flash-politics or media-parties). This further weakened the existing precarious system and opened the opportunity for presidential manipulation of congressional votes. It brought about the institutionalization of what Colombians historically call *lentejismo*, referred to in other countries as transhumance, or *camisetazo* (to change one's T-shirt or allegiance), where candidates seek office under one party or political group to later become affiliated with an artificial majority in Congress favoring presidential wishes in exchange for political favors (positions, contracts, etc.)

2. It politicized the judicial branch by replacing the existing co-opting system, which isolated and created cliques within the judicial sector, with a system of appointments, permitting the influence of the president and Congress on the election process of most of the Superior Judiciary Council magistrates (Consejo Superior de la Judicatura): seven judges of a total of thirteen; of the remaining six, two are chosen by the Supreme Court, one by the Constitutional Court, and three by the Administrative Court (Consejo de Estado).

3. It brought about a fiscal crisis as a result of the creation of new institutions (Attorney General, General Auditor, General Accountant, Constitutional Court, Superior Judiciary Council, National Television Commission, several regulatory commissions) and the introduction of an automatic system that transfers almost 50 percent of ordinary rev-

enues from the national budget to the municipalities and provincial departments.

4. It contributed to an even greater fragmentation of political forces.

Both the overt and the covert antagonism within the mostly anti-1991-constitution Congress and the political crisis of Ernesto Samper's administration (1994–98) contributed to the creation of laws and regulations that, although based on the new constitution, were perverse or failed to produce the legal underpinnings, leaving fundamental ordinances or arrangements in limbo, as will be pointed out later. There were also constitutional reforms that changed the spirit of the 1991 constitution, including the introduction of a system of substitutes for temporary absences (Legislative Act 3 of 1993), permanent salaries and the right to special privileges in the social security system for the assembly deputies of the provincial departments (Legislative Act 1 of 1996), and the failed attempt to control the transfers to the territorial entities (Legislative Act 1 of 1995).

The unfortunate fact that the "spirit of the 1991 Constituent Assembly" was not maintained largely explains why its weaknesses were not corrected and why some of its virtues were perverted. The failure of the attempted political reforms in 1995, 1999, and 2000 should come as no surprise.

Weaknesses of the Responses

The quid pro quo decision to revoke the 1991 Congress, which opposed the Constituent Assembly, was a diabolical one. As a result of new electoral rules such as a nationwide constituent district for the election of senators, the Congress was comprised of over 50 percent of new members in both chambers. Ninety-three percent of the senators had to look for new jobs as a result of the elections of 1991 and 1994. Yet the change in personnel did not translate into a change of habits. In fact, some believe that the situation actually got worse. The national district mechanism was gravely distorted from the start because the list apportionment clearly benefited the owners of regional electoral machines. The same mechanism applied for chamber elections, in which the district is not national but departmental.[8]

In a study on the political reforms in Colombia commissioned by the Colombian government (1999), Arturo Valenzuela, Joseph M. Colomer, Arend Lijphart, and Matthew Shugart concluded that by assigning values to different alternatives and adding them together to get an index which can be standardized at +100 (maximum partyocracy) and −100 (maximum individualism), the current system in Colombia gets the maximum individualism score of −100. The political parties have lost control over candidacies for Congress and other offices. This translates into a multiplicity of lists that makes the voter's decision more difficult and stimulates party indiscipline. Thus, Congress becomes a collection of individuals that increasingly represent themselves rather than their electoral districts or their parties. In this manner, governability suffers. In the case of the Senate, the magnitude is so high (100 seats) that it produces the highest imaginable degrees of individualist competition. This has engendered what the government itself calls "the abundance of electoral micro-enterprises" for a "retail clientelism of small and medium dominions."

In this manner, the system is mobilized at the service of special interests. The absence of a debate on national issues leaves the process of public policy consensus-building, essential for democratic governance, in a vacuum. The citizenry, therefore, does not feel represented because the agenda of the political leadership does not correspond to the social agenda.[9]

The majority of the post-1991 Congress, as has been mentioned, did not share the reformist spirit of 1991. The new constitution was the target not only of reforms that betrayed its spirit but also of precarious and perverse legal maneuverings that more often than not contradicted it outright. Some of the more deplorable cases follow:

- statutory Law 130 of 1994 that regulated political parties and movements as well as party and campaign financing
- the laws that regulated the National Electoral Council, the organism that controls political developments
- the statutory law regulating multiple forms of political participation (Law 134 of 1994). The same thing happened to other areas, such as territorial organization, the justice system, and so on.

To make matters worse, many issues were left unfinished, such as territorial organization, for example.

Another factor was the "clientelization" of two institutions that were of key importance for governability. One was the Superior Judiciary Council, which has the responsibility of administering the whole system of justice, including proposing candidates for magistrates and judgeships and exercising disciplinary power. A collegiate body was not the best formula to correct the serious administrative flaws of the judiciary, especially because the interests of partisan factions mediated it. The same thing happened with the National Electoral Council. It is telling that, thus far, the institution has yet to figure out how to work with diligence in the execution of its duties to assure the transparency of the political process.[10]

Regarding the strengthening of the other institutions that are in charge of public order, the expected results did not materialize. The significant budget increases for the military—very fair, to be sure—were channeled into pay raises distributed equally to retired personnel. Very little was left for equipment, intelligence gathering, and the training and restructuring of the different forces. The National Police, however, prompted by serious incidents, was able to institute reforms that have improved the institution and made it more effective, particularly in the fight against drugs.[11] The prison system, manipulated perversely by guerrillas, drug traffickers, and illegal self-defense groups, has not been able to overcome its incompetent administration and endemic corruption.

There were other factors that impeded the full materialization of the 1991 constitutional reforms. The least reformist part of the 1991 constitution deals with political parties and movements. Intended to dampen the powerful bipartisan system and given that the Constituent Assembly was made up principally of three major political forces (the Liberal Party, the Conservative Party, and the AD-M19), decisions regarding political parties and movements would henceforth require a consensus, tending to weaken the power of the traditional majority—the Liberal Party—and advance the cause of minority political parties and movements. Several institutions were introduced with the deliberate purpose of weakening the majority Liberal Party, particularly in the presidential election. To this effect, the institution of the vice-presidency and the system of runoff elections were introduced. The former facilitates the selection of a Liberal vice-presidential candidate by a minority candidate in order to split the Liberal Party and thus gain an electoral majority. In the two presidential elections that followed, the ability of these two institutions to accomplish these goals was amply proven. In 1994 and in 1998 the Liberal Party won in the first elections but not by enough to avoid the runoffs. In 1994 they won the runoffs by a narrow margin (first round: Ernesto Samper 45.10 percent, Andrés Pastrana 44.75 percent; runoffs: Ernesto Samper 50.27 percent, Andrés Pastrana 48.15 percent). In 1998 the Liberal Party won the first round by a narrow margin but lost the runoffs by a wide margin (first round: Horacio Serpa 34.38 percent, Andrés Pastrana with a Liberal candidate for the vice-presidency, Gustavo Bell, ex-governor of the department of the Atlantic, a Liberal stronghold, 33.98 percent; Noemí Sanín 26.47 percent; runoffs: Andrés Pastrana 49 percent, Horacio Serpa 45.97 percent). The same has not been true of elections for Congress, assemblies, town councils, mayorships, and governorships, where the Liberal Party maintains its majority at the cost of enormous factionalism that has dampened all possibility of party discipline and has had the dangerous tendency to produce splinter groups or mini-parties. This hampers governability at the national level as well as in provincial departments and municipalities. Andrés Pastrana became president without a majority in either the Senate or the Chamber. Noemí Sanín did not have representation in Congress from 1998 to 2002 and in the March 10, 2002 elections, she was the presidential candidate that had the least congressional representation.

Amid this anarchy, coarse forms of clientelism have been revived, causing further government inefficiency and corruption: a masterful recipe for ungovernability. In addition, the constitution that encourages and mandates citizen participation in both the governmental and private sectors—public and private universities, for example—exempts political parties from this obligation (Article 108 of the national constitution).

A New Governability Crisis

Another factor was the political crisis that characterized Ernesto Samper's government (1994–98) as a result of the Cali Cartel's $U.S.6 million donation used to finance the runoff presidential election. This situation divided the Liberal Party and generated both overt and latent confrontation between two factions, the gaviristas and the samperistas.[12]

The 1991 constitution was the subject of numerous reform proposals that neither materialized nor were conducive to a normal and orderly legislative follow-up. The political polarization in Colombia that started in 1994, fringed by social polarization and aggravated by the coercive public diplomacy of the U.S. government, fatally interrupted the transition toward greater democratic governability and an appropriate insertion into the new global economy. At the same time, it exacerbated problems of public order.

The 1991 institutions were especially useful in revealing the ties that existed among the drug mafia, the political sector, the economy, and society. At least three of them—the General Prosecutor's Office (Procuraduría General); the Supreme Court's special judicial privilege to investigate Congress members, eliminating congressional immunity; the loss of office (*pérdida de investidura*) in conflict of interest cases, as well as other disciplinary measures that are now processed in a summary trial before the Administrative Court—have allowed for the effective punishment of more than thirty members of Congress. This phenomenon would have been impossible or very difficult—and never at this scale—if these new institutions and tools had not existed.[13]

The effective judicial prosecution of Congress members and high officials was a good example of governability in an area once characterized by impunity. Since the 1991 constitution, the Administrative Court has prosecuted over 153 cases, resulting in the removal from office on cases presented by the Senate itself, the General Prosecutor's Office, or private citizens. Over twenty members of Congress have been convicted. The Supreme Court itself has convicted at least four members of Congress on criminal grounds. The General Prosecutor and ordinary judges have also prosecuted several Congress members who have renounced their right to the Supreme Court's special judicial privilege, hoping for greater leniency.

New Frustrated Responses

The flaws of the 1991 constitution regarding political parties, the electoral system, the functioning of Congress, and campaign finance could have been mitigated with appropriate legislation and the opportune intervention of entities like the National Electoral Council. But the opposite occurred. A first attempt to correct these flaws involved the creation of the "Commission to Study Political Party Reforms" (Decrees 763 and 842 of 1995)[14] that worked between May 15 and July 13, 1995, finishing only a few days before the scandalous news of the mafioso financing of Ernesto Samper's presidential campaign, based on the broadly diffused testimony of Santiago Medina, the campaign treasurer.

The Commission achieved an unexpected consensus among the official representatives of the Liberal and Conservative parties, AD-M19, independent political movements, civil society, trade unions, and the academic community. The recommendations, directed at "giving politics back to the citizens,"[15] required some minor modifications to the 1991 constitutional text but preserved and praised it as "the most significant legacy, in the country's recent history, for current and future generations."[16] "The work of the Commission—as described in the general considerations section of the report—is inspired by the loyalty and respect it accords the constitutional framework, understanding that it is rich with opportunities for development."[17] The recommendations sought to correct the defects already mentioned within Congress and the party system.

In spite of the consensus, this political reform was thwarted by the political crisis brought about by the scandal, and further aggravated by the public testimony of former Minister of Defense Fernando Botero in January 1996.[18] The political reform thus began the painful journey that had afflicted attempts at constitutional reform prior to 1991.

Andrés Pastrana's victory in June of 1998 created a difficult situation in terms of governability. The Liberal Party, target of tough prosecutions for corruption, had won 19 governorships while the Conservative Party had only 3. Other political groups won 9. The Liberal Party had 45.6 percent of the mayorships, the Conservative Party 33.1 percent, and other parties 14.2 percent. The Liberal Party won 48 seats in the Senate, the Conservative Party 25, Liberal Oxygen Movement 2, Christians 2, ethnic movements 3, other political movements 15, and coalitions 7, for a total of 102 senators. In the Chamber of Deputies, the Liberals obtained 87 seats; the Conservatives 38, the Christians 2, the ethnic movements 2, coalitions 14, and other political movements 18. And as already mentioned, Pastrana's electoral performance in both of the presidential election rounds was not catastrophic, as was expected. The Liberal candidate, Horacio Serpa, won the first round by a small margin. In the runoffs, faced with the impossibility of picking up dissident Liberal votes or independent votes, he lost by a 3.3 percent margin.[19] President Pastrana, represented by the minority party in Congress, had two alternatives:

1. Respect the Liberal majority and establish common ground rules to ensure the passage of fundamental legislation; or
2. Seek to put the Liberal majority into disarray and build his own majority, which is what he did. This assured him, despite the ups and downs characteristic of parliamentary life, the passage of his legislative proposals—with the glaring exception of the political reform package that he had promised during his campaign. The reform collapsed in the second to last debate due to a complex process. Fundamentally, there was skepticism over the peace process. The first article of the reform (that was never published in the media) granted President Pastrana extraordinary constitutional powers (dictatorial some would say) to do whatever was necessary to negotiate a peace treaty. It was a hard blow to the government's coalition. They lost this important issue by a single vote.

Another Crisis in Governability: The Relationship Between the Executive and Congress

The executive and the legislative branches of government have a distorted and impaired relationship. This has been especially true since the National Front (1958). What has existed since then is what I have described elsewhere as a "presidential party" consisting of a majority in Congress with diverse political roots, but who support the president for better or for worse. This relationship is not free of crises, friction, and difficulties. Toward the end of each administration, the "presidential party" begins to weaken as it seeks to renew itself based on the results of the upcoming electoral process that reshapes Congress and chooses a new president. It is noteworthy that, with the single exception of President Barco's administration, all the governments since 1958 have been coalitions.[20]

The main flaw of the Colombian Congress is its inability to independently exercise its power (legislate, debate on issues of national concern, exercise political control, seek an equal distribution of benefits and development among the nation's regions and sectors). Colombian congresspersons prefer to use their power as a tool to obtain bureaucratic positions and other advantages and privileges. Public policy is really not their main concern. To be sure, there are exceptions in terms of personalities and time periods. As the government itself recognized in the declaration of motives for the proposed referendum of April 5, 2000, "the great forum of political debate, bereft of its underpinning as a true representative body, loses itself in the urgencies of the moment, leaving only the executive to hold the political system together. In this environment, the needs of governance must accommodate the machinery of clientelist benefits as a pre-condition for the legislature to give the executive whatever it may require. This scenario weakens the system's capacity for self-control. Political control ceases to operate, opening the way to an incestuous relationship between the executive and Congress wherein festers the constant danger of systemic corruption."[21]

Nothing is more disconcerting to members of Congress than an administration that declares its intent to respect the autonomy of the legislature as an independent branch of government. Given this state of affairs, the government has the capacity to guide legislative behavior. There is a price to pay—at times, very high. But that is the only barrier.

The roles of both the executive and the legislature have been distorted by this clientelist paradigm, which has become the perverting factor hampering the functioning of public administration at all levels. This behavior is also replicated in municipal assemblies and town councils.

In essence, the struggle for a representative Congress, sensitive to the needs and aspirations of the citizenry, with the capability and the will to exercise authentic political control, has been frustrated by the clientelist relationship between the executive and legislative branches. This relationship has reached unimaginable levels, engendering gross corruption—at times scandalous—as well as the gross inefficiency of these institutions. In the bill proposal that accompanied the referendum project, the government itself described this relationship as pernicious. The opposition calls it the "corrupt marriage" between the legislative and executive. This clientelist relationship has stymied an appropriate separation of powers. But it does mean that, in the end, both the administration and Congress members, representatives and councilmen, get what they want: positions, favors, contracts through the "right" connections, cushy jobs, preferential treatment for their relatives, and so on.

Political control has almost become moot. The same is true of public expenditure control or the management of public entities. The effectiveness of motions to censor ministers is a telling example: it has never been approved although it has been introduced several times. The ease with which the Pastrana administration disrupted the Liberal majority reveals the weakness of most Congress members when faced with the enticements of the clientelist and kinship system.

Another Governability Crisis

The frustrated political reform initiative of 1995, reattempted in 1998, was again revived on March 30, 2000, giving rise to a serious and unprecedented crisis in the executive-legislative relationship.

After a deplorable scandal regarding the handling of the Chamber of Deputies budget by a directive panel controlled by the government's coalition (and after a harsh exchange of recriminations between the government and the Liberal opposition lasting several months), Pastrana called for a referendum to change political practices and control and punish corruption. On Wednesday, April 5, the text of the referendum was sent to Congress without prior consultation with the political establishment or even with the government's own coalition.[22] The text had seventeen articles of constitutional reform to be voted on by the citizenry on July 16, 2000. This political reform called for a reduction in the number of congresspersons in both chambers; a reduction in the number of members that would replace the departmental assemblies and the municipal town councils; the adoption of a new electoral system of proportional representation (the D'Hondt) that favored large parties and large minorities; the introduction of the single-party list; the reform of the campaign financing system; the introduction of compulsory voting for only one instance; the annulment of the current congressional mandate by calling new elections on October 29, 2000 (the same day as the territorial elections); and the introduction of a Public Ethics Tribunal, among others.

This proposal eliminated most of the "great alliance for change" (the government's coalition) and it reinstated the Liberal Party's majority status. Obviously, the Congress rebelled. The Liberal Party threatened to devise another proposal that included revoking the president's mandate.

In effect, President Pastrana sacrificed the governability that the old strategy (that had squashed the Liberal majorities) had given him in order to hoist the anti-corruption flag and to eventually build new, more coherent majorities, guided by the spirit of 1991. The presidential proposal enjoyed broad public support (68 percent would vote, and 92 percent of those would cast a "yes" vote) although the president's popularity and his job approval ratings were very low (67 percent disapproved, 83 percent believed that the country was on the wrong path, 81 percent believed that the peace process was on the wrong path). These results were based on a random nationwide telephone survey conducted by *El Espectador* on April 6 and 7. Experts say that this proposal had a negative impact on Colombia's economic reactivation and on international markets by creating uncertainty through a deteriorated political environment that made the fulfillment of commitments with the IMF more difficult.[23]

Once again (as in 1990), a necessary constitutional reform for the democratic governability of the country had to be decided by the electorate in order to overcome the barriers put up by Congress and the courts. It is noteworthy that the 1991 constitution sets up mechanisms to unblock eventual impasses between the executive and the legislature.

The political crisis forced the president to take back his referendum initiative; the attempts to reach an agreement with the Liberal Party did not work out. The president appointed Juan Manuel Santos, a Liberal, to his cabinet as minister of the treasury in the hope of obtaining the programmatic cooperation of the Liberal Party regarding the approval of the economic package.

Decentralization

An ambitious strategy of decentralization intended to strengthen governability was advanced involving the transfer of almost 50 percent of the national budget's ordinary revenues. However, neither the institutions necessary to administer these considerable sums efficiently nor the mechanisms of institutional or civilian control to assure effectiveness and transparency were in place. A great squandering of funds inevitably ensued, causing much of the fiscal deficit and irresponsible indebtedness of municipalities and departments. As a result, this issue was addressed in the legislative package agreed to with the IMF in December 1999. The IMF went so far as to demand a constitutional amendment to correct the system of transfers. Bad regional management, waste, the absence of effective controls, and a clientelist system had given corruption free rein.[24] In addition, the guerrillas had successfully set up extortion schemes in some municipalities to skim off a percentage of revenues or to secure municipal contracts and bureaucratic positions.

It is a clear case of how the interrelationship among institutional ineptness, a crisis of representation, public disorder, impunity, and corruption can bring down an ambitious decentralization plan. The lack of insight into these situations and, on occasion, the monumental naiveté of many of its bureaucrats was behind the World Bank's 1996 proposal to introduce legislation to deepen the process of decentralization!

Public Order

The entire institutional framework in charge of maintaining public order and civilian security in a country disrupted every day by powerful organizations (guerrillas, self-defense organizations, mini drug cartels, organized crime, kidnappers, extortion rings) was severely crippled after the 1991 constitution. As a result, the strategy of "selective governability" that was popular during the Cold War had to be replaced by strategies that seek to make the entire system governable—within the state, the government, and civil society.

A handful of islands of efficiency in fighting the illicit drug problem within the justice system is not the recipe to strengthen the entire administration of justice. Islands of efficiency in the military (anti-drug battalions) do not strengthen the military as a whole. Islands of efficiency in the National Police (anti-drug units) do not contribute to the safety of the population in its daily life. Islands of efficiency in intelligence agencies do not assure the preservation of public order. Special prisons for drug dealers do not improve the integrity of the penitentiary system. Likewise, the islands of technocratic governability championed by the multilateral financing agencies have not helped democratic governability in Colombia, but rather weakened it.

Plan Colombia is, once again, structured around this selective governability focus that results in partial successes and greater disasters in the long run. As indicated in the report produced by the Council on Foreign Relations and the Inter-American Dialogue,[25] the Colombian armed forces need to be professionalized across the board. The same realities must be preached regarding the other institutions linked to public order and security, whose notorious weakness has contributed to the crisis of governability.

This is a fundamental consideration for the future of democratic governability in Colombia. The strategies that have been put in place do not appear to be the appropriate ones. Admittedly, the emergency situation, for now, does not encourage longer-term measures. In order to recover democratic governability in Colombia, however, the solutions must be inspired by an integrated approach that will look at each institution individually and its interrelationship with the multiplicity of crises. Selective prescriptions translate into apparent healings that actually end up aggravating the crisis.

The interrelationship of guerrillas, illegal self-defense groups, and narco-financing is responsible for the astonishing strength of the insurgencies and armed counterinsurgencies in Colombia. The ongoing "peace process," started in 1980, has unwittingly contributed to this situation. The result has been the demoralization and quasi-paralysis of an already weak institutional apparatus in charge of public order. This, together with the other institutional and social weaknesses mentioned above, comprise the Gordian knot that has severely eroded Colombian governability. It bears repeating: strategies of selective governability do not lead to a sustainable democratic governability on a national, departmental, or municipal level. The state, the government, and society as a whole must be strengthened. That is the challenge for the next few years.

The Political System

Colombia has had a traditional two-party system since the middle of the nineteenth century. Conservatives and Liberals have alternatively governed the nation, at times under hegemony, at others, in coalition. The Conservative Party predominated from 1886 to 1930. Since then, the Liberal Party has held a majority. This correlation of forces—a Liberal majority and a Conservative minority—has been decisive in the political history of Colombia over the past seventy years. The Liberal republic (1930–46); the Conservative minority governments, with their crises of violence and ungovernability (1946–53); and the suspension of the democratic regime between 1953 and 1957 are intimately related to the attitude of a Conservative Party that will not abide with its minority status and a Liberal Party that counts on almost unbeatable majority support.[26]

The National Front settled this argument via plebiscite (December 1, 1957), by virtue of which the two parties agreed to equal treatment, initially through the sharing of power at all levels, including the judicial branch, for twelve years. Later, this equal distribution was extended to the presidency of the Republic, resulting in the need to extend the National Front to sixteen years so that each party could alternate the presidency every eight years. Because the Conservatives were in power when this arrangement was made, it was further agreed that the Conservatives would occupy the presidency in the final period, that is to say, between 1970 and 1974. As a result of this and other reasons, the Liberals held the presidency during the first term of the National Front (1958–62). The constitutional reform of 1968 created the mechanism to dismantle this particular system. This led to a new agreement (Article 120 of the national constitution) for an "adequate and equitable" participation of the party that came in second to that of the president of the Republic, with this second party having the privilege of deciding whether it wanted to participate in the government for that term or not. In this manner, the government's structure—single party or coalition—was not determined by the majority party but by the losing party.

This arrangement was unsustainable when Virgilio Barco won by a landslide victory (4,215,510 votes versus 2,588,050) against the Conservative candidate Alvaro Gómez, who declined to participate in President Barco's government. This decision was also influenced by presidential candidate Virgilio Barco's announcement during the campaign that he would prefer to govern within a more typically democratic structure in which the winning party assumes the responsibility of governing and the loser or losers, the role of the opposition. President Barco, however, did not have the power to impose his will in this matter. He picked three Conservative Party ministers and extended similar participation in governorships, mayorships, and the diplomatic corps, and guaranteed that by virtue of the distinction between government and administration, the latter would see no variations in the existing presence of the losing party. This was the only time since 1945 that Colombia experienced a government-opposition system. There is no need to mention the enormous difficulties that surrounded this experiment.[27] The following administrations (César Gaviria, Ernesto Samper, and Andrés Pastrana) returned to coalition governments with an even greater flexibility than those of the National Front.

President Pastrana faced a crisis of governability after summoning the referendum to revoke Congress members from the same legislative body where he had built a majority coalition that he now consciously sought to eliminate. This reinstated the government-opposition system and again posed the political predicament of a minority government that must deal with a Congress dominated by the opposition majority.

This majority-minority correlation is, therefore, the main characteristic of the Colombian two-party system. Both parties include various social segments and have witnessed the gradual fading of their ideological differences as a result of the combined exercise of power, among other reasons. The changes brought about by the end of the Cold War have greatly contributed to this fading and have also spurred the formation of new factions and coalitions. In addition, political parties—especially after the National Front—experienced increasing intraparty, rather than interparty, competition (which had been made unnecessary due to the power-sharing scheme). This led to a culture of party factionalism that has resulted in the near absence of a national organization with any real directive and disciplinary capability. There are a multiplicity of movements and micro-parties, for example, at the municipal, departmental, and national levels that cater to an enormous variety of coalitions, sometimes dispensing with the names and symbolic colors of the traditional collectives. In the October 26, 1997 elections there were 125 candidates for 32 governorships, 3,416 candidates for 1,004 mayorships, 1,895 lists for 502 seats in the regional assemblies. The same occurred in the territorial elections of October 29, 2000.[28] The number of lists and candidates for Senate and Chamber seats completely overwhelmed any possibility of control by the parties or political movements. The numbers speak for themselves: in 1991, only 24 of the 100 Senate lists were able to meet or exceed the votes needed for the electoral quotient; in 1994, only 13; and in 1998, barely 10. The study that analyzes the electoral system, done by Valenzuela and others, concludes that the result has been an impressive factionalism of political parties and a resurgence of local clientelism. The ensuing parliamentary fragmentation has produced a weak government and a crisis of governability. This situation is duplicated at the departmental and municipal levels.[29]

This internal lack of discipline has even reached the presidential elections, particularly in the Conservative Party. For example, Andrés Pastrana (1998–2002) did not register in 1994 or in 1998 as a Conservative Party candidate, although he had the backing of the party. In the October 29, 2000 elections for the mayorship of Bogotá, neither the Liberals nor the Conservatives presented a party candidate that could wave the party flag. This also reflects the need to appeal to the non-partisan or undecided vote. This has not yet happened within the Liberal Party ranks for the presidential elections. The Conservative Party's minority status, however, has induced this situation.

On the other hand, unaffiliated candidacies and anti-political or anti-party movements, such as that of Noemí Sanín (26.47 percent of the votes in the first presidential round at 2,845,750, almost identical to that of César Gaviria, the winning Liberal candidate in 1990, who got 2,891,808 votes, and almost double that of the Conservative and well-known candidate during that same election at 1,433,913 votes), have become a force to be reckoned with and a real threat to the predominance of the two-party system.[30]

In fact, the intent of the political reforms previously described was to strengthen big parties without canceling or diminishing the opportunities for small parties or emerging political movements—a daunting task at best. The referendum proposed by President Pastrana reasonably seeks to strengthen political forces, rationalize the operation of Congress, and thus assure governability without having to exchange favors, a system that inevitably leads to administrative inefficiency and corruption. This is the challenge that Colombia now faces.

The need to build disciplined parliamentary majorities becomes more urgent as the splintering of political parties and the mechanisms introduced by the 1991 constitution make it possible for political movements with weak or nonexistent representation in Congress to pursue the presidency of the Republic realistically. For example, if Noemí Sanín had won the presidency, she would have lacked a base of support in Congress because her anti-politics strategy meant that she would not have participated in the elections of senators and representatives. Given the new playing field and the political forces and opportunities that the 1991 constitution has helped to unleash, there is an urgent need for governability in the executive-legislative relationship, at the national, departmental, and municipal levels. The referendum proposed by President Pastrana sought to achieve exactly that. The issue of whether the formulas are appropriate is now precariously being confronted in Colombia. There is, however, no doubt that the political reform agenda is an indispensable and urgent complement to the advances achieved by the constitution of 1991.

During the National Front it was argued that the governability pact was exclusive, in spite of the fact that, as Francisco Gutierrez affirms in his essay

"Rescate por un elefante, congreso, sistema y reforma política" ("Rescued by an Elephant, Congress, System and Political Reform") after analyzing presidential elections from 1962 to 1990, third parties such as the Liberal Revolutionary Movement (MRL) and the Popular National Alliance (ANAPO) in 1966 and 1974, respectively, experienced what he calls "their golden era."[31] Some even go so far as to call the National Front the raison d'être of the armed insurgencies. Likewise, there are those that say that the 1991 constitution and the legislation that emerged from it regarding political parties and movements, campaign finance, and the like has contributed to ungovernability because it has stimulated internal party factionalism and the proliferation of what has been called "electoral micro-enterprises." They also point to the creation of a legal framework that stimulates the emergence of political movements that take advantage of short-lived situations and circumstances, which can be expertly exploited with the help of political consultants (particularly from the United States) to mount successful electoral campaigns, like Collor de Mello's, for example.

The effect of the electoral rules established by the 1991 constitution are very clear: they limited the hegemony of the Liberal Party and opened opportunities so that others may effectively challenge and defeat it. This has indeed been the case, particularly in the last elections. The strength of the Liberal Party, however, cannot be taken lightly. The 1998 elections came after one of the biggest crises of any Liberal administration. Nevertheless, the presidential candidate that was identified with that administration won a first-round victory with the biggest voter turnout, in absolute terms, in the history of the Liberal Party.

It is also necessary to recognize that the existing electoral rules have given rise to a representation deficit because Congress is a battleground where mini-parties and electoral micro-enterprises vie for their very survival, and expediency will often outweigh principle or political responsibility to the nation. This is another way in which the executive-legislative relationship is further corrupted. It produced the governability crisis that prompted President Pastrana to call for the referendum.

Still, the existing electoral rules are basically fair and permit and even stimulate the participation of emerging and competing forces in the political arena. This has been amply proven in the post-1991 elections at all levels. Yet, independents and other small political groups continue to push for favorable legislation, increasing the tension among governability, electoral rules, and campaign finance reform that favor newly formed or minority views.

Victories, such as Antanas Mockus' in Bogotá in 1995 and 2000, did not count on the backing of any traditional political party and were precariously financed. They were the result of a well-organized media effort crafted by consultants who portrayed their candidate as a great "media figure." This strategy has been repeated successfully in other cities of Colombia like Barranquilla, Cali, and Manizales. Andrés Pastrana Arango's victory in 1998, with the biggest numerical turnout in the history of Colombia, is also an example of the possibilities offered by the new ground rules. The case of Noemí Sanín is illustrative. A Conservative, who was a minister in both Belisario Betancur's Conservative administration and in César Gaviria's Liberal administration, she was able to launch an anti-political movement against Andrés Pastrana and Horacio Serpa that brought her to the threshold of the presidency. Just as representatives of small independent movements like Ingrid Betancourt and Antonio Navarro (former guerrilla and presidential candidate of AD-M19), Noemí Sanín supported the referendum proposal and its content. Evidently, the fight for fair rules subject to modifications that attempt to make them even more favorable to small political groups is still on the agenda. This is the basis for the fear of the Liberal Party that perceives all this reformist activity as a way to destroy or block the Liberal majority. This is the central issue.

Civil Society

The role of political parties as entities that articulate and aggregate interests has been systematically vanishing. Independent civil society organizations have emerged representing the environment, indigenous affairs, corruption, human rights, and other issues. Some of these are financed by foreign governments or agencies, giving them a unique capacity to gather and distribute information that the political parties themselves do not enjoy. During the Samper administration, associations representing the production sectors assumed a role usually reserved for political parties. They submitted proposals in the United States on how to manage the crisis and went as far as to ask for the president's resignation. Their initiative failed in the end due to the lack of a coherent political strategy. This, along with the three-year economic crisis, has significantly weakened these associations to the point that several have disappeared and others are barely surviving. Another contributing factor to the weakening of the associations—which apparently represent the most powerful sector—has been the emergence of economic groups that have substituted them in their effective communication with high government officials. This is a topic that has not been analyzed in depth but that is having a major impact on the roles of unions such as the National Industrial Association (ANDI), the Banking Association, the National Association of Financial Institutions, and even the National Council of Associations that represents the seventeen principal production-sector associations. The new 1991 constitution, without a doubt, offers the most participation scenarios at all levels (with the exception, as mentioned before,

of the major political parties). Participation is the hallmark of the 1991 constitution and is based on the notion that sovereignty resides with the people. This is a radical change. It is evident that there are all types of networks,
movements, and organizations struggling to influence public opinion and
public policy. However, a long learning process lies ahead on how to participate and gain influence. Individualism and the inability to build coalitions
still undermine the efforts of many of these civil society organizations. Yet,
there is a sharp contrast between the pre- and post-1991 scenarios.

The referendum itself (as a tool to arbitrate the disagreement between the
executive and the legislative branches of government) is indicative of the decisive importance that the mechanisms of popular participation have attained. Civil society participation in the peace process, for example, has been
decisive in the advances achieved so far. This is particularly true in the case of
the negotiations with the ELN, which were practically promoted by a civil society group in which, it must be recognized, the Catholic Church has played
a major role in combination with German religious authorities. It has even
had the unintended consequence of delaying some agreements with the ELN
because it has not been easy for the government to align its expectations with
those of civil society. But as of April 2002, this has largely been overcome.
Other civil society organizations such as unions, however, are showing signs
of weakness. Recent data indicate that the Unified Workers' Union (CUT)
only represents 8 percent of the working population. Union leaders argue
that there are no guarantees given to union activism. The International
Labour Organization (ILO) has made an inspection visit to examine the situation. It is common knowledge that the exacerbated violence in the country
has claimed the lives of a substantial number of union leaders. Others feel
that the pervasive informality of the Colombian economy contributes to the
weakness of the union movement. The employed population in the seven
largest cities in Colombia is 5.8 million. In a country of 40 million inhabitants, the total membership of the three labor unions (CUT, General Confederation of Democratic Workers [CGTD] and Workers' Confederation of
Colombia [CTC]) barely adds up to 743,000. The unions have not been
spared from the confidence crisis that grips the country.

A survey carried out recently by the managerial sector (Fundación Corona
y Confecámaras) ranks the official unions as the least qualified of the twenty-
eight public entities surveyed. The president of the CUT, Luis Eduardo
Garzón, stated: "we must accept that there have been cases of corruption
which we must combat, we have to carry out purges."[32] The statement by the
excellent French expert on Colombia, Daniel Pécaut, that the only existing
civil society in Colombia is an armed civil society—referring to the guerrillas
and the illegal self-defense groups—overlooks other organizations (albeit
less effective ones than the armed insurgencies).

Colombia has a rich and varied media. Traditionally, newspapers and broadcasters would ally themselves with one of the different political parties or their factions. *El Tiempo* and *El Espectador* were identified with the Liberal Party and on occasion expressed the positions and ambitions of different factions. *El Siglo* always represented the most recalcitrant extreme of the Conservative Party. *La República*, the Ospinista faction of that party, was less militant in the radically conservative areas. In the French tradition, the first requirement for building a political faction with national ambitions was to create or acquire communications media. In the 1960s, the liberal revolutionary movement of Alfonso López Michelsen, for example, founded a weekly publication, *La Calle*. A conservative faction founded *La Gente*. Former presidents maintained their political presence through their own writings: Carlos Lleras Restrepo founded and wrote most of the articles in *La Nueva Frontera*. Misael Pastrana Borrero did the same in *Guión Magazine* and Julio César Turbay in *Consigna Magazine*. The advent of television created an unwritten law in politics giving each one of the former presidents a television newscast. Only President Barco declined. Today, for professional and commercial reasons, the major newspapers have distanced themselves from the political parties and their factions. This is particularly true in the case of *El Tiempo* and *El Espectador*. Many regional newspapers still maintain partisan loyalties; the most typical of these are *El Colombiano* in Medellín and *El País* in Cali, both of conservative leanings. There is a new tendency for powerful economic conglomerates to gain control of the media. The Bavarian Group, for example, owned by Julio Mario Santodomingo, controls Caracol, the biggest radio chain in Colombia, a nationwide television channel, magazines, and the *El Espectador* newspaper. The Ardila Lulle group is another, if somewhat smaller, example. In general, the assignment of publicity gives these and other groups significant influence.

Broadcast media, especially television, has become more important than the printed page. But an orchestrated effort between the two translates into a very real capacity to influence events, both during political campaigns and in the formulation of public policy. In addition, the media has increasingly become a kind of refuge for personalities with political aspirations whose bids for Congress, a governorship, or a mayorship did not quite succeed. In this manner, journalists have conquered political arenas, placing them in direct competition with the public entities that do indeed have a constitutionally mandated representative function. Congress, departmental assemblies, and municipal town councils are no match against the immediacy and penetration power of the electronic media. As a result, the role of the media has become a predominant and crucial factor in the management of corruption scandals and of other topics that have a great impact on public opinion. This was the case during "the 8,000 process," the judicial scandal that uncovered the ties among the mafia, politics, and society, as well as other specific cases of corruption.

Even Congress has adjusted its work schedule around the news programs. It has become routine for the official channel, SEÑAL COLOMBIA, to air congressional debates on live TV. This practice, which has given the public access to real information as to what actually occurs in Congress, has also contributed to the discredit of Congress members. Rules such as those adopted by the British Parliament which regulate the handling of television cameras have not been established. The absenteeism, vulgarity, waste of time, old-fashioned, annoying, endless, and pointless rhetoric transmitted faithfully by the electromagnetic spectrum has conveyed a most unflattering picture of Congress.

Jaime Bermúdez, an excellent media and public opinion analyst, produced as his doctoral thesis at the University of Oxford a careful comparative work on the role of the media in the scandals surrounding the administrations of Carlos Andrés Pérez in Venezuela (second term), Ernesto Samper in Colombia, and William J. Clinton in the United States. Regarding Colombia he concludes: "It is clear that for some years now the media has been very critical of the traditional political classes and of Congress. They have analyzed their absenteeism and their inefficiency, their clientelism and their estrangement from representing the interests of those that elected them. But they have also begun to unveil the corruption that was displayed most dramatically in 'the 8,000 process.' The affected politicians and senators have in turn reacted to this changed relationship with the media. There have been some obvious attempts to retaliate. During the debate on television legislation (in the Samper administration) for example, several Congress members, among them the Liberal María Izquierdo (an important player in 'the 8,000 process') initiated a debate against the media, advocating regulatory and control measures."[33]

Public opinion has acquired special prominence due to a polling-obsessed media. At times, unscientific polls have been taken on a daily basis by radio stations to ascertain public opinion on some topic of the day. This technique has also been utilized by some television programs. The written media carry out monthly surveys on the government's situation and the public's attitude on specific subjects such as the peace process, employment policies, and international issues. This is a new phenomenon that did not even exist ten years ago.

An analysis of the polls has allowed Carlos Lemoine, an opinion poll expert, to identify how Colombians feel about their institutions: only 24 percent of Colombians trust the state and 39 percent trust NGOs. Trust in the armed forces runs high at over 60 percent in various surveys. Only 26 percent believe that elections are free and fair. And only 16 percent believe that the country is governed by the will of the people. Trust in political parties and in Congress is the lowest, at 8 percent and 16 percent, respectively. Trust in private corporations, television, and the press is high at 62, 54, and 51 percent, respectively. The presidency has lost importance in the public's perception: 30 percent consider it important. Only 17 percent believe that the main problem that affects the country is the political problem. They point rather to crime and unemployment. Sixty-five percent believe that human rights are not respected in Colombia. Only 6 percent believe that the revolution is the way to change the country.[34]

In conclusion, in spite of the efforts by several administrations to strengthen institutions and guarantee democratic governability, the results have been a growing institutional weakness that has continued to undermine the ability of the government and society to overcome the most serious problems: armed insurgencies, illegal self-defense groups, illicit drugs, human rights and international humanitarian law violations, corruption, high homicide rates, kidnappings, impunity, and the very serious current economic crisis, to mention the most salient.

There is a key date. Since 1980, the problems of violence, drugs, and kidnappings have grown enormously. Undoubtedly, the illicit drugs factor has been the catalyst that strengthened the armed insurgencies (guerrillas and illegal self-defense groups), catapulted all forms of violence (homicides, kidnappings), and destroyed a traditional society's system of values, substituting it for a get-rich-quick mentality, bringing corruption to such an alarming level that Andrés Pastrana's government has identified it as systemic.

Colombia faces multiple crises. The armed conflict and the drug problem are addressed through the peace strategy and Plan Colombia; the economic crisis through an agreement with the IMF. The rest, through precarious strategies designed to combat corruption and kidnapping, and to offer protection against human rights violations. There are many agendas on the table that on occasion reinforce, interfere, or even collide with each other.

The Strategy to Recover Democratic Governability

The government, at the beginning of the new millennium, has taken a series of initiatives that, if implemented appropriately and in spite of some contradictory elements, should put Colombia on the right path, reinstating democratic governability and assuring its integration into a competitive global economy. These initiatives represent an integrated and comprehensive response to the governability crisis:

1. *The agenda with the United States and the European Union,* the so-called Plan Colombia, seeks to strengthen the government, the economy, and the armed forces and therefore increase their capacity to effectively

control the national territory, eradicate the cultivation of coca and poppy, implement a crop substitution program, reactivate the economy, protect human rights, and mitigate impunity. The strong human rights conditions required by U.S. law and reflected in Plan Colombia assure substantive progress by the armed forces and the self-defense forces in this area. Military reform began on September 15, 2000, with eleven decrees going into effect. The most relevant of these authorizes the use of discretionary disciplinary powers, including the immediate dismissal of soldiers from the service for serious violations. This procedure permitted a massive housecleaning within the ranks of the national police (10,000 policemen were sanctioned) during the administrations of Gaviria and Samper.

2. *The agenda with the IMF* to correct macroeconomic problems such as the fiscal deficit, bankrupt territorial entities (departments and municipalities), the pension funds, and territorial funds crises, among others. It includes the modification of the generous and uncontrolled current system that transfers almost 50 percent of national ordinary revenues to the territorial entities.

3. *A common agenda with the FARC* (and eventually with the ELN) to build a new society politically, economically, and socially. This agenda, agreed to in May 1999, had twelve topics and forty-seven subtopics that may be expanded. It is hard to say how long it will take to negotiate agreements in so many matters. Suffice it to say that the first round of economic issues occupied the attention of the negotiators and society for almost all of 2000. The challenge for the government is to reach substantive agreements. Although the possibility of reaching those agreements is not out of the question, the complexity of the agendas does not guarantee certainty in this respect.

It is crucial for the government negotiators to use Plan Colombia as a "powerful negotiation card" to overcome the obstacles in the peace process so that it can proceed at an acceptable pace. As U.S. Ambassador Thomas Pickering put it, "if the Pastrana government feels that the process is approaching a solution and it wants to look at alternative or different methods (to those contemplated in Plan Colombia) to accelerate the peace negotiations, we would study the possibility of assisting, provided that it contributes to the ultimate goals that the government has set." And later he adds, "history has shown that the absence of the Plan would not imply a positive change by the FARC. On the contrary, we believe that at this time the Plan is the government's most powerful tool on the negotiating table and that its successful implementation will bring the process closer to a resolution" (*El Tiempo*, August 26, 2000, page 1–1-2).

The peace negotiations are intimately linked to the eradication of coca and poppy cultivation. It is known that the FARC, the ELN, and the self-defense groups are financed in good part by illicit drug money through "cultivation" taxes or some other extortion mechanism from this lucrative business (in the style of what Paul Collier of the World Bank has described as the contemporary financing of the insurgencies, either by means of the so-called blood diamonds, or petroleum, gold, timber, etc.).

Given this state of affairs, the attempt was made to add military pressure or force to the incentives offered by the original Plan Colombia, which was presented in December 1998 in Puerto Wilches, Colombia. These incentives included a generous plan for social development and crop substitution with the voluntary and effective participation of the guerrilla groups. The 2000 version of Plan Colombia incorporates the United States' military assistance factor. This is the "powerful negotiation card" referred to by Ambassador Pickering. Initially, the FARC rejected Plan Colombia as being an anti-insurgency strategy disguised as an anti-narcotics plan, and the idea of using it as a negotiation tool was declared an unacceptable ultimatum. The negotiators must find a way out of this impasse to unblock the negotiations.

4. *The government's ordinary agenda* (education, health, exports, anti-corruption, etc.), which has been forever hobbled and delayed by the pre-eminence of the other agendas.

The more or less successful handling of these agendas will determine the future of Colombian democracy.

10

Peru

The Vanishing of a Regime and the Challenge of Democratic Rebuilding

Carlos Iván Degregori

"All that is solid melts into air." Marshall Berman used this phrase, penned by Marx, to title his renowned book on modernism. This phrase, slightly varied, can aptly be used to define Peruvian politics in the past decade. For in these years, although never quite achieving total solidity, everything in Peru's political system ended up vanishing into thin air.

Alberto Fujimori was an unknown candidate in February 1990 with just a little over one percent of voter support. Two months later he was headed for runoff elections and in June he won the presidency, heralding an auspicious decade of hope. Over the next several years, with Vladimiro Montesinos by his side, he was able to monopolize a level of power unheard of in Peru in decades, which ultimately collapsed in an equally quick and astonishing manner. It is not surprising that in February 2000 more than two-thirds of Peruvians, irrespective of their personal preference, were convinced that Fujimori would be reelected to a third term in office. He indeed achieved it, but in November, he and his adviser fled the country while a transitional government scheduled new elections for 2001. In the meantime, while fujimorismo vanished into nothingness and returned with one percent voter support, the APRA, the most important Peruvian party of the twentieth century, considered dead in 1995, was reborn. It reemerged with such force that it lost the runoff elections with barely a 6 percent margin against Alejandro Toledo, the candidate who had mobilized against the irregular elections in 2000.

Marx's metaphor and Berman's book title allude to the transforming power of modernism. Peru's vanishing political system, however, is a consequence of the extremely fragile political institutions formed during the first transition (1978–80), which were incapable of engendering or sustaining a viable democratic political system. Confronted with the Shining Path (SP) terrorist offensive and the economic debacle of the Aprista government, the system imploded in the late 1980s. This ruined landscape was fertile ground for the rise of anti-politics, which can be understood as the "demonization" of politics as an institutionalized public activity and the attempt to replace it with mechanisms considered to be "natural," such as market forces. These natural mechanisms would be under the supervision of technicians responsible for working up practical solutions to specific problems. Political parties were specifically targeted with the intention of replacing them with politically uncommitted independents, touting a redemptive and plebiscitary leadership style that actively encouraged the masses to identify personally with the leader, downplaying the role of institutions. This personal identification was intended to create the illusion of participation in a time of crisis, dilute socioeconomic class differences, collapse political representation, and blur identities.[1]

In general terms, anti-politics is a volatile and short-lived beast. Its survival depends on de facto powers that lay outside the political system. This essay attempts to understand the persistence of anti-politics in Peru throughout the 1990s. How was it able to survive for so long? Furthermore, if the party system is the backbone of a democratic system, what was and how did that spineless body function? More urgently, do the flights of Fujimori and Montesinos and the installation of a transitional government of impeccable democratic behavior really signify the decline and fall of anti-politics and authoritarianism?

The present chapter recounts the Fujimori decade, describing three major stages: early fujimorismo or protofujimorismo, which from 1990 to 1992 operated within constitutional democratic boundaries. Classic or victorious fujimorismo, authoritarian but maintaining a high degree of popular support, started with the April 1992 self-coup and lasted through mid-1996. Finally, a late fujimorismo, a decomposition that began in August 1996 with the approval of the so-called law of authentic interpretation of the constitution, intended to pave the way for Fujimori's second reelection. Finally, there is a brief analysis of the fall of the regime, its orderly and peaceful replacement by a transitional government in charge of calling for new elections, and the challenges facing Alejandro Toledo's new government.

An Outsider within a Democratic Framework (1990–1992)

The landslide victory of Alberto Fujimori in the June 1990 presidential elections will be remembered as the greatest electoral upset in contemporary Peruvian history.[2] When Fujimori took office, he found a country in shambles: an annual hyperinflation rate of over 7,000 percent; tax revenues under 4 percent of GNP; unemployment and underemployment affecting over 70 percent of the workforce; and a collapsing infrastructure. This was exacerbated by widespread corruption throughout all levels of government, the lack of credibility of the political parties, and the onslaught of the SP.

Fujimori initially capitalized on his outsider status, touting his independence and promoting his image as an "effective technician." His slogan was "honesty, technology, and work." He borrowed everything else, including the Democratic Front's (FREDEMO)[3] economic program and the armed forces' anti-subversive strategies. The triumphant candidate had promised not to apply the economic shock measures announced by Mario Vargas Llosa. But only two weeks into his new government, Fujimori appropriated a good part of his defeated rival's programs and applied them anyway, without riots or civil unrest, and with favorable results in the country's opinion polls. Paradoxically, one of the central reasons for this sort of anticlimax was the SP. The economic adjustment measures were applied on the empty streets of a country traumatized by violence, where any mobilization might be treated as a terrorist act. The relief felt when hyperinflation ended compensated for the rigors of the subsequent recession. The opening of the economy aroused expectations. In addition, Fujimori's measures attacked the corruption and inefficiency rampant throughout government, as well as the "mercantilist" executives accustomed to state subsidies.[4] Exhausted by the crisis, neither the politicians, nor the unions, nor civil society organizations were able to mount a concerted and coordinated opposition to the government's policies or offer concrete alternatives.

As Romeo Grompone points out, the fujimorista regime had to invent its own style.[5] International financial organizations and the Peruvian technocrats in charge of implementing the economic adjustment programs were the main endorsers. The rise of Vladimiro Montesinos, surreptitious at that point, was the dark side of that configuration.[6] The government also drew strength from a diffuse feeling of hope revealed in surveys, as well as from the global hegemony achieved by neoliberal ideology after the downfall of populism and Marxism. This relative political vacuum provided Fujimori with a large degree of autonomy, and a fork in the road. One path would focus on the president himself, relying heavily on his popular appeal in the midst of the terrorist violence, to seal a definitive alliance with the armed forces. The more progressive path would seek to invigorate democratic institutions and, given the lack of a clear majority in Congress, rely on negotiation and consensus-building between the executive and the legislative branches of government. This path implied the self-reform of the political system, thus granting a central role to political parties.

The Parties: An Unexpected Implosion

The crisis at the end of Alan García's government (1985–90) was not limited to the economy. It was a crisis of political representation, cultural isolation, and moral authority as well. One of the central consequences of the crisis was the anemic condition of political parties, which were unable to embody the aspirations of the public or find ways to connect with other social actors who were also in crisis.

As bad as the crisis of the political parties was at the time, it was greatly overshadowed by the dual scourges of hyperinflation and terrorism, even in the minds of the party leaderships. Ricardo Belmont's 1989 victory as an independent mayoral candidate for Lima should have set off alarm bells, but it passed unnoticed. On the other hand, the 1989 splintering of the Izquierda Unida (United Left), the second strongest force in politics during the entire decade, seemed understandable in light of the emergence of FREDEMO. It was, apparently, simply a shift of the political spectrum to the right.

Between August 1990 and March 1992, motivated by their survival instinct and their bewildered condition, political parties began to change and adopted an attitude of cooperation with the new government. The APRA and the left-wing parties reacted prudently to the government's economic measures. During those first twenty months, the opposition majority in Congress delegated legislative powers to the executive fifteen times through 158 legislative ordinances.[7]

In contrast with other countries of the region, such as Ecuador, the crisis did not hinge on economic belt tightening but rather on pacification policy. When this issue brought the executive and the legislature into confrontation, it became obvious that the self-coup was a strategy that had been simmering on the back burner for quite a while. The countdown began in November 1991, when the executive sent to Congress fifteen legislative ordinances on pacification with an unmistakably military slant.[8]

Congress, from fredemistas to left-wingers, surprisingly agreed on a series of modifications to the executive's proposals that changed the center of gravity of the anti-subversive strategy against the SP toward a *political* struggle, giving the civilian government and civilian organizations important roles in the fight against terrorism. The armed forces would be required to coordinate and participate with democratically elected authorities and civilian organizations. The amended law was sent back to the executive for approval. Fujimori made some technical objections and returned the package to Congress, but Christmas was near and the debate was postponed until after the recess.

In the first few months of 1992, a series of events inflamed tensions between the executive and Congress. To mention only one: the approval of a

Law of Executive Control that attempted to constrain the normative acts of the president. Unaware of their own fragility, the political parties tried to limit the authority of a president who intended to outdistance their reach. Fujimori responded by accusing Congress of being "irresponsible, sterile, anti-historic and anti-national."[9]

We will never know whether worn-out political parties opposed by the executive and the armed forces would have been able to implement the legislative pacification package that would probably have been approved by a majority in Congress. Two days before the new legislative session, Alberto Fujimori burned his bridges and took the authoritarian path. On April 5, 1992, he dissolved Congress and took control of the regional governments, the judiciary, the Tribunal of Constitutional Guarantees, the National Board of Elections (JNE), and the Treasury. The executive now had total control and became, from that day on, an Emergency Government of National Reconstruction.

Self-Coup: Increased Military Prerogatives

The interruption of the constitutional regime was Fujimori's second great surprise in less than two years. The most revelatory phenomenon, however, was the massive public support for these actions, a support born out of a universal disgust with widespread immorality, inefficient democratic institutions, and politicians who, acting through anti-democratic party structures, engaged in endless Byzantine disputes. This disenchantment was to surface repeatedly throughout the decade in several Latin American countries. Seen in a positive light, it was a demand for efficiency, morality, and participation. Adding to this was the need for order in a country at war against terrorism and the illusion that the executive could more easily solve the crisis without what appeared to be the obstruction of the other branches of government.

The September 12, 1992 capture of Abimael Guzmán, supreme leader of the Shining Path, consolidated Fujimori's popularity and led, in succession, to the November 1992 electoral victory creating a new Constituent Congress and the October 1993 referendum victory approving the new constitution drafted by this new Congress.

In addition to his charisma and lack of party affiliation, several factors worked in Fujimori's favor. The most important was the increasing terrorist activity. Another factor was fear of APRA and Alan García.[10] In general terms, the discredit of political parties favored the president's projects decisively. That discredit and the subsequent collapse of the parties occurred, among other reasons, because attempts at self-reform were weak and did not command the same degree of urgency across the political spectrum. Only after the coup was the magnitude of the parties' crisis made visible.

The lack of consensus on certain basic national issues—whose definition had always been impeded by the president—made Congress appear unnecessarily polarized in the eyes of the public. Debates were not seen as an exchange of ideas to find solutions, but as sterile conflicts over petty interests. Oversight was confused with obstructionism.[11] Given this scenario and considering that the same person elected in 1990 was still at the helm of government, the events did not appear to be a coup at all but rather a needed untangling, a possibility to deliver on the election's promises. The absence of massive repression, facilitated in turn by the public's support and the capture of Guzmán, favored this perception.

The collapse of the party structure was not all self-inflicted. On the one hand, the decline of the so-called real socialism and Latin American populism dragged down with it the Left-of-Center parties. On the other hand, hyperinflation, terrorism, and belt-tightening accelerated the erosion of institutions. It was becoming more difficult for the parties to engage with an increasingly disjointed society in which too many avenues led to extreme poverty. In addition, parties, as a group, were subjected to incessant attacks from outside the political system, including many lethal incursions by the SP. However, the government's ideological battle, taking advantage of the obsolescence of the old parties, was the most damaging, as it instigated a general rejection of politics. Finally, the decision of the most important parties—APRA, Popular Action (AP), United Left (IU)—not to participate in the November 1992 elections for a new Constituent Congress further deepened the crisis by leaving the stage open for the independents.

Let us return now to April 5, 1992, that locus or primordial scene that defined the rest of the decade. The 1979 constitution, which ushered in the first democratic transition, severely curtailed the prerogatives of the armed forces in comparison with, for example, those of Brazil, Chile, or Guatemala.[12] Throughout the 1980s, however, the government's response to the expansion of the SP was to increase the armed forces' political responsibilities in areas declared to be in a state of emergency, without concurrently increasing a series of prerogatives demanded by the military.[13]

Given this evolving situation and the ongoing debate over pacification ordinances, two possibilities emerged: either the civilian government needed to restrain the military and take leadership of the war against terrorism, as was insinuated in the modifications proposed by Congress, or the military's prerogatives had to be recognized politically and legally. With the coup, Fujimori took the second option. The prior succession of events, the makeup of the advisers surrounding him, and the president's own personality favored this outcome. The central issue, however, was that Fujimori did not have an organized civilian base and, therefore, could not allow the anti-subversive strategy on which his alliance with the armed forces was based to be modified.

By this time, Vladimiro Montesinos, principal mediator between the president and the armed forces, had General Hermoza Ríos installed as commander-in-chief. Almost unnoticed, the National Intelligence Service (SIN) slowly began to swallow the armed forces.

Authoritarianism with Inter/National Legitimacy (1993–1996)

The authors of the coup apparently had not given much thought to the existing international environment. In 1991, the General Assembly of the OAS passed Resolution 1080, known as the Santiago Declaration, that excluded from the inter-American system those countries that underwent abrupt interruptions of their democratic regimes. On April 13, 1992, the hemisphere's foreign ministers gathered in Washington and rejected the coup unanimously, calling for the "urgent reestablishment" of the democratic constitutional regime.[14]

From the Self-Coup to Its Legitimization at the Ballot Box (1993–1995)

Giving in to international pressure, Fujimori convened elections to establish a new Constituent Congress in the midst of an especially difficult moment. The country had suffered the most violent offensive to date in the Shining Path's twelve-year "popular war." But, on September 12, the National Police captured Abimael Guzmán as well as the main political leaders of the SP. The captures assured Fujimori's victory, and an opaque majority rushed to draw up a new constitution enthroning neoliberal principles, increasing the military's prerogatives, and accentuating presidentialism and centralism.

After completion of the project, the government called for a referendum to legitimize the regime, especially at the international level. The opposition was in disarray. Furthermore, surprisingly, one month before the referendum, Abimael Guzmán began sending letters to the president requesting peace talks. Everyone expected an overwhelming victory that would pave the way for Fujimori's reelection in 1995. In another surprise, however, the October 1993 referendum ratified the new constitution by a slender 52 percent majority.

The referendum proved that reelection could not be taken for granted. With tenacity and tactical ability, Fujimori decided to improve the odds. He first ratified his alliance with the armed forces, defending the immunity of military personnel who violated human rights. Furthermore, with the Shining Path virtually bankrupt, the SIN went to work on nailing down the reelection, counting on the support of a congressional core that advocated what Alfred Stepan calls an "unequal civilian accommodation," in other words, the subordination of the civilian government to the armed forces.[15]

With a consolidated alliance and with financial resources pouring in from privatization and international financial institutions, the government went on a social spending spree. With $4.6 billion earmarked for social spending through organizations dependent on the Ministry of the Presidency, Fujimori intensified his visits to the provinces and the poorer neighborhoods of Lima, inaugurating school buildings, launching infrastructure projects, giving away computers, and deploying what some analysts have called "neopopulism."[16] The government squandered fiscal resources in an "electoral binge" that was paid for by all Peruvians after the elections with a new round of belt-tightening and a recession in 1996. With the judicial branch under his thumb, Fujimori began to clip the wings of the municipality of metropolitan Lima whose mayor, Ricardo Belmont, was mentioned as a possible rival in the 1995 presidential elections. The central government was able to suffocate and eliminate Belmont's candidacy by postponing the recovery of the city, which continued to deteriorate.

This is how Fujimori was able to salvage a situation that, only one year prior to the elections, was considered adverse. In April 1994, surveys gave Javier Pérez de Cuéllar 44 percent of the vote against Fujimori's 38 percent. One year later, in April 1995, the incumbent candidate swept the first-run elections with 64.4 percent of the vote against Pérez de Cuéllar's 22.8 percent.

The dual victories over hyperinflation and terrorism were the two pillars supporting Fujimori's electoral triumph, which culminated in the national and international legitimization of a government born out of a coup. The president cashed in on the capital he had accrued between 1990 and 1993. Added to this was the need for order. The opposition was unable to offer convincing economic or democratic alternatives. The electorate chose the authoritarian alternative that dared to appear both politically competitive and honest. Except for his marital problems, no major scandal had yet to taint either Fujimori or his cohorts.

There were also favorable signs that encouraged the population to look the other way rather than cast a wary eye on the increasingly presidentialist, centralist, and authoritarian regime: even if there was corruption, the economy was growing and the government was "doing public works." Every socioeconomic group had hopes for the future. GNP growth for 1994 was, at 12.5 percent, the highest in the world, although this statistic was not all that meaningful given the depth of the country's crisis. These were the glory years for Lima's stock market. Peru was then considered one of the most attractive emerging markets. Privatization attracted capital, and low import tariffs resulted in a veritable flood of imported goods. In spite of criticisms over the manner in which certain privatizations were handled and the growing trade deficit, Peru had its honeymoon with globalization: reengineering was the fashionable euphemism, nationalism an unspeakable word.

In addition, social spending, which began a slow increase in 1993–94, was strongly concentrated in the Ministry of the Presidency, giving the appearance that the president was the great and only constructor. Nothing, therefore, seemed to tarnish him. Criticism would smash into his countless suits[17] and slide off; his was the "Teflon presidency."

Authoritarian Governability

According to O'Donnell, lengthened temporal perspectives and invigorated social and political institutions are the keys that enable "representative democracies" to climb out of black holes. The temporal perspectives in Peru had evidently been lengthened after 1992 for Fujimori and his associates, but the will to invigorate social and political institutions was absent from his perspective. Fujimori continued to preside over a country of weak and incoherent institutions, forging ahead with an internationally accepted economic program and a more than minimal level of governability. By exhibiting concrete results, he had so far avoided the "vertiginous political consumption" that Marcelo Cavarozzi correlated with the collapse of institutions and the party system.[18]

Fujimorismo could lay claim to being the authoritarian road to recovery for semi-collapsed countries. Not in vain did the World Bank and the IMF seek to showcase Peru as an example of guided recovery, at a time in which international players became internal players in the globalization process and in the rescaling of national sovereignty. The business community and the fujimorista press postulated that democracy would materialize as a natural by-product of a burgeoning market economy. Faced with a contest between democracy and efficacy, they opted for the latter and accepted what we might call an authoritarian governability.

Several pundits were convinced that after such a comfortable victory the president would loosen up a bit, encourage greater dialogue, and finally create a political party. They were wrong. Fujimori wasted no time in retaking the offensive against his opponents.[19] After winning with a two-thirds majority and with the party system in ruins, it was reasonable to think that the government might aspire to build a sort of Peruvian Revolutionary Institutional Party (PRI), yet nothing was farther from the president's mind. 'Cambio 90' (C90, Change 90), the party that brought him to power in 1990, ceased to exist the day after he won office. Nueva Mayoría (NM, New Majority) was an acronym created to bring together the technicians and personalities that ran for the Constituent Congress in 1992. CM-C90, the algebraic formula with which he ran for reelection in 1995, was really just the president himself. Opposed to any type of organization, the leader preferred to rule over an amorphous political scenario, based on pragmatic alliances with the powerful: intelligence services, armed forces, businessmen, the media, and professionals linked to international financial institutions.

Classic Fujimorismo

I am inventing a country . . .
    —Alberto Fujimori[20]

If a system of political parties is the backbone of democracy, what we have in 1995 is a spineless political body, victorious in its war against hyperinflation and terrorism, validated by an overwhelming majority of votes, accepted by the international community, and marching toward what the majority imagined would be a brilliant future. How could this happen?

Presidentialism

First, although the spine was shattered, the head continued working and growing, converting the regime into a hydrocephalic entity. Not only did the executive grow, but literally, the head of the state itself; the omnipresent, hyperactive, and indefatigable president who never stopped campaigning. The Ministry of the Presidency had the lion's share of the budget. The presidency became a high-profile institution at the expense of a deteriorated Congress and judicial system. The capture of the latter began during the April 5 coup. In the years that followed, a series of laws would subjugate the courts and turn them into an instrument to persecute opponents, becoming a rubber stamp for the executive's whims.[21] With the judicial under control, the JNE soon followed.

Congress after the coup was reduced to a single 120-member chamber representing a single National Electoral District. This arrangement distanced the legislators from their constituents, practically eliminating accountability, and brought them ever closer to an executive that subordinated them. In exchange for the abrogation of their oversight responsibilities, the executive granted members of Congress a series of privileges previously unthinkable in contemporary Peru.[22] Thus, between 1992 and 2000, the pro-government majority in Congress legitimated the regime, validating it through a series of mechanisms, such as:

- *Subordination rituals,* willingly undercutting their official powers, delegating legislative functions to the executive in the name of efficiency, and blocking any oversight initiatives from the opposition minority, especially the traditional parties, branded as disloyal to the political system.

- *Legitimization speeches,* notably those on democracy, defined unilaterally as a discretionary government of the majority and not as a building of alliances or respect for minority rights, and "uses of the past" speeches, aggrandizing and legitimizing the current Congress while badmouthing prior legislatures (1980–92).
- *Closely choreographed intermediation,* which reinforced the president's personal connection to the population. Some Congress members used the media. Others accompanied the president to places where they had a constituent base, linking the president directly with those "regional fiefdoms" and helping to organize the different ad hoc political nuclei that the government built for each election.

Extra-Systemic Support

This spineless, big-headed body was able to stand and even walk forward thanks to a support structure from outside the political system that propped it up from above, from its sides, from behind, and from below. These were the powerful institutions and individuals,[23] the de facto powers that replaced the traditional components of a political system and acted as trusses and braces in lieu of a spine.

From above, multilateral institutions provided the financial backing and the loan guarantees that allowed Fujimori to carry out economic reforms and the initial phase of government reform. They also downplayed the 1992 coup, expressing satisfaction that "democratic minimums" were being met: elections, freedom of the press, a Congress (even if lobotomized), and judicial reform, understood as an increase in procedural effectiveness rather than independence.

From the sides, businessmen and the armed forces became the regime's right and left arms. The military brass supported the government from the moment that Fujimori adopted the anti-subversive package that they had designed in the late 1980s, and even more so after the coup. This resulted in the legal blessing of their new prerogatives,[24] which were the broadest in the region and on a par with those of the armed forces of Chile and Ecuador.

The business community, on the other hand, was encouraged by the government's adoption of a significant part of FREDEMO's pro-business economic program, which, albeit with some reservations over certain details, received widespread support. Several issues affected this decision, among them a legitimate desire to modernize and become competitive in an open economy as well as hopes of being the main beneficiaries of the reforms that also included the strong anti-labor policies of the regime. With a few exceptions—and to Mario Vargas Llosa's chagrin—the coup did not bother them, revealing that political freedoms were not a high priority on their agenda.

From behind, the hidden advisers replaced the original intellectuals and ideologists, and the militants and loyal followers of the past.[25] Some of these advisers were technicians with working experience in international institutions, returning to create what they themselves called "pockets of excellence" in certain public institutions, with salaries that were disproportionate for the sector. There was yet another group that acted behind the scenes. Several in this group were family members of the president, others, high school or university buddies. And finally, the covert inner circles of advisers,[26] answerable to no one except the president. Up to 1996, the government insisted that Vladimiro Montesinos, an ex-army captain dishonorably discharged for spying for the Central Intelligence Agency (CIA) in the 1970s, and by then the number-two man of the regime, was an ad honorem adviser to the SIN and, therefore, outside the scope of any investigation.

Looking back, it is astonishing that anyone could think that it was possible to modernize the country with teams built on such base loyalties, outside of institutional bounds or accountability, with styles reminiscent of the old personalized dictatorships of the first half of the twentieth century.

Starting with the November 1991 legal amendment allowing General Hermoza Ríos to stay on as commander-in-chief of the armed forces after his retirement,[27] and through the April 5, 1992 coup and the failed countercoup later that year on November 13,[28] Montesinos and the SIN stopped sustaining the spineless body from behind and ascended to the hydrocephalic head. Thus, they became embedded, acting like some sort of cerebellum that grew alongside the SIN's personnel, power, and budget. If the function of the cerebellum is to ensure the body's balance, the growing control of Montesinos and the SIN over the armed forces, the media, and the judicial system was the chosen method of preserving that balance (read governability) of the spineless body.

From below was the solid ground of constant public support between 1992 and 1996, without which the spineless body would probably not have survived. The mixture of a presidentialist tradition and a new pragmatism explains this rather passive support that did not quite solidify into a durable political identity. This was due to the fact that, beyond loyalty to the leader, there was no political institution to channel that sympathy and transform it into active support. This forced the government to legitimate itself through its performance and thus have to ratify its trustworthiness repeatedly and through plebiscite (*plebiscitariamente*), rather than counting on a blank check.

Other than the ballot box, vertical accountability was scarce. The social movements of the 1970s and 1980s whose agendas were capable of influencing national policy were replaced in the 1990s by a vague public opinion that only had a sort of selective and occasional veto power to limit government excesses.

The Nontransferable Charisma

This unusual political creature had, however, several Achilles' heels. The most important was not in the foot, but in the head, which was unique and nontransferable, so much so that rumors of a presidential illness elicited shivers not only in Peru but in the international press as well. Menem in Argentina had the Justicialista Party. In Peru nobody knew who the first vice-president was, let alone the second. Congress was a lackluster entity. The model, therefore, condemned Fujimori to frantic activism. "I never rest," claimed the president, and nobody could deny his amazing capacity for work.

With only one head and no backbone, the fujimorista creature was unable to present a list of candidates for the 1992 municipal elections, not even for Lima. In the 1995 municipal elections, at the peak of his success, Fujimori concentrated forces on Lima and freed his sympathizers to make their own lists and vote for their preferred candidates in the rest of the country. Taking advantage of the second honeymoon after the reelection, Fujimori sought to install Jaime Yoshiyama, another nisei (Japanese-Peruvian), in Lima's mayoral office. There were two objectives: block Alberto Andrade, the successful mayor of Miraflores[29] and potential rival in the 2000 elections, and groom a possible successor. Yoshiyama was defeated. The charisma of "el chino"[30] was not transferable.

Those elections made it perfectly clear that the concentration of power in the figure of the president may have been the regime's greatest strength, but it was also its greatest weakness. In a sense, it was a mirror image of the Shining Path, which concentrated enormous symbolic power in its boss, and was unable to survive after his capture. It was becoming clear that Fujimori was sentenced to perpetual reelection, thus condemning the country to circle about itself as it obsessively relived the founding moments of fujimorismo. The decision not to allow even a minimal look into the human rights violations perpetrated by the government in those years further revealed the two other congenital flaws of the paradigm: the militarization of politics and its lack of transparency.

With political parties in shambles and the SIN and the armed forces replacing them as the de facto party of the government, the strategies of war moved to the political arena. Psychosocial operatives replaced old-fashioned political campaign tactics with ambush tactics. Anything could be labeled a military secret. The regime was forced to show some sort of proof of compliance with democratic formalities, but it managed to cover everything in a fog through pro-government congressional fact finding committees. Such committees did not actually investigate, but accused the whistleblowers or simply refused to even hear controversial accusations. This method was justified due to a state of emergency or of permanent war, dissolving into blatant cynicism and dissociation in the final days.

The Permanent Reelection (1996–2000)

Around 1995, at the zenith of his power, Alberto Fujimori was personally building the cage, invisible at first, which would trap the country in the past. First bar: the electoral "fiscal binge" proved that clinging to power was much more important to the administration than economic modernization or state reform. Second bar: the clear-cut refusal to build a political organization ratified the autocratic form in which this power would be exercised. Third bar: the July 1995 amnesty law confirming that human rights violations by the government would go unpunished was the foundation of this autocracy. Fourth bar: indifference in the face of the public's rejection of the amnesty law revealed that one of the few dikes shoring up the exercise of arbitrary power was crumbling.[31] The president's ratification of this state of affairs immediately following his comfortable victory also confirmed the confrontational rather than hegemonic style of his government.

Montesinos: A Mole in Broad Daylight

The opening months of the second term found the president "inventing a country," exercising his power, dictating laws, and moving his pawns without encountering resistance. The most valuable pawn was Jaime Yoshiyama, part of Fujimori's inner circle, businessman, head of the C90-NM list in the 1992 constituent elections, president of the Constituent Congress up to 1995, and rumored to be the presidential dauphin. His mission was to checkmate the last important bastion of the opposition: the municipality of Lima.

As we have already mentioned, in spite of Fujimori's best efforts, 52.2 percent of the electorate chose Alberto Andrade over Yoshiyama in the November 1995 elections. The 1993 plebiscite had been a narrow victory, but this time the presidency was not at stake and that fact possibly encouraged enough timid voters to contradict the president's wishes and tip the balance. In 1993, economic and regional redress were important issues, in 1995 it was local redress. Lima was in chaos and Andrade had had a successful administration in Miraflores. This time, however, there was a noticeably more explicit rejection of the president's steamroller tactics.

The defeat of Yoshiyama seems to have pulverized any remaining scruples regarding the second reelection. In August 1996, Congress amended Article 112 of the 1993 constitution[32] and passed the "law of authentic interpretation," establishing Fujimori's right to run for a third term in office. According to Sally Bowen,[33] the decisive factor prompting the government to approve the "law of authentic interpretation" was the scandal caused by Demetrio Chávez Peñaherrera, alias "Vaticano," the most important Peruvian drug lord. Vaticano had testified the previous week in a public hearing that he had paid Vladimiro Montesinos $50,000 a month from July 1991 to August 1992, and that he stopped making payments because the adviser had demanded $100,000 instead.

The mole was now irreversibly exposed, and in the worst possible way. His enormous power was also exposed: in the days following Vaticano's revelations, the top officials in the country closed ranks in his defense. The commander-in-chief of the armed forces said that Vaticano's declarations were laughable, the minister of the economy called them abominable, and the attorney general asserted that they were a "a lie, an outrageous fabrication."[34] Montesinos then decided that the best defense was to counterattack, and he chose the most favorable arena (the United States' anti-drug policy) and the most favorable moment (the visit to Lima of Barry McCaffrey, the U.S. drug czar). Therefore, in the last week of October 1996, the "Doctor," as he liked to be called, was seen in public for the first time next to the czar. By the time he was photographed openly on the steps of the government palace, his notoriety had reached, Bowen affirms, "the rural farmer and the illiterate peasant in the most remote corner of Peru."[35]

Coincidentally, by this time several key figures had been left out of the game. A little after the "authentic interpretation" and the Vaticano scandal, Yoshiyama went back to managing his business interests, never to return to politics. Shortly before, Santiago Fujimori had fallen into disgrace and had been left out of the presidential environment. Around this time, the first cabinet of Fujimori's second term, which had lately been displaying progressive tendencies, handed in their resignations. Montesinos was clearing the way toward the summit of power, but he continued to be bombarded by questions from all sectors.

The country was approaching a turning point at the end of 1996. A persistent economic recession began to erode confidence in the economic model. In 1994 the GNP grew more than 12 percent, in 1995 only 6 percent, and in 1996 it was down to 2 percent. It was the hangover from the electoral fiscal binge—a hangover from which the economy never fully recovered throughout the five-year period. The Tequila effect, El Niño (1998), and the Asian crisis hit the government, an administration in which the will to reform was subordinate to the political interests of the people in power. The leadership did not have any original ideas to undertake the so-called second-generation reforms in any case.

Fissures and Alterations in Authoritarian Governability

The government's confrontational style began to prove counterproductive in the atmosphere of an economic crisis. Throughout 1996, public opinion in Lima was consistently in favor of the municipal David in its struggle against the presidential Goliath. On the other hand, a government that, up until then, had not been widely perceived as corrupt, was now mired in the Vaticano scandal; and the paramilitary actions of the SIN, which had seemed a thing of the past, had sprung back to life. The regime's obstinacy in maintaining and exhibiting Montesinos began to irritate a growing number of citizens.

Seizing the moment, the opposition awakened from its long catatonia, rallying around a campaign to gather signatures demanding a referendum to annul the "authentic interpretation" and stop Fujimori's candidacy in 2000. Opinion polls showed that the government's popularity was slowly declining. In November, for the first time in four years, the administration's approval rating crossed over into negative territory. The government seemed to be on the defensive. Then, suddenly on December 17, a commando of the Tupac Amaru Revolutionary Movement (MRTA) burst spectacularly onto the complex scenario, reconfiguring the positioning of the political players in a matter of minutes. A small subversive group thought to be virtually extinguished assaulted the Japanese ambassador's residence, totally taking by surprise not only the hundreds of guests celebrating Emperor Akihito's birthday, but the entire nation as well.

The taking of the residence forced the opposition to close ranks with the government and contributed to the rebound of the president's popularity.[36] The MRTA's act made security a central issue once again, giving the president the opportunity to reenact his role as a tough and effective leader against terrorism. Yet after the initial shock, the residence with its seventy-two hostages and the last of the MRTA holdouts was understood for what it was: a terrible act, but one at the fringes of the country's social and political dynamics. Four months later, the "hostage crisis" had been bumped off the front pages by a series of conflicts within the intelligence services that came to light when an agent, having been tortured by her own colleagues, decided to hold a televised press conference revealing the existence of plans to intimidate the press, opposition politicians, and local governments. The revelations took a terrifying turn with the appearance in early April 1997 of the dismembered body of another intelligence agent.[37] Shortly after, Frecuencia Latina, a popular television station, obtained a copy of Vladimiro Montesinos' income tax statements. The U.S.$80,000 in monthly income contrasted sharply with Fujimori's prior assertions that Montesinos was an ad honorem adviser to the SIN, as well as with his later admission that he was indeed on the payroll, making about U.S.$600 a month.

These revelations shocked the nation on an almost nightly basis. Then, on April 22, using a tunnel dug out during the government's ongoing negotiations with the kidnappers, an elite army commando stormed the ambassador's residence and rescued the hostages. The president's approval rating jumped only temporarily, yet long enough to allow Congress to approve accusations against three members of the Constitutional Guarantees Tribunal (TGC) that had declared the law of "authentic interpretation" inapplicable,[38] which would have prevented Fujimori's candidacy in 2000. Soon after, the three magistrates were removed from office.

The response to the TGC members' dismissal signaled that business as usual was over. In the first week of June, students, workers, and opposition party members took to the streets to express their rejection of the dismissal, not through opinion polls, but for the first time that decade, massively, publicly, and in plain sight of the OAS, which happened to be holding its General Assembly meeting in Lima at the time. This event opened up a first line of attack against the regime, what we might call a low-intensity resistance, spearheaded by students and centrally concerned with democracy. The expropriation of Frecuencia Latina in September 1997 after having stripped its owner, Baruch Ivcher,[39] of his Peruvian nationality resulted in renewed public demonstrations.

One year later a concerned citizens' movement, the Democratic Forum, presented more than a million and a half signatures (as specified by Fujimori's own 1993 constitution) calling for a referendum on Fujimori's candidacy in 2000. Congress, however, rushed to pass an unconstitutional law requiring the support of forty-eight Congress members, in addition to the signatures. The government then used sticks and carrots to prevent the opposition from gathering the forty-eight votes. Some of the broadcast television stations had not been bought off by the government, and the country was able to follow the voting in Congress on live TV. This time, the marches and demonstrations overflowed from Lima, flaring up across the nation.

One year earlier, in September 1997, a group of mayors from Huancavelica, the poorest department in Peru, had ridden into Lima on horseback, capturing the public's imagination and opening up another front of low-intensity resistance opposed to centralism, which spread rapidly to other departments, especially those of the Greater South and the East. The country was definitively not allowing itself to be invented so easily. The economic success of the first period was not reoccurring and the government continued to draw on the capital accumulated with the defeat of hyperinflation and the first privatizations. GNP growth was rather mediocre and the economic plan was not creating employment. In 1998, remnants of the organized labor movement opened a third front, which expressed itself on the streets. Unrest over the employment situation, however, went far beyond work stoppages and street marches, becoming the primary concern for most of the country.

The greatest, if unavoidable liability of the second fujimorismo was Vladimiro Montesinos—unavoidable because as the five-year term progressed, it became increasingly obvious that Fujimori and Montesinos were inextricably bound to each other. With this in mind, Fujimori's second term can be understood as a constant flight forward. Montesinos' first appearance with McCaffrey was followed by another Montesinos/Fujimori joint photo-op walk among the MRTA's cadavers in a visit to the recaptured Japanese ambassador's residence. McCaffrey's April 1998 visit to Lima was used to produce a video in which the czar seems to further legitimize Montesinos.[40] Then there is the famous April 1999 television interview in which Fujimori and Montesinos, in what was by then old news, recounted their version of the hostage rescue.

It was now clear, however, that in spite of having been declared the "victorious General" in the 1995 conflict with Ecuador[41] and having rumbled through Lima's streets in his intimidating tanks on a couple of occasions, General Nicolás Hermoza Ríos was the weakest link in the triumvirate. In August 1998, after months of wrangling about each other's roles in the "hostage crisis" and in the middle of peace negotiations with Ecuador, Hermoza was removed from office. His removal was apparently induced by his militaristic posture and pressured by the treaty guarantors, especially the United States. Fujimori and Montesinos now held all the power, and the latter took the opportunity to seize total control of the armed forces, filling all key positions with his old colleagues from the military academy's class of 1966.

The combination of economic crisis, authoritarianism, and growing corruption threatened to crack the laboriously crafted internal and external legitimacy of the regime. It was not the best of preambles to a successful electoral campaign. In October 1998, Andrade won a second term as mayor of Lima. The novelty was yet another new political group from the president's inexhaustible sleeve called Vamos Vecino (VV, Come Along, Neighbor), which was extended to the last corners of the country in a matter of months. Never had a Peruvian political organization covered the national landscape so densely and with so many resources at its disposal. Finally, after eight years and two defeats in municipal elections—1992 and 1995—the government had apparently realized that it needed something more than an acronym to assure governability.

Vamos Vecino picked up on the vitality of an important sector of new local leaders that emerged in the 1990s. That vitality, coupled with the massive use of the government's apparatus, allowed the government to obtain decent returns for the first time in municipal elections: 25.2 percent at the national level, only 4 points behind Somos Peru (We are Peru) (29.2 percent), Mayor Andrade's incipient national movement.[42] Nevertheless, the fact that the candidates were not able to obtain a higher percentage in spite of having the government's backing and given the opposition's weakness, revealed the government's significant deterioration. The decent percentages, however, also proved the resilience of a retrenched state apparatus. VV was born out of that state apparatus. It had no stable structures, no regional or national Congress, only local leaders without channels to ascend on nonexistent partisan steps, without the least security in their positions and always dependent on the nucleus of high state officials in charge of the movement's national organization.

In other words, this political creature of the 1990s refused to develop a backbone. Instead of creating a real political party, fujimorismo created a government spin-off in the form of operative nuclei meant to compete politically. This concept was shipwrecked in early 2000 when it was discovered that Peru al 2000, another new fujimorista organization created for that year's elections, had registered with the JNE by handing in more than a million falsified signatures.

It was definitively another type of power—different from democratic regimes or those of the classic Latin American dictatorships—but effective in its own way. If we look back to the December 1998 voter intention polls for the 2000 presidential elections, Fujimori was a distant third place with 12.8 percent, behind Andrade (34 percent) and another independent candidate, Castañeda Lossio (17.3 percent).[43]

Towards the Re-Reelection: The Spillover of Authoritarianism and Corruption

Fujimori's recovery in 1999 was one of the most astonishing political feats of the decade, especially considering that he pulled it off in the middle of an unrelenting economic crisis. But if he did indeed recover the possibility of being reelected a second time, it was primarily due to a very unimpressive opposition consisting of either stale political parties or "independent groups" built around "caudillos" surrounded by a thin core of relatives and friends leading a periphery that was often recruited at random. The success of the government's campaign against the mayors of Somos Peru should come as no surprise. Between August and September 1999, twenty-three mayors resigned.

Understanding its adversaries, the government concentrated its efforts on the poorest social strata, what demographers label sectors D and E. The idea was to capture these sectors by increasing and manipulating social assistance programs.[44] The capture strategy required the manipulation of public opinion in general and public opinion in sectors D and E in particular. To this end, the government developed several tactical objectives: first, to control the media and, consequently, to stoke fears of a return of terrorism or the loss of social assistance programs, and to unfold a show of opportunistic nationalism, turning the international community's growing dissatisfaction with the regime's increasingly authoritarian style to the president's advantage.

Manipulation of social programs and control of the media were key elements in the recovery of the government's electoral possibilities. After the expropriation of Frecuencia Latina in 1997, the onslaught against the independent press continued unabated. It is now known that the submission of the broadcast TV stations was achieved through enormous cash payments to the station owners, many of whom were in financial straits due to the economic crisis. In December 1998, the last independent opinion program disappeared off the air. Seemingly, the electorate was being depoliticized, but in fact it was more a repoliticization through other channels (for example, the politicization of some reality shows in favor of Fujimori). Well-known comedians and impersonators were hired by the government's channel and directed against Fujimori's opponents. It was the *chicha*, or yellow press, however, that was in charge of demolishing the opposition. Up until 1997, the popular press had stuck to the classic combination of crime, sports, and entertainment. The yellow press, however, was now part of Fujimori's reelection strategy, and to this end they were co-opted, bought outright, or created by the SIN to crush opposition candidates, especially Andrade. The front pages were politicized with a synchronized daily chorus, with regular, almost identical headlines directed at one or another opposition candidate.

With a playing field swept clean of opposing voices,[45] the government embarked on an unlimited propaganda campaign, supported by the armed forces and reaching into every corner of the nation. They also set out to construct a "salvation memory" of the terrorist nightmare according to which Fujimori and Montesinos had masterminded the defeat of the subversives and pacified the country both internally and externally. The contribution of others was erased from the official version, whose construction culminated on Army Day, December 9, 1999, with the observance of a minute of silence in memory of the 25,000 victims of terrorist violence throughout the country. This act was an attempt to whitewash any government responsibility in the violence.

The arbitrariness of the electoral process, however, was just too visible.

Added to the aforementioned falsification of over a million signatures was the flagrant control of the JNE, as well as the mass media's refusal to accept political advertisement from opposition candidates, even those willing to pay exorbitant prices. In the three months prior to the 2000 elections, three facts changed the course of events. First, the social movements that had been slowly regrouping since 1997 reached critical mass and along with their demands for employment and decentralization, there were forceful demands for democracy, accountability, and respect for human rights. This brings up an interesting difference with the first transition (1978–80), during which even larger national movements were major factors in the military government's retreat. Those movements, however, were fundamentally about socioeconomic demands. Democracy itself was not a high priority, which was one of the causes of the subsequent weakness of democracy in Peru throughout the 1980s.

Second, the appearance of new and unexpected players was also important. Civilian groups comprised of intellectuals, students, and artists were active participants in the mobilizations, displaying creative forms of so-called performative politics, which was previously unheard of in the Peruvian political scene. New mass media outlets also appeared, such as cable channel 'N', which brought about an exponential increase in cable connections in those months, both formal and informal. In another venue, Transparencia, a civilian association that concerned itself with monitoring elections and had played a modest role in 1995, became a magnet for thousands of young people, giving them an opportunity to channel their instinct for civic participation,[46] a role formerly played by the now moribund political parties. Finally, the Office of the Ombudsman, created in 1997, became, to the government's surprise, the only important governmental organization that maintained its independence. During those months, this institution, while staying within legal bounds, gave a voice to many civilian claims.

Among the most important of the new and unexpected players were the OAS electoral monitoring mission and Alejandro Toledo. It should be mentioned, however, that the key role played by the OAS mission, an organization normally characterized by a certain bureaucratic stiffness and extreme circumspection, was due in great part to the outstanding performance of its leader, Eduardo Stein. But that is another story. What must be highlighted here is that, faced with the media's character assassination campaigns against the main opposition candidates, in the middle of an economic crisis, and lacking democratic institutions to fall back on, the electorate constructed its own candidate for the second time in a decade. Fujimori got a taste of his own medicine. In 1990, an electorate, dissatisfied with its political options, propelled Fujimori to victory in a matter of weeks. This time it was Toledo following that same trajectory. Three months before the April 2000 elections, Toledo's projections were in the single digits. In the few remaining weeks, the candidate of indigenous roots and a very poor upbringing, the Harvard graduate of economics with a better command of English than Spanish, became another success story and role model, breaking Alberto Fujimori's monopoly among the poorest voters, especially in the departments with large indigenous populations and in the Amazon region.

Given this state of affairs, the international legitimacy of the regime finally began to crack, including the support of the United States. For the first time in eight years, the U.S. Congress and Department of State began to prevail over other U.S. government agencies such as the Drug Enforcement Administration (DEA) and the CIA, which favored Vladimiro Montesinos' effectiveness over respect for democratic ideals until the very end. Multilateral financial institutions and investment banks began to distance themselves from a regime that no longer offered the same stability as in the past.

Compounding this situation was a partially estranged business community, disappointed by the stagnant economy rather than by the regime's arbitrary excesses. The network of extra-systemic support was collapsing. The only remaining solid support was that of the armed forces, controlled more than ever by the SIN and, from 1999, by Vladimiro Montesinos, whose class of 1966 colleagues seized all the top positions in the army, the most powerful of the three military establishments.

This also helps to explain the apparent paradox of a besieged government that was nonetheless able to hold on to more than 40 percent of the votes in the 2000 elections, and that in August of that year, one month after Fujimori's third inauguration, had a 53 percent approval rating. It is one thing to have a 53 percent approval rating in 1996, with a nonexistent opposition and no storms on the horizon, and quite another to have it in 2000, with half of the country actively against the regime, and with an opposition that had achieved a certain measure of a so-called strategic majority. This sector included the younger, urban, and educated segment of a population that had become, at least to some extent, "well-informed citizens." The half that supported Fujimori, on the other hand, was concentrated in the rural, less educated areas that were more dependent on the social giveaways and benefits of the Ministry of the Presidency, and now found themselves on the defensive, lending a passive support at best.[47] It was not possible to mobilize this support in a context in which mobilization had become a central factor of the political battle plan.

For that reason, just as the third fujimorista regime seemed to be riding out the storms of popular protests and international pressure, the September 14, 2000 broadcast of a video showing an elected Congress member receiving U.S.$15,000 from the hands of Vladimiro Montesinos in his office at the SIN precipitated the collapse of the regime. This was due to the fact that the armed forces high command—the regime's only fundamental bastion of support—was totally under the control of Montesinos. The attack on Montesinos was a missile that hit under the water line.[48] But the video was not the main cause. In fact, its broadcasting "was the pretext sought after the decision had already been made" ("Fue el pretexto buscado cuando ya se le había bajado el dedo al asesor").[49] In addition, the United States had finally turned its back on the adviser, apparently for his role in the smuggling of weapons to the Colombian FARC. The motivations behind this act remain a mystery as these lines are written.

Conclusion

The transitional government installed after Alberto Fujimori and Vladimiro Montesinos fled the country was presided over by Valentín Paniagua between November 2000 and July 2001. It was faultlessly democratic and finished with an approval rating of over 70 percent. Paniagua, a "traditional politician," proved that the authoritarian decade was not a product of a "political culture" that condemned Peru to gravitate eternally around personalist commanders. The transitional government embodied the best Peruvian political tradition as well as the vitality of the civilian movements of the previous months and their democratic demands. The transitional government proceeded to act upon and institutionalize these demands by organizing the most transparent and effective elections in the contemporary history of the nation, by restoring the independence of the judiciary, press freedoms, and even the independence of Congress, even though the latter had been born out of an irregular fujimorista electoral process. Congress has been forced to behave democratically not only in emulation of the executive but bowing to the pressure of a mobilized citizenship.[50] But perhaps the most important measure has been the replacement of the armed forces high command and the capture and trial of Vladimiro Montesinos. Many key figures in the network of corruption—military officers, policemen, judges, media owners and congress members—are now behind bars, in a scene reminiscent of Operation Clean Hands after the fall of the Italian pentaparty.

The transitional government achieved these dramatic changes in only nine months, supported by a mobilized civil society, the collapse of both the SIN and the armed forces, and international legitimacy earned with the restoration of democratic institutions. If Fujimori and Montesinos were able to stay in power with the support of organizations like the CIA and the DEA, the transitional government connected with the spirit of democracy and human rights that was not only emerging among other international actors, but was also gaining strength on the world political stage after Pinochet's capture in London. Thus, Alejandro Toledo's election in April and June 2001 opens a chapter of fragile hope. Fragile because the regional scenario, especially the economy, is not very favorable, and because the personalist traditions and the havoc of anti-politics will not be conquered overnight. Hopeful, because politics, understood as an exercise in agreement, alliances, and the search for consensus, has stopped being a dirty word. The fact that Toledo's party does not have a majority in Congress forces it to "do politics," even as the sword of Damocles of the past hangs over its head, because no government without a partisan majority in Congress has finished out its term since 1963.

11

Argentina

From Crisis to Consolidation (and Back)

Steven Levitsky

For most of the twentieth century, Argentina was one of the world's leading democratic under-achievers. Despite its high levels of wealth and education, large middle-class, and relatively egalitarian social structure, civilian regimes repeatedly broke down between 1930 and 1976.[1] Beginning with the second government of Hipólito Yrigoyen (1928–1930), every civilian government that came to power through elections—including those of Juan Perón (1946–55), Arturo Frondizi (1958–62), Arturo Illia (1963–66), and Juan and Isabel Perón (1973–76)—ended in a military coup.

This regime trajectory changed markedly in the 1990s. During this more recent period, elections and civil liberties were institutionalized, the military disappeared from the political scene, and macroeconomic stability was achieved for the first time in decades. Democratic institutions also proved remarkably robust: they survived a hyperinflationary crisis, the implementation of radical economic reforms, and the often marginally constitutional behavior of the government of Carlos Menem (1989–99). Indeed, by the late 1990s, Argentine democracy was widely viewed as consolidated. Beginning in late 2001, however, Argentine democracy again fell into crisis. An unprecedented economic collapse, the successive resignation of two presidents, and a massive rebellion against the entire political elite raised the specter of a return to regime instability. Given Argentina's troubled democratic past, it is tempting to view the 2001–2 crisis as evidence of the persistently dysfunctional character of the country's political and economic institutions, and to view the achievements of the 1990s as little more than a temporary deviation from the norm.

This chapter offers a different view. It argues that Argentina's democratic success during the 1990s was the product of a relatively strong democratic foundation. Entrenched civil rights, a vibrant media and civil society, and strong political parties enhanced democratic governance and provided a critical buffer against authoritarian encroachment. Although the 2001–2 crisis had devastating political consequences, its causes were primarily *economic*: a prolonged recession, followed by an unprecedented depression. Thus, rather than treating Argentina as a case of a weak democracy in crisis (again), the chapter treats it as a case of a moderately successful democracy that encountered something approaching the perfect storm.

The Foundations of Democratic Stability

Argentina's new democracy confronted a set of severe challenges during the 1980s and 1990s. One challenge was economic. The disastrous economic legacies of the 1976–83 dictatorship, combined with the debt crisis and mounting crisis of the import-substituting industrialization model, created an economic environment that was hardly propitious for democratic stability. A second challenge was political: decades of regime instability had left a legacy of widespread and persistent institutional weakness.[2] For much of the twentieth century, whenever the political or economic "rules of the game" were perceived to harm the short-term interests of those in power, they were circumvented, changed, or simply broken. Thus, despite a system of fixed presidential terms, only one elected president (Juan Perón) completed his mandate between 1928 and 1989. Similarly, despite a formal guarantee of lifetime tenure security for Supreme Court justices, virtually every change of government or regime after 1946 was accompanied by court stacking.[3] This institutional fluidity had far-reaching and negative implications for democratic governance. The absence of stable and accepted rules of the game created high levels of uncertainty, shortened actors' time horizons, and eroded trust and cooperation.[4] Political and economic actors routinely pursued their objectives through extra-institutional (and often non-democratic) means. The result was frequent cycles of praetorianism, economic failure, and regime breakdown.

Yet Argentina's new democratic regime also benefited from some important strengths. In particular, three developments distinguished post-1983 Argentina from previous periods of civilian rule. The first was the emergence of an unprecedented consensus around democratic rules of the game. The failures of the 1976–83 military dictatorship led business and conservative leaders to reassess the value of democracy, and many of them began to invest seriously in electoral politics.[5] The (Peronist) Justicialista Party (PJ) also underwent an important transformation. Able to participate freely and consistently in elections for the first time since the 1950s, the PJ abandoned anti-system politics, and with the ascent of the Renovation faction in 1987, the party leadership fell into the hands of professional, territorially based politicians with a strong stake in democratic politics. Similar changes could be observed at the mass level. Not only did a large majority of Argentines consistently reject authoritarian alternatives after 1983,[6] but the traumatic experience of the 1970s gave rise to new public demands for the protection of civil liberties. The emergence of what Enrique Peruzzotti calls "right-oriented politics" helped to entrench civil liberties to a degree that was unprecedented in modern Argentine history.[7]

A second development was the emergence of a vibrant civil society. The human rights movement of the late 1970s and early 1980s gave birth to a "second wave" of rights-oriented organizations aimed at combating state abuses, strengthening citizenship rights, and fostering civic participation.[8] Civil society was strengthened by a vigorous media. Argentine media organizations, which were among the most independent and sophisticated in Latin America, played a critical role as government watchdogs after 1983.[9] Civil society demonstrated a striking capacity to handle abuses of state power during the 1980s and 1990s. Sustained civic and media campaigns not only brought state abuses to national attention but also kept them on the public agenda, thereby compelling government officials to undertake serious investigations.[10] In this sense, civic and media organizations functioned as agents of what Catalina Smulovitz and Peruzzotti call "societal accountability," or "societal watchdogs" that "expose and denounce wrongdoings" by state actors and thereby raise the reputational costs of abuses.[11]

A third development took place in the party system. The Argentine party system has been widely cited as a source of regime instability, largely due to its failure to integrate powerful economic actors into the electoral arena. The absence of a viable conservative party left the economic elite unable to defend its interests via electoral politics.[12] The labor movement was also poorly integrated into the party system, due to both the post-1955 proscription of Peronism and the weakly institutionalized nature of the Peronist Party.[13] The combination of a weak electoral Right and a powerful, but banned, populist party created an unstable dynamic in which civilian governments were highly vulnerable to military intervention.[14]

During the 1980s and early 1990s, the party system transformed in ways that were more favorable to democratic governance. For one, the Right was better integrated into electoral politics. The initial vehicle for this integration was the Center Democratic Union (UCEDE), which emerged as the country's third leading party in the late 1980s.[15] Although the UCEDE failed to consolidate as a major party, conservative elites nevertheless gained a stake in electoral politics through ties to conservative provincial parties and Center–Right factions of the PJ and the middle class Radical Civic Union (UCR). An even more significant change took place within Peronism. During the 1980s, PJ leaders built a strong territorial organization and sharply reduced trade union influence in the party. By the end of the decade, the PJ had transformed into a moderate and predominantly patronage-based party in which unions were at best junior partners.[16] As a result, Argentina's long "stalemated" party system took on features of what Ruth Collier and David Collier call an integrative party system.[17] Such a party system, in which labor is linked to a moderate, multiclass party that plays an important role in governing coalitions (as in post-1940 Mexico and post-1958 Venezuela), has been associated with governability and regime stability.[18]

The emergence of a broad democratic consensus, a vibrant media and civil society, and a stable and integrative party system provided a strong foundation for democratic governance during the 1990s. Although hardly a guarantee of regime stability, these conditions almost certainly enhanced the capacity of Argentine democracy to weather the storms that lay ahead.

The Relative Success of Argentine Democracy in the 1990s

Argentina entered the 1990s in a state of profound political and economic crisis. As elsewhere in Latin America, the crisis eroded representative institutions, or what Guillermo O'Donnell has called "horizontal accountability."[19] Hyperinflation atomized and demobilized civil society. It also weakened the established political parties, giving rise to political outsiders, including sports and music personalities (such as pop singer Ramón "Palito" Ortega and auto racer Carlos Reutemann) and former military leaders with distinctly authoritarian profiles (such as Antonio Bussi and Aldo Rico). Finally, the crisis generated a societal demand for decisive executive action and dulled public opposition to abuses of power, reinforcing patterns of "hyperpresidentialism" or "delegative democracy."[20] These patterns were clearly seen in the Peronist government of Carlos Menem.

Yet Argentina under Menem differed in important ways from other crisis-ridden regimes in Latin America. First, its core democratic institutions remained intact throughout the 1990s, despite a profound economic crisis and radical neoliberal reforms. Second, the erosion of horizontal accountability was far less extensive than in other so-called delegative democracies, such as Peru and Venezuela (see Degregori and Coppedge chapters, respectively). Third, Argentina diverged substantially from other crisis-ridden cases in the latter half of the 1990s. Rather than experiencing an institutional breakdown (as occurred in Peru, Ecuador, and Venezuela), Argentine democracy became increasingly routinized.

What Menemism Was (and Was Not)

During his first term in office, President Menem governed in a highly unilateral manner. This concentration of power was widely perceived to violate the spirit—if not the letter—of the constitution. For example, the government made repeated use of ambiguously constitutional prerogatives, such as executive decree authority and the partial veto, in an effort to circumvent the legislative branch.[21] Prior to the 1994 constitutional reform, the authority to issue so-called Necessity and Urgency Decrees (NUDs) was not explicitly granted by the constitution, and legal experts and politicians disagreed over whether such decrees were constitutional.[22] Presidents used them sparingly: fewer than 20 NUDs were issued by constitutional presidents between 1853 and 1983. Between 1983 and 1989, President Alfonsín issued just 10. By contrast, President Menem issued 335 NUDs between July 1989 and the 1994 constitutional reform and a total of 545 during his 10 years in office.[23] The 1994 constitution permitted NUDs, but only under "exceptional circumstances" and never on fiscal matters.[24] After 1994, Menem issued 210 NUDs, at least 15 of which were related to fiscal policy.[25]

The Menem government also undermined judicial independence. In 1990, for example, the government pushed through legislation (over the objections of the UCR and with a contested quorum) expanding the size of the Supreme Court from five to nine and then stacked it with Menem loyalists. The new Court rarely ruled against the executive branch during Menem's first term in office,[26] and several of its decisions were critical to the success of the government's economic reforms. For example, the 1990 Peralta decision upheld the constitutionality of Menem's use of decree authority in carrying out economic policy. The cozy relationship between the executive and many judges seriously eroded the judiciary's legitimacy. Indeed, surveys carried out in the mid-1990s found that between 70 and 80 percent of Argentines did not trust the judicial branch or believe it to be independent.[27]

More generally, the Menem government showed little interest in multiparty consensus-building—even on matters of rather fundamental importance to democracy. This was made manifest by the government's reckless pursuit of constitutional reforms permitting Menem's reelection. In 1994, Menem bullied the UCR into agreeing with the reform by threatening to hold a referendum on the issue. Confronted with opinion polls showing overwhelming support for reelection, ex-president Alfonsín negotiated what became known as the Olivos Pact, which included the reelection clause as part of a larger package of constitutional reforms. Four years later, despite the clear unconstitutionality of running for a third term, Menem toyed publicly with the idea of another plebiscite and even sought to gain a court ruling permitting his candidacy.

A major consequence of weak executive accountability was corruption. Several top government officials, including Labor Minister and Sociedad Mixta Siderúrgica Argentina (SOMISA) steel plant "intervenor" Jorge Triaca, Public Works Minister Roberto Dromi, National Administration of Health Insurance (ANSSAL) director Luis Barrionuevo, Environment Minister María Julia Alsogaray, and Programa de Atención Médica Integral (PAMI) directors Matilde Menendez and Victor Alderete, were implicated in corruption scandals. None were brought to justice during the Menem administration. Even more alarming was the degree to which the late mafia boss Alfredo Yabran penetrated the political establishment during the 1990s. Although the full extent of Yabran's political influence has yet to be ascertained, it is clear that he maintained close ties with top government officials and financed a large number of legislators in both major parties.

Yet the scope of abuse under Menem should not be overstated. Unlike most Latin American countries (including Chile), Argentina's core democratic institutions were never seriously violated during the 1990s. The fairness of elections was unquestioned, and civil liberties were broadly protected. Government opponents of all ideological stripes enjoyed substantial freedom, and the state intelligence apparatus was not used to harass opposition or media figures. Despite a few notable attacks on journalists,[28] particularly the 1997 killing of news photographer José Luis Cabezas, press freedom remained among the most extensive in Latin America. Although government officials launched a handful of libel suits against journalists and media outlets, they lost the most important of these cases.

Critical to the protection of civil liberties was civil society's vigorous response to abuses or attempted abuses. For example, efforts to limit press freedom, such as the 1992 "Truth in Press" bill and Menem's 1997 proposed "law of the stick" (which encouraged citizens to take matters into their own hands when offended by the media), generated substantial public opposition and were quickly abandoned. In the latter case, the public response was so intense that Menem was forced to apologize publicly to journalists ten days after his initial declaration.

When abuses did occur, effective mobilization by civil society frequently imposed heavy political costs on government officials, compelling them to investigate crimes committed by figures with ties to the state. A clear example was the 1990 rape and murder of teenager María Soledad Morales in the northern province of Catamarca, apparently by members of the dominant

Saadi clan. When the Saadi government moved to cover up the crime, local residents, backed by the Church, student organizations, and the local bar association, organized a series of "marches of silence" that drew nationwide attention to the case. A total of 82 marches, some mobilizing as many as 30,000 people (nearly 15 percent of Catamarca's population), were held.[29] The movement provoked a federal intervention of the provincial judiciary, a nationally televised trial, and an eventual conviction. Effective societal accountability could also be seen in the aftermath of the 1997 Cabezas killing (whose author, mafia boss Alfredo Yabran, maintained close ties to the government), during which the journalists' union, media outlets, and human rights organizations organized a massive campaign to bring the perpetrators to justice. Throughout 1997, Buenos Aires was flooded with "Who killed Cabezas?" posters, fliers, and television, radio, and newspaper ads. The civic campaign transformed the Cabezas case into a central issue in the 1997 midterm elections, forcing Buenos Aires governor Eduardo Duhalde to push the investigation forward. (Yabran committed suicide in the face of imminent arrest.)

The Menem government also asserted an impressive degree of civilian control over the military. In contrast to neighboring countries such as Chile (see Agüero chapter), Ecuador, Paraguay, and Peru (see Degregori chapter), the military's presence in Argentine politics in the 1990s was virtually nil. The armed forces had no role in the cabinet, military officers did not issue independent proclamations, and there were no military shows of force in the streets of the capital. President Menem, whose reputed ties to former military rebels and 1990 pardon of top military officers made him an unlikely candidate to advance civilian supremacy, played a major role in reining in the military. After crushing a military rebellion in 1990, he reduced the size of the army by a third, abolished the draft, slashed the military budget (from 18.2 percent of total government expenditure in 1989 to 10.6 percent in 1993),[30] and privatized military-owned enterprises. By the end of Menem's term, military spending was under the exclusive control of the Economic Ministry, responsibility for military deployment was in the hands of the Foreign Ministry, and external peacekeeping missions had come to "occupy the bulk of serious military effort."[31]

Even on the dimension of horizontal accountability, the Menem government's abuses were comparatively limited and short-lived. Notwithstanding his plebiscitarian rhetoric, President Menem did not routinely bypass parties or the legislature after 1990. Nearly all of the government's major post-1990 reform measures were approved by Congress, including the 1991 Convertibility Law, the currency peg system that put an end to hyperinflation. Most of the post-1990 reforms were the product of extensive negotiations with Congress, governors, and business and labor leaders. Many reform bills, including those to privatize social security and the gas and petroleum sectors, were substantially modified by the legislature.[32] Others were blocked entirely. For example, it took several years of tripartite negotiations with business and labor leaders, as well as extensive congressional deliberation, to approve even a limited labor market reform bill.[33] Hence, although Argentine democracy showed delegative tendencies in the early 1990s, both the margin for executive abuse and the scope of actual abuse were narrower than in many of the region's other crisis-ridden democracies.

Combining Democracy and Radical Economic Reform

What was perhaps most striking about Argentina's post-1983 democracy was its robustness. Democratic institutions survived not only the 1989 hyperinflationary crisis but also a series of market-oriented reforms that were considered among the most far-reaching in the world.[34] Virtually none of the most radical economic reforms in post-1973 Latin America were undertaken in a fully democratic context. In Chile and Mexico, economic reforms were carried out under authoritarian regimes (see Agüero and Dresser chapters, respectively). In Peru, they were accompanied by a presidential self-coup. Even in Bolivia, which is generally viewed as a democracy, orthodox stabilization was accompanied by a state of siege and labor repression. By contrast, in democracies such as Costa Rica, Uruguay, Venezuela, and Brazil, economic reform was slower and less extensive. Hence, Argentina arguably combined radical economic reform and democracy in a way that was unparalleled in Latin America.

The Menem government's capacity to combine democracy and radical reform was rooted, in large part, in the Justicialista Party. Given its close ties to organized labor and deep roots in working- and lower-class society, the PJ represented many of the potential losers under neoliberalism. Its capacity to deliver these sectors on behalf of economic reform was therefore critical to the reform's success.[35] This was most clearly seen with respect to the unions, whose repeated protests had helped to derail the Alfonsín government's comparatively mild heterodox stabilization policies. Through a deft combination of persuasion, threats, and side payments, the Menem government gained a remarkable degree of labor acquiescence. The Peronist-led General Labor Confederation (CGT) did not carry out a single general strike during Menem's first three and a half years in office, and it led only one general strike during his entire first term. Moreover, sector-level unions cooperated with every major privatization, including electricity, telecommunications, petroleum, and social security.[36]

Democratic reform implementation was also facilitated by the PJ's capacity to retain the support of its traditional working- and lower-class base. The party's powerful subculture and extensive linkages to working- and lower-class society helped it to retain the support of a large number of activists and voters who might otherwise have actively opposed neoliberal reforms.[37] The activities of grassroots Peronist networks, which included operating soup kitchens, distributing clientelistic goods, organizing social and cultural events, and occasionally intimidating left-wing activists,[38] helped to prevent the kind of mass looting and rioting that shook the Alfonsín government.

The PJ's capacity to deliver its traditional base contributed to democratic governance in two ways. First, it meant that relatively few working- and lower-class voters were available for anti-reform or anti-system appeals. Anti-reform electoral appeals by leftists, nationalists, and dissident Peronists failed repeatedly to capture working- and lower-class votes during the 1990s. Second, the PJ's capacity to retain its traditional voters helped the party score the electoral victories needed to maintain control of the legislature. Combining its traditional base with an important fraction of the independent and conservative electorate, the PJ easily won both 1991 and 1993 legislative elections and the 1995 presidential elections. These victories enabled the PJ to maintain a majority in the Senate and a near-majority in the legislature, which—with the votes of a handful of conservative and provincial parties—ensured the passage of the bulk of Menem's reform agenda. This legislative strength, which distinguishes Argentina from other cases of delegative democracy or "neopopulism," was critical to the government's capacity to carry out radical reforms in a democratic context.

It is worth noting that democratic institutions also imposed important limitations on economic policy. For example, although it is widely believed that the fixed exchange rate should have been abandoned in the mid-1990s, widespread public support for convertibility (up to 90 percent, according to some surveys) and the repeated electoral failure of convertibility critics created a broad political consensus against such a move. Opposition to convertibility came to be viewed as political suicide, and the issue disappeared from the debate. Democratic constraints also may have inhibited provincial-level administrative reform. Because most PJ legislators' political loyalties lay with their governors (who controlled access to legislative candidacies), President Menem needed the governors' support to get his economic program through Congress. Because fiscal reform in the provinces entailed politically costly public-sector layoffs, such policies would clearly have jeopardized that support. Indeed, the non-reform of the provinces has been cited as a critical ingredient of the Menem government's legislative success.[39] Hence, the failure to abandon convertibility or reduce provincial spending may have been the price the Menem government had to pay to carry out its radical reform program under democracy.

Menem's Second Term (1995–1999): The Routinization of Democratic Politics

Democratic politics became increasingly routinized during Menem's second term, largely because the political-economic crisis that had given rise to hyperpresidentialism diminished. As fears of hyperinflation faded, new issues, such as corruption and public accountability, became increasingly salient. One manifestation of this changing political climate was the rapid rise of the Front for a Country in Solidarity (FREPASO), a progressive Center clean government party that captured 30 percent of the presidential vote in 1995. The passing of the crisis also permitted the resurgence of the middle-class opposition. Widely viewed as incapable of either winning or governing during the early and mid-1990s, anti-Peronist forces undertook two strategic changes after 1995. First, FREPASO and the UCR accepted the core elements of the neoliberal economic model, including fiscal balance, privatization, trade openness, and convertibility. Second, in August 1997, the UCR and FREPASO formed the Alliance for Jobs, Justice, and Education. These changes transformed what had been a weak and discredited opposition into a viable alternative to Menemism. The Alliance easily won the 1997 midterm legislative elections, handing the PJ its first electoral defeat in more than a decade.

The post-1995 change in the balance of political forces substantially reduced President Menem's capacity to govern unilaterally. In contrast to the 1989–95 period, much of the Menem government's post-1995 legislative agenda was stymied by Congress. Beginning in 1997, a group of approximately 40 PJ legislators loyal to Buenos Aires governor Eduardo Duhalde routinely joined the opposition in blocking much of the executive's proposed legislation. As a result, legislation to "flexibilize" labor markets and privatize the airports, the postal system, and the national mortgage bank were stalled for several years. Although Menem threatened to impose many of these reforms by decree, such threats were rarely carried out. Indeed, Menem's use of executive decrees declined by nearly 50 percent between 1993 and 1998.[40] Judicial rulings against the government also increased. In 1999, for example, the Supreme Court voted, for the first time, to limit executive discretion in issuing NUDs.[41]

The resilience of Argentina's democratic institutions was made particularly manifest in 1998, when President Menem engaged in a reckless, if half-hearted, effort to run for a third term. In contrast to 1994, Menem's "re-

reelection" bid was opposed by a strong and united opposition, as well as by much of the PJ. Although Menem sought to obtain a favorable ruling from the Supreme Court, his allies on the Court, aware of the potential consequences of such an illegitimate ruling (including impeachment and prosecution if Menem were to lose the election), made it clear that they would take no such action.[42] As a result, Menem was left with no alternative but to hand over the presidency, as scheduled, in December 1999.

The Legacies of Menemism

When Carlos Menem left the presidency, Argentine democracy was more stable than at any time in the country's history. The core elements of democracy were institutionalized, the armed forces had disappeared from the political scene, and macroeconomic stability had reduced the likelihood of regime-threatening distributive conflict. The 1999 electoral process was a highly routinized affair. The president-elect, Alliance candidate Fernando De la Rúa, was a career UCR politician, and established party politicians captured nearly all of the country's governorships. The transfer of power from Menem to De la Rúa was also highly routinized. Whereas in 1989 the hyperinflationary crisis had forced Alfonsín to abandon the presidency six months before the end of his mandate, the 1999 transition took place virtually without a hitch. The transition marked the first time that the Argentine presidency had twice consecutively passed between elected presidents from different parties, as well as the first time that Peronism had ever been peacefully removed from power.

Yet the Menemist period also left several legacies that would later prove problematic for democratic governance. The first was a failure to invest seriously in institution-building. Although core democratic institutions were respected during the 1990s, patterns of bending or changing politically inconvenient rules of the game persisted. A clear example was Menem's widespread use of executive decrees. Although the 1994 constitution legalized decrees in cases of "public emergency," Menem's liberal use of that authority set a low threshold for what constitutes an emergency (a precedent that was followed by his successors). Menem's reelection bids were similarly deinstitutionalizing. The 1994 constitutional reform was a clear case of the rules being changed in line with the short-term interests of powerful actors, and although Menem's second reelection bid failed, it nevertheless revealed a strikingly low level of commitment to the constitutional rules of the game. Rule-bending in the judicial arena was manifested not only in Menem's 1990 stacking of the Supreme Court, but also in the 1993 Menem–Alfonsín agreement (as part of the Olivos Pact) to reshuffle the Court. Although aimed at creating greater political "balance" on the Court, the 1993 pact nevertheless reinforced existing patterns of political intervention.

Politicians also did little to strengthen institutions of horizontal accountability. For example, congressional leaders took few significant steps to develop the skills and resources necessary to effectively oversee the executive. Whereas the executive branch (particularly the Economic Ministry) took major steps toward staff professionalization, the legislature lagged behind.[43] Congressional staff positions continued to be filled by patronage appointees whose primary responsibility was to maintain local clientelist networks. As a result, legislators remained ill-equipped to oversee (or negotiate policy with) the executive. Similarly, in the area of civil-military relations, little progress was made in developing civilian oversight capacity or defense policymaking expertise in either the legislature or the Defense Ministry.[44] Thus, even though military influence in politics was low during the 1990s, civilian control over the military was not institutionalized.

The Menem period also left difficult socioeconomic legacies. One was a doubling of the public debt, which was partly a product of the economic reform process (particularly social security privatization, which meant that the state lost contributors but continued to make payments to pensioners).[45] Another problematic economic legacy was the Convertibility Law. Convertibility was a classic double-edged sword, for although it had been critical to ending hyperinflation and restoring credibility with foreign investors and lenders, it also deprived governments of macroeconomic policy tools necessary to combat economic downturns. Finally, the Menem reforms resulted in severe economic dislocation. The unemployment rate rose from 7.1 percent in 1989 to 18.6 percent in 1995, creating a new class of structurally unemployed or marginal poor. Many middle-class Argentines (public employees, pensioners, small shop owners) also experienced declining—and increasingly precarious—living standards.

The combination of political shenanigans and economic insecurity eroded public trust in elected leaders, particularly among the (historically anti-Peronist) middle sectors. This increase in voter alienation was not necessarily fatal for the political class. During the late 1990s, the Alliance offered disaffected middle-sector voters a clear partisan alternative. Modeling itself on the Chilean Democratic Concertation, the Alliance offered a "new way of doing politics" that, while preserving the economic gains of the 1990s, would restore confidence in public institutions. At the core of the Alliance platform lay two promises: (1) greater public accountability; and (2) greater attention to the social costs of neoliberalism, particularly unemployment. Had the De la Rúa government been able to even minimally fulfill these promises, public disaffection might have remained at a level similar to that of neighboring countries.

Back to the Brink? Economic Collapse and Its Political Consequences, 1999–2002

The De la Rúa government failed to deliver on either the political or economic fronts. On the political front, the Alliance quickly unraveled. De la Rúa invested little in the governing coalition, bypassing the FREPASO and UCR leaderships and governing with a small circle of friends and family. However, the most devastating blow to the Alliance came in the wake of August 2000 allegations that government officials had paid bribes to several senators—most of them Peronist—to gain support for labor market reform legislation. Vice-President Carlos "Chacho" Álvarez, whose FREPASO had made anti-corruption its central plank, called for an aggressive investigation and the immediate resignation of those implicated in the scandal. This stance met stiff resistance within the government and both leading parties. Faced with the prospect of an investigation that could implicate not only top government officials but also much of the political class, De la Rúa balked. Although key government officials (Labor Minister Alberto Flamarique, intelligence chief Fernando de Santibañes, and Senate President José Genoud) were forced to resign, the government did not pursue a serious investigation into the scandal. The case was eventually dismissed—by a judge who himself was being investigated for illicit enrichment—for lack of sufficient evidence.

The senate scandal had severe political consequences for the Alliance. When it became clear that there would be no serious investigation, Álvarez stunned the country by resigning the vice-presidency, which effectively destroyed the governing coalition. Although FREPASO remained in the government, it suffered a debilitating wave of defections, and within a year, it had virtually disappeared. More important, the scandal shattered the Alliance's claim to represent a "new way of doing politics," convincing many middle-class Argentines that *none of the major parties* effectively represented them.

But the roots of De la Rúa's failure lay in the economic realm. After averaging 6.2 percent annual growth between 1991 and 1998, the economy fell into a protracted recession from which—as of June 2002—it never recovered. The economic collapse was the product of a convergence of external shocks and domestic policy constraints. The Argentine economy suffered a series of external shocks beginning in 1997. First, in the wake of the Asian and Russian financial crises of 1997–98, foreign investment dried up. Second, a strong U.S. dollar reduced the competitiveness of Argentine exports to Europe and Latin America. Third, and crucially, Brazil's devaluation in 1999 delivered a major blow to Argentina's export competitiveness. These shocks sent the economy into a prolonged recession beginning in 1998.

Argentina's difficulties would be compounded by an additional external shock: a major shift in U.S. and IMF policy following the election of George Bush. The Bush administration combined a deep skepticism toward bailouts —made manifest by Treasury Secretary Paul O'Neill's declaration that "America's plumbers and carpenters" would not "pay for someone else's bad decisions"[46]—with a narrow *realpolitik* foreign policy vision. A primary goal of both the Treasury Department and the IMF became avoiding "moral hazard," or the encouragement of bad investments and policies via bailouts. Consequently, the prospects for a large-scale international rescue package—along the lines of the 1995 Mexican bailout—diminished substantially after 2000.

Argentina's capacity to dig itself out of recession was limited by two domestic constraints: convertibility and debt. Convertibility prevented the government from using either monetary or exchange rate policies to reactivate the economy. In other words, governments could neither expand the money supply nor devalue the currency (as Mexico and Brazil did in 1994 and 1999, respectively) as a means of stimulating growth. To make matters worse, the debt burden effectively ruled out Keynesian anti-cyclical spending. Due to a combination of declining tax revenues (a product of recession) and increased debt payments, governments faced a growing fiscal crisis, which accentuated their dependence on debt financing through bonds. But the fiscal crisis eroded investor confidence in the government's capacity to make its debt payments, and as a result, interest rates on Argentine bonds soared. To shore up investor confidence, governments were forced to continually offer evidence of fiscal solvency, generally by reducing budget deficits. Thus, rather than combating the recession through deficit spending, as most industrialized countries do, Argentine governments were forced to implement *pro-cyclical* austerity measures that could only be expected to prolong the recession.[47]

One way out of this dilemma would have been to abandon the fixed exchange rate system. However, public support for convertibility remained so strong that such a move remained virtually unthinkable. It would have required bold leadership and an unusually strong government to end convertibility in 1999. The Alliance met neither of these criteria. Wedded to convertibility, the De la Rúa government fell into a vicious recessionary circle: recession eroded the tax base and exacerbated the fiscal crisis, which undermined investor confidence in the government's capacity to pay the debt, which created further pressure for austerity, which only prolonged the recession.

The Alliance's two years in power were characterized by repeated economic adjustments and prolonged recession. The government's initial program, including the January 2000 *impuestazo* (tax hike), failed to revive the economy, and subsequent austerity measures led to a steady erosion of public support. In March 2001, Economic Minister José Luis Machinea was replaced by orthodox economist Ricardo López Murphy, whose draconian austerity package (including $4.5 billion in spending cuts) generated such widespread public opposition that he was forced to resign after just two weeks. López Murphy was replaced by Domingo Cavallo, who by now had reemerged as something of a savior figure. Cavallo's status as the father of convertibility might have given him the credibility to dismantle the currency peg. However, Cavallo rejected such a move (perhaps because he was considering a presidential bid) in favor of a set of heterodox reactivation policies that included tax cuts, subsidies and protection for selected industries, and a planned transition from a pure U.S. dollar basket to a mixed dollar-euro peg. Financial markets responded unfavorably, forcing Cavallo to shift back in a more orthodox direction. In July, he launched a draconian "zero-deficit" policy in which the government committed, on a month-to-month basis, to spending only what it raised in taxes. The zero-deficit policy required immediate cuts of up to 13 percent in pensions and public-sector wages.

Two years of austerity and recession generated severe social and political costs. The unemployment rate reached 18.3 percent by October 2001, and more than three million people fell below the poverty line in 2001 alone.[48] As a result, public support for the government plummeted from 70 percent in December 1999 into the low teens. Social protest rose sharply. Organized labor led six general strikes during 2000 and 2001, compared to just one during Menem's entire first term. Provincial protest also picked up, and groups of unemployed people—known as *piqueteros*—escalated an emergence practice of blocking roads and highways throughout the country. In August 2001, a nation-wide street picket blocked an estimated 200 roads in sixteen provinces.[49]

The depth of public disaffection was made manifest in the October 2001 midterm legislative elections. The Alliance was soundly defeated (falling from 49 percent of the vote in 1999 to just 23 percent), allowing the PJ to regain control of Congress. More ominously, the election made it clear that public dissatisfaction extended beyond the De la Rúa government to the entire political class. Voter abstention skyrocketed, and the number of blank and spoiled ballots nearly quintupled. At the national level, the total blank and null vote was greater than that of the governing Alliance, and in the capital and the province of Santa Fe, it surpassed that of all parties.

The Descent into Chaos

De la Rúa never recovered from the 2001 election. As the economy slipped deeper into recession, fears of a default and devaluation triggered a financial panic. In November, in a desperate attempt to stave off a financial collapse, Cavallo froze bank deposits, limiting withdrawals to $250 a week. Popularly known as the *corralito*, the freeze on deposits enraged the middle classes and brought economic activity to a standstill. A final blow was delivered by the IMF, which announced on December 5 that it was suspending $1.3 billion in loan payments due to the government's failure to comply with its zero-deficit policy.

On December 18 and 19, Argentina exploded in protest. Massive riots and protests broke out on several fronts. In the working- and lower-class suburbs surrounding Buenos Aires, as well as in several provinces, crowds blocked highways and looted supermarkets and neighborhood grocery stores. In the capital, middle-class protesters took to the streets banging pots and pans in protests known as *cacerolazos*. The government responded by declaring a state of siege, and the ensuing police repression resulted in more than two dozen deaths. The repression destroyed the last vestiges of De la Rúa's presidential authority. Protests multiplied. On December 20, after a last-minute call for a national unity government was rebuffed (by both the PJ and the UCR), De la Rúa resigned.

De la Rúa's resignation triggered a massive political rebellion from below. Although originally rooted in opposition to the De la Rúa government, protests quickly extended into a rebellion against the entire political class. Protesters surrounded each branch of government, banging pots and pans and demanding the resignation of all of the members of Congress and the Supreme Court. The public mood was crystallized in an extraordinary slogan: *que se vayan todos* ("throw everyone out"). Public anger reached such an extreme that politicians were frequently attacked—verbally, and in some cases, physically—when they ventured out into public spaces. On downtown streets, in restaurants, and in airports, and even in their own neighborhoods, politicians were targets of spontaneous assaults known as *escraches*.

The rebellion threw Argentina into a state of near-anarchy. Because the vice-presidency had been vacant since Álvarez's resignation in 2000, it fell to a joint session of Congress to choose an interim president. But the dominant force in Congress, the PJ, was in a state of internal chaos. Power lay in the hands of Peronism's provincial bosses, particularly governors such as José Manuel De la Sota of Córdoba, Carlos Ruckauf of Buenos Aires, and Carlos Reutemann of Santa Fe. Because the PJ lacked a central bureaucracy capable of imposing internal discipline, the governors faced problems of collective action. Many of them had their eyes on the presidency, and the uncertainty surrounding who was in power and when new elections would be held dramatically reduced their time horizons. The Peronists initially chose San Luis governor Adolfo Rodriguez Saa as interim president and scheduled elections for March. The decision was a disastrous one. Soon after announcing a default on Argentina's $140 billion debt, Rodriguez Saa fell victim to another round of mass protests (including a storming of the Congress) and severe Peronist infighting. Amid signs that Rodriguez Saa sought to stay in power beyond March, the PJ governors withdrew their support, and on December 30 Rodriguez Saa became the second president in two weeks to resign.

The Political Class under Siege

When Congress convened on New Year's Day to select yet another interim president, the Argentine political class made what many viewed as its last stand. Radicals, Peronists, and a faction of FREPASO came together in a broad legislative coalition to elect Peronist Senator Eduardo Duhalde—the PJ's losing candidate in 1999—interim president. Duhalde possessed two potential advantages in terms of restoring governability: (1) he enjoyed a broad coalition of support in Congress; and (2) he was a Peronist. Although eroding, the PJ's links to the labor movement and organized presence in working- and lower-class zones provided critical resources with which to contain popular-sector protest.

Yet Duhalde confronted a nearly impossible situation. On the one hand, he faced the largest and most sustained wave of protest seen in Latin America in nearly two decades. Although mass looting had subsided, *cacerolazos*, *escraches*, and highway blockades continued to mount. The middle classes remained hypermobilized. In the capital, dozens of radicalized grassroots block organizations, or neighborhood assemblies, emerged in the aftermath of the December protests. Many of the assemblies combined participatory forms of democracy with maximalist demands in a way that provoked comparisons to Russian Soviets. Outside the capital, militant unions and left-wing activists stitched together local *piquetero* networks into a national *piquetero* movement. During the first two months of 2002, *piqueteros* carried out 488 highway blockades—a rate of nearly 10 a day.[50] In this context, mainstream politicians began to describe Argentina as being in a state of "social revolution."[51]

However, the new government was in no position to meet any of the protesters' demands. By January 2002, the paralysis of the banking system had brought the economy to the brink of depression. A solution to the financial crisis was virtually impossible without external assistance, but no such help was on the horizon. The IMF ruled out an immediate rescue package and insisted that future assistance would hinge on the development of a "sustainable" economic program—a central component of which was deep spending cuts. The IMF demanded a 60 percent reduction in provincial budget deficits, and IMF officials suggested that fiscal balance would require the elimination of up to 450,000 public-sector jobs.[52] Not only did such policies run directly counter to *piquetero* demands for jobs and unemployment subsidies, but a strategy of cutting spending to combat a depression was also questionable from an economic standpoint.[53] Thus, whereas an international rescue package might have provided Duhalde with the space to restore political and economic order, IMF policy did just the opposite: it created conditions that virtually doomed Duhalde to failure.

The Duhalde government's first five months in office were marked by repeated policy failures and a deepening political and economic crisis. On January 6, Congress put an end to more than a decade of convertibility. The move triggered an intense distributional struggle, as banks, industrialists, privatized companies, and even foreign governments lobbied ferociously to defend their interests. Unable to effectively mediate these interests, the government responded with a series of contradictory signals and a staggering succession of policy reversals. The peso depreciated from $1.00 to more than $3.00, pushing up prices and triggering fears of a return to hyperinflation. Meanwhile, the extended paralysis of the financial system brought economic activity to a standstill. As contracts were broken and the commercial chain of payments collapsed, Argentina fell into the deepest depression in its history. Although the government met a series of IMF demands (including a floating exchange rate, an austere national budget, and an agreement with the governors to reduce provincial deficits), Argentina received no help from the international community. When it became clear that Duhalde would be unable to deliver either an economic recovery or external assistance, support for the interim government eroded. By May, public support for Duhalde had fallen into single digits, and speculation was rampant that he, too, would soon be forced out of office.

Assessing the Damage (Midstorm)

The political and economic consequences of the crisis were enormous. By mid-2002, the economic collapse had begun to rival the worst depressions of the 1930s. In April, the IMF estimated that the economy would contract by up to 15 percent in 2002.[54] The social costs of the collapse were staggering. The unemployment rate reached 22 percent. More than 1.5 million people fell into poverty between October 2001 and March 2002.[55] The poverty rate, which had been as low as 22 percent in 1994, soared to nearly 50 percent.[56]

A second casualty of the crisis was Argentina's fragile institutional structure. The crisis triggered another round of institutional collapse. Economic institutions that had been the centerpiece of the Menem reforms, such as the

Convertibility Law and central bank autonomy, were swept away in a matter of hours. In the political realm, the rules of the game governing the electoral cycle, executive-legislative relations, the judiciary, and the federal system were essentially up for grabs. During the first half of 2002, it was unclear when the next election would be held and which offices would be up for election.[57]

A third casualty of the crisis was the party system. A striking number of Argentines began to reject all of the established parties—and all politicians in general—in 2001. As a result, the party system began to melt down. As FREPASO—and quite possibly the UCR—headed toward collapse, a plethora of anti-political establishment outsiders emerged and ascended in the polls. The growing list of outsider candidates included Luis Zamora, a previously marginal left-wing politician; Elisa Carrió, a congressional backbencher who left the UCR to create Argentines for a Republic of Equals (ARI); businessman Mauricio Macri, the president of the popular Boca Juniors soccer club; orthodox economist Ricardo López Murphy, who abandoned the UCR to launch an independent presidential bid; and ex-labor minister Patricia Bullrich, a former Peronist who created her own "Now Argentina" party. Ex-interim president Rodriguez Saa, who retained strong support in the interior, was also reported to be considering an independent presidential bid. In May, former military rebel leaders Aldo Rico and Mohammad Ali Seineldín both stood higher in the polls than any member of the UCR or FREPASO. As of mid-2002, then, the future of the political class was very much in doubt. Surveys suggested that if an election were held, the party system would suffer a collapse comparable to those of Peru in 1990 and Venezuela in 1993.

Finally, there was at least some evidence that the crisis had begun to erode support for the democratic regime. For the first time in more than a decade, mass support for democracy declined in 2001–2. According to a 2001 Latinobarómetro survey, the percentage of Argentines who agreed that "democracy is preferable to any other kind of government" fell from more than 70 percent during the 1990s to just 58 percent in 2001.[58] Perhaps even more threatening was evidence of disloyal or semi-loyal regime behavior.[59] In February 2002, newspapers reported a series of meetings—behind the back of the president—between top business leaders and military officers, including armed forces chief Ricardo Brinzoni.[60] Several weeks later, another military official declared that—notwithstanding its illegality—military action "cannot be ruled out" in the event of a social crisis.[61] As of mid-2002, a military coup remained unlikely, due to both strong public opposition and the military's extreme reluctance to engage in such action. Nevertheless, it was clear that for the first time in more than a decade, a democratic rupture had became "thinkable" in Argentina.

Given the depth of the crisis, the fact that democracy survived through mid-2002 was a remarkable achievement. Not only did a coup not take place, but the military refused to intervene to repress protests (even during moments of extreme chaos and uncertainty, such as December 2001), made no independent proclamations or shows of force, and did not work behind the scenes on behalf of a particular outcome. The strikingly robust nature of Argentina's democratic institutions represented one of the few silver linings to emerge from the crisis.

Explaining the Meltdown: Are the Politicians to Blame?

Explanations of the 2001–2 crisis vary considerably. However, many explanations—both within and outside Argentina—have converged around the idea that the crisis is rooted in politics. Argentine politicians and political practices have emerged as a central target of criticism from U.S. and IMF officials, many international analysts, and the vast majority of Argentines themselves. According to these explanations, the roots of the crisis lie in pervasive corruption, clientelism, runaway political spending, and a closed or cartel-like party system that has been described as "partyarchy."[62] These phenomena are said to be major causes of both Argentina's profound crisis of representation and its recurrent fiscal problems.

There are reasons to doubt such explanations. By any comparative measure, the levels of corruption, clientelism, and fiscal profligacy in Argentina were moderate during the 1990s. Between 1995 and 2000, Argentina was consistently located in the middle of the pack on Transparency International's annual Corruption Perception Index: more or less on par with Brazil and Mexico, only a notch below the Czech Republic, Greece, Italy, and South Korea, and substantially better than China, India, and Thailand. Moreover, there is little evidence clientelism and patronage politics was any more pervasive in Argentina than in countries like Brazil or Mexico. Although these were a source of fiscal strain, particularly in the provinces, it is difficult to attribute the post-1998 economic crisis to political overspending. Argentina's fiscal deficits during the 1990s were relatively small (never surpassing the level required for entry into the Maastrict Treaty), and much of the public debt accumulated during the 1990s was a product of internationally backed economic reforms (such as bank restructuring and social security privatization).[63]

Finally, the Argentine party system was far from closed during the 1990s. The legal requirements for forming a party were relatively minimal, and a low threshold proportional representation system allowed a variety of small parties to gain election to Congress. Indeed, the post-1983 Argentine party system was one of the most open, competitive, and ideologically diverse in

Latin America. The PJ and UCR faced significant electoral challenges on several fronts, including the Intransigent Party (PI), FREPASO, and ARI on the progressive left and the UCEDE and Domingo Cavallo's Action for the Republic on the conservative Right, as well as the ultranationalist Movement for National Dignity and Independence (MODIN).

In sum, political inefficiencies in Argentina did not exceed those found in most middle-income countries. Given that corruption, clientelism, and patronage politics were no worse than in Brazil and Mexico (and were substantially better than in many other Latin American countries), it is difficult to attribute the crisis primarily to political factors. In fact, a more compelling explanation is the reverse one. The roots of Argentina's political crisis were primarily economic: a seemingly endless recession, followed by a seemingly bottomless economic collapse. By 2002, the economic crisis reached depths that historically had destroyed all but the world's most established democracies. Hence, although it may be tempting to characterize Argentina as a case of a persistently dysfunctional political system that fell into yet another crisis, it may be more accurate to view it as a case of a moderately strong democratic regime that was hit by enormous economic shock. Had Argentina experienced even slow to moderate growth between 1998 and 2001 (as did Brazil and Mexico), there almost certainly would have been no political crisis to explain.

Problems and Prospects: Three Dilemmas

As of mid-2002, it was impossible to see just how far down Argentina would descend. With no signs of imminent economic recovery or forthcoming external assistance, the crisis appeared virtually bottomless. More than anything else, the future of democratic governance—indeed, democratic survival—hinges on economic recovery. However, at least three political issues will also be critical to the short- to medium-term fate of Argentine democracy: (1) institutional instability; (2) the fate of the party system; and (3) the political representation of the Right.

The Dilemma of Institutional Change: Innovation or Continued Weakness?

As might be expected, the 2001 crisis gave rise to a plethora of institutional reform proposals from across the political spectrum. These included electoral and campaign finance reform, a revamping of the judiciary (including reducing the size of the Supreme Court), the downsizing (or elimination) of the Senate, and the establishment of a parliamentary system of government. Whatever the technical merit of these proposals, it is worth remembering that historically, the central problem with Argentine political institutions has been not their design but their *weakness*. Argentine governments have experimented with a great variety of political and economic institutions—many of which were praised by international observers—during the latter half of the twentieth century. What is most striking about these institutions, however, is their failure to take root. Indeed, throughout most of the twentieth century, whenever the political and economic rules of the game got in the way of groups or actors powerful enough to change them, the rules were changed. Constitutions were reformed; Supreme Courts were stacked; presidents were forced to resign before the end of their mandates; elections were rescheduled. The political and economic costs of this institutional fluidity were enormous.

A major problem in contemporary Argentina is that many of its democratic institutions have again become broadly discredited. This has (again) generated widespread public demands that the slate be wiped clean: protesters demand new elections; a new Supreme Court; a new constitution. Given the depth of public anger, some bending or changing of the rules— calling early elections or impeaching some Supreme Court justices—may well prove to be a "least bad" alternative. Yet there are serious costs to another round of institutional change. Institution-building is a long-term and arduous process. To take root, political institutions often have to survive a few major storms, which generally means periods of suboptimal performance. Another round of institutional destruction and reconstruction, even if done for the most noble of reasons, will reinforce the dominant pattern of the past seventy years: whenever the going gets tough, the rules get changed. An example of this dilemma is the Supreme Court. In early 2002, many Argentines complained about the absence of judicial independence and yet at the same time called for the impeachment of the Supreme Court. Whatever its benefits in terms of political legitimacy, impeachment would come at the cost of another blow to the institution of tenure security, which would reinforce existing patterns of judicial weakness.

The Crisis of the Political Class: Party System Renewal or Collapse?

The Argentine political class entered into a serious—and potentially terminal—crisis in 2001. Widespread rejection of established parties and politicians suggests that the potential for a full-scale meltdown of the party is great. Indeed, many Argentines on the Left, Center, and Right view the wholesale removal of the existing partisan elite and the election of a new political leadership as the only way to restore public trust in democratic institutions. A model for such a scenario might be Italy in the early 1990s.

However, recent Latin American history suggests the possibility of a darker path: that of Peru and Venezuela in the 1990s. In those countries, the collapse of established parties resulted not in democratic renewal but in party system decomposition, the rise of anti-political establishment outsiders, and democratic breakdown. Outsider politics is often dangerous for democracy. Outsiders tend to be political amateurs, with little experience with (or patience for) the negotiation, compromise, and coalition-building that is inherent to democratic institutions. As a result, they are more likely to enter into conflict with—and in some cases, seriously assault—those institutions. Because institutions of horizontal accountability tend to be weakened during periods of system collapse, these assaults often pose a serious threat to democracy.

Party system crisis thus poses a difficult dilemma. If the established parties have lost public trust, their persistence in power could erode democratic legitimacy. But in the contemporary period, in which the influence of mass media technologies has reduced politicians' incentives to invest in parties, stable party systems are extremely difficult to rebuild. Indeed, of all the new parties that emerged in Argentina during the 1980s and 1990s, none established a national structure that linked the country's wealthy metropolitan centers to its peripheral provinces. Hence, although a collapse of the UCR and the PJ could trigger an Italian-style democratic renewal, a more likely outcome is a fragmented universe of provincial parties, narrowly based Buenos Aires-centered parties, and outsiders. At best, such party system fragmentation would make democratic governance more difficult. At worst, it could push Argentina farther down the road of a Peruvian- or Venezuelan-style democratic collapse.

The Political Representation of the Right

A third and related problem has to do with the political representation of the Right. As noted above, a major Achilles' heel of modern Argentine democracy has been the absence of an electorally viable conservative party. Unable, after the extension of full suffrage, to defend their interests in the electoral arena, economic elites never developed an effective stake in democratic institutions.[64] On several occasions, they turned to the military to defend their interests. During the 1990s, the problem of a weak electoral Right was temporarily resolved by Menemism, which linked the PJ's mass base to a market-oriented government. However, in the wake of the 2001–2 crisis, conservative sectors again grew estranged from the major parties. Moreover, none of the independent Center–Right candidates who emerged in anticipation of the 2003 election (most notably, Patricia Bullrich and Ricardo López Murphy) appeared likely to appeal to a broad electorate.

It is encouraging that, at least though mid-2002, much of the Right continued to invest seriously in electoral politics. One emerging right-of-center alternative was businessman Mauricio Macri, whose ties to Peronism and the Boca Junior soccer club could potentially provide him with a broader base of support. Other options included business-friendly Peronist governors such as De la Sota, Reutemann, and perhaps Juan Carlos Romero of Salta. However, as the February 2002 conversations between business and military leaders made clear, sectors of the Right could begin to explore other avenues if these alternatives falter.

Conclusion

Argentine democracy remained intact as this book went to press. This chapter has argued that regime stability was rooted in a relatively strong democratic foundation. During the 1990s, a broad democratic consensus, a vibrant media and civil society, and a stable and integrative party system enhanced democratic governance and helped democratic institutions survive a severe economic crisis and radical economic reform. But that foundation is now eroding. Given the depth of the crisis, the virtual absence of near-term economic solutions, the potential for mass mobilization, and the U.S. government's growing disinterest in democracy in the region, the potential for a democratic rupture is high. Regime stability may ultimately depend on the depth and duration of the crisis.

Here the role of international actors may be decisive. Had the U.S. government and the IMF responded to the December 2001 crisis with a strategy aimed at avoiding a financial collapse and shoring up democratic institutions, a political and economic meltdown might have been avoided and Argentine history might have taken a different path. Six months later, after an unprecedented economic collapse and amidst a full-scale rebellion against the political elite, external assistance is more critical than ever.

For the United States and the IMF, this may mean having to choose, in the short term, between democracy and economic orthodoxy. The international community could respond to the Argentine crisis in one of three ways: (1) it could support democracy by acting to shore up the elected government, even if that means a bailout and toleration for short-term heterodox policies; (2) it could promote orthodox economic policies at the cost of democracy by tolerating a coup that facilitates the implementation of such policies; or (3) it could continue the strategy that the United States and the IMF followed through mid-2002, which is to act as if there is no choice to be made. The rationale behind this third strategy is that the refusal to bail out Argentina is a response to the country's *economic* sins, and that it had nothing to do with democracy. However, in punishing Argentina for its economic sins, the international community may be allowing the country's democratic institutions to erode to the point of collapse.

Such an outcome would be tragic. Strong democratic institutions take years—even decades—to build. During the 1980s and 1990s, Argentina's democratic institutions weathered a series of extraordinary political and economic crises, and in the process, strengthened considerably. If democracy were to succumb to the latest storm, two decades of institution-building would be wiped out, raising the specter of a violence that once seemed confined to Argentina's darkest past.

12

Brazil

An Assessment of the Cardoso Administration

Bolívar Lamounier

Early in his first term President Fernando Henrique Cardoso told an Italian newspaper that "Brazil [is] an easy country to govern." At first glance, one is tempted to think he was right. Setbacks there certainly were, but the achievements of the Cardoso administration are quite impressive. First and foremost, the Brazilian government managed to keep inflation under control (in itself a major feat, given Brazil's long record of currency instability), despite the three severe blows that originated in Mexico in 1994, in Asia in 1997, and in Russia in 1998. Despite some initial confusion due to the precipitous devaluation of January 1999, the country successfully moved from its traditionally rigid to a floating exchange rate system. Reform of the banking system—including privatization of banks owned by the member-states and opening up the market for foreign banks—was another important achievement of the Cardoso administration, one that partly explains why Brazil was quickly able to overcome the devaluation crisis of 1999. In fact, progress in privatization includes sectors such as telecoms and the mining giant, Companhia Vale do Rio Doce (CVRD), once regarded as nearly sacred public monopolies. Fiscal performance also improved markedly in terms of both government attitude and legal framework, the latter including the adoption in 1998 of an ambitious Fiscal Responsibility Law. Substantial progress was also made in social policy, notably in land reform and in the quality of government spending in education. In order to achieve his policy goals, Cardoso managed to get the country's notoriously cumbersome legislature to approve a remarkable number of bills and constitutional amendments.

But clearly, Cardoso's record and his remark about how easy it is to govern Brazil are rather like that glass that may be half-empty or half-full, depending on how we look at it. Economic growth rates for the six-year period considered above were quite modest in view of the country's needs, reflecting persistent constraints due to inadequate infrastructure, fiscal imbalances (notably in the financing of social security), and external vulnerabilities (with mediocre export performance, despite the substantial devaluation of early 1999). Rather than promoting tax reform, the administration chose to increase tax collection on the basis of the existing flawed taxation framework and specifically on "cascading" taxes that seriously hinder the economy's efficiency and external competitiveness. Last but not least, the administration took a lot of blame for the energy crisis of 2001, interpreted by most Brazilians as a result of under-investment combined with poor short-term management.

On a broader historical canvas, not limited to Cardoso's presidency, the fact is that from 1986 to 1993 Brazilians witnessed the dramatic failure of five successive attempts to stabilize their economy, chronic super-inflation aggravating the country's steep social inequalities, the impeachment of the first elected president in twenty-nine years, numerous corruption scandals and serious clashes between the branches and levels of government. This alternative picture suggests that Brazil is anything but "easy to govern." More than anything else, Cardoso's success may reflect the high caliber of his personal leadership and the inevitability of much of his reform agenda; indeed, plausible as that evaluation may have sounded at the beginning, Cardoso would later publicly admit that that was not a felicitous statement.

Cardoso's administration may well turn out to be seen as one of the most effective in Brazilian history, but the extent to which it will leave irreversible improvements in Brazil's governance patterns is a moot point. The performance of individual presidents will of course vary over time, but the quality and effectiveness of the Brazilian political system as such remain open to question. The key point seems to be that it is a system structurally geared toward dispersing and diluting political power, constantly eroding the strength and cohesion of any majority. Not by chance, this description strongly evokes Arend Lijphart's consensus model of democracy, which he opposes to the majoritarian or Westminster one.[1] In his study of thirty-six countries, Lijphart claims that Westminster democracies do not perform better than consensus democracies in terms of macroeconomic management.[2] Important as his study is, the policy process under the majoritarian model tends to be more effective and intelligible to the common citizen than under the consensus model. This is because the need to include and obtain the consent of many actors and veto players to make relevant decisions is more manageable under the majoritarian system. The consensus model, Lijphart argues, is more adequate for some types of societies:

In the most deeply divided societies, like Northern Ireland, majority rule spells majority dictatorship and civil strife rather than democracy. What such societies need is a democratic regime that emphasizes consensus instead of opposition, that includes rather than excludes, and that tries to maximize the size of the ruling majority instead of being satisfied with a bare majority. . . . The consensus model is obviously appropriate for less divided but still heterogeneous countries, and it is a reasonable alternative to the Westminster model even in fairly homogeneous countries.[3]

Is Brazil a "deeply divided" society in this sense—and hence one in need of a consensus democracy?[4] Let us first look at the cleavages structuring political conflict in the country. Political conflict in Brazil is clearly unidimensional, centered on the distribution of wealth and income among social classes and regions, the latter pitting the richer regions of the South and Southeast against the poorer of the North, Northeast, and Center-West. There are marked differentials by race in a variety of social indicators associated with upward social mobility, but few analysts would include race among the main determinants of political behavior and open political conflict. Social inequality is obviously steep, but ethnic and religious (not to speak of linguistic and cultural) cleavages are mild in comparison with other large countries. It is a heterogeneous society, but one with a much simpler cleavage structure than India, South Africa or Indonesia, or even the United States, to name but a few of the world's big countries. In short, it is not a divided society in the sense emphasized by Lijphart. I would wholeheartedly grant that Brazil's heterogeneity justifies some measure of "consensus" democracy, but not the extremely "consociational" (to use Lijphart's original terminology)[5] character of the country's existing political arrangements. In this sense, President Cardoso got it right by saying it wrong. What he probably meant to say was that, given its comparatively simpler cleavage structure, Brazil should be easier to govern than it has been during the whole of the twentieth century.

This chapter begins with an evaluation of Brazil's political system—a combination of presidentialism and consociationalism, which ultimately hinders democratic governance. A highly fragmented political party system with loose party discipline, as well as a cumbersome judiciary and an extremely federative structure, further complicate governability. The chapter analyzes the implications of "provisional measures" for democratic governance—a policy instrument utilized by the Brazilian executive to bypass the legislature. The second part of the chapter explores the effects of plebiscitarian democratic regimes on Brazil's political system, with a special emphasis on Cardoso's ability to improve the presidentialist/consociationalist system through a broad-based legislative coalition. In particular, it delineates Cardoso's strategies for navigating Brazil's multiple economic and political challenges, showing how Cardoso's patient and skillful political management style (as well as changes in the global political and economic context) helped to facilitate effective policymaking. Finally, the chapter analyzes the development of Brazil's political system during the Cardoso presidency and the challenges that lie ahead for future administrations.

Brazil's Political Structure: Much Ado About Little

Consociationalism cum Presidentialism

The dispersion of political power in Brazil is generated by the combination of multipartyism, coalition governments, strong bicameralism, robust federalism, judicial review, and an extensive and detailed constitution protected by supermajority amendment rules. It would take us far afield to inquire into why the 1987–88 Constitutional Assembly chose to greatly reinforce the consociational character of the political system—but the fact is that it did. When the constitution-makers set about to reorganize the country's political institutions after twenty-one years of military rule, they came close to turning the country into a full-fledged consensus democracy. But perhaps aware that they were going too far, they chose at the same time to keep a key anti-consociational feature: the pure presidential system of government established in the early days of the Republic, at the end of the nineteenth century. I have elsewhere argued that this combination of consensus institutions with presidentialism is at the root of Brazil's institutional difficulties.[6] In the case of Brazil, as in much of Latin America, presidentialism *cum* consociationalism further weakens already fragile institutions because, as soon as presidents begin to face the complexities of faltering party and legislative support, they tend to bypass the legislature and appeal directly to "the people." Populism, or plebiscitarianism, as I prefer to call it, is a constant temptation in systems characterized by a low level of institutional consolidation and where the executive must somehow overcome the hurdles posed by consociationalism. To this structural feature some historians often add the "Iberian authoritarian legacy,"[7] an argument which I prefer not to take up here. My point is simply that, in the institutional context just described, the executive seeks to outflank the legislative and the judicial branches (notably by abusing the prerogative of issuing decree-laws), while these and the whole myriad of "consociational" institutional agents react, attempting to rein in the executive using the give-and-take of legislative and party politics, pork-barrel, and power-sharing, or else by attempting altogether to undermine and delegitimize presidential power.

Plebiscitarianism is obviously not a Latin American invention. Even in the United States and Europe presidents and party leaders occasionally resort to plebiscitarian appeals. But in Brazil and in Latin America, the formal institutions of government, the party system, and the civil society organizations that together should temper and countervail such appeals are far weaker. Conflicts thus tend to occur more frequently and to be sharper and more dangerous. Under such conditions, presidentialism *cum* consociationalism does not seem conducive to democratic stability and effectiveness.

Political Parties and the Party System

Political parties played a key role in Brazil's transition to democracy by mobilizing popular opposition to the military regime (1964–85). This task, however, was facilitated by the structure of the party system imposed by the military in 1965, which allowed the existence of only two parties, one to support and the other to oppose the government. In 1979 an electoral reform enacted by the government of General João Figueiredo, the last military president, and designed to divide the opposition, made room for the emergence of new parties. Table 12.1 shows that five parties obtained lower chamber seats after the 1982 elections. Yet communist parties were still legally banned. With the formal return to civilian rule in 1985, all restrictions to the formation of parties were lifted. This resulted in the proliferation of many new parties, which contested the 1986 election for Congress, which would become a Constitutional Congress in 1987–88. Seven new parties entered the Brazilian Congress, although six of them held one percent or less of lower chamber seats, and the largest party, the Brazilian Democratic Movement Party (PMDB), commanded a majority of seats (53.4 percent).

At this juncture, Brazil's party system seemed more manageable. However, during the workings of the Constitutional Congress, the PMDB would prove to be a fissiparous party, and would suffer a major breakaway (today's Brazilian Social Democracy Party [PSDB]) in 1988. The decline of the PMDB, the standard-bearer of the opposition to the military, coupled with the defeat of all major parties by the outsider Fernando Collor de Mello in the 1989 presidential race, constituted a turning point in the evolution of Brazil's post-authoritarian party system, which became highly fragmented and volatile. As shown in Table 12.1, twenty-one parties entered the Congress after the 1990 elections, eighteen of them obtaining legislative seats in the 1994 and 1998 general elections, thus greatly increasing the dispersion of legislative power.

The nominal number of parties, however, is not the best indicator of legislative fragmentation because it overstates the weight of tiny labels. The best measure available of legislative fragmentation is Marku Laakso and Rein Taagepera's effective number of parties (N).[8] By squaring parties' seat shares, N assigns more weight to larger parties, thus providing a politically more valid indicator than a simple count. Amorim Neto calculated N for

Table 12.1. Seat Shares per Party in the Chamber of Deputies After Five Elections, 1983–1999 (in percents)

Party	1983	1987	1991	1995	1999
PDS/PPR/PPB	49.1	6.8	8.3	10.1	11.7
PMDB	41.8	53.4	21.5	20.9	16
PDT	4.8	4.9	9.1	6.6	4.9
PTB	2.7	3.5	6.8	6	6
PT	1.7	3.3	7	9.6	11.3
PFL		24.2	16.5	17.3	20.7
PDC		1	4.4		
PSB		0.2	2.2	2.9	3.7
PC do B		0.6	1	1.9	1.4
PCB/PPS		0.6	0.6	0.4	0.6
PL		1.2	3	2.5	2.3
PSC		0.2	1	0.6	0.4
PSDB			7.4	12.1	19.3
PRN			8.2	0.2	
PMN			0.2	0.8	0.4
PRP			0.2	0.2	
PTR			1		
PSD			0.2	0.6	0.6
PRS			0.8		
PRT			0.2		
PST			0.4		0.2
PP*				7	
PRONA					0.2
PV				0.2	0.2
PSL					0.2
Total (= 100%)	479	487	503	513	513

Source: Jairo Marconi Nicolau, *Multipartidarismo e Democracia* (Rio de Janeiro: Fundação Getúlio Vargas, 1996), 78; and Brazil—Tribunal Superior Eleitoral, available at www.tse.gov.br.
*The PP merged with the PPR to form the PPB.

every year from 1985 to 1999.[9] The reason for this year-by-year count is that party switching (*troca-troca*, in Brazilian political parlance) has become rampant in Brazil, particularly from 1985 on.[10] Brazilian deputies change parties either to go to older labels or to form new ones. By doing so, they alter the party membership of the Congress many times within a single legislature. (Table 12.2 below provides the values of N for Brazil in 1985–99.)

The 1988–90 period marks the transition from a moderately fragmented party system to a highly fragmented one. In 1992 Brazil was certainly one of the most fragmented democracies in the world. From this year on fragmentation declined a bit, but Brazil's party system remained highly fragmented throughout the 1990s.[11]

Table 12.2. Effective Number of Legislative Parties, 1985–1999

1985	1986	1987*	1988	1989	1990	1991*	1992	1993	1994	1995*	1996	1997	1998	1999*
3.2	3.3	2.8	4.1	5.5	7.1	8.7	9.4	8.5	8.2	8.1	7.1	6.9	6.8	7.1

Source: Adapted from Octavio Amorim Neto, "Gabinetes Presidenciais, Ciclos Eleitorais e Disciplina Legislativa no Brasil," *Dados* 43, no. 3 (2000): 491.
*First year of a new legislature elected in the last quarter of the previous year.

In addition to legislative fragmentation, Brazil's largest parties (PSDB, PMDB, Liberal Front Party [PFL], Brazilian Progressive Party [PPB], and Brazilian Labor Party [PTB]), especially those making up Cardoso's governing alliance, are loosely disciplined in contrast with the left-wing opposition, which is fairly disciplined. Although some authors contend that Brazil's larger governing parties are actually disciplined and that their behavior is predictable rather than chaotic,[12] the fact that there is within them approximately a 10 to 15 percent minority consistently voting against the majority on key roll call votes further aggravates the problems inherent in high legislative fragmentation. This is particularly true if we consider that in Brazil harnessing legislative majorities requires complex coalition arrangements. A significant defection in any of the largest parties creates a high risk of defeat for an executive-initiated bill. On December 2, 1998, for example, an executive-initiated proposal (indeed, a decree-law!) on social security reform was unexpectedly voted down, producing a major scare among investors and accelerating the exchange rate crisis. Supported by large but loosely disciplined parties, presidents have no alternative but to assemble fiscally costly, oversized multiparty coalitions.

Legislative fragmentation *cum* loose party discipline also creates serious problems for the electorate. The Brazilian voter is clearly faced with too many options, due to the fact that there are too many parties and not even the larger ones behave consistently, whether in the electoral or in the legislative arena. By raising voters' information costs, legislative fragmentation *cum* loose party discipline also blurs the accountability lines between voters and Congress. The high and increasing number of blank and null votes cast in congressional elections in the transition period from a moderately fragmented party system to a highly fragmented one may well have been due to such faulty accountability lines. In the 1986 elections 28.6 percent of the votes for congressional seats were either blank or null. In 1990 those figures jumped to 43.7 percent, and stayed close to that level in 1994 (41.2 percent). Interestingly, in the 1998 race the percent of blank and null votes went down to 20 percent. However, turnout rates have consistently been declining since 1986. In this election year 95 percent of registered voters went to the polls.

In 1990 this figure was 85.8 percent, going down to 82.3 percent in 1994 and to its lowest point in 1998, 78.5 percent.

A Cumbersome Judiciary

The difficulties stemming from Brazil's consociational model are compounded by some specific features of the country's federation and judiciary. By Third World standards, the Brazilian judiciary and federation are both deeply rooted and important institutions. Developments since the 1988 constitution have on the whole been quite positive for democracy, with the justice system becoming more independent and the federation more decentralized. Combined with the sharply consociational nature of the political system, both can and do, however, give rise to additional problems, as we shall now briefly indicate.

At the federal level, Brazilian courts are generally respected for their independence vis-à-vis the executive and legislative branches of government; but the whole system and especially the state courts have been sharply scrutinized in recent years in view of their many organizational flaws, including corruption and nepotism. These problems are partly explained by the fact that the supply of material and human resources, particularly new judges, has not kept pace with demands created by the 1988 constitution, which greatly broadened access to the justice system. Broadened access, as Sadek points out, does not necessarily mean democratic access, but rather the multiplication of points of pressure for a few, still leaving out many who never take their grievances to court.[13] But the most significant part of the problem seems to derive from some basic institutional features. Castelar Pinheiro claims that judicial malfunctioning—especially slowness and unpredictability (high probability of different outcomes in similar cases)—significantly affects economic performance, raising transaction costs and discouraging investment.[14] The freedom that individual judges, even those at the lowest level, have to reach very different decisions on similar cases and the power granted to them to paralyze government policies have encouraged society to seek in the judiciary the solution to its social and political conflicts. This has led to the twin evils referred to in public debate as the "judicialization of politics" and the "politicization of the judiciary," which overload the courts and compromise their ability to remain impartial. The demands on the judiciary have also increased as a result of market-oriented reforms, which brought complex new issues to the courts. In this environment, the important increase in public resources allocated to the judiciary has not been sufficient to allow the adequate management of the numerous cases that are initiated each year.[15]

Perhaps even more important in an institutional perspective, as pointed out by Rogério Arantes, and Arantes and Fábio Kerche Nunes,[16] the Brazilian judicial review mechanism is a complex hybrid, combining features of both the U.S. and the European systems. It is neither a pure diffuse system, as the American one, in which the (un)constitutionality of laws can be declared by any judge or lower court anywhere in the country, nor a centralized system, as the European one, in which unconstitutionality can only be declared by constitutional courts, at the top of a judicial hierarchy. "In fact," Arantes and Kerche Nunes write, "the 1987–88 Constituent found itself faced with a dilemma: on the one hand, as an important part in the liberalization process, it was necessary to restore the judiciary's independence and autonomy. In this sense, reaffirming the diffuse principle—allowing every judge to exercise judicial review—was one of the most important points. On the other hand, the experience had demonstrated that the increasing centralization of the judicial review in a special body, although associated with authoritarianism, was more conducive to efficiency and stability of the political system."[17] The consequence, they go on to say, is that today the Brazilian system is not diffuse, as the Supreme Federal Court (SFC) can directly declare unconstitutionality with *erga omnes* (against all) effect; from this point of view, the SFC is a quasi-constitutional court. On the other hand, the system is not centralized, because the SFC does not hold a monopoly: it shares the prerogative of declaring (un)constitutionality with lower courts and judges throughout the country. From this perspective, when the SFC receives appeals from the lower courts regarding constitutional issues, it will manifest itself only as the judiciary's highest body: contrary to the U.S. case, its decisions are not binding on the lower courts. This hybrid judicial review system is extremely permeable to demands and non-uniform in its responses. Moreover, the scope of judicial review is such that the courts are inevitably brought into the political arena. The judiciary can control the constitutionality not only of ordinary and organic laws passed by the legislatures and of extraordinary measures enacted by the executive through *provisional measures* (i.e., decree-laws), but even of *constitutional* amendments, given its power to question any of these with regard to substantive merit or to the deliberation method through which they come into being.

An Unbalanced Federation

The federative nature of the Brazilian republic also contributes decisively to the complexity of the country's political system. In the late nineteenth century, the highly centralized monarchy inherited from Portuguese colonization gradually gave way to an unstable federation in which state governors often challenged presidential authority. The federative ideal as such was seldom questioned, but the extent and form of decentralization were matters of contention until recently. Authoritarian arguments demanding concentration of power at the federal level remained strong until the transition from military to civilian rule in 1985, and at least one governor (Itamar Franco, of Minas Gerais) gestured defiantly against the president as late as 1999, when he defaulted on his state's foreign debts, adding momentum to the exchange crisis that took place early that year.

Federal arrangements are inherently consociational, and a strong case can of course be made for them in a country of continental size. But at least two features deserve particular attention with regard to the Brazilian case. One is that the 1988 constitution reacted against the centralization carried out by the military dictatorship in a radically decentralizing way. In addition to transferring a substantial part of tax revenues to the lower levels, it gave full political and administrative autonomy to the municipalities, not only to the states, thus turning Brazil into a full-fledged, three-layer federation. From the political and electoral point of view, then, Brazil is a composite of one national, twenty-seven state, and some 5,500 local constituencies. Healthy as this arrangement may be in abstract democratic terms, the sad truth is that some states and about half of the local governments lack revenues to sustain themselves adequately. One consequence of this discrepancy between local political autonomy and actual financial dependency is of course that the quality of local democracy is often not as high as one would desire.

While it is undeniable that federal arrangements are inherently consociational, in some federations the consociational argument is further invoked to justify the under-representation of electoral majorities, through the over-representation of the less populated states. In Brazil this has long been a matter of contention, especially in view of the sharp under-representation of the largest state, São Paulo, and the over-representation of the sparsely populated states of the Center-West and North-West regions. Alfred Stepan refers to this feature somewhat awkwardly as "demos-constraining," but provides important comparative evidence of the extent to which this majority-constraining effect takes place in the Brazilian federation:

> Brazil is the most *demos*-constraining federation in the world. . . . In Brazil, the overrepresentation is even more extreme [than in the United States]. One vote cast for senator in Roraima has 144 times as much weight as a vote for senator in São Paulo. Moreover, Brazil and Argentina are the only democratic federations in the world that replicate a version of this overrepresentation in the lower house. With perfect proportional representation, São Paulo should have 114 seats. It actually has 70. With perfect representation, Roraima should have one seat. It actually has eight. The Brazilian Constitution, inspired by the ideology of territorial representation, specifies that no state can have more than 70 seats in the lower house (thereby partially disenfranchising São Paulo) and that no state can have fewer than eight.[18]

Provisional Measures: A Doubtful Democratic Instrument

In a nutshell, Brazil has a political system geared more to blocking than to making decisions. Healthy as this may sound in terms of abstract democratic theories concerned with the limits of government, the cost in terms of democratic effectiveness is undoubtedly high. Insofar as executive-legislative relations are concerned, the chief means by which the near-impasse embedded in the country's institutional structure has been managed is the sweeping presidential prerogative of issuing "provisional measures"—a rose that smells very much like the old "decree-laws" of the military regime. Once adopted by the 1987–88 Constitutional Congress, this legislative instrument quickly became an overwhelming source of power to which the executive resorts in order to overcome the obstacles posed by the country's weak and fractionalized party and legislative systems. It is important to remember that, from 1988 on, every conceivable obstacle to economic stabilization and reform became entrenched in the new constitution, which could only be amended with the approval of 60 percent of the total membership of each house of Congress, twice and separately. Considering that the largest parties hardly get 20 percent of the seats each, this means that during this period the executive was at the mercy of Congress in the numerous matters that demanded constitutional change. Operating in the opposite direction, the prerogative of legislating by very broadly defined emergency decrees (the above-mentioned "provisional measures") place the executive in a paramount position with regard to ordinary legislation. Viewed from this angle, it is not far-fetched to say that the pattern of executive-legislative relations in Brazil is one in which Congress is hostage to the executive in matters subject to ordinary legislation (i.e., decree-law regulation), while the president is hostage to the Congress in matters demanding constitutional reform. Since both are quite elastic realms, due to sweeping decree-law prerogatives given to the president and the detailed nature of the constitution, this perverse mutual dependence is clearly a matter for serious concern.

Some authors contend that the issuance of decree-laws does not necessarily mean that the executive has usurped congressional powers,[19] but the fact remains that the civilian presidents since the late 1980s have resorted all too often to this arguable form of legislative initiative. As established by the 1988 constitution, "provisional measures" (MPs) go immediately into effect with force of law, and can be issued to regulate an enormous variety of subjects—as long as they fulfill the conditions of being "urgent and relevant" matters. Here, of course, is where the difficulty lies. From 1988 up to now, presidents have overstepped these loosely defined bounds of constitutional authority, legislating by decree in areas that seemed neither appropriate nor urgent enough for this kind of legislative decision making. From fishery in the Amazon River to sweeping economic measures (the "Real Plan" of 1994 itself being a case in point), an impressive spectrum of policy-making has been dealt with by means of decree-laws. But this is not all. Already in early 1989, a Supreme Court ruling allowed the executive to reissue MPs not voted upon in due time by Congress. Presidents swiftly took advantage of this opportunity, to the point even of reissuing decree-laws with changes in the original content.

Table 12. 3 reports original decree-laws, decree-laws reissued with changes in the original text, and decree-laws reissued without changes. It is clear that the total number of decree-laws per year has increased sharply since the 1988 constitution was adopted. It was only in August 2001 that the Brazilian Congress finally passed a constitutional amendment tightening the criteria for the issuance of decree-laws.

Cardoso ranks first among post-1988 presidents in terms of the total number of decree-laws they signed. Of the 5,764 decree-laws issued in 1988–2000, he signed no less than 4,951, that is, 86 percent of the total. However, if we look only at original decree-laws issued per year, he no longer holds the first position. In 1989, 1990, 1993, and 1994, the incumbent president(s) issued more original decree-laws than in any year of Cardoso's six years in office. Yet, as regards the reissuance of decree-laws without changes in the text of the original decree, every year of Cardoso's first term constituted a new record.

Cardoso is also the winner in terms of decree-laws reissued with changes in the original text. Amorim Neto and Tafner argue that the high number of reissued decrees is not evidence of congressional passivity. As the Brazilian Congress lacks staff, information, and expertise to assess policy decision in a timely fashion, it lets the executive reissue decree-laws so it can have more time to ponder their effects on the different constituencies. In case the latter are eventually hurt by a decree, legislators press the executive to reissue it with changes so as to redress their constituencies´ demands. According to this view, decree politics involves a lot of inter-branch bargaining, not just unilateral decision making.[20]

It is also noteworthy that in the final two years of the aborted Collor presidency the issuance of decree-laws witnessed its lowest rates (1988 cannot be compared to the other years because only from October on President Sarney could start signing decree-laws): nine and seven original decree-laws in 1991 and 1992, respectively. This is evidence that without stable majority legislative support, no president can implement his or her policy agenda via decree for a long period of time. As Collor was never able or willing to form a legislative majority, his decree-based policymaking strategy was tolerated by Congress as long as the "honeymoon" phase of his presidency lasted. In the second year of his term Congress threatened to pass a law restricting resort to

Table 12.3. Decree-Laws (DLs) per Year, 1998–2000

Year	Incumbent President(s)	Original DLs	DLs Reissued with Changes	DLs Reissued without Changes	Total Number of Reissued DLs	TOTAL
1988*	Sarney	6	2	7	9	15
1989	Sarney	92	0	11	11	103
1990	Collor/Sarney	88	20	55	75	163
1991	Collor	9	0	2	2	11
1992	Collor/Franco	7	1	2	3	10
1993	Franco	57	1	48	49	106
1994	Franco	92	36	277	313	405
1995	Cardoso	29	90	318	408	437
1996	Cardoso	38	89	521	610	648
1997	Cardoso	35	142	543	685	720
1998	Cardoso	56	132	615	747	803
1999	Cardoso	45	108	973	1,081	1,126
2000**	Cardoso	25	114	1,078	1,192	1,217
Total		579	735	4,450	5,185	5,764

Source: Brazil—Senado Federal. *Levantamento e Reedições de Medidas Provisórias: Dados Atualizados em 28 de Fevereiro de 1999* (Brasília: Senado Federal–Subsecretaria de Informações and www.planalto.gov.br,1999).
*Presidents were constitutionally granted the right to issue decree-laws in October 1988. Thus, this row covers only the last three months of the year.
**Updated to December 17, 2000.

decree power, thus sending him a clear sign that it was no longer willing to be outflanked.[21] No wonder, in 1991 and 1992 Collor issued far fewer decrees.

The Cardoso presidency is the reverse image of Collor's. Cardoso has been able to keep using decrees throughout his two terms precisely because he counts on majority legislative support. Such support allows him to initiate policy safely by standard legislative procedures such as bills and constitutional amendments, all requiring congressional approval. This is why the number of original decree-laws he issued per year is lower than that of Presidents Sarney, Collor, and Franco, all three politically weaker than him. And the high number of decree-laws reissued by Cardoso, as mentioned above, should be seen as a mechanism chosen by the executive and the legislative majority to accommodate the former's need for timely policymaking and the latter's concern with the effects of decrees on their constituencies.

Even granting that resort to decree-laws does not ipso facto imply emasculation of Congress, as some authors claim, the over-abundance of MPs is a serious distortion in the democratic legislative process, which can only be understood and accepted as a means to bypass some deeper flaws in the Brazilian institutional structure. It would take us too far afield to assess how much instability the abuse of this legislative instrument has brought to

Brazil's legal order. The fact that legal codes regulating key aspects of social life can be changed overnight by executive fiat and *ex post* legislative consent is undoubtedly a threat to individual rights and the predictability required by the normal operation of a complex economy.

The Plebiscitarian Pseudo-Solution to a Flawed Institutional Structure

In the late 1980s and early 1990s, legislative fragmentation, loose party discipline, and steep inflation eroding popular support of the presidency had the effect of rendering the Brazilian political system unable to aggregate issues for negotiation and decision. Caught in the vicious circle of political disarray and monetary instability, Brazil seemed doomed to lag behind the rest of Latin America in the path to structural economic reform. During the 1980s and early 1990s, Brazil's nightmarish legislative fragmentation problem was compounded by two other factors: the resilience of the statist economic ideological legacy (much of which had been entrenched in the 1988 constitutional text) and weak presidential leadership under the last military and the initial three civilian presidents (João B. de Oliveira Figueiredo [1979–85], José Sarney [1985–90], Fernando Collor [1990–92], and Itamar Franco [1992–94]).

Contrary to what happened in Argentina or Chile, in Brazil the state-centered industrialization model continued to be perceived by many as successful until the early 1990s, causing the Brazilian business and technocratic elites to send Congress contradictory signals as to which route it should take. This is why the Constitutional Congress of 1987–88 paid little attention to the deep fiscal crisis underlying Brazil's chronic super-inflation and wrote much of the economic model inherited from the Vargas era (1930–54) into the new constitution. To make things worse, the executive leadership provided by the three first post-transition presidents was weak and not always wise with regard to economic stabilization. President Sarney, who unexpectedly ascended to the presidency when president-elect Tancredo Neves died before his inauguration in 1985, never fully understood the need to control inflation and promote comprehensive reforms in the public sector. Fernando Collor did understand that, but saw the popular support he initially enjoyed vanish as his stabilization plan quickly failed, and ended up impeached on charges of corruption in September 1992. Itamar Franco, the ill-tempered vice-president who took office after Collor's impeachment, zigzagged quite a bit in both policy orientation and cabinet appointments at the beginning, but was wise enough to recognize his own weakness in 1993, when he appointed Fernando Henrique Cardoso to a key ministerial position.

Collor epitomizes the difficulties inherent in Brazil's pattern of executive-legislative relations and the risks involved in the attempt to overcome them by means of direct plebiscitarian appeals to "the people."[22] Although he faced a highly fragmented Congress, and his party, the Party of National Reconstruction (PRN), commanded only about 5 percent of lower chamber seats, Collor thought he could govern without a coalition agreement with the largest parties, which would imply a measure of "parliamentarization" of the political process, so he could count on stable legislative support. His strategy was, on the one hand, to try to stabilize the currency by means of a major heterodox shock, blocking some 70 percent of the country's financial liquidity by decree-law, and, on the other, resorting to wildly theatrical appeals to the citizenry as a way of compensating his weakness in the legislative arena. Except for the final chapter—the congressional impeachment vote against him on grounds of corruption—the results of Collor's strategy were quite predictable: three months after his attempt to stabilize the economy by means of an heterodox shock, inflation was already making a robust comeback and support for him in public opinion began to plummet.

President Franco (1992–94) also began his caretaker administration trying to keep political parties at arms' length, but to a lesser extent than Collor. The problem was again popular dissatisfaction due to high inflation and the widely disseminated perception among the elites that he was ideologically and psychologically unprepared to take up the urgent tasks of stabilization and economic reform. After six months of populist gesturing, he had managed to fire three finance ministers and Brazil's economic prospects once again seemed somber. It was at this juncture, in May 1993, that Franco took the country by surprise, appointing his then foreign relations minister, Fernando Henrique Cardoso, as finance minister. This step was key in reducing the dangers inherent in Brazil's combination of extreme plebiscitarianism and extreme consociationalism: as an experienced senator, Cardoso fully understood that broad congressional support was essential to pass the legislation the country badly needed and to withstand the difficulties likely to arise when popular support falls sharply.

Cardoso's Rise to Center Stage

From the very beginning after Fernando Henrique Cardoso's appointment to the Finance Ministry, President Itamar Franco placed him in the role of a de facto prime minister, thus turning his administration into an informal parliamentary government. From this point on, executive-legislative relations improved markedly. Cardoso's ambitious objectives as finance minister were also helped by a corruption scandal involving the lower chamber budget committee, which further reduced whatever intent Congress might have harbored to resist the fiscal measures required prior to the launching of a new stabilization plan. Brazil's protracted vicious circle of economic and political disorganization—or what I have elsewhere dubbed as the country's "hyper-active paralysis syndrome"[23]—thus began to be broken from the economic end. On July 1, 1994, the Real Plan came fully into effect and monthly inflation rates came down from something like 50 percent to 3 percent. Within four weeks, Cardoso, as the presidential candidate of a large coalition, had overtaken the front-runner, Lula (of the Workers' Party), and emerged clearly as Franco's successor, winning the election already in the first round.

Despite the institutional shortcomings analyzed in previous sections, there can be little doubt that Cardoso will go on the record as one of the most effective presidents in Brazilian history. Triggered, as indicated above, by the "parliamentarist" twist that consciously or unconsciously President Itamar Franco gave to the Brazilian political system, this positive turn was extended in time by a conjunction of several favorable factors. Prominent among them was undoubtedly the end of the Cold War, which reduced ideological distances and the range of economic policy choices, thus helping Cardoso to put together an unprecedentedly large electoral and governing party coalition. Another significant factor was that Brazilian society, still plagued by high inflation after the failure of five successive heterodox stabilization plans, was ready to support a credible new effort. Fourth, this new effort was now embodied in a political leader endowed with substantial credibility, strong academic credentials, a known ability to form and work with first-rate technical teams, and of course significant political experience. Cardoso's affable personality and strong analytical skills surely go a long way toward explaining his conscious choice of an oversized legislative coalition model as an alternative to the country's ill-starred tradition of plebiscitarian executives in a minority position and at loggerheads with fragmented legislatures. In a nutshell, Brazil's crisis-prone blend of presidentialism *cum* consociationalism started to work better under Cardoso, from 1995 on. This was made possible, on the one hand, by the less polarized atmosphere brought about by the end of the Cold War and the new worldwide agenda, and, on the other, by the rise to the presidency of a skilled consensus-builder with a firm sense of priorities regarding inflation and economic reform.

Cumbersome and contradictory as it certainly was (is), Cardoso's large legislative coalition cannot be said to have been (be) "consociational," if by this term we understand a skew toward blocking rather than toward facilitating the task of legislative decision making. This was signaled from the beginning of Cardoso's first term (1995–98), as Deputy Luís Eduardo Magalhães, the speaker of the lower house, firmly led the government majority in an effort to pass a series of important constitutional amendments quickly.

An evidence of Cardoso's penchant for consensus-building is that, when appointing his inauguration cabinet, he drafted not only politicians from the parties that had joined his electoral coalition (PSDB, PFL, and PTB) but also from the PMDB, Brazil's largest party at that moment, which had endorsed the candidacy of São Paulo's former governor, Orestes Quércia, an adversary of Cardoso's in that state. This step was decisive in providing the new administration with the 3/5 majority required to enact constitutional reforms, which were at the top of Cardoso's legislative agenda. In April 1996 Cardoso would include politicians from the PPB, a medium-size rightist party, in his cabinet, thus adding one more bloc of seats to his legislative majority.

Brazil's combination of pure presidentialism with consociationalism was historically aggravated by short terms of office and a rigid ban on reelection for executive offices. In early 1997, the Congress lifted that ban, passing a constitutional amendment that allowed Cardoso to become the first Brazilian president to run for a consecutive term. In October 1998, having Lula again as his main opponent, Cardoso would again win in the first round, scoring 53.1 percent against Lula's 31.7 percent. In January 1999, Cardoso began his second term, backed by the same multiparty coalition that had supported him in the previous four years.

Backed by an oversized legislative coalition cemented by key cabinet and subcabinet appointments, Cardoso's relations with Congress throughout his first term were on the surface smooth. If an approval rate of executive-initiated bills is used to measure Cardoso's legislative performance, we come to the conclusion that he was very successful indeed. Moreover, a very high share of the bills enacted by the Brazilian Congress were sponsored by the executive. Pereira shows that of the 805 bills passed by the Congress between 1995 and 1997, 80.5 percent were sponsored by the executive.[24] But useful as aggregate measures of legislative performance may be, they do not tell the whole story of executive-legislative relations under Cardoso. Persistent fiscal pressure and an overvalued exchange rate (dubbed by some critics as exchange rate populism) were among the risks incurred by Cardoso as he strove to hold his multiparty coalition together. Another significant cost was the watering down or the sheer abandonment of important executive proposals, as well as a few devastating setbacks. Prominent among these was the defeat of three executive-sponsored proposals to reform the social security system, which seriously compromised the administration's efforts to place the country's fiscal accounts on a firmer long-term footing. As already mentioned, one of these votes in which the majority helped defeat an executive-sponsored bill took place in December 1998, severely affecting the country's credibility vis-à-vis foreign investors and mightily compounding the exchange rate crisis that led to the precipitous devaluation of January 1999.

Indeed, by the time of Cardoso's reelection (October 1998), Brazil already faced a mounting exchange rate crisis. In mid-January 1999, only two weeks after Cardoso's reinauguration, the government was forced to devalue the

Real to stem a massive outflow of resources. As one should expect, the devaluation severely undermined the president's popularity. Cardoso's reelection bid had been strongly staked on the promise to keep the *Real*'s domestic and foreign exchange value. The sudden collapse of the *Real* brought back a sense of frustration, distrust, and pessimism that Brazilians apparently thought they had exorcised forever. In the wake of the devaluation, key opinion leaders and economic pundits began to voice doomsday forecasts predicting that the Brazilian economy would dramatically recede, inflation would soar, and unemployment would skyrocket, therefore bringing about social unrest and political instability. But the devaluation's actual impact was much more moderate: the GDP growth rate in 1999 was low, but still slightly above zero; the inflation rate stood at 8.3 percent and unemployment at 7.6 percent (as compared to 8.4 percent in 1998!).

As pointed out, Cardoso's popularity did plummet in the wake of the exchange crisis, and particularly after the January 1999 devaluation, dropping again a few months later as a consequence of popular discontent with public utility and fuel price hikes. Without underestimating Cardoso's qualities as a political leader, it is worth noting that he was also quite lucky in 1998: if the Russian crisis of August had taken place a few months earlier, the exchange rate crisis and its negative impact on Cardoso's popularity might well have occurred before the October presidential election. But between January and March 1999, market confidence began to be restored as Congress swiftly approved an array of emergency measures demanded by Brazil's agreement with the IMF. Already by mid-March the exchange rate began to appreciate and the business climate started to improve. But as often happens in Brazilian party politics, something strange then began to take place. Instead of going along with improving economic prospects, the political picture quickly worsened. As soon as the situation of financial emergency that had prompted Congress to come to the aid of the executive was over, key party leaders engaged in a fierce struggle in the Senate, thus engendering an atmosphere of political crisis that proved quite detrimental to short-term economic recovery.

From March through September 1999, a great deal of prudence and tolerance was required from Cardoso and his ministers to prevent the development of a fairly artificial political crisis—artificial in the sense that it derived from gross miscalculation on the part of key party leaders, who apparently began to take it for granted that Cardoso would quickly become a lame duck, and also in the sense that those leaders' bleak prospects ran counter to the very plausible indications that Brazil would not take too long to recover from the devaluation.

To make sense of the negative political scenario that prevailed in Brazil in 1999, it should first be noted that the executive, for the first time since Cardoso's inauguration in 1995, had temporarily lost its tight grip on the country's political agenda. Constrained by the IMF agreement and with his political authority undermined by the loss of popularity, Cardoso was drawn into a defensive position vis-à-vis public opinion and Congress. Having given passage to the IMF emergency package, the legislature was left with an empty agenda. Also, new governors had just taken office, one of them Itamar Franco, the governor of Minas Gerais who defaulted on his state's foreign debts on January 4, 1999, speeding up the exchange rate crisis. It was in the wake of these events that several political leaders, some of them key figures of the governing alliance itself, badly miscalculated and started behaving as if Cardoso's second term had a high probability of collapsing. Worth recalling in this respect is that Senators Antonio Carlos Magalhães (the strong man of the PFL and then chair of the Senate) and Jader Barbalho (Senate leader of the PMDB) then started a fierce struggle for political space. This was typically a position-taking battle, each attempting to out-maneuver the other in search of media exposure; a banal episode, one might say, were it not for the fact that it prolonged the crisis atmosphere from which the country had begun to reemerge. Given the fact of Cardoso's loss of popularity, this position-taking struggle between the two senators was part and parcel of a movement to distance their respective parties from what they seem mistakenly to have perceived as an irreversible decline in presidential power. In their outbidding tactical maneuvers, Magalhães and Barbalho led their parties to establish investigative committees on corruption in the judiciary and on the financial system, respectively. Needless to say, the hearings captured public attention, and thus made it more difficult for the executive to keep Congress and the media focused on its priorities—social security and public administration reforms, both related to the administration's intent to improve the country's fiscal picture.

This pattern of unrestrained position-taking and competition among Cardoso's key coalition partners put the administration under increasing pressure, forcing Cardoso to display extra initiative and authority at a time when he lacked the means (notably public opinion support) to do so. This created the impression that the governing coalition would not support additional fiscal measures, and might even fall apart. This chain of events and misperceptions was among the reasons why the economic optimism emerging around March 1999 submerged again and did not reappear until mid-2000.

By early 2001, halfway down the road in his second term, Cardoso's popularity had begun slowly to recover from the very low point it reached after the January 1999 devaluation crisis. Not only this, he had undoubtedly recovered much of his strength vis-à-vis the political elite and the media; instead of a lame duck, he had again begun to be regarded as an important potential influence shaping the game of his own succession in the presidency. On the economic side, adoption of the floating exchange rate and effective management of monetary policy by the central bank were the initial stepping stones toward Brazil's comparatively quick recovery. On the political side, an important factor was Cardoso's patience and skill in diluting the then prevailing self-fulfilling prophecy of a mounting crisis. With hindsight, there can be no question that he adequately handled challenges from allies such as Senators Magalhães and Barbalho and from determined opponents such as former president Itamar Franco, now governor of Minas Gerais, as well as from a myriad of protest movements, notably the Landless Workers Movement (MST), inclined to see Cardoso as a precocious lame duck and his second term as an opportunity to stage major and ever more aggressive demonstrations.

Restocking the legislative agenda, empty after the more urgent part of the IMF package was approved in early 1999, was also an important step. Given the bargain and collective action problems faced by Brazil's fragmented Congress, vigorous presidential leadership is key to providing the country with a measure of effectiveness in policymaking. In April 1999, the executive sent Congress an ambitious Fiscal Responsibility Bill, which would be finally approved in 2000, and which thus became the framework for managing public finances at federal, state, and municipal levels of government. The budget proposal and a Pluriannual Investment Plan (PPA) were also shuttled to Congress in August, along with other matters relevant for fiscal adjustment, including a new proposal through which the administration succeeded in indirectly introducing a minimum age requirement into the social security system. With improved political coordination and a substantial legislative agenda, the executive was thus able, contrary to the doomsday forecasts of the previous year, to gradually sterilize a long series of disruptive initiatives and pass relevant fiscal policy measures. The energy shortage of 2001 again hurt Cardoso's popularity quite badly, but fortunately enough for him, not too late for him to recover and still play a relevant role in the nomination process toward the 2002 presidential race.

Conclusion

The shortcomings of Brazil's extreme consociational model and particularly of its pathetically weak party system have long been prompting calls for institutional reform. The key issue in institutional reform debates has been the perceived need to make Brazil's multiparty presidentialism more wieldy by reducing the number of parties, strengthening party discipline, creating more efficient mechanisms to coordinate executive-legislative relations, and establishing stronger accountability lines between voters and their representatives. Yet, despite widespread discontent with the functioning of political institutions, attempts at political reform have always failed. Even under Cardoso—who, together with his party, had previously advocated profound changes in the political system—political reform has stalled. The one important exception to this statement was the approval of the constitutional amendment allowing presidents to run for a consecutive term.

Paradoxical as it may sound, failure of political reform during the 1990s was caused by two remarkable success stories: the orderly impeachment of President Collor and Cardoso's record in economic stabilization and public-sector reform. Successful management of the Collor crisis led many to think that the country's political institutions were not that flawed after all, and Cardoso's rise to center stage added further "proof" that this new diagnosis should be right. As pointed out earlier, the launching of the Real Plan in 1994 began to break Brazil's long-drawn vicious circle of economic and political debilitation from the economic end. As the Cardoso administration draws to a close, there is also plenty of room for the hypothesis that, although political reform has not taken place, the functioning of the political system has been changed indirectly and in practice, as a consequence of economic and public-sector reform. Privatization of state banks and the recently approved Fiscal Responsibility Law are important illustrations of this new reasoning, as both have come to be regarded as severe blows to Brazil's deep-rooted practices of clientelism and corruption. According to this hypothesis, political reform *strictu sensu* has not taken place, but the conditions under which parties and politicians must act have changed. Not much has been done toward reforming formal political institutions, but a great deal has been accomplished that may become permanent and thus change their functioning over the medium term.

The apparently irreversible impact of Cardoso's reforms and the fact that he was able to launch them despite the manifest dysfunctionality of the political system will of course require much scholarly analysis in years to come. But the starting point of such analysis will undoubtedly be the new worldwide agenda, with the end of the Cold War, globalization, the narrower range of viable economic policy choices, widespread acceptance of market-oriented reforms, and, in the case of Latin America, the high priority given to inflation control by governments as well as citizens. Cardoso's caliber as a political leader is one side of the coin, but the other was the previous ripening of this mighty public agenda, which gave the unprecedented chance of launching a whole range of important initiatives in the legislative as well as in the executive arenas.

Whether and to what extent Cardoso's achievements will become permanent gains for the political system, making Brazilian democracy as such more effective over time, is a key but probably premature issue to raise. A word of

caution may be useful at this point. Globalization and free market economics may be here to stay, but hardly as a worldwide, wholehearted consensus.
Specifically with regard to the Brazilian case, support for stabilization and reform in the early 1990s, remarkable as it was, was perhaps more negative than
positive—an immediate mandate to end inflation and a stock of good will
would of course lose density and become contradictory as the whole range of
structural reforms and their differentiated impact on various social groups
unfolded. Powered by the clear understanding that chronic super-inflation
had just about disorganized the economy and brought the country to the
brink of serious social conflict, this "negative" consensus was more than
enough to catapult Cardoso to the presidency in 1994. The fact that he over-
took Lula a few weeks after the launching of the Real Plan and got the absolute majority of the vote already in the first round bear out this statement
beyond any reasonable doubt. The reverse side of the coin was the formidable agenda that Cardoso faced, including the need to pass a string of important constitutional amendments. This complex task worked in his favor, giving him the time and the staff he needed to outmaneuver the other relevant
political actors, including quite a few in his own congressional coalition.

As has been the case since he was appointed as a de facto prime minister
in 1993, Cardoso has been drawing on the strength of the administration's
reform program and on the inability of various branches of the left-wing
opposition to unite and offer viable alternatives. This fact was clearly illustrated in 1999 by the behavior of the Workers' Party (PT) in the episode involving the Supreme Court ruling against a bill requiring retired and inactive civil servants to pay social security contributions. The PT initially tried
to forbid state governors affiliated with the party from entering into political negotiations with the federal government in an effort to devise alternative legislative proposals. However, these same PT governors, directly in con-
tact with the fiscal realities of their respective states, chose not to abide by
the party's attempted veto. The national leadership of the PT was therefore
forced to beat a retreat.

But the agenda for the 2002 presidential race and the remainder of the
decade will of course be different in many ways. Currency stability, fiscal discipline, and public-sector modernization came to be highly valued in the
public's mind, but law and order on the Right and redistributive policies on
the Left will also loom large. The several important victories scored by the
left-wing opposition in the local elections of 2000, local and international
attempts to mobilize against globalization (vide the "anti-Davos" demonstrations staged in both Davos itself and Porto Alegre in early 2001), and
other relevant media events suggest that, like the *oeuvre au noir* of ancient
alchemy, the new agenda, no matter how diffuse, may well be something
new in the making. It is premature to say whether the presidential succes-

sion of 2002 will again be a bipolar race between two "natural" candidates as Cardoso and Lula were in 1994 and again in 1998—battles almost entirely focused on inflation and the newly gained satisfaction with stability. Without inflation as an overriding issue and hence a "great elector," the 2002 presidential succession looks more open and uncertain.

The issue now seems to be not so much the direction, but the scope and the pace of change. Assuming that Cardoso's economic reform program will stick and that the presidency will retain the strength gained under his leadership, it is quite plausible to argue that the party system will be simplified over the next decade or so—in practice, if not also in terms of nominal labels. As many of the parties currently represented in the Congress only voice personal ambitions or narrow regional or sectoral interests, they may sooner or later vanish as the bipolar competition between Cardoso's Center–Right coalition and the Left-to-Center one spearheaded by the PT takes hold of the electoral and governmental arenas. This trend is being reinforced by the concurrence of presidential and congressional elections since 1994, and should also be favored if the de facto single-member district pattern of electoral competition that already prevails in many regions becomes more widespread.[25] By this logic, Brazil's party system may formally continue to display a relatively high effective number of parties, but with a simpler pattern of actual functioning, based on a few parties, perhaps even a two-bloc competition roughly like that of Chile or France.

13

Chile

Unfinished Transition and

Increased Political Competition

Felipe Agüero

Since the resumption of democracy in 1990, Chile has been haunted by the specter of an unfinished political transition. The regime that emerged was hindered by lingering authoritarian enclaves that imposed constraints upon successor democratic administrations. Unable to find congressional majorities for reform, these administrations focused during the 1990s on the agendas of growth and modernization, and were gradually led to act as if authoritarian enclaves had been swept under the carpet. They decreed the end of the transition and disseminated this impression down to the rest of society. However, the obstinacy with which pressing issues of the transition regularly surfaced, especially in the areas of human rights and civil-military relations, made these issues an inescapable feature of the new Chilean democracy.

These issues pervaded the political process and impacted the calculations of all actors influencing the national agenda. They obdurately imposed themselves over the wishes of many high-level officials who would have preferred that attention fall exclusively on the dynamism of economic growth, the stability of institutions, or the challenges of state modernization. The new millennium, and the third Concertación[1] administration, had to begin with this still pending task of ending a transition that had started more than a decade earlier. It was not merely symbolic that President Ricardo Lagos concluded his first year in office in March 2001 simultaneously with the twentieth anniversary of the constitution passed under Pinochet's auspices and the tenth anniversary of its full implementation.

In hindsight, one may view the past political decade in Chile as movement channeled along separate and often uncoordinated tracks. On one track, the economy moved in a rather steady fashion, displaying high rates of growth that allowed for serious progress in the reduction of poverty levels. While policy disagreements surfaced in this track, it generally operated under consensus over the broader policy orientations, at least among government, business, and most of the political elites. Consensus over these broad orientations remained essentially unshaken even during the slowdown that started in 1999, induced by the Asian economic crisis.

On a second track, governance and sectoral public policy occasionally saw major achievements when political support could be garnered across the political divide. Decentralization, municipal policy, and judicial reform are good examples. Government policies took important steps in the fields of educational reform and state modernization. Other areas, such as tax and labor reform, took a longer and divisive debate to produce bare majorities, while health reform awaited the formation of minimal bases of congressional support. This second track lacked the level of consensus attained in the former, and was relatively much less steady.[2]

On a third track, political-institutional progress remained behind that of the other two, being immobile for most of the decade. However, actually dropped from the agenda for lack of consensus, it boomeranged in full force toward the end of the 1990s, placing again all the divisive issues—human rights and constitutional issues—before political elites and the country as a whole. It became apparent, at the outset of the new decade, that these elements could no longer be bypassed. The political-institutional track not only had some catching up to do; it also became the critical track around which significant progress in the other ones hinged.

This chapter argues that the persistence of an incomplete transition to a full-fledged democracy has coexisted with progress in the advancement of democratic governance in specific areas. Stress created from disagreement on pressing transition issues did not prevent the Concertación administrations of the 1990s from working with the opposition and obtaining legislative approval for critical reforms in several other areas. This progress was possible because of agreements attained in areas not directly connected to conflict around the authoritarian enclaves. Pressures mounting from the unresolved issues of the incomplete transition itself also helped to instigate this progress, as crises and tension at times energized the demand for reform.

This chapter also maintains that the continued inability to put an end to the transition, and especially to settle the constitutional differences, may harden the obstacles to progress in democratic governance and economic development. The divisive impact of these unresolved issues may hamper otherwise healthy debates on policy options and orientations toward the betterment of state and economic institutions.

The line of interpretation adopted here draws attention to the fact that authoritarianism and the manner of transition have ultimately had a greater impact upon the successor regime in Chile than in other cases in the region. Redemocratization in other Latin American cases could resume under the auspices of previous democratic constitutions, proceed via a new constitution, or produce a new democratic constitution not long after the inauguration of a post-authoritarian regime. Chile, in contrast, stands out in the stickiness of its authoritarian constitution. It would be inappropriate, therefore, to ignore those elements in the current Chilean political process that highlight the weight of the past and that prevent an imaginable earlier end to the transition.[3]

A decidedly new feature of Chilean politics at the turn of the decade was increased political competition. The undisputed majority support for the Concertación, which seemed a reasonable certainty until the very end of Frei's administration, turned into a fierce battle for each individual vote in the presidential election of December 1999. For the first time, the constitutional proviso of a second ballot had to be set in motion. The Concertación, in January 2000, emerged victorious once again, but now faced a significantly strengthened rightist opposition that was a few votes away from winning the presidency. Increased political competition may have a positive impact on solving end-of-transition issues, if it encourages the parties of the Right to advance more Center-leaning positions on human rights violations and constitutional reform.

This chapter will proceed as follows. The following section addresses the meaning of the transition's incompleteness and the impact of its discussion among relevant political actors. Then it addresses the development of seemingly contradictory tendencies that, on one hand, reaffirm a cleavage around this incompleteness (the authoritarian/democracy cleavage) and, on the other, lead to intensified centripetal competition. Trends in electoral competition, especially those leading to the close presidential elections of 1999–2000, are specifically discussed. In addressing these questions, the Pinochet case, changing roles of the judiciary, civil-military relations, and the impact of the Mesa de Diálogo (a roundtable that brought together officials from the military and the human rights lobby to set mechanisms for the pursuit of information on the disappeared), are given special emphasis. The final sections address progress and problems of democratic governance in specific areas, such as judicial reform, educational reform, and the mobilization of ethnic conflict. At the end of the chapter, comments on the challenges facing the Lagos administration inaugurated in March 2000 are provided.

The Incomplete Transition

At the turn of the decade, at least three implications emerged from the idea that the transition remains incomplete. The simplest one points to the constraints on the democratic process imposed by some key clauses in the inherited constitution. These clauses speak primarily to the institution of non-elected senators; the role and composition of the National Security Council; the selection of the Constitutional Court; and the electoral system.[4] The National Security Council has twice been the subject of reforms that have softened, albeit not eliminated, its restrictive features. An important constraint outside the constitution is the organic law of the armed forces, which forbids the president to dismiss the top commanders of the armed services. Under this meaning, the transition will be completed only when those laws and aspects of the constitution are reformed.

Another implication of the idea of an unfinished transition has to do with the pressing human rights problems. The most important of these problems is the continued silence about the fate of large numbers of the disappeared. In January 2001, the armed forces' chiefs, following a commitment before the Mesa de Diálogo (Dialogue Roundtable), gave the government all the information they could collect within their services about these cases. The eerie report, referred to the courts with guarantees for the anonymity of the sources of information, told of bodies dropped on mountains, in rivers, and in the ocean. But it came short of expectations as it only covered about 200 cases. Other pressing human rights problems demand the expansion of investigation of crimes beyond disappearances. Only by solving these problems can the transition be completed.

A third, more complex, meaning focuses on the idea of reconciliation, and involves the development of a shared interpretation of the events and circumstances that led to the 1973 coup. The convergence of self-critical views about the past behavior of different political actors would lead to demands for, and expressions of, pardon and apologies, as well as preventing those behaviors and crimes in the future. These views have been offered in different ways, but they have yet to be articulated by those primarily responsible for human rights violations.[5]

These three views about what is needed to finish the transition emerged mostly as a result of the climate created by Pinochet's arrest in London, which permitted the surfacing of previously suppressed divisive issues. Different sectors advocated one or another of these meanings.[6] The first two meanings were dominant within the Center–Left coalition—the Concertación. The coalition insisted on constitutional reforms, and most within it emphasized the pressing problems in the human rights area.

The discourse of an unfinished transition that emerged toward the end of the 1990s also permeated the coalition of Right parties in the opposition, which had previously refused to admit the incompleteness of political democratization. With the climate created following Pinochet's London affair, these parties reconsidered and began to realize that closure of the transition required a solution to the most egregious pressing human rights problem, the fate of the disappeared. This need emerged primarily to keep the armed forces buffered from the demands of relatives of the victims. However, parties in this coalition have been reluctant to consider constitutional reforms a necessary condition for finishing the transition, although minority liberal sectors within it had long advocated some of these reforms. The military, under pressure to placate demands from human rights groups, now more actively processed by the courts, adopted a similar stance. The Catholic Church, in turn, adopted all three implications, distinctively emphasizing reconciliation while maintaining a pragmatic orientation. Civil society groups, particularly human rights organizations, were keen on the first two implications.

This chapter will consider the question of the transition's incompleteness from two angles. The first one, at the level of discourse, views the unfinished transition as a specter that waxes and wanes, with different degrees of urgency, in the actors' discourse. This influences actors' outlook, behavior, and strategic assessments. The second one views the question in the light of the implications noted above, which highlight lingering elements of the transition that significantly affect the quality of democratization. The notion of an incomplete transition has instrumental uses, as it enhances or reduces the visibility of specific areas or tasks related to the quality of democracy. This dual manner of considering the question concedes the unfinished character of the transition while viewing the Chilean situation as one that has completed a transition to a stable, albeit of lesser quality, democracy. The pervasiveness of the notion of an incomplete transition in the actors' discourse in the past few years makes this incompleteness an unavoidable part of the study of democratic governance in Chile.

Ending and Restarting the Transition

Government officials wished, at the outset of the new democracy, to focus on forward-looking tasks and not be hindered by institutional traps of the past. The elimination of these traps via constitutional reform was sought and agreed upon with representatives of the Right that, mainly in Renovación Nacional (the National Renovation Party, one of the two parties on the Right), were more removed from the Pinochet legacy. This path, however, hit a dead end when these representatives were unable to deliver the votes in

Congress. Unwilling to live perennially under the self-imposed priority of finishing the transition, the Aylwin government (1990–94) decided to move on and declare the transition over.[7] The government wanted to promote broad policy initiatives and avoid paralysis from an intractable opposition to institutional reforms. It also wished to benefit from the vast area of consensus that it had helped develop around economic policy that kept substantial continuity with the policies of the previous regime. A seemingly all-embracing consensus in this area helped to push the constitutional divide to the wayside.[8] This consensus facilitated the view that the transition was over, and thus led the government to give in to the Right's discourse on the matter.

The administration's view on this issue had important consequences because it was regarded as *the* transition government, the one whose task was to carry the transition through to its end. The fact that a special constitutional reform had turned this first post-Pinochet administration into a four-year mandate, while the constitution contemplated eight-year presidential periods,[9] reaffirmed its transitional character and focus. If the government charged with ending the transition declared the mission accomplished, there was little to prevent this view from becoming dominant.

An important consequence was the emergence of a climate that discouraged divisive views and issues, which were perceived like skunks at a garden party.[10] Even the recalcitrant surfacing of confrontational episodes such as acts of military indiscipline were turned, as a result of their negotiated resolution, into occasions for reaffirming the appearance of consensus. The military's discontent with the way that government officials and members of Congress handled problems of corruption, human rights, or budgetary issues affecting the armed forces, especially the army, would lead to military demonstrations of sorts (i.e., the *boinazo*, the *ejercicio de enlace*).[11] These would force negotiations with government authorities. Agreements meant to appease the military would be used to reinforce the view of the Chilean transition as a pacted transition that had reached closure.[12]

Electoral dynamics further strengthened the dominant perception of a completed transition. The Concertación candidate for the 1993 presidential elections, Eduardo Frei Ruiz-Tagle, arranged his campaign around the catchphrase that while the outgoing administration had been a transition government, his would be the modernization government. Frei (1994–2000) was in fact not confronted with any of the demonstrations that a discontented military had staged against Aylwin's government. Minister of Defense Edmundo Pérez Yoma developed such relations with the military that General Pinochet declared him the best minister in the cabinet, and awarded him the highest army decoration. With no overt military contestation, with lessened visibility of human rights problems (Frei could afford to postpone meeting with representatives of the relatives of the disappeared until his final year in office), and with the economy maintaining high growth rates, the administration made no reference to pressing problems of the transition. The latter could effectively be perceived as over, even if constitutional reform remained pending after failed attempts in Congress by the administration itself.[13]

That perception began to crack with the surprising results of the December 11, 1997 congressional elections, which shook the heretofore overconfident Concertación.[14] The share of the vote for this coalition declined 5 points from the previous election to 51 percent. A bare majority was not what the coalition had been used to since the sound vote against Pinochet in the 1988 referendum (57 percent). More important, the major parties in the Right coalition, Renovación Nacional (National Renovation, RN) and the UDI obtained 36 percent of the vote, up 3 points from the 1993 congressional elections. Together with independents, with whom they formed the Unión por Chile (Union for Chile) coalition, the Right's total share went up to over 38 percent. Within the Right, the momentum was with UDI, the party closest to Pinochet and his legacy. RN, with whose leadership the Concertación sought support for constitutional reforms, began gradually to weaken. Making matters worse, the Right had a number of former Pinochet direct hard-line collaborators and even a former Junta member elected to Congress. And, against the hopes of government officials, General Pinochet decided to take up his seat in the Senate, as his 1980 constitution enabled him to (a privilege denied former President Aylwin for having served only a four-year period). Having designated his own successor in the top army post in October 1997, it was assumed that he would step down before entering the Senate. Instead, he chose to remain army chief until the very day he was sworn in in the Senate in March 1998. The electoral strengthening of the more hard Right and the prospects of a Pinochet role in the Right's political leadership made it difficult to simulate the kind of democratic normalcy that the "end of the transition" was supposed to grant.[15]

The elections brought to the surface another important expression of dissatisfaction: abstention reached 13.7 percent of registered voters, and 13.5 percent of ballots cast were voided, a significantly higher proportion than in previous elections. Over a million Chileans among the newly eligible voting-age population failed to respond to a vastly publicized preelection voter registration campaign. In all, about 3.7 million people, of a total of 9.6 million of voting age, chose not to express any preference. Among the explanations to account for these figures was the infelicitous incentive structure that the electoral legislation presented prospective voters: while registration is not mandatory, voting is. Another explanation pointed to the public's sense of a lack of alternatives. In this view, votes have little impact on policy, either because the electoral system tends to split district representation between the two leading blocs regardless of vote shares, or because the direction of social and economic policy is so determined that it is perceived as unchangeable. Finally, the government's technocratic orientation to problems, in the midst of heightened income inequality and increased social and sectoral protest mobilization, became a source of frustration for many of the supporters of Concertación. In fact, some of that support went to the pact led by the Communist Party, which received 7.5 percent of the vote, up 3 points from the previous elections, and the Humanist Party, which received a 3 percent share of the vote.[16]

The election results made it clear that the chances of constitutional reform had become even more elusive. The hope that the right-wing opposition would at some point consent to reform after several years of economic growth and consensual politics—the mound from which the transition was decreed over—began to fade quickly. The prospects of an electorally empowered and ideologically belligerent right-wing opposition revived the feeling that divisive postures on regime issues were still around and that critical elements of the transition would remain pressing for longer than initially anticipated.[17]

The Impact of Pinochet's Arrest

The final and definitive blow to the idea that the transition had ended was delivered by Pinochet's arrest in London on October 16, 1998.[18] The series of decisions and reversals by the courts in London until the final decision by the British Home Secretary to allow his return to Chile early in 2000 on the grounds that he was medically incapable of facing trial following extradition to Spain initiated an animated and veritable debate in Chilean political circles and civil society. This debate definitely ended, or significantly toned down, the promotion of a Pinochet image of a true statesman and contributor to a smooth transition, an image to which *The New Yorker* had contributed in an interview published—ironically—only a few days before his arrest.[19]

As the Chilean government reacted by denying jurisdiction to Spanish courts on the case and claiming diplomatic immunity for Pinochet, Chilean political society plunged into a cathartic debate. Human rights issues were widely voiced in international legal documents and in the British House of Lords, and they made a full reentry onto the Chilean scene with renewed legitimacy.[20] The skunk had managed to make its way into the garden party after all, albeit in the guise of a more respectable animal. Despite the vitriolic reaction of rightist nationalistic sectors, almost the entire political class began talking about the need to solve pressing human rights issues, particularly those relating to the disappeared, the need to try Pinochet at home, and the need to initiate a review of proposed reforms to the constitution.

The debate was back to the transition, and the suppression of divisive issues was now clearly out of place.[21]

The Pinochet case coincided with significant changes in the attitudes and behavior of the judiciary that led to a more active role in the investigation of human rights cases. These changes were the product of shifts in the composition of the courts, which in turn were the result of new legislation on this composition, new appointments of court members by the government, and the influence of public opinion. The courts began, only in 1998, to adopt the government's view on the application of the amnesty law: the existence of a crime had to be established before amnesty could be applied; that is, that the amnesty law did not prevent investigation.[22] And, perhaps more important, the highest court adopted the doctrine that the cases of disappearances, as long as there was no evidence of death, should be viewed as ongoing cases of kidnappings. These changes led to a more active stance involving interrogation and detention of high-ranking, mostly retired, military officers, and would allow later for the actual continuation of the case against Pinochet in Chile.[23]

The Pinochet case also affected, unexpectedly, the relationship of the military and the parties of the Right. These parties rallied around the defense of "Chilean sovereignty" over the Pinochet case, but at the same time began to distance themselves from his record and to accept the inevitability of a solution to the human rights issues.[24] All now spoke of the problems of an unfinished transition. The saga of Pinochet in London had started a mere fourteen months before the scheduled elections for president, and electoral motives influenced the Right to take a more moderate position and to gain distance from Pinochet's image, especially under the de facto leadership of its presidential candidate, UDI's Joaquín Lavín. This scenario, the one least desired by the military, deprived it of powerful allies.

A growing sense of isolation developed in the military, which had up until this point counted on three strong protective shields. The first was the strong position that the constitution gave it. Pinochet had remained as head of the army for eight years after the inaugural democratic elections of 1989, and, in justification, he had declared that he would stay on so that his men would not be touched. A second shield had been the judiciary, and the third was the weight of the parties of the Right. All these protective shields appeared to evaporate or weaken. Pinochet was in detention, the judiciary had changed its stance and actually began to prosecute cases involving high-ranking military officers, and the parties of the Right now focused principally on the presidential elections of 1999.

The military, then, while delivering a strong corporatist reaction in defense of its former chief, began to admit that gross violations of human rights had indeed occurred under the Pinochet regime, and gradually moved closer to accepting the need to face the human rights problems. The military was caught in this situation at the same time that it faced critical challenges for its institutional development and modernization plans, for which budgetary levels were perceived as vastly insufficient. All three services faced what they regarded as the need for urgent renovation of military hardware. In this context, seeking a way out of political isolation and initiating a move that would begin to solve problems that kept it from concentrating on its professional mission, the military accepted the proposal put forth by Defense Minister Edmundo Pérez Yoma to join the human rights lobby around the Mesa de Diálogo. The primary purpose was to find a solution to the problem of the disappeared.[25]

The Mesa de Diálogo was a bold initiative that simultaneously signaled the enhanced legitimacy of the human rights groups and the significant shift in the military's approach to the human rights problems. For the human rights groups, primarily consisting of lawyers who represented the relatives of the disappeared and who had been longtime activists, this meant the recovery of recognition and legitimacy, which had paradoxically weakened since the inauguration of democracy. For the military, this meant accepting responsibility for its part in the human rights problems and a commitment to meet with groups it had uninterruptedly derided for a long time. In doing so, the military ended up going much farther than the Right was willing to go, and accepting a degree of responsibility that civilian allies of the military government never have. The Mesa de Diálogo, since its first session in August 1999, began to confront pressing issues involved in the view of the transition's incompleteness: the disappeared, which required the most attention, human rights violations, and reconciliation. The very summoning of the Mesa de Diálogo gave formal recognition to the fact that the transition was not over.

Despite the impact of the evolution of the Pinochet case, the Mesa concluded its deliberations in June 2000 with a statement expressing the priority of finding the remains of the disappeared or, at least, of learning about their fate. It also called for society as a whole to assume responsibility in the solution of this problem, through its civil, political, and military institutions. Specifically, in the Mesa's final statement the armed forces took on a commitment to making every possible effort to obtain information about the remains or fate of the disappeared. Through proposed legislation subsequently passed by Congress that provided guarantees for informants, the armed forces committed themselves to turn in to the president information collected within six months of that legislation.[26]

In January 2001, the armed forces top commanders officially delivered this information. The episode was both remarkable and disappointing. It was remarkable because of the enormous change it signified in the position of the armed forces, which was in stark contrast to their overt rejection of the Rettig report issued in March 1991. Their willingness to collaborate in the solution of the problem was also noteworthy. The incident was at the same time disappointing, because information was provided on only about 200 of the nearly 1,000 pending cases, and it confirmed that most remains would actually never be found.[27]

Thus, closure on this issue had not been possible, and it continued to appear elusive and unlikely to be attained. While more information on the disappeared may emerge in the future, despite the apparent unwillingness of former members of the security forces to cooperate, demands for truth and justice in other areas of repression are likely to strengthen. The government rejected suggestions of a political agreement to force closure on the issue on grounds that they were unrealistic, and President Lagos maintained his stance about not interfering with judicial matters. In turn, the archbishop of Santiago, Francisco Javier Errázuriz, confirmed, shortly after his appointment as cardinal, his continuing respect for those demanding justice in court.[28] The view prevailed that there would be no foreseeable closure on these matters.[29]

However, both the work of the Mesa de Diálogo and the legal evolution of the Pinochet case provided some relief to those seeking some kind of satisfaction to their demands for justice. Since his return to Chile in March 2000, Pinochet nurtured a legal drama through carefully staged steps. A few days after his return, Judge Guzmán requested the withdrawal of his parliamentary immunity, which the Court of Appeals granted on June 5 by a vote of 13 to 9. On appeal, the Supreme Court ratified that decision on August 8 by 14 to 6 votes. Following medical examinations that failed to determine mental illness—the only criterion outlined in Chilean legislation that could exempt him from prosecution—Pinochet was interrogated by Judge Guzmán, who then decided to arrest him and charge him with the murders of fifty-seven individuals and eighteen kidnappings.[30] At the defense's request, the Court of Appeals and then the Supreme Court temporarily suspended Judge Guzmán's decision. The judge, however, finalized it on January 29, 2001, decreeing house arrest on one of his rural properties. Subsequently, Pinochet was freed on bail, awaited a decision on a date to be booked, was photographed and fingerprinted, which never materialized, and was granted, on medical grounds, a temporary suspension of proceedings against him.

Abortive Constitutional Reform

While visible progress had been made, it became clear that the open-ended character of the human rights problems would keep this area from playing any role in marking the end of the transition. Clearly, only constitutional reform held the capacity to herald this landmark event. What had happened in this area? Despite the absence of reform twenty years after the constitution's inauguration, and ten years since it became fully implemented, leaders of the Right began advancing views on constitutional reform. These views, many of which had been discussed in the Senate's constitution committee, were aired in a seminar on the constitution's anniversary. Possibilities of agreement existed on reforming key clauses, such as on the Constitutional Court, regarding its composition, manner of appointment, and powers; the National Security Council, regarding powers and composition; presidential powers of removal of the armed forces' chiefs, and the mission assigned the armed forces; the elimination of the non-elected senators, both the designated senators and the senators for life; redressing the imbalance in the executive-congressional powers; and other clauses.[31] However, no agreement developed on reforming the electoral system, with the Right strongly opposed to any changes. Concertación leaders would have liked to introduce some measure of proportionality to the current "binomial" system, which would return the power to effect representational changes to voters. In the current system, significant changes in the share of the vote do not, for the most part, alter the government-opposition split in representation in the two-member districts.[32]

The greater consensus on the need to reform had not led, and may not necessarily lead, to actual reform. While the opposition may consent to some of the reforms, the Concertación will want to include electoral reforms as part of the package. This difference in strategies of reform may in fact delay progress for a long time.[33] The conclusion of the December 2001 congressional elections led to no appreciable changes in the differences separating government and opposition on this subject. However, uncertainty surrounding the outcome of the next presidential elections, to be held in 2005, should encourage all sides of the political spectrum to operate, at least partially, as if covered by a "veil of ignorance." This situation may just be the condition to help rid the constitution of its biases and enclaves, and via these reforms, to finally put an end to the transition.

Presidential Elections and Increased Centripetal Competition

The first Concertación government, led by Patricio Aylwin, succeeded in attaining high levels of growth, reducing poverty levels, and advancing democratic stability. These achievements assured the coalition a second term. This second term started in 1994 with much higher levels of electoral support than had been obtained in the 1988 referendum on Pinochet and the subsequent elections. Enhanced electoral support for the Concertación owed much to the high prestige of candidate Eduardo Frei Ruiz-Tagle and to the disarray in the leadership of the opposition's presidential campaign.

Table 13.1. Presidential Election Results (in percents)

Candidate	1989	1993	First Round, 1999	Second Round, 2000
Concertación	55.2	58.0	48.0	51.3
(Aylwin, Frei, Lagos)				
Unión por Chile	29.4	24.4	47.5	48.7
(Büchi, Alessandri, Lavín)				
Unión de Centro-Centro	15.4	—	0.4	—
(Errázuriz, Frei, Bolívar)				
José Piñera	—	6.2	—	—
Total Right	44.8	30.6	47.9	48.7
Partido Comunista	—	4.7	3.2	—
(Pizarro and Marín)				
Partido Humanista	—	1.2	0.5	—
(Reitze and Hirsch)				
Manfred Max Neef	—	5.6	—	—
Sara Larraín		0.4		
Total Left	—	11.5	4.1	—
(Extra-Concertación)				

Source: Patricio Navia and Alfredo Joignant, "Las elecciones presidenciales de 1999," in *Nuevo Gobierno: Desafíos de la Reconciliación, Chile 1999–2000* (Santiago: Flacso-Chile, 2000). For the second round, 2000, www.elecciones.gov.cl.

The context of the 1999 presidential elections was quite different, and so were the results. (See Table 13.1.) The winner, Ricardo Lagos, came in only half a percent point ahead of runner-up Joaquín Lavín of the Unión por Chile (Right). This led to a runoff election between the two leading candidates in January 2000.[34]

Lavín's strong showing and his near victory over the Concertación candidate were major surprises. Although the strong lead that Lagos had clearly held until the primaries of his coalition in May 1999 had visibly eroded as election day approached, very few actually expected the virtual tie that the tallies finally yielded. Lavín improved the Right's share of the vote by 17 percent points relative to the previous presidential election, and by about 10 points relative to the 1997 congressional elections. Most important, he managed to surpass the mark set by supporters of Pinochet in the 1988 referendum (43 percent). Indeed, Lavín obtained the highest percent of the vote of any single presidential candidate of the Right since 1938.[35]

A complex set of circumstances combined to produce these extremely competitive electoral results.[36] First, there was the natural erosion of the government coalition after ten years in power. In the previous years, sectoral social conflict increased dramatically, leaving numerous groups (ethnic groups, student organizations, professional associations, labor unions) disaffected with a government policy that was constrained by the strict boundaries set by conservative fiscal policies and influenced by technocratic policymaking styles. Second, the electoral campaign coincided with a significant contraction of the economy as a result of the crisis in Asia, whose markets are critical for the export-oriented Chilean economy. This contraction led to the first recession in sixteen years, a phenomenon to which Chileans had grown vastly unaccustomed. GNP growth receded to −1.1 percent in 1999, after staying at very high rates the previous years (10.6 in 1995; 7.4 in 1996; 7.4 in 1997; 3.9 in 1998), and the rate of unemployment grew from 6.4 percent in 1998 to 9.8 percent in 1999.[37] Support figures for the government and the opposition candidate neatly evolved following the signals of the recession. Lastly, after Lagos won an impressive and vastly unexpected 70 percent in the coalition's primaries with a very large turnout, precious time was wasted in trying to forge a campaign team that included all coalition partners. Under the impression that his overwhelming lead in the polls would remain unchanged, his post-primaries campaign took too long to resume in full force. It was at this time that the recession began to reflect negatively in the opinion polls.

On the other side, Lavín ran a remarkably smart campaign. Early on, he organized a campaign team that relied on personal loyalists with backgrounds in efficient administration, instead of relying on leaders of his supporting parties—the Pinochet-prone UDI and RN. His campaign slogan advocated change and catered to the youth vote by utilizing appealing campaign symbols. Instead of focusing on large constitutional and other divisive policy issues, he centered on "solving the people's real problems." While Lagos felt overconfident with the results of the opinion polls following the May primaries, Lavín adopted a platform based on a "call for change" in policies, in style, in government officials that hit a cord with voters. Lagos could never soundly counter the effectiveness of the "for change" sound bite. Lavín adopted a populist campaign style—dressing up in the local manner everywhere he went, staying at supporters' modest homes rather than hotels, announcing that he would not incur waste by traveling as much as President Frei had, and so on. In contrast with the more technocratic style of government officials, and in the midst of economic recession, his style touched a soft spot among the Chilean electorate.

It was to the benefit of Lavín's campaign that this was the first election of the decade in which a single candidate represented the Right. In previous elections, independent Francisco Javier Errázuriz weakened Hernán Büchi's bid in 1990, just as José Piñera, a former minister of Pinochet, weakened Arturo Alessandri's in 1993. It also helped Lavín that his campaign outspent his opponent's by 15 to 1. The huge imbalance in resources was a new element in Chilean politics, as was the extent of personalization that he brought in.

Due to the enormous popularity that he had gained as mayor of one of the wealthy Santiago districts, Lavín managed to outshine his opponents.

Two factors greatly helped Lavín's strategists attain the goal of leaving the ideological baggage of the parties of the Right behind. First, this election was the first not to be held concurrently with elections for Congress. This allowed Lavín to personalize the campaign, without having to share the limelight with party leaders and candidates who would have curtailed Lavín's flexibility to move toward centrist stands. Second, Pinochet was removed from the campaign simply by being kept in detention far away in England. This allowed Lavín to detach himself from an otherwise sticky connection to Pinochet's legacy and influence, and freed him to focus on his preferred campaign issues. The insignificance of the Pinochet detention issue to the election was not even altered by Britain's Home Secretary Jack Straw's well-publicized decision to stop the extradition process only a few days before the vote, which sent the general back to Santiago. If the public had ceased paying attention to developments in London and Madrid, the Lavín campaign did nothing to remind voters of Pinochet, let alone of the candidate's associates' previous militant allegiance to him. Lavín's most remarkable achievement indeed was to rid the Right, at least during the campaign, of its connection with Pinochet and his regime. Pinochet's remoteness, the personalization of the campaign, and the Center-prone dynamics of the competition, all combined to present the semblance of a renewed Right ready to take charge of the government.

The Center-prone dynamics of the campaign led to a blurring of differences in the candidate's platforms. Lavín, for instance, campaigned for increased spending for pensioners, for student aid in higher education, and for educational and health policies. He described the debate about further shrinking the state sector as passé, and argued for reorganizing rather than reducing the state. He offered to help in solving pressing human rights issues, and hinted at favoring constitutional reforms. The Right could not have attained the strong showing in the polls without airing these more moderate views. The Center-prone dynamics were well depicted by the accusation of "Lavinization" which the Lavín camp threw at Lagos for shifting to a focus on "solving the people's real problems," and by the counteraccusation against Lavín of shifting to a focus on social policies, greater equality, human rights, and other issues that had been alien to the Right throughout most of the decade.

The second round saw a transfer of the votes of the Left outside the Concertación to its candidate and the affirmation of its first-round voters. The latter were not guaranteed, given the momentum reached by Lavín. Lagos gave a stronger role to Christian Democrats in the campaign for the January 2000 runoff election, in the hope of appealing to middle-class female Christian democratic sympathizers who had fallen for the allure of Lavín and feared the first socialist candidate of the Concertación. The competitive nature of the 1999–2000 elections resulted in increased electoral participation, especially relative to the 1997 congressional elections, reaching levels comparable to those of the 1988 referendum and inaugural democratic elections of 1989.

Change and Continuity

The vote for Lavín rose by about 5 percent points over the vote for Pinochet in the 1988 referendum. Lagos' vote descended by a similar magnitude from the vote against Pinochet in that referendum and the Aylwin vote in 1989, movements that are accounted for by the factors mentioned above.[38] Enhanced competition and participation; moderation of and increasing support for the Right; personalization of the campaign were all novel elements introduced in the political scenario by this election. However, the elements of continuity—the affirmation of trends that started with the new democracy—have had equal if not more weight. Continuity is marked by the renewed vitality, and strengthening, of the two-bloc division of political competition. This division started with the first elections in the successor post-Pinochet democracy, which followed patterns determined by the binomial electoral system that created two-member districts encouraging a bipolar competition. This pattern was reinforced by the actual cleavage generated by the authoritarian regime and which crystallized in the yes-no choice of the 1988 referendum that rejected Pinochet's claim to a renewable eight-year presidential term.[39] All elections since 1990 have been structured around the Concertación versus the Right's opposition coalition. This bipolar configuration has clearly obscured the tripolar Left–Center–Right political division of the pre-authoritarian democratic period.

Underneath the apparent changes from the previous presidential election, well-structured features in the character of supporters of each side are clearly discernible. There remained a hard-core, non-transferable basis of support for each side, which came from identities developed around the positions of support or rejection of the Pinochet regime. Tables 13.2 to 13.4 shed light on the profile of both coalitions' voters. While appreciable differences exist in the share of each coalition's voters according to income, the ideological/cultural identification appears most relevant.[40]

Despite the Center-prone campaign dynamics and the actual convergence in the discourse of both candidates during the campaign, survey respondents revealed clear positioning in the Left–Right scale (Table 13.2). Lavín voters identified the position of their own ideas to the Right in almost the same proportion as Lagos voters did so to the Left, sharing a similar proportion in the Center.

Furthermore, respondents clearly revealed the existence of a substantial

Table 13.2. Self-placement According to Political Ideas

	Lavín	Lagos
Left	2.7	61.1
Center	37.0	36.0
Right	60.3	2.8

Source: Patricio Navia and Alfredo Joignant, "Las elecciones presidenciales de 1999," in *Nuevo Gobierno: Desafíos de la Reconciliación, Chile 1999–2000* (Santiago: Flacso-Chile, 2000).

Table 13.3. Regime Preferences According to Voters

With which of these statements are you most in agreement?

	Democracy is preferable to any other form of government.	Sometimes a military government is preferable.	There is no difference between these two forms of government.
Lavín	41.2	40.9	15.6
Lagos	85.7	4.4	9.8

Source: Patricio Navia and Alfredo Joignant, "Las elecciones presidenciales de 1999," in *Nuevo Gobierno: Desafíos de la Reconciliación, Chile 1999–2000* (Santiago: Flacso-Chile, 2000).

gap in their regime preferences (Table 13.3). Lavín voters' preference for democracy as a form of government was quite feeble, while it was strong among Lagos voters. Almost the same proportion of Lavín voters that support democracy admit to a preference for military government under certain circumstances.

Finally, respondents revealed a clear pattern of prior political allegiance by their immediate family group (Table 13.4). Lavín voters supported the military regime in a somewhat similar proportion to the Lagos voters who opposed it. Chileans have in fact had their political preferences formed by experiences of support and opposition to the military coup of 1973, the 1973–90 military regime, and the 1988 referendum, which defeated Pinochet.

The above data reveal a contrast between the positioning of the leadership during the campaign—a clear move to Center-leaning positions—and the general public. The latter has shown substantial continuity in their political allegiances, supporting the existence of a regime cleavage (authoritarianism/democracy) behind their choice of coalition.[41]

The Municipal and Congressional Elections

The third Concertación government faced municipal elections in October 2000, only seven months after taking over. Voters validated then the majority they had given the coalition in the January runoff election, and even improved it slightly to 52 percent of the vote (see Table 13.5). In terms of non-presidential elections, the government coalition dropped 4 percent points from the previous municipal elections of 1996, but improved over the 50.6 obtained in the 1997 congressional elections. The Right, running as Pacto Alianza por Chile (Alliance for Chile Pact), dropped to 40 percent. Although this was significantly lower than Lavín's performance the previous January, the Right attained its best result of the decade in non-presidential elections, and ratified its electoral empowerment.

The Right did much better still in the number of municipalities it controlled. While the government coalition got 169 mayors elected—a drop of

Table 13.4. Family Political History

	Lavín	Lagos
Unidad Popular	66.0 (against)	41.1 (in favor)
Military coup	62.6 (in favor)	56.8 (against)
Military government	63.2 (in favor)	70.4 (against)

Source: Patricio Navia and Alfredo Joignant, "Las elecciones presidenciales de 1999," in *Nuevo Gobierno: Desafíos de la Reconciliación, Chile 1999–2000* (Santiago: Flacso-Chile, 2000).

Table 13.5. Congressional and Municipal Election Results (in percents)

Party Coalition	Municipal			Congressional		
	1992	1996	2000	1993	1997	2001
Concertación[a]	53.3	56.1	52.1	55.3	50.6	47.9
Right Coalition[b]	29.6	32.5	40.1	36.6	36.3	44.3
UCC[c]	8.1	2.8	1.2		2	
PC[d]	6.6	5.9	4.1	6.4	7.5	5.2
PH[e]		1.6	0.9	1.4	2.9	1.1
Ind. And others[f]	2.1	1.1	1.4	0.1	0.7	1.5

Source: For 1992, 1993, 1997, Patricio Navia and Alfredo Joignant, "Las elecciones presidenciales de 1999," in *Nuevo Gobierno: Desafíos de la Reconciliación, Chile 1999–2000* (Santiago: Flacso-Chile, 2000). For the 2000 and 2001 elections: www.elecciones.gov.cl.
[a]1992 and 1996: Concertación por la Democracia / 2000: Pacto para la Concertación de Partidos por la Democracia / 2001: Concertación de Partidos por la Democracia.
[b]1992: Participación y Progreso / 1996: Unión por Chile / 2000: Pacto Alianza por Chile / 2001: Alianza por Chile.
[c]1992: Unión de Centro Centro / 1996: Independientes Progresistas por Centro Centro / 2000: Pacto Centro Centro.
[d]1992: Partido Comunista / 1996: La Izquierda / 2000: Pacto Izquierda / 2001: Partido Comunista.
[e]1996: Opción Humanista / 2000: Pacto Humanista y Ecologistas / 2001: Partido Humanista.
[f]2000: Independientes fuera de Pacto / 2001: Independientes fuera de Lista / partido Liberal.

about 15 percent from the 1996 elections—the Right placed 165 mayors at the helm of their municipalities, an increase of about 22 percent from the previous elections. Tensions within the government coalition impeded the kind of intra-coalition agreements that would have helped translate the share of the vote more proportionally into control of municipalities. The large increase in the number of mayors from the opposition was also important symbolically: it attained control of many municipalities in low-income districts that had a leftist tradition, and controlled a majority of municipalities in nine of the country's twelve administrative regions. Observers were right in forecasting that this distribution would have a favorable impact for the Right in the congressional elections held in December 2001: its share of the vote increased to 44.3 percent, while the Concertación dropped for the first time below the 50 percent mark to 47.9 percent (see Table 13.5).

The 2001 congressional elections were the tenth elections held since the inauguration of democracy and the sixth to be held since 1996.[42] In all of them the primary contenders were the Concertación and the rightist opposition pact formed by RN and UDI. The party and its coalition systems thus displayed a remarkable stability, a stability sustained by the coalitional imperatives of the electoral system and by the weight of the regime cleavage that has continued to influence voters even as competition turns more centripetal. Forecasts of a collapse of the system have turned out to be premature.[43] However, two developments could conceivably weaken the system significantly. One is electoral reform that substitutes a proportional representation system that withdraws or weakens the current incentive to form electoral pacts.[44] Other kinds of alliances and coalitions could then be envisioned. The other is the completion of the transition, which via constitutional reform, the finalization of the legal cases against Pinochet, and a lessened presence of pressing human rights issues, could significantly weaken the regime cleavage that originated in the dictatorship period and the 1988 referendum. Both developments are on the horizon, but may for a long time remain no more than possibilities.

Nurturing those possibilities is the existence of what is referred to as the coexistence of two different souls within the Concertación. One is more Left-prone, critical of the poor achievements in social policy and in lessening inequality, as well as in promoting more democratic and participatory institutions. The other one is more willing to stand by the achievements of economic growth and liberalization as the pillars of a vastly modernized society that may create better opportunities for all. Also in the opposition there have coexisted different souls—one more oriented toward liberal democratic tenets, the other still hooked to the authoritarian past albeit aggressively liberal in its economic orientations.

Another element that could weaken the current system is the development of significant, undesired change within one of the coalitions. A noticeable change has occurred within the Concertación: the relative weakening of the Christian Democratic Party. This Center party, crucial for the transition and pivotal in the Alliance, provided the first two presidents of the new democracy. However, it lost its relative majority in the share of the vote over the combined strength of the Socialist Party and the Party for Democracy for the first time in the 1997 congressional elections. Almost two years later, Ricardo Lagos, of PS-PPD, defeated overwhelmingly his Christian Democratic competitor in the May 1999 primaries for the presidential candidacy, with 70 percent of the vote. Later, the Christian Democrats suffered the most losses in elected mayors in the 2000 municipal elections, and in the 2001 congressional elections they lost to UDI the symbolic title of being Chile's largest party. Still, the possibility of a substantial change in the system continued to be premature.

With substantial support, Lavín, the former presidential candidate of the Right, was elected mayor of Santiago. From the municipality's headquarters Lavín expected to coordinate the activities of a large number of young new mayors around the metropolitan region and the country. By emphasizing a commitment to "solving the people's real problems" through specific policies, he sought to keep active his enormous electoral capital for a second attempt in 2005. But caught in the specifics of municipal policies and conflicts, the national limelight returned to the parties and their leadership engaged in organizing their opposition to the Lagos administration. The promises of support for constitutional reforms and other centrist policies made during the 1999 campaign ceded ground to a more confrontational approach, which was reflected in the opposition to some of Lagos' major legislative initiatives such as tax reform and labor reform. (These initiatives are discussed again below, toward the end of the following section.)

Conflict, Public Policy, and Democratic Governance

In the midst of Frei's modernization government, new conflicts emerged out of the mobilization of social groups that placed demands on the state or opposed specific policies or proposals. Sectoral mobilization included students against the university modernization law, groups with environmental concerns, coal mine workers, teachers, health care workers, municipal workers, bus drivers, dock workers, and others. These mobilizations revived those that had occurred in the twilight of the dictatorship, but that paradoxically had been weakened with the resumption of democracy. They reemerged with a sense of contestarian urgency, although lacking permanence or intersectoral connections of the type that encompassing organizations had provided in the pre-authoritarian democracy. They very well reflected, in this regard, the social disarticulation created by market principles of social co-ordination and the weakened links of political parties to social organizations. Nevertheless, they occasionally succeeded in influencing responses from state officials and the political agenda.[45]

Mobilization of Indigenous Groups

The most important conflict and mobilization was staged by indigenous groups. Signs of awakened mobilization had surfaced toward the end of the dictatorship and the transition. Patricio Aylwin, as presidential candidate, signed an agreement with representatives of the indigenous peoples for the promotion of an indigenous law that would recognize their ancient and cultural rights.[46] This promise was fulfilled: President Aylwin passed the Ley Indígena (Indigenous Peoples Act) in 1993, which created the National Corporation for the Development of Indigenous People (CONADI) and the Fund for Indigenous People's Land and Water Resources. The law established protections for indigenous lands, in the context of state duty to respect, protect, and promote the development of indigenous communities, families, and their culture, as well as the expansion of their properties.[47] This approach began to take up long-delayed responsibility and reparation by Chilean state and society for a history of seizures of indigenous lands. In addition, indigenous rights were especially mistreated under the military dictatorship. Thus, ethnic mobilization strongly surfaced during democracy in reaction to a century of suppressed claims that worsened in the years of military rule.[48]

Ethnic mobilization is plural, with variegated leaderships and locations. The most active leadership resides with the Council of All Lands, and demands include claims for land, for national political recognition, for constitutional reform that would accept the recognition of a people and culture and their rights within the Chilean state. Demands for land are combined with extreme levels of poverty in rural communities. Meeting these demands would necessitate a complex package of assistance to accompany land distribution, which in itself demands resources that have not yet been made available by the Chilean state.

Mobilization in pursuit of these demands has laid bare problems and contradictions with the Ley Indígena, which in practice is not fully enforced. Mobilization has lately developed violent overtones, in turn generating extreme reactions from landowners and some members of the press.[49] As with other areas, such as in human rights more generally or the state of the press, domestic developments have reached international courts or demanded action from international organizations. Chile's absence from the International Labour Organization's Convention 169 on Indigenous and Tribal Peoples has become noted internationally. Ethnic conflict also has led to action by the OAS Inter-American Committee on Human Rights.[50]

The Concertación administrations have set up committees of notables to study the complex set of issues and reforms involved in providing an integral long-term solution to the demands of indigenous peoples. President Lagos created in 2001 the Committee on Historic Truth and New Treatment of Indigenous Peoples, and appointed former President Aylwin to lead it. The committee, as well as actual ongoing mobilization, should continue to expand awareness of the magnitude of the historic ethnic problem and the corresponding solutions. As in other areas, the Chilean polity and society are faced with the challenge of tolerance of diversity, and are urged to speedily catch up with situations that other countries have faced earlier. The disjuncture noted at the beginning of this chapter between different tracks in Chilean development becomes quite apparent in this connection.

Human rights, the press, the judiciary, are all areas in which liberalization and modernization have lagged far behind similar processes in the economy. Large segments of Chilean society have been only recently awakened to the realization that modernization also entails diversity, tolerance, and inclusion.[51]

Judicial Reform

In terms of public policy, one of the most important areas of change and modernization has been the judiciary, the site, according to the press, of the "reform of the Century." This characterization highlights the backward state in which the judiciary, the most unreformed institution in the Chilean state, was found at the start of the new democracy. The lamentable performance and obsequious behavior of the courts during the Pinochet regime made it a prime candidate for reforms. Reforms did in fact sweep through this ancient and ossified institution. In 1990, all seventeen members of the Supreme Court had been appointed by Pinochet; ten years later, only three of them remained. During the democratic decade, four Court members, including its president, were the object of constitutional accusations, and one of them was successfully dismissed in a political trial by the Congress. The Court itself expelled another of its members in 2001 for influence trafficking. The number of Supreme Court members was expanded to twenty-one, and the century-old procedure for their appointment was reformed. The Court's duties and assignments were reduced and changed, and a new penal system (*sistema procesal penal*) along with new courts were introduced.[52]

The impetus for reform came, on one hand, from the interests of Concertación leaders, rooted in their bitter experience under the repression of the military regime, and on the other, from business and opposition leaders who realized that the judiciary had become too dysfunctional to meet the needs of a modernized economy confronting new issues at a faster pace. Aylwin's government started with an ambitious agenda that included the creation of a National Council of Justice with oversight powers, a Judicial School, and changes in the composition of the higher court. The Supreme Court reacted vigorously against these proposals, which it perceived as invasion of its autonomy. The Court also was feeling threatened by the increasing number of human rights cases presented to the judiciary, and the criticisms, including the very overt criticism by President Aylwin, about its past behavior and its continued inability to handle these cases adequately. The parties of the Right also felt threatened and shifted from a position of sympathy for reforms to a staunch rejection of the executive's proposals. The government lowered its aim and settled for the Judicial Academy, a reform of the judicial career and evaluation structures, and a reorganization of the operations of the Court around specialized subcommittees (*salas*). All of them pointed to greater efficiency, a change in career incentives, and a specification of the power of the higher court, away from the broad discretionary revision powers it had held. These goals were acceptable to the Right, and the reforms passed early in the following administration of President Frei.

However, the Frei administration's most remarkable success was its ability to press forward for a consequential reform of the penal justice system and of the Supreme Court. For the ambitious enterprise that the former signified, Minister of Justice Soledad Alvear was able to put together a broad coalition of experts and political support. This was possible as a result of several episodes that had further weakened the powers of the courts to resist change, episodes that were related to corruption trends in the courts, to the justice system's blatant inability to accommodate itself more responsively to the greater demand for justice in human rights cases,[53] and to difficulties in coping with increases in criminality in large cities. The reform coalition included *El Mercurio* (Chile's oldest functioning newspaper), the Fundación Paz Ciudadana (Citizen's Peace Foundation), linked to the former, other NGOs and a group of young legal scholars in the Universidad Diego Portales' Law School, and even the Finance Ministry, which was willing to support the increased funds needed for such reforms.

The reform proposal, introduced in 1998, passed in different phases and consists of assigning penal investigation to a national prosecution agency (Ministerio Público), separate from the judiciary. This office decides on priorities for prosecution, and guarantees the indicted person a public and oral trial and his or her rights. The reform also passed a new penal code (Código Procesal Penal) in 2000, which introduced oral and public trials and created new courts.

Fiscal Nacional (attorney general) Guillermo Piedrabuena was appointed by President Lagos, and two regions (La Araucanía and Coquimbo) were selected to start the implementation of the process that should be completed in 2005. This will demand a staff of 642 district attorneys and 782 new judges, almost half of whom will be in charge of supervising the process and protecting the rights of victims and accused. The other half will staff sentencing courts in oral and public trials.[54] In April 2001, President Lagos promulgated the final leg of this reform with the creation of the Defensoría Penal Pública, which will guarantee a fair defense for all those accused who are unable to provide themselves with legal counsel.[55]

Equally important were the changes introduced in the Supreme Court in 1997. Following an accusation against the president of the Supreme Court by a UDI deputy, the conditions were created for a swift and important reform of the Court. The reform did away with a transitory norm that allowed the older members to stay past the age of 75. This change rid the Court of reform-resistant Pinochet-appointed judges, and cleared the way for new appointments. It expanded membership to twenty-one judges, and allowed for the appointment of five members from outside the judiciary, to instill fresh air and innovation. The reform also stipulated that appointments to the higher court, made by the president from among five names submitted by the Court, had to have the approval of the Senate. This was necessary to get the support of the Right.[56]

These reforms—the first major reforms in a century of this state power—are critical to the advancement of democratic governance. For their successful implementation, it will be necessary that they be accompanied with the development of a new culture among its members that is receptive to societal demands, prone to efficiency, and permeated by an ethos of defending citizens' rights.[57] The reforms also highlighted that, despite the differences stemming from the transition's pending issues, good public policy could occasionally be pursued in important areas with a broad across-the-aisles consensus. It should also be noted that those reforms would not have been possible without the obduracy with which human rights issues were kept alive, despite enormous obstacles, throughout the democratic decade.

Improvement of liberties and rights, such as those promoted by judicial reform, were also advanced in a few other important areas. One of them was the attainment of constitutional equality for men and women, which permitted consistency with international treaties that do not tolerate discrimination. This constitutional reform, opposed by only three members of the Right in a vote of a plenary session of Congress, substituted the word "persons" for "men" in Article 1 of the constitution that establishes that they "are born free and equal in dignity." It also added, in Article 19, that "men and women are equal before the law."[58]

Freedom of the press and of expression are another critical area in which important progress was made very recently. Chilean state security legislation treated contempt of authority (*desacato*) as an offense to national security that could carry a prison sentence of up to five years. Clauses such as this had led the special rapporteur for freedom of expression of the OAS to state that Chile has tighter legal restrictions on free speech than any other Latin American country except Cuba.[59] More than thirty individuals have been prosecuted under this statute since the return to democracy. The most recent episode occurred in February 2001, when Air Force Chief of Staff General Gabrielli used it against those who had identified him as torturer in 1973. Supreme Court Judge Servando Jordán applied it against journalist Alejandra Matus, and had her book confiscated. In her *The Black Book of Chilean Justice,* Matus exposed corruption in the judiciary and had to leave the country to avoid detention. In a telling commentary about speech restrictions in Chile, the U.S. government granted her asylum. Attempts to repeal this clause had been sitting for seven years in Congress. The Lagos government, responding to pressure from many, mostly international, quarters took the initiative to push the legislation forward and successfully had the repeal approved by both chambers of Congress. The bill also protects journalists from any obligation to reveal their sources. Prosecution for press offenses will be conducted solely by civilian courts, ending the power of military courts to try journalists for sedition.[60] These reforms, important as they are, are only partial steps. Clauses on contempt of authority, for instance, will remain in the penal code and the code of military justice.[61]

Another important initiative was the elimination of film censorship after the government submitted a bill in March 2001. The government was responding to pressure from the Inter-American Human Rights Court, which requested that legislation be modified to make it consistent with the American Convention on Human Rights. This international court had in turn responded to a case submitted before it in 1997 for Chile's censorship of the film *The Last Temptation of Christ.*[62] A plenary session of Congress approved in July 2001 the constitutional reform allowing for the end of film censorship and affirming the right to freedom of artistic expression. These reforms have been especially welcome in a context where there has been little pluralism in the press. Most of the country's newspapers, like many television stations, are aligned with the conservative opposition.[63]

Education Reform

The educational sector was a focus of attention and resources for the government throughout the 1990s. Perhaps more so than with judicial reform, the focus on education has been able to attract more of a consensus among competing political groups. Just as the Right perceived that judicial reform was a means of elementary modernization necessary for economic development, it equally perceived educational improvement as essential for reaching that goal. The 1980s under the military regime had witnessed important changes in primary and secondary education, through policies aimed at promoting efficiency and decentralization (municipalization). The goal of the governments of the 1990s was the promotion of quality and equity on top of the previous goal of efficiency.

A team of experts in the Ministry of Education has, since democratization, provided continuity in the development of plans for the betterment of educational quality and the expansion of coverage and equity, with support of sizable grants from multilateral financial institutions and the support of the Ministry of Finance. An important achievement has been the formation of inclusive committees bringing all sectors together in the discussion of educational goals. An example was the "Framework Agreement for the Modernization of Chilean Education," signed by the government and all political parties with congressional representation.[64] Increased expenditure has led to substantial improvement in the equipment of schools, particularly in rural areas, and in curricula, with the goal of providing more flexible learning processes in tune with changing contexts. Still, the modernization promoted had a long way to go in transforming content, resources, and institutional change into actual results vis-à-vis the goals of quality and equity.[65]

The Lagos Administration and the Future of Democratic Governance

Lagos and his coalition stated that he would be the third Concertación president and not the second socialist president (Salvador Allende [1970–73] being the first). Still, the symbolic import of the election of a socialist was not lost on him or his followers. His victory speech in January 2000 before thousands of supporters on Constitution Square, albeit conciliatory, rejoiced in this symbolism by opening with a tribute to Salvador Allende's widow—"representative of Chile's dignity."

Lagos came to power following a technocratically oriented Frei administration that had lifted the economy to high growth rates, but that confronted new levels of conflict-prone social mobilization. He also inherited the revival of the end-of-transition tasks. Lagos' principal orientations were to provide some form of democratic political rationale to the unrestrained market orientations that pervaded all areas. His emphases were on "growth with equity" and on advancing a society of citizens, not of consumers. Following the governments of transition and modernization led by Aylwin and Frei respectively, Lagos' government wanted to posit itself as the government of reforms. Ambitiously, as he stated in his speech of May 21, 2000, the goal is to make of Chile a fully developed country by 2010.[66]

Lagos outlined seven great reforms that would accompany the full implementation of the judicial and educational reforms: health reform to guarantee expanded coverage and efficient treatment; access to and dissemination of information technologies; labor reform; fiscal reform, to attain a structural surplus of one percent of the GDP; political and constitutional reforms; state reform, including decentralization; and urban reform to allow greater integration and enhanced coexistence in city life. Since that speech, major aspects of labor and fiscal reforms successfully passed in Congress.

However, two important problems stood in the way of fully attaining such ambitious goals. One was the economy, which grew at 5.4 percent in 2000, surmounting the −1.1 percent figure of the previous year. This was the best result in South America, and the third best in Latin America, but below the expectations that government officials had held. More important, however, economic growth proved unable to reduce the high levels of unemployment. The rate of unemployment reached 9.3 percent in 2000, and the first quarter of 2001 showed no significant decline at 8.8 percent. The estimates of growth for 2001 kept being revised downward to about 4 percent or less, in light of the international downturn.[67] These rates would simply not permit the ambitious goal of full development by 2010.

The other difficulty was the succession of elections—the 2000 municipal elections and the December 2001 elections for Congress—which kept the political elite focused more on campaigns than policy. Perhaps this disposition stood behind what many observers criticized as the government's inability to turn ideas into actual policies and implementation.[68] At the conclusion of his first year in government, President Lagos could claim success in restarting economic growth and in advancing cultural development and freedoms. Lagos also took credit for affirming the republican institutions by letting them do their work, that is, letting the courts pursue the human rights cases and the Pinochet case without political interference or undue military influence. In fact, the government had managed to assert its supremacy over the military symbolically and to induce cooperation in human rights problems and other areas.[69] But it had difficulty pushing its reform agenda.

The government put much emphasis on labor reform, which would expand the conditions for collective bargaining and strengthen the right to strike by making it costly to replace workers. While considering demands for flexibility in the labor market, the government saw this reform as critical to the modernization of employment institutions and the economy with a long-term perspective. The proposals would perhaps have faced more promising prospects in the context of the higher growth rates to which economic actors had grown accustomed. They faced, however, strong opposition from the Right and business. It did not help that these sectors were embittered by the government's stance on letting the legal case against Pinochet follow its course. The government moderated its reform proposals in the attempt to open ways for negotiation. In the end, it managed to pass the reforms but without the support of the right-wing opposition.

The pursuit of these issues reflected well the dilemma facing government policy and democratic politics. The development of an agreement on the pending transition issues, primarily constitutional reforms, would greatly clear the way to work out legislative agreements on other sectoral policy areas, as was possible with judicial and educational reform. Agreement on those larger issues thus demands priority attention. However, lingering disagreements or tactical delays on those broader issues should not detract the government from advancing specific sectoral policy. It is conceivable that the calmer waters of the post-electoral period may create the appropriate environment for the development of such broad agreements. The reasonable expectation of the opposition that it might win the government in 2006 should help nurture the state of uncertainty—the veil of ignorance—propitious for constitutional agreement, on which much has already been advanced in informal across-the-aisles negotiations. The Right might also be called to face up to the promises made during the presidential campaign. However, important remaining differences could still prevent constitutional reform for some time.

With or without reforms, and with or without resumption of the spectacular growth rates of the 1990s, the government will also be called to face up to its campaign promises.[70] They relate to solving the pressing human rights issues and advancing a positive state role in the promotion of fairer conditions in labor relations, higher education, the media, the environment, social security and health, and state reform. Policies will also be demanded for advancing the liberties and mechanisms for increased participation, in the face of social conflict, particularly ethnic conflict. Finally, a more coherent model of insertion in the international network of trade alliances and economic and political integration will be needed. In this area, the government actively pursued integration agendas with Mercosur, the European Union, and the United States in ways that were not always consistent.[71]

There were, at the start of the century, great opportunities to make significant strides toward improved democratic governance. On the one hand, there was the government intent on advancing equity and fairness in all areas of policy and promoting cultural change and participation in accordance with its view of a society of citizens. On the other hand, sectors of the

Right had taken sizable, albeit hesitating, steps in the direction of severing ties with its recent authoritarian past. Opportunities for finally ending the transition (or greatly advancing democratization) were *ad portas*. The post-electoral scenario to begin in 2002 would put to test the willingness and abilities of contending actors to seize those opportunities.

14

Mexico

From PRI Predominance

to Divided Democracy

Denise Dresser

The loss of the presidency by the PRI in July 2000 has laid to rest fierce debates over the Mexican transition to democracy. For some, Mexico's transition had taken place years ago and although fine-tuning was still required, the basic institutional changes for democratic rule were in place. The 2000 election simply confirmed Mexico's democratic credentials. Others argued, however, that a true transition would only materialize if and when the PRI lost the presidential chair. As a result of Vicente Fox's victory, both sides now agree that Mexico is a functioning electoral democracy.[1] Mexico underwent a "voted transition."

The election revealed that the ballot box, revised electoral laws, and refurbished electoral institutions were capable of eroding the PRI's dominance and dislodging the party from the presidency. In the electoral arena, Mexico proved that it had the essential components of a democracy: real voters with real choices, political parties with national representation, autonomous electoral institutions, an impartial media, and an independent public opinion.[2] The contest was uncertain and had clear rules, voters punished the incumbent and brought a different party into power, the winner was recognized by his adversaries, and civic normalcy prevailed throughout.

The debate over Mexico's political system has now shifted to the adjectives that should characterize its new democratic regime: "fledgling," "unconsolidated," "skin-deep," "fragile," "divided." Arguments abound because of the nature of the political process that ousted the ruling party from power. Over the past decade, Mexico experienced a transition from a hyperpresidentialist regime to a presidentialist system. Political and economic decentralization led to a transfer from the federal government to state governments, from the PRI to opposition parties, and from political parties to civil society. Mexico became a country in which power was divided in a complex way, ceased to be concentrated in the hands of the president, and flowed to other actors within and without the party system. Vicente Fox and his Alliance for Change capitalized on the changes produced by power-sharing, but the division of power itself will constrain the new government's room to maneuver. What follows is an initial overview of key themes that will shape Mexico's new politics and affect the country's prospects for democratic governance.

The conditions that enabled Vicente Fox's broad-based coalition to defeat the PRI—and the political landscape the 2000 election produced—may make it difficult for him to govern and deepen the democratic agenda. Fox assembled a politically heterogeneous and ideologically divergent coalition; now he will have to negotiate and share power with it. Mexico still is a presidentialist system of government, but it is also a multiparty system. Fox won a majority of votes, but not enough of them to avoid the emergence of a divided government, wherein his party does not control Congress. The future of democratic governance will be limited and shaped by a constrained executive, a divided Congress, a party system built on parties in disarray, and a decentralized political geography in which the PRI still exerts a large amount of influence.

Democratic governance will also be complicated by the weight of the past and by inertia rooted in the country's political culture and institutional arrangements. Traditional political alignments have been swept away and yet many of the old institutions and rules—including dysfunctional constitutional provisions such as the non-reelection of legislators—remain in place. Major components of the system, such as PRI patronage, have been weakened, but others, such as PRI veto power, remain in place. Empowered new actors in the media and civil society coexist, side by side, with aging attitudes and authoritarian practices.[3] But perhaps the most daunting challenge for democratic rule will be institutional renovation to address the precarious nature of the judiciary, the absence of the rule of law, the persistence of age-old impunity. Many of Mexico's institutions are ill-equipped to meet the ongoing challenge of democratic consolidation. The country has no strong and rooted tradition of democratic institutions, and its main task will be to build them.[4]

The chapter begins by examining the historic changes that have taken place at the executive level of government, that is, the absence of key elements of old presidentialism in Mexico's post-PRI era. In this context, I analyze President Fox's challenges regarding executive-legislative relations as well as the nature of the new president's political style. The second part of the chapter focuses on Mexico's political party system with a special emphasis on the breakdown of PRI hegemony and the challenges that lie ahead for party institutionalization and party politics. The chapter later evaluates the divided nature of Mexico's political power and demonstrates the extent to which this dispersion can be attributed to the development of a stronger and more active civil society as well as a more independent media. The chapter follows with an assessment of Mexico's perennial challenge of building effective institutions and practices that assure the rule of law, especially in areas related to judicial reform, law enforcement, drug trafficking, and corruption. I conclude with an analysis of Mexico's future challenges based on an initial assessment of Fox's administration. I argue that although the country has undergone a profound and positive democratic transition, the extent to which democratic governance will be truly institutionalized and consolidated remains to be seen.

The New Presidency: Fox in a Box

In Mexico the days of omnipotent presidentialism have come to an end. Since 1988 the Mexican presidency has lost or voluntarily ceded control over key areas of its traditional domain due to a combination of political will, partisan negotiations, and public pressure.[5] The country moved slowly away from an interventionist executive who exercised meta-constitutional powers to a restrained executive restricted to his formal role. Through successive electoral reforms enacted since 1990, the executive abandoned control over the organization of federal elections. Reforms carried out in 1993 established that the president could no longer name the mayor of Mexico City, who would be elected by the popular vote. Also in that year the Bank of Mexico formally became an autonomous institution, thus limiting the president's capacity to dictate the country's monetary policy. Since 1995, executive nominations for Supreme Court justices have to be ratified by two-thirds of the Senate, instead of a simple majority. In the 1997 midterm election, the PRI lost control of the lower house, and as a result, the president could no longer get legislation approved without building coalitions with the opposition. Ernesto Zedillo (1994–2000) offered a republican presidency, detached from the ruling PRI, and he frequently kept his word, leaving decisions to Congress and relinquishing his capacity to hand-pick his successor.

The 2000 election eliminated the three conditions—unified government, strong discipline within the majority party, and presidential leadership of the PRI—that enabled Mexican presidentialism to exist and flourish.[6] Given the absence of the key instruments of presidentialism, Vicente Fox has less room to maneuver than post-electoral euphoria had first suggested. Mexico's president is governing in a box, under siege, and within the confines of a contested Congress. More people voted for Fox than for the PAN: the difference between voting percentages at the party level was not as big as the PAN wanted or the PRI feared; the "Fox effect" allowed a charismatic candidate to win, but was not enough to guarantee a unified Congress headed by the president's party.[7] Fox obtained 5.5 percent more of the vote than his party and its allies did for Congress. Fox's coalition, the Alliance for Change, won 43.7 percent of the vote in the presidential race, followed by the PRI with 36.91 percent, and Cuauhtémoc Cárdenas' Alliance for Mexico with 17.02 percent. But in the congressional races the Alliance for Change garnered only 2 percent more votes than the PRI.[8] Beyond the elusive desire for change, Mexico's newly elected executive was not endowed with a forceful mandate.[9] He has to construct one on an ongoing basis, and that endeavor will not be an easy one due to the unprecedented division of power in the Mexican Congress.[10]

Executive-legislative relations prior to the 2000 election cannot be compared to the new challenges Fox and a divided Congress face. After the PRI lost its majority in the lower chamber in the midterm election of 1997, a true revolution in parliamentary organization and practices emerged during the second half of the Zedillo administration.[11] The Mexican legislature turned into a battlefield, replete with frontal attacks, strategic retreats, seemingly endless negotiations, and frequent stalemates. In contrast with past passivity, budgets for the fiscal years 1998 and 1999 were heavily modified in committees. Opposition deputies challenged both taxes and spending, took the budget negotiations into overtime, and achieved some of their goals.[12] The executive was responsible for only 11 percent of all legislation that reached the Chamber of Deputies, lower than any point in the three previous congresses, and deputies presented a record number of bills.[13] The president was less influential than in the past, and congresspersons were more so.

But certain trends were proven and predictable: high party discipline remained in full force, last-minute deals brokered between the PAN and the PRI—such as those relating to the bailout of the banks and a set of electoral reforms—became the norm.[14] On economic and political issues, the PRI-PAN cufflink set the agenda, rounded up the votes, and frequently won the day, despite the recalcitrance of the leftist PRD. PRI control of the Senate meant that many PAN-PRD initiatives never saw the light of day. Although highly visible bickering in Congress was frequent, in the end at least two-party consensus assured the passage of key bills and assured governability. Party cohesiveness prevailed.[15]

The results of the 2000 election, in contrast, have created a new context for practices and alliances in the Chamber of Deputies and the Senate. Mexico is moving into a fluid, unpredictable situation where no single party has the majority to approve legislation on its own, and ad hoc coalitions will have to be built on a case by case basis. Unholy alliances between traditional archenemies like the PRI and the PRD may be forged, and even the president and his party could have very different legislative agendas. In order to pass a constitutional reform in the lower house that requires a two-thirds majority or 333 votes, the PAN—with 206 deputies—would need an additional 127 votes.[16]

In Mexico's new legislative landscape, government officials are being forced to defend their proposals, and congressional lobbying has become an integral part of daily politics. The real battles over Mexico's destiny are being fought not in Los Pinos (the presidential residence) but in San Lázaro (the congressional building). Therefore, the kind of rapid change the Fox team envisioned upon arrival into office has been difficult to bring about. Ordinary laws and constitutional reforms have become contested and combative affairs in Congress, in the Senate, and in local legislatures.[17] The election produced a weaker president who will have to negotiate with a divided Congress. And given the composition of Congress itself, some have suggested that although Mexico is a presidentialist system, in coming years, the country will function with a parliamentary logic.[18]

Mexico's Congress changed since the 2000 election, but so did the executive. Fox's victory brought an end to the presidency as Mexicans had known it. During the PRI's reign, Mexican presidents wielded great power with little accountability.[19] Their personal styles diverged but they shared a common purpose: to preserve the PRI-dominated system through discretionary presidential intervention. In a break with the past, Vicente Fox inaugurated a new era in which the president is viewed less as a totemic figure and more as a temporary occupant of a post that can be won or lost at the polls. The imperial presidency has ended and the informal presidency has begun. Instead of imposing from above, the president now has to engage in bargaining and deal brokering in order to generate support from below.

As part of the new government's approach, the president perceives the country as divided into two different dimensions: the green circle, composed by the majority of the population, and the red circle, composed by elites who form opinion and make decisions.[20] The first circle is where the votes are; the second circle has the capacity to influence them. The green circle encompasses the beneficiaries of the president's promised programs, whereas the red circle includes the legislators who can veto them. The green circle includes those who approve of Vicente Fox, and the red circle incorporates those who have less lofty opinions about him.

Fox has tried to govern by "going public," jumping over the red circle in order to convince the green circle, using his personality to generate popularity.[21] Instead of locking himself in to negotiate, the president delegates that task to others. Instead of encouraging mobilization via political parties, the president appeals to the media. Instead of working within institutions, the president jumps over them. Vicente Fox has transformed the Mexican presidency into a public affair. By doing so, he is adapting the Mexican presidency to the Information Age, wherein via the media, presidents speak directly to the public and appeal to millions of voters instead of convincing hundreds of congresspersons.

As governor of the state of Guanajuato, Fox set a precedent, a blueprint for current executive actions.[22] Fox did not exercise power sitting behind a desk, reading policy briefs. He governed on the streets and on the screens, consulting and asking, listening and deciding. He traveled through the countryside, eliciting public support for his policies.[23] In the presidency he has adopted the same activist stance vis-à-vis Congress. His presidency is media-driven and television-based. He appears frequently on television, he has a weekly radio show, he promotes his programs and responds to his critics.

Fox triumphed over the PRI due to a successful campaign based on "The Millennium Project," a political manual and roadmap.[24] Devised by one of Fox's closest friends and former Coca-Cola colleague, José Luis González, the document set forth how Fox, "the product," would be sold, and what would compel Mexicans to buy him. The Millennium Project gave Fox precise instructions on how to steal banners from the Left and contain the Right, how to take advantage of his height and how to comb his hair, what to say and what to wear. Advised by a team of expert marketers, Fox learned how to develop a winning persona: stubborn and persistent, charismatic and contradictory, informal and intemperate, simple and sincere. Vicente Fox toppled the PRI by gambling on the formula: "Marketing + Money = Presidency."

Since the beginning of his term in December 2000, Fox has used the same credo to govern the electorate he courted in an assiduous fashion. Just as he did during his three-year-long campaign, Fox constructs his image deliberately and carefully. He knows that 69 percent of Mexicans who wanted "change" voted for him, and therefore the word has become his sound bite of choice. He is aware that a majority of voters between the ages of 18 and 34 are his natural constituency, and he wants to speak as colloquially as they do. He understands that the majority of Mexicans relate to politics through television, and consequently he appears onscreen as frequently as he can. Fox ran a personality-driven campaign and now he is running a personality-driven presidency. Day after day, event after event, Mexicans are treated to the presidency as a spectacle in which the president himself occupies center stage.

Vicente Fox has inaugurated a new way of doing politics in Mexico, based largely on the techniques he applied to propel himself to office, including polls, data processing, image management, and marketing. Polls discover what the population thinks, data processing reveals the depth of those beliefs, image management builds upon detected desires, and marketing inserts the product into the media. Behind Fox's carefully crafted persona, an army of advisers carries out polls and discusses their results, designs media strategies, and evaluates their impact. At the helm of the Office of the Presidential Image, Francisco Ortiz, a former marketing executive with Procter and Gamble, takes the country's pulse through weekly opinion polls. When the president's popularity dips, quick measures—including a televised marriage ceremony—are taken to counteract the downward trend.

Vicente Fox appeals to public opinion at large, at times bypassing political parties and their congressional representatives, because he won the presidential election in that fashion. The president believes that the successful promotion of himself and his policies will lead to key legislative victories in a divided government, thus assuring democratic governance. But the use of public relations to determine presidential success is fundamentally incompatible with bargaining, and without it, the Mexican Congress may not respond to the president's demands. Ultimately, the media-driven, peripatetic, and public style that enabled Fox to win the office of president may be counterproductive for executive-legislative relations.

The presidential campaign produced a president who has a great deal of media experience but little political experience, who can speak in front of cameras but has trouble convincing congresspersons, who speaks to the masses but does not understand the country's institutional elite. A recalcitrant, divided Congress routinely trips the president at every turn. Because he and members of his team believe in "going public," Fox fought for negotiations with the Zapatista rebels and the indigenous rights bill in the initial months of his presidency before building support for them in Congress. Fox also launched a massive media campaign to advertise the need for fiscal reform in the spring of 2000, before having constructed consensus for it in his own party. Ultimately, Congress passed an indigenous rights bill that was not to the president's liking, and fiscal reform languished in the legislature for months.

"Going public" is a strategy for presidential leadership that frequently works well in consolidated democracies, but does so less effectively in their incipient counterparts. In the United States—for example—the green circle can and does influence the red circle, but in Mexico, the green circle has very little engagement with the red circle. In the United States, the population can and does pressure political elites, but in Mexico elites routinely ignore the population. In full-fledged democracies, citizens know who their congresspersons are and how to communicate with them, but in Mexico the majority of the people do not even know their congressperson's name, let alone how he or she votes. Whereas in the United States, a congressperson who ignores his or her base runs the risk of losing reelection, in Mexico congresspersons as a rule ignore their constituencies and pay no political price for doing so. North of the Río Grande, the president can use the bully pulpit to pressure recalcitrant adversaries in the legislature, but in Mexico, presidential popularity is irrelevant for lawmakers that do not face reelection. The future of a PAN congressperson hinges more on the goodwill of the party's leadership than on the good image of the president.

"Going public" in Mexico has created congresspersons who are ill-disposed to a president who prefers to deal with them indirectly. Fox's strategy entails posturing, and has frequently fixed the president's bargaining position, making it difficult to reach subsequent compromises. As a form of presidential leadership, the public route undermines the legitimacy and the pride of other politicians. So when Fox has attempted to jump over Congress, he has won the popularity contest, but has lost legislative battles. What the president perceives as persuasion, congresspersons perceive as coercion. When Fox appeals to the public at large, he places obstacles along the road of concertation.

By adopting a final position on the stage, the president has limited his room to maneuver behind it. By using public strategies, the president has jeopardized private negotiations. By appealing to the silent majority, Fox has often alienated the powerful minority. Jumping over the heads of party politicians—in order to sway public opinion—functions effectively in countries where elected representatives are responsive to their constituencies. But in Mexico, where congresspersons cannot be reelected, and their destinies depend less on the will of the people and more on their party's executive committee, "going public" may exacerbate problems instead of solving them.

Going public cannot solve the structural problem the new government faces: Mexico has a presidential system of government in which the president's powers have been reined in by divided government. This combination has created unprecedented challenges of political and economic management, and may lead to the postponement of pending economic and political reforms. The Fox team promised a six-year term of increased competitiveness in telecommunications, stronger public finances, weakened media monopolies, reforms to the electricity, micro-credits for mini-businesses, and negotiations on immigration with the United States.[25] And throughout his first year in office, Fox underscored his commitment to assure that these changes took place. But Fox's lack of congressional support within his own party (and outside of it) has hampered the government's capacity to construct stable coalitions of support for its reform agenda.

In the Mexican case, the combination of presidential popularity and political will has not been enough to assure the passage of key reforms. The government had hoped to take advantage of the *bono democrático* (the democratic bonus produced by the transition from authoritarian rule). However, government elites overestimated the president's popularity and underestimated congressional opposition. Prospects for economic reform—including the privatization of the electricity sector—have been delayed due to the lack of congressional support, and this problem may continue until and unless the Fox government can build reform coalitions in a divided Congress. A weak president faced with a divided Congress could be a recipe for governmental paralysis.

In the 57th Legislature under Ernesto Zedillo—Fox's predecessor—23 percent of bills that were sponsored by opposition parties that included the PRI were approved. Broad-spectrum alliances occurred in a divided Congress in the past and may happen again if the new executive demonstrates good negotiating skills in the future. Despite a fractured Congress, a limited common legislative agenda could be feasible if the Fox government is able to assure the support of his own party and successfully woo moderate fractions of the opposition, particularly in the PRI. Yet bargaining may come at a price: in an effort to obtain the PRI's collaboration, the Fox government could face the dilution of reforms to a degree that hampers their effectiveness.

Political Parties: Shaken to the Core

The 2000 election marks the end of hegemonic party rule by the PRI and confirmed how substantially the PRI's predominance had eroded since the turbulent elections of 1988. The Mexican transition to democracy was built election after election through a gradual, evolutionary process wherein the PRI lost power with the passage of time.[26] Prior to 1982, the PRI vote stood at 70 to 90 percent. In the 1997 congressional election PRI support fell to a historic low point of 39.1 percent, and in 2000 the ruling party's vote decreased to an unprecedented 36.91 percent. Increased electoral competitiveness and several significant electoral reforms took their toll and led the PRI to ultimately lose the last crucial bastion: the presidency.[27]

The breakdown of PRI hegemony poses significant challenges for party institutionalization, largely because the election has left the party system in a state of disarray. Prior to the 2000 presidential race it seemed that despite internal turbulence, Mexico's three main parties were fairly consolidated.[28] Party officials projected an ideologically stable image even though voters— as public opinion polls revealed—did not have strong ideological orientations compatible with those supported by party leaders. In the case of the privatization of government enterprises, for example, the attitude of PAN and PRI voters ran across the entire ideological spectrum. As a result, the PAN and the PRD alternated as the PRI's main competitor approximately once every three years from 1985 to 2000. On the other hand, voter profiles were comparatively stable: there were PRI voter profiles, PRD voter profiles, and strategic-voter profiles, and these had not changed much over time.[29]

Fox's victory rocked the foundations of the country's party system. In the 2000 election, for many voters the choice was for an individual rather than a party. Fox lacked the constraints of a clear party platform and his pragmatic, shifting stance blurred the PAN's ideological profile.[30] In a political system characterized by widely prevalent cynicism toward parties, Mexican voters voted more for the candidate and less for his party, more for change and less for its specific content.[31] Electoral dealignment from traditional party bases took place and was enough to create a broad-based coalition of Mexicans from all walks of life in favor of Vicente Fox.

The profile of the electorate in the aftermath of the election poses challenges for both winners and losers. Voters did not vote for policy issues but for the prospect of better government. They did not vote for broad-based political reform but for better economic management, less crime, and less corruption. The electorate decided to "toss the bums out" with the prospect that the newly elected government would do better. Partisan positions and policy issues mattered less and empowering a forceful politician who promised to govern more effectively than the PRI mattered more.[32] Many voters abandoned their party affiliations and took risks, and in the future may do so again if government performance falls below their expectations. Mexico's main parties thus face a scenario of potential electoral volatility and lukewarm partisan loyalties. In the aftermath of the 2000 election, the PAN, the PRI, and the PRD have problems of identity and strategy.

Although the PAN had made important electoral inroads in the 1990s through a "creeping federalist" strategy, and had steadily increased its congressional representation, the party could not have won the presidency without Vicente Fox and the political phenomenon he unleashed.[33] Yet the nature and characteristic of Fox's victory create future dilemmas for a party that was conceived and has operated largely as an opposition force. The PAN was created to oppose what its founders perceived as the populist excesses of Lázaro Cárdenas in the 1930s. During the 1980s it functioned as a "loyal" opposition and during the 1990s it was rewarded—via recognition for its local electoral victories—by a larger slice of the political pie. Yet despite its strategic collaboration with the PRI, the PAN remained a party defined by distance, opposition, separateness. Historically, the PAN has distrusted presidential power, and now finds itself in the unprecedented situation of having to exercise it.

The PAN had frequently been described as the only democratic party in Mexico because of its long tradition of internal primaries, of rules and regulations, of time-honed methods to elect and rotate its leadership. Yet the PRI was defeated by the ultimate "outsider," even to his own party, the PAN.

Fox won because he did not play by the rules of the game. Instead of waiting for the National Action Party to nominate him, he began his campaign before the nomination period and then presented PAN leaders with a fait accompli. Instead of relying exclusively on the PAN's campaign organization, he created a parallel fundraising and electoral mobilization agency known as "Amigos de Fox" (Friends of Fox). Instead of using the PAN's Center–Right agenda as the basis for his presidential bid, he devised his own pragmatic platform.[34] Fox's victory brought an end to the PAN's "long march" to conquer the presidency, but it also raised questions regarding the party's future course.

Fox's reliance on Mexico's first Political Action Committee—"Friends of Fox"—postponed a necessary organizational rehaul and encouraged split-ticket voting in favor of the party's candidate. Post-electoral surveys underscored that the majority of the population did not vote for a shift to the right, or for the ideological position of the PAN's elite, or for social conservatism. The country voted against PRI incompetence but not in favor of PAN's platform. The PAN has always been the party of "political reform," yet the electorate did not endow it with a mandate for further political change.

PAN core supporters tend to be religious but are essentially heterogeneous on economic and cultural issues.[35] The party has many right-wing and liberal supporters among professionals, the upper class, and highly educated voters. But the PAN also garners support among left-wing groups that encompass housewives and people with lower education and lower income. Thus the challenge for the Fox government will be to govern at the center but without alienating the Right or the Left. The center of Mexico's political spectrum is occupied largely by voters with weak or nonexistent party identifications, whose political support Fox will need to retain while reining in more intemperate stances.

Relations between Fox and the PAN since the 2000 election have exhibited a marked level of conflict, particularly when the president has adopted stances that contradict the views of PAN elders. In terms of public rhetoric, PAN leaders and Fox are frequently at odds with each other. The PAN itself has yet to adjust to the imperatives, constraints, and responsibilities of a party in power. At times PAN congresspersons have exhibited an extraordinary amount of anti-Fox discipline, as they did when they opposed the president's stance on the indigenous rights bill. Animosity between key members of the PAN hierarchy and Vicente Fox runs deep, and frequently PAN leaders have seemed more intent on sabotaging the president than on working with him. Many traditional *panistas* feel that the party is slipping through their fingers; they reject the replacement of traditional *panismo* by pragmatic *fox-ismo;* they fought for power and now do not know exactly how Vicente Fox should enact his agenda without selling the party's soul.

The party has confronted recurrent challenges created by a savvy politician who reaches out to constituencies directly, and has sought to establish ties with a wide variety of citizen organizations. Fox's advocacy of the style and instruments of direct democracy goes against the grain of the PAN's vision of political parties as the only acceptable mediation between citizens and the state. The PAN has yet to find a way to govern in tandem with a president who has publicly declared that he will govern alone.[36] It remains to be seen whether in light of their mutually agreed dependence, and with future elections looming large, Fox and the PAN will develop a mutually supportive arrangement.

On the left of the political spectrum, the PRD emerged from the 2000 election in a weakened position in comparison with its electoral gains in 1997.[37] The Left won once again the mayorship of Mexico City but performed badly at the national level and lost over half of its congressional seats. Cuauhtémoc Cárdenas, in his third bid for the presidency, became a victim of the "useful vote" as traditional leftist voters abandoned the PRD's fold to vote for a candidate—Vicente Fox—who actually had a chance of defeating the PRI. Even the PRD's victory in the country's capital was clouded by the PAN's unprecedented gains that forced the PRD to co-govern with its historic enemy in the city's legislative assembly.

The PRD's electoral fracas was due to Cuauhtémoc Cárdenas' bad performance in office compounded by strategic miscalculations during his presidential campaign. After a brief honeymoon in office as mayor of Mexico City, Cárdenas experienced a steady erosion of support as his government flailed and media attacks mounted. Cárdenas' political fortunes also suffered collateral damage from his party's tumultuous election for party leadership and the exit of party founder, Porfirio Muñoz Ledo. Once again, divisions in the PRD seemed more pervasive, more constant, and more public than divisions in its rivals. Internal splits tarnished the party's image as the standard-bearer of democracy.

As it had in the past, the party suffered due to its reliance on the leadership of a single individual, Cuauhtémoc Cárdenas, who continuously displayed his personal preference for confrontational tactics. As the presidential race evolved, Cárdenas campaigned on the proposition that a true transition to democracy would not take place unless the Left won, and therefore was not concerned about becoming the "spoiler." Instead of resurrecting the moderate stance that had served him so well in 1997, Cárdenas remained entrenched in a recalcitrant leftist identity that appealed to core PRD voters but alienated everyone else.

Cárdenas refused Fox's offer to assemble an electoral alliance and instead gambled that his candidacy would be enough to assure between 20 and 25 percent of the vote—enough to sabotage a Fox victory—and thus guarantee the PRD a solid representation in Congress.[38] From that foothold the PRD would groom Cárdenas' political protégés, Andrés Manuel López Obrador or Rosario Robles, for the presidential race in 2004. Cárdenas, however, misunderstood the significance and weight of the "useful vote" and overestimated his capacity to retain popular support.[39] Electoral results revealed that the independents who had cast their lot with him in 1997 defected and even leftist voters left the fold: Cárdenas received significantly fewer votes than his coalition did for Congress. His failed crusade left the PRD in a beleaguered and embattled state. The true tragedy for the PRD has been that the democratic transition it was created to bring about has already occurred.

The PRI did not understand the election and underestimated the desire for change.[40] Party leaders believed that they could only win by resorting to the party's traditional modus operandi—and they were wrong. Instead of building on the political capital produced by the PRI's first-ever presidential primary in November 1999, the PRI squandered it. Instead of committing themselves to the "new PRI" announced by presidential candidate Francisco Labastida, regional powerbrokers returned to clientelistic practices.[41] Instead of reinventing itself, the PRI mimicked itself. The party relied on the old voices, on the old machinery, on the old forms of intimidation.[42] The PRI looked to the past and discarded modern campaign methods that might have assured its future.

The 2000 presidential election revealed that clientelism was no longer enough to guarantee the PRI's electoral dominance. One of the key contributing factors to the PRI's defeat was the decline of the "mobilized" voter whose vote was bought, coerced, or induced. Vote-buying did not disappear, but its impact on electoral behavior was less significant than in the past, proving that old-style machine politics in Mexico had reached their limits. Throughout the country many Mexicans accepted the PRI's gifts—bicycles, washing machines, foodstuffs, basic grains—and still voted against the ruling party. The PRI bought, spent, distributed, and doled out but was unable to convince.[43]

Overall voter turnout was lower than during the 1994 presidential election, but the machine-driven voter turnout favorable to the PRI decreased, while the citizen-motivated vote favorable to Fox increased. In southern Mexico the PRI machine malfunctioned: the party was not able to mobilize the "green," rural vote as it had in the past. The levels of voter turnout in southeast Mexico were lower than in the rest of the country.[44] In contrast, urban, educated Mexico turned out in droves to vote for change and against the PRI.[45] Voters between 18 and 34 years of age gave Vicente Fox a 15 point advantage over the PRI's candidate Francisco Labastida.[46] Fox won with a 20 point advantage over Labastida in the cities.

Fox successfully turned the election into a referendum about change versus continuity: 69 percent of Mexicans who wanted change voted for Fox while only 13 of those who favored change cast their ballots for Labastida. Fox also won because many undecided voters—who made up their minds in the last two weeks of the campaign—voted for the Fox–PAN formula. Fox and the PAN's strong showing in Mexico City and the state of Mexico, where the Left-leaning PRI had made important electoral inroads since the mid-1990s, revealed that Fox's appeal to the *voto útil* (the useful vote) of the Left ultimately did work in his favor.[47] Fox also received electoral support from Mexicans who voted for Roberto Madrazo—Labastida's unruly rival in the PRI primary in November 1999—and from every one in four people who had voted for Ernesto Zedillo in 1994. By waving the banner of change and promising to "kick the PRI out," Fox was able to assemble a heterogeneous coalition that encompassed the country's ideological spectrum, from left to right.

The Fox coalition in effect stole the PRI's identity as multiclass organization that had the capacity to be all things to all people. The identity of the PRI was defined by not having an identity at all. The party had functioned successfully since its inception in 1929 as a pragmatic coalition of interests. Over the years, the PRI was able to unite in a single political force the interests of most social groups: conservatives and revolutionaries, peasants and agro-industrialists, workers and patrons. Its ideological arch was so wide, so broad, and so encompassing that it could embrace most political stances. The PRI was an emblematic "inclusionist" coalition. But in order to survive the loss of the presidency and compete successfully, the PRI will be forced to define itself. Definition, however, implies exclusion, and it is unlikely that in the future the PRI will be able to maintain its diffuse ideology and multifaceted constituency.

Despite its defeat, the PRI was not destroyed; it became an opposition party, but it did not disappear. The once ruling party still controls 59 percent of the states, it is still a majority in 65 percent of the local legislatures, and it still has the strongest national presence.[48] In the past, the PRI had the power to impose its will; in the aftermath of the 2000 election it has the power to veto the government's initiatives. The PRI could become the ultimate "spoiler," the volatile veto, the hangman of any constitutional reform. Mexico's congressional institutional dynamics will depend on what happens to the PRI, on whether the party divides and/or disintegrates, regroups and rebounds, decides to collaborate with the Fox government or hampers it at every opportunity.

The PRI has yet to develop a new identity in the aftermath of the election. Some factions want the PRI to go back to its nationalist-populist-revolutionary roots, while others still support market-led reforms and the technocratic tilt the party took during the past decade.[49] The PRI's legislative behavior is a central question mark, and underscores Mexico's curious paradox: the future dynamics of the country's legislative life depend on a divided and downtrodden party that does not really know how to behave as one. The future of Fox's legislative agenda is in the hands of a disorganized organization with no direction, no leadership, no ideology, and no clear course.[50]

Up until the 2000 election the PRI was a highly disciplined party in Congress. The prohibition on consecutive reelection of deputies meant that congresspersons were loyal to party leaders but detached from their constituencies. Candidacies were decided by the PRI's top brass, not by open primaries. Party loyalty was actually rewarded with a candidacy, a bureaucratic position, a senate seat, or a governorship. Congresspersons followed the party line, and the president and his men delivered on their promises. The *dedazo*—the president's capacity to hand-pick his successor—kept this system alive and well for decades, as the incoming president protected the interests of the former president, including all promises made to PRI legislators who voted the party line.[51]

That era has ended. In all probability, a constitutional amendment that would allow the reelection of congresspersons will be approved during the Fox term. PRI deputies will listen more to the demands of their constituencies and have fewer incentives to obey orders from above. As the PRI struggles to rebuild its bases of support and democratize internally, open primaries will become the rule instead of the exception. PRI discipline will decrease. The PRI's loss of the presidency also entails the loss of a large bureaucracy whose posts can no longer be offered as a political reward. As a consequence, party loyalty will no longer be a foregone conclusion. For seventy-one years the PRI was the party of organized Mexico and most major unions, peasant organizations, and professional associations swelled its ranks. But after the 2000 election it is unlikely that the PRI will be able to count on its past pillars of support and traditional strategies to win the vote.

During hegemonic rule, the PRI could always rely on vote-buying in rural areas to assure electoral success. But in coming years, the real political battleground will be the cities, where votes can be garnered more efficiently and other parties can engage in clientelist practices as well. The problem for the PRI is that urban areas are highly competitive in electoral terms, and the PAN, as the party in power in many cities, has the upper hand. The PAN has also developed clientelist strategies with a national coverage, and in the 2000 election the party relied on them to mobilize its own voters with a greater degree of effectiveness: 82 percent of those targeted by the PAN voted for Vicente Fox. Not only has clientelism declined; its effectiveness as a method for voter mobilization by the PRI has also decreased.

The PRI is divided and chaotic; it lacks autonomous organizations and routinized procedures; its mere survival is unclear. Yet the PRD also faces its own travails stemming from relatively weak organizational links to civil society and organizational mishaps, that have earned it a well-deserved reputation for divisiveness and disorganization. Both parties have lost the driving forces that fueled their electoral behavior and assured their unity. The PRI has lost the presidency and the power and resources that came with it, and the PRD has been confronted with the irrefutable fact that a democratic transition has already taken place. Both parties now face the tasks of ideological redefinition and leadership renovation. Perhaps, as Andreas Schedler has suggested, Mexico will witness the birth of "a two-and-a-half" party system, with one of them reduced to a miniscule presence."[52]

The party system that has emerged from the 2000 election confirms several past trends, but also faces new uncertainties. The system is highly competitive and is centered on the three main parties, all of which face uncertain futures and hard choices. The PRI as a state party must learn how to become an opposition party. The PAN as a former opposition party must learn how to become a party in government. The PRD as a party of the old Left must learn how to become a party of the new Left. While the parties resolve their crises of identity, one thing is clear: none of them show great appetite for congressional cooperation. All three—the PRI, the PAN, and the PRD—are thinking about the midterm election to renew the lower house in 2003 and the next presidential race in 2006, and will structure their future strategies accordingly.

The PRD will continue to vote against most of the Fox government's legislative initiatives for rational reasons. The electoral base of the Left—comprised largely of low-income voters with lower levels of education—may swell if former members of the PRI switch over in light of the party's defeat. The PRD will continue to decry the negative impact of economic neoliberalism, and argue that the new administration is merely more of the same. Meanwhile, the PRI's ad hoc cooperative strategy will enable the PRD to articulate a political discourse that blames the PAN and the PRI for persistent social inequalities. The PRD knows that crucial legislative decisions, such as the budget, will ultimately be approved by the combined votes of the PAN and the PRI. The Left can maintain a purist, opposition stance without jeopardizing governability, but pay no political cost for its strategic stance.

In Mexico's new political context, opposition parties will play predictable roles dictated by the libretto of their current circumstances. They know that they will not be able to obtain all their demands at the negotiating table, but nonetheless hope to make a dent in the government's armor. The PRD consistently voted against most economic initiatives put forth by PRI regimes, and will do the same under Fox. The PRI supported political and fiscal centralization when the party was in power, and will now demand devolution to the states it still governs. The PRI does not have the credibility to provoke governmental paralysis, and the PRD—as a free rider—does not have to face the prospect of provoking it. Political compromise may occur, but the Fox government may have to pay for it via budgetary allocations to its only feasible congressional ally, the PRI. Fox may promote a policy of appeasement toward the PRI throughout his tenure in order to garner the party's legislative support for key presidential initiatives.

Political Power: Dispersed and Divided

The July 2000 election confirmed that politically speaking Mexico is many Mexicos.[53] The decentralization of power, begun under President Carlos Salinas de Gortari, accelerated by Ernesto Zedillo, and reinforced by electoral results throughout the 1990s, had consolidated a political landscape where PAN and PRD governments share power with their PRI counterparts. Parties other than the PRI now govern in thirteen of thirty-one entities, with over half the population. Divided governments, once the exception, have become the norm at the national and subnational levels. The results revealed a political system where many states are strongly competitive, and have been competitive for over a decade. By 1994, the PRI faced electoral threats in all 300 electoral districts. Democratization had already taken place at the local level, and the national transfer of power from the PRI to the opposition merely reinforced a preexisting trend.

Over the past decade, state and municipal governments slowly became laboratories of local democracy, due to the onset of divided governments. State governors learned how to deal with local congresses dominated by opposition parties, and the increased competitiveness of political processes in the provinces led to increased responsiveness and accountability among public officials. Particularly in northern states, citizens became accustomed to rewarding or punishing parties at the polls. Party organizations learned how to compete, draft better candidates, and wage better battles.

Divided government was accompanied over the past decade by decentralization, and the two tandem trends have led to the emergence of checks and balances and rowdy battles over the budget. Decentralization has entailed the substantial and rapid devolution of financial—and political—resources from the federal to the state to the municipal governments, thus shifting political power to the states, away from the federal bureaucracy and away from Mexico City-based politicians. Governors and municipal presidents are becoming powerbrokers in their own right, and are participating in national coalition-building in a way that will create future challenges for democratic governance.

Decentralization may breathe new life into the PRI, as the party struggles to regain the power it lost and preserve the power it has. The 2000 election left many members of the PRI without a map, without a compass, without a leader, without a job. After the party's national defeat, many of its members migrated to the periphery, to the states they still controlled. From there they have emulated the PAN's past strategies and have become the most vociferous advocates of economic and fiscal decentralization. Fueled by the PRI's diaspora to the provinces, Mexico is experiencing a vigorous, combative, demanding, and possibly anti-democratic federalism.[54]

During the Zedillo term decentralization opened spaces for subnational politics that were promptly occupied by old-guard *priistas*. In states and localities still controlled by the PRI, modernizers and traditional party leaders constantly struggled over issues ranging from electoral fraud and unfair electoral competition to human rights violations and unresolved labor disputes.[55] Even in the afterglow of an exemplary election, Mexico is witnessing a growing gap between the national-level democratization process and what occurs in PRI-controlled authoritarian archipelagos at the state and local levels. PRI members may copy the PAN's longtime strategy and use the periphery as a way of regaining the center.[56] The PRI may become a major migraine for the Fox government as it attempts to rebuild itself by challenging the central government from the periphery, using every means at its disposal.

In the long term, however, the possibility that regional *caciques* continue to control the population through fraud and coercion has decreased. The PRI no longer has access to the presidential pocketbook, and therefore can no longer buy political support at the local level through federal government spending. In addition, divided governments will increasingly act as a counterweight to provincial powerbrokers. Clientelism may not disappear but it will be harder to enact at the national level. And although local patronage machines may subsist, *caciques*—in states like Tabasco and Yucatán —will increasingly become the exception instead of the rule.[57]

In light of this new landscape, the PRI has faced three choices: retrench and regroup at the local level as a nationalist, center-left, anti-government force; succumb to internal cannibalism; or thoroughly reinvent itself as a moderate, centrist alternative to the Fox government. The "state-within-a-state" scenario appeals to some of the hard-line governors who foresee the maintenance of authoritarian archipelagos as their only route to survival. However, a scenario whereby the PRI succumbs to gradual self-destruction or to an implosion provoked by an internal split should not be discounted. Cleavages within the PRI run deep, particularly the divide between those who supported Francisco Labastida during the PRI primary and the presidential race, and those who sided with his main rival, Roberto Madrazo. Some factions have called for thorough internal democratization, while others continue to resist it. Without an ideology to defend, without bureaucratic positions to offer, without goods to distribute, without the presidency to lean on, the PRI may be no more than a hollow man.

If the August 2000 defeat of the PRI in the southern state of Chiapas is any indication, the party has found it more difficult to deal with the sort of electoral competitiveness at the local level that is here to stay.[58] Political decentralization coupled with competition has created an unprecedented situation wherein the PRI's staying power depends on how well it performs in state and local elections, without federal support. Politics for the PRI has become local. In some areas, like Tabasco, the PRI has been able to retain its hold, but in others, like Yucatán, the party's political predominance has come to an end due to popular resistance and the growing political strength of the PAN. The PRI's salvation will ultimately depend on the party's ability to use its positions of power in the states and in Congress to construct a real alternative to the Fox government.

The dispersion of political power in Mexico during the 1990s has also been fueled by the continued empowerment of civil society. Approximately 15 percent of the urban adult population consider themselves participants in civic associations, excluding religious and recreational groups. This is a surprisingly high figure for a country without a civic tradition.[59] The process of democratization has created new local governments more open to societal initiatives related to the struggle for justice, democracy, and human rights.[60] The late 1990s also mark the beginning of greater NGO interest and focus on matters of public policy. Women's groups and environmental NGOs were particularly successful in promoting the adoption of new laws and obtaining greater public recognition. The efforts of some groups in recent years have centered on improving public accountability, including the legal suit against President Zedillo in order to force him to make information public regarding his salary.

The indigenous uprising in Chiapas in 1994 also became a catalyst for the formation and strengthening of pro-democracy movements and networks of *zapatista* solidarity. For many NGOs, the main form of civic mobilization was the popular *consultas* held in 1995 and 1999, on the issue of indigenous rights and the future of the Zapatista Army of National Liberation (Ejército Zapatista de Liberación Nacional—EZLN). Sporadic violence in the state—including the Acteal massacre in 1996—kept public interest focused on the issue of authoritarian enclaves and indigenous demands. Heightened civic consciousness combined with the electoral alliance of the PAN and the PRD behind a single candidate led to the PRI's historic loss of the governorship of Chiapas.

Beyond grassroots activism related to accountability, human rights, women's rights, and Chiapas, Mexico has also witnessed the emergence of new actors with new roles, including the Catholic Church and the Mexican media. In the aftermath of President Carlos Salinas' historic decision to reestablish the government's diplomatic ties with the Vatican, the Catholic Church has developed a more visible and potent profile. Over the past decade, some progressive sectors of the Church became a force for democratization through their calls for voter participation during electoral contests. The Catholic Church also contributed to the emergence of urban cultural groups working outside the framework of the state.[61] During the Zedillo period, some members of the Church's hierarchy engaged in vocal criticism of the neoliberal components of economic policy, and may continue to do the same if Fox's decisions do little to improve the lot of the poor. Yet at the same time, the Church could view Fox's conservative stance on social issues as a window of opportunity to engage in public and political activism related to its own agenda. For better or for worse, the Church has become a key—albeit controversial—actor in Mexico's political process.

Significant changes have also taken place in the realm of the media, whose reporters have metamorphosed from government scribes into members of a burgeoning fourth estate. Objective reporting, critical journalism, and government bashing are now daily routines instead of episodic occurrences.[62] The media's political subservience has largely become a relic of the past, and today Mexican journalism can be criticized more for its lack of professionalism than for its pro-government stance. During the 2000 election, coverage provided by the country's main television networks still displayed a PRI bias, but was much more plural and inclusive than in prior contests. The pressure to increase ratings guides more content and editorial decisions than does the desire to please the Office of the Presidency. Print journalism increasingly functions as a political watchdog, and has uncovered key stories on corruption and government malfeasance. The media's evolution is both cause and effect of greater electoral competition, given the key role that television plays in political campaigns.

For many Mexicans, campaigns have ceased to be ritualistic forms of behavior with foreseeable results. American-style campaigns in which key battles are waged in the media have now become everyday forms of political performance. Mexicans make up their own minds after viewing the screen, instead of following the PRI's explicit or implicit instructions. As a result, political participation is more open-ended and less predictable. Government accountability is becoming an important facet of Mexican political culture, and explains the sort of retrospective voting that forced the PAN out of the governorship of Chihuahua in 1996.

Over the past two decades, Mexican political culture has undergone important transformations, leading to what Vikram Chand has called "Mexico's political awakening."[63] Whereas corruption was once tolerated as an unavoidable component of the political system, today it is increasingly denounced. Clientelism was an effective strategy to garner support, but the PRI's decline underscores its terminal weakness. Gift giving affected the vote, but today its use by the PRI has little impact on electoral outcomes. Government accountability was an elusive goal, but now it is increasingly perceived as a public right. The road from clientelism to citizenship has been hard to build, but in the aftermath of the 2000 election, it will be easier to follow.

After the contested election of 1988, political debates among elites in Mexico centered on the essential unfairness of the electoral process, on the lack of impartiality of electoral authorities, and on the improper tallying of the votes. As electoral fraud subsided, subsequent political negotiations shifted to the need to assure a level playing field among contenders and address issues of electoral credibility. As those problems were gradually resolved via successive rounds of electoral reform, new items emerged on the public agenda, including campaign financing and party coalitions. Mexico's democracy has not arrived at a final, pristine destination.[64] It is a work in progress. As democratic consolidation proceeds, public debates on pending issues such as redistribution and economic well-being, public insecurity, minority rights, indigenous rights, and women's participation must be addressed.[65] For years Mexicans debated whether or not democracy had arrived; now they will need to argue over its content.

The Rule of Law: Unenforceable and Elusive

The main challenge to democratic governance in Mexico lies not only in the realm of executive-legislative relations, party politics, or civil society. The highest hurdle the new regime faces is the establishment of institutions and practices that assure the rule of law. Mexico's transition has cast a glaring light on the country's "precarious, uneven, and limited rule of law."[66] Crime has been on the upswing since the 1995 crisis, and public insecurity is now an integral part of the country's psyche.

But perhaps even more troublesome than increased criminality is the government's incapacity to deal with it in an effective fashion. Overwhelmed by its caseload and saddled by inefficiency and corruption, the Mexican judiciary cannot establish, ensure, or enforce the rule of law.[67] Plagued by financial and institutional deterioration, courts frequently cannot process cases quickly or effectively enough to deal with Mexico's growing wave of criminality.

As a result of judicial inefficiency, impunity runs rampant. In Mexico City in 1997, of the 95 cases processed out of every 100 reported crimes, 72 were tossed out due to insufficient evidence, 23 were actually resolved, and only 4 of those 23 actually culminated in conviction and detention. Cases of official corruption—those of former governors accused of drug trafficking abound—and the credibility of public institutions has suffered when even those proven guilty have eluded punishment. The Fox government has underscored its commitment to transparency and accountability, but its effort may be undermined by judicial institutions that cannot assure those goals.

Mexico's culture of illegality is not only the result of government inaction and institutional dysfunctionality. In Mexico the lack of respect for the rule of law is "encrusted in the heart of citizen beliefs."[68] In a poll conducted in 1999, 49 percent of Mexicans believed that laws should not be obeyed if they are unfair. Circumventing the law has become an old tradition. Mexicans partially follow laws, negotiate their implementation, tolerate illegality, and justify it with economic, political, or practical reasons. As long as ambiguity persists—among the government and the governed themselves—regarding the rule of law, legality will be subject to negotiation. Justice or injustice will be the result of "influence, pressure, public opinion or the conciliation of interests."[69] An unhealthy skepticism regarding rules has become entrenched and is exacerbated by societal distrust of the state.[70]

The precarious nature of Mexico's rule of law is compounded by drug trafficking, a pervasive and growing problem.[71] The DEA believes that Mexico earns more than $7 billion a year from the drug trade, and that the drug business provides employment to roughly 200,000 people. As much as 70 percent of the South American cocaine bound for the United States market enters through Mexico; Mexico also supplies between 20 and 30 percent of the heroin consumed in the United States and up to 80 percent of the imported marijuana.

Mexico's weak and malfunctioning judicial and law enforcement institutions have been unable to withstand the corrupting influence of the drug trade, as illustrated by the series of high-profile murders and scandals— involving public officials—in recent years. Enormous profits provide the means to buy political protection. Cocaine traffickers spend as much as $500 million a year on bribery, which is more than double the budget of the Mexican attorney general's office. Oftentimes it becomes difficult to distinguish those charged with policing smuggling from the smugglers themselves. A report by Mexico's Interior Ministry estimates that by 1995 there were approximately 900 armed criminal bands in the country, and that 50 percent were comprised of current or former law enforcement agents. Policemen frequently play dual roles: they act as drug enforcers and as drug-smuggling protectors.

Under President Zedillo, drug control dominated the Mexican judicial system, with the majority of the federal budget for the administration of justice devoted to the effort. But corruption within Mexican law enforcement itself also burgeoned: in 1996 the attorney general estimated that 70 to 80 percent of the judicial police were corrupt. Police corruption, in turn, has generated growing pressures to turn to the military to take on more drug control tasks, and currently about one-third of the military's budget is devoted to the anti-drug effort, with some 25,000 Mexican soldiers involved in drug control operations.

As a result of its anti-drug role, the military has become the supreme authority—or in some cases the only authority—in parts of some states such as Oaxaca, Sinaloa, Jalisco, and Guerrero. While the military has traditionally concentrated on crop eradication, its anti-drug mission has expanded significantly in recent years. But greater militarization has also led to greater corruption in the military. When Sinaloa drug cartel leader Hector "El Güero" Palma was arrested in 1995, he was at the home of a local police commander and the majority of the men protecting him were federal judicial police whom he had bought off. The lucrative payoffs from the drug trade also fuel intense competition within and between law enforcement. Violent conflicts often erupt between police and military personnel operating as law enforcers and police and military personnel acting as lawbreakers.

According to Peter Andreas,[72] drug corruption in Mexico reflects a paradox: the government's drug enforcement effort is undermined by the corrupting influence of the drug trade, yet the drug trade cannot survive without the protection of compromised elements within the government. When drug corruption scandals have erupted in Mexico, the official response has been to fire or transfer individual officers and at times disband entire agencies and create new ones. A report by the attorney general's office indicates that over 400 agents of the federal judicial police (more than 10 percent of total personnel) were fired or suspended between 1992 and 1995 on drug-related charges. Such mass firings, however, only begin to make a dent in the problem. Moreover, many fired police officers were simply rehired in other regions of the country and hundreds of other officers were reinstated after challenging their dismissals in court.

The prospects for effective democratic governance in Mexico will be contingent on the country's capacity to hold all significant actors—inside the state and beyond it—accountable to the rule of law.[73] This development, in turn, would require a clear hierarchy of laws, interpreted by an independent judicial system and supported by a strong legal culture in society.[74] In concrete terms, that goal would require a major overhaul of Mexico's judiciary and its law enforcement apparatus. In addition, corrupt practices would have to be sanctioned in a clear, non-partisan, and legitimate fashion. Government institutions would have to be reinvented to resist the temptations of the illicit activities related to the drug trade. Accountability would have to become, in a nutshell, "the only game in town."

The turn to transparency has already taken place in the electoral realm, and the government can learn lessons from the renovation of the country's electoral institutions in the 1990s. The institution in charge of organizing and supervising elections—the Federal Electoral Institute (IFE)—emerged from the 2000 election as a consolidated and strengthened entity. Its electoral counselors demonstrated impartiality and intelligence, prudence and professionalism. Electoral booths were installed on time, electoral representatives were generally well trained, data flowed in a normal fashion, and the Institute proved that it was capable of running an impeccable contest. Parties competed on a largely level playing field, electoral results were viewed as legitimate, electoral authorities were recognized as impartial and fair, and the election itself empowered new faces with new political stripes. Real *alternancia*—taking turns in office—took place. Electoral authoritarianism came to an end.[75] These dramatic changes to the IFE and the rules governing electoral competition were brought about by ongoing, intense negotiations over time among the country's main political forces. They were the product of political agreements and pacts undertaken to transform the system. This past history of pact-making could set a precedent for future negotiations on what remains to be done to enable democratic governance in the future.

Institutional reform will be crucial to address the pressing items of Mexico's democratic transition. The retreat of the state in the 1980s and 1990s was not accompanied by the construction of a new, democratic, institutional structure aside from the electoral arena. The privatization of state enterprises did not bring about the desired transparency of economic transactions. The turn toward neoliberalism did not remedy dramatic disparities and income inequalities. The weakening of state control over security forces left an open field for the burgeoning of crime and corruption. Mexico is a more democratic country, a more open society, a more competitive economy, but it is not a safer or a more equal place.

Conclusion

As an astute analyst predicted, Mexico's classic hegemonic party system ended not with a bang, but with a whimper.[76] The country was blessed with unexpected good fortune: a resounding victory by an opposition candidate, a long-standing ruling party that lost and had no choice but to recognize its defeat, a sufficiently large margin of victory that allowed for a surprisingly peaceful passing of the torch. For once, after a long history of bloody battles, Mexicans enjoyed the best of all worlds and experienced a peaceful transition of power. Longtime union leader and PRI icon Fidel Velazquez had declared: "We [the PRI] arrived shooting and we'll leave shooting." Yet voters, electoral officials, pollsters, the media, and Mexicans at large proved him wrong.

Mexico has become a country of exiled PRI dinosaurs, an empowered PAN, and intense legislative negotiations. Mexico now has a Congress that acts as a counterweight, a media that functions as a watch-dog, and a civil society that demands more and accepts less. Mexico today looks more like a democracy that has arrived, warts and all, and less like a democracy in waiting. Suddenly the challenges for democratic governance—a constrained executive, a divided government, an increasingly decentralized political system—have become proof of Mexico's great leap forward.

Yet post-PRI Mexico will not be an untroubled place. The challenges are significant and should not be underestimated. Forty percent of the population lives in poverty. Drug trafficking continues apace. An ineffective judiciary and a corrupt police force create more problems than they solve. Some of these hurdles are inherited, but the Fox government also faces new ones created by the conditions under which it was elected. The peculiar nature of the political process that ousted the ruling party from power may make future political and economic reforms more difficult to carry out. In the future, democratic governance in Mexico will be hampered by the fact that Vicente Fox arrived in office on the shoulders of a disparate array of forces, many of which do not support the president's initiatives.

As a result of contending imperatives, instead of rapid change, inertia has prevailed. Since the 2000 election, the president has attempted to govern at the center without alienating the Right or the Left. In an effort to straddle both ends of the ideological spectrum and address the concerns of disparate groups, the new government has often diluted reforms or accepted their postponement. Necessary transformations in the areas that Mexicans want and the country needs will only occur when the government defines a clear set of priorities, follows them consistently, and forges consensus in the legislature.

This will not be easy to accomplish in a divided democracy. President Fox's ambitious agenda has frequently been sabotaged by a recalcitrant Congress. Opposition parties have often blocked the government's plans for reform without producing alternative proposals of their own. Post-PRI Mexico is saddled with a divided government and a fragmented legislature, making legislative coalitions difficult to create and difficult to sustain. Parties in opposition have no incentives to carry out responsible policies, because either they are in crisis or they are without any prospects of governmental responsibilities. The enactment of "second-stage" reforms—including further economic liberalization—faces staunch opposition from both the PRI and the PRD. The PRD exercises permanent veto power in an effort to solidify support among its electoral base, while the PRI exacts a high price for its ad hoc collaboration.

The president has attempted to govern in a divided democracy by "going public" and using presidential popularity to bring about legislative victories. But in cases like Mexico, where presidential and congressional reelection is prohibited by law, courting public opinion to pressure Congress does not work effectively as a method to enact the executive's reform agenda. The future of congresspersons depends more on party leaders than on the president's political fortunes, and this will only change when congressional reelection is allowed.

Most Mexicans who voted for Vicente Fox endowed him with the mantle of change—better economic management, less crime, less corruption—and they expect the new government to ensure it occurs. High expectations that often accompany new democracies are a source of political capital, and Mexico is no exception. If expectations are left unmet, however, support may be withdrawn and a "punishment vote" could ensue in the 2003 legislative elections. Mexican voters are rewarding and punishing parties and presidents at the polls, and will continue to do so.

Mexicans today expect democratic governance to be about performance. As Roderic Camp's World Values poll suggests, Mexicans perceive democracy as *bienestar social* (social well-being), and although citizens celebrate the arrival of liberal/procedural democracy, they will continue to demand the material benefits they believe it affords. In the long run, sustained and equitable economic growth, coupled with greater government transparency and less public insecurity, may be the best way to bolster confidence in the virtues of democratic governance.

A democratic transition undoubtedly has occurred in Mexico, but the country still needs to establish institutions and cultivate habits and attitudes that will allow democracy to thrive and flourish. Mexico has an increasingly free and lively civil society, but citizens have yet to be fully represented in a Congress where reelection assures responsiveness. Mexico exhibits a relatively autonomous political society, but the terms *institutional routinization* and *compromise* have yet to become part of the country's daily vocabulary, particularly where relations between the executive and the legislature are concerned. And most important, Mexico still lacks a critical component of democratic consolidation: a rule of law. The future of democratic governance will hinge on the interaction of the following conditions: divided government, diminished presidential power in a former presidentialist regime, a party system in flux, political and economic decentralization, and the absence of an institutional framework that assures the rule of law.

Yet despite the enormity of the task at hand, the possibility of incremental change and institutional renewal—in wake of the PRI's defeat—is real. During the PRI's uninterrupted reign, politics in Mexico had become a fig leaf for corruption and complicity. Vicente Fox's victory entails more than the arrival of an opposition government to power, more than another landmark in Mexico's tortuous transition to democracy. When Fox won, the PRI lost its capacity to buy and sell factories and favors, banks and businesses, drug routes and political protection. *Alternancia* has opened the door for greater accountability, the stuff of which democratic governance is made of. Old institutions have collapsed and new ones have yet to be built, but the country has the building materials and the appropriate site to do so. As Mexican historian Héctor Aguilar Camín has suggested, Mexico is simultaneously treading on "ashes and seeds."[77]

PART IV

Conclusion

15

Constructing Democratic Governance in Latin America

Taking Stock of the 1990s

Jorge I. Domínguez

The practice of democratic governance improved in most Latin American countries during the second half of the 1990s, in comparison to the circumstances prevailing during the first half of the 1990s (analyzed in the first edition of this book).[1] Constitutional governments survived; many became stronger. All but one military coup attempt failed. Political parties became more reliable and responsible in most countries. Societal changes led to new roles for labor unions and for women in politics and in the workforce. Congressionally approved laws, rather than presidential decrees, were used increasingly to enact the principal economic and other policy reforms. Various Supreme Courts displayed greater independence and assertiveness. In 2000, an opposition candidate was elected president of Mexico for the first time since that country's revolution early in the twentieth century, and Alberto Fujimori was compelled to resign as president of Peru, as his third consecutive reelection was marred by electoral fraud, vote-buying, and rampant abuse of power.

And yet, this improvement was highly uneven among countries. The setbacks to democratic governance in the late 1990s were pronounced in the Andean region. Especially troubling was the decay of constitutional government in Colombia and Venezuela, two of Latin America's longest-lived democracies, as well as the abuse of presidential power in Alberto Fujimori's Peru and the fragility and instability of the democratic regime in Ecuador (where the region's only successful coup against a freely elected president in two decades took place also in 2000). Disastrous economic performance hurt Argentine political stability in 2002. The improved quality of constitutional governance did not reach acceptable standards of democratic performance in many countries as the 1990s ended. For example, in the mid-1990s Guatemala at long last overcame decades of brutal civil war—an important accomplishment—but Guatemala's armed forces remain weakly subordinated to civilian authorities, parties are unstable and poorly organized, and the rule of law has yet to serve broad segments of the indigenous population. Moreover, the conditions that affect the daily lives of most citizens in nearly all Latin American countries improved too little from the first to the second half of the 1990s.

Therefore, a majority of Latin American citizens deemed constitutional government broadly unsatisfactory, as evidenced in many public opinion polls.[2] In more general terms, the inner workings of constitutional government remained defective in many countries where presidents tended still to lord it over Parliaments. The rule of law remained precarious wherever the application of the law was unpredictable, varying in time and by case. The courts also remain slow and are at times unprofessional. Corruption remained the bane of much of the region; in too many cases market reforms lacked transparency. The challenges for the construction of effective democratic governance persisted, therefore, into the twenty-first century.

In this chapter, however, I will argue that the net effect of the patterns of the 1990s was to strengthen the performance and the prospects for effective democratic governance in most Latin American countries. I distinguish between levels and trends. The level of democratic governance, in many although not all respects, remains poor not just in the Andean region but also throughout much of Latin America. The trends toward better democratic governance are more hopeful throughout the region, except in some Andean countries and Nicaragua, Paraguay, and Cuba. In arguing that the trend is positive, I am comparing Latin American countries to their own history, not to some set of idealized categories. Nor am I comparing the performance of Latin American democracies to the hopeful expectations that many citizens and analysts held in the early 1990s for the region's political trajectory for the remainder of the decade; those expectations were understandably inflated but also unreasonable, given the region's context and circumstances.

The Survival of Constitutional Government: Coup and Impeachment Attempts

In the 1990s, constitutional government was resilient throughout the world even when its performance left much to be desired. The armed forces did not overthrow a single constitutional government in former communist Europe. The frequency of military coups against constitutional governments fell as well in East Asia; the armed forces did not overthrow any East or Southeast Asian constitutional government even in the midst or aftermath of the subregion-wide financial crash of 1997. In Latin America, only one constitutionally elected civilian president was overthrown by the armed forces (Ecuador's Jamil Mahuad in January 2000). Even in this case, domestic and international pressure quickly forced the military plotters to turn over power to Ecuador's constitutionally elected vice-president and Congress. Despite the region-wide repercussions of the Mexican financial panic of 1994–95 and the Brazilian financial panic of January 1999, or the prolonged economic decline begun in Argentina in the late 1990s, the armed forces overthrew no other Latin American civilian president. In decades past, these economic disasters would have toppled various governments.[3]

The frequency of presidential-led military coups against Congress declined in Latin America. In 1992, Peru's President Alberto Fujimori secured military support to shut down the Congress and purge the courts of his enemies. In May 1993, Guatemala's President Jorge Serrano unsuccessfully attempted a similar coup. No such attempt was tried in Latin America during the second half of the 1990s.

The frequency of unsuccessful coup attempts seems to have declined over the 1990s, although not all such attempts may have become public. In the first half of the 1990s, coups aimed at elected civilian authorities were attempted or extensively plotted in Argentina, El Salvador, Paraguay (1989), and Venezuela. All failed. In the second half of the 1990s, by contrast, only Paraguay witnessed repeated (1996, 1999, 2000), albeit unsuccessful, coup attempts. In Peru, there were two unsuccessful coup attempts associated with the breakdown of President Alberto Fujimori's corrupt regime in late 2000. The former chief of the intelligence service, Vladimiro Montesinos, attempted to launch a coup in September 2000 when President Fujimori dismissed him; the military leadership refused to back Montesinos. In October 2000, two mid-ranking military officers, the brothers Ollanta and Antauro Humala, launched a brief rebellion in a remote area of Peru to press for Fujimori's resignation. In April 2002, a military coup attempt failed in Venezuela.

Coups are not the only threats to the survival of constitutional government. Severe conflicts between president and Congress, as John Carey's chapter shows, also pose serious challenges even if the constitutional procedures for presidential impeachment and removal are followed to the letter. Impeachments have occurred for very different reasons. In the first half of the 1990s, President Fernando Collor de Mello in Brazil and President Carlos Andrés Pérez in Venezuela were removed from office through constitutional processes. The Guatemalan Congress removed President Serrano after his failed coup against the Congress, but Congress also dissolved itself and called for early elections. In the second half of the 1990s, the Congress impeached and removed President Abdalá Bucaram in Ecuador, accusing him of mental illness, and President Raúl Cubas in Paraguay, charging him with violating the constitution and complicity to murder. The Peruvian Congress insisted on rejecting President Fujimori's resignation in late 2000 in order to impeach and remove him, a moot although symbolic point; the Peruvian Congress also dissolved itself and called for early elections. Although the number of actual presidential impeachments and removals was the same during both halves of the 1990s, the frequency of impeachment activity increased somewhat during the decade. Serious although ultimately unsuccessful attempts to impeach and remove the president were also launched against Ernesto Samper in Colombia and Arnoldo Alemán in Nicaragua in the later 1990s. (There was probable cause for the president's removal from office in all of these cases; the more constitutionally doubtful cases were the removals of Pérez in Venezuela and Bucaram in Ecuador.)

The Problem of Civilian Supremacy

The Americas may not yet sigh with relief, however. The trend toward civilian supremacy over the armed forces is positive but the level of performance in effectively exercising such control remains poor throughout most Latin American countries, as Rut Diamint makes clear in her chapter. Constitutional government will not be secure until civilian supremacy is unquestioned. Constitutional government remains in peril in Ecuador, Paraguay, and Venezuela, where there have been coup attempts (one, successful in Ecuador) and presidential impeachments. In addition, the armed forces still intervene in the day-to-day politics of several Latin American countries. Persistent violence from drug traffickers, guerrillas, and paramilitaries wracks Colombia, as Fernando Cepeda shows in his chapter, necessarily endowing Colombia's security forces with a significant political role (Colombia's forces remain subordinate to civilian authorities, however). Diamint's chapter also shows that military expenditures, not surprisingly, rose in Colombia, Ecuador, and Paraguay from the mid-1980s to the late 1990s.

Peru continued to face the remnants of terrorist groups that, in the early 1990s, had threatened to overwhelm enfeebled national institutions. By the late 1990s, this political violence had become a task that the police could handle but, as Carlos Iván Degregori shows in his chapter, the armed forces retained significant political clout through the end of Alberto Fujimori's presidency in late 2000. Chile is a model of progress on various dimensions of politics, economics, and society as it enters the twenty-first century but, as Felipe Agüero demonstrates in his chapter, very high military prerogatives remain embedded in Chile's constitution many years after the transition from General Pinochet's dictatorship to constitutional government. The Chilean armed forces retain discretionary budget and political entitlements guaranteed by the constitution; these authoritarian entitlements would be considered "unconstitutional" in any other democratic political system. Repeated acts of coordinated military indiscipline occurred, especially in the first half of the 1990s. Nonetheless, in 1999–2000 the Chilean armed forces voluntarily participated in dialogues with civilians regarding violations of human rights committed in the 1970s and 1980s and provided more information on some of the "disappeared."[4] In Venezuela, failed coup-maker Hugo Chávez was elected president in 1998. Chávez appointed military officers to hitherto civilian posts and increased the military budget deliberately and enthusiastically, as Michael Coppedge and Diamint explain in their chapters, at times despite the reluctance of professional military officers to assume roles outside of strict military arenas.

In contrast, institutionalized civilian control over the military proceeded farthest in Argentina and Uruguay. In the late 1990s, Brazilian President Fernando Henrique Cardoso also made progress in this direction. In Central American countries, as Diamint notes, the downsizing of the armed forces as a result of the various transitions to civilian rule and the end of civil wars were not generally accompanied by the emergence of effective civilian control over the military. The level of performance remains low. Moreover, increased crime added greatly to citizen insecurity. Nonetheless, the trend toward significant demilitarization in Central America is a stunning accomplishment for a region that long symbolized military tyrannies and that was wracked by civil war from the 1960s to the early 1990s.[5]

Explaining Patterns in Civil-Military Relations

Two patterns need explanation. Why the trend toward fewer coups? What explains the level of military clout? In the first edition of this book, Domínguez and Giraldo identified two factors to account for the decline in the frequency of coups.[6] On the one hand, the propensity toward, and frequency of, military coup attempts seems to be related to the level of professionalization of the armed forces: the lower the level of professionalization (Ecuador, Paraguay, for example), the more likely coup attempts would be. This pattern differs from what had prevailed in Latin American countries in the late 1960s and early 1970s, when the more professional the military, the greater the likelihood and success of coup attempts.[7] What explains the inversion of this pattern? Their professionalism notwithstanding, the militaries for the most part governed badly, often damaging the military institutions in the process. As a result, most seem to have been vaccinated against attempting coups. The "supply" of coups declined. Only time will tell whether the effect of these vaccines will last forever.

The "demand" for coups also fell. Except for General Augusto Pinochet's

Chile and, thanks to the oil boom, the Ecuadorian military government in the 1970s, no authoritarian regime that yielded power during the democratizing "moment" (1979–90) managed the economy well; they presided over declining living standards. All authoritarian regimes repressed public liberties and persons; some committed acts of appalling cruelty. The demand for coups was also reduced thanks to the evident strength of parties of the Right; many business elites no longer rely on military coups to advance their objectives because they have direct influence under civilian rule. For example, Center–Right and right-wing parties, alone or in coalition, consistently won the much freer elections held in Brazil since the transition from military rule in 1985, and in El Salvador, Guatemala, and Nicaragua since the end of their respective civil wars in 1992 and 1996, respectively.[8] The end of Fujimori's regime also supports this argument. Despite political uncertainty and a power vacuum, there was no "demand" in Peru for a military coup as the Fujimori regime unraveled in late 2000; thus the attempted coups fizzled.

Yet the worldwide regularity of the decline in the frequency of coups suggests that international factors constitute a third explanation. The end of the Cold War deprived would-be coup-makers of anti-communist "national security" rationales and U.S. support for possible coups. The United States became much more likely to support democratic governments. The European Union also took an interest in the consolidation of constitutional government in Eastern Europe. Argentina, Brazil, and the United States helped to prevent the success of coup attempts in Paraguay. The OAS, with support from the United States and most members, has helped to thwart some military coup attempts since the adoption of new policies (the Santiago Declaration 1080) in 1991. In general, efforts by various governments, groups of governments, and NGOs strengthened the worldwide efficacy of international democratic norms, with salutary effects in Latin America as well.

The level of military influence over politics, the second pattern to be explained, is unrelated to the factors just cited, however. Two elements cited for the trends toward fewer coups (demand reduction and international factors) have converging and uniform effects across countries. They explain the absence of variation: there are virtually no coups against constitutional governments. But as a consequence, they cannot explain the differences and variation in the level of military influence.

Nor do supply-side factors—the relative degree of military professionalism—explain the relative clout of the armed forces in a country's democratic politics (see Table 15.1). The armed forces of Argentina, Brazil, and Chile are among the most professional in Latin America; their levels of professionalism are fairly similar. In all three countries, the trend has been in the direction of greater civilian control over the military, but there is still

Table 15.1. Military Professionalism and Political Influence in the 1990s

		Extent of Military Professionalism	
		High	Low
Extent of	High	Chile	Peru
Military	Medium	Brazil	Colombia
Political	Low	Argentina	Mexico
Influence			

wide variation in the extent of military prerogatives.[9] The military prerogatives of the Chilean armed forces are very high, of the Brazilian armed forces medium, and of the Argentine military low. Lower and fairly similar levels of military professionalism prevail in Colombia, Mexico, and Peru, where the armed forces have been dragged into counternarcotics operations and become vulnerable to corruption. Yet military prerogatives have been very high in Peru, medium in Colombia, and much lower in Mexico.[10] Military professionalism and military influence seem unrelated to each other.

Diamint insists correctly that the key to explaining the level of military influence is the relative degree to which military subordination to civilian authority is institutionalized. In some countries, civilian politicians have failed to expend their political capital to institutionalize civilian control in part because they seem satisfied so long as the military does not threaten a coup and in part because they believe they have more pressing governing priorities. The varying effective civilian demand for military subordination explains varying levels of military influence. Where civilian authorities have demanded military subordination and have had the power to enforce it (Argentina, Mexico), they have succeeded.

In sum, the military has not toppled constitutional governments as it once did. The frequency of coup attempts declined despite new economic crises that might have triggered coups in the past. But it remains an arduous task to ensure that constitutional government will endure effectively, not just nominally, and that requires more capable, institutionalized civilian control over the armed forces than all but a few Latin American governments have accomplished. Civilian control requires systematic, recurrent steps from civilian authorities to implant civilian supremacy over the armed forces, and equally systematic, recurrent steps of due obedience from military officers to civilian constitutional officials.[11] Deepening constitutional government necessarily requires time and its effective use for these purposes. Yet most Latin American governments have failed to institute processes to strengthen civilian control even a decade or two after transiting from dictatorship. The level of civilian control, in short, remains weak, but the trends toward fewer coups are positive.

Responsible and Reliable Parties and Politicians

Parties matter for democratic politics. They are the most effective instruments for articulating and aggregating societal demands, setting priorities among them, and taking steps to respond to some of those demands. Parties are essential to the organization of parliamentary life in both support and opposition to the executive branch. Bargaining between political parties serves to reduce the intensity of acute conflicts and may create non-partisan political spaces to permit "neutral" institutions, such as the courts, to function more effectively.

Nearly a half-century ago, Anthony Downs identified two traits that all democratic political parties in any country require in order to succeed in winning elections. Arguably, political parties should also have these qualities to foster the consolidation of democracy. "A party is reliable," Downs argued, "if its policy statements at the beginning of an election period—including those in its preelection campaign—can be used to make accurate predictions of its behavior." In addition, a "party is responsible if its policies in one period are consistent with its actions (or statements) in the preceding period, i.e., if it does not repudiate its former views in formulating its new program."[12] By these standards, many Latin American politicians and parties were unreliable and irresponsible in the late 1980s and early 1990s. By the later 1990s, in contrast, winning presidential candidates in most Latin American countries were less likely to announce policies that flatly contradicted campaign promises, and consecutive parties of the same administration were generally likely to pursue similar policies.[13] Voters came to rely on a party's and a politician's reputation to obtain important information to vote.

As Susan Stokes has ably shown, in the late 1980s and early 1990s there was a shockingly wide gap between a presidential candidate's campaign promises and his policy choices as president.[14] There are, to be sure, always gaps between campaign promises and subsequent policy implementation. Stokes rightly calls attention to dramatic departures not just from the details of policies but also from the entire general orientation promised for a new government. Parties were not reliable, Downs would have concluded. The economic policies promised by Carlos Andrés Pérez in Venezuela in 1988, Carlos Menem in Argentina in 1989, or Alberto Fujimori in Peru in 1990 during their respective campaigns for the presidency bore little relationship to the market-reliant neoliberal policies that they implemented once in office. The policy reputations of Pérez's party, AD, and Menem's party, the Justicialistas (Peronists), were closely associated with strong state intervention in the economy and import-substitution industrialization, not with trade liberalization, deregulation, privatization, and monetary stability that the respective Pérez and Menem administrations carried out. Similarly, the winning candidates for the presidency of Ecuador in both the 1988 and 1992 elections promised a strong role for the state in the economy, but followed instead much more market-reliant policies.[15]

The region-wide embrace of more market-conforming policies was also evident in ruling parties that retained the presidency from one term to another but dramatically changed economic policies and shocked their voters. For example, Venezuela's AD government under President Jaime Lusinchi (1984–89) followed the party's traditional statist economic policies. Voters who supported AD's candidate Carlos Andrés Pérez in the 1988 presidential election were surprised that Pérez, one of the pillars of past AD economic policies, returned to the presidency as a born-again freer-market advocate. Mexico's PRI was the decades-long architect of import-substitution industrialization and state intervention in the economy—until 1982. The PRI administration of Miguel de la Madrid (1982–88) turned toward greater reliance on markets. These parties were irresponsible in Downsian terms.

In the late 1990s, this behavior became less common. The change of trend was evident already in the early 1990s according to Stokes' evidence. Seven of fifteen presidential elections held between 1988 and 1991 in fifteen Latin American countries featured a switch from the general programmatic orientation promised during the campaign to another quite different orientation actually implemented once in office. Between 1992 and 1995, however, only three out of fourteen presidential elections featured such a dramatic change.[16] Employing Stokes' criteria for the same fifteen countries for the period (1996–2000) subsequent to her study, none of the fifteen presidential elections was followed by such a drastic change from campaign promises to implementation (see Table 15.2). Party responsibility increased.

Latin America ended the twentieth century, therefore, with more responsible and reliable political parties. In Argentina, Menem (1989–95, 1995–99) ran for reelection on his record in 1995 and persevered in similar policies during his second term. In Brazil, Cardoso (1994–98, 1998–2002) ran first on his record as finance minister in 1994 and then for reelection on his record as president in 1998. Cardoso followed through on his campaign promises after his first election and on his policies after his reelection, as Bolívar Lamounier notes in his chapter. In Peru, Fujimori (1990–95, 1995–2000) ran for reelection in 1995 on his record, as Degregori shows, and again in 2000 and persisted in similar economic policies during his second term.[17]

Economic policies came to persist between ruling administrations of the same party, or the same coalition of parties, but under a different president, signaling Downsian party responsibility. In Mexico, the economic policies of the PRI administration of President Ernesto Zedillo (1994–2000) continued those of his PRI predecessor, Carlos Salinas de Gortari (1988–94). In El Salvador, the economic policies of three consecutive presidents from the Na-

Table 15.2. Increasing Reliability of Political Parties in the 1990s

Do parties implement campaign promises once in office?

	Yes	No	Total
1988–91	8	7	15
1992–95	11	3	14
1996–2000	15	0	15

tionalist Republican Alliance (ARENA) party were consistent, namely, those of Alfredo Cristiani (1989–94), Armando Calderón Sol (1994–99), and Francisco Flores (1999–2004). In Colombia, César Gaviria (1990–94) in 1990 announced during his campaign that he would deepen policies begun during his Liberal Party predecessor, Virgilio Barco (1986–90), specifically proposing a wider market opening as well as constitutional reform.[18] In Chile, the economic policies of the three administrations of the Concertación Democrática coalition—Christian Democrats Patricio Aylwin (1990–94) and Eduardo Frei R. (1994–2000) and Socialist Ricardo Lagos (2000–2006)—built upon each other.

Voters still complain that politicians do not live up to everything they promised. Running for office differs from governing. What stopped happening by the mid-1990s was a shocking wholesale betrayal of the entire general orientation of a campaign program. The gaps between promises and performance in contemporary Latin America are no longer wider than in the long-democratic North Atlantic democracies.

Opposition presidential candidates also became more reliable and responsible in Downsian terms when they won the presidency. In Argentina, Fernando de la Rúa (1999–2001) announced economic policies that he went on to implement once elected. In Mexico, Vicente Fox ran for the presidency successfully in 2000 campaigning on, rather than repudiating, his past as a Coca-Cola executive. Arnoldo Alemán was elected president of Nicaragua in 1996 openly on a pro-market platform, which he went on to attempt to implement. In Peru, Alejandro Toledo accepted the market economy as the framework for the policies he hoped to implement, if elected president. He lost to Alberto Fujimori in 2000 in elections broadly perceived as unfair but won the presidency in June 2001 on a similar platform.

Increased responsibility and reliability is not the exclusive property of proponents of a market economy. Hugo Chávez was elected president of Venezuela in 1998 promising to enact his cherished Bolivarian revolution, overhauling the entire political system, and emphasizing a number of statist economic policies. He delivered once elected, as Coppedge makes clear in his chapter. There was comparable transparency in economic-policy responsibility and reliability on the political Left among such unsuccessful presidential candidates as Cuauhtémoc Cárdenas in Mexico (1988, 1994, 2000 elections), Daniel Ortega in Nicaragua (1990, 1996, 2001 elections), and Luiz Inácio da Silva (Lula) in Brazil (1989, 1994, 1998 elections). Each of these three candidates became perceptibly market-friendlier, however, in time for the most recent presidential election.

Explaining Increased Party Reliability and Responsibility

In the late 1980s and early 1990s, "unreliable" and "irresponsible" presidents felt, as Javier Corrales has noted, that they had no other choice: betray their campaign promises and the records of their parties in order to enact policies that they deemed essential but for which there was little popular support, or watch the country plunge into an economic abyss. Politicians also thought they had to shock the system to gain the confidence of skeptics. Presidents subsequently had to work hard to transform their initial laborite/populist bases of support into new coalitions to back and sustain economic reforms. Latin America's economic performance in the 1990s was not stellar; politicians and parties had to build support for the new policies. In the 1990s, these new reformist coalitions explain the return of the same party to the presidency for at least two consecutive terms in Argentina, Brazil, Chile, Colombia, El Salvador, and Mexico.

Certainly, two of the more dramatic campaign "liars," Menem and Fujimori, faced a catastrophic economic situation upon taking office at their first inaugurations in 1990. Latin America had suffered a region-wide economic depression in the 1980s, triggering these spectacular instances of trust breaking between politicians and citizens. Latin America's economic situation stabilized, for the most part, in the early to mid-1990s. Despite numerous problems in economic performance in the 1990s, the economies of most countries grew, enabling politicians and parties in office to become more reliable and responsible, as Downs would have predicted. Moreover, the choices among economic policy frameworks became clearer. Market-oriented economic policies polarized party politicians and, to a lesser extent, the electorate. Government and opposition politicians demarcated lines of policy cleavage and explained them to the voters, thereby enhancing reliability and responsibility.

Some might object that Cardoso, Menem, and Fujimori were just dominant individuals; their parties had little to do with the outcomes generated by their administrations. That is true with regard to Fujimori who, as Degregori shows, destroyed existing parties and built none of his own. But in Argentina and Brazil, the comprehensive economic policy changes were enacted through acts of Congress in democratic contexts. In Brazil, unlike in Peru, the legislative votes were not in the president's pocket. No Latin American president had to work as hard as Cardoso to sustain his congressional majorities. Cardoso required super-majorities to enact constitutional amendments that permitted the implementation of his economic program. In Argentina, the Justicialistas put aside their fatal attraction for the state and voted, beginning in 1991, for the Convertibility Law, one after another privatization, and similar market-promoting policies. In 1999, with Menem no longer a candidate, the Justicialista presidential candidate, Eduardo Duhalde, retained a market-conforming economic platform. Under Radical Civic Union President De la Rúa, faced with a dangerous decline in the economy in 2000–2001 that in decades past might have triggered a military coup, Justicialista members of Congress voted time and again for market-conforming economic policies proposed by the government, despite their new role in the opposition. In 2002, the two main parties in Congress provided essential support for Eduardo Duhalde, who was elected president by Congress in January 2002 (de la Rúa had resigned). Argentina began the twenty-first century with severe troubles, but Downsian party irresponsibility was no longer one of them.

In some countries, constitutional amendments that permit the president's immediate reelection contributed to partisan and candidate responsibility and reliability. Carlos Menem and Alberto Fujimori lied once but could not lie twice. When they ran for reelection, they had to run on their records in office. Fernando Henrique Cardoso ran also for immediate reelection but, in this case, this was his second successful presidential campaign on a similar broad program of government.

The analytic and normative importance of parties for effective democratic governance is poignantly demonstrated in Steven Levitsky's chapter on Argentina. From the late 1920s to the late 1980s, Argentina had been the hemisphere's best example of sustained bad governance. Neither liberty, nor equality, nor prosperity was well served by its dictators or its democrats. Yet in the 1990s, Argentina reconstructed a democratic political system, strengthened protections of civil rights, permitted the growth of powerful independent media, and hosted a newly vibrant civil society, thanks to a large extent to the transformation of its two large and long-lived parties. Argentine parties moved toward the political Center, where the largest number of votes was to be found. Argentine parties rediscovered the utility of democratic institutions to save themselves and, in so doing, to provide for better public goods.

The main Argentine parties adopted three compatible fundamental policy frameworks in issue areas that had long divided the nation. One was a market-oriented economic policy framework even though, for the 1999 elections, the contenders swung slightly to the Left, promising more social programs. Parties continued to differ over specific economic policies but did not seek to re-create the entire economic system upon each accession to presidential power. These decisions had vast consequences for political life, the economy, and the labor union movement (chapters by Levitsky, Corrales, and Murillo). The second was consensus on the significance of civilian supremacy over the armed forces, a process that built upon gains begun during the presidency of Raúl Alfonsín. The third was agreement on the basic outlines of Argentina's foreign policy, including dramatically improved relations with Brazil, Chile, and the United States. Argentina's foreign policy came to emphasize cooperative security with its neighbors and international institutions, commitments to regional integration (especially in the southern common market, MERCOSUR), and collaboration with the United States over many global issues. These three shared policy frameworks made it easier for the political system, not just for individual parties, to become more reliable and responsible. These three frameworks endured despite Argentina's economic crisis in 2002.

In short, many Latin American politicians and political parties became more responsible and reliable in the sense defined by Downs. The trend was positive. They acted in this way to compete effectively in elections but, in so behaving, they improved the quality and scope of democratic politics.

The Partisan Democratic Deficit

The story of political parties in Latin America is, however, less cheerful than the preceding section would imply. Along the seismic Andean mountain chain (Bolivia excepted), political earthquakes brought down the party systems. Parties can be neither responsible nor reliable in most Andean countries because they barely exist. The partisan democratic deficit has long been severe also in Brazil. Candidates for office seek electoral labels that prove ephemeral, are committed to no discernible program, and are incapable of enforcing party cohesion or discipline in the legislature. Internal party life is weak. The level of contribution of parties to democracy remains poor.

Venezuela and Peru ended the twentieth century with much weakened party systems, as Coppedge and Degregori show in their respective chapters and their broader work. Venezuela's historically powerful parties, AD and COPEI, long held more than four-fifths of the seats in Congress. Their influence declined dramatically in the early 1990s, giving rise to an amalgam of supporters for the wildly popular but weakly institutionalized political forces backing President Chávez and amorphous opposition political groupings. At the end of the 1990s, AD held only about a sixth of the seats in the National Assembly and COPEI held a much smaller fraction. During the 1990s, President Fujimori systematically undermined even the embryonic political parties he had established as vehicles to gather electoral support. Peru's APRA party was one of Latin America's strongest and best institutionalized from the 1920s to the 1980s, but the disastrous administration of APRA President Alan García (1985–90) gravely weakened the party. APRA recovered only after Fujimori's demise when Alan García, again its presidential candidate in the 2001 elections, won a quarter of the votes in the first-round elections and APRA won 28 of 120 parliamentary seats.

In Colombia, as Cepeda observes with distress, the Liberal and Conservative parties weakened and fragmented during the second half of the 1990s. Early in the new century, these parties risk a fate similar to what befell their neighbors in Venezuela and Peru. The Colombian Conservative Party found it difficult to win office even in former bastions of political support. The fragmentation of the Liberal Party proceeded far beyond its past experiences. Non-party politicians won important subnational posts, such as the mayoralty of Bogotá, the capital city. And in 2002, non-party candidate Álvaro Uribe (a former liberal legislator and governor) won the presidency.

Brazil and Ecuador have long shared a dubious honor in terms of the partisan democratic deficit. On average, in the 1980s and 1990s approximately one-third of the members of Congress elected for any given term switched political parties by the end of the term. Although at any given moment the legislators of these parties are capable of united behavior, their propensity to partisan defection over time greatly complicates the task of governing, as Lamounier notes.[19] There are many parties in each country; some last just for a few years, and then disintegrate and recombine into new parties.

Some Brazilian political parties are internally cohesive, however. In general, the closer to the ideological Left, the greater the extent of party discipline; among large Brazilian parties, the most cohesive is the left-wing PT. Even among other Brazilian parties, there is a generally consistent policy orientation present even among politicians who shift allegiances among weakly disciplined parties.[20] Party switching occurs mainly within "ideological families" so that there is substantial ideological-bloc legislative cohesion. Thus even a number of Brazilian party switchers in Congress may themselves be reliable and responsible in policy terms, although their non-policy political behavior makes the task of governing more difficult. Indeed, the overall level of party discipline displayed by members of the Brazilian Congress increased somewhat in the 1990s because parties of the Left were better represented in Congress and these parties were the most disciplined and also because in the second half of the 1990s the Center and Right parties in President Fernando Henrique Cardoso's coalition behaved with greater party discipline.

The partisan democratic deficit is also not of recent vintage. Venezuela's AD and COPEI parties, and Peru's APRA party, collapsed in the early to mid-1990s although, as noted, AD retained about a sixth of the seats of the National Assembly elected in late 1999 and APRA staged a comeback in the

2001 national elections. The conditions of indiscipline in political parties in Brazil and Ecuador were present well before the 1990s; they were not caused by the democratic transitions of the late 1970s and 1980s or by the economic reforms their governments attempted during the 1990s.

More generally, parties tended to become stronger in some countries of "late" transition to democracy especially in Central America. Nicaragua ended the 1990s with a stronger set of parties than at the decade's beginning (the Liberals and the Sandinistas);[21] so did El Salvador, around the ruling ARENA party and the civilian reconstitution of the former guerrillas of the Farabundo Martí National Liberation Front (FMLN). As Denise Dresser argues in her chapter, the consolidation of Mexico's three-party system in the 1990s is one of the keys to its transition to democracy. The PRI learned that it had to appeal to voters, not just lord it over them. The National Action Party reached out to a much more heterogeneous electorate. And the Party of the Democratic Revolution learned the importance of uniting the various forces and factions on the political Left. In these ways, Mexican parties strengthened themselves, the party system, and their capacity to represent more effectively the interests and values of Mexican voters. These trends toward stronger parties, and their persistence in countries where parties had long been strong such as Argentina, Chile, Uruguay, Bolivia, Costa Rica, and the Dominican Republic, bode well for democratic politics.

Explaining the Partisan Democratic Deficit

Why, then, did Colombia's ancient and time-tested two-party system disintegrate in the late 1990s? In the first edition of this book, Domínguez and Giraldo offered explanations for the breakdown of AD, COPEI, and APRA in the early 1990s that also help to explain the breakdown of the Colombian party system in the late 1990s. They argued that AD and APRA suffered from retrospective voting, that is, voters assessed their performance in government and pronounced it dismal. Cepeda's chapter provides a trenchant analysis of Colombian politics, pertinent to this analytic point. Colombia had been the best long-term economic performer in Latin America during the second half of the twentieth century. In the second half of the 1990s, its economy plunged. Retrospective economic voting punished the Colombian Liberal Party government of Ernesto Samper (1994–98) and the Conservative Party government of Andrés Pastrana (1998–2002). Just as important, accusations of corruption swirled about the Samper administration, discrediting Liberal Party officials and contributing to Andrés Pastrana's victory heading an opposition coalition built around the Conservative Party. Moreover, levels of violence escalated significantly during the second half of the 1990s, weakening allegiance to governing politicians from the two traditional parties: it seemed as if they could no longer govern the country effectively.

Domínguez and Giraldo had pointed to a second factor, drawing from Coppedge's earlier work: the persistence of a preexisting party establishment that embodies a duopoly of power and employs the electoral laws to sustain its grip on public office, defying shifts in popular preferences. Colombia had long been the principal example of coalescent behavior between its two leading political parties—no Latin American country had ever featured such a stable duopoly. Alone, this factor had never in the past unraveled Colombian politics. Combined with hard times in terms of economics, corruption, and violence, this factor weakened AD and COPEI in Venezuela in the first half of the 1990s and the Liberals and Conservatives in Colombia in the second half. Partyarchical trends also hurt Costa Rica's party system, where collaboration between the two largest parties over economic policy increased during the second half of the 1990s. In the 2002 elections, the two largest parties won only 63 percent of all legislative seats compared to 88 percent in 1998.

At the start of the twenty-first century, the partisan democratic deficit remains severe, and arguably worse in Colombia. Countries that witnessed the collapse of long-powerful parties (Peru and Venezuela) in the early 1990s were slow to build up new successful parties. On the other hand, despite many problems that persist, in the late 1990s parties became stronger in Brazil, Mexico, Nicaragua, and El Salvador. Parties remained strong in Argentina, Bolivia, Chile, Costa Rica, and the Dominican Republic (party life changed little in Guatemala, Ecuador, and Paraguay). The partisan democratic deficit marked especially the Andean region, where it weakened the capacity of institutions to represent and serve the interests of the governed and elicit their consent.

Societal Transformations

Democratic politics requires effective constitutional government, with due obedience from the military to civilian authorities, based on free elections in which parties compete for public office. Democratic politics requires as well the free and effective exercise of citizen rights. In order to deepen democratic politics, workers should have rights to help shape the conditions in which they work. This is why democratic politics is impossible without labor unions (although the mere presence of unions is an insufficient guarantee of democratic politics). Citizen rights imply, of course, that women as well as men are equal before the law and can actively seek and hold public office and advance general as well as gender-specific interests. Most Latin American countries are undergoing extraordinary changes with regard to the roles of workers and women.

The Political Role of Labor Unions

Labor unions in Latin American countries, as elsewhere in the world, have played key roles in political democratization. Unions contributed to the widening of the right to suffrage, promoted effective rights to political, economic, and social participation, and demanded policies on behalf of the interests of most citizens. They also benefited from political democratization that permitted unions to carry out their tasks. By the mid-twentieth century, as Victoria Murillo indicates, Latin American labor unions had developed a preference for government regulations and state intervention in industrial relations to advance their social and political interests, and for import-substitution industrialization as a means to defend the economic conditions of their members. Many labor unions were not internally democratic. The spread of harsh dictatorships from the mid-1960s to the late 1970s, and the subsequent collapse of the import substitution model and the opening of economies, battered organized labor power. Governments were hostile to labor; real wages dropped. Unemployment and underemployment rose everywhere in the region while union membership fell in most countries.

To explain the response of labor unions, Murillo calls attention to political alignment as it relates to the extent of interpartisan competition in the labor movement and the extent of interunion competition. Interpartisan competition weakened the incentives for labor union leaders to cooperate with their partisan allies for fear of being outflanked by a partisan adversary within the labor movement. Thus labor unions allied to Venezuela's AD Party often opposed the policies of the AD government of Carlos Andrés Pérez in order not to be outflanked by Causa R or other parties that competed for labor support. Interunion competition, in contrast, weakens unions in their relationship with any given political party or the government because officials from these organizations play off one union against the other. Thus Mexico's PRI found it easier than other Latin American parties to manage the divided labor movement despite government policies that weakened labor union power in the 1990s.

Murillo analyzes new labor union strategies to cope with the new configurations of politics and with more open market economies. The first strategy —the attempt to form new political and social alliances—has not been very successful, although these alliances are discussed often. The Brazilian PT is the only example of the creation late in the twentieth century of an alliance between a party and labor unions, but it was forged as far back as the late 1970s. A second union strategy is the search for organizational autonomy. That has long been a strategy in Brazil and it has become more important in Argentina and Mexico. The third strategy is less common for nationwide union federations but increasingly common for certain sectoral labor union federations, namely, industrial participation linked to new commitments to enhance productivity and the competitiveness of firms in open economies.

In sum, societal transformations have been generally adverse to labor unions. Whether the setbacks for the labor movement are also setbacks for democratic politics varies more. For example, the highly authoritarian labor union structure in Mexico had long been an impediment to democracy in the political system and in society, as Dresser notes; the breakdown of that structure is a step toward democratization. The Chilean labor movement, in contrast, had been badly battered by the Pinochet dictatorship. The reconstruction of Chile's democratization requires a greater capacity for labor unions to represent the interests of their workers. Agüero shows that President Ricardo Lagos' government took various steps to strengthen labor rights. The choice of labor union strategy, in turn, will help shape an important aspect of each country's political economy. Will labor unions oppose open economies, or will they operate within the context of the new market-oriented economic policies?[22]

Gender and Politics

The trends in women's roles in politics are clearer and generally positive thanks to converging social, economic, and political trends over time. As Mala Htun argues in her chapter, democracy expanded women's opportunities to participate in politics as elected officeholders, through their actions in social movements and interest group organizations and as voters. By the end of the 1990s, at least fifteen governments had enacted initiatives to counter domestic violence. Nearly all had eliminated some effects of discrimination based on gender, especially with regard to matrimonial property and parental rights. During the last three decades of the twentieth century, women's share of national legislatures, Htun finds, grew from one-twentieth to one-seventh. In countries as varied as El Salvador, Chile, Costa Rica, and Colombia, women made up a quarter of the members of the cabinet as the twentieth century ended. Mireya Moscoso had become president of Panama and women were credible presidential candidates in several other countries. Women mayors governed Mexico City and São Paulo in the late 1990s. Women's groups and women participants in various social movements had also become part of the landscape of civil society of all Latin American countries.

These changes were caused in part by democratic politics—few dictatorships have national legislatures, for example—but broader social changes, Htun argues, also account for these outcomes. The life expectancy of women in Latin America lengthened by eighteen years during the second half of the twentieth century; women's participation in the labor force widened by a dozen percentage points. Women's fertility was cut in half, to just three children per woman in 1995. Women were better educated, healthier, and more economically independent and, therefore, could perform more effective roles in politics.

It may thus be surprising that laws and policies governing women's reproductive health changed so slowly in the region, and hardly at all with regard to abortion (for the most part, a tribute to the Roman Catholic Church's continuing clout) despite various political battles over it during the closing third of the twentieth century. Countries with very liberal abortion laws, such as Cuba, and countries with absolute bans on abortion, such as Chile, made no legal changes at all despite other changes in their social and political contexts. It is also somewhat surprising that women in such countries as Brazil, Chile, and Mexico, as Htun demonstrates, are consistently somewhat less likely to vote for Left than for Right presidential candidates. In Chile's presidential election in 2000, for example, Joaquín Lavín, the candidate of the right-wing parties, defeated Ricardo Lagos, the candidate of the Center–Left Concertación Democrática coalition, among women voters in both the first and the second rounds; Lagos won thanks to a solid majority among male voters.[23] These gender differences in voting behavior have narrowed over time, and may narrow even farther as women gain in education and labor force participation.

The circumstances of labor unions and women changed considerably in the closing quarter of the twentieth century. Changes in the labor market affected both kinds of persons, and especially women workers. Trends with regard to women as citizens were generally positive, widening effective social, civic, and political rights, even though the level of women's participation in politics remains modest in most countries. Trends with regard to labor unions were more troubling. The capacity of unions to defend collective rights, never strong, weakened by century's end. Only a few labor unions had been able to cope with the fury of social, economic, and political transformations swirling all around them.[24]

Assessing Institutional Reforms

In the 1980s and 1990s, among many Latin American politicians reforming the constitution became almost as popular as playing soccer. Each of the seven countries analyzed in this book reformed the constitution at some point during those years, with mixed results. Institutional reform-mongering was often a symptom of the broad dissatisfaction with governance. Politicians believed that the fundamental rules had to be changed in order to cope with deep and widespread crises during the last quarter of the twentieth century.[25]

Key amendments enacted to the constitutions of Chile and Mexico during these years, and to Brazil's in the 1990s, sought to strengthen property rights and the constitutional context for market-friendly policies; this was also the thrust of many institutional reforms enacted through law. Constitutional reforms in Argentina, Peru, Colombia, and Venezuela were not principally focused on economic themes. However, Argentina and Peru, and to some extent Colombia, instituted by law far-reaching institutional changes already permitted by their constitutions, to the same effect. Only in Venezuela in the 1990s did constitutional reform represent a setback for market-conforming policies. The pro-property rights changes in all but one of these countries should be seen as part of the broad international movement in the same direction, backed as well by the U.S. government and the international financial institutions. The general shift in macroeconomic policy orientation explains the timing of the adoption and the content of these new rules.

Consider some examples. In Chile, constitutional reforms such as securing the independence of the central bank were part of the bargain to permit the transition to democracy. The Brazilian Constituent Assembly of 1988 produced a gigantic text that sought to prescribe so much of social and economic life that hardly a year would pass in the decade that followed when Congress did not attempt to amend it. Brazil's democratically elected government in the mid- and late 1990s succeeded in enacting market-opening constitutional and other institutional changes. In Mexico, similar changes took place in a democratizing political context. The Mexican constitution of 1917, heir to one of the hemisphere's most intense social revolutions, has been amended at various times. In the late 1980s and early 1990s, however, there was a systematic pattern to the many amendments adopted: to eliminate its statist economic norms. Corrales' chapter explains the politics of the arduous road to the market.

In the 1990s, constitutional amendments in Argentina, Brazil, Peru, and Venezuela were principally motivated by the incumbent president's wish to remove the formal prohibition against immediate reelection. In Peru and in Venezuela, as Degregori and Coppedge note in their chapters, many other changes were enacted to strengthen disproportionately the powers of Presidents Alberto Fujimori and Hugo Chávez, weakening the democratic credentials and practices of both political systems. In no country did constitutional reforms strengthen the capacity of legislative institutions to represent more effectively the consent of the governed, but during this decade only in Peru and Venezuela was there an evident authoritarian design in the motivations and processes for revising the constitution.

John Carey's chapter analyzes the effects and utility of various significant

institutional changes. Some of these were parts of more encompassing constitutional reforms; others were adopted by law, or within party organizations. Carey's empirical analysis finds that the following institutional changes
generally fostered or deepened democratic governance when they were implemented in Latin America:

1. The adoption of primary elections to choose presidential candidates, as in Argentina, Chile, the Dominican Republic, Mexico, and
Uruguay (presidential primary elections in Venezuela in the past had also
provided for a measure of democratic competition within the major parties),[26] fosters both competition and partisan commitment.

2. The spread of technology makes it easier to conduct legislative
business in public, to disseminate reports and other information, and to
record legislative votes with full transparency, avoiding the veil of anonymity that often in the past obscured legislative behavior from citizen
scrutiny.

3. Aggregate budget ceiling procedures maximize legislative discretion over the distribution of funds across government programs while retaining a general incentive for budget restraint, thereby fostering both
constitutional government and fiscal prudence.

Carey also finds that several well-publicized institutional changes had
virtually no significant effects:

1. The creation of first ministers and of limited requirements for parliamentary confidence in cabinets has had negligible effects, as in Argentina, Peru, or Venezuela.

2. The shift toward unicameralism has had very few consequences, as
in Peru or Venezuela.[27]

3. The budget item veto has no measurable effect on deficits.

Finally, Carey identifies some bad ideas that persist in many constitutions:

1. Term limits reduce the learning time horizon as well as the efficacy
of presidents and legislators; they impede the exercise of the power of
democratic majorities.

2. Prohibiting immediate presidential reelection but permitting it subsequently gives incentives to internal party fratricide between the outgoing president and his former allies, who suddenly become potential challengers for renomination.

3. Majority runoff presidential elections enhance the unpredictability
of presidential elections and encourage divided government.[28]

This analysis highlights the complexity of constitutional revision and the need to examine the variation among institutions in democratic contexts, to distinguish between the worth of specific institutional changes and their abuse by prospective authoritarians, and to identify the structural conditions that permit presidents to abuse their powers. Presidential reelection has gotten a bad name among democrats because of examples of abuse and tampering with electoral procedures, such as Alberto Fujimori's in Peru, and the fear of similar abuses in the future by Hugo Chávez. But Fernando Henrique Cardoso won reelection in Brazil in clean and fair elections, deepening democratic governance and continuing a program of macroeconomic policy reform. The democratic worth of immediate reelection, therefore, is highly variable and uncertain.

Comprehensive versus Incremental Constitutional Reform-mongering

From the perspective of democratic government, the comprehensive constitutional revisions carried out in Colombia in the early 1990s and in Venezuela in the late 1990s illustrate the perils with such exercises: they weakened constitutional democracy or governability. The Venezuelan case, ably described in Coppedge's chapter, exemplifies the concentration of political power in the hands of President Hugo Chávez. From his first election in December 1998, President Chávez and his allies worked to disempower constitutional organs that were not yet under their control, such as the Congress and the Supreme Court. They undercut support for the Roman Catholic Church and fought the organized labor movement. Contrary to Venezuela's political tradition since the end of dictatorship in 1958, President Chávez appointed many military officers to his cabinet and entrusted important civilian tasks to the armed forces. The old Venezuelan constitution had created a powerful presidency; the new one retained those powers. The main difference was the collapse of organized party opposition that could counter the president's power. The key effect of the new constitution was evident through a political process: the dissolution of the preexisting constitutional institutions, through the mechanism of approving a new constitution, enabled Chávez and his allies to purge all branches of government of officials whom they disliked. Venezuela remained a democratic political system as the twentieth century ended, but the prospects for its survival had not been so weak since the late 1950s.

The comprehensive revision to Colombia's constitution, approved in 1991, and associated enabling laws illustrates different problems. As Cepeda argues in his chapter, governability was weakened by constitutional reforms that intensified the preexisting pattern of personalist politics. The parties have no control over the use of the party label. The national party cannot prevent a party "list" with just one person, who runs based on a personal electoral machine, from appearing on the ballot competing with the party's main multicandidate list. In the new Senate, all members are elected from the same single national district, intensifying incentives for cultivating a personalist vote in competition with all other candidates from allegedly the same party. The insertion of second-round electoral procedures made it easier to fragment the nominally larger Liberal Party and facilitated Conservative Andrés Pastrana's victory in the second round in 1998 as head of a broad coalition (having lost the first round). Not all of the ills of party fragmentation were invented by the 1991 reform, to be sure. Colombia's National Front experiment (1958–74) mandated coalition government between Liberals and Conservatives. The political habits of perpetually coalescent parties severely weakened party cohesion and discipline. As Cepeda comments, since 1945 Colombia was governed by just one of the two big political parties only once and then very briefly, during Virgilio Barco's presidency (1986–90). The 1991 constitution contributed to the worsening of the preexisting level of party fragmentation. The constitutional reform could be made to work in Colombia's political context only through more frequent recourse to clientelist practices, one of the evils that the reform of 1991 had sought to curtail.

The counterproductive effects of the 1991 Colombian constitutional reform are evident in other ways. The constitution mandated fiscal transfers to subnational governments equal to nearly half of the ordinary revenues in the national budget, without providing equally for institutional support for the effective use of those resources at the subnational level. Colombia found it more difficult to manage its budgets also because the new constitution created new institutions with considerable autonomy such as the office of the general prosecutor, various regulatory commissions, and the constitutional court. Decentralization with weak means for accountability to constituents and toward national institutions impairs governability.

A principal explanation for outcomes that weakened Colombia's governability was the composition of the 1991 constituent assembly. Its members included representatives from the former guerrilla movement, the M-19, in addition to members of the already deeply fractured Conservative and Liberal parties. The assembly protected the rights of factional politicians and the prospects for coalitions among factions as well as the rights of minority political forces. The assembly was also under intense mass media and public pressure to devolve effective authority to subnational governments or to autonomous decentralized entities at the national level. These multiple "pushes" to weaken central power succeeded, alas, on the eve of an intensification of political violence derived from guerrilla, drug-trafficker, and paramilitary activity. Colombia's capacity to govern itself weakened at the very moment when the prospects for its future became most dire.

In contrast, an example of effective reform was the Argentine constitutional revision of 1994. The 1993 Olivos Pact between the leadership of the country's two largest parties—specifically President Carlos Menem and former President Raúl Alfonsín—limited the scope of the reform. The subsequent constitutional convention met under party discipline and focused on this agreed upon agenda. As Levitsky notes in his chapter, many of these reforms improved the quality of Argentine democracy, such as the direct election of the president (abolishing the electoral college), senators (previously elected by provincial legislatures), and the mayor of the federal capital (previously appointed by the president). Other democratizing reforms included the creation of an ombudsman and a general auditor, both of whom would be selected by opposition parties, and the establishment of an independent Magistrates' Council to oversee the selection and disciplining of federal judges.

On balance, Latin America's experiences with systematic constitutional reform-mongering were not good. The adverse trends were especially distressing because the region did not begin with a good level of effective democratic governance. From the late 1980s to the late 1990s, the most far-reaching constitutional assemblies in Brazil, Colombia, Peru, and Venezuela produced new constitutions that either weakened liberal democracy (Peru, Venezuela) or governability (Brazil, Colombia). The construction of constitutional democracy was more likely through incremental reforms (Argentina, Mexico, or Brazil in the second half of the 1990s). The latter were fashioned by wizened members of Congress, conscious of ongoing political habits and limitations, and knowledgeable about practical issues of government. They were likely to behave under party or presidential discipline, and they were better focused on a key set of problems.

Legislatures and Courts

In the 1990s, the cross-national variation in the performance of Latin America's national legislatures and Supreme Courts increased. At the start of the decade, these were weak institutions everywhere, often badly staffed, poorly funded, and inept at making effective decisions. Subsequently, the power of legislatures and Supreme Courts weakened markedly only in Peru and Venezuela, threatening the prospects for democratic governance, while it strengthened to varying degrees in the five other countries included in this book. Presidential initiative and the collapse of political parties explain Peru's and Venezuela's distinct experiences.

In general, party competition makes it more difficult for the presidency to impose its will on the other constitutional organs. Competition between parties and party discipline within parties helps create "political space" required for Parliaments to exercise their constitutional autonomy. Imperfect party discipline, on the other hand, lets individual parliamentarians retain a margin of autonomy from party leaders (although at the risk that they would use this independence for personal gain rather than in the public interest), but it thwarts the ability of congressional party leaders to mobilize party leverage against the executive.

Competition between parties is also the key explanation for Supreme Court independence. Supreme Courts are political institutions. They are likely to defer to the presidency when only one party is likely to win elections for the foreseeable future; the long-term subordination of the Mexican Supreme Court to the presidency is a noteworthy example. Supreme Courts follow public opinion polls and election returns; they begin to tip against long-dominant presidents and parties only when they anticipate the replacement of these politicians in office. In situations of high party competition, the Supreme Court can expect to find political support for its rulings in large and well-organized segments of society when it rules against the presidency. Competitive parties have an incentive to preserve the independence of the Supreme Court as a neutral arbiter.

El Salvador provides a good example of these Supreme Court patterns. All justices of the Supreme Court of El Salvador belonged to the same party as the president's until 1994. Its constitutional replacement in 1994 took place after the 1992 peace accords in circumstances of high partisan competition. The new Supreme Court drew justices from various parties, with greater professional experience than in the past. The new Court began to behave with greater independence from both the president and Parliament.[29]

Presidents Hugo Chávez and Alberto Fujimori weakened national legislatures, Supreme Courts, and political parties in Venezuela and Peru. Their methods differed; the results were comparable, as Coppedge and Degregori show. In both countries, old-line political parties crumbled; no new ones were born, other than personalist vehicles for Chávez and Fujimori. Chávez deployed his popularity through plebiscitary means to rid himself of a Congress where his opponents had held a majority and to intimidate the Supreme Court and gut its powers. He packed the new National Assembly and the new Supreme Court with his supporters. Fujimori led a coup against Congress and the Supreme Court in 1992. He, too, built political support through plebiscites, sponsoring constitutional reforms to his liking, in effect preventing the legislature from holding the executive accountable thereafter. When in 1996 the Constitutional Court dared to act independently (attempting to deny Fujimori the opportunity to run for president for the third consecutive time), the fujimorista majority in Congress sacked the offending justices. Fujimori's key political agent, Vladimiro Montesinos, co-opted and literally bought members of Congress elected on opposition lists to augment the fujimorista base in Congress. In many instances, Montesinos filmed these transactions; the videotapes were eventually made public in late 2000 and in 2001. Such scandalous behavior was possible because, as already noted, Peru had no effective political parties in the 1990s. Chávez and Fujimori concentrated power in their own hands; party competition declined markedly. The autonomy of legislature and court from the executive consequently declined in both Venezuela and Peru. (The successor government to Fujimori's, led by interim President Valentín Paniagua, removed corrupt justices from office and greatly strengthened the judiciary's independence.)

The next most timid Parliaments and Supreme Courts were those in Argentina and Mexico. Levels of party discipline have been very high, thereby limiting the extent of parliamentarian autonomy from party leaders. The Argentine example, however, shows how party-led constitutional organs can construct greater independence from the presidency, and it may point to Mexico's future. The Argentine Congress played a modest role during the first two years of Carlos Menem's presidency, when the executive ruled through issuing presidential Necessity and Urgency Decrees (NUDs). After 1990, however, as Levitsky's chapter argues, the vast majority of Menem's economic reform proposals were channeled through Congress, including laws on monetary and exchange rate policy, social security reform, and the privatization of the gas and petroleum sectors. Congress forced the executive to withdraw and rethink its various proposals for labor law reform. The number of NUDs per year fell from sixty-eight to thirty-six from 1989–93 to 1994–98. Congress became more influential as Argentine politics became more competitive during the 1990s, culminating with the Justicialista Party defeat in 1999, while the new presidential coalition failed to win control of both chambers of Congress.[30]

The pattern is similar with regard to the Supreme Court. President Menem entertained the same thought as President Fujimori: to get the Supreme Court to interpret the constitution to permit a third consecutive presidential term. In Peru, Fujimori compelled the Court to cave in because organized partisan opposition was so weak; in Argentina, as Levitsky reminds us, the Supreme Court, taking note of Menem's weakness in public opinion polls, refused to comply with Menem's wishes and was broadly supported by political parties (including a wing of the Justicialistas). And, in 1999, no doubt anticipating a new presidency after the elections late that year, the Supreme Court declared unconstitutional a presidential decree extending the sales tax and, for the first time, limited presidential discretion in issuing decrees that have the force of law (NUDs). The Court's growing independence was tied to a more competitive electoral process.

Mexico's Congress and Supreme Court, as Dresser demonstrates, have been learning to become more independent. In 1997, for the first time ever, no political party had a majority in the Chamber of Deputies, creating a much more complex political dynamic and making it possible for Congress to exercise independent influence at last. Budgets for the following fiscal years were modified in committees, and substantive changes were enacted. Executive initiation of bills in Congress dropped to an all-time low. In 2001, no political party had a majority in either chamber of the Mexican Congress, permitting thereby an array of political combinations and hence greater parliamentary autonomy. In the early months of Vicente Fox's presidency, Congress modified every presidential bill in some significant way and forced the president to negotiate extensively. Similarly, the Mexican Supreme Court, appointed during the long PRI rule, no longer felt the same deference toward presidents of other political parties.

National legislatures and courts matter more in the three other countries under analysis. In the Chilean Congress, the close division of highly disciplined political parties made it prudent for the executive to negotiate to enact major changes. This pattern began soon after the transition to constitutional government. For example, the key 1990 fiscal reform resulted from explicit negotiations to generate an over-sized majority, involving the government parties and the largest opposition party, to ensure that the reform would last even if the presidency were to change partisan coloration in the future.[31]

The Chilean Senate, however, as Agüero reminds us in his chapter, embodies some of the most striking anti-democratic legacies from the Pinochet dictatorship, namely, unelected senators. The people directly elect thirty-eight senators but another nine are appointed by the president (two), the Supreme Court (three), and the National Security Council (four); the Chilean armed forces obtain senatorial representation through this last vehicle. (In addition, every past president of Chile who has served six years becomes a senator for life.)

The Supreme Court of Chile acted with greater independence by the late 1990s, especially through its rulings on human rights issues, thanks to a reform of the Supreme Court and the fact that, in 2000, only four out of twenty-one Court members were legacies from the Pinochet dictatorship. The Court's reform, Agüero points out, stemmed from agreements between government and opposition parties to ensure the Court's role as an impartial arbiter with broad support. In the late 1990s, the Court ruled that cases of "disappearances" for which there was yet no accountability should be considered kidnappings still under investigation; consequently, the amnesty law could not apply to cases that had not been resolved yet. And on August 8, 2000, the Supreme Court ruled that former dictator and senator-for-life Augusto Pinochet be stripped of his congressional immunity and prosecuted in court for crimes committed during his dictatorship.[32]

The Supreme Courts of Brazil and Colombia, and the Colombian Constitutional Court, as Lamounier and Cepeda note in their respective chapters, are no longer shy. They have ruled unconstitutional some major economic reform proposals in each country. The Brazilian Supreme Federal Court and the other federal courts have generally become respected for their independence relative to the executive and legislative branches of government. The Supreme Court, for example, declared unconstitutional the proposed significant reform of the social security system. The Brazilian state court system retains many organizational flaws, however, and it is much more vulnerable to corruption. The Colombian Supreme and Constitutional Courts have ruled extensively as well on issues pertaining to extradition of drug traffickers, personal safety, and various attempts to curb violence in the country. The greater extent of political competition in both countries, including but not limited to competition between parties, widened the space for such behavior by the courts. Indeed, as Lamounier suggests, some worry about the "judicialization of politics," that is, the overload of tasks imposed on the courts as citizens and organizations ask them to solve ordinary political problems, risking new forms of politicization of the judiciary. The burdens on these courts have also risen as a result of market-oriented reforms that require courts to uphold laws on contracts and other market-conforming rules.

The Brazilian and Colombian Congresses have the greatest political autonomy and the lowest party discipline of those considered in this book, two traits that reinforce each other.[33] The executive cannot rely on the votes of members of Congress from its own party or an allegedly supportive coalition of parties because members can exercise their individual autonomy. To secure support for its programs, the executive, in effect, "buys" votes from members of Congress from its own and opposition parties through extensive clientelist practices: favors are traded in exchange for votes. In Brazil, these practices occur member by member. These practices enable the president to govern, as Lamounier observes, with considerable legislative support. In Colombia, the clientelist exchange occurs sometimes through the factions into which Colombian parties are formally organized. Members of Congress employ their relative independence to obtain material benefits for their constituents or themselves, not to monitor the president's behavior or focus on public policy issues. Clientelist practices are a perverse form of congressional autonomy, fostering corruption and weakening the prospects for democratic rule. The pork-barrel-seeking behavior of politically autonomous, clientelist-motivated individual legislators is more pernicious in Parliaments without disciplined parties precisely because such behavior is less restrained.

In Latin America, the likelihood of effective democratic governance—the representation of public interests and purposes—is greater under Parliaments with high levels of party discipline and competition and appreciably lower individual member political autonomy, such as Argentina, Chile, and at long last Mexico, among those studied in this book. High Supreme Court political autonomy seems to increase the prospects for democratic liberty in Latin America but, at the start of the twenty-first century, often at the cost of delaying and increasing the costs of economic policy reforms. The dilemma is that the operation of these fundamental constitutional organs seems to require the sacrifice of some worthwhile value for the sake of maximizing the accomplishment of another significant value. In actual practice in Latin America, individual member parliamentary autonomy is at odds with parliamentary support for effective democratic governance, and Supreme Court institutional autonomy may safeguard liberty at the expense of needed economic reforms.

Democracies without Democrats?

There are some notable puzzles in the attitudes of the public in some Latin American countries. For example, consider the evidence presented in the chapter by Marta Lagos concerning two countries—Chile and Uruguay —with a long experience of constitutional government that was interrupted by respective military coups in the early 1970s. In the late 1990s, the Chilean public's preference for democracy as a form of government was only about 55 percent, in contrast to democratic preference levels above 80 percent in Uruguay. This difference is difficult to explain because the annual average growth rate of gross domestic product was twice as high in Chile than in Uruguay during those years. Why did Chileans think less well of democracy even when it seemed to be performing better in their country than in Uruguay?

Another puzzle is the attitudes of Venezuelans. In 2000, Venezuelans expressed the highest levels of optimism for the economic future of their country and for their own economic future, clearly a tribute to President Chávez's ability to charm Venezuelans during the first two years of his presidency. And yet in 1999–2000, the trends in gross domestic product per capita in Venezuela were the second worst in Latin America; there was little basis to expect that the economic future would be rosy.[34]

There are, however, some general patterns. A majority of Latin Americans supported democracy as the preferred form of government by high and stable margins throughout the late 1990s, as Marta Lagos' chapter makes clear, but levels of democratic support dropped at the start of the twenty-first century.[35] In the late 1990s, Latin Americans preferred democratic to authoritarian rule by a margin of nearly 4 to 1. On the other hand, comparably consistent majorities of Latin Americans were dissatisfied with the way democracy worked in their respective countries. By huge margins, as Lagos shows, they were deeply worried about crime, drug abuse, and corruption. They had shockingly low confidence in the key institutions of democratic governance. In the second half of the 1990s, confidence in the national Congress for the region as a whole did not rise above 10 percent in any of the four Latino-barómetro surveys carried out during those years; confidence in political parties never exceeded 7 percent. Yet, as Lagos points out, confidence in Parliaments in Europe typically hovered around 50 percent during the same time. Fortunately for democratic governance in Latin America, in the second half of the 1990s confidence in the armed forces never reached 20 percent, decreasing the temptation for potential coup-makers.

The public opinion evidence does not suggest that Latin Americans are authoritarian. On the contrary, it indicates that they prefer democratic governance but also have high expectations about performance (expectations in Chile may be too high, however). Latin Americans look for better results from the governments of the moment, and they are understandably critical because these fall short. Their attitudes respond mainly to the low level of democratic governance in the region. For the most part, these publics are unresponsive to trends, that is, to subtle changes in the level of effective democratic governance because the problems facing democracies remain so great that the little improvements are often difficult to perceive.

The circumstances of democratic rule are not good in many Latin American countries. Latin America still suffers from weak civilian control over the military, from serious instances of malperformance by political parties, and from weakened party systems in Colombia, Peru, and Venezuela. Some constitutional revisions reduced the prospects for governability in Colombia and for democratic practices in Venezuela. Societal transformations weakened organized labor and its capacity to represent the interests of workers at the workplace and in politics. Some national Parliaments retained clientelist practices that impair the likelihood for democratic governance, as in Brazil, Ecuador, and Colombia. The level of effective democratic governance, in general, remains poor.

And yet, from the early to the late 1990s, the trends toward more effective democratic governance in Latin America, warts notwithstanding, improved in more countries than not. The improvement is clearer if the effectiveness of democratic governance in the late 1990s is compared to the grave politico-economic crises of the 1980s. In the late 1990s, constitutional government typically prevailed over military coup attempts; even the frequency of those attempts declined. Many political parties became more reliable and responsible than they were when the decade began. Some countries reformed their institutions and basic laws to deepen democratic governance and effectiveness. More Parliaments and Supreme Courts behaved with greater independence according to constitutional prescriptions. Significant societal transformations took place; in some respects, such as the changing role of women in politics, these changes empowered citizens to exercise their rights. As the twentieth century ended, Mexican voters confirmed the country's transition to constitutional government, electing the first president from an opposition party since the Mexican Revolution. And Peruvian citizens celebrated the return of constitutional democracy.

As the twenty-first century began, effective democratic governance, despite fits and starts, had improved during the preceding decade in Brazil, Chile, and Mexico, among the countries studied specifically in this book. Governance had improved markedly in Argentina in the 1990s but the economic implosion in 2002 put it at grave risk. It deteriorated in Colombia and Venezuela. The quality of Peru's democratic life worsened during the second half of the 1990s, but the end of Fujimori's decade-long rule in 2000 gave basis for democratic hope. But the record of more effective democratic governance is evident as well in other countries. Democratic governance improved in all Central American countries except Nicaragua. (The improvement in Guatemala stemmed principally from the 1996 peace accord, putting an end to decades of internal war, but Guatemala's democratic institutions remain weak otherwise.) Democratic governance improved as well in Panama, where citizens were free enough to defeat an incumbent president's attempt to modify the constitution to permit his reelection, the Dominican Republic, Uruguay, and Bolivia; in all four countries, opposition parties were able to win the presidency, and in all four, Congress played a significant role in shaping public policy. The record worsened markedly in Ecuador; it remained approximately the same and quite poor in Nicaragua[36] and Paraguay. Cuba experienced little change in the authoritarian structures of its political system.

On balance, most Latin Americans lived in more open societies and were freer to exercise their political rights, including the right to protest against the government. Their governments worked more effectively. In nearly all countries, these tasks could and still should be performed better. And Latin Americans remained skeptical that the positive changes were real enough or would endure. Democratic pessimism still colored the perspectives of many citizens of the Americas. It is the challenge of the new century to make democratic governance in Latin America more credibly and truly effective.

Notes

Chapter 2. Presidentialism and Representative Institutions

1. Adam Przeworski, Michael Álvarez, José Antonio Cheibub, and Fernando Limongi, "What Makes Democracies Endure?" *Journal of Democracy* 7, no. 1 (January 1996): 39–55; Karen Remmer, "The Political Impact of Economic Crisis in Latin America in the 1980s," *American Political Science Review* 8, no. 3 (September 1991): 777–800; and "The Sustainability of Political Democracy: Lessons from Latin America," *Comparative Political Studies* 29, no. 6 (December 1996): 611–34.

2. J. Samuel Fitch, *The Armed Forces and Democracy in Latin America* (Baltimore: Johns Hopkins University Press, 1998).

3. Susan C. Stokes, *Mandates and Democracy: Neoliberalism by Surprise in Latin America* (New York: Cambridge University Press, 2001).

4. Matthew Soberg Shugart and John M. Carey, *Presidents and Assemblies: Constitutional Design and Electoral Dynamics* (New York: Cambridge University Press, 1992); Mark P. Jones, "Evaluating Argentina's Presidential Democracy," in *Presidentialism and Democracy in Latin America,* ed. Scott Mainwaring and Matthew Soberg Shugart (New York: Cambridge University Press, 1997); Gary W. Cox, *Making Votes Count: Strategic Coordination in the World's Electoral Systems* (New York: Cambridge University Press, 1997); Michael J. Coppedge, "Presidential Runoffs Do Not Fragment Legislative Party Systems," paper presented at the American Political Science Association conference, Washington, D.C., August 2000. In the most rigorous empirical test of the effects of presidential runoffs to date, Coppedge finds evidence for greater fragmentation of legislative party systems in runoff systems only relative to the format in which legislative elections are held concurrent with a plurality election for president. That is, presidential runoffs do not fragment legislative party systems when elections to the two branches are decoupled.

5. Gregory Schmidt, "Fujimori's 1990 Upset Victory in Peru: Electoral Rules, Contingencies, and Adaptive Strategies," *Comparative Politics* 28, no. 3 (April 1996): 321–54.

6. Scott Mainwaring and Matthew Shugart, eds., *Presidentialism and Democracy in Latin America* (New York: Cambridge University Press, 1997).

7. Costa Rica's system has been in place since 1949, and its first-round threshold is low enough to approximate the effects of a plurality system; Shugart and Carey, *Presidents and Assemblies.* Argentina's reform, in 1994, and Nicaragua's, in 1995, were evidently attempts to split the difference between the Costa Rican threshold and the standard majority runoff format.

8. Jones, "Evaluating Argentina's Presidential Democracy."

9. Arturo Valenzuela, "Party Politics and the Crisis of Presidentialism in Chile: A Proposal for a Parliamentary Form of Government," in *The Failure of Presidential Democracy*, ed. Juan J. Linz and Arturo Valenzuela (Baltimore: Johns Hopkins University Press, 1994).

10. John M. Carey, "Partidos y coaliciones en el Congreso Chileno," *Política y gobierno* 6, no. 2 (Mexico City: Centro de Investigaciones y Docencia Económicas, 1999): 365–406.

11. John M. Carey, "Los efectos del ciclo electoral sobre el sistema de partidos y el respaldo parlamentario al ejecutivo," *Estudios Públicos* (Santiago, Chile) 55 (Winter 1994): 305–14.

12. "Lavin Opines on Pinochet Trial and Poll Results," *Santiago (Chile) Times*, April 27, 2000, Electronic listerve newsletter, @santiagotimes.chip.mic.cl.

13. "Zaldívar destaca clima político para analizar posibles reformas constitucionales," *La Tercera*, on-line edition, April 17, 2000, http://www.tercera.cl/diario/2000/04/17/extras/t- 17.12.3a.EXT.ZALDIVAR.html.

14. NotiSur, "Chile: Socialist Ricardo Lagos is Concertación Candidate for President," *Latin American Political Affairs* 9, no. 22 (June 11,1999): http://jukebox.ucsd.edu/news.

15. Jeffrey Cason, "Electoral Reform and Stability in Uruguay," *Journal of Democracy*, 11, no. 2 (April 2000): 85–98.

16. I thank the editors of this volume for this insight.

17. Although not explicit, concessions from President Zedillo allowing Madrazo to resume his post as governor of Tabasco state, and to name the PRI's candidate to succeed him, almost certainly were key to his acquiescence as well (Jeffrey Weldon, personal communication with the author, April 25, 2000). However, it is difficult to imagine Madrazo having accepted Labastida's candidacy under any circumstances had the nomination been made through the traditional *dedazo* method, by which the incumbent president names the party's anointed.

18. Julia Preston, "Ruling Party Gets a Lift in Mexico as Foes Disagree," *New York Times*, on-line edition, September 29, 1999.

19. Paul Berman, "Mexico's Third Way," *The New York Times Magazine*, on-line edition, July 2, 2000.

20. In Costa Rica, non-consecutive reelection was prohibited by constitutional amendment in the 1970s, after the third presidency of José Figueres Ferrer. In 2000, former president Oscar Arias proposed removing the lifetime prohibition and allowing non-consecutive reelection once again. The idea attracted attention but also, predictably, criticism as self-serving, given the source. Arias, in turn, complained that prominent politicians had *approached him* with the idea and encouraged him privately, then betrayed him once he went public. At the time of this writing, prospects for the reform appear bleak.

21. Juan J. Linz, "Presidentialism or Parliamentarism: Does It Make a Difference?" in *The Failure of Presidential Democracy: The Case of Latin America*, ed. Juan J. Linz and Arturo Valenzuela (Baltimore: Johns Hopkins University Press, 1994).

22. On the other hand, recent work by Stokes (*Mandates and Democracy*, 2001) confronts us with the puzzle that Latin American presidents who flagrantly violated their own campaign promises have subsequently been rewarded at the polls (either personally, if reelection is allowed, or through their parties) *if* their policy switches yielded good macroeconomic results. In short, the relationships among citizen preferences, presidential performance, and electoral responses in Latin America are complex, and we are only just beginning to understand them.

23. Jones, "Evaluating Argentina's Presidential Democracy."

24. Michael Coppedge, *Strong Parties and Lame Ducks: Presidential Partyarchy and Factionalism in Venezuela* (Palo Alto, Calif.: Stanford University Press, 1994).

25. *El Universal* (Caracas, Venezuela), March 6, 2000, 1–10.

26. John M. Carey, *Term Limits and Legislative Representation* (New York: Cambridge University Press, 1996).

27. Centralization of authority is a double-edged sword, however, and Chávez's over-reaching generated serious problems within his broader coalition. Governor Francisco Arias Cárdenas, of Zulia state, a former Chávez ally, justified his decision to mount an opposition campaign for president in part by decrying "the old practice of party bosses designating candidates by 'dedo'" as proof that the MVR is no more internally democratic than the traditional parties had been: I say that if there has not been a change, on the part of the President and his organization, for democracy and participation, they don't deserve our support." Other erstwhile Chávez allies agreed, including Governor Yoel Acosta Chirinos ("The MVR is worse than the AD") and leaders of the PPT party, who stormed out of meetings to discuss nominations with top MVR officials, slamming the door and shouting, "There is complete lack of respect!" José Marin, "Chávez tendrá que venir al Zulia a levantar las manos a sus candidatos," *El Nacional* (Caracas, Venezuela), March 7, 2000, sec. D-2.

28. Coppedge, *Strong Parties and Lame Ducks.*

29. NotiSur, "Brazil: Former President Fernando Collor de Mello Acquitted on Corruption Charges," *Latin American Political Affairs* 4, no. 46 (December 16, 1994): http://jukebox.ucsd.edu/news/.

30. NotiSur, "Venezuela: Former President Carlos Andrés Pérez Sentenced to 28 Months for Misappropriation of Funds," *Latin American Political Affairs* 6, no. 23 (June 7, 1996): http://jukebox.ucsd.edu/news; Maxwell A. Cameron, "Political and Economic Origins of Regime Change in Peru: The *Eighteenth Brumaire* of Alberto Fujimori," in *The Peruvian Labyrinth: Polity, Society, and Economy,* ed. Maxwell A. Cameron and Philip Mauceri (University Park: Penn State Press, 1997), 28–70.

31. NotiCen, "Nicaragua: Legislature Passes Bill to Privatize Pensions Over Strong Union Opposition," *Latin American Political Affairs* 5, no. 11 (March 23, 2000): http://jukebox.ucsd.edu/news.

32. José Antonio Cheibub, "Presidentialism and Democratic Performance," in *The Architecture of Democracy: Constitutional Design, Conflict Management, and Democracy,* ed. Andrew Reynolds (Oxford University Press, 2002).

33. Mainwaring and Shugart, eds., *Presidentialism and Democracy.*

34. Larry Rohter, "Venezuela's Leader Is Seeking Decree Powers to Speed Changes," *New York Times,* November 5, 2000, 22.

35. Catherine Conaghan, "Polls, Political Discourse, and the Public Sphere: The Spin on Peru's Fuji-golpe," in *Latin America in Comparative Perspective: New Approaches to Methods and Analysis,* ed. Peter H. Smith (Boulder, Colo.: Westview, 1995), 227–56.

36. Linz, "Presidentialism or Parliamentarism."

37. Przeworski, Álvarez, José Cheibub, and Limongi, "What Makes Democracies Endure?"

38. Linz, "Presidentialism or Parliamentarism"; Alfred Stepan and Cindy Skach, "Constitutional Frameworks and Democratic Consolidation," *World Politics* 46, no. 1 (October 1993): 1–22.

39. Shugart and Carey, *Presidents and Assemblies.*

40. Many authors refer to hybrid regimes, in which cabinet responsibility is shared between assemblies and directly elected presidents, as "semipresidential." Shugart and Carey suggest that this nomenclature hides more than it illuminates because differences in the specifics of appointment and dismissal generate fundamentally different structures of

cabinet responsibility and patterns of conflict between presidents and assemblies; Shugart and Carey, *Presidents and Assemblies*. On these grounds, we distinguished between "premier-presidential" and "presidential-parliamentary" configurations in hybrid systems. These catchy labels mysteriously failed to enter common parlance, however, so I defer here to common usage, sticking with the generic "hybrid" label. For the record, however, Latin American and post-Soviet regimes tend toward president-parliamentarism in their arrangements regarding cabinet appointments and confidence, whereas European hybrids are mostly premier-presidential.

41. Charles de Secondat baron de Montesquieu, *The Spirit of the Laws* (New York: Cambridge University Press, 1989); Alexander Hamilton, James Madison, and John Jay, *The Federalist* [1787–88] (New York: Signet, 1961).

42. Ricardo Combellas, interview by author, Caracas, Venezuela, March 8, 2000.

43. Ecuador limited legislative reelection after the return to democracy in the late 1970s, but the restriction was overturned by a popular referendum in the early 1990s. Many U.S. states attempted to impose term limits on their delegations to Congress in the early 1990s, but these were ruled unconstitutional by the Supreme Court in 1995.

44. Jeffrey Weldon, personal communication with the author, April 25, 2000.

45. John M. Carey, Richard G. Niemi, and Lynda Powell, *Term Limits in the State Legislatures* (Ann Arbor: University of Michigan Press, 2000); Carey, *Term Limits and Legislative Representation*.

46. Carey, Niemi, and Powell, *Term Limits in the State Legislatures*.

47. Carey, *Term Limits and Legislative Representation*.

48. Quoted in ibid., 153.

49. In Chile, moreover, if Congress does not pass a final version of the budget within a set time period (sixty days), the president's proposal takes effect.

50. Lisa A. Baldez and John M. Carey, "Presidential Agenda Control and Spending Policy: Lessons from General Pinochet's Constitution," *American Journal of Political Science* 43, no. 1 (January 1999): 29–55; John M. Carey, "Consequences of Institutional Design: Term Limits and Budgetary Procedures in Presidential Systems," in *El gobierno en América Latina: Presidencialismo o parlamentarismo?* ed. Diego Valadés and José María Serna (Mexico City: Universidad Nacional Autónoma de México, 1999), 167–98.

51. Closer to home, the analogous situation is the rule for splitting a candy bar between two children. Let one (the president) divide the candy bar, thereby setting the "consumption ceiling," or the size of the largest piece; and let the other (the legislature) decide who gets which piece. The equilibrium in this game is an equitable distribution of the candy bar, which should be instructive for designers of budgetary procedures.

52. Baldez and Carey, "Presidential Agenda Control."

53. This example demonstrates that legislative voting records are salient to politicians. Their salience to voters is more difficult to discern. Among the Brazilian deputies belonging to Cardoso's coalition, those who were the least loyal to the executive had a lower reelection rate in 1998 than the loyalists (Octavio Amorim Neto, personal communication with author, 1999). This suggests either that the attack advertisements did not work, or that the concessions Cardoso provided to his supporters more than offset any electoral damage from the controversial votes.

54. As Jeff Smith trenchantly pointed out to me, votes by handraising provided the political equivalent of the old "Saturday Night Live" routine in which Joe Piscopo reported (roughly) as follows: "Good evening. It was a *great* day in sports. Scores were 7–3; 4–1; and, in a real cliffhanger, 12–11. For *Weekend Update*, this is Joe Piscopo. Good night" (*SNL* around 1980).

55. *Diario de los Debates* (Perú): Primera Legislatura Ordinaria de 1998, 11a Sesión, Congreso de Perú (Caracas, September 24, 1998).

56. Alexis Murillo, interview by author, Caracas, Venezuela, March 8, 2000.

57. *Diario de los Debates* (Perú), 169–71.

58. NotiSur, "Colombia: Scandal in Congress Prompts Call for Referendum," *Latin American Political Affairs* 10, no. 13 (April 7, 2000): http://jukebox.ucsd.edu/news.

59. Elisabeth Ungar, personal communication with the author, November 7, 2000.

Chapter 3. The Military

1. See Alfred Stepan, *Rethinking Military in Politics: Brazil and the Southern Cone* (Princeton: Princeton University Press, 1988).

2. Wendy Hunter, "State and Soldier in Latin America," *Peaceworks*, no. 10 (Washington, D.C.: U.S. Institute of Peace); Wendy Hunter, "Conflicto civil-militar y acomodación en las nuevas democracias latinoamericanas," *Fuerzas Armadas y Sociedad* (Santiago, Chile), 10, no. 4 (October–December 1995): 27–32.

3. Hunter, "Conflicto civil-militar y acomodación," 30.

4. For other research showing the incomplete character of analysis based on the *rational choice* theory used by Wendy Hunter, see Rut Diamint, "Militares y Democracia en Argentina," in *Argentinien nach zehn Jahren Menem—Bilanz und Perspektiven*, ed. Peter Birle (Berlin: Preußischer Kulturbesitz Ibero-Amerikanischen Institut, forthcoming); Claudio Fuentes, "After Pinochet: Civilian Unity, Political Institutions, and the Military in Chile (1990–1998)," working paper, Department of Political Science, University of North Carolina-Chapel Hill, North Carolina, 1999.

5. David Pion-Berlin and Craig Arceneaux, "Decision-Makers or Decision-Takers? Military Missions and Civilian Control in Democratic South America," *Armed Forces and Society* (Spring 2000): 146.

6. Fitch agrees with Brian Loveman on this point. See J. Samuel Fitch, "Civil-Military Relations in the 21st Century: Implications for DOD Policy," in *Defense Strategy at the Crossroad: Insights from a Changing Security Environment* (Washington, D.C.: National Defense University, 2001).

7. David Pion-Berlin, "Between Confrontation and Accommodation: Military and Government Policy in Democratic Argentina," *Journal of Latin American Studies* 23, no. 3 (October 1991); Hunter, "State and Soldier in Latin America."

8. Consuelo Cruz and Rut Diamint, "The New Military Autonomy in Latin America," *Journal of Democracy* (October 1998): 115–27.

9. Edward Luttwak, "From Geopolitics to Geoeconomics," *The National Interest*, no. 20 (Summer 1990): 17–23.

10. Ole Wæver, "Securitization and Desecuritization," in *On Security*, ed. Ronnie D. Lipschutz (New York: Columbia University Press, 1995), 46–58.

11. See John R. Redick, "Latin America's Emerging Non-Proliferation Consensus," in *Arms Control Today* (Washington, D.C.: March 1994), 4–8; and Rut Diamint, "Esquemas de seguridad en América Latina. Las medidas de fomento de la confianza," working paper, Universidad Torcuato Di Tella, Buenos Aires, Argentina, 1988, 4–9.

12. Suzeley Kalil Mathias, "Pensamiento y papel militar en América Latina en el umbral del siglo XXI," in *Control civil y fuerzas armadas en las nuevas democracias latinoamericanas*, ed. Rut Diamint (Buenos Aires: Editorial GEL, 1999), 169; Jorge Zaverucha, "A Constituição brasileira de 1988 e seu legado autoritário: formalizando a democracia

mas retirando sua essência," in *Democracia e instituições políticas brasileiras no final do século XX,* ed. Jorge Zaverucha (Brasil: Coordenação Editorial, 1998), 124.

13. "A Pirâmide Militar," *Jornal do Brasil,* December 27, 1998, 8.

14. Thomaz Guedes da Costa, "Brazil in the New Decade: Searching for a Future," *CSIS Report* (September 2000): 21.

15. Complementary Law No. 97, enacted on June 9, 1999, created the position of defense minister. The Ministry itself was created on September 2, 1999, with constitutional amendment No. 23.

16. News published on *Folha de São Paulo* and *Jornal do Brasil* (December 18, 19, 22, 1999).

17. Bolívar Lamounier affirms in this book "the resilience of the statist ideological legacy."

18. "Informe de Atividades da Secretaria de Assuntos Estratégicos (SAE)," *Parcerias Estratégicas* (Brasilia, Brazil) 3 (June 1997): 228–34.

19. See Alberto Cardoso, "Amazônia é Prioridade da Política de Defesa," in *Parcerias Estratégicas* (Brasilia, Brazil) 2 (December 1996): 19–21.

20. See Carlos Iván Degregori in this book, and also Carlos Basombrío Iglesias, "Hacia el 9 de abril . . . y después," *Revista Ideele* (Lima, Peru), 126 (March 2000).

21. Carlos Iván Degregori in this book.

22. Report to Brigadier General (Ret.) Daniel Mora, in *Perú Hoy* (Lima: Desco, December 1999), 52.

23. See Juan Rial, "Las fuerzas armadas y la cuestión de la democracia en América Latina," in *Los militares y la democracia. El futuro de las relaciones cívico-militares en América Latina,* ed. Louis Goodman, Johanna Mendelson and Juan Rial (Uruguay: Peitho, 1990), 6–7.

24. *El Universo* (Quito, Ecuador), December 2, 1999.

25. Fitch, "Civil-Military Relations in the 21st Century," to be published in *Defense Strategy at the Crossroad.*

26. *Diario Hoy* (Quito, Ecuador), November 26, 1999.

27. Juan Ramón Quintana and Raúl Barrios, "Las Relaciones Civiles-Militares en Bolivia: Una Agenda Pendiente," in *Control civil y fuerzas armadas,* ed. Rut Diamint, 251.

28. In Bertha García Gallegos, "El 21 de enero de la democracia ecuatoriana: el asalto al poder," paper presented at the seminar on *Gobernabilidad, seguridad e instituciones militares en las democracias,* Partnership for Democratic Governance and Security, Buenos Aires, Argentina, April 2000.

29. Francisco Leal Buitrago, "Relaciones civiles militares y seguridad nacional en Colombia," paper, December 1999.

30. Andrés Pastrana, "Colombia no puede sola," *La Nación* (Buenos Aires, Argentina), July 11, 2000.

31. Fernando Cepeda Ulloa in this book.

32. See "El conflicto en Colombia: ¿Hacia la intervención?" *IRELA* (Madrid), September 16, 1999. *The Economist* reports that FARC has 17,000 warriors. "Colombia's War, Rights, Wrongs and Powers," *The Economist,* July 28–August 3, 2001, 39.

33. Gabriel Marcella and Donald Schulz, *Colombia's Three Wars: U.S. Strategy at the Crossroads* (Washington, D.C.: Strategic Studies Institute, March 1999), 14.

34. Data from the *Miami Herald,* December 25, 1998, quoted in Marcella and Schulz, *Colombia's Three Wars,* 8–9.

35. Andrés Dávila Ladrón de Guevara, "Dime con quién andas: las relaciones entre

civiles y militares en la Colombia de los años 90," in *Control civil y fuerzas armadas,* ed. Rut Diamint, 366, 382–86.

36. In "El conflicto en Colombia: ¿Hacia la intervención?" *IRELA* (Madrid), September 16, 1999, and *El Tiempo* (Bogotá, Colombia), November 20, 1999.

37. Michael Coppedge in this book; Francine Jâcome, "Las relaciones cívico-militares en Venezuela (1992–1997)," in *Control civil y fuerzas armadas,* ed. Rut Diamint, 424; Jennifer McCoy, "Demystifying Venezuela's Hugo Chávez," *Current History* (February 2000): 67.

38. McCoy, "Demystifying Venezuela's Hugo Chávez," 70.

39. In *El Mercurio* (Santiago de Chile), February 14, 2000.

40. Juan Ramón Quintana and Raúl Barrios, "Las relaciones civiles-militares en Bolivia: Una agenda pendiente," in *Control civil y fuerzas armadas,* ed. Rut Diamint, 252–54.

41. Adrián Bonilla, "The Andean Security Agenda at the Beginning of the Century," paper presented at the LASA XXII International Congress, Miami, Florida, March 2000.

42. Carlos Martini told Radio Uno that the attempted coup against the new president, González Macchi, "means that the Paraguayan president does not exercise an unquestioned leadership of the armed forces." Both news items appeared in *Diario Hoy* (Asunción, Paraguay), November 23, 1999.

43. *Strategic Survey 1998/1999* (London: International Institute for Strategic Studies, 1999), 87–88.

44. The following day the president of the Republic, Dr. Jorge Batlle, made his displeasure known to the minister of national defense. The armed forces chiefs met with Fernández, who was arrested for ten days and removed from his duties. *Búsqueda* (Montevideo, Uruguay), April 6, 2000.

45. Diamint, "Militares y Democracia en Argentina."

46. See Steven Levitsky in this book, on the institutionalization of civil rights, freedom of the press, and party transformation.

47. "The military's malaise is expressed continuously, not as a challenge to authority but by letting it be known that the army will not be left out of the Pinochet process." *El Mercurio* (Santiago, Chile), May 2, 2000.

48. Claudio Fuentes, "Militares en Chile: ni completa autonomía ni total subordinación," *Chile 96. Análisis y opiniones* (Santiago, FLACSO-Chile, 1997), 167–70.

49. Guillermo A. Pacheco Gaitán, "Las relaciones civiles-militares en las democracias emergentes de Centro América: entre olvido a la esperanza," paper presented at the LASA XXII International Congress, Miami, Florida, March 2000.

50. Alejandro Bendaña, *Demobilization and Reintegration in Central America: Peace-Building Challenges and Responses* (Managua, Nicaragua: Centro de Estudios Internacionales, 1999), 23–34.

51. Roberto J. Cajina, *Transición política y reconversión militar en Nicaragua, 1990–1995* (Managua, Nicaragua: CRIES, 1996), 334.

52. Ibid., 342.

53. On May 25, 1993, well into the democratizing process, President José Luis Serrano decreed the suspension of the constitution, dissolved Congress and the Supreme Court, removed both the attorney general and the civil rights advocate from office, and suspended the Electoral and Political Party Laws.

54. The armed forces were responsible for 93 percent of the abuses while the URNG guerrillas were responsible for 3 percent. *La Nación* (Guatemala), February 15, 2000.

55. Quoted by Bernardo Arévalo, "Bases para la consideración de la cuestión militar en Guatemala," working paper, FLACSO, Guatemala, December 1999.

56. Córdova further states that "the negotiating process stopped being about who was going to hold power and focused on the ways and means of access to power," which implies that at least institutional rules of the game were established. This is reflected in the 1992 national constitution, where military roles are restricted. See Ricardo Córdova Macías, "El Salvador: Los acuerdos de paz y las relaciones cívico-militares," in *Control civil y fuerzas armadas,* 549.

57. The death rate was even higher than during the dictatorship. See "Building Peace and Democracy in El Salvador: An Ongoing Challenge," *Policy Paper* (Ottawa, Canada, FOCAL, April 2000).

58. National Security Law, Article 48, National Civil Defense Directorate (Quito, Ecuador, 1993).

59. García Gallegos, "El 21 de enero de la democracia ecuatoriana."

60. Army Industries Directorate, brochure, 1999.

61. Ibid.

62. Arnoldo Brenes and Kevin Casas, eds., *Soldados como empresarios. Los negocios de los militares en Centroamérica* (San José, Costa Rica: Ed. Fundación Arias para la Paz y el Progreso Humano y Agencia Suiza para el Desarrollo y la Cooperación, 1998), 14.

63. See ibid., 37.

64. Leticia Salomón, *Poder civil y fuerzas armadas en Honduras* (Tegucigalpa, Honduras: CEDOH-CRIES, 1997), 162.

65. Brenes and Casas, *Soldados como empresarios,* 95–119. The case of joint personal and institutional wealth-building in the armed forces also occurs in El Salvador: 158–60.

66. *El Nuevo Diario* (Managua, Nicaragua), February 28, 2000.

67. *Diario HOY* (Lima, Peru), September 24, 1999.

68. Lieutenant Colonel Ollanta Moisés Humala Tasso, "Manifesto to the Peruvian Nation" (October 29, 2000). Information from the office of the Peruvian ombudsman.

69. *Liberación* (Lima, Peru), December 17, 1999, 3.

70. *El Comercio* (Lima, Peru), November 2, 2000.

71. Bruno Masi, "Los militares y la política en el Paraguay," *Masinformes* (Asunción, Paraguay), August 8, 1996.

72. Statement from the president of the Industrial Union of Paraguay (UIP), Ing. Guillermo Stanley, *ABC* (Asunción, Paraguay), July 23, 2000.

73. Bruno Masi, *Masinformes* (Asunción, Paraguay), December 12, 1995.

74. *Clarín* (Buenos Aires, Argentina), April 24, 1996, 3.

75. *Jane's Defense Weekly,* June 21, 2000.

76. Felipe Agüero, *Militares, Civiles y Democracia. La España postfranquista en perspectiva comparada* (Madrid: Alianza Editorial, 1995), 41–52.

77. J. Samuel Fitch, *The Armed Forces and Democracy in Latin America,* (Baltimore: Johns Hopkins University Press, 1998), 188.

78. Juan Ramón Quintana and Raúl Barrios, "Las relaciones civiles-militares en Bolivia: Una agenda pendiente," *Control civil y fuerzas armadas,* ed. Rut Diamint, 246.

79. *La Prensa* (Honduras), August 5, 1999.

80. Ministry of Defense, Uruguay, May 1999.

81. *La República* (Montevideo, Uruguay), January 6, 2000, 4, 5.

82. Suzeley Khalil Mathias and Iara Beleli, "Os militares e as eleições de 1994 (notas de pesquisa)," *Premissas no. 8* (Campinas, Brazil: NEE-UNICAMP, November 1994), 62.

83. Ministry of Defense, Chile, *Libro Blanco de la Defensa de Chile* (Chile, 1998); Ministry of Defense, Argentina, *Libro Blanco de la Defensa Nacional* (Argentina, 1999).

84. Kristina Mani Clark, "Concepciones de la defensa nacional en Argentina y Chile: Una comparación de los libros de la defensa," *Fuerzas Armadas y Sociedad* 15, no. 2 (Santiago, Chile: FLACSO-Chile, April–June 2000): 42, 45–49; Ministry of Defense, Argentina, *Libro Blanco de la Defensa de Argentina*, 107.

85. Buitrago, "Relaciones civiles militares y seguridad nacional."

86. "Argentina: Dismantling an Authoritarian Legacy" *NACLA Report on the Americas* 33, no. 5 (March–April 2000): 1. Also in *La Nación* (Buenos Aires, Argentina), February 14, 2000.

87. ABIN was created on December 7, 1999. See João Roberto Martins Filho, "Focos armados e serviços de informação no governo Cardoso," paper presented at the LASA XXII International Congress, Miami, Florida, March 2000.

88. *Diario HOY* (Caracas, Venezuela), July 7, 1999.

89. One of the best studied cases is that of Colombia; see Yaneth Giha Tobar, Héctor Riveros Reyes, and Andrés Soto Velasco, "El gasto militar en Colombia: Aspectos macroeconómicos y microeconómicos," *Revista de la CEPAL* (Santiago, Chile), December 1999.

90. See Francisco Rojas Aravena, ed., *Gasto Militar en América Latina. Procesos de decisión y actores claves* (Chile: CINDE-FLACSO, 1994).

91. This topic is developed in Kanti Bajpai, "Human Security: Concept and Measurement," working paper, Joan B. Kroc Institute for International Peace, Notre Dame, August 2000.

92. Jorge Domínguez, "The Future of Inter-American Relations," working paper, Inter-American Dialogue, Washington, D.C., 1999, 8.

93. *Hoy* (Asunción, Paraguay), March 23, 1994.

94. "Profile of the United States Southern Command," working paper, Public Affairs Directorate, Panama Headquarters United States Southern Command, Quarry Heights, Panama, June 20, 1994.

95. In Richard Downes, *Landpower and Ambiguous Warfare: The Challenge of Colombia in the 21st Century* (Washington, D.C.: Strategic Studies Institute, Conference Report, March 10, 1999), 5.

96. In *Clarín* (Buenos Aires, Argentina), December 17, 1996, 16.

97. In *Folha de São Paulo y O Estado de São Paulo* (November 23, 24, 26, 30, 1999).

98. As Stepan explains, the Brazilian constitution is ambiguous regarding armed forces participation in internal affairs. See Stepan, *Rethinking Military in Politics*, 103–14.

99. See *La República* (Montevideo, Uruguay), February 5, 2000.

100. Pion-Berlin and Arceneaux, "Decision-Makers or Decision-Takers?" 417, 432.

101. Fitch, "Civil-Military Relations in the 21st Century."

102. Raphael F. Perl, "The Andean Drug Initiative: Background and Issues for Congress" (Washington, D.C.: Congressional Research Service, February 13, 1992), 15.

103. Michael Shifter, "Central America: Current Trends and Recommendations for U.S. Policy," *Policy Brief*, Washington, D.C., Inter-American Dialogue, June 25, 1997.

104. In December 2000, the U.S. Army School of the Americas officially closed. The Western Hemisphere Institute for Security Cooperation (WHINSEC) was established under the Floyd D. Spence National Defense Authorization Act for fiscal year 2001 in October 2000, and formally opened on January 17, 2001.

105. *Defense Issues* 12, no. 12 (Washington, D.C.: American Forces Information Service, April 1998).

106. Christopher P. Gibson and Don M. Snider, "Civil-Military Relations and the Ability to Influence: A Look at the National Security Decision-Making Process," *Armed Forces & Society* 25 (Winter 1999).

107. Rut Diamint, "El proceso de toma de decisión. Algunas experiencias comparadas," working paper no. 39, Universidad Torcuato Di Tella, Buenos Aires, Argentina, 1997.

108. Peter Feaver and Richard Kohn, "The Gap: Soldiers, Civilians and Their Mutual Misunderstanding," *The National Interest* (Fall 2000): 29–37.

109. Patrice McSherry, "The Emergence of 'Guardian Democracy,'" *NACLA Report on the Americas* 32, no. 3 (November–December 1998): 18.

110. Karl W. Deutsch et al., *Political Community and the North Atlantic Area* (Princeton: Princeton University Press, 1957), 5–7.

Chapter 4. Market Reforms

1. Francis Fukuyama, "The End of History?" *The National Interest* (Summer 1989):10.

2. Max Weber, *Economy and Society: An Outline of Interpretive Sociology,* ed. Guenthyer Roth and Claus Wittich (New York: Bedminster, 1968); Charles Tilly, "War-Making and State-Making as Organized Crime," in *Bringing the State Back In,* ed. Peter B. Evans, Dietrich Rueschemeyer, and Theda Skocpol (New York: Cambridge University Press, 1985); Theda Skocpol, *State and Social Revolutions: A Comparative Analysis of France, Russia, and China* (New York: Cambridge University Press, 1979); Peter A. Hall, *Governing the Economy: The Politics of State Intervention in Britain and France* (New York: Oxford University Press, 1986).

3. Alexander Gerschenkron, *Economic Backwardness in Historical Perspective* (Cambridge, Mass.: The Belknap Press of Harvard University Press, 1962).

4. See Albert O. Hirschman, "The Political Economy of Import-Substituting Industrialization in Latin America," *Quarterly Journal of Economics* 82, no. 1 (February 1968): 1–32; John Sheahan, *Patterns of Development in Latin America: Poverty, Repression, and Economic Strategy* (Princeton: Princeton University Press, 1987); Rosemary Thorp, *Progress, Poverty and Exclusion: An Economic History of Latin America in the 20th Century* (Washington, D.C.: Inter-American Development Bank, 1998), 127–57.

5. Economics was not the only justification for state intervention. Politicians also invoked other goals, such as maximizing social welfare, incorporating labor, consolidating territorial unity, conciliating class divisions, developing backward regions, reducing inequality, and asserting sovereignty in the international arena.

6. Werner Baer, "Import Substitution and Industrialization in Latin America: Experiences and Interpretations," *Latin American Research Review* 7, no. 1 (Spring 1972): 95–111.

7. James E. Mahon Jr., "Was Latin America Too Rich to Prosper? Structural and Political Obstacles to Export-led Industrial Growth," *Journal of Development Studies* 28, no. 2 (January 1992): 241–63; Robert R. Kaufman, "How Societies Change Developmental Models or Keep Them: Reflections on the Latin American Experience in the 1930s and the Postwar World," in *Manufacturing Miracles: Paths of Industrialization in Latin America and East Asia,* ed. Gary Gereffi and Donald L. Wyman (Princeton: Princeton University Press, 1990), 110–38.

8. Carol Wise, "Reinventing the State: Economic Strategy and Institutional Change in Peru," Washington, D.C., SAIS, manuscript.

9. Sylvia Ann Hewlett, *The Cruel Dilemmas of Development: Twentieth Century Brazil* (New York: Basic, 1980), 110.

10. Victor Bulmer-Thomas, *The Economic History of Latin America since Independence* (New York: Cambridge University Press, 1994), 356.

11. Marcelo Cavarozzi, "Politics: A Key for the Long-Term in South America," in *Democracy, Markets, and Structural Reform in Latin America: Argentina, Bolivia, Brazil, Chile, and Mexico,* ed. William C. Smith, Carlos H. Acuña, and Eduardo A. Gamarra (New Brunswick, N.J.: North-South Center/Transaction, 1994).

12. Douglas Bennett and Kenneth Sharpe, "The State as a Banker and Entrepreneur: The Last Resort Character of the Mexican State's Economic Intervention, 1917–1970," in *Brazil and Mexico: Patterns in Late Development,* ed. Sylvia Ann Hewlett and Richard S. Weinert (Philadelphia: Institute for the Study of Human Issues, 1982).

13. On how politicians easily gravitate toward granting rents to special groups, see Anne O. Krueger, "Government Failures in Development," *Journal of Economic Perspectives* 4, no. 3 (Summer 1990): 9–23.

14. Robert R. Kaufman and Barbara Stallings, "The Political Economy of Latin American Populism," in *The Macroeconomics of Populism in Latin America,* ed. Rudiger Dornbusch and Sebastian Edwards (Chicago: University of Chicago Press, 1991).

15. Luiz Carlos Bresser Pereira, "Economic Reforms and Economic Growth: Efficiency and Politics in Latin America," in *Economic Reforms in New Democracies: A Social-Democratic Approach,* ed. Luiz Carlos Bresser Pereira, José María Maravall, and Adam Przeworski (Cambridge: Cambridge University Press, 1993).

16. Barbara Stallings and Wilson Peres, *Growth, Employment, and Equity: The Impact of Economic Reforms in Latin America and the Caribbean* (Washington, D.C.: Brookings Institution, 2000), 17–34.

17. Argentina, Brazil, Nicaragua, Peru, and Suriname experienced triple-digit inflation rates or higher in the 1980s and early 1990s.

18. Gerschenkron, *Economic Backwardness,* 24.

19. Sebastian Edwards, *Crisis and Reform in Latin America: From Despair to Hope* (New York: Oxford University Press, 1996), 29.

20. Roberto Cortés Conde, "Growth and Stagnation in Argentina," in *Towards a New Development Strategy for Latin America: Pathways from Hirschman's Thought,* ed. Simón Teitel (Washington, D.C.: Inter-American Development Bank, 1992).

21. For a full description of the reforms, see Inter-American Development Bank, *Economic and Social Progress in Latin America, 1997 Report: Latin America After a Decade of Reforms* (Washington, D.C.: Inter-American Development Bank, 1997); Edwards, *Crisis and Reform;* and Stallings and Peres, *Growth, Employment and Equity.*

22. Evelyne Huber, "Assessing State Strength," in *Latin America in Comparative Perspective: New Approaches to Methods and Analysis,* ed. Peter H. Smith (Boulder, Colo.: Westview, 1995).

23. Jorge I. Domínguez, "Technopols: Ideas and Leaders in Freeing Politics and Markets in Latin America in the 1990s," in *Technopols: Ideas and Leaders in Freeing Politics and Markets in Latin America in the 1990s,* ed. Jorge I. Domínguez (University Park: Penn State Press, 1997), 29.

24. Anne O. Krueger, "Problems of Liberalization," in *World Economic Growth,* ed. Arnold C. Harberger (San Francisco: Institute for Contemporary Studies, 1984), 404.

25. John Williamson, *Latin American Adjustment: How Much Has Happened?* (Washington, D.C.: Institute for International Economics, 1990).

26. William C. Smith and Roberto Patricio Korzeniewicz, "Latin America and the Second Great Transformation," in *Politics, Social Change and Economic Restructuring in Latin America,* ed. William C. Smith and Roberto Patricio Korzeniewicz (Miami, Fla.: University of Miami, North-South Center Press, 1997).

27. See William P. Glade, "Latin American Economies Restructure, Again," in *Latin*

America: Its Problems and Its Promise, ed. Jan Knippers Black (Boulder, Colo.: Westview, 1998).

28. See Carlos H. Acuña and William C. Smith, "The Political Economy of Structural Adjustment: The Logic of Support and Opposition to Neoliberal Reform," in *Latin American Political Economy in the Age of Neoliberal Reform: Theoretical and Comparative Perspectives for the 1990s,* ed. William C. Smith, Carlos H. Acuña, and Eduardo Gamarra (Miami, Fla.: North-South Center, 1994); Juan Carlos Torre, *El proceso político de las reformas económicas en América Latina* (Buenos Aires: Paidós, 1998).

29. See, for example, Robin Broad and John Cavanagh, "The Death of the Washington Consensus?" *World Policy Journal* (Fall 1999): 79–88; Benjamin R. Barber, "Jihad vs. McWorld," *The Atlantic Monthly* (March 1992).

30. See Stephen M. Walt, "Fads, Fevers, and Firestorms," *Foreign Policy* (November–December 2000): 34–43; Kurt Weyland, "Learning from Foreign Models in Latin American Policy Reform," Woodrow Wilson International Center for Scholars, Washington, D.C., August 2000, mimeo.

31. Domínguez, *Technopols.*

32. See Stallings and Peres, *Growth, Employment, and Equity;* Javier Corrales, "Coalitions and Corporate Choices in Argentina, 1976–1994: The Recent Private Sector Support of Privatization," *Studies in Comparative International Development* 32, no. 4 (Winter 1998): 24–51.

33. Jeffrey Sachs, "Keynote Address," in *Credible Signals of Reforming Governments: What to Believe?* rapporteur's report by Karissa Price, conference sponsored by Baring Asset Management Inc. and the Center for International Affairs, Harvard University, Cambridge, Mass., February 6, 1995; Guillermo A. Calvo, "Incredible Reforms," in *Debt Stabilization and Development: Essays in Memory of Carlos Díaz-Alejandro,* ed. Guillermo Calvo, Ronald Findley, Pentti Kouri, and Jorge Braga de Macedo (London: Blackwell, 1989).

34. See Peter Kingstone, *Crafting Coalitions for Reform: Business Preference, Political Institutions, and Neoliberal Reform in Brazil* (University Park: Penn State Press, 1999), 19–22; Arnold C. Harberger, "The Other Side of Tax Reform," in *Policymaking in the Open Economy: Concepts and Case Studies in Economic Performance,* ed. Rudiger Dornbusch (New York: Oxford University Press for the World Bank/EDI Series in Economic Development, 1993).

35. Stephan Haggard, *Pathways from the Periphery: The Politics of Growth in the Newly Industrializing Countries* (Ithaca: Cornell University Press, 1990); Robert R. Kaufman, "How Societies Change Developmental Models or Keep Them: Reflections on the Latin American Experience in the 1930s and the Postwar World," in *Manufacturing Miracles: Paths of Industrialization in Latin America and Asia,* ed. Gary Gereffi and Donald L. Wyman (Princeton: Princeton University Press, 1990); Kaufman and Stallings, "The Political Economy."

36. Joan M. Nelson, "Conclusion," in *Economic Crisis and Policy Choice: The Politics of Adjustment in the Third World,* ed. Joan M. Nelson (Princeton: Princeton University Press, 1990); Joan M. Nelson, "Poverty, Equity, and the Politics of Adjustment," in *The Politics of Economic Adjustment,* ed. Stephan Haggard and Robert R. Kaufman (Princeton: Princeton University Press, 1992); Stephan Haggard and Robert R. Kaufman, "Introduction," in *The Politics of Economic Adjustment,* ed. Stephan Haggard and Robert R. Kaufman (Princeton: Princeton University Press, 1992); and Carlos H. Acuña and William C. Smith, "The Political Economy," in *Markets and Democracy in Latin America: Conflict or Convergence,* ed. Philip Oxhorn and Pamela K. Starr (Boulder, Colo.: Lynne Rienner, 1999).

37. Rudiger Dornbusch, "The Case for Trade Liberalization in Developing Countries," *Journal of Economic Perspectives* 6, no. 1 (Winter 1992): 69–85.

38. Álvaro Díaz, "New Developments in Economic and Social Restructuring in Latin America," in *Politics, Social Change and Economic Restructuring in Latin America,* ed. William C. Smith and Roberto Patricio Korzeniewicz (Miami, Fla.: University of Miami, North-South Center Press, 1997).

39. Raquel Fernández and Dani Rodrik, "Resistance to Reform: Status Quo Bias in the Presence of Individual-Specific Uncertainty," *American Economic Review* 81, no. 5 (December 1991): 1146–55.

40. For an explanation of why reforms usually produce short-term losses followed by recoveries, see Adam Przeworski, *Democracy and the Market: Political and Economic Reforms in Eastern Europe and Latin America* (New York: Cambridge University Press, 1991); Martha de Melo, Cevdet Denizer, and Alan Gelb, "Patterns of Transition from Plan to Market," *The World Bank Economic Review* 10, no. 3 (September 1996): 397–424; Acuña and Smith, "The Political Economy." In disagreement, Dani Rodrik argues that short-term losses are insignificant, probably nonexistent, when the starting inflation is very high because ending high inflation yields benefits to many groups, at least in the short term. See "Understanding Economic Policy Reform," *Journal of Economic Literature* 34 (March 1996): 9–41.

41. Dani Rodrik, "The Rush to Free Trade in the Developing World: Why So Late? Why Now? Will It Last?" in *Voting for Reform: Democracy, Political Liberalization, and Economic Adjustment,* ed. Stephan Haggard and Steven B. Webb (New York: Oxford University Press, 1994).

42. Kurt Weyland, "Risk Taking in Latin American Economic Restructuring: Lessons from Prospect Theory," *International Studies Quarterly* 40 (1996): 185–208; Guillermo O'-Donnell, "Delegative Democracy," *Journal of Democracy* 5, no. 1 (January 1994): 55–69; John T. S. Keeler, "Opening the Window for Reform: Mandates, Crises and Extraordinary Policy-making," *Comparative Political Studies* 25 (1993): 433–86; Aaron Tornell, "Are Economic Crises Necessary for Trade Liberalization and Fiscal Reform?" in *Reform, Recovery, and Growth,* ed. Rudiger Dornbusch and Sebastian Edwards (Chicago: University of Chicago Press, 1995); Karen L. Remmer, "The Politics of Neoliberal Economic Reform in South America, 1980–1994," *Studies in Comparative International Development* 33, no. 2 (Summer 1998): 3–29.

43. Javier Corrales, "Do Economic Crises Contribute to Economic Reforms: Argentina and Venezuela in the 1990s," *Political Science Quarterly* 132 (1997–98); Remmer, "The Politics of Neoliberal Economic Reform."

44. Leslie Elliott Armijo, "Inflation and Insouciance: The Peculiar Brazilian Game," *Latin American Research Review* 31, no. 3 (1996): 7–46.

45. In federal systems such as Argentina, Brazil, Mexico, and increasingly Colombia, the conflict of interest between national and subnational authorities can become quite serious. In these systems, subnational authorities enjoy enormous spending discretion, resulting in a built-in incentive for provincial agents to overspend and then pass the bill to central authorities. Central governments may have no option other than to relax budget constraints, bail out provincial banks, and offer debt relief. Eduardo J. Gómez, "Decentralization and Sub-National Governance," paper prepared for the World Bank Thematic Seminar Series on Decentralization and Sub-National Governance, Washington, D.C., April 11, 2002. A significant cause of the Brazilian crisis of 1999 and the Argentine crisis of 2000–2001 was the result of provincial overspending. See Karen L. Remmer and Erik Wibbels, "The Subnational Politics of Economic Adjustment: Provincial

Politics and Fiscal Performance in Argentina," *Comparative Political Studies* 33, no. 4 (May 2000): 419–59.

46. Javier Corrales, "Why Argentines Followed Cavallo: A Technopol Between Democracy and Economic Reforms," in *Technopols,* ed. Domínguez.

47. *Época* (Mexico City), July 17, 2000, 8–13.

48. Jeanne Kinney Giraldo, "Development and Democracy in Chile: Finance Minister Alejandro Foxley and the Concertación's Project for the 1990s," in *Technopols,* ed. Domínguez.

49. Moisés Naím, "Latin America: Post-Adjustment Blues," *Foreign Policy* 92 (Fall 1993): 133–50.

50. Javier Corrales, "Presidents, Ruling Parties and Party Rules: A Theory on the Politics of Economic Reform in Latin America," *Comparative Politics* 32, no. 2 (January 2000): 127–50.

51. Barbara Geddes, *Politician's Dilemma: Building State Capacity in Latin America* (Berkeley: University of California Press, 1994); and "The Politics of Economic Liberalization," *Latin American Research Review* 30 (1995): 195–214.

52. For the reaction of labor unions to market-oriented reforms, see M. Victoria Murillo, "From Populism to Neoliberalism: Labor Unions and Market Reforms in Latin America," *World Politics* 52, no. 2 (January 2000): 135–74; and Katrina Burgess, "Loyalty Dilemmas and Market Reform: Party-Union Alliances Under Stress in Mexico, Spain, and Venezuela," *World Politics* 52, no. 1 (October 1999): 105–34.

53. For an explanation of this paradox, see Mariano Tommasi and Alex Cukierman, "When Does It Take a Nixon to Go to China?" *American Economic Review* 88, no. 1 (March 1998): 180–98.

54. Dani Rodrik, "Promises, Promises: Credible Policy Reform Via Signaling," *The Economic Journal* 99 (1989): 756–72.

55. Consistent with this, Karen Remmer has found that the weaker the base of domestic support, the higher the chance that a president will launch a far-reaching reform package. See Remmer, "The Politics of Neoliberal Economic Reform."

56. "Big bang packages" refer to reform efforts that seek deep changes in multiple domains almost simultaneously. It differs from gradualist approaches (which introduce reforms in an incremental fashion) or piecemeal approaches (which seek change in a few, focalized domains); see Anders Åslund, "The Case for Radical Reform," *Journal of Democracy* 5, no. 4 (October 1994): 63–74.

57. Carol Wise, "Introduction," in *Exchange Rate Politics in Latin America,* ed. Carol Wise and Riordan Roett (Washington, D.C.: Brookings Institution, 2000).

58. Pablo Guerchunoff and Guillermo Cánovas explain that most Latin American nations began to privatize by targeting public utilities, rather than industrial firms. This choice cannot be explained by economic rationality. Public utilities SOEs are risky, symbolic, hard-to-manage firms. The only explanation for selecting these firms to kick off privatization was for signaling purposes: a privatized public utility firm, unlike a privatized industrial firm, produces widespread and visible improvements to wide sectors of the public, and thus, holds the promise of generating support. See "Privatization: The Argentine Experience," in *Bigger Economies, Smaller Governments: Privatization in Latin America,* ed. William Glade and Rossana Corona (Boulder, Colo.: Westview, 1996).

59. Verónica Montecinos, "Economic Policy Elites and Democratization," *Studies in Comparative International Development* 28, no. 1 (1993): 25–53; John Williamson, "In Search of a Manual for Technopols," in *The Political Economy of Policy Reform,* ed. John Williamson (Washington, D.C.: Institute for International Economics, 1994); Domínguez,

Technopols; Merilee Grindle, *Challenging the State* (New York: Cambridge University Press, 1996); Miguel Ángel Centeno, *Democracy Within Reason: Technocratic Revolution in Mexico* (University Park: Penn State Press, 1994); Miguel A. Centeno and Patricio Silva, eds., *The Politics of Expertise in Latin America* (New York: St. Martin's, 1998); Arnold C. Harberger, "Secrets of Success: A Handful of Heroes," *American Economic Review* 83, no. 2 (May 1993): 343–50.

60. Mark Eric Williams, "Market Reforms, Technocrats, and Institutional Innovation," *World Development* 30, no. 3: 395–412.

61. Ben Ross Schneider, "The Material Bases of Technocracy: Investor Confidence and Neoliberalism in Latin America," in *The Politics of Expertise in Latin America*, ed. Miguel A. Centeno and Patricio Silva (New York: St. Martin's, 1998).

62. Remmer, "The Politics of Neoliberal Economic Reform."

63. See Nicolas Van de Walle, "Privatization in Developing Countries: A Review of the Issues," *World Development* 17, no. 5 (1989): 601–15.

64. Guerchunoff and Cánovas, "Privatization."

65. Javier Corrales, "Coalitions and Corporate Choices in Argentina, 1976–1994: The Recent Private Sector Support of Privatization," *Studies in Comparative International Development* 32, no. 4 (Winter 1998): 24–51.

66. Héctor E. Schamis, "Distributional Coalitions and the Politics of Economic Reform in Latin America," *World Politics* 51 (January 1999): 236–68.

67. Carol Graham, *Safety Nets, Politics, and the Poor: Transitions to Market Economies* (Washington, D.C.: Brookings Institution, 1994).

68. See Gibson, "The Populist Road."

69. Denise Dresser, "Bringing the Poor Back In: National Solidarity as a Strategy of Regime Legitimation," in *Transforming State-Society Relations in Mexico: The National Solidarity Strategy*, ed. Wayne A. Cornelius, Ann L. Craig, and Jonathan Fox (San Diego: Center for U.S.-Mexican Studies, University of California, 1991).

70. Most social spending was conveniently allocated to regions where Fujimori needed an electoral boost. See Bruce H. Kay, "Fujipopulism and the Liberal State in Peru, 1990–1995," *Journal of Interamerican Studies and World Affairs* 38, no. 4 (Winter 1996): 55–98; Kenneth M. Roberts, "Neoliberalism and the Transformation of Populism in Latin America: The Peruvian Case," *World Politics* 48, no. 1 (October 1995): 82–116.

71. An example of a policy that entailed favors to both winners and losers without impairing market forces was Bolivia's 1994 decision to "capitalize" rather than privatize. The government offered private investors the opportunity to invest 100 percent in the market value of the targeted SOEs, thereby obtaining 50 percent ownership, while the state retained the other 50 percent. The government then distributed its shares among the population, free of charge.

72. World Bank, "Educational Change in Latin America and the Caribbean" (Washington, D.C.: Latin America and the Caribbean, Social and Human Development, The World Bank, 2000), 66–67.

73. Social spending per capita increased by 38 percent in the 1990s, and social spending as a percentage of GDP increased from 10.1 percent in 1990 to 12.4 percent in 1997. CEPAL, *Panorama Social de América Latina, 1998* (Santiago, Chile: CEPAL, 1998).

74. This use of funds is populist because, like traditionalist populist measures, the goal is to mobilize support among marginalized masses; it is "neo" because spending not always compromised fiscal health. On neopopulism, see Kurt Weyland, "Neopopulism and Neoliberalism in Latin America: Unexpected Affinities," *Studies in Comparative International Development* 31, no. 3 (Fall 1996): 3–32; Roberts, "Neoliberalism"; Edward Gibson,

"The Populist Road to Market Reform: Policy and Electoral Coalitions in Mexico and Argentina," *World Politics* 49, no. 3 (April 1997): 339–70; Eduardo A. Gamarra, "Market-Oriented Reforms and Democratization in Latin America: Challenges of the 1990s," in *Latin American Political Economy in the Age of Neoliberal Reform*, ed. William C. Smith, Carlos H. Acuña, and Eduardo A. Gamarra (New Brunswick, N.J.: Transaction, 1994).

75. Corrales, "Presidents, Ruling Parties and Party Rules"; Gibson, "The Populist Road"; Edward L. Gibson and Ernesto Calvo, "Federalism and Low-Maintenance Constituencies: Territorial Dimensions of Economic Reform in Argentina," *Studies in Comparative International Development* 35, no. 3 (Fall 2000): 23–55.

76. Eduardo Silva, "Business Elites, the State, and Economic Change in Chile," in *Business and the State in Developing Countries*, ed. Sylvia Maxfield and Ben Ross Schneider (Ithaca: Cornell University Press, 1997).

77. In Mexico in 1987, the state (under President Miguel de la Madrid) negotiated with labor unions and business groups the Pacto de Solidaridad Económica (Pact of Economic Solidarity), in which business agreed to restrain prices of goods, and unions, restrain the price of labor (wage demands). Blanca Heredia, "Making Economic Reform Politically Viable: The Mexican Experience," in *Democracy, Markets, and Structural Reform in Latin America: Argentina, Bolivia, Brazil, Chile, and Mexico*, ed. William C. Smith, Carlos H. Acuña, and Eduardo A. Gamarra (New Brunswick, N.J.: North-South Center/Transaction, 1994).

78. See Torre, *El proceso político*, 58; Haggard and Kaufman, *The Political Economy*, 340–45.

79. Pacts between the state and business groups were more successful, however, as instruments for generating support for trade liberalization. States that negotiated trade liberalization directly and transparently with business groups were able to obtain business cooperation even from non-competitive firms. See Kingstone, *Crafting Coalitions;* and Javier Corrales and Imelda Cisneros, "Corporatism, Trade Liberalization, and Sectoral Responses: The Case of Venezuela, 1989–1999," *World Development* 27, no. 2 (December 1999): 2099–2122.

80. Charles H. Blake, "The Politics of Inflation-Fighting in New Democracies," *Studies in Comparative International Development* 31, no. 2 (Summer 1996): 37–57.

81. In 1985, after "exerting considerable control over his own party," Bolivian President Víctor Paz Estenssoro sealed an agreement between his own party and the main opposition party, Acción Democrática y Nacionalista (Democratic and Nationalist Action). This so-called Pact for Democracy stipulated party cooperation with the reforms. Catherine M. Conaghan and James M. Malloy, *Unsettling Statecraft, Democracy and Neoliberalism in the Central Andes* (Pittsburgh: University of Pittsburgh Press, 1994), 189–93; Eduardo A. Gamarra, "Crafting Political Support for Stabilization: Political Pacts and the New Economic Policy in Bolivia," in *Democracy, Markets and Structural Reform in Latin America: Argentina, Bolvia, Brazil, Chile, and Mexico*, ed. William C. Smith, Carlos H. Acuña, and Eduardo A. Gamarra (New Brunswick, N.J.: North-South Center/Transaction, 1994).

82. Stephan Haggard and Robert R. Kaufman, *The Political Economy of Democratic Transitions* (Princeton: Princeton University Press, 1995).

83. See Peter R. Kingstone, "Party Politics and Policy Performance: Evaluating the Impact of Party System Design," paper presented at the Latin American Studies Association XXII International Congress, Miami, Florida, March 2000.

84. Javier Corrales, *Presidents Without Parties* (University Park: Pennsylvania State University Press, 2002).

85. Trade liberalization entails reduction in tariffs on imports and non-tariff barriers.

By 1995, no country (except Brazil in the automobile sector) used tariffs to protect domestic business. Domestic financial liberalization entails decontrolling interest rates and abandoning direct credit. See Samuel A. Morley, Roberto Machado, and Stefano Pettinato, "Indexes of Structural Reform in Latin America," *Serie Reformas Económicas,* no. 12 (Santiago: CEPAL, 1999).

86. Javier Corrales, "Reform Lagging States and the Question of Devaluation: Venezuela's Response to Exogenous Shocks of 1997–98," in *Exchange Rate Politics in Latin America,* ed. Carol Wise and Riordan Roett (Washington, D.C.: Brookings Institution, 2000).

87. Argentina, Peru, and Brazil fit this list because prior to 1991, 1992, and 1994, respectively, they were reform-lagging states experiencing the "ax-relax-cycle" pattern of policy implementation.

88. See also Carol Wise, "Latin America and the State-Market Debate: Beyond Stylized Facts," paper presented at the LASA XXII International Congress, Miami, Florida, March 2000.

89. However, recent research shows that this acceptance of neoliberalism by Latin America's new converts is more precarious than originally believed, likely to erode if the popularity of incumbents or the health of the economy declines. For Brazil, see Timothy J. Power, "Brazilian Politicians and Neoliberalism: Mapping Support for the Cardoso Reforms, 1995–1997," *Journal of Interamerican Studies and World Affairs* 40, no. 4 (Winter 1998): 51–72. For Argentina, see Javier Corrales, "The Political Determinants of Argentina's Recession," Washington, D.C., Woodrow Wilson International Center for Scholars (Summer 2001), mimeo.

90. For an explanation of why market economics, and especially capital flows, can intensify the economic insecurity of citizens, see Geoffrey Garrett, *Partisan Politics in the Global Economy* (New York: Cambridge University Press, 1998); and Dani Rodrik, "¿Por qué hay tanta inseguridad económica en América Latina?" *Revista de la Cepal* 73 (April 2001): 7–31.

91. Joseph E. Stiglitz, "Some Lessons from the East Asian Miracle," *The World Bank Research Observer* 11, no. 2 (August 1996): 151–77.

92. Products of the mind consist of intangible, knowledge-based goods such as research and development, product design, financing, marketing, transport, insurance, and legal services. According to Richard Rosecrance, "products of the mind" is the trademark of modern states. See Richard Rosecrance, *The Rise of the Virtual State: Wealth and Power in the Coming Century* (New York: Basic, 1999).

93. Financial liberalization is not entirely a curse. No doubt, financial liberalization creates volatility, but it can also have democratizing effects because it helps to disperse capital among actors other than the state, and to dismantle oligopolistic corporate structures in host countries. For a review of the differing impacts of capital flows, see Sylvia Maxfield, "Globalization, Economic Policymaking, and Democratization," keynote address delivered at the Conference on Technocratic Policymaking and Democratization, United Nations Research Institute for Social Development, Geneva, Switzerland, April 27–28, 2000.

94. Michael Gavin and Roberto Perotti, "Fiscal Policy in Latin America," *NBER Macroeconomics Annual 1997* (Cambridge, Mass.: The MIT Press, 1997).

95. One of the positive results achieved by aggressive reformers is an increase in fiscal revenues. Nevertheless, compared to industrialized countries, Latin American states have trouble collecting taxes and securing stable revenues. In addition, even though foreign debt has declined since the early 1980s, interest and principal payments on the remaining

debt remain high, and are prone to increase during hard times. Elizabeth McQuerry, Michael Chriszt, and Stephen Kay, "Patterns in Latin American Public Sector Accounts," in *Sustainable Public Sector Finance in Latin America* (Atlanta: Research Department, Federal Reserve Bank of Atlanta, 1999).

96. Manuel Pastor Jr. and Carol Wise, "The Politics of Second-Generation Reform," *Journal of Democracy* 10, no. 3 (July 1999): 34–38.

97. World Bank, *World Development Report: The State in a Changing World* (New York: Oxford University Press, 1997).

Chapter 5. Latin American Labor

I thank Steve Levitsky, Hector Palomino, Francisco Zapata, and the editors of this book for their comments on previous versions of this chapter.

1. For an analysis of Morones' political strategy to compensate for industrial weakness with political influence, see Graciela Bensusán, "Institucionalización laboral en México. Los años de la definición (1917–1931)" (Mexico, DF: Facultad de Ciencias Políticas y Sociales, Universidad Nacional Autónoma de México, 1992); Marjorie Ruth Clark, *Organized Labor in Mexico* (Chapel Hill: University of North Carolina Press, 1934); and Kevin Middlebrook, *The Paradox of Revolution* (Baltimore: Johns Hopkins University Press, 1995). They also describe the expansion of unionization and CROM influence in the labor movement thanks to Morones' tenure as minister of trade, industry, and labor.

2. Organized labor provided Cárdenas with a political base of support in his rivalry with Calles. Cárdenas, in turn, gave political power to labor leaders, expanded labor rights, established mandatory payment of wages for the seventh day of the week, set up commissions to establish the ability of companies to pay wage hikes, and threatened noncompliance with expropriation. See Alberto Aziz Nassif, *El estado mexicano y la CTM* (Mexico, DF: Editorial La Casa Chata, 1989), 47–89; and Ruth Berins Collier and David Collier, *Shaping the Political Arena* (Princeton: Princeton University Press, 1991), 241.

3. Different views on alliance between labor unions and Perón are provided by Gino Germani, "El surgimiento del peronismo: el rol de los obreros y de los migrantes internos," *Desarrollo Económico* 13, no. 51 (October–December 1973); Torcuato Di Tella, "Working-class Organization and Politics in Argentina," *Latin American Research Review* 16, no. 2 (1981): 61–95; Miguel Murmis and Juan Carlos Portantiero, *Estudios sobre los orígenes del peronismo* (Buenos Aires: Ediciones Siglo XXI, 1971); Hiroshi Matsushita, *Movimiento Obrero Argentino 1930/1945. Sus proyecciones en los orígenes del Peronismo* (Buenos Aires: Siglo Veinte, 1983); David Tamarin, *The Argentine Labor Movement, 1930–1945: A Study in the Origins of Peronism* (Albuquerque: University of New Mexico Press, 1985); and Juan Carlos Torre, *La Vieja Guardia Sindical y Perón* (Buenos Aires: Editorial Sudamericana e Instituto Torcuato Di Tella, 1990).

4. Author's interview with union leader Juan Carlos Taccone (Buenos Aires, 1995). The strategy served Argentine workers whose real income, social benefits, and labor rights increased during Perón's tenure and labor leaders who gained political influence in executive and legislative positions. See James W. McGuire, *Peronism Without Perón: Unions, Parties, and Democracy in Argentina* (Stanford: Stanford University Press, 1997).

5. Francisco Zapata, *El conflicto sindical en América Latina* (Mexico, DF: El Colegio de Mexico, 1986) and Collier and Collier, *Shaping the Political Arena* (1991), analyze the institutionalization of industrial relations. Collier and Collier label the process as labor incorporation by the state. Depending on the strength of organized labor and the need of politicians for labor constituencies, incorporation involved different terms in the ex-

change and different degrees of subsidies and controls to labor as shown by Ruth Berins Collier and David Collier, "Inducement versus Constraints: Disaggregating 'Corporatism,'" *American Political Science Review* 73 (1979): 967–86.

6. Ian Roxborough, "Urban Labour Movements in Latin America since 1930," in *Latin America: Politics and Society since 1930,* ed. Leslie Bethell (Cambridge: Cambridge University Press, 1988).

7. Carlos Díaz-Alejandro, "Latin America in the 1930s," in *Latin America in the 1930s,* ed. Rosemary Thorp (Oxford, U.K.: Macmillan, 1984).

8. Elizabeth Jellín, "Orientaciones e ideologías obreras en América Latina," in *Fuerza de trabajo y movimientos sociales en América Latina,* ed. Rubén Kaztman and José Luis Reyna (Mexico, DF: El Colegio de México, 1979), provides a good summary of the ideologies appealing to workers in Latin America.

9. Silvia Sigal and Juan Carlos Torre, "Una reflexión en torno a los movimientos laborales en América Latina," in *Fuerza de trabajo y movimientos sociales en América Latina,* ed. Ruben Kaztman and José Luis Reyna (Mexico, DF: El Colegio de México, 1979), 142.

10. J. Samuel Valenzuela, "Labor Movements in Transitions to Democracy: A Framework for Analysis," *Comparative Politics* 21, no. 4 (1989): 445–72, provides an insightful analysis of labor unions and democratic transitions.

11. Paul Drake, *Labor Movements and Dictatorships: The Southern Cone in Comparative Perspective* (Baltimore: Johns Hopkins University Press, 1996), and Manuel Barrera and Gonzalo Fallabella, eds., *Sindicatos bajo regímenes militares. Argentina, Brasil, Chile* (Santiago: CES Ediciones, 1990), provide analyses of labor under military rulers in the Southern Cone, whereas Patricio Frias, *El movimiento sindical chileno en la lucha por la democracia* (Santiago: PET, 1989), and Margaret E. Keck, "The New Unionism in the Brazilian Transition," in *Democratizing Brazil,* ed. Alfred Stepan (Oxford: Oxford University Press, 1989), describe the role played by organized labor in pressuring for political liberalization in Brazil and Chile, respectively.

12. Economic liberalization was not immediate and followed an initial protectionist reaction and several failures with heterodox attempts at macroeconomic stabilization. By the late 1980s and 1990s, fiscal deficits and macroeconomic instability spread market reforms throughout the region. See Sebastian Edwards, *Crisis and Reform in Latin America* (New York: Oxford University Press, 1995), and Juan Carlos Torre, *El proceso político de las reformas económicas en América Latina* (Buenos Aires: Paidós, 1998).

13. According to Dani Rodrik, *Has Globalization Gone Too Far?* (Washington, D.C.: Institute for International Economics, 1997), capital mobility increases the elasticity of labor demand, making workers' labor market positions more uncertain. Dani Rodrik, "Why Is There So Much Economic Insecurity in Latin America?" (unpublished manuscript, Harvard University, Cambridge, Mass., 1999), adds that capital mobility and responsiveness to domestic productivity magnifies the fluctuations in workers' income, particularly in countries with fixed exchange rates.

14. Rodrik (unpublished manuscript) reports a growth in the proportion of Latin American workers not "protected" by formal written contracts or included in social benefits programs, which he claims shows the increasing insecurity provoked by economic liberalization in the region. In a similar vein, Adriana Marshall, "Labor Market Regulation, Wages and Workers' Behavior: Latin America in the 1990s," paper presented at the Latin American Studies Association XXII International Congress, Miami, Florida, March 2000, argues that the growth of unemployment in the informal sector increases the insecurity of workers in the formal sector and makes labor markets more flexible even without legal reforms.

15. Additionally, legal and contractual arrangements, such as Mexican closed shops that forced all workers in a unionized company to become union members in order to keep their jobs, may be distorting these figures. This distortion is likely to diminish because the Mexican Supreme Court ruled the unconstitutionality of closed shops in 2001.

16. For instance, Ana Margheritis, "Implementing Structural Adjustment in Argentina: The Politics of Privatization" (Ph.D. diss., University of Toronto, 1997), 137, reports interviews where union leaders Julio Guillán (telephone workers' union) and Antonio Cassia (oil workers' union) recalled a 1989 meeting with president-elect Carlos Menem. In this meeting, he explained to them that the central bank had run out of reserves, the country was bankrupt, and there was no alternative to structural reforms to "save democracy."

17. I elaborate this argument in M. Victoria Murillo, "Labor Parties and Partisan Labor," paper presented at the LASA XXII International Congress, Miami, Florida, March 2000.

18. After the Peronists lost power, Radical President Fernando de la Rúa passed a labor reform that facilitated the decentralization of collective bargaining in 2000.

19. See René Cortázar, "Chile: The Evolution and Reform of the Labor Market," in *Labor Markets in Latin America: Combining Social Protection with Market Flexibility,* ed. Sebastian Edwards and Nora Claudia Lustig (Washington, D.C.: Brookings Institution, 1997), and Alejandra Mizala, "La regulación del mercado laboral en Chile: 1975–1995," *Perspectivas en Política, Economía y Gestión* 1, no. 2 (1998): 185–214. Kurt Weyland, "Economic Policy in Chile's New Democracy," *Journal of Interamerican Studies and World Affairs* 41, no. 3 (Fall 1999): 67–96, points out CUT support for the Aylwin administration and describes his social and labor policies as a reward for their support.

20. I develop this argument and provide empirical evidence for a variety of cases in Venezuela, Mexico, and Argentina in M. Victoria Murillo, *Labor Unions, Partisan Coalitions and Market Reforms in Latin America* (Cambridge: Cambridge University Press, 2001).

21. Jorge I. Domínguez and Jeanne Kinney Giraldo, "Conclusion: Parties, Institutions, and Market Reforms in Constructing Democracies," in *Constructing Democratic Governance,* ed. Jorge I. Domínguez and Abraham Lowenthal (Baltimore: Johns Hopkins University Press, 1996), describe the simultaneity of both processes in the region. Adam Przeworski, *Democracy and the Market* (Cambridge and New York: Cambridge University Press, 1991), provides a theoretical discussion of the challenges created by this simultaneity for policy makers.

22. See Guillermo O'Donnell and Phillipe Schmitter, *Transitions from Authoritarian Rule: Tentative Conclusions About Uncertain Democracies* (Baltimore: Johns Hopkins University Press, 1986) on political liberalization and transitions to democracy.

23. For a discussion on the weakness of Latin American institutions, see Guillermo O'Donnell, "Illusions about Consolidation," *Journal of Democracy* 7, no. 2 (April 1996): 34–51, and "Delegative Democracy," *Journal of Democracy* 5, no. 1 (January 1994): 55–69. Kenneth Roberts, "Neoliberalism and the Transformation of Populism in Latin America," *World Politics* 48 (October 1995): 82–116, Alan Knight, "Populism and Neo-Populism in Latin America, Especially in Mexico," *Journal of Latin American Studies* 30, part 2 (May 1998): 233–46, and Kurt Weyland, "Clarifying a Contested Concept: 'Populism' in the Study of Latin American Politics," paper presented at the workshop "New Populism, Old Populism in Latin America," Yale University, April 7–8, 2000, discuss the concept of "new populism" linking charismatic leadership with market reforms in Latin America. Paul Drake "Conclusion: Requiem for Populism?" in *Latin American Populism in Comparative Perspective,* ed. Michael Conniff (Albuquerque: University of New Mexico Press, 1982), and Collier and Collier, *Shaping the Political Arena* (1991), provide definitions of the traditional "populism" as a labor-based movement.

24. Causa R, in fact, split into two parties along the lines of its labor and political factions.

25. M. Victoria Murillo, "Union Politics, Market-Oriented Reforms, and the Reshaping of Argentine Corporatism," in *The New Politics of Inequality in Latin America,* ed. Douglas Chalmers et al. (Oxford: Oxford University Press, 1997).

26. "Quality circles" are teams of labor and management to improve the phases of production for which they are responsible. Enrique De La Garza, *Restructuración productiva y respuesta sindical en México* (Mexico, DF: UNAM-UAM-Itzpalapa, 1993), describes the evolution of this strategy in the interaction between the Mexican telecommunications' union and the privatized state-owned monopoly in telecommunications.

27. Margarita López Maya, "The Rise of Causa R in Venezuela," in *The New Politics of Inequality in Latin America,* ed. Douglas Chalmers et al. (Oxford: Oxford University Press, 1997), describes the practices of the Venezuelan "new unionism."

28. Scott Martin, "Beyond Corporatism: New Patterns of Representation in the Brazilian Auto Industry," in *The New Politics of Inequality in Latin America,* ed. Douglas Chalmers et al. (Oxford: Oxford University Press, 1997), provides an account of this process.

29. The symbolic effect of this labor victory is largely due to the weakness of Venezuelan civil society. Chávez called for union elections controlled by the state and supervised by the Supreme Electoral Commission for the end of 2000. To win the control of the unions he had demanded Congress that elections be open to the workforce rather than unionized workers.

30. Those rules include union registration and monopolies of representation, union electoral systems and procedures, as well as the governance structure of the union.

31. Bruce E. Kaufman, "The Early Institutionalists on Industrial Democracy and Union Democracy," *Journal of Labor Research* 21, no. 2 (2000): 189–210, 205, argues that although union leaders tend to be less radical than the rank-and-file due to their responsibilities and their direct engagement in negotiations with employers, internal political competition within the union or a bitter strike with an employer may cause leaders to become more radical than members to whip up support for their position.

32. Michael J. Piore and Charles F. Sabel, *The Second Industrial Divide* (Boston: Basic, 1984), introduce the new technologies of work organization derived from the Japanese experience as part of the process of flexible specialization that displaced Fordist mass production. Flexible specialization is based on multi-use equipment, skilled workers, and the creation, through politics, of an industrial community that restricts the forms of competition to those favoring innovation (p. 17). Joseph Stiglitz, "Democratic Development as the Fruits of Labor," keynote address, Industrial Relations Research Association, Boston, January 2000, 14–15, argues that the "high road" industrial relations system created by high worker involvement in workplaces is based on the trust between managers and employees and is associated with higher levels of human capital and lower costs for internal equity.

33. George Strauss, "What's Happening Inside U.S. Unions: Democracy and Union Politics," *Journal of Labor Research* 21, no. 2 (2000): 211–46.

Chapter 6. Women and Democracy

1. The data and analysis in this section are drawn from Mala Htun, "Women and Power in the Americas: A Report Card," Inter-American Dialogue, April 2001; Mala Htun, "Women's Leadership in Latin America: Trends and Challenges," in *Politics Matter: A Dialogue of Women Political Leaders* (Washington, D.C.: Iner-American Development Bank/Inter-American Dialogue, 2001); Mala Htun and Mark Jones, "Engendering the

Right to Participate in Decisionmaking: Electoral Quotas and Women's Leadership in Latin America," in *Gender and the Politics of Rights and Democracy in Latin America,* ed. Nikki Craske and Maxine Molyneux (London: Palgrave, 2002).

2. Inter-American Development Bank, *Facing up to Inequality in Latin America, Economic and Social Progress in Latin America: 1998–1999 Report* (Washington, D.C.: IADB, 1999); FLACSO, *Mujeres latinoamericanas en cifras* (Santiago: FLACSO, 1995); World Bank, *Gender Status: A Database of Gender Statistics* (http://genderstats.worldbank.org/menu.asp).

3. Marta Suplicy, "Ações afirmativas e novos paradigmas nas esferas de poder," *Estudos Feministas* (June 1996).

4. "Report of the Fourth World Conference on Women, Beijing, September 4–15, 1995, United Nations Document No. A/CONF, 177/20," in *Covenant for the New Millennium* (Santa Rosa: Free Hand Books, 1996).

5. Marta Suplicy, interview by the author, Brasília, Brazil, August 7, 1997.

6. In Argentina, for example, the support of President Carlos Menem was decisive for approval of the quota law. Although the law enjoyed the support of women from all major political parties, resistance from male legislators made passage unlikely. At the last minute, Menem's interior minister, José Luis Manzano, was called to Congress to convince recalcitrant legislators to vote in favor of quotas.

7. Women's representation also jumped by 11 percentage points in Ecuador, although Htun and Jones note that "this gain is largely attributable to voters' lack of familiarity with the new electoral system, not the success of the quota. Instead of utilizing the preference aspect of Ecuador's block voting method, voters tended to vote for a party's entire slate of candidates, a behavior encouraged by the parties who strategically placed their most popular candidates at the top, middle, and bottom of their respective lists. For example, in the province of Guayas where 18 Deputies were elected, the Partido Social Cristiano (Social Christian Party) won twelve seats with a mere 29 percent of the overall vote, while two other parties each won 25 percent of the vote but only three seats each." See Htun and Jones, "Engendering the Right to Participate in Decisionmaking."

8. "If a district elects ten members to Congress, for example, each party is permitted to offer 15 candidates to the electorate. The quota law requires that a party *reserve* five of these slots for women. If a party is unable or unwilling to recruit women, it may offer 10 male candidates to the electorate without any women on the ticket" and still comply fully with the law. Htun, "Women's Leadership in Latin America," 7.

9. Jacqueline Peschard and Eduardo Ramírez, interview by the author, Instituto Federal Electoral, Mexico City, Mexico, July 2000. I thank Jacqueline and Eduardo for providing me with data on the July 2000 elections.

10. Twenty-one of Argentina's twenty-three provinces, as well as the city of Buenos Aires, use quotas in elections for provincial legislators. In 2000, women held, on average, 25 percent of seats in provincial legislatures.

11. Ana Isabel García, "Guía para entender y aplicar los mecanismos de acción afirmativa para mujeres," unpublished paper.

12. Joe Foweraker, "Ten Theses on Women in the Political Life of Latin America," in *Women's Participation in Mexican Political Life,* ed. Victoria Rodríguez (Boulder, Colo.: Westview, 1998), 65.

13. Marysa Navarro, "The Personal is Political: *Las Madres de la Plaza de Mayo,*" in *Power and Popular Protest,* ed. Susan Eckstein (Berkeley: University of California Press, 1989); Solange de Deus Simões, *Deus, pátria e família: as mulheres no golpe de 1964* (Petrópolis, Brazil: Vozes, 1985); Jane Jaquette, ed., *The Women's Movement in Latin Amer-*

ica (Boulder, Colo.: Westview, 1994); Jane Jaquette and Sharon Wolchik, eds., *Women and Democracy: Latin America and Central and Eastern Europe* (Baltimore: Johns Hopkins University Press, 1998); Lisa Baldez, *Why Women Protest: Women's Movements in Chile* (New York: Columbia University Press, 2002).

14. Sonia E. Alvarez, "Latin American Feminisms 'Go Global': Trends of the 1990s and Challenges for the New Millennium," in *Cultures of Politics, Politics of Cultures,* ed. Sonia Alvarez, Evelina Dagnino, and Arturo Escobar (Boulder, Colo.: Westview, 1998); Margaret Keck and Kathryn Sikkink, *Activists Beyond Borders* (Ithaca: Cornell University Press, 1998).

15. Sonia E. Alvarez, *Engendering Democracy in Brazil: Women's Movements in Transition Politics* (Princeton: Princeton University Press, 1990).

16. Adriana Muñoz, interview with author, Santiago, Chile, April 1998.

17. Alvarez, "Latin American Feminisms 'Go Global'"; Barrig, "De cal y de arena. ONGs y movimiento de mujeres en Chile."

18. Ronald Inglehart and Pippa Norris, "The Developmental Theory of the Gender Gap: Women and Men's Voting Behavior in Global Perspective," *International Political Science Review* 21, no. 2 (October 2000): 441–63, Table 1.

19. Pippa Norris, "The Gender Gap: Old Challenges, New Approaches," in *Women and American Politics: Agenda Setting for the 21st Century,* ed. Susan Carroll (New York: Oxford University Press, forthcoming), 4.

20. Marysa Navarro and Susan C. Bourque, "Fault Lines of Democratic Governance: A Gender Perspective," in *Fault Lines of Democracy in Post-Transition Latin America,* ed. Felipe Agüero and Jeffrey Stark (Miami, Fla.: North-South Center Press, 1998).

21. Armand and Michèle Mattelart, *La mujer chilena en una nueva sociedad* (Santiago, Chile: Editorial del Pacífico, 1968).

22. The gender gap was calculated as the average difference between women and men on a 10-point voting scale (with negative numbers indicating women's preferences to the Right and positive numbers to the Left). The gender gap in Chile was −0.32; in Mexico, −0.12; in Brazil, −0.01; and in Argentina, 0.19 (meaning that more women expressed preferences for parties of the Left).

23. Data are from the Chilean government's election site (www.elecciones.gov.cl). Other studies report that 62 percent of the members of the Right Renovación Nacional party are women. See Nikki Craske, "Mexican Women's Inclusion into Political Life: A Latin American Perspective," in *Women's Participation in Mexican Political Life,* ed. Victoria Rodríguez (Boulder, Colo.: Westview, 1998), 62, n. 19.

24. Jorge Domínguez and James McCann, *Democratizing Mexico* (Baltimore: Johns Hopkins University Press, 1996), 38.

25. Chappell Lawson, "Why Cárdenas Won: The 1997 Elections in Mexico City," in *Toward Mexico's Democratization,* ed. Jorge Domínguez and Alejandro Poiré (New York: Routledge, 1999), 171, n. 24.

26. *Folha de São Paulo,* October 4, 1998.

27. As previously mentioned, the average difference between women's and men's positions on a 10-point voting scale was 0.19 in the early 1990s (women slightly to the Left of men). Scores on a separate indicator, a 10-point Left-Right "ideology scale," confirmed the direction of the gender gap. The ideology data show that Argentine women have become more left-wing than men over time. Whereas the mean difference between men and women was −0.11 in 1981, it was reduced to −0.03 in 1990 and then moved to 0.05 in 1995. Inglehart and Norris, "The Developmental Theory of the Gender Gap," 21.

28. Anna-Lizbeth Alatorre, "Parties, Gender, and Democratization: The Causes and

Consequences of Women's Participation in the Mexican Congress" (bachelor's thesis, Harvard University, 1999).

29. Anna Greenberg, "Deconstructing the Gender Gap" (working paper 98–14, Politics Research Group, John F. Kennedy School of Government, Harvard University, 1998), 4. Greenberg remarks further that not only did the "soccer mom" story refer "inconsistently to a variety of women" and fail to "tap a recognized identity group in American politics," it also obscured the fact Clinton tended to attract "economically vulnerable women and women with working class sensibilities," while Dole attracted "socially and economically secure women." Suburban residence, moreover, was not a significant predictor of women's vote (1, 13).

30. Ibid., 15.

31. Cecilia Blondet Montero, "El poder político en la mira de las mujeres," in *Poder político con perfume de mujer: Las cuotas en el Perú* (Lima: PROMUJER, 1998).

32. See Alvarez, "The Rise and Fall of a United Women's Movement," in *Engendering Democracy in Brazil;* and Nancy Saporta Sternbach et al., "Feminisms in Latin America: From Bogotá to San Bernardo," *Signs* 27, no. 2 (Winter 1992).

33. Edward G. Carmines and James A. Stimson, "The Two Faces of Issue Voting," *American Political Science Review* 74, no. 1 (March 1980): 78.

34. Jorge I. Domínguez, "The Transformation of Mexico's Electoral and Party Systems, 1988–1997," in *Toward Mexico's Democratization,* ed. Jorge Domínguez and Alejandro Poiré (New York: Routledge, 1999), 11.

35. Ibid., 15.

36. Quoted in Norris, "The Gender Gap," 5.

37. Cecilia Blondet Montero, "El poder político en la mira de las mujeres," 54.

38. Mala Htun, *Democracy, Dictatorship, and Gender Rights in Latin America* (New York: Cambridge University Press, forthcoming).

39. Lisa Baldez, "Democratic Institutions and Feminist Outcomes: Chilean Policy Toward Women in the 1990s" (working paper no. 340, Department of Political Science, Washington University, 1998).

40. Because of internal disagreements, the DC failed to endorse divorce explicitly, although DC deputies had introduced the divorce bill. Most RN deputies voted against divorce, but the party did not adopt an explicit position in order to maintain a "liberal" image and to accommodate dissenting views within its ranks.

41. For more information on these policy initiatives and policy changes, see Mala Htun, "Advancing Women's Rights in the Americas: Achievements and Challenges" (working paper, Leadership Council for Inter-American Summitry, North-South Center, University of Miami, 2001).

42. See, for example, Michele Swers, "From the Year of the Woman to the Republican Ascendancy: Evaluating the Policy Impact of Women in Congress" (Ph.D. dissertation, Harvard University, 2000); Sue Thomas, *How Women Legislate* (Oxford: Oxford University Press, 1994); Mark P. Jones, "Legislator Gender and Legislator Policy Priorities in the Argentine Chamber of Deputies and the United States House of Representatives," *Policy Studies Journal* 25, no. 4 (1997).

43. Linda S. Stevenson, "Gender Politics in the Mexican Democratization Process," in *Towards Mexico's Democratization,* ed. Jorge Domínguez and Alejandro Poiré (New York: Routledge, 1998).

44. "Legislators make requests to the leader of their party's congressional delegation regarding which committees they want to serve on. While legislators do not always receive assignments on their preferred committees, with the exception of assignments on the

most prominent committees (e.g., Budget, Constitutional Affairs, Foreign Affairs), legislators generally obtain assignments on the committees they requested." Htun and Jones, "Engendering the Right to Participate in Decisionmaking."

45. "Relatório preliminar da pesquisa de opinião com parlamentares federais sobre os direitos das mulheres, previstos na Plataforma de Ação da IV Conferência Mundial sobre a Mulher—Pequim/1995," CFEMEA, Brasília, March 2000.

46. Victoria Rodríguez, "The Emerging Role of Women in Mexican Political Life," in *Women's Participation in Mexican Political Life,* ed. Victoria Rodríguez (Boulder, Colo.: Westview, 1998), 8.

47. Alatorre, "Parties, Gender, and Democratization."

48. Htun and Jones, "Engendering the Right to Participate in Decisionmaking."

49. Interview by the author, Buenos Aires, Argentina, August 4, 1998.

50. Rodríguez, "The Emerging Role of Women in Mexican Political Life," 8.

51. Kristin Luker, *Abortion and the Politics of Motherhood* (Berkeley: University of California Press, 1984); Jane J. Mansbridge, *Why We Lost the ERA* (Chicago: University of Chicago Press, 1986).

52. It is interesting, however, that whereas the vast majority of bills in Latin America proposing the decriminalization of abortion or the expansion of conditions of legal abortion are presented by female deputies, most of the bills calling for greater restrictions on abortion have been introduced by men.

53. Htun, "Women's Leadership in Latin America: Trends and Challenges."

54. Senator Beatriz Paredes, interview by the author, Mexico City, Mexico, July 2000.

55. Htun, *Democracy, Dictatorship, and Gender Rights in Latin America.*

Chapter 7. Public Opinion

1. There is extensive literature on the transition to democracy: Julián Santamaría, ed., *Transiciones a la democracia en Europa del Sur y América Latina* (Madrid: Centro de Investigaciones Sociológicas, 1981); John H. Herz, ed., *From Dictatorship to Democracy: Coping with the Legacies of Authoritarianism and Totalitarianism* (Westport, Conn: Greenwood, 1982); Enrique Baloyra, ed., *Comparing New Democracies* (Boulder, Colo.: Westview, 1987); Guillermo O'Donnell, Philippe C. Schmitter, and Laurence Whitehead, eds., *Transiciones desde un gobierno autoritario* (Buenos Aires: Paidós, 1988); Giuseppe di Palma, *To Craft Democracies* (Berkeley: University of California Press, 1990); Samuel P. Huntington, *The Third Wave: Democratization in the Late Twentieth Century* (London: University of Oklahoma Press, 1991); Richard Gunther, P. Nikiforos Diamandouros, and Hans-Jürgen Puhle, eds., *The Politics of Democratic Consolidation: Southern Europe in Comparative Perspective* (Baltimore: Johns Hopkins University Press, 1995); Klaus von Beyme, *Systemwechsel in Osteuropa* (Frankfurt: Suhrkamp, 1994).

2. Alain Rouquié, *Poder militar y sociedad política en la Argentina hasta 1943* (Buenos Aires: Editorial Sudamericana, 1981).

3. Huntington, *The Third Wave.*

4. Dankwart A. Rustow, "Transition to Democracy," *Comparative Politics* 2 (April 1970): 337–63.

5. Robert A. Dahl, *Polyarchy* (New Haven: Yale University Press, 1971).

6. For example, Colombia had military regimes for about five years, but they were "small tyrannies ruled by large landowners." Venezuela developed a democracy where the political parties exercised all the power with a high degree of corruption. Other countries

such as Argentina developed democracies in the 1920s, but their political history has been 'caudillo'-driven, preventing strong institutional development. It is a fact that present democracies are being judged harder than past democracies in Latin America, giving the impression of democratic regression with respect to the past. We believe that this analysis is rather nostalgic and romantic, and that closer looks at those democratic periods in some countries reveal that they were not as democratic as their image.

7. On consolidation of democracy: Juan Linz and Alfred Stepan, *Problems of Democratic Transition and Consolidation: Southern Europe, South America, and Post-Communist Europe* (Baltimore: Johns Hopkins University Press, 1996); and Leonardo Morlino, *Democracy between Consolidation and Crisis* (Oxford: Oxford University Press, 1998).

8. Globalization and communication have produced virtual international monitoring of political process, where the international community reacts almost instantly. Military and social actors are well aware of the costs of going against the international tide.

9. The military was also restrained in the Bucaram crisis of 1997.

10. Dahl, *Polyarchy*.

11. For more on the concept of superimposition and the intensity of social conflict, see Ralf Dahrendorf, *Class and Class Conflict in Industrial Society* (London: Allen & Unwin, 1958).

12. David Collier, ed., *The New Authoritarianism in Latin America* (Princeton: Princeton University Press, 1979).

13. The case of Alan García in Peru is similar.

14. Nancy Birdsall and Carol Graham, *New Markets, New Opportunities? Economic and Social Mobility in a Changing World* (Washington, D.C.: Brookings Institution, 2000), 5.

15. Hans-Dieter Klingemann and Dieter Fuchs, *Citizens and the State* (Oxford: Oxford University Press, 1995).

16. www.latinobarometro.org. Samples of approximately 1,000 cases per country representing mostly urban populations.

17. A good example is the Venezuelan 2000 data gathered after the Chávez election, showing high satisfaction.

18. Karl Popper, *In Search of a Better World* (London: Routledge, 1994).

19. Elias Norbert, *Du temps* (Paris: Fayard, 1984).

20. Argentina had democratic moments in the 1920s, Brazil and Bolivia in the 1950s, the Dominican Republic in the 1980s.

21. Juan Linz, "Transition to Democracy," *Washington Quarterly* 13 (1990): 48.

22. Seymour Martin Lipset, *American Exceptionalism* (New York: W. W. Norton, 1996).

23. Larry Diamond, *Political Culture and Democracy in Developing Countries* (London: Lynne Rienner, 1994), 2.

24. Pippa Norris, *Critical Citizens: Global Support for Democratic Governance* (Oxford: Oxford University Press), 26.

25. Seymour Martin Lipset, "Some Social Requisites of Democracy: Economic Development and Political Legitimacy," *American Political Science Review* 53, no. 1 (March 1959): 69–105.

26. The importance of cultural factors is considered in Lipset's article, "The Social Requisites of Democracy Revisited," *American Sociological Review* 59 (1994): 1–22.

27. Emile Durkheim, "Cours de Science Sociale: Leçon d'Ouverture," *Revue Internationale de l'Enseignement* 15 (1888): 23–48.

28. Ronald Inglehart, *Culture Shift in Advanced Industrial Society* (Princeton: Princeton University Press, 1990) and *Modernization and Postmodernization: Cultural, Economic, and Political Change in 43 Societies* (Princeton: Princeton University Press, 1997). See also

Robert D. Putnam, *Making Democracy Work: Civic Traditions in Modern Italy* (Princeton: Princeton University Press, 1993).

29. Latinobarómetro applies the trust indicator developed by Ronald Inglehart in the World Value Study.

30. Karl Popper, *Open Society and its Enemies* (London: Routledge & Kegan Paul, 1966).

31. Inglehart, *Culture Shift.*

32. Hans Dieter Klingeman, *The Citizens and the State* (Oxford: Oxford University Press, 1995), 304.

33. The data quoted show that decline in Europe during the 1980s is low on average where data are available. The most salient case of decline is therefore in the United States.

34. Norris, *Critical Citizens.*

35. Juan J. Linz, *Crisis, Breakdown and Reequilibration* (Baltimore: Johns Hopkins University Press, 1978).

36. Juan J. Linz, "Legitimacy of Democracy and the Socioeconomic System," in *Comparing Pluralist Democracies: Strains on Legitimacy,* ed. M. Dogan (Boulder, Colo.: Westview, 1988).

37. Leonardo Morlino and José Ramón Montero, "Legitimacy and Democracy in Southern Europe," in *The Politics of Democratic Consolidation,* ed. Gunther, Diamandouros, and Puhle, eds., 233.

38. This question was designed by Juan Linz and has been widely used to measure transitions to democracy in Europe and around the world, having the widest range of comparative data in the past decade.

39. The 1992 results show Spain and Portugal with 9 percent and Greece with 4 percent; José Ramón Montero, Richard Gunther, and Mariano Torcal, "Actitudes hacia la democracia en España: legitimidad, descontento y desafección," *Revista Española de Investigaciones Sociológicas* (Spain), no. 83 (July–September 1998): 9–50.

40. These data are from January 2000, so that the effect of the change in power that took place in July 2000 is not included.

41. Afrobarometer data from IDASA Cape Town, directed by Robert Mattes and Michael Bratton; Eastern European Barometer from the University of Strathclyde, directed by Richard Rose; and also data available in Larry Diamond, "Political Culture and Democratic Consolidation," working paper no. 118, Table 4, Centro de Estudios Avanzados, Instituto Juan March de Estudios e Investigaciones, Madrid, Spain, 1998.

42. Robert Dahl, *On Democracy* (New Haven: Yale University Press, 1998), 3.

Chapter 8. Venezuela

1. Allan Randoph Brewer Carías, "Reflexiones críticas sobre la Constitución de Venezuela de 1999," paper prepared for the conference on "The New Venezuelan Constitution: A New Political Model for Latin America?" Georgetown University, Washington, D.C., February 2, 2000, 4.

2. Hugo Chávez Frías, "Palabras al dar inicio al desfile militar con motivo del 188º aniversario de la Independencia," *Paseo de Los Próceres,* July 5, 1999, in the on-line library of *Venezuela Analítica* at http://www.analitica.com/bitblioteca/hchavez/99–07–05.asp.

3. Guillermo O'Donnell, "Delegative Democracy," *Journal of Democracy* 5, no. 1 (January 1994): 55–69.

4. Michael Coppedge, "Instituciones y gobernabilidad democrática en América Latina," *Síntesis* 22 (July–December 1994): 63.

5. In order to meet this standard, a government would actually have to do what most citizens want it to do, not merely *claim* to act in their interests. Of course, in practice it is difficult to know what most citizens want on every issue. Contemporary procedural definitions of democracy specify institutions and processes that help reveal the will of the people, but in reality these rules are sufficient for only a rough and sporadic alignment of government policy with public opinion. The older ideal of popular sovereignty is a more demanding standard, even if it is vague on the process that would come close to achieving it.

6. Robert A. Dahl, *A Preface to Democratic Theory* (Chicago: University of Chicago Press, 1956), especially chapter 3 (pp. 63–89) on "Polyarchal Democracy," which proposes a reconciliation of the tensions between the "Madisonian democracy" outlined in chapter 1 (pp. 4–33) and the "populistic democracy" discussed in chapter 2 (pp. 34–62).

7. Margarita López Maya and Luis Lander, "La popularidad de Chávez: ¿Base para un proyecto popular?" unpublished manuscript, Caracas, February 6, 2000, 6.

8. Ibid.

9. "Sondeos de opinión," *El Nacional* (on-line archive), May 10, 2000, at http://www.el-nacional.com/megaelecciones/Encuestas/.

10. Maya and Lander, "La popularidad de Chávez," 14.

11. Some of the text in this section is taken from an earlier version of this article: Michael Coppedge, "Venezuela: The Rise and Fall of Partyarchy," in *Constructing Democratic Governance: South America in the 1990s*, ed. Jorge I. Domínguez and Abraham F. Lowenthal (Baltimore: Johns Hopkins University Press, 1996), 3–19.

12. This concept is fully developed and contrasted with Dahl's concept of polyarchy in my book, *Strong Parties and Lame Ducks: Presidential Partyarchy and Factionalism in Venezuela* (Stanford: Stanford University Press, 1994). This section summarizes arguments developed at length in chapter 2 (pp. 18–46).

13. Daniel H. Levine, *Conflict and Political Change in Venezuela* (Princeton: Princeton University Press, 1973).

14. Angus Maddison, *Monitoring the World Economy, 1820–1992* (Paris: Development Centre of the Organisation for Economic Cooperation and Development, 1995), Table D-1d, 203.

15. Terry Lynn Karl, *The Paradox of Plenty: Oil Boom and Petro-States* (Berkeley: University of California Press, 1997).

16. "New Venezuelan President Sworn In," Associated Press report, February 2, 1999.

17. See Charles D. Kenney, "Reflections on Horizontal Accountability: Democratic Legitimacy, Majority Parties and Democratic Stability in Latin America," paper presented at the conference on "Institutions, Accountability, and Democratic Governance in Latin America," Kellogg Institute for International Studies, University of Notre Dame, May 8–9, 2000, 5, for an eloquent application of this idea to both Chávez and Fujimori.

18. However, Lijphart has argued that the more the rules require the inclusion of as many political tendencies as possible, as opposed to narrow majorities or even minorities, the more democratic the system is. Arend Lijphart, *Patterns of Democracy: Government Forms and Performance in Thirty-Six Countries* (New Haven: Yale University Press, 1999), 275–300.

19. Alexis de Tocqueville, *Democracy in America*, trans. George Lawrence, ed. J. P. Mayer (Garden City, N.Y.: Doubleday, 1969), 246–61.

20. Robert A. Dahl, *Democracy and Its Critics* (New Haven: Yale University Press, 1989), 220–22. Here, I am equating the "minimal standards for democracy" with polyarchy.

21. The electoral system used in 2000 was a version of the increasingly popular mixed

member proportional system, in which some seats are filled in single-member districts by plurality and others are filled in multi-member districts by proportional representation (PR). Venezuela's version deviated from the basic German system in two ways. First, 60 percent of the seats were filled by plurality and 40 percent by proportional representation (d'Hondt), instead of the usual 50–50 split. Second, some of the plurality districts were multi-member districts, which made the rule there, in effect, a bloc vote. For these seats, each voter cast a number of votes equal to the number of seats to be filled, and the most-voted candidates were elected until all the seats were filled. This system had a strong tendency to exaggerate the margin of victory of the largest party due to most voters' tendency to vote a straight ticket. For example, in the first district of Zulia state, MVR candidates won all four seats with less than 40 percent of the votes cast. Nationally, however, most of the plurality districts were single-member districts, and the overall allocation shifted partially toward proportionality because each party's plurality seats were subtracted from the number of PR seats to which it was entitled.

22. Coppedge, "Instituciones y gobernabilidad democrática en América Latina," 61–88.

23. "Evangelicals Bring Chávez's Message to the People," *Oxford Analytica* (January 28, 2000). I thank David Smilde, Department of Sociology, University of Chicago, for this piece.

24. Ibid.

25. Andrew Webb-Vidal, "Exodus from Venezuela," *Business Latin America,* reprinted in *The Economist Intelligence Unit,* May 8, 2000; David J. Myers, unedited submission for "Venezuela," *Encyclopedia Britannica Online Yearbook 2000,* supplied personally to the author.

26. Larry Rohter, "A Divided Venezuela to Vote on New Constitution," *New York Times,* December 15, 1999.

27. "Gobierno presiona a la CTV para producir cambios," *El Nacional,* February 3, 2000.

28. Ibid.

29. Gustavo Méndez, "[Chávez:] Nadie evitará la demolición de la CTV," *El Universal,* November 12, 2000, on-line at http://noticias.eluniversal.com/2000/11/12/12114AA.shtml.

30. Website of the Comité de Familiares de las Víctimas de los Sucesos de Febrero y Marzo de 1989, at http://www.cofavic.org.ve/lista.htm.

31. Margarita López Maya, "El ascenso en Venezuela de La Causa R," paper presented at the XVIII International Congress of the Latin American Studies Association, Atlanta, Georgia, March 10–12, 1994.

32. Julia Buxton, *The Failure of Political Reform in Venezuela* (Burlington, Vt.: Ashgate, 2001), 82–104.

33. "CNE desincorporará a 138 funcionarios adscritos a nómina de partidos políticos," *El Nacional,* January 4, 2000.

34. "Reestructurada directiva del Consejo Nacional Electoral para actuar bajo consenso," *El Nacional,* February 7, 2000.

35. AD won governorships in Amazonas, Apure, Mérida, and Monagas; COPEI in Miranda and Táchira; Unión Nuevo Tiempo (a COPEI offshoot) in Zulia; Proyecto Venezuela in Carabobo; Convergencia in Yaracuy. Patria Para Todos, which supported Chávez, won in Guárico and Nueva Esparta. The remaining twelve governorships were won by MVR. A very similar distribution prevailed in the election of mayors of the state capitals.

36. "Agreden a periodistas junto a sede del Consejo," *El Universal,* May 31, 2000.

37. Others that allied with MVR for the 1998 presidential election were the Venezuelan

Communist Party, the People's Electoral Movement (MEP), and four other tiny parties (IPCN, GE, SI, and AA—meaning of acronymns unknown), none of which contributed as much as 2 percent of the vote to Chávez.

38. Steve Ellner, "Polarized Politics in Chávez's Venezuela," *NACLA Report on the Americas* 33, no. 6 (May–June 2000): 29–33.

39. Ludmila Vinogradoff, "La creciente presencia militar marca los 100 primeros días de Chávez," *El País,* May 15, 1999.

40. Ibid.

41. Alicia La Rotta Morán, "Roche Lander califica al actual gobierno como el más corrupto," *El Universal Digital,* April 1, 2000, at http://universal.eud.com/2000/04/01/01102F F.shtml; Florángel Gómez, "En este gobierno faltan sanciones ejemplares," *El Universal Digital,* 14 April 2000, at http://politica.eud.com/informespecial/corrupcion/eltrabajo.html.

42. Vinogradoff, "La creciente presencia militar."

43. Arguments and evidence for this paragraph come from Harold Trinkunas' excellent analysis, "The Crisis in Venezuelan Civil-Military Relations: from 'Punto Fijo' to the Fifth Republic," *Latin American Research Review* (forthcoming 2002).

44. Nevertheless, there could be other motives for dissolving the assembly, such as eliminating the inviolability and immunity of deputies or preventing impeachment.

45. "Chávez to Return Enabling Law to Congress," *Agence France Press* report, April 6, 1999, translated by *World News Connection* (FBIS-LAT-1999–0406).

46. Agence France Press, August 25, 1999, reported and translated by World News Connection (FBIS-LAT-1999–0825).

47. The text approved in the April referendum authorizing the ANC read in part, "Once the ANC is installed, it must dictate its own operating statutes. Its limits will be the values and principles of our republican history, as well as the fulfillment of international treaties, accords, and commitments validly signed by the Republic; the progressive character of the fundamental rights of man and democratic guarantees; within the most absolute respect for the commitments assumed" ("Proceso Constituyente," at http://politica.eud.com/procesoconst/referendo.html). If this is read as a *complete* listing of the limits on the ANC's authority, it supports the view of its absolute sovereignty; if it is read as a *partial* listing of limits, then it supports a more conservative view. Considering the magnitude of the consequences of readings of this pivotal passage, a more explicit statement would have been desirable. However, the revolutionary mood prevailing in April 1999 probably would have made it possible to approve even a completely unrestricted grant of authority to the ANC.

48. "Decreto de regulación de las funciones del Poder Legislativo," August 30, 1999, text published at http://politica.eud.com/1999/08/31/250899d.html.

49. Andrew Reynolds and Ben Reilly, *The International IDEA Handbook of Electoral System Design* (Stockholm: International Institute for Democracy and Electoral Assistance, 1997), 36. The variant used in Venezuela was that 104 seats were filled in statewide districts and twenty-four were filled in a single national district. Four of the six independents were elected in the large national district.

50. María Pilar García Guadilla and Mónica Hurtado, "Participation and Constitution Making in Colombia and Venezuela: Enlarging the Scope of Democracy?" paper presented at the XXII International Congress of the Latin American Studies Association, Miami, Florida, March 16–18, 2000, 19.

51. Ibid., 20–22.

52. The Bolivarian constitution defined the state as "federal and decentralized"; permitted states to adopt their own constitutions; recognized regional powers between the

states and the federal government; established a "Federal Council of Government"; established the right to local and state-level referendums and recalls; and delegated certain minor taxation powers to states and municipalities (as contemplated in legislation under the 1961 constitution). However, the federal government retains control over the bulk of the financing for state and local governments and in 1999 and 2000 was dispensing it in a discriminatory way in order to undermine regional regime opponents. William Dávila Barrios, "Crisis fiscal y poder central," *El Universal,* November 6, 2000, at http://noticias.eluniversal.com/2000/11/06/OPI9.shtml.

53. "Decreto mediante el cual se dicta el Régimen de Transición del Poder Público," *Gaceta Oficial* Número 33,859, published at http://politica.edu.com/1999/12/26/231299b.html.

54. This percentage, unlike the one reported earlier, is based on the total membership of the ANC, including the three indigenous delegates.

55. Corte Suprema de Justicia, "Fallo 17 [de la Corte Suprema de Justicia de Venezuela sobre el referendo para convocar a una Asamblea Constituyente]," January 19, 1999, from chapters IV and VIII, published in *Venezuela Analítica* at http://www.analitica.com/bitblioteca/csj/fallo17.asp#introduccion [my translation].

56. This Tribunal was to be renewed in late 2000 by the National Assembly, which was to choose from a larger number of nominees composed by citizen dialogue groups (*mesas de diálogo*). However, the assembly's MVR majority reappointed most of the incumbent justices.

57. "Tribunal Supremo absuelve al presidente de la Comisión Legislativa," *El Universal,* June 9, 2000, at http://noticias.eluniversal.com/2000/06/09/09062000_16059.html.

58. Irma Alvarez, "Suspenden 83 jueces y destituyen a 28," *El Universal,* March 30, 2000.

59. Florángel Gómez, "Esperemos colocar un puñado de buenos jueces en el sistema judicial," *El Universal Digital,* April 14, 2000, at http://politica.eud.com/informespecial/corrupcion/.

60. Jesús Urdaneta charged that new technicians were incompetent because they were chosen for their political loyalties: "From Miquilena's daughter on down, they are all [Chávez's] people and serve his interests." Larry Rohter, "Critics Question Legitimacy of Venezuelan Election Process," *New York Times,* May 23, 2000. Also, one CNE technician dismissed after the postponement quoted his boss telling him not to trust certain other technicians, who were alleged to be supporters of Francisco Arias. Finally, the head of the U.S. firm contracted to supply electronic equipment for the voting machines charged that he had been instructed by the CNE to ensure that all votes for any party in the pro-Chávez alliance would count as votes for Chávez in the presidential race even though PPT had formally withdrawn its support for him (Alcides Castillo, "El CNE planteó a ES&S que los votos favorecieran al candidato Chávez," *El Nacional,* June 1, 2000).

61. "Los cinco principales del CNE" and "Los cinco suplentes," *El Universal,* June 4, 2000.

62. Cenovia Casas, "Congresillo decide hoy sobre destitución de siete alcaldes," *El Nacional,* March 30, 2000; Luisana Colomine, "Sólo el gobernador de Cojedes será destituido," *El Universal,* April 5, 2000.

63. "Congresillo intervendrá las gobernaciones de Cojedes y Amazonas," *El Nacional,* March 26, 2000.

64. Eleonora Delgado and Alonso Zambrano, "Denunciarán ante la OEA allanamiento de la Disip a la Gobernación de Mérida," *El Nacional,* May 25, 2000; Deisy Martínez and Solbella Pérez, "Eliézer Otaiza: No hubo allanamiento," *El Nacional,* May 25, 2000.

65. President Chávez tended to complain loudly whenever his government's actions

were criticized in the media, calling on editorialists to report news with a more optimistic and "patriotic" slant. In December 1999, Teodoro Petkoff was fired from the board of the Caracas daily *El Mundo* in response to such official pressure. In February 2000, Interior Minister Luis Alfonso Dávila blamed the media for the criminality rampant in the country. Ernesto Villegas Poljak, "Denuncian amenazas a libre expresión," *El Universal,* February 23, 2000, at http://noticias.eluniversal.com/2000/02/23/23111AA.shtml.

66. There were signs that expectations had changed already. To whom, for example, did Governor Dávila complain when the DISIP raided his office? He complained to the Organization of American States, an international organization, because he could not expect an impartial, much less sympathetic, hearing from any politically relevant actor inside Venezuela. He no longer had the protection of a party with clout; the electoral council was in disarray at the time; judges would risk dismissal if they protected him; the comptroller was the one auditing his books; and the executive and legislature were on Chávez's side.

Chapter 9. Colombia

1. Fernando Cepeda Ulloa and Christopher Mitchell, "The Trend towards Technocracy: The World Bank and the International Labor Organization in Colombian Politics," in *Politics of Compromise,* ed. R. Albert Berry, Ronald G. Hellman, and Mauricio Solaun (New Brunswick: Transaction, 1980), 237–55.

2. William J. Clinton interview published in *Cambio Magazine* (Bogotá: August 30, 2000).

3. Defensoría del Pueblo, *Los cultivos ilícitos* (Bogotá: Imprenta Nacional, August 2000), 19–49.

4. Manuel José Cepeda, *La constituyente por dentro: mitos y realidades* (Bogotá: Imprenta Nacional, 1993).

5. Manuel José Cepeda, *Introducción a la Constitución de 1991* (Bogotá: Imprenta Nacional, 1993), 173–251.

6. Fernando Cepeda Ulloa, *Dirección política de la reforma económica en Colombia* (Bogotá: Fonade-DNP, 1994).

7. Manuel José Cepeda, *La Constitución de 1991 ante nuestra realidad: respuesta a algunas críticas* (Bogotá: Folletos Esap, 1992); Manuel José Cepeda, *El derecho a la Constitución en Colombia entre la rebelión pacífica y la esperanza* (Madrid: Revista Epsilon de Derecho Constitucional, 1995). There have been many critiques of the 1991 constitution over the past ten years in newspapers and magazines.

8. Fernando Cepeda Ulloa, "La representatividad del Congreso," *Revista Foro* (Bogotá: Ed. Foro Nacional por Colombia, 2000), 3–11.

9. Arturo Valenzuela et al., "Sobre la reforma política en Colombia, informe de la Consultoría Internacional," in *Reforma política un propósito de nación,* ed. República de Colombia, Ministerio del Interior (Bogotá: Oficina de Publicaciones del Ministerio del Interior, Serie Documentos 17, November 1999), 209–311.

10. Fernando Cepeda Ulloa, *Financiación de campañas políticas* (Bogotá: Ariel, Colombiana Editorial, 1997), 55, 141–48.

11. Camilo Granada, "La evolución del gasto en seguridad y defensa en Colombia 1950–1994," in *Reconocer la guerra para construir la paz,* ed. Malcolm Deas and María Victoria Llorente (Bogotá: Ediciones Uniandes-Cerec-Editorial Norma, 1999), 537–97.

12. Francisco Leal Buitrago, ed., *Tras las huellas de la crisis política* (Bogotá: Tercer

Mundo Editores-Fescol-Iepri [UN], 1996).

13. Fernando Cepeda Ulloa, *Corrupción y gobernabilidad* (Bogotá: 3R Editores, 2000), 132–34.

14. Ministerio del Interior, *Comisión para el estudio de la reforma de los partidos políticos, Memoria de trabajo* (Bogotá: Publicaciones del Ministerio de Interior, 1996).

15. Ibid., 35.

16. Ibid., 23.

17. Ibid., 24.

18. Fernando Cepeda Ulloa, "Origen, desarrollo y desenlace del Caligate," in *Colombia Contemporanea* (Bogotá: Ecoe ediciones-Iepri, 1996), 299–338.

19. Ana María Bejarano and Andrés Dávila, *Elecciones y democracia en Colombia* (Bogotá: Universidad de los Andes, 1998), 297.

20. Fernando Cepeda Ulloa, "El Congreso Colombiano ante la crisis," in *Tras las huellas de la crisis política*, ed. Francisco Leal Buitrago (Bogotá: Tercer Mundo Editores-Fescol-Iepri [UN], 1996), 95–97.

21. *Gaceta del Congreso* 9, no. 98 (Bogotá, April 5, 2000): 9.

22. Proyecto de Ley No. 261, 9, no. 98 (Cámara: Gaceta del Congreso, 2000).

23. The Extended Fund Facility for Colombia, IMF Press Release no. 99/63, December 20, 1999.

24. Ulloa, *Corrupción y gobernabilidad*, 19–28, 61–73.

25. Bob Graham and Brent Scowcroft, *Toward Greater Peace and Security in Colombia* (Washington, D.C.: Council on Foreign Relations and the Inter-American Dialogue, October 2000).

26. Olivier Duhamel and Manuel José Cepeda, *Las democracias entre el derecho constitucional y la política* (Universidad de los Andes: TM editors, 1997), 253–80.

27. Fernando Cepeda Ulloa, "Una Colombia nueva: la visión política de Barco," in *El gobierno Barco política, economía y desarrollo social 1986–1990*, ed. Malcolm Deas and Carlos Ossa (Bogotá: Editorial Nomos, 1994), 49–78.

28. Bejarano and Dávila, *Elecciones y democracia en Colombia*, 297.

29. Valenzuela, "Sobre la reforma política en Colombia," 257, 286.

30. Bejarano and Dávila, *Elecciones y democracia en Colombia*, 396–99.

31. Ibid., 223.

32. *El Tiempo*, May 1, 2000, 9A.

33. *Opinión pública: encuestas y medios de comunicación. El caso del 8.000* (Fescol, 1997), 61.

34. Carlos Lemoine, *Nosotros los colombianos del milenio* (Bogotá: Tercer Mundo, 2000).

Chapter 10. Peru

1. We use the term *anti-politics* as defined by Nicolás Lynch; Nicolás Lynch, *La antipolítica en el Perú* (Lima: DESCO, 2000). For the Bolivian usage, see René Antonio Mayorga, *Antipolítica y neopopulismo* (La Paz: Centro Boliviano de Estudios Multidisciplinarios, 1995).

2. For information on the 1990 elections, see, among others, Sally Bowen, *El expediente Fujimori: El Perú y su presidente 1990–2000* (Lima: Perú Monitor S.A., 2000); Carlos Iván Degregori and Romeo Grompone, *Elecciones 1990: Demonios y redentores en el Nuevo Perú* (Lima: IEP, 1991); Mario Vargas Llosa, *El pez en el agua* (Madrid: Seix Barral, 1993). For in-

formation on the political career and personality of Alberto Fujimori, see Luis Jochamowitz, *Ciudadano Fujimori: La construcción de un político* (Lima: Peisa, 1993); Bowen, *El expediente Fujimori*.

3. FREDEMO, a liberal alliance, was formed of Acción Popular, the Partido Popular Cristiano, and the Movimiento Libertad. The writer Mario Vargas Llosa, who was also its presidential candidate, founded it.

4. Hernando de Soto popularized the term *mercantilists* in his best-seller *El otro sendero*, which played an important role in bringing about the intellectual hegemony of neoliberalism.

5. Romeo Grompone and Carlos Mejía, *Nuevos tiempos, nueva política. El fin de un ciclo partidario* (Lima: IEP, 1995).

6. For information on the rise of Montesinos and his influence in the armed forces, see Bowen, *El expediente Fujimori*; Francisco Loayza, *El rostro oscuro del poder* (Lima: Ediciones Referéndum, 1998); Fernando Rospigliosi, *Las Fuerzas Armadas y el 5 de abril: La percepción de la amenaza subversiva como una motivación golpista* (Lima: IEP, 1996).

7. Samuel Abad and Carolina Garcés, "El gobierno de Fujimori: antes y después del golpe," in *Del Golpe de Estado a la Nueva Constitución* (Lima: Comisión Andina de Juristas, 1993), 85–190. This is the way in which much legislation was enacted, for example, the new Penal, Penal Procedural, and Civil Procedural Codes; the Juridical Organic Law, tax reform, banking, financial institution and insurance laws, job creation and private investment stimulus packages, various labor regulations, and a package of ordinances on pacification.

8. The ordinances greatly enhanced the power of the SIN and the political-military authorities in areas declared to be in a state of emergency; they imposed new obligations on the citizens to keep the National Intelligence Service (SIN) informed and support the armed forces when requested; they established draconian penalties for journalists who published information considered secret by the military authorities or the intelligence services; it became possible to accuse someone who published an article criticizing the counterinsurgency program abroad of treason. See Bowen, *El expediente Fujimori*, 108–10. On the debate surrounding these ordinances, see Rospigliosi, *Las Fuerzas Armadas y el 5 de abril*; Carlos Tapia, *Las Fuerzas Armadas y Sendero Luminoso: Dos estrategias y un final* (Lima: IEP, 1996).

9. See Bowen, *El expediente Fujimori*, 115.

10. In early 1992, the former president, Alan García, was elected general secretary of the APRA. He intensified his opposition to the regime from that moment on.

11. This in no way condones Congress' shortcomings, its inefficiency and tendency to favor "special interests," or the growth of its bureaucracy as a way to reward favors and maintain clienteles, to mention some examples.

12. On military prerogatives in Brazil and Chile, see Alfred Stepan, *Rethinking Military Politics: Brazil and the Southern Cone* (Princeton: Princeton University Press, 1988). On civilian-military relationships between 1980 and 1992, see Carlos Iván Degregori and Carlos Rivera, *Perú 1980–1993: Fuerzas Armadas, subversión y democracia* (Lima: IEP, 1994); Philip Mauceri, *Militares: Insurgencia y democratización en el Perú, 1980–1988* (Lima: IEP, 1988); Enrique Obando, "Las relaciones civiles-militares en el Perú 1980–1996: Sobre cómo controlar, cooptar y utilizar a los militares (y las consecuencias de hacerlo)," in *Los senderos insólitos del Perú: Guerra y sociedad en el Perú, 1980–1995*, ed. Steve Stern (Lima, IEP/UNSCH 1999). On the November 1991 legislative package and on the armed forces and the self-coup: Rospigliosi, *Las Fuerzas Armadas y el 5 de abril*; Tapia, *Las Fuerzas Armadas y Sendero Luminoso*.

13. Some examples of the prerogatives that the armed forces got after the self-coup were greater financial resources, expanded areas subject to military justice, and, especially, virtual immunity from human rights violations, among others.

14. DESCO, *Resumen Semanal* 15, no. 665 (April 10–14, 1992).

15. See Stepan, *Rethinking Military Politics*.

16. For an analysis of the use of the term *neopopulism,* see Nicolás Lynch, "Neopopulismo: Un concepto vacío," *Socialismo y participación,* no. 86 (1999).

17. An elusive ethnic factor also played in favor of the president. A migrants' son, the president was representative of the sociocultural makeup of contemporary Peru, which is composed in great part by migrants that are well established in the old Creole cities. A nikkei, as Japanese-Peruvians are called, in contrast with the old creole-mestizo political class, made Fujimori appear to be closer to the Andean population, and he exploited that impression, becoming the man of a thousand costumes. There wasn't a typical set of clothes that he hadn't worn in his costume of neopopulism. The masquerade and the corporal language would reach their climax five years later with "el Chino's boogie" that the president popularized in his 2000 electoral campaign. For further on this, also see Patricia Oliart, "Fujimori: El hombre que el Perú necesitaba," in *Los senderos insólitos del Perú: Guerra y sociedad en el Perú, 1980–1995,* ed. Steve Stern (Lima: IEP/ UNSCH, 1999), 358–420. On the ethnic-cultural factor in Fujimori's triumph over Vargas Llosa in 1990: Degregori and Grompone, *Elecciones 1990.*

18. Marcelo Cavarozzi, "Transformación de la Política en la América Latina Contemporanea," *Análisis Político,* 19, Bogotá, 25–40.

19. He incarcerated a number of retired military officials who disagreed with the way the 1995 conflict with Ecuador was handled. Congress, doing its part, raised the required number of signatures that political parties needed for reinscription; after decreeing the reorganization of the National Board of Elections (JNE), Fujimori put delegates of the executive and Congress, rather than JNE members, in charge of the reorganization; and he promulgated a law reorganizing national universities. And that was only the beginning ...

20. Declarations to the media chain; *O'Globo,* May 22, 1995.

21. The main links of the subordination chain were the creation of intervention commissions in the judiciary and the Public Affairs Ministry; cutting of the attributes of the latter, which were given to a new Executive Committee whose president was a submissive district attorney; amputation of the functions of the National Council of Magistrates; and above all, the keeping of an overwhelming majority of judges and attorneys, including entire sections of the Supreme Court, on a provisional status and therefore, very sensitive to pressure from the executive.

22. Very high salaries, bonuses, offices, advisory staff, trips, and communications. Technical modernization was thus put at the service of very traditional political objectives.

23. On the role of the de facto powers in contemporary Peru, see Sinesio López, "Estado y ciudadanía en el Perú: Vuelcos y revuelcos de una relación tormentosa," *Cuestión de Estado,* no. 17 (1995): 13–18.

24. On prerogatives, see Stepan, *Rethinking Military Politics*. On the armed forces and democracy: Carlos Iván Degregori and Carlos Rivera, *Perú 1980–1993: Fuerzas Armadas, subversión y democracia* (Lima: IEP, 1994); Mauceri, *Militares*; Rospigliosi, *Las Fuerzas Armadas y el 5 de abril.*

25. Romeo Grompone and Carlos Mejía, *Nuevos tiempos, nueva política. El fin de un ciclo partidario* (Lima: IEP, 1995), 31.

26. Notable among these was the president's brother, Santiago Fujimori, who was thought to be a precocious boy because the only photo that came out in the media, taken before he decided to hide his face, was that of his electoral identification card; and the person that would soon become the most important adviser: Vladimiro Montesinos.

27. On November 12, 1991, a law was passed granting the president the authority to name the heads of the armed forces, which also rescinded mandatory retirement after thirty-five years of service. The first beneficiary was General Nicolás Hermoza Ríos, who was named comander-in-chief of the army on December 19, 1991. Shortly thereafter he became eligible for retirement but was ratified repeatedly as head of the armed forces until the end of 1998. Bowen, *El expediente Fujimori*, 72; Rospigliosi, *Las Fuerzas Armadas y el 5 de abril.*

28. On that day, a group of generals, unhappy with Hermoza Ríos' continuation as head of the armed forces because it blocked their own path to the coveted position, and frustrated with the overall manipulation and growing politicization of the military, tried to overthrow Fujimori and reinstate the institutional framework that existed before the coup. Montesinos had a stellar role in the quelling of the countercoup that allowed him to consolidate his power within the armed forces and his influence on the president.

29. A district that is emblematic of Lima's middle class.

30. Fujimori's nickname but one that is generally used to designate Peruvians of Asian origin, either Chinese or Japanese.

31. According to Apoyo, Inc., 87 percent of those interviewed were not in agreement with the Congress' actions to prevent the judiciary from prosecuting military personnel implicated in human rights violations; and 78 percent rejected the Amnesty Law favoring accused military personnel and the very few people previously convicted of human rights violations.

32. Article 112 states: "the presidential term is five years. The president can be reelected immediately for an additional period. After another constitutional term as a minimum, the ex-president can again seek office subject to the same conditions." In spite of the spirit of the 1993 constitutional debate, the pro-government faction adduced that the 1995–2000 period was Alberto Fujimori's first term under the new constitution.

33. Bowen, *El expediente Fujimori.*

34. Bowen, *El expediente Fujimori*, 269; Rospigliosi, *Las Fuerzas Armadas y el 5 de abril.*

35. Bowen, *El expediente Fujimori*, 56.

36. Several pollsters show that the president recovered between 6 and 12 approval points between December and January. IMASEN found a 42 percent approval rating for the president in December, but measured 50.3 percent one month after the crisis began.

37. For further information on the agents Leonor la Rosa and Mariela Barreto, as well as the student massacre at the "La Cantuta" University in 1992 and the 1997 expropriation of Frecuencia Latina, the TV channel that revealed these crimes, see Alvaro Vargas Llosa, *En el reino del espanto* (Mexico: Grijalbo, 2000).

38. On the positions of the four members of the TGC against the "law of authentic interpretation" and the details of their removal from office, see Marcial Rubio, *Quítate la venda para mirarme mejor: La reforma judicial en el Perú* (Lima: DESCO, 2000); Enrique Chávez Molina, *Mi voto singular* (Lima: Editorial Horizonte, 2000).

39. A Peruvian businessman born in Israel.

40. Soon after his return to Washington, McCaffrey pointed out that Montesinos "is a figure that seeks legitimacy through manipulation" (*El Comercio*, May 15, 1998).

41. Between February and March 1995, the Peruvian and Ecuadorian armies clashed in an area of the border deep in the Amazon jungle, where a problem of territorial demar-

cation had festered for several decades. After a cease fire was achieved with the participation of the original 1942 peace treaty guarantors (the United States, Brazil, Chile, and Argentina), a period of negotiations ensued culminating in October 1998 with a definitive peace agreement between the two countries.

42. Vamos Vecino actually won more mayoral seats than Somos Peru nationally. Soon after, VV was able to win the leadership of the Peruvian Association of Municipalities (AMPE), which then lapsed into a vegetative state that was very convenient for the government.

43. Source: Analistas y Consultores, December 29, 1998.

44. Sinesio López has concluded that those socioeconomic sectors put more emphasis on social issues than on the strictly political ones; Sinesio López, "El Perú entre el continuismo autoritario y la transición democrática," *Cuestión de Estado*, no. 26 (2000): 22–28. Yusuke Murakami looks into a similar topic from another angle. The author finds that social demands are uppermost, pragmatism is favored, and there is a willingness to exchange political freedoms for security; Yusuke Murakami, *La democracia según C y D: Un estudio de la conciencia y el comportamiento político de los sectores populares de Lima* (Lima, IEP/JCAS, 1999). In an ambitious critique of Latin American democratic transition theories, Carlos Franco calls attention to these aspects and affirms that the hegemonic theories put excessive emphasis on politics as an independent sphere, ignoring the history of its rules, institutions, and players; underestimating the structural factors that circumscribe the action of the players; Carlos Franco, *Acerca del modo de pensar la democracia en América Latina* (Lima: Friedrich Ebert Stiftung, 1998), 24. In our case, poverty was underestimated, as well as the barrier it creates in popular sectors that keeps its citizens from being "well informed" and who then become easy targets of patronage. See also Fernando Coronil, "De transición en transición: Democracia y nación en Latinoamérica," *Anuario Mariateguiano* 10 (1998): 54–63.

45. Except one cable channel that started transmitting a few months before the 2000 elections, two newspapers, *El Comercio* and *La República*, one weekly, *Caretas* magazine, some Lima radio stations, CPN, and several others spread throughout different cities of the country. Except for the provincial radios, the target audience of the rest is concentrated in socioeconomic sectors A, B, and the educated portion of sector C, while the government concentrated its efforts on the poorest but demographically more important sectors.

46. On election day, *Transparencia* had voluntary observers in all of the country's provinces and the results of its quick count gave Fujimori less than 49 percent of the votes. This was fundamental in order to stop the executive-controlled National Board of Elections (JNE) from claiming that the president-candidate had obtained 50 percent plus one vote, that being the necessary minimum, according to law, to win the elections and avoid a runoff.

47. In the 2000 elections, one of the most respected pollsters, Apoyo, Inc., tried to explain the difference in the numbers between the exit polls that gave Fujimori around 42 percent and the actual vote count, which gave the president-candidate over 48 percent, according to Transparencia. They reasoned that there existed a segment of the population that had cast a "shameful ballot," that is to say, that although they had voted for Fujimori, they were ashamed to admit it.

48. On fujimorism's final days, see also Julio Cotler, "La gobernabilidad en el Perú: entre el autoritarismo y la democracia," in *El fujimorismo: Ascenso y caída de un régimen autoritario*, ed. Julio Cotler and Romeo Grompone (Lima: IEP, 2000).

49. On the various factors that contributed to the fall of the regime—recession, fraud,

corruption, civil unrest, partial estrangement of the business community, distancing of foreign investors, and mainly the confrontation with the United States and the international community—see Julio Cotler, "La gobernabilidad en el Perú: entre el autoritarismo y la democracia," in *El fujimorismo: Ascenso y caída de un régimen autoritario*, ed. Julio Cotler and Romeo Grompone (Lima: IEP, 2000); Romeo Grompone, "Al día siguiente: El fujimorismo como proyecto inconcluso de transformación política y social," in *El fujimorismo: Ascenso y caída de un régimen autoritario*, ed. Julio Cotler and Romeo Grompone (Lima, IEP, 2000), 153; Martín Tanaka, *Perú, 1980–2000 ¿Crónica de una muerte anunciada? Determinismo, voluntarismo, y poderes estructurales* (Lima: IEP, 2001); Jane Marcus-Delgado, *The Fall of Alberto Fujimori: A Study of Presidential Legitimacy* (forthcoming).

50. That was seen clearly, for example, when in December 2000, Congress decided that the 2001 elections were to be conducted using the single electoral district (national). The immediate and massive outcry by the citizens, civilian institutions, and the media forced Congress to vote again and reinstate the departmental electoral districts that had existed up to 1992.

Chapter 11. Argentina

The author thanks Javier Corrales, Jorge Domínguez, Sebastián Etchemendy, James McGuire, and María Victoria Murillo for comments on earlier versions of this chapter.

1. Guillermo O'Donnell, *Modernization and Bureaucratic-Authoritarianism: Studies in South American Politics* (Berkeley: Institute of International Studies, 1973); Carlos Waisman, *Reversal of Development: Postwar Counterrevolutionary Politics and their Structural Consequences* (Princeton: Princeton University Press, 1987).

2. See Pablo T. Spiller and Mariano Tomassi, "Los determinantes institucionales del desarrollo argentino: Una aproximación desde la Nueva Economía Institucional," Centro de Estudios para el Desarrollo Institucional Working Paper no. 33 (Buenos Aires: CEDI, May 2000).

3. Gretchen Helmke, "Ruling Against the Rulers: Insecure Tenure and Judicial Independence in Argentina, 1976–1995" (Ph.D. dissertation, Department of Political Science, University of Chicago, 2000). As a result, the average tenure of Supreme Court justices between 1960 and 1999 was less than four years, compared to nine years in Chile and thirteen years in the United States (Spillar and Tomassi, "Los determinantes institucionales del desarrollo argentino,"22–23, table 2).

4. Guillermo O'Donnell, "Delegative Democracy," *Journal of Democracy* 5, no. 1 (January 1994): 57–59; Spillar and Tomassi, "Los determinantes institucionales del desarrollo argentino."

5. Edward Gibson, *Class and Conservative Parties: Argentina in Comparative Perspective* (Baltimore: Johns Hopkins University Press, 1996).

6. Edgardo Catterberg, *Argentina Confronts Politics: Political Culture and Public Opinion in the Argentine Transition to Democracy* (Boulder: Lynne Rienner, 1991).

7. Enrique Peruzzotti, "Towards a New Politics: Citizenship and Rights in Contemporary Argentina," *Citizenship Studies* 6, no. 1 (March 2002): 77–93.

8. Ibid.

9. Silvio Waisbord, *Watchdog Journalism in South America: News, Accountability, and Democracy* (New York: Columbia University Press, 2000).

10. Catalina Smulovitz and Enrique Peruzzotti, "Societal Accountability in Latin America," *Journal of Democracy* 11, no. 4 (October 2000): 147–58.

11. Catalina Smulovitz and Enrique Peruzzotti, "Societal and Horizontal Controls: Two Cases about a Fruitful Relationship," paper presented at the conference "Institutions, Accountability and Democratic Governance in Latin America," The Helen Kellogg Institute for International Studies, University of Notre Dame, May 8–9, 2000, 2–6.

12. Gibson, *Class and Conservative Parties.*

13. James W. McGuire, *Peronism without Perón: Unions, Parties, and Democracy in Argentina* (Stanford: Stanford University Press, 1997).

14. O'Donnell, *Modernization and Bureaucratic Authoritarianism,* 166–96; Ruth Berins Collier and David Collier, *Shaping the Political Arena* (Princeton: Princeton University Press, 1991).

15. Gibson, *Class and Conservative Parties.*

16. Steven Levitsky, *Transforming Labor-Based Parties in Latin America: Argentine Peronism in Comparative Perspective* (New York: Cambridge University Press, forthcoming).

17. Collier and Collier, *Shaping the Political Arena.*

18. Ibid.

19. O'Donnell, "Delegative Democracy."

20. Carlos S. Niño, "Hyper-Presidentialism and Constitutional Reform in Argentina," in *Institutional Design in New Democracies,* ed. Arend Lijphart and Carlos H. Waisman (Boulder: Westview, 1996); O'Donnell, "Delegative Democracy."

21. Niño, "Hyper-Presidentialism and Constitutional Reform in Argentina"; and Delia Ferreira Rubio and Matteo Goretti, "When the President Governs Alone: The Decretazo in Argentina, 1989–93," in *Executive Decree Authority,* ed. John M. Carey and Matthew Soberg Shugart (New York: Cambridge University Press, 1998).

22. Rubio and Goretti, "When the President Governs Alone"; Mark Jones, "Evaluating Argentina's Presidential Democracy," in *Presidentialism and Democracy in Latin America,* ed. Scott Mainwaring and Matthew Soberg Shugart (New York: Cambridge University Press, 1997), 285–90.

23. Delia Ferreira Rubio and Matteo Goretti, "Executive-Legislative Relationship in Argentina: From Menem's *Decretazo* to a New Style?" paper presented at the conference "Argentina 2000: Politics, Economy, Society and International Relations," Oxford University, May 15–17, 2000, 1, 4

24. Ibid., 3.

25. Ibid., 7.

26. Christopher Larkins, "The Judiciary and Delegative Democracy in Argentina," *Comparative Politics* 30, no. 4 (July 1998): 423–42; Helmke, "Ruling Against the Rulers."

27. Emilio Jorge Cárdenas, "Refurbishing the Argentine Judiciary: A Still-Neglected Theme," in *Argentina: The Challenges of Modernization,* ed. Joseph Tulchin (Wilmington: Scholarly Resources, 1998), 155; Larkins, "The Judiciary and Delegative Democracy in Argentina," 429.

28. According to journalist union leaders, between July 1989 and December 1992, 139 journalists received death threats and fifty journalists suffered physical attacks. McGuire, *Peronism without Perón,* 259.

29. Smulovitz and Peruzzotti, "Societal and Horizontal Controls," 13–14.

30. Harold Trinkunas, "Crafting Citizen Control in Emerging Democracies: Argentina and Venezuela," *Journal of Interamerican Studies and World Affairs* 42, no. 3 (Fall 2000): 100.

31. Ibid.

32. Mariana Llanos, "Understanding Presidential Power in Argentina: A Study of the Policy of Privatization in the 1990s," *Journal of Latin American Studies* 33, no. 1 (February 2001): 85–96.

33. Sebastián Etchemendy and Vicente Palermo, "Conflicto y concertación: Gobierno, Congreso y organizaciones de interés en la reforma laboral del primer gobierno de Menem," *Desarrollo Económico* 37, no. 148 (January–March 1998): 559–90.

34. Inter-American Development Bank, *Latin America after a Decade of Reforms: Economic and Social Progress* (Washington, D.C.: IDB, 1997), 96. According to one study, the Argentine reforms were the second and most radical in the world during the 1990–95 period. See James Gwartney, Robert Lawson, and Walter Block, *Economic Freedom of the World, 1975–1995* (Vancouver, British Columbia: The Fraser Institute, 1996).

35. Dani Rodrik has called this the "Nixon in China syndrome." See Dani Rodrik, "Comment," in John Williamson, *The Political Economy of Policy Reform* (Washington, D.C: Institute for International Economics, 1994).

36. María Victoria Murillo, "From Populism to Neoliberalism: Labor Unions and Market Reforms in Latin America," *World Politics* 52, no. 2 (January 2000): 135–74.

37. Levitsky, *Transforming Labor-Based Parties in Latin America*.

38. Steven Levitsky, "An Organized Disorganization: Informal Organization and the Persistence of Local Party Structures in Argentine Peronism," *Journal of Latin American Studies* 33, no. 1 (February 2001): 53.

39. Pablo Gerchunoff and Juan Carlos Torre, "La política de liberalización económica en la administración de Menem," *Desarrollo Económico* 36, no. 143 (October–December 1996): 733–68; and Edward L. Gibson and Ernesto Calvo, "Federalism and Low Maintenance Constituencies: Territorial Dimensions of Economic Reform in Argentina," *Studies in Comparative International Development* 35, no. 3 (Fall 2000): 32–55.

40. Rubio and Goretti, "Executive-Legislative Relationship in Argentina," 8.

41. Gretchen Helmke, "Checks and Balances By Other Means: Strategic Defection and the 'Re-Reelection' Controversy in Argentina," paper delivered at the Annual Meeting of the American Political Science Association, Washington, D.C., August 31–September 3, 2000), 21–22.

42. Ibid.

43. Javier Corrales, "Technocratic Policy-Making and Parliamentary Accountability: The Argentine Case," paper presented at the XXIII International Congress of the Latin American Studies Association, Washington, D.C., September 6–8, 2001.

44. Trinkunas, "Crafting Civilian Control in Emerging Democracies." Also Rut Diamint, this volume.

45. Hector Schamis, "Argentina: Crisis and Consolidation," *Journal of Democracy* 13, no. 2 (April 2002): 84–85.

46. *New York Times*, January 2, 2002, A1.

47. See Joseph E. Stiglitz, "Argentina, Shortchanged: Why the Nation that Followed the Rules Fell to Pieces," *Washington Post*, May 12, 2002.

48. *Clarín*, December 20, 2001.

49. *Clarín*, August 1, 2001; *Página 12*, August 1, 2002.

50. *La Nación*, March 8, 2002.

51. UCR Senator Rodolfo Terragno, quoted in *Clarín*, January 28, 2001.

52. *Clarín*, April 18, 2002.

53. Stiglitz, "Argentina, Shortchanged."

54. *Clarín*, April 18, 2002.

55. *Clarín*, April 30, 2002.

56. *Clarín*, May 10, 2002.

57. Praetorianism extended all the way to the Supreme Court, whose members, under threat of impeachment, used their capacity to declare the *corralito* unconstitutional

(which, it was widely acknowledged, would trigger a collapse of the financial system) as a bargaining chip to ensure their survival.

58. *The Economist,* July 28, 2001, 37.

59. These terms are taken from Juan Linz, *The Breakdown of Democratic Regimes: Crisis, Breakdown, and Reequilibration* (Baltimore: Johns Hopkins University Press, 1978).

60. See *Página 12,* February 25–28, 2002.

61. General Hernán Guillermo Olmos, quoted in *Clarín,* April 5, 2002.

62. See, for example, Mariano Grondona's column in *La Nación,* March 31, 2002.

63. Schamis, "Argentina," 84–85.

64. Gibson, *Class and Conservative Parties.*

Chapter 12. Brazil

Although the final responsibility for this text is exclusively mine, I wish here to acknowledge the substantial and substantive help I received from my friend Octavio Amorim Neto while working on it.

1. Arend Lijphart, *Patterns of Democracy: Government Forms and Performace in Thirty-Six Countries* (New Haven: Yale University Press, 1999).

2. Ibid., 258–74.

3. Ibid., 33.

4. For a background of Brazilian politics, see Bolívar Lamounier, "Brazil: Inequality against Democracy," in *Democracy in Developing Countries: Latin America,* ed. Larry Diamond, Jonathan Hartlyn, Juan Linz, and Seymour Martin Lipset (Boulder, Colo.: Lynne Riener, 2nd ed., 1999), also published in *Politics in Developing Countries: Comparing Experiences with Democracy,* ed. Larry Diamond, Juan Linz, and Seymour Martin Lipset (Boulder, Colo.: Lynne Riener, 1995); idem, "E no Entanto se Move: Formação e Evolução do Estado Democrático no Brasil, 1930–1994," in *50 Anos de Brasil, 50 Anos de Fundação Getúlio Vargas,* ed. Bolívar Lamounier, Dionísio Dias Carneiro, and Marcelo de Paiva Abreu (Rio de Janeiro: Fundação Getúlio Vargas Editora, 1994); Bolívar Lamounier and Edmar Lisboa Bacha, "Democracy and Economic Reform in Brazil," in *A Precarious Balance: Democracy and Economic Reforms in Latin America and Eastern Europe,* vol. II, ed. Joan Nelson (Washington, D.C.: Overseas Development Council, 1994).

5. See Arend Lijphart, *Democracy in Plural Societies: A Comparative Exploration* (New Haven: Yale University Press, 1977).

6. Bolívar Lamounier, "Estrutura Institucional e Governabilidade na Década de 1990," in *O Brasil e as Reformas Políticas,* ed. João Paulo dos Reis Velloso (Rio de Janeiro: José Olympio Editora, 1992).

7. This argument underlines the persistence and endurance of cultural practices and values that derive directly from the tradition of Spain and Portugal. These tend to favor authoritarian characteristics that pose an obstacle to moving toward the sort of modern, liberal democracy associated with the tradition that shaped the United States and Great Britain.

8. Marku Laakso and Rein Taagepera, "Effective Number of Parties: A Measurement with Application to West Europe," *Comparative Political Studies* 12, no. 1 (April 1979): 3–27.

9. Octavio Amorim Neto, "Gabinetes Presidenciais, Ciclos Eleitorais e Disciplina Legislativa no Brasil," *Dados* 43, no. 3 (2000): 479–517.

10. Carlos Ranuldo Felix de Melo, "Partidos e Migração Partidária na Câmara dos Deputados," *Dados* 43, no. 2 (2000): 207–38.

11. For an in-depth analysis of the evolution of Brazil's party system from 1979 to 1996, see Scott Mainwaring, *Rethinking Party Systems in the Third Wave of Democratization: The Case of Brazil* (Stanford: Stanford University Press, 1999).

12. Argelina Figueiredo and Fernando Limongi, "Partidos Políticos na Câmara dos Deputados: 1989–1994," *Dados* 38, no. 3 (1995): 497–524; idem, *Executivo e Legislativo na Nova Ordem Constitucional* (Rio de Janeiro, Editora FGV, 1999); Carlos Pereira, "What Are the Conditions for the Presidential Success in the Legislative Arena: The Brazilian Electoral Connection" (unpublished Ph.D. dissertation, New School University, New York, 2000).

13. Maria Teresa Sadek, "A Crise do Judiciário e a Visão dos Juízes," Universidade de São Paulo, *Revista USP*, no. 1 (March–May 1994); idem, ed., *Justiça e Cidadania no Brasil* (São Paulo: Editora Sumaré, 2000); idem, "O Judiciário Brasileiro em Números" (typescipt, IDESP, São Paulo, 2001).

14. Armando Castelar Pinheiro, "Judiciário e Economia: Evidência Empírica para o Caso Brasileiro," in *O Judiciário e a Economia no Brasil,* ed. Armando Pinheiro Castelar (São Paulo: Editora Sumaré, 2000).

15. An estimated 40,000 cases per year have arrived in the Supreme Court in recent years—about 8 times the annual load of the U.S. Supreme Court. This compares to the 6 million arriving at the lower courts, 2 million of which are in the Labor Courts.

16. Rogério B. Arantes, *Judiciário e Política no Brasil* (São Paulo: Editora Sumaré, 1997); Rogério B. Arantes and Fábio Kerche Nunes, "Judicial System and Democracy in Brazil," paper presented at the XXIst International Congress of the Latin American Studies Association, Chicago, September 25, 1998.

17. Arantes and Kerche Nunes, "Judicial System and Democracy in Brazil."

18. Alfred Stepan, "Federalism and Democracy: Beyond the U.S. Model," *Journal of Democracy* 10, no. 4 (October 1999): 24–25.

19. Octavio Amorim Neto and Paulo Tafner, "O Congresso e as Medidas Provisórias: Delegação, Coordenação e Conflito," paper presented at the conference on "Congress and the Provisional Measures," Instituto Universitário de Pesquisas do Rio de Janeiro, Rio de Janeiro, April 26, 1999.

20. Amorim Neto and Tafner, "O Congresso e as Medidas Provisórias."

21. Timothy J. Power, "The Pen is Mightier Than the Congress: Presidential Decree Power in Brazil," in *Executive Decree Authority,* ed. John M. Carey and Matthew S. Shugart (New York: Cambridge University Press, 1998), 197–230.

22. On the Collor presidency and his impeachment, see Bolívar Lamounier, *Depois da Transição: Eleições e Democracia no Governo Collor* (São Paulo: Edições Loyola, 1991); Keith Rosenn and Richard Downes, eds., *Corruption and Political Reform in Brazil: The Impact of Collor's Impeachment* (Miami, Fla.: North-South Center Press at the University of Miami, 1999).

23. Bolívar Lamounier, "Brazil at an Impasse," *Journal of Democracy* 5, no. 3 (July 1994): 72–87.

24. Pereira, "What Are the Conditions."

25. For an analysis of patterns of electoral competition in Brazil, see Barry Ames, "Electoral Strategy Under Open-List Proportional Representation," *American Journal of Political Science* 39, no. 2 (May 1995): 406–33.

Chapter 13. Chile

1. Concertación (Concertación de Partidos por la Democracia) refers to the government coalition in power since the inauguration of democracy in 1990, which includes the

Christian Democratic Party, the Socialist Party, the Radical Party, and the Party for Democracy. The coalition was formed to compete in the national elections of 1989, and replaced the coalition organized to defeat Pinochet in the referendum of 1988.

2. Labor reform sought by the Concertación was finally passed by Congress in September 2001 in a divided vote. Tax reform, reducing personal tax in exchange for an increase in corporate tax and stringent rules against evasion, was similarly passed in August 2001.

3. For relevant literature on the impact of transitions and the authoritarian past on successor regimes, see Juan J. Linz and Alfred Stepan, *Problems of Democratic Transition and Consolidation: Southern Europe, South America, and Post Communist Europe* (Baltimore: Johns Hopkins University Press, 1996); Yossi Shain and Juan J. Linz, *Between States: Interim Governments and Democratic Transitions* (Cambridge: Cambridge University Press, 1995); Felipe Agüero, "Legacies of Transitions: Institutionalization, the Military, and Democracy in South America," *Mershon International Studies Review* 42 (1998): 383–404; Ellen Comisso, "Legacies of the Past or New Institutions?" *Comparative Political Studies* 28 (1995): 200–238; Beverly Crawford and Arend Lijphart, "Explaining Political and Economic Change in Post-Communist Eastern Europe: Old Legacies, New Institutions, Hegemonic Norms, and International Pressures," *Comparative Political Studies* 28 (1995): 171–99; Barbara Geddes, "A Comparative Perspective on the Leninist Legacy in Eastern Europe," *Comparative Political Studies* 28 (1995): 239–74; Daniel V. Freidheim, "Bringing Society Back into Democratic Transition Theory after 1989: Pact Making and Regime Collapse," *Eastern European Politics and Societies* 7 (1993): 481–512. For a look at changes in the Chilean Left as a result of authoritarianism, see Katherine Hite, *When the Romance Ended: Leaders of the Chilean Left, 1968–1998* (New York: Columbia University Press, 2000).

4. The extent to which the electoral system significantly distorts democratic representation is certainly debatable. But the fact that it was part of the non-negotiated constitution makes it part of the unfinished transition. On the electoral system, see, for instance, Peter Siavelis and Arturo Valenzuela, "Electoral Engineering and Democratic Stability: The Legacy of Authoritarian Rule in Chile," in *Institutional Design in New Democracies*, ed. Arend Lijphart and Carlos Waisman (Boulder, Colo.: Westview, 1996); Rhoda Rabkin, "Redemocratization, Electoral Engineering, and Party Strategies in Chile: 1989–1995," *Comparative Political Studies* 29 (1996): 335–56; and J. Samuel Valenzuela and Timothy Scully, "Electoral Choices and the Party System in Chile: Continuities and Changes at the Recovery of Democracy," *Comparative Politics* 29, no. 4 (July 1997): 511–27.

5. Manuel Antonio Garretón, *La sociedad en que vivi(re)mos: Introducción sociológica al cambio de siglo* (Santiago, Chile: Lom Ediciones, 2000), 170.

6. With this, actors in the Chilean political process and scholars who were troubled by the constraints on the successor regime, began to coincide in its characterization. Scholars emphasized that the persistence of authoritarian enclaves impeded the characterization of the Chilean transition as having attained closure. Only ridding the new regime of those enclaves would render the transition over, at which point consolidation, given the strength of political institutions, would also be attained. For this view of Chilean democratization as incomplete, see Linz and Stepan, *Problems of Democratic Transition and Consolidation*. Other views captured the trouble facing scholars with the characterization of the Chilean regime, by addressing it as "moving towards consolidation." See Richard Gunther, Hans-Jürgen Puhle, and P. Nikiforos Diamandouros, "Introduction," in *The Politics of Democratic Consolidation: Southern Europe in Comparative Perspective*, ed. Richard Gunther, P. Nikiforos Diamandouros, and Hans-Jürgen Puhle (Baltimore: Johns Hopkins University Press, 1995).

7. Several government officials and the president himself stated that the transition was over, even though they kept insisting on constitutional reform. The view of a finished transition was aided by some accomplishments. In the realm of human rights, by the Rettig Commission reports and by the committees created to compensate the victims of human rights violations. (The Rettig Comission was named after Raul Rettig, who chaired the National Committee on Truth and Reconciliation created by President Aylwin in April 1990.) In the realm of the military, by the Constitutional Court's ruling in favor of the president's power to deny promotions of general officers submitted by the chief service commander. The ruling came in the early 1990s when General Pinochet was still the head of the army.

8. The climate of consensus was animated by substantial and symbolic rituals, some truly unprecedented, such as the business-oriented presidential trips abroad that included delegations with large numbers of representatives of business and the opposition.

9. This became the subject of another constitutional reform right before the end of Aylwin's term that set a presidential period of six years. This, however, had the consequence of breaking the simultaneity of elections for president and Congress.

10. Human rights issues, painful memories of the past, or use of terms such as "dictatorship" to refer to the military government were discouraged by the dominant discourse of elites and the media. Underneath, there also was a deep fear of conflict among the public. See Norbert Lechner and Pedro Güell, "Construcción social de las memorias en la transición chilena," in *La Caja de Pandora: El retorno de la transición chilena,* ed. Alfredo Joignant and Amparo Menéndez Carrión (Santiago, Chile: Editorial Planeta, 1999).

11. *Boinazo* (from *boina,* which means beret) referred to the mobilization and display of troops in combat gear, wearing berets. *Ejercicio de enlace* (coordination exercise) was the way the army officially described another overtly irregular Boinazo-like mobilization. See Claudio Fuentes, "Militares en Chile: ni completa autonomía ni total subordinación," in *Chile 96: Análisis y Opiniones* (Santiago, Chile: Nueva Serie Flacso, 1997).

12. The Chilean transition did involve a number of partial agreements, the most important of which was the agreement reached in 1989, prior to the transfer of power, to partially reform the constitution. However, this reform left outside all the major aspects which later made for the incompleteness of the transition. See Felipe Agüero, "¿Transición Pactada?" *El Mercurio* (Chile), November 20, 1998, A2. See also Jorge Correa Sutil, "'No Victorious Army Has Ever Been Prosecuted . . .': The Unsettled Story of Transitional Justice in Chile," in *Transitional Justice and the Rule of Law in New Democracies,* ed. A. James McAdams (Notre Dame: University of Notre Dame Press, 1997).

13. Negotiations with the Renovación Nacional leadership advanced successfully to promote constitutional reforms, but this party's leadership failed to secure the support of its congressional representation. With the negative vote of Renovación Nacional and UDI senators, the reforms were rejected in the Senate in April 1996. See Andrés Allamand, *La travesía del desierto* (Santiago, Chile: Aguilar Chilena de Ediciones, 1999).

14. Manuel Antonio Garretón, "Balance y perspectivas de la democratización política chilena," in *La Caja de Pandora: El retorno de la transición chilena,* ed. Alfredo Joignant and Amparo Menéndez Carrión (Santiago, Chile: Editorial Planeta, 1999), and Alfredo Joignant and Amparo Menéndez-Carrión, "De la 'democracia de los acuerdos' a los dilemas de la polis: ¿transición incompleta o ciudadanía pendiente?" in *La Caja de Pandora: El retorno de la transición chilena,* ed. Alfredo Joignant and Amparo Menéndez Carrión (Santiago, Chile: Editorial Planeta, 1999). Cracks in this perception had in fact already surfaced during the difficulties that the government and the judiciary found in actually implementing the sentence against former DINA chief, General Contreras, which put him in prison in 1995.

15. Felipe Agüero, "Chile's Lingering Authoritarian Legacy," *Current History* 97, no. 616 (February 1998): 66–71.

16. An important part of the dissatisfaction was captured in Programa de las Naciones Unidas para el Desarrollo, *Desarrollo humano en Chile-1998. Las paradojas de la modernización* (Santiago, Chile: PNUD, 1998). For the ensuing debate, see José Joaquín Brunner, "Malestar en la sociedad chilena: ¿de qué, exactamente, estamos hablando?" *Estudios Públicos* 72 (1998): 173–98.

17. Different interpretations of the new situation circulated among Concertación officials. For many, it was time to confront squarely the pressing issues. A change in the language became noticeable: the "military regime" was now referred to as the "dictatorship." Pinochet was received in the Senate by Concertación representatives holding banners with pictures of the disappeared, and in the lower chamber by a constitutional accusation against him presented by a small group of young Concertación deputies (which did not succeed). Others, however, hoped that Pinochet would not heighten divisive issues of the past. They thought that the fact that he had stepped down as president in 1990 and as chief of the army in 1998 gave him gradually less relevance. In addition, he could surprise the Right parties by acting autonomously from them. His decision to negotiate with the president of the Senate and leading Christian Democratic presidential hopeful, Andrés Zaldívar, the end of the holiday that commemorated the coup on September 11, supported just that view.

18. Alexandra Barahona de Brito, "The Europeans, the Latin Americans, the Chileans and their General: The Case for an International Criminal Court," unpublished manuscript, 1999. See also José Luis Díaz, "Las agendas del sector Defensa y Pinochet," and Manuel Antonio Garretón, "Chile 1997–1998. Las revanchas de la democratización incompleta," in *Entre la II Cumbre y la detención de Pinochet, Chile 1998* (Santiago, Chile: Flacso-Chile, 1998).

19. Jon Lee Anderson, "The Dictator," *The New Yorker,* October 19, 1998. The article's subtitle was: "Augusto Pinochet ruled Chile ruthlessly, but he left behind a democracy. Now he wants history's blessing." In the opening paragraph, Pinochet hinted that he had never been truly a dictator, he had merely been an aspiring dictator, and then added: "And history teaches you that dictators never end up well" (p. 44).

20. The enormous impact which the Pinochet case, from his arrest in London through the legal battles in Chile, had in redrawing the political scenario owes a debt of gratitude to the consistent and persistent role played by human rights organizations and movement inside the country and internationally. For an approach that is sensitive to this role, see Thomas Risse, Stephen C. Ropp, and Kathryn Sikkink, eds., *The Power of Human Rights: International Norms and Domestic Change* (Cambridge: Cambridge University Press, 1999).

21. Initially, many, including within the Concertación, criticized the interference of a foreign court with that critical aspect of the "transition pact" that had kept Pinochet from legal responsibility for past crimes. ("The cornerstone of 'consensus politics' is the impunity of the military," wrote *Latin American Weekly Report* on October 20, 1998, in its front-page article entitled "Pinochet's arrest could be the death knell for 'consensus politics' in Chile.") The idea of an implicit pact may have flowed from the acceptance by all sectors of the actual validity of the constitution, by going along with the 1988 referendum and the 1989 constitutional reforms, and from the partial, and secret, agreements/appeasements reached with the military after acts of insubordination during the Aylwin administration. However, either those agreements had actually not explicitly existed or were no longer valid. The very idea of a pacted transition (such as it had occurred in Spain and other places) was no longer sustainable in the face of growing acceptance across the po-

litical spectrum of the need for constitutional reforms, that is, the need to make progress toward a still pending pact to finish the transition. For different views by Concertación figures, see Enrique Correa Ríos, "Razones y Pasiones," *El Mercurio* (Chile), October 27, 1998; José Zalaquett, "Pinochet y la Fuerza del Derecho," *La Tercera*, October 20, 1998; Ricardo Lagos and Heraldo Muñoz, "Pinochet y la Transición Incompleta," *El País*, February 24, 1999. Some of the leaders of RN had sustained this position for some time, but now even UDI leaders, and particularly its presidential hopeful, began to accept this view.

22. Jorge Correa, "Cenicienta se queda en la fiesta: El poder judicial chileno en la década de los 90," in *El modelo chileno: Democracia y desarrollo en los noventa*, ed. Paul Drake and Iván Jaksic (Santiago: Lom Ediciones, 1999), 300.

23. The principal case against Pinochet in Chile, the one leading to his detention, was based on the caravan of death in 1973, which resulted in remains unaccounted for, and thus was deemed to be a case of kidnappings. For a thorough account, see Patricia Verdugo, *Chile, Pinochet, and the Caravan of Death* (Miami, Fla.: North-South Center Press, 2001). For an account of the evolution of the courts on human rights, see Correa, "Cenicienta se queda en la fiesta." See also José Zalaquett, "Balance de la política de derechos humanos en la transición chilena a la democracia," in *Entre la II Cumbre y la detención de Pinochet, Chile 1998* (Santiago: Flacso-Chile, 1998); Elizabeth Lira and Brian Loveman, "Derechos humanos en la transición 'Modelo': Chile 1988–1999," in *El modelo chileno: Democracia y desarrollo en los noventa*, ed. Paul Drake and Iván Jaksic (Santiago, Chile: Lom Ediciones, 1999).

24. In an isolated but courageous gesture, RN Deputy Pía Guzmán apologized for her position under the military government, which had ignored human rights problems. Other leaders in the opposition, however, such as UDI Senator Evelyn Matthei and UDI Deputy Julio Dittborn, rejected her move. See "Pía Guzmán queda aislada tras mea culpa," *La Tercera*, February 28, 2001; "Evelyn Matthei rechazó un 'mea culpa' por tema de DD.HH.," *La Segunda* (Chile), March 6, 2001, and Julio Dittborn, "No pisaremos el palito," *La Tercera* (Chile), February 25, 2001.

25. The Mesa's first session convened on August 21, 1999, and brought together representatives from churches, the Jewish community, the masonry, human rights lawyers, the armed forces, academics, and the Ministry of Defense. See Elizabeth Lira, "Mesa de diálogo de derechos humanos en Chile, 21 de agosto 1999–13 de junio de 2000," in *Chile: Nuevo gobierno, desafíos de la reconciliación, Chile 1999–2000*, ed. FLASCO (Santiago, Chile: Flacso-Chile, 2000).

26. José Zalaquett, "La mesa de diálogo sobre derechos humanos y el proceso de transición política en Chile," *Estudios Públicos* 79 (2000).

27. The president spoke about 151 detained and disappeared persons that were dead, having been thrown in the ocean, rivers and lakes; 29 others who were buried in different parts of the territory, and 20 others unidentified by name who were buried somewhere in the Santiago metropolitan area. See Francisco Rojas, "Las Fuerzas Armadas reconocen a detenidos desaparecidos," *Nueva Mayoría*, January 12, 2001, and "Extractos del Discurso del Presidente Lagos," *La Segunda* (Chile), February 10, 2001. Despite the remarkable shift in the position of the armed forces, the information delivered did not provide accompanying details about agencies involved in the crime or the specific procedures utilized. Also, some of the information provided on the identity of victims and location of remains proved to be inaccurate.

28. Cardinal Errázuriz addressed the "deep wound that still bleeds in our society and that comes from the violation of the right to life and to physical integrity during the recent past." See Cardenal Errázuriz, "La justicia no lo es todo, no se trata del olvido sino

del perdón," *El Mercurio* (Chile), March 5, 2001. On the 10th anniversary of the Rettig Report, President Lagos stated that "truth is the only way to overcome the wounds that each society carries," and that "there is no one particular moment in which societies close the past," and added that truth, justice, reconciliation, and forgiveness do not constitute "well delineated and successive stages in time." See "Lagos abre seminario sobre informe Rettig y destaca logros en DD.HH.," *La Tercera* (Chile), April 10, 2001.

29. See statements by Senator Edgardo Boeninger in "Borrón y Agenda Nueva: Otra Propuesta sobre Derechos Humanos," *El Mercurio* (Chile), February 25, 2001, Reportajes section.

30. Carlos Vergara, "Reacciones del gobierno chileno durante el caso Pinochet," in *Chile: Nuevo gobierno, desafíos de la reconciliación, Chile 1999–2000*, ed. FLASCO (Santiago, Chile: Flacso-Chile, 2000); Mariela Herrera Muzio, "El año que vivió en peligro. Los tragos amargos de Pinochet," *El Mercurio*, April 3, 2001, Reportajes section. The charges, recently changed from authorship to accessory to murder and kidnappings, are contested in court.

31. See Cristián Larroulet, "La Constitución 20 años después: Evaluación y propuestas," *El Mercurio*, March 11, 2001, D26.

32. See Sergio Bitar, "Por el bien de Chile," and Hernán Larraín, "¿Una última oportunidad?" both in *La Tercera*, March 24, 2001; "Las 'movidas' de Diez para reformar la Constitución," *Radio Cooperativa*, April 2, 2001; and Sebastián Valenzuela, "Tan cerca, tan lejos. El adiós de las reformas constitucionales," *El Mercurio*, April 8, 2001, Reportajes section.

33. Andrés Allamand has argued that those who promoted the current constitution have faced a "boomerang effect," that is, the extraordinary powers assigned the presidency are now controlled by the Concertación. This, in his view, would discourage the Concertación from really pushing for reforms. See Andrés Allamand, "Chile: La transición empantanada," in *Chile-México: Dos transiciones frente a frente*, ed. Carlos Elizondo and Luis Maira (Mexico City: Editorial Grijalbo, 2000).

34. This was the first time that a runoff election was held in Chile. It is a novelty introduced by Pinochet's 1980 constitution. The previous 1925 constitution, which ruled until the 1973 coup d'etat, had stipulated that a full session of Congress would elect the president from among the two highest pluralities should none of the candidates obtain a majority. Former presidents Alessandri (1958–64) and Allende (1970–73) were elected this way.

35. In 1938, Gustavo Ross, of the Liberal party, obtained 49.2 percent against Pedro Aguirre Cerda of the Popular Front, who won with 50.1 percent. In 1946, however, the candidates from the Right Eduardo Cruz-Coke (conservative) and Fernando Alessandri (liberal) obtained a combined 56.9 percent, but lost to Gabriel González, who obtained 40.1 percent. See Arturo Valenzuela, "Party Politics and the Crisis of Presidentialism in Chile: A Proposal for a Parliamentary Form of Government," in *The Failure of Presidential Democracy: The Case of Latin America*, ed. Juan J. Linz and Arturo Valenzuela (Baltimore: Johns Hopkins University Press, 1994).

36. On the elections, see Felipe Agüero, "Second Round Needed to Break Virtual Tie in Chilean Presidential Elections," *North-South Center Updates* (January 2000), and "Second Round in Chile: Lagos wins third consecutive presidential term (2000–2006) for Concertación," *North-South Center Updates* (January 2000). Also, Manuel Antonio Garretón, "Cambio, continuidad y proyecciones de las elecciones presidenciales de fin de siglo," in *Chile: Nuevo gobierno, desafíos de la reconciliación, Chile 1999–2000*, ed. FLASCO (Santiago: Flacso-Chile, 2000), and Patricio Navia and Alfredo Joignant, "Las elecciones presidenciales de 1999: la participación electoral y el nuevo votante chileno," in *Nuevo go-*

bierno: Desafíos de la reconciliación, Chile 1999–2000, ed. FLASCO (Santiago: Flacso-Chile, 2000).

37. The annual average GDP growth rate for the 1991–2000 period was 6.6 percent, and 5 percent for GDP per capita. In 1999 GDP per capita fell by 2.4 percent. On GDP growth data, see *ECLAC Notes,* no. 14 (January 2001): 1, 11. For unemployment, see ECLAC, *Preliminary Overview of the Economies of Latin America and the Caribbean* (Santiago: United Nations/ECLAC, 2000), 38.

38. The 1988 referendum should be the standard for comparison for the vote on both sides. The Frei election in 1993 is a bit of a distortion—an inflation—of the Concertación vote, as is the weakened vote for a split right in post-referendum elections.

39. Felipe Agüero, Eugenio Tironi, Guillermo Sunkel, and Eduardo Valenzuela, "Votantes, partidos e información política: La frágil intermediación política en el Chile post-autoritario," *Revista de Ciencia Política* 19, no. 2 (1998); Eugenio Tironi and Felipe Agüero, "Sobrevivirá el nuevo paisaje político chileno?" *Estudios Públicos* 74 (1999); Mariano Torcal and Scott Mainwaring, "The Political Recrafting of Social Bases of Party Competition: Chile 1973–1995," *British Journal of Political Science* (forthcoming). See also J. Samuel Valenzuela, "Reflexiones sobre el presente y futuro del paisaje político chileno a la luz de su pasado: respuesta a Eugenio Tironi y Felipe Agüero," *Estudios Públicos* 75 (1999).

40. More of the lower-income groups vote for Concertación candidates. This would suggest the continuing importance of the class cleavage in Chilean politics. For a discussion of survey data on this and the other features, see Eugenio Tironi, Felipe Agüero, and Eduardo Valenzuela, "Clivajes políticos en Chile: Perfil sociológico de los electores de Lagos y Lavín," unpublished manuscript, 2000, and Carla Lehmann and Ximena Hinzpeter, "Del surgimiento de un nuevo mapa político en Chile: ¿Adiós al Sí y al No?" working paper no. 314, Centro de Estudios Públicos, Santiago, Chile, February 2001. Also, Timothy R. Scully, "Reconstituting Party Politics in Chile," in *Building Democratic Institutions: Party Systems in Latin America,* ed. Scott Mainwaring and Timothy R. Scully (Stanford: Stanford University Press, 1995).

41. Beyond the leadership positions during the campaign, the contrast between the leadership and the public is confirmed from data on parliamentary elites. See Leticia M. Ruiz-Rodríguez, "Clivajes y competencia partidista en Chile (1990–1999)," in *Chile: Nuevo gobierno, desafíos de la reconciliación, Chile 1999–2000,* ed. FLASCO (Santiago: Flacso-Chile, 2000).

42. An important constitutional reform entertained by leaders in the government and the opposition would shorten the presidential term so that presidential and congressional elections are held concurrently.

43. For a stimulating reflection on such a possibility, see Genaro Arriagada, *¿Hacia un Big Bang del sistema de partidos?* (Santiago, Chile: Editorial Los Andes, 1997). See also Peter M. Siavelis, "Continuidad y transformación del sistema de partidos en una transición 'modelo,'" in *El modelo chileno: Democracia y desarrollo en los noventa,* ed. Paul Drake and Iván Jaksic (Santiago, Chile: Lom Ediciones, 1999).

44. For a debate, see Mario Fernández Baeza, "El sistema electoral chileno," and Eugenio Guzmán A., "Apariencia y realidad: Comentarios al sistema electoral chileno de Mario Fernández," in *Democratizar la democracia: Reformas pendientes,* ed. Agustín Squella and Osvaldo Sunkel (Santiago, Chile: Lom Ediciones, 2000). Fernández rightly points out that three different electoral systems operate for presidential, congressional, and municipal elections.

45. Manuel Antonio Garretón, *La sociedad en que vivi(re)mos,* 173, and Gonzalo de la Maza E., "Los movimientos sociales en la democratización de Chile," in *El modelo chileno:*

Democracia y desarrollo en los noventa, ed. Paul Drake and Iván Jaksic (Santiago, Chile: Lom Ediciones, 1999). Women played important roles in these mobilizations. See Lisa Baldez, "La política partidista y los límites del feminismo de Estado en Chile," in *El modelo chileno: Democracia y desarrollo en los noventa,* ed. Paul Drake and Iván Jaksic (Santiago, Chile: Lom Ediciones, 1999), and the chapter by Mala Htun in this volume.

46. Florencia Mallon, "Cuando la amnesia se impone con sangre, el abuso se hace costumbre: El pueblo mapuche y el estado chileno, 1881–1998," in *El modelo chileno: Democracia y desarrollo en los noventa,* ed. Paul Drake and Iván Jaksic (Santiago, Chile: Lom Ediciones, 1999), 436.

47. José María Bulnes, "La causa mapuche y el caso Ralco en su contexto histórico y presente," in FLASCO, *Chile: Nuevo gobierno y desafíos de la reconciliación,* 348–49.

48. José Bengoa, *Historia de un conflicto: El estado y los Mapuches en el siglo XX* (Santiago, Chile: Planeta/Ariel, 1999).

49. "Se acabó la tregua: Dura crítica al manejo del conflicto Mapuche," *El Mercurio,* March 11, 2001, D5.

50. "Compensarán a Mapuches condenados," *El Mercurio,* March 4, 2001. See also Enrique Correa Ríos, "Conflictos indígenas," *El Mercurio,* February 5, 2001; "El conflicto en Arauco. Opinan interesados y experto," *El Mercurio,* February 4, 2001, and "Notable comisión. Aprontes para resolver el problema indígena," *El Mercurio,* July 11, 1999.

51. For a thought-provoking piece on issues of morals and secularization, see Merike Blofield, "La excepcional moral de Chile," *La Tercera,* March 22, 2001.

52. An excellent account of these changes, which I follow here, is Jorge Correa, "Cenicienta se queda en la fiesta." See also Hugo Frühling, "Judicial Reform and Democratization in Latin America," in *Fault Lines of Democracy in Post-Transition Latin America,* ed. Felipe Agüero and Jeffrey Stark (Miami, Fla.: University of Miami, North-South Center Press, 1998).

53. In 1992, for instance, three senators of the Right gave their votes to a successful constitutional accusation against a Supreme Court judge for dereliction of duties in a human rights case. Felipe Agüero, "Chile: South America's Success Story?" *Current History* 92, no. 572 (March 1993): 130–35. See also Lisa Hilbink, "Un estado de derecho no liberal: La actuación del Poder Judicial chileno en los años 90," in *El modelo chileno: Democracia y desarrollo en los noventa,* ed. Paul Drake and Iván Jaksic (Santiago, Chile: Lom Ediciones, 1999).

54. See "De 75 a 782 aumentarán los jueces," *El Mercurio,* July 5, 1999; Pamela Aravena Bolívar, "La revolución de la justicia: Piedrabuena y el debut de la reforma judicial," *El Mercurio,* December 17, 2000, Reportaje section; and "Reforma penal ya opera en dos regiones," *El Mercurio,* December 7, 2000.

55. "Lagos firma decreto que crea Defensoría nacional," *El Mercurio* (Chile), April 5, 2001.

56. Correa, "Cenicienta se queda en la fiesta," 311–13.

57. The Court was still hesitant in fully taking responsibility for its appalling behavior under the military regime that permitted, and ended up encouraging, massive crimes against human rights. Different interpretations on this matter continued to elicit debate. See, for instance, the speech by the president of the Supreme Court, Hernán Alvarez, on March 1, 2001, that was contested by Concertación leaders and former President Aylwin. Alvarez admitted limitations to justice under the Pinochet regime but blamed the regime for not providing information. See "Hernán Alvarez reconoció limitaciones a la justicia durante régimen militar," *El Mercurio* (Chile), March 1, 2001.

58. "Congreso Pleno ratificó igualdad hombre y mujer," *La Tercera,* May 16, 1999, (tercera.copesa.cl).

59. *The Economist,* April 12, 2001 (From *The Economist* print edition).

60. *Human Rights Watch,* Press Release, March 15, 2001, and April 14, 2001.

61. *The Economist,* April 12, 2001, and Rafel Otano, "Ley de prensa: La transparencia que no fue," *El Mostrador* (Chile), April 12, 2001.

62. "Comenzó ofensiva contra la censura cinematográfica," *El Mostrador* (Chile), March 16, 2001.

63. There is no question that this uneven situation has a cultural impact in the formation of public opinion. However, studies of voters in political intermediation processes found that most perceived the press as neutral. See Felipe Agüero, Eugenio Tironi, Guillermo Sunkel, and Eduardo Valenzuela, "Votantes, partidos e información política," and Felipe Agüero, Eugenio Tironi, and Eduardo Valenzuela, "Medios de comunicación y elecciones presidenciales en Chile 1993–1999: Informe descriptivo," unpublished manuscript, 2001.

64. Cristián Cox and María José Lemaitre, "Market and State Principles of Reform in Chilean Education: Policies and Results," in *Chile: Recent Policy Lessons and Emerging Challenges,* ed. Guillermo Perry and Danny M. Leipziger (Washington, D.C.: The World Bank, 1999), 173.

65. Ibid., 185–86. See also Juan Eduardo García-Huidobro, "La educación en 1999: Memorándum para el 2000," in *Chile: Nuevo gobierno, desafíos de la reconciliación,* ed. FLASCO (Santiago, Chile: Flacso-Chile, 2000); Isidora Mena and Cristián Bellei, "El desafío de la calidad y la equidad en la educación," in *Chile en los noventa,* ed. Cristián Toloza and Eugenio Lahera (Santiago, Chile: Presidencia de la República, Dolmen Ediciones, 1998), and Raúl Atria, "La educación superior en Chile: la demanda por regulación," in *Chile en los noventa,* ed. Cristián Toloza and Eugenio Lahera (Santiago, Chile: Presidencia de la República, Dolmen Ediciones, 1998). For a somber assessment of results in Chile from a comparative study of literacy, see Organisation for Economic Co-operation and Development, *Literacy in the Information Age: Final Report of the International Adult Literacy Survey* (Paris: OECD Publications, 2000).

66. Mensaje Presidencial, May 21, 2000.

67. On growth, figures are from *Banco Central de Chile;* on unemployment, from *Instituto Nacional de Estadísticas, Chile.*

68. Manuel Antonio Garretón, "El primer año: Avance con contradicciones," March 24, 2001.

69. *Qué Pasa,* no. 1560, March 3, 2001, 16–20.

70. Garretón, *La sociedad en que vivi(re)mos,* 195–96.

71. Ricardo Lagos Escobar, "Chile en un mundo en cambio. Los énfasis de la política exterior," *El Mercurio* (Chile), March 4, 2001, Reportaje section, reprinted from *Foreign Affairs,* Spanish version, 1, no. 1. See also, Alberto van Klaveren, "La inserción internacional de Chile," in *Chile en los noventa,* ed. Cristián Toloza and Eugenio Lahera (Santiago, Chile: Presidencia de la República, Dolmen Ediciones, 1998), and David R. Mares and Francisco Rojas Aravena, *The United States and Chile: Coming in From the Cold* (New York: Routledge, 2001).

Chapter 14. Mexico

1. According to survey data collected and analyzed by Roderic Camp, after Vicente Fox's victory, two-thirds of Mexicans now say that Mexico is a democracy.

2. Héctor Aguilar Camín, *México: La ceniza y la semilla* (Mexico City: Cal y Arena, 2001), 21.

3. Sergio González Rodríguez, "La vida nueva (sin el PRI)," *Letras Libres* (Mexico) (August 2000): 30.

4. José Woldenberg, "La transición a la democracia," *Nexos* (Mexico) (September 1, 1999).

5. See Alonso Lujambio, "Adiós a la excepcionalidad," *Este País* (Mexico) (February 1, 2000).

6. For an analysis of these three conditions, see Jeffrey Weldon, "The Political Sources of Presidencialismo in Mexico," in *Presidentialism and Democracy in Latin America,* ed. Scott Mainwaring and Matthew Soberg Shugart (Cambridge: Cambridge University Press, 1997).

7. The "Fox effect," the candidate's personal popularity, contributed to the PAN's 2 to 1 electoral victory in the gubernatorial races in the states of Guanajuato and Morelos, and also helped the PAN's candidate in Mexico City to finish a close second, although he had trailed far behind in the polls prior to election day.

8. María Amparo Casar, "México: Las elecciones federales del 2000 y la LVII legislatura," paper presented at the conference "The 2000 Elections and Mexico's Political Transition," Center for U.S.-Mexican Studies, University of California, San Diego, September 8, 2000.

9. Vicente Fox is the first Mexican president to be elected with less than 50 percent of the vote. See Juan Romero and Emilio Zebadúa, "Geografías de la alternancia," *Letras Libres* (Mexico) (August 2000): 58.

10. Beatriz Magaloni and Alejandro Poiré, "The Issue, the Vote and the Mandate for Change," paper presented at the XXIII International Congress of the Latin American Studies Association, Washington D.C., September 6–8, 2001.

11. Jeffrey Weldon, "Executive-Legislative Relations in Mexico in the 1990s," paper presented at the conference, "Dilemmas of Change in Mexican Politics," Center for U.S.-Mexican Studies, University of California, San Diego, October 8–9, 1999.

12. Ibid., 17–18.

13. In the 57th Congress, deputies presented bills at twice the rate of any of the three previous legislatures, and over 3 times the rate compared to the first three years of the Zedillo term. Ibid., 23.

14. On political and economic issues, the most frequent coalition in the 57th Legislature was between the PRI and the PAN (47.4 percent and 48.6 percent, respectively). On security and judicial issues the most frequent coalition involved all the parties (33.3 percent and 83.3 percent, respectively). See María Amparo Casar, "Coaliciones y cohesión partidista en un congreso sin mayoría: La Cámara de Diputados de México, 1997–1999," *Política y Gobierno* 7, no. 1 (1994).

15. The PRI congressional fraction had the lowest level of dissidence at 1.2 percent while the PRD had the highest at 12.7 percent. Casar, "Coaliciones y cohesión partidista," 197.

16. Casar, "México: Las elecciones federales," 7.

17. Constitutional reforms must also be approved by state legislatures.

18. Camín, *México*, 41.

19. See Enrique Krauze, *La presidencia imperial* (Mexico: Tusquets, 1977).

20. José Luis González, interview by the author, August 15, 2001.

21. For an analysis of this strategy in the U.S. context, see Samuel Kernell, *Going Public: New Strategies of Presidential Leadership* (Washington D.C.: Congressional Quarterly Inc., 1997).

22. See Vicente Fox, *A Los Pinos: Recuento autobiográfico y político* (Mexico: Editorial Océano, 1999).

23. For a sampling of books on Fox's presidential campaign and his tenure in Guana-

juato, see Miguel Ángel Granados Chapa, *Fox & Co.* (Mexico: Editorial Grijalbo, 2001); Arturo Miranda Montero and José Argueta Acevedo, *YA, Fox 2000 al natural* (Mexico: Ediciones ABC, 2000); César Leal, *Fox populi* (Mexico: Disem, 1999); Bruce Fielding Tipton and Hilda Rico Llanos, *El amanecer* (Mexico: Ediciones 2000, 2000); Guillermo Rivera, *2 de julio, La historia no narrada* (Mexico: Ediciones 2000, 2000).

24. Guillermo Cantú, *Asalto a palacio: Crónica de una guerra* (Mexico City: Grijalbo-Raya en el Agua, 2001).

25. See *Vicente Fox Propone* (Mexico: Ediciones 2000, 2000).

26. Increased competition and electoral transparency led to greater power sharing over time. In 1988 only 3 percent of the country's population lived in municipalities governed by an opposition party. In 1990, that figure rose to 10.45 percent; in 1992 to 14.4 percent; in 1995 to 24.3 percent; in 1996 to 37.5 percent; and in 1997 to 44.2 percent. See Lujambio, "Adiós a la excepcionalidad."

27. As Juan Molinar Horcasitas, former electoral counselor of the Federal Electoral Institute, puts it: "El sistema se cayó a pedazos" (the system fell apart in chunks, little by little). Alonso Lujambio also makes the same argument in *El poder compartido: un ensayo sobre la democratización mexicana* (Mexico: Editorial Oceano, 2000).

28. Kathleen Bruhn, "The Emergence of Party Competition in Mexico," paper presented at the Annual Meeting of the American Political Science Association, September 2–5, 1999. See also Alejandro Moreno, "Ideología y voto: Dimensiones de competencia política en México en los noventa," *Política y Gobierno* 6, no. 1 (1999): 45–81. Moreno argues that in the 1990s, electoral competitiveness and the evolution of the party system in Mexico were accompanied by a hardening of political-ideological tendencies.

29. See Jorge Buendía, "The Unchanging Mexican Voter," paper presented at the conference "Dilemmas of Change in Mexican Politics," Center for U.S.-Mexican Studies, University of California, San Diego, October 8–9, 1999.

30. In an interview prior to the election Fox declared that he was "un poquito a la izquierda" (a little toward the Left). See Raymundo Riva Palacio, "Vicente Fox cambia de piel," *Milenio* (Mexico), April 17, 2000, 35–39.

31. Casar, "Coaliciones y cohesión partidista."

32. Magaloni and Poiré, "The Issues."

33. During the 1980s, the PAN progressively accumulated electoral victories at the state and municipal levels. In 1987, the PAN governed less than one percent of the Mexican people. By the late 1990s, the PAN's municipal governments alone governed nearly a quarter of the national population. See David A. Shirk, "The Rise of the PAN," *Journal of Democracy* 11, no. 4 (October 2000): 27. See also Soledad Loaeza, *El Partido Acción Nacional: La larga marcha, 1939–1994* (Mexico: Fondo de Cultura Económica, 1999).

34. For an analysis of the evolution of the PAN's ideological stance, see Soledad Loaeza, *El Partido Acción Nacional.*

35. PAN elites are relatively compact in ideological terms, and support conservative positions on abortion and social issues. But at the mass level ideological heterogeneity prevails, so the PAN cannot really be defined as a typical Christian Democratic Party. See Beatriz Magaloni and Alejandro Moreno, "Catching All Souls: Religion and Ideology in the PAN," *Working Papers in Political Science WPPS-06* (Mexico: Instituto Tecnológico Autónomo de México, 1999).

36. "Vicente Fox: Gobernaré yo y no el PAN," *La Jornada* (Mexico), July 5, 2000.

37. For an account of the PRD's successful performance in the 1997 midterm elections, see Kathleen Bruhn, "The Resurrection of the Mexican Left in the 1997 Elections: Implications for the Party System," in *Toward Mexico's Democratization: Parties, Campaigns,*

Elections and Public Opinion, ed. Jorge I. Domínguez and Alejandro Poiré (New York: Routledge, 1999).

38. Cárdenas' working assumption was that a divided opposition could not defeat the PRI, and even some of Fox's closest advisers shared that view. After Fox's closing campaign rally, Jorge Castañeda expressed the view that "if Cárdenas obtains 18 percent of the vote Fox will lose."

39. Jaime Sánchez Susarrey, "Por qué perdió el PRD," *Reforma* (Mexico), August 15, 2000.

40. Elba Esther Gordillo, former head of the National Teachers' Union, interview by author, July 30, 2000.

41. See articles in the *Wall Street Journal* and the *Financial Times* on Victor Cervera Pacheco's campaign practices in the southern state of Yucatán prior to the 2000 election.

42. In May 2000, after Francisco Labastida's lackluster performance in the first televised debate, the PRI made last-minute changes in campaign strategy that entailed the incorporation of longtime political operators with a questionable past. See Julia Preston, "For First Time, Mexican Election is a Real Race," *New York Times,* May 16, 2000; Denise Dresser, "Francisco Labastida: Muerto en Vida," *Proceso* (Mexico) (May 21, 2000).

43. Schedler has described four strategies used by the PRI to exploit material resources for electoral purposes: (1) courting voters; (2) bribing voters; (3) coercing voters; and (4) threatening voters. See Schedler, *El Partido Acción Nacional,* 13.

44. *Reforma* (Mexico), July 4, 2000.

45. Ibid.

46. Demographic trends hurt the PRI and benefited Fox. Between 1985 and 2000 over 26 million new voters were incorporated into the Padrón Federal Electoral (the voter registration list). New citizens comprised 40 percent of the almost 60 million voters who could vote in the 2000 election. See Emilio Zebadúa, "La nueva geografía electoral," *Letras Libres* (Mexico) (August 2000): 58.

47. Vicente Fox spent the final weeks of his campaign trying to convince Cárdenas supporters to switch over and vote for change. Fox argued that he, not Cárdenas, had a real chance to win and that a vote in favor of the Alliance for Change coalition would be a "useful" vote, whereas a vote for the Cárdenas coalition would be useless. As a campaign adviser to Fox, prominent leftist Jorge Castañeda articulated this argument in numerous publications and public forums in Mexico and abroad.

48. Alain de Remes, "Mexican Federalism and the New Electoral Geography," paper presented at the conference "The 2000 Elections and Mexico's Political Transition," Center for U.S.-Mexican Studies, University of California, San Diego, September 8, 2000.

49. The option of "el regreso a los orígenes" (a return to the roots) might prove difficult for the PRI given that in the 1990s the party experienced a loss in the ideological diversity of its voters. Its electoral support came mainly from citizens who placed themselves at the right of the political spectrum. Curiously, in the 1997 election PAN supporters identified themselves as "centrists." See Moreno, "Ideología y voto," 47.

50. Luis Rubio, "Las contradicciones del PRI," *Reforma* (Mexico), August 6, 2000.

51. Weldon, "Executive-Legislative Relations," 4–5.

52. Schedler, *El Partido Acción Nacional,* 19.

53. Alberto Díaz Cayeros, for example, argues that regional diversity never disappeared. Before the consolidation of the PRI's hegemony, Mexican federalism was vigorous and active. See "Diez mitos sobre el federalismo mexicano" (mimeo).

54. Mexico's federalism will only be truly effective if the federal government is capable of creating and implementing compensatory schemes that benefit the country's poorest

regions. It will only flourish if local governments are capable of providing goods and services to the citizens under their jurisdiction. During the next several years Mexican federalism will face three key challenges: (1) how to strengthen states' fiscal capacities; (2) how to establish a politically acceptable and economically viable transfer of federal resources—especially those targeted to combat poverty—to local governments, and (3) how to devise a system that allows state and municipal governments to contract debt. See ibid., 144.

55. For a prelude of trends to come, see Wayne A. Cornelius, Todd A. Eisenstadt, and Jane Hindley, eds., *Subnational Politics and Democratization in Mexico* (La Jolla: Center for U.S.-Mexican Studies, University of California, San Diego, 1999).

56. Throughout the 1990s the PAN enacted a deliberate electoral strategy of winning congressional seats, municipal presidencies, and state governorships in an effort to lay the groundwork that would allow them to win the presidency subsequently. See Alonso Lujambio, *Federalismo y congreso en el cambio político en México* (México: UNAM, 1997).

57. Díaz Cayeros, "Diez mitos," 144.

58. In August 2000, a PRD-PAN coalition led by Pablo Salazar Mendiguchía won the governorship of Chiapas, a state that had been a PRI stronghold for over sixty-five years. For an analysis of the election, see Juan Pedro Viqueira, "Las elecciones en Chiapas," *Letras Libres* (Mexico) (August 2000): 52–55.

59. Alberto Olvera, "Civil Society in Mexico at Century's End," paper presented at the 20th Anniversary Conference, Center for U.S.-Mexican Studies, University of California, San Diego, October 1999, 18.

60. See the chapters contained in the section, "Popular Movements and Democratization" in Cornelius, Eisenstadt, and Hindley, *Subnational Politics*, 107–268.

61. The Church's Social Secretariat has been the driving force behind the formation of numerous specialized associations, created largely to address specific development problems at the micro level with the financial help of the clergy.

62. See Chappell Lawson, "Building the Fourth Estate: Media Opening and Democratization in Mexico," paper presented at the conference "Dilemmas of Change in Mexican Politics," Center for U.S.-Mexican Studies, University of California, San Diego, October 8–9, 1999.

63. Vikram K. Chand, *Mexico's Political Awakening* (Notre Dame: University of Notre Dame Press, 2001).

64. José Woldenberg, "El ancla de la democracia," *Voz y Voto* (mimeo).

65. Moreno, "Ideología y voto," 46.

66. "Mexico Transforming" (Los Angeles: The Pacific Council on International Policy, 2000): 30.

67. Guillermo Zepeda Lecuona, "Expectativas de justicia defraudadas: la actuación de las procuradurías de justicia en el esclarecimiento y persecución de los delitos" (Mexico: Centro de Investigación Para el Desarrollo, 1997).

68. Camín, *México: La ceniza y la semilla*, 62.

69. Ibid., 63.

70. Enrique Krauze, "Priismo mental," *Reforma* (Mexico), October 8, 2000.

71. Peter Andreas, "The Political Economy of Narco-Corruption in Mexico," *Current History* 97 (April 1998): 160–65.

72. This section draws from Peter Andreas, *Border Games: Policing the U.S.-Mexico Divide* (Ithaca: Cornell University Press, 2000), and Peter Andreas, "The Paradox of Integration: Liberalizing and Criminalizing Flows Across the U.S.-Mexico Border," in *The Post-NAFTA Political Economy*, ed. Carol Wise (University Park: Penn State Press, 1998).

73. The conditions for democratic consolidation are explored in Juan J. Linz and Al-

fred Stepan, "Toward Consolidated Democracies," *Journal of Democracy* 7, no. 2 (April 1996).

74. Ibid.

75. I borrow the term *electoral authoritarianism* from Andreas Schedler, who defines it as a regime type that reproduces and legitimizes itself through periodic elections that show some measure of pluralism but fall short of minimum democratic standards. See "Mexico's Victory: The Democratic Revelation," *Journal of Democracy* 11, no. 4 (October 2000): 6.

76. Bruhn, "The Emergence of Party Competition in Mexico," 23.

77. I borrow this imagery from the title of Héctor Aguilar Camín's book, *México: La Semilla y la Ceniza.*

Chapter 15. Constructing Democratic Governance in Latin America

1. This chapter is the successor to "Conclusion: Parties, Institutions, and Market Reforms in Constructing Democracies," in *Constructing Democratic Governance: Latin America and the Caribbean in the 1990s*, ed. Jorge I. Domínguez and Abraham F. Lowenthal (Baltimore: Johns Hopkins University Press, 1996). I co-authored that article with Jeanne Kinney Giraldo. All of the good ideas in that article were hers. I am also grateful to her for saving me from my worst errors in this chapter.

2. This is not a freestanding chapter. Instead, it calls attention to, and to some degree summarizes, themes that emerge in the chapters of this book. There are occasional textual references to other chapters, but my debt to the authors in this book is much greater than these citations suggest. The views expressed here are mine alone, however. The Inter-American Dialogue and the authors are free to claim that all the errors in this chapter are mine and all the insights are theirs.

3. For an assessment of some of the most worrisome events in the 1980s and early 1990s, see Deborah Norden, "The Rise of the Lieutenant Colonels: Rebellion in Argentina and Venezuela," *Latin American Perspectives* 23, no. 3 (Summer 1996): 74–86. For a summary of earlier examples, see Robert Dix, "Military Coups and Military Rule in Latin America," *Armed Forces and Society* 20, no. 3 (Spring 1994): 439–56.

4. See also Brigadier Juan Carlos Salgado, "La participación del ejército de Chile en la mesa de diálogo sobre los derechos humanos," and Elizabeth Lira, "Mesa en diálogo de derechos humanos en Chile," both in *Nuevo gobierno: Desafíos de la reconciliación. Chile 1999–2000* (Santiago, Chile: FLACSO, 2000).

5. A. Douglas Kincaid, "Demilitarization and Security in El Salvador and Guatemala: Convergences of Success and Crisis," *Journal of Interamerican Studies and World Affairs* 42, no. 4 (Winter 2000): 39–58. See also Cynthia J. Arnson, ed., *Comparative Peace Processes in Latin America* (Stanford: Stanford University Press, 1999).

6. Domínguez and Giraldo, "Conclusion," 33–35.

7. For a discussion of the earlier pattern, see Alfred Stepan, "The New Professionalism of Internal Warfare and Military Role Expansion," in *Armies and Politics in Latin America*, ed. Abraham Lowenthal and J. Samuel Fitch (New York: Holmes & Meier, 1986), 134–47.

8. For a discussion of right-wing parties, see Kevin Middlebrook, ed., *Conservative Parties, the Right, and Democracy in Latin America* (Baltimore: Johns Hopkins University Press, 2000).

9. Wendy Hunter has analyzed this process well in her "Civil-Military Relations in Ar-

gentina, Chile, and Peru," *Political Science Quarterly* 112, no. 3 (Fall 1997): 453–75. See also Wendy Hunter, *Eroding Military Influence in Brazil: Politicians Against Soldiers* (Chapel Hill: University of North Carolina Press, 1997).

10. For information on one of the least well-studied military organizations, see Mónica Serrano, "The Armed Branch of the State: Civil-Military Relations in Mexico," *Journal of Latin American Studies* 27, no. 2 (May 1995): 423–48.

11. For a comprehensive study, see J. Samuel Fitch, *The Armed Forces and Democracy in Latin America* (Baltimore: Johns Hopkins University Press, 1998), especially chapters 5 and 6.

12. Anthony Downs, *An Economic Theory of Democracy* (New York: Harper & Row, 1957), 104–5.

13. For general background, see Scott Mainwaring and Timothy R. Scully, eds., *Building Democratic Institutions: Party Systems in Latin America* (Stanford: Stanford University Press, 1995).

14. Susan Stokes, *Mandates, Markets, and Democracy: Neoliberalism by Surprise in Latin America* (Cambridge: Cambridge University Press, 2001).

15. For an analysis of aspects of these problems, see Kenneth Roberts and Erik Wibbels, "Party Systems and Electoral Volatility in Latin America: A Test of Economic, Institutional, and Structural Explanations," *American Political Science Review* 93, no. 3 (September 1999): 575–90.

16. Stokes, *Mandates, Markets, and Democracy*, Table I.2.

17. As with sausage making, the outcome is much nicer looking than the process. See Edward Gibson, "The Populist Road to Market Reform: Policy and Electoral Coalitions in Mexico and Argentina," *World Politics* 49, no. 3 (April 1997): 339–70; and Kenneth Roberts, "Neoliberalism and the Transformation of Populism in Latin America: The Peruvian Case," *World Politics* 48 (October 1995): 82–116.

18. Fernando Cepeda, *La dirección política de la reforma económica* (Bogotá: Fonade y Tercer Mundo, 1994).

19. See Scott Mainwaring, *Rethinking Party Systems in the Third Wave of Democratization: The Case of Brazil* (Stanford: Stanford University Press, 1999), 142–47.

20. See, for example, Timothy J. Power, *The Political Right in Postauthoritarian Brazil: Elites, Institutions, and Democratization* (University Park: Pennsylvania State University Press, 2000).

21. On the development of the Liberal and Sandinista parties, see David R. Dye, *Patchwork Democracy: Nicaraguan Politics Ten Years After the Fall* (Cambridge, Mass.: Hemisphere Initiatives, 2000), 12–18, 34.

22. For comparative perspectives, see Ruth Berins Collier and James Mahoney, "Adding Collective Actors to Collective Outcomes: Labor and Recent Democratization in South America and Southern Europe," *Comparative Politics* 29, no. 3 (April 1997): 285–303.

23. Indira Palacios and Teresa Valdés, "Las mujeres en las últimas elecciones presidenciales," in *Nuevo gobierno: Desafíos de la Reconciliación. Chile 1999–2000* (Santiago, Chile: FLACSO, 2000).

24. For discussions of social movements in other Latin American settings, see Henry Veltmeyer, "New Social Movements in Latin America: The Dynamics of Class and Identity," *Journal of Peasant Studies* 25, no. 1 (October 1997): 139–69; Jean-Pierre Bastian, "The Metamorphosis of Latin American Protestant Groups," *Latin American Research Review* 28, no. 2 (1993): 33–61; and Deborah Yashar, "Contesting Citizenship: Indigenous Movements and Democracy in Latin America," *Comparative Politics* 31, no. 1 (October 1998): 23–42.

25. For a general analysis of executive-legislative relations, see Matthew Soberg Shugart and John M. Carey, *Presidents and Assemblies: Constitutional Design and Electoral Dynamics* (Cambridge: Cambridge University Press, 1992). For comparative studies, see Arend Lijphart and Carlos H. Waisman, *Institutional Design in New Democracies: Eastern Europe and Latin America* (Boulder, Colo.: Westview, 1996). For a closer focus on similar issues in Latin America, see Scott Mainwaring and Matthew Soberg Shugart, eds., *Presidentialism and Democracy in Latin America* (Cambridge: Cambridge University Press, 1997).

26. See John D. Martz, "Political Parties and Candidate Selection in Venezuela and Colombia," *Political Science Quarterly* 114, no. 4 (Winter 2000): 639–59.

27. There is one difference between the upper and lower house of Parliament. As in nearly all countries, the extent of malapportionment is much more marked in the upper chamber. See Richard Snyder and David Samuels, "Devaluing the Vote in Latin America," *Journal of Democracy* 12, no. 1 (January 2001): 147–59. The political behavior of the two chambers and the relations between the chambers and the executive are, however, nearly identical.

28. Divided government, of course, has other institutional and political foundations. See Mark P. Jones, "Presidential Election Laws and Multipartism in Latin America," *Political Research Quarterly* 47, no. 1 (March 1994): 41–57; and Matthew Soberg Shugart, "The Electoral Cycle and Institutional Sources of Divided Presidential Government," *American Political Science Review* 89, no. 2 (June 1995): 327–43.

29. Margaret Popkin, "Building the Rule of Law in Post-War El Salvador," in *El Salvador: Implementation of the Peace Accords,* ed. Margarita Studemeister (Washington, D.C.: United States Institute of Peace, 2001), 16.

30. For a convergent analysis, see Javier Corrales, "Presidents, Ruling Parties, and Party Rules: A Theory on the Politics of Economic Reform in Latin America," *Comparative Politics* 32, no. 2 (January 2000): 127–49.

31. Delia Boylan, "Taxation and Transitions: The Politics of the 1990 Chilean Tax Reform," *Latin American Research Review* 31, no. 1 (1996): 7–31.

32. For the text of the Supreme Court decision, see Francisco Rojas Aravena and Carolina Stefoni Espinoza, eds., *El "caso Pinochet." Visiones hemisféricas de su detención en Londres* (Santiago, Chile: FLACSO, 2001), 273–320.

33. For a nuanced debate on the extent of partisan legislative cohesion and discipline in Brazil, see Argelina Cheibub Figueiredo and Fernando Limongi, "Presidential Power, Legislative Organization, and Party Behavior in Brazil," *Comparative Politics* 32, no. 2 (January 2000): 151–70; and Scott Mainwaring and Aníbal Pérez Linan, "Party Discipline in the Brazilian Constitutional Congress," *Legislative Studies Quarterly* 22, no. 4 (November 1997): 453–83.

34. Data on growth rates from Comisión Económica para América Latina y el Caribe, *Balance preliminar de las economías de América Latina y el Caribe, 2000* (Santiago, Chile: Naciones Unidas, 2000), 85–86.

35. See report of Latinobarómetro results for 2001 in "An Alarm Call for Latin America's Democrats," *The Economist* (July 28, 2001): 37–38.

36. Dye, *Patchwork Democracy: Nicaraguan Politics.*

Index

Page numbers in *italics* refer to figures and tables.